FOR VALOUR

The Complete History of the Victoria Cross

VOLUME 3

The Colonial Wars (1860 – 1889)

0000846

DEDICATION

This book is dedicated to all members of the British armed forces, past, present and future.

Our thanks and gratitude is extended, to all those who have served, for the services that they have provided to ensure the welfare, independence and security of our nation.

FOR VALOUR

The Complete History of the Victoria Cross

VOLUME 3

The Colonial Wars (1860 – 1889)

Michael Charles Robson

UNIFORM

Published in 2018 by
Uniform, an imprint of Unicorn Publishing Group LLP
101 Wardour Street
London W1F 0UG
www.unicornpublishing.org

The author asserts the moral right to be identified as the author of this work
A catalogue record for this book is available from the British Library

ISBN 978 1 910500 93 4

Typeset in Minion Pro

Design by Nick Newton Design

Printed and bound in Poland

The author would be grateful for any information that may add to the further enhancement, accuracy or development of this title or others in the series. Please contact the publisher in the first instance.

CONTENTS

ILLUSTRATIONS

Main Illustrations and Portraits
1 Public Domain
2 Michael Charles Robson
3 John Fawkes
4 Garen Ewing
9 No Image

Graves and Memorials
A Memorials to Valour
B Public Domain
X No Image
Z Copyright by named people
105 – Patrick Hugh Lynch
125 – Geoff Andrews
133 – Dundas Family
134 – Jean-Philippe Boulet
159 – Brett Hendy
171 – Surenda Singh
174 – Anthony Cope
196 – Clan McCrea

PREFACE

This is the third volume of what will be an eight volume set, providing a full history of the Victoria Cross, the first volume covered how and why the Victoria Cross was instigated and detailed the first 111 recipients who received the award for deeds performed during the Crimean War. The second volume covered the 181 awards during the Indian Mutiny.

In a similar fashion to the first two volumes, this book contains three parts; the first part covers introductory material such as how the original Victoria Cross Royal Warrant was changed to accommodate the situations following the Indian Mutiny.

The second part covers the wars, battles and deeds of the recipients who were awarded the Victoria Cross for actions during the colonial wars between the Indian Mutiny and the First World War. The deeds which resulted in the award of the Victoria Cross are detailed within the narrative of a condensed history of the various colonial wars to provide an enhanced context for these extraordinary and brave actions.

The third part contains biographies of the recipients, so that we may obtain a better understanding of the lives of these brave and gallant men.

The colonial wars are covered by two volumes; this volume covers the period between 1860 and 1889 and covers the Zulu Wars and other conflicts.

Volume 4 will cover the period from 1890 until 1904 and will include the Boer War and other conflicts up until the last award prior to the Great War.

PART ONE
INTRODUCTION

Wherever possible I have used contemporary sources during the research of this book.

It should be noted that I have used the regimental designations in use at the time of the narrative and no attempt has been made to bring them up to date.

For the spelling of place names and the names of people I have used the common spellings in use at the time the events occurred and no attempted had been made to update them to their modern names where they may have changed. It should be noted that the spelling of names for foreign people and places was based upon British phonetic interpretations of these names and often had several different spellings – I have tried to maintain a single consistent spelling in these circumstances.

The Colonial Wars

During the reign of Queen Victoria the British Empire rose to its peak, it was not until after her death and the end of the First World War that the Empire began its decline.

This book covers the wars during this period, where at least one Victoria Cross was awarded, that were fought to defend or expand the borders of the Empire; which I have collectively called the "Colonial Wars".

1

THE VICTORIA CROSS WARRANT CHANGES

During the period covered by this book (1858 to 1889), the Originating Royal Warrant issued on 29th January 1856, which established the Victoria Cross, had to be amended to cater for changing circumstances.

Not Before the Enemy

On the 10th August 1858, the Royal Warrant was amended to *"Extend the Victoria Cross to Cases of Conspicuous Courage and Bravery Displayed under Danger but not before the Enemy".*

Originally the request for this amendment was raised in response to the bravery of men on board the troopship *Sarah Sands* which caught fire on 11th November 1857.

A large detachment of men from the 54th Regiment of Foot were onboard the ship bound for India as reinforcements to help quell the mutiny. The ship caught fire while 800 miles off the coast of Mauritius and most of the crew took to the boats, however, some men of the 54th bravely tackled the fire in a ship full of gunpowder and other munitions. Private No. 3190 Andrew Walsh was singled out, together with Mr Welch the Chief officer of the *Sarah Sands*, and they were eventually recommended for the Victoria Cross after the amendment was ratified by Queen Victoria.

Ironically, these men did not receive the Victoria Cross as the award was refused on the grounds that the amended warrant could not be applied retrospectively.

Only 6 awards (5 in one incident) were made under this ruling, which was eventually scrapped in 1881.

Victoria Cross extended to New Zealand local forces

On the 1st January 1867, eligibility for the award of the Victoria Cross was extended to *"the Local Forces in New Zealand and in the Colonies and their Dependencies Generally".*

Under the terms of the originating royal warrant, it was only men of the British Army and Navy that were eligible for an award of the Victoria Cross, this change extended the eligibility to men of the New Zealand Militia and colonial forces. The change was implemented as a result of the recommendations for Major Heaphy and Sergeant Kenrick of the New Zealand Militia to be awarded the Victoria Cross.

After the amended warrant came into force, the application for Major Heaphy was resubmitted and it was subsequently approved, for some unknown reason, the recommendation for Sergeant Kenrick was not resubmitted so he did not receive an award.

Victoria Cross extended to Auxiliary and Reserve Forces

On the 23rd April 1881, the Royal Warrant was changed once again to extend the eligibility for the award of a Victoria Cross to the men of Auxiliary and Reserve Forces.

This warrant also removed the *"not in the face of the enemy"* clause introduced in the amendment of 1858.

Indian Ecclesiastical Establishments

On the 6th August 1881, the eligibility for the award of the Victoria Cross was extended to men of the Indian Ecclesiastical Establishments.

Clergymen who were commissioned officers acting as Chaplains in the British Army were already eligible, this amendment extended eligibility to Clergymen of the various Indian Ecclesiastical Establishments who performed a similar role in the Indian Army, often without the benefit of a commission.

2

THE BRITISH EMPIRE

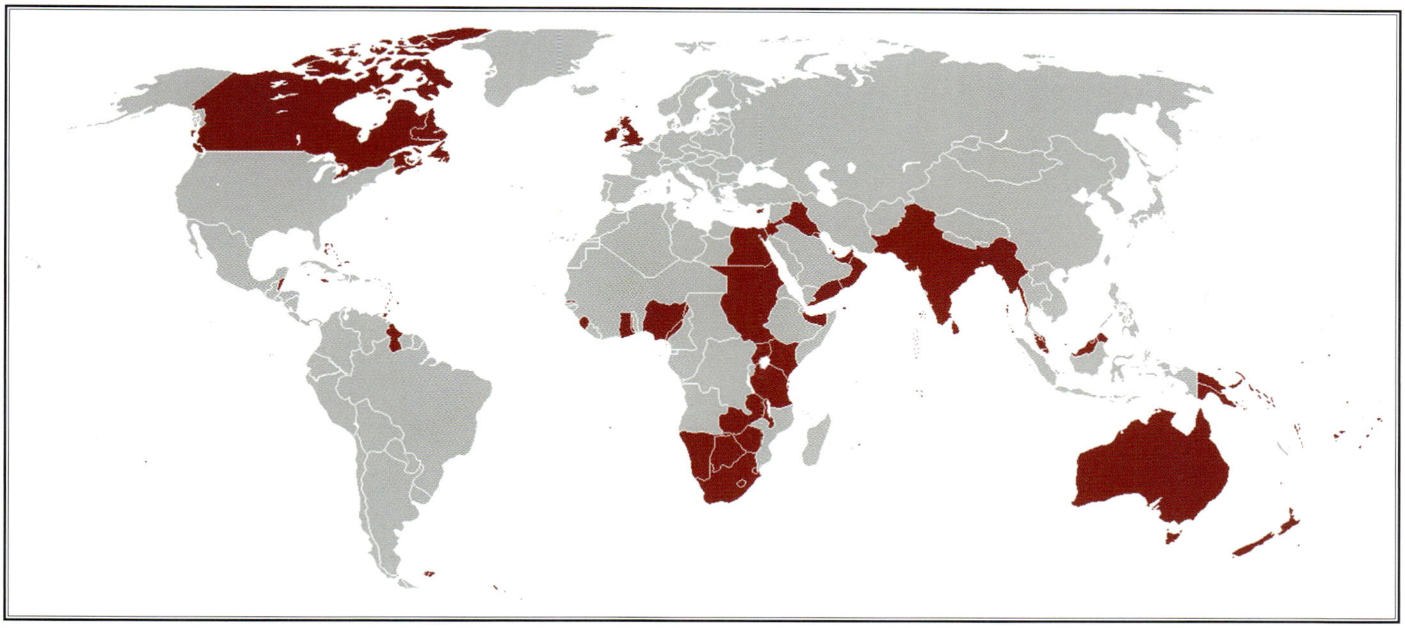

Figure I. British Empire at its peak

As this and the next volume cover conflicts that were mainly fought to extend or protect the borders of the British Empire, I have included this short history to provide a background to later events.

The start and end dates of the British Empire are somewhat fluid, with divided opinions in the academic community. In line with the majority of historians, I have taken the start of Empire to be 1497, when the first substantial colony of Newfoundland was founded, and the end of Empire to be 1997, when the last major colony of Hong Kong was handed back to China.

Using these dates, the Empire lasted for 500 years and the last Colonial War was the Falklands war fought in 1982.

What constitutes a "Colony"?

There were five main categories of 'Colony':

Company Rule – this was where a private company, capitalised in Britain, set up a colony as a private commercial enterprise; the most famous of these being the "Honourable East India Company".

Colony – ruled by a governor, representing the Crown on behalf of the British Government. The governor, though responsible to the Colonial Office, usually had wide discretionary powers.

Protectorates – were territories where local rulers continued to have control of domestic issues but had ceded Foreign and Defence issues to the British government. Although, theoretically, the local rulers had full autonomy of domestic affairs, British advisers often exercised considerable influence over a wide range of policies.

Dominions – were former settler colonies, granted significant authority for self rule; after the 1931 statute of Westminster, Dominions became fully independent countries, although their Head of State continued to be the British sovereign.

Mandates – set up after the Great War, as German and Turkish colonies were handed over to Britain and France, to prepare them for self government on behalf of the League of Nations. After World War II, this concept was continued under the United Nations, however, the mandates were designated "Trust Territories".

In addition to these five, formal elements of Empire, there were many informal arrangements made by individuals or groups to exercise commercial supremacy over a territory, that in many cases resulted in some form of British government control.

Motivation for colonisation

The motivation for establishing any form of colony, generally fell into one, or more, of the following reasons:

Trade: As England became more and more industrialised, the need to extend the geographical area for the source of raw materials and as a market place for their goods became evermore necessary.

Religion: Missionaries used the process of colonisation to extend Christianity to more and more areas of the globe.

Settlement: As opportunities for new entrants into the commercial world, in England, became increasingly difficult many entrepreneurs saw colonisation and the creation of a settlement in a far off land, as the only way to acquire land and make their fortune.

Defence: As the extent of the colonies expanded, the motivation of defence, to protect, retain and expand the Empire became more and more prevalent.

The age of Exploration

Despite being a maritime nation, with a formidable navy, England was slow to take part in global exploration. This tardiness was mainly as a result of the fact that in England, voyages of exploration were thought to be the preserve of private individuals rather than the state.

With the support of their monarchy and governments, it is therefore of no surprise that the early leaders of the voyages of discovery were from Portugal and Spain. Towards the end of the fifteenth century, two major discoveries were made during voyages sponsored by these countries, which heralded the age of discovery.

Discovery of America[1]

In 1485 and 1488 Christopher Columbus (an Italian) tried to gain support from King John II of Portugal for an expedition to sail westward across the Atlantic and find a sea route to the East Indies.

Failing to obtain the support of the king of Portugal for his expedition, Columbus sent his brother Bartholomew to the court of King Henry VII, to obtain the support of the English king for his voyage.

After being unsuccessful in obtaining the support of the English, Columbus turned his attention to Spain, and on 1st May 1486 he was granted a charter of discovery by King Ferdinand II of Aragon and Isabella I of Castile.

It was not until January 1492 that Columbus eventually received the funding for his voyage. After protracted negotiations and after setting sail on 3rd August 1492, he discovered land on 12th October 1492.

Figure 2. Christopher Columbus

1 It is now generally accepted that America was discovered much earlier by Viking explorers, however, at this time it was accepted that Columbus had discovered new lands across the Atlantic.

After discovering the current land of the Bahamas, Columbus was convinced that he had achieved his objective of finding a sea route to the East Indies. Further voyages, with the discovery of more land, consolidated this view, resulting in the naming of the area as the West Indies.

Sea Route to India via Cape of Good Hope

In 1482 and 1484–1486, with support from King John II of Portugal, Diogo Cão a Portuguese explorer carried out two voyages south down the west coast of Africa.

Another Portuguese explorer, Bartolomeu Dias, building on the knowledge from Diogo Cão's earlier voyages, and again with support from King John II of Portugal, set off on a voyage to discover an eastern sea route to the East Indies.

Setting sail in October 1487, Bartolomeu sailed down the west coast of Africa and managed to round the southernmost tip of the continent, discovering the Cape of Good Hope in the process, thus opening up a sea route to the East Indies.

British Colonisation

The First British Colony

In 1493, Pope Alexander VI issued a papal Bull to the effect that Spain could lay claim to all newly discovered lands up to 100 leagues to the west and south of a line drawn from pole to pole between the islands of the Azores and the Cape Verde Islands. Although not explicitly stated, it was inferred that Portugal could lay claim to all of the newly discovered lands east of this line.

The treaty of Tordesillas, signed on 7th June 1494, formalised this understanding but moved the line to 370 leagues west and south of the Azores and Cape Verde Islands.

Despite the papal bull and treaty, Henry VII , perhaps spurred on by the success of the Portuguese and Spanish voyages, was ready to support an expedition by John Cabot to explore an Atlantic route to Cathay (China) and Tartary (Northern and Central Asia).

On 5th March 1496, Henry VII granted letters patent to John Cabot, an Italian living in Bristol, and his three sons for exploration with "*... free authority, faculty and power to sail to all parts, regions and coasts of the eastern, western and northern sea, under our banners, flags and ensigns, with five ships or vessels of whatsoever burden and quality they may be, and with so many and with such mariners and men as they may wish to take with them in the said ships, at their own proper costs and charges, to find, discover and investigate whatsoever islands, countries, regions or provinces of heathens and infidels, in whatsoever part of the world placed, which before this time were unknown to all Christians.*"

Figure 3. John Cabot

Very little information is available, regarding this very important voyage, however, it appears that John Cabot set sail from Bristol on 2nd May 1497 and after sailing across the Atlantic landed on the coast of north America on 24th June 1497, St John the Baptist's day.

John Cabot, landed at what became known as St John's in Newfoundland and after taking on water and claiming the lands for the British Crown, soon began his return journey, arriving back at Bristol on 6th August 1497.

Following on from this success, William Weston also setting sail from Bristol crossed the Atlantic and landed on the north American continent at Newfoundland, and became the first Englishman to set foot in America.

Colonial Expansion

Following on from establishing the first colony in 1497, expansion of the Empire was carried out at a slow pace and suffered a major setback in 1776 with the loss of the American colonies following the American War of Independence.

Loss of the American colonies, seemed to act as a spur for further expansion of the Empire; the Royal Navy, now the unchallenged sea power controlled most of the key maritime trade routes and with the Industrial Revolution in full swing Britain was establishing a dominant position in world trade.

By the 1850s the Empire consisted of colonies in Canada, the West Indies, Guiana in South America, Africa, India and Australasia and occupied 9.5 million square miles of the earth's surface (approximately 18%).

During the period from 1815 to 1914, often referred to as Britain's *"Imperial Century"* the empire would be extended to cover 10 million square miles (approximately 25% of the earth's surface) and a quarter of the world population, about 400 million people, lived under some form of British rule. Due to the geographical distribution of these colonies it was true to say that *"the sun never sets on the British Empire"*.

The Empire would reach its peak in 1920, when it covered about 12.7 million square miles with a population of almost 460 million people.

Pax Britannica

The nearly 100 years between the end of the Napoleonic Wars in 1815 and the start of the Great War in 1914, is also known as *"Pax Britannica"* or British Peace, during which there was a relative peace between Britain and the other great powers.

However, Pax Britannica is somewhat of a misnomer, as during this period Britain fought over 40 campaigns with over 200 battles and there were only six years (1820, 1829, 1830, 1833, 1907 and 1909) during which the British Army was not involved in some conflict; there was military action during each year of Queen Victoria's extensive reign.

Not all of these conflicts were what are commonly known as "Victoria's Little Wars" as during this period three major conflicts also took place; the Crimean War, the Indian Mutiny and the Second Boer War.

It is these conflicts, which I have called "The Colonial Wars", that are covered by this and the next volume of my History of the Victoria Cross.

PART TWO

WARS, BATTLES AND DEEDS

THE COLONIAL WARS

3

THE PERSIAN WAR (1856–57)

Figure 4. Persia

Build-Up to War

In the early 1800s (1801, 1809 and 1813), Britain signed treaties with Persia, mainly to ensure that there was a friendly state to act as a buffer with Afghanistan and the route to British India.

Following the loss of lands to Russian, Persia signed the so called "Definitive Treaty" with Britain on 25th November 1814. Under the terms of this treaty, Persia was required to annul all alliances with states hostile to Britain and would not permit Britain's enemies to cross their lands on the way to India. Persia would also supply troops to aid Britain, in the event that the Afghans attacked British India. Britain was also permitted to be involved in discussions about issues arising from the newly established Russian-Persian border.

In return, Britain would supply instructors for the Persian army and would supply troops from India if Persia was attacked by any European Power. Britain also promised not to interfere in internal Persian affairs and would remain neutral in the event of war between Afghanistan and Persia.

In 1825, after launching an attack against Russian forces, while attempting to recover some of their lost lands, the Persian army was defeated and tried to invoke the 1814 treaty. Britain, refused to get involved as Persia had acted as the initial aggressor and after some negotiations Persia was given a one off payment and Britain was freed of most of the obligations of the 1814 treaty.

After concluding a treaty with Russia, Persia now looked towards Afghanistan as a place to extend its borders and with the support of Russian advisors to the Persian court began to plan a campaign of invasion. The British were, quite naturally, opposed to a move against Afghanistan as it could effectively bring Russia to the gates of British India. Despite British protest, Persia invaded Afghanistan and in November 1837, lay siege to the fortified city of Herat, however, with the help of several British officers in the city, the Persians were held at bay.

The British envoy Sir John McNeill tried to convince Mohammad Shah to lift the siege, however, the Shah cited the 1814 treaty which stated that Britain would remain neutral in the event of Persia invading Afghanistan. In violation of the 1814 treaty, the British occupied Karg Island in the Persian Gulf and informed the Shah that Britain considered the occupation of Herat as a hostile act. In order to avoid a war with Britain, the Persian forces were forced to withdraw from Herat and adding insult to injury, Persia was forced to sign a trade treaty on terms favourable to Britain.

As Russia, France, Turkey and Britain became embroiled in the activities which would lead to the Crimean War; Russia tried to enlist the support of Persia by offering them the Ottoman territories of Baghdad and Erzerum. Mirza Aqa Khan Nuri, the grand vizier, persuaded the Shah that it would do more for Persian interests to side with the British, French and Turks rather than Russia. The Shah entered into negotiations with the British in the hope of getting assistance to recover their lands in the Caucasus. Being already at war with Russia in the Crimea, Britain declined to provide the requested assistance much to the disappointment of the Persians.

Troubles with the Persian government began to deepen when they objected to the appointment on 15th June 1854 of Meerza Hashim Khan as the first Persian secretary to the British Mission in Tehran, which resulted in the Persians confining Meerza Khan's wife to prison. Unable to resolve the issues, relationships between the British envoy Mr Murray and the Persian officials rapidly deteriorated until on the 17th November 1855, Mr Murray issued the ultimatum that if Meerza Khan's wife was not released by the 20th November, then he would break off diplomatic relations and evacuate the British Mission. Without an appropriate response from the Persians, true to his word, Mr Murray struck the flag at the mission on the 20th November and on 5th December 1855 withdrew the mission from Tehran.

With relations between Persia and Britain at an all time low and the Persian court buoyed up by the apparent success of the Russians at Kars in the Crimea, a new Persian mission against Herat was launched in February 1856. The Afghans were defeated at Ghosrian and Herat was once again besieged.

On the 11th July 1856, Lord Clarendon wrote to the Persian Prime Minister demanding that Persian troops be immediately withdrawn from Herat or the British Government would adopt other measures. At the same time, the Governor-General of India was instructed to assemble a force at Bombay suitable to occupy the island of Karrack and the city and district of Bushire in Persia.

On the 17th October, Ferokh Khan the Persia ambassador arrived at Constantinople and began negotiations with Lord Stratford de Redcliffe regarding the situation in Herat and after reaching broad agreement an ultimatum was issued to the Persian Government on 22nd November 1856. The ultimatum required Persia to evacuate Herat immediately, withdraw her troops and pay compensation for any damages done. A further demand was for a treaty where Persia recognised the independence of Afghanistan, would enter into a new trade agreement and recognise the right of Britain to appoint consuls in any part of Persia. It was also demanded that Sadr Azim, the Prime Minister, be replaced by a minister more likely to foster good relations between the two countries.

However, before the agreement, which had been agreed by Ferokh Khan, could be communicated to Tehran news of two significant events reached Constantinople that made this agreement null and void. The first was that Herat had fallen to the Persian forces on 20th October and was now occupied; the second was, that as a result of the occupation of Herat, following instructions from London, the Governor-General of India had on the 1st November 1856 declared war on Persia.

Britain and Persia at War

As early as July 1856, the Government in India had been requested to make ready a force for the invasion of Persia. London had considered two options; a land assault via Afghanistan was rejected in favour of on attack by sea via the Persian Gulf. With the general plan already agreed, by the time the declaration of war was issued preparations for the campaign only required the finishing touches.

The Quartermaster General in India, with a great deal of audacity had even sent Lieutenant J. Ballard, a superintendant of the Intelligence Department, to carry out an initial reconnaissance. The Lieutenant landed quite openly at Bushire and brazenly carried out a survey of the fortifications using a compass and measuring chains until he was asked to leave by the Persian Authorities.

The initial Expeditionary Force (later referred to as the 1st Division) was assembled at Bombay under the command of Major-General Foster Stalker and comprised 2,300 British Soldiers and 3,400 native Sepoys all from the Bombay Presidency Army and some men of the 64th Regiment of Foot. Brigadier Stopford and Brigadier Honnor commanded the two Infantry Brigades (H.M. 64th Foot, 2nd Bombay European Light Infantry, 2nd Balooch Battalion, 4th Bombay Native Infantry and 20th Bombay Native Infantry), Brigadier Tapp commanded the Cavalry (3rd Bombay Native Cavalry and Poona Horse) and Brigadier Trevelyan the Artillery (1st and 4th Company 1st Battalion Bombay Artillery, 3rd Troop Bombay Horse Artillery and 2nd and 4th Company Bombay Sappers & Miners).

Final instructions to despatch the force arrived at Bombay on the 9th November and due to the extent of the prior preparations, the Expeditionary Force left from Bombay and Karachi only four days later. They departed on board a flotilla, of seven steamships towing 30 sailing ships, commanded by Commodore Young, and by the 21st November the lead ship had reached the straits of Hormuz where over the next four days the transports assembled. It was agreed that the fleet would next assemble off the shore near Bushire; this was accomplished by the 30th November.

On the 4th of December, a small force was landed and captured the island of Kharag in the Persian Gulf, about 16 miles from the mainland.

On the 7th December, the Expeditionary Force landed almost completely unopposed at Halilah Bay a few miles south of the main Persian port at Bushire, where there was a plentiful supply of fresh water and over the next three days the troops were disembarked. By the evening of 7th December, the advance party had established a base at Halilah village and by the 8th December, sufficient forces and materials had been landed to commence operations on the next day.

Battle of Reshire

On the morning of the 9th December, the advanced guard began their march towards Bushire and by 9:30 a.m. had reached the village of Imamzadeh and the old Dutch fort of Reshire which was nearby.

Much to the surprise of the British advanced guard, the fort was occupied by a force of about 500 Persian troops, so they took up position on broken ground about 400 yards from the fort to await the arrival of the main force. The cavalry was posted to the right of their position in order to cut off any retreat towards Bushire and the guns were unlimbered to be ready for action.

After spotting the small British force, some of the Persians left the fort taking up positions in nearby ruined buildings and then began to advance in skirmishing formation on the British lines, however, with the arrival of the main British force they retreated back inside the fort.

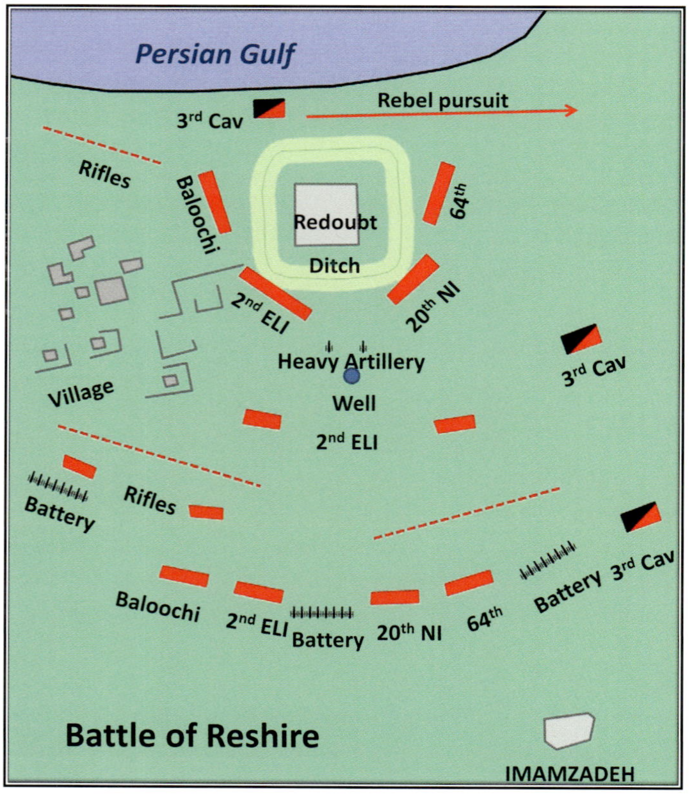

Figure 5. Battle of Reshire

Captain John Augustus Wood – Victoria Cross No. 112

Following a brief bombardment of the fort by the British artillery and the men-of-war, a frontal assault with fixed bayonets was made on the fort. To gain the walls, the force had to cross a ditch and climb an embankment of loose sand and stones; leading his brigade from the front Brigadier Stopford was shot dead by enemy fire just as he reached the crest of the embankment but undeterred, his men continued with the assault.

Captain Wood, leading a company of Grenadiers was one of the first men to reach the parapet of the fort where he was immediately attacked by a large group of the defenders. The enemy fired a musket volley at short range towards Captain Wood and his assault party but despite having been hit by seven musket balls, the Captain continued the charge and killed the leader of the group with his sword.

For this action Captain Wood was later awarded the Victoria Cross; two native soldiers, Subedar Major Mohamed Sherif and Sepoy Beer Bhut (who supported Captain Wood in his charge) were also recommended for the award, however, at this time they were ineligible and were both awarded the Indian Order of Merit instead.

The charge of the 64th Regiment of Foot, 20th Bombay Native Infantry and the 2nd European Bombay Infantry continued unabated and the enemy were driven from the fort and down the cliffs where many lost their lives trying to escape through the ravines. The British cavalry also gave chase to the fleeing enemy, killing many as they tried to make their escape, unfortunately a well loved officer Colonel G. G. Malet of the 3rd Bombay Cavalry was killed during this action.

After the battle, the Balooch regiment were left to guard the fort, while the remainder of the British force encamped at the village of Imamzadeh where they rested for the night.

Battle of Bushire

At 8 a.m. on the 10th December, while the fleet began to bombard the town, the British force began their advance on Bushire and it was not until they reached a point about a mile from the town that they came across any of the enemy.

As the British advanced the Persians abandoned their outer defences and retreated behind the walls of the town. After advancing to within 500 yards of the town walls, the British cavalry was deployed near the creek to cut off the most likely route of retreat but before an assault was mounted, the Persian garrison of about 2,000 men marched out of the town and surrendered their arms without firing a shot.

After leaving a small force to guard the Persians who were imprisoned in the town, the British force returned to their encampment at Imamzadeh.

Extended Reconnaissance

On the 20th December 1856, a small force was sent off to reconnoitre inland and by the 25th December had collected information that a Persian force of 4,000 men was gathered at Shiraz and that supply depots of food and ammunition had been established at Borazjun and Chah Kutah.

On the 1st January a British cavalry force, supported by Horse Artillery attacked and destroyed the enemy supply depot at Chah Kutah.

Further intelligence was gathered that a force of about 10,000 Persians with artillery support was being assembled with the intention of retaking Bushire. With the news of these large Persian forces it was agreed that the British should not move inland from the coast without reinforcements which were duly requested from Bombay.

The 2nd Division Campaign

At the outbreak of the war with Persia, Major-General Sir James Outram, of the Bombay Army, was in England on sick leave, however, when a request for reinforcements was made, he rapidly proceeded to India to take command of the new forces and assume overall command of operations in Persia.

On the 10th January 1856, Sir James Outram was given the temporary rank of Lieutenant-General while in charge of the Persian forces, Brigadier Tarol was appointed to the command of Cavalry for both divisions, Major-General Stalker retained his command of the 1st Division, already in Persia while Brigadier-General Havelock was appointed to the command of the new 2nd Division. General Havelock's second division was organised as follows; the first Infantry Brigade was commanded by Brigadier Hamilton (78th Highlanders and the 26th Bombay Native Light Infantry), the second Infantry Brigade was under the command of Brigadier Hale (23rd Bombay Native Light Infantry), Colonel Stuart commanded the Cavalry (14th King's Light Dragoons and Scinde Horse) while Brigadier Hill commanded the Artillery (4th Troop Bombay Horse Artillery and 2nd and 4th Bombay Foot Artillery).

The 78th Highlanders were stationed at Poona when the call to arms arrived and on the 7th & 8th January they began their journey to Bombay, halting at Khandalla from the 10th until the 18th awaiting transportation to complete their journey.

At the same time the various native regiments were also moving towards their embarkation ports. On the morning of the 19th January the 78th Highlanders were embarked upon the steamers *Precursor* and *Pottinger* with the light company on board the transport *Kingston*. The *Precursor* was set up to tow the *Earl of Clare* with the 26th Bombay Native Infantry on board and the *British Queen* which was loaded with artillery and stores. The *Pottinger* towed the *Kingston* with the 78th Light Company on board and the *Futteh Mombarrack* which was loaded with horses and forage. In the late afternoon of the 19th January, the ships had put to sea and by nightfall were well clear of the harbour and by daybreak on the 27th January had reached the Gulf of Ormuz.

The small flotilla was off the coast at Bushire on the 30th January and by the 1st February all troops had been disembarked and were warmly welcomed by their comrades of the 1st Division. Sir James Outram, who had travelled separately, with his staff, had arrived a few days earlier on the 20th January.

Attack on Borazjun

With his forces having arrived, General Outram decided to make an attack on Borazjun, where intelligence suggested the Persians were assembling a force to retake Bushire.

On the evening of the 3rd February, the General left Bushire with the 1st and 2nd Infantry Brigades of the 1st Division, all of the 2nd Division, 400 Cavalry, 18 artillery pieces and a detachment of 120 men from the Sappers and Miners; about 2,000 men were left to guard the camp at Bushire. The force travelled light without tents but with each man carrying cooked rations for two days, a further three days rations were carried by the commissariat. On the 4th February the force reached Chah Kutah, where there was plenty of fresh water, and rested for the day.

On the 5th February the force passed by Khush Ab and approached Borazjun from the south east in preparation for their attack and after gaining heights which overlooked the town observed the enemy force retreating to the north east with their departure being covered by the cavalry. Apart from some minor skirmishes between the opposing cavalry units, the town of Borazjun was taken unopposed and large quantities of stores and ammunition were captured.

With the enemy escaping to the Mulleh Pass and being short on provisions, General Outram decided not to pursue the Persians but instead ordered the force to return to Bushire. On the 7th February, after the captured powder and ammunition had been destroyed, the force began the march back towards Bushire but after advancing over difficult ground only managed to reach Khush Ab before being forced to call a halt.

Hearing that his rear guard was being attacked, General Outram rode back to investigate and when his horse fell he was slightly injured and incapacitated for a few hours and as the light was fading, the force moved off to a position about four miles from Khush Ab, where there was plenty of water, and set up camp for the night.

Battle of Khushab

During the night, the British camp was surrounded and the enemy, kept up a fusillade with their cavalry charging up to the line and firing before moving away. The British troops adopted a square formation with guns placed at regular intervals with the baggage and followers secured in the centre, and rested while they could until daylight. In the early hours of the morning on the 8th of February, there was a short exchange of artillery fire but to little effect.

At daybreak, the enemy were drawn up in line, on rising ground to the rear of the British position. The enemy who numbered 6,000 infantry and 2,000 cavalry had their left flank on the walled city of Khush Ab and their left flank on a hamlet. The British guns were moved to the front and fired on the enemy while the cavalry swept around the base of the hill and charged the Persian cavalry on the left of their line. The Persian cavalry did not wait to engage their British counterparts but instead retreated back towards the Mulleh Pass.

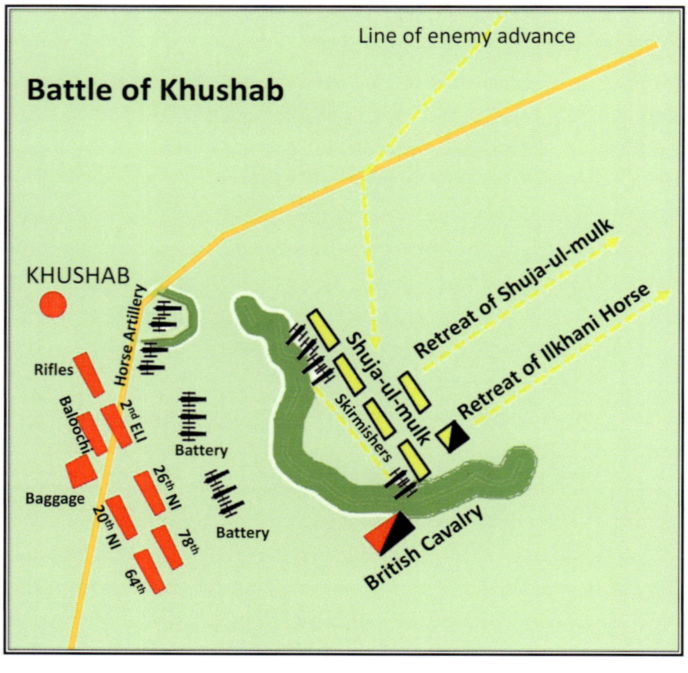

Figure 6. Battle of Khushab

The first line of British infantry managed to scale the hill almost without loss and after some close order fighting managed to silence the enemy artillery, but not before damage had been done to the second lines who were hit by shot fired over the heads of the first line.

Lieutenant John Grant Malcolmson – Victoria Cross No. 113
Lieutenant Arthur Thomas Moore – Victoria Cross No. 114

With the enemy cavalry having fled the field, the attention of the British Cavalry became focused on the infantry who were drawn up in square formations, the appropriate way to fend off a cavalry charge. Undeterred, Captain Forbes ordered his squadrons to charge the square of about 500 Persian soldiers.

The charge was vividly described by an officer in a letter to a Calcutta newspaper: '*When Forbes, who commanded this regiment, gave the order to charge, he and his adjutant, young Moore, placed themselves in front of the 6th troop, which was the one directly opposite the nearest face of the square. The other Moore [Ross], Malcolmson, and Spens came the least thing behind, riding knee to knee, with spurs in their horses flanks, as if racing after a hog.*

In the rear of them rushed the dark troopers of the 3rd, mad to avenge the death of poor Malet at Bushire. In spite of steel, fire, and bullets they tore down upon the nearest face of the devoted square. As they approached, Forbes was shot through the thigh and Spens horse wounded; but, unheeding, they swept onward.

Daunted by the flashes, and the fire, and the noise, and crackle of the musketry, the younger Moore's horse swerved as they came up. Dropping his sword from his hand and letting it hang by the knot at his wrist, he caught up the reins in both hands, screwed his head straight, and then coolly, as if riding at a fence, leapt him at the square.

If, therefore, any man can be said to have been the first, the younger Moore is that man. Of course the horse fell stone dead upon the bayonets; so did his brother's, ridden with equal courage and determination. The elder Moore – 18 stone in weight, and 6 ft. 3 in. or thereabouts, in height – cut his way out on foot.

Malcolmson took one foot out of his stirrup when he saw his brother officer down and unarmed (for his sword had been broken to pieces by the fall), and, holding on to that, the younger Moore escaped.

The barrier once broken, and the entrance once made, in and through it poured the avenging troopers. On and over everything they rode, till, getting clear out, they re-formed on the other side, wheeled, and swept back – a second wave of ruin.

Out of 500 Persian soldiers of the 1st Regular Regiment of Fars, who composed that fated square, only twenty escaped to tell the tale of its destruction. Thus the 3rd Light Cavalry, to use their own phrase, gave our enemies a jewab (answer) for the death of Malet Sahib Bahadur.'

For their part in this almost unique successful cavalry charge against and infantry square, Lieutenants Malcolmson and Moore were both awarded the Victoria Cross.

The enemy infantry was much shaken up by the charge of the British cavalry and together with the effective fire of the British artillery this broke the enemy ranks and they fled after throwing down their arms. The enemy were pursued by the cavalry and horse artillery for several miles before returning back to camp.

The Persians lost about 700 men killed during the battle, with British casualties being two officers and 18 men killed and four officers and 60 men wounded.

After the battle heavy rain began to fall, which continued for several days, forcing the British to establish a camp near the battlefield before marching back to the base at Bushire. The remainder of February was spent at Bushire, awaiting the arrival of the remainder of the 2nd Division who had been delayed by the bad weather, however, the time was spent in improving the defences and planning for an expedition to Muhammareh.

In the first week of March 1856, a small force consisting of a troop of horse artillery, a troop of 14th Dragoons, a wing of the 26 Bombay Native Infantry and detachment of the 64th Regiment and 78th Highlanders boarded ships for the 36 hour sea voyage to Muhammareh.

On the 14th March, General Stalker committed suicide and was replaced by General Jacob as the commander at Bushire, while General Outram took command of the expedition to Muhammareh.

On the 19th March a further force set sail from Bushire bound for Muhammareh bringing the total expeditionary force to a total of nearly 4,900 men, including 1,500 European Infantry, 2,400 Native Infantry and 340 artillerymen with 12 guns. The force was conveyed on 21 transports and 8 steamers with four armed steamers and two men of war in support.

After all of the delays, the expeditionary force eventually came together off the coast of Muhammareh between 21st and 23rd March. On the 24th March, the fleet moved off to the second rendezvous point off Hartheh and preparations were made for the bombardment of Muhammareh, which included the construction of a raft on which were placed several mortars.

Action at Muhammareh

At daylight on the 26th March, the bombardment of the town commenced and when the guns were silenced the transports moved in to disembark a landing force. When the 78th Highlanders, Grenadiers of the 64th, Scinde Horse, 14th Dragoons and some horse artillery had been landed, General Outram decided to begin the advance against the Persian positions, men of the 23rd and 26th Native regiments would soon join them. As the British advanced, their naval war ships began a bombardment of the town with their 68 pounder guns, to devastating effect.

When the British infantry got within range of the Persian lines, the enemy literally vanished and the British advanced into the Persian camp unopposed. In the camp, the tents were still standing and the ground was strewn with arms and ammunition that had been abandoned; large quantities of grain, flour and 18 brass guns were also captured.

The lack of sufficient cavalry prevented the British force from pursuing the fleeing Persians so they occupied the town instead.

Action at Ahwaz

The Haffar channel to the north of Muhammareh was navigable to some of the smaller British vessels, but the shore was very difficult terrain for cavalry and artillery. It was therefore decided to pursue the enemy and destroy their magazines at Ahwaz by an expedition up the river by steamer. On the 28th March, 150 from the 64th regiment and 150 men from the 78th Highlanders were boarded on three steamers, 100 men to a boat, and set off up river at sunset the steamers anchored off the ruined fort at Kutal-al-Abd where the men rested for the night.

Setting off again on the 30th March, the force halted for a second time off the village of Ismaini where they received news that a Persian force of 7 regiments with 2,000 cavalry and four guns had passed through on the previous day. On the next morning the force set off again and when they reached Kut-al-Amaireh in the evening, they received the news that the Persians had reached Ahwaz on the 30th March but had not yet crossed the river. The British force set off again in the early morning of the 1st April and by first light were within sight of Ahwaz where the Persian army was sighted drawn up on the right bank of the river behind a ridge.

After closing to within 3,000 yards of the village some of the locals advised the British that the village was guarded by a garrison of only 500 men. At 10 o'clock in the morning, the British landed their men at three locations and advancing in a single line, to confuse the Persians that their number was greater than it was, approached the enemy lines.

With covering fire from the boats, the advance continued and instead of engaging in battle the Persians fled abandoning their supplies. A large amount of flour was captured, much of it placed on the boats to be carried away while the remainder was distributed to the villagers. Fifteen cases of flintlocks, 56 mules and a large number of sheep were also taken.

At about noon, the British fired shells at a nearby mosque where the main enemy force of about 10,000 men was located, the Persian commander, taking this small British force to be the advance guard of General Outram's main force decided to retire and moved off towards Shushtar. As the British steamer could progress no further up the river, due to some bunds, they could not pursue the rebels further and the next day headed back down river to Muhammareh.

The War Ends

On the 4th April, when General Outram arrived back at Muhammareh with his force, he received the news that a peace treaty had been signed on the 4th March in Paris and that hostilities were to be ended.

At the end of April, General Outram, after leaving his troops at Muhammareh, visited Kharag and Bushire and after receiving the consent of General Jacob to take over command of the troops set out for Baghdad to make arrangements for the Persian exit from Herat. Outram finally left Persia on 17th June to return to India. In early May, the troops at Muhammareh began their return to India, however, Bushire was occupied until October and Kharag was not evacuated until February 1858.

Under the terms of the Paris treaty, Persia agreed to withdraw her troops from Herat and relinquish all claims to sovereignty over the region and abstain from any interference in the internal affairs of Afghanistan. The Persians also agreed to suppress their slave trade on the Persian Gulf.

From a British perspective the war in Persia provided officers and men with valuable experience which was soon employed to fight the Indian Mutiny.

4

THE WAGHER UPRISING IN KATHIAWAR

The Wagher uprising is often included within accounts of the Indian Mutiny, probably for reasons of convenience more than anything else. A close examination of the events makes it clear that despite occurring in the same timeframe, the uprising was unconnected with the Indian Mutiny and should therefore be handled separately.

At the time of these events, the Kathiawar peninsular, which was sub divided into the regions of Halar, Jhalaad, Sorath and Gohelwad, was part of Western Gujarat. Most of the princely states of Kathiawar had been part of a British Protectorate since 1820 and was populated by various Rajput clans, collectively known as the Kathi, hence the name of the region.

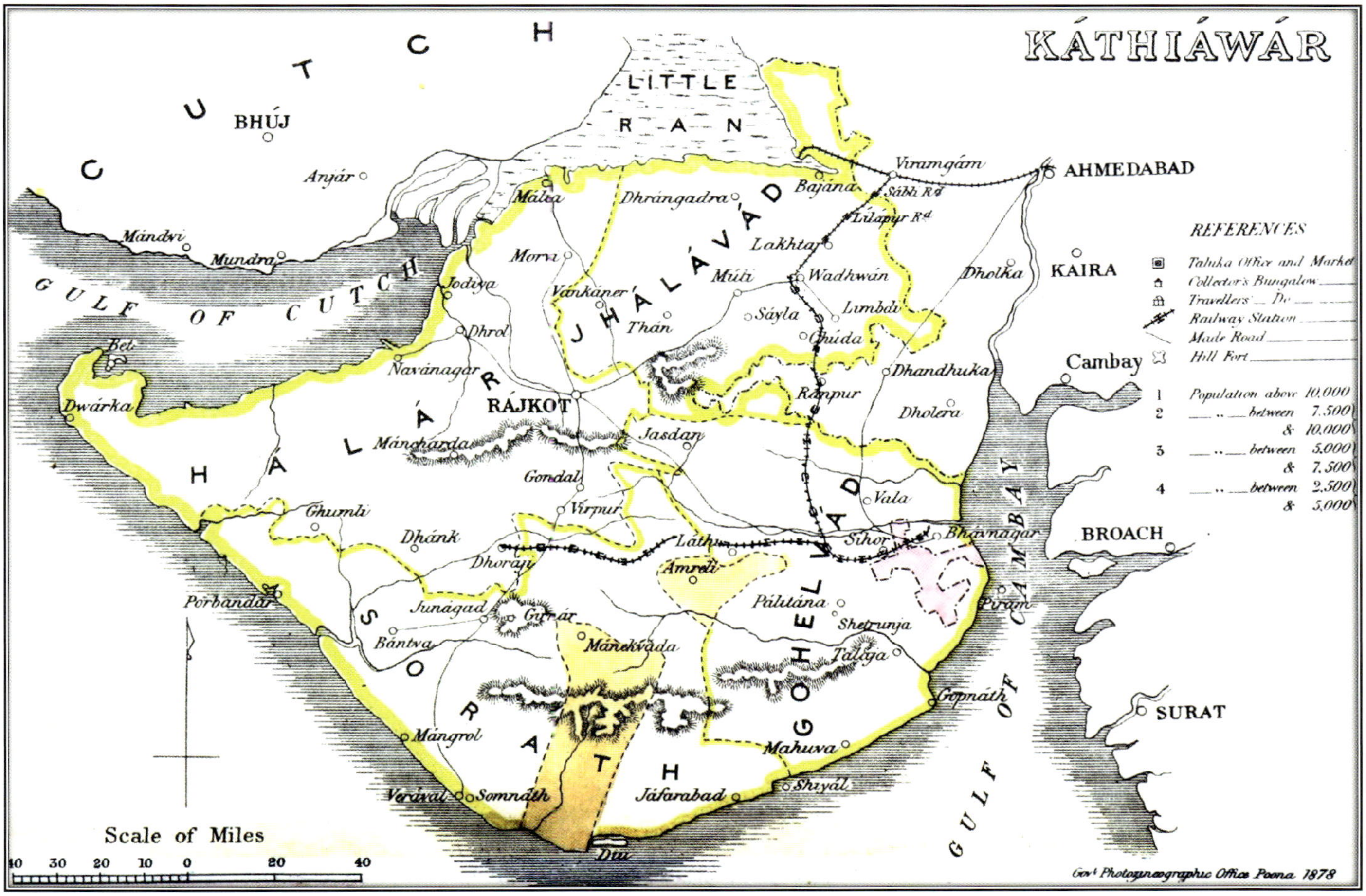

Figure 7. Kathiawar

For many decades the peninsular was thought to be the most lawless region in the whole of India with various clans operating as outlaws marauding against the other clans, who would counter with revenge raids. To some extent, the presence of British forces helped to quieten things down as the bandits knew that if they were captured then they would face harsh punishments. The days of the freebooters were over but three main bands of bandits still existed.

The first was the Kathi, who used the Gir Forest as a place of refuge but after the capture of their leader Sadul Khasia in 1838 they ceased to exist as a force. The other two groups were the Waghers of Okhamandal and the Mianas of Malia.

The Waghers had always been a race of robbers and when the British outlawed and abolished piracy they became highwaymen. In 1817, the British handed over Okhamandal to the Gaewad of Baroda and the leading Waghers who had been deprived of their lands were given a pension. However, in 1857 when the Baroda Government caused some disruption to the pension, the recipients were only too pleased to create a disturbance. This uprising was only put down after the arrival of British troops under the command of Lieutenant Barton. After this action, it was decided that the Government of Baroda should be responsible for conducting its own operations against future disturbances of the peace and Lieutenant Barton's force was withdrawn.

In early 1858, the Waghers rose again and occupied the fort on the island of Beyt. A small force of men from the 10th and 16th Bombay Native Infantry under the command of Captain Bayly was despatched from Karachi on board the HEIC steamer *Prince Arthur*. An attempted to dislodge the rebels from the fort was carried out on the 3rd April. The force was unable to take the fort, however, after some negotiations the rebels surrendered the fort and moved off during the night.

In September 1859, perhaps emboldened by the British occupation with the mutiny, the Waghers rose en masse under the leadership of Jodho Manik and seized the whole of Okhamandal.

Once again a British force was despatched from Karachi, the Okhamandal Field Force under the command of Colonel Donovan. The field force with a total of 1,350 men was made up of a wing of the 28th Regiment of Foot, wings of the 6th and 17th Bombay Native Infantry, a detachment of the Marine Battalion and No. 4 Company of the Bombay Sappers and Miners under the command of Lieutenant Goodfellow. A secondary force under the command of Colonel Scribe was ordered to march from Rajkot to Dwarka, however, they were delayed.

On reaching the island of Beyt, a major offensive was launched from both sea and land, with the warships *HMS Empress of India*, *HMS Victoria* and *HMS Clive* laying down a heavy bombardment on the fort.

Lieutenant Charles Goodfellow – Victoria Cross No. 296

Despite the heavy naval bombardment of the fort, the walls remained surprisingly intact due to their massive structure, being between 18 to 40 feet thick and between 30 and 40 feet high. The British assault force was also hampered by the fact that their scaling ladders were too short for the task at hand.

During the unsuccessful assault, on the 6th October 1859, Lieutenant Goodfellow, under heavy musket fire from the fort rushed to the walls to bring a wounded soldier of the 28th Regiment to safety (unfortunately the soldier later died of his wounds).

For this action Lieutenant Goodfellow was later awarded the Victoria Cross.

The failed assault was at a heavy cost to the British force with two officers and 22 men killed and two officers and 45 men wounded. The rebel leader Deva Chhabani was also killed and with the death of their leader, the Waghers abandoned the fort and moved off to Dwarka where they took up refuge in another fort. The British force occupied the fort at Beyt and over the next few days this was reduced to rubble by the Engineers.

Colonel Donovan now moved his force towards the fort at Dwarka and after a heavy bombardment from the warships *HMS Zonabia* and *HMS Firoz* on the 31st October 1859 the rebels were defeated, however, a large force of rebels, under the leadership of Jodha Manek and Mulu Manek, escaped to the Abhapara hills where they continued the fighting.

A force under the command of General Honner, comprising men from the 1st Grenadiers, 11th, 14th and 17th Bengal Native Infantry, the Marine Battalion and detachments from the 2nd Bombay Light cavalry and the Bengal Sappers and Miners was sent against the rebels and by the end of the year had dispersed them.

After being dislodged from the hills a small force of the rebels escaped by sea and made their way to Sutrapada where they were joined by other outlaws and malcontents who continued to ravage the Gaewad territory and on 8th October 1860 captured Kodinar. Soon afterwards, the rebel leader Jodha Manek died from a fever. The rebels continued to cause minor acts of banditry until they were finally eliminated in 1868.

5

TARANAKI WAR, MAORI, NEW ZEALAND (1860–61)

Reasons for the War

As the 1850s were drawing to a close, the number of settlers on the North Island of New Zealand was approaching that of the indigenous Maori population; and they were becoming desperate for more land to farm. With the withdrawal of the 58th Regiment of Foot from the colony in October 1858, the military forces in New Zealand were limited to one regiment of troops, the 65th Regiment of Foot.

Figure 8. New Zealand (North Island)

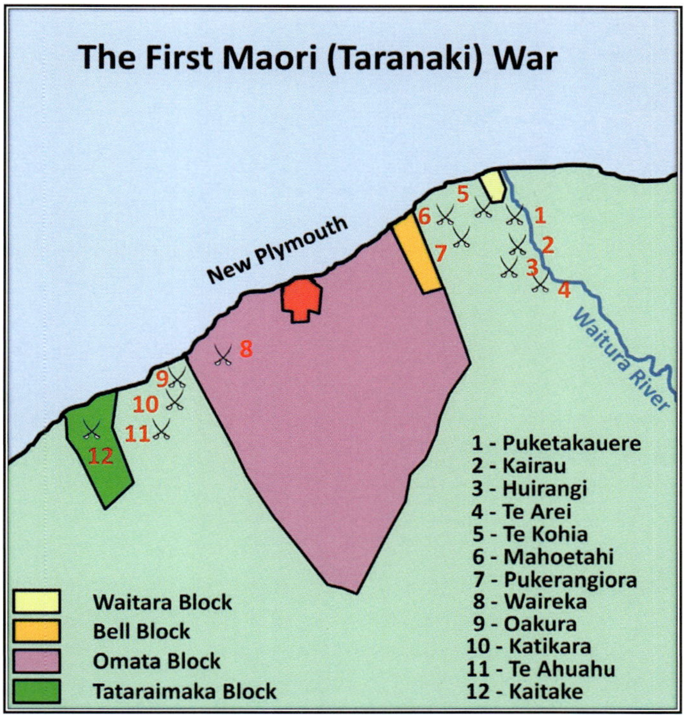

Figure 9. First Maori War

In 1859, a minor Maori chief, Te Teira, offered the Pekapeka block of land at Waitara for sale to the British Government, which in principle was accepted by Governor Gore Browne despite the fact that the sale had not been approved by the paramount chief William King.

After some initial skirmishes in February 1860, Governor Browne declared martial law in Taranaki and initiated the sale of the land block. On 4th March Governor Browne ordered Colonel Charles Emilius Gold, the commander of the British troops (65th Regiment), Taranaki Militia, and Rifle Volunteers, to occupy the block and prepare for surveying.

On the night of 15th March the Maoris built a Pa (defensive stockade) on the land, the Te Kohia which became known as the 'L' shaped Pa.

Start of Hostilities

On March 17th, without determining whether the Maoris had the right to build this defensive fort or not, Colonel Gold ordered his men to open fire on the Pa, using shot, shell and rockets.

There were few casualties, however, as the British forces had initiated the use of force, under Maori law they were deemed to be in the wrong and this encouraged many of the other Maori chiefs to join in the conflict. In response to their ill treatment at the 'L' shaped Pa, a force of about 500 Maori marched to the New Plymouth area and built the Kaipopo Pa near the Waireka river, about six miles from New Plymouth.

On 5th March 1860, prior to the arrival of the Maoris, a force of about 200 men from the 65th Regiment of Foot under the command of Colonel Murray was landed at New Plymouth by *HMS Niger* and her Captain Peter Cracroft, left some of his men to help with the operation of artillery.

HMS Niger, returned to Auckland to pick up more supplies but when they arrived back at New Plymouth on 28th March, Captain Cracroft was requested by Governor Gore Brown to land a party of his men to help defend the town. Captain Cracroft willingly acceded to the Governor's request and landed an impromptu "Naval Brigade" of about 60 sailors and marines.

Soon afterwards, Colonel Murray and his men left on a mission to bring outlying settlers back to the safety of the town. However, it was not long before Captain Cracroft received a request from Colonel Murray for reinforcements and ammunition, as he had been attacked by a band of Maoris soon after setting out on his mission.

Captain Cracroft and his naval brigade set out for the blockhouse at Omata, to await the arrival of ammunition and here they came across some of the men from *HMS Niger*, who had been with the mission. One of the men, Lieutenant William Hans Blake was badly wounded by a musket ball in the chest which had struck him near the heart. After sending on the requested ammunition to Colonel Murray, Captain Cracroft, who had a commanding view of the Kaipopo Pa from his position at the blockhouse, began to formulate a plan to assault the Pa.

Assault on the Kaipopo Pa

At about 5:30, just as the light was beginning to fade, Captain Cracroft moved his men to within 800 yards of the Pa and set up his rocket tube which was used to fire on the stockade. After having fired about six rockets, to little effect, a messenger arrived from Colonel Murray, stating that he was withdrawing back to the town and because of the failing light, suggested that he did the same. However, instead of retiring, the Captain decided to mount an assault on the Pa, despite the arrival of night and the lack of support.

Leading Seaman William Odgers – Victoria Cross No. 297

After advancing to within 60 yards, the naval brigade, armed with cutlass and revolver, charged at the heavily fortified Pa, using the cover of darkness to surprise the Maori warriors.

Seaman Odgers was involved in a flanking attack and was the first man to breach the palisades, and strike down one of the enemy flags. Once inside the compound, the small force, who were experienced in close quarter combat after their time in China, caused mayhem and the Maori fled the Pa and escaped into the darkness.

For his part in the action Leading Seaman Odgers was later awarded the Victoria Cross.

With insufficient men to hold onto the Kaipopo Pa, Captain Cracroft returned with his men to New Plymouth.

Destruction of Warea Pa

On 30th March 1860, again at the request of Governor Gore Browne, *HMS Niger* sailed 20 miles south to destroy the Warea Pa, where the fugitives from the Kaipopo Pa were thought to be sheltering. After finding a suitable anchorage *HMS Niger*, at a range of 2,000 yards, fired one of her 68 pounder cannons at the Pa. The first shot fell short, which warned the Maoris and allowed them to escape before the second shot fell on target and set fire to the Pa.

General Pratt's Expedition

With less than 1,000 men to defend the whole of the New Zealand North Island, Colonel Gold could do little in the way of proactive operations against the Maori, until the arrival of the requested reinforcements from Australia.

The request for reinforcements was directed to General Thomas Simpson Pratt, commander of British forces in the Australian colonies.

On April 5th 1860, the Governor General of New South Wales, Sir William Denison, telegraphed to Melbourne that he was willing to lend some of his troops, should General Pratt require them. The colony of Victoria, placed the *HMS Victoria* at the General's disposal, for use in the transportation of troops. General Pratt was very quick to respond to the request for reinforcements and on the 10th April, a small detachment of the 12th Regiment of Foot, with some artillery, set sail from Sydney. A week later the *SS City of Hobart* left Melbourne with two companies of the 40th Regiment.

The arrival of these new troops in May 1860, increased the British strength in the Taranaki district to about 1,700 men. Major Nelson commanded the largest detachment, based at camp Waitara, which comprised 300 men of the 40th Regiment of Foot plus a few men of the Royal Artillery and Royal Engineers. The Maoris occupied the Puketakauere Pa, about 2,000 yards from the British camp.

Believing that the Maoris were intruding on the British land, Major Nelson ordered an attack on the Pa, which took place with disastrous results on the morning of 27th June.

Despite the bravery of the men and officers involved, the British force was completely defeated leaving about 30 men, missing, killed or wounded on the field; they returned to camp with a further 32 wounded men. After receiving news of the disaster on 12th July, General Pratt immediately ordered the despatch of further reinforcements from Sydney and resolved to go to New Zealand and take direct control of operations.

Leaving from Melbourne with his staff, on board *HMS Victoria* on 24th July, the General arrived at New Plymouth on 3rd August and took control of the British forces, which by now included almost 3,500 men from Australia, however these were distributed across all of the North Island of New Zealand.

As soon as he landed, General Pratt set about improving the defences of New Plymouth, surrounding the town with a ditch and parapet. On the 22nd August, the General set sail on board *HMS Victoria* bound for Auckland, for discussions with the Governor regarding the best way to bring the war to a conclusion.

One of the General's aims was to get help from the Governor in removing the settlers from New Plymouth, as they were hindering military operations and were reluctant to leave. After some help in this matter, a steamer was eventually provided and 600 women and children were moved to Nelson.

On 27th August, Major Hutchins, the commander at Waireka, reported that the Maori had abandoned the Pa opposite his camp and that he had destroyed it. With the threat at Waireka no longer present, on his return to New Plymouth on 28th August, General Pratt ordered Major Hutchins and his men to return, to bolster the garrison of the town.

On the 29th August, news was received that the Maori had also abandoned the Puketakauere Pa at Waitara, however, intelligence was received on 3rd September, that the Maori had established a new Pa at Burton's Hill near Omata and General Pratt decided that an attempt should be made to try and surround them.

Accordingly three columns, with about 250 men in each column, were despatched at midnight on the 3rd September, one to advance on the Pa by daybreak and the other two set out to cut off the likely routes of retreat. However, when the force reached the Pa, they found it to have already been abandoned, foundations has been dug and building material collected but the Pa had yet to be constructed. The work had been abandoned when news of the advancing British force reached the Maori.

On the 8th September 1860, further intelligence was received that a large body of Maori, William King's Waitara tribe reinforced by the Ngatiruanui from Taranaki, had occupied three Pas at Ngatiparirua, Kairau and Huirahgi. The Huirahgi Pa was located in the midst of almost impenetrable jungle, however, the other two were in the open on a plain in front of the jungle.

After leaving a garrison to guard New Plymouth, General Pratt set off with a force of 750 men and after camping for the night at Mahoetahi, the Pa of a friendly chief, he was joined by a force of 300 men from the camp at Waitara. Moving off the next night the force arrived at the location of the two Pas and instead of finding an open plain, found broken ground situated between two rivers that was crossed by deep gullies and covered by marsh and a tangle of ferns and brambles.

Despite the poor ground, the men of the 65th Regiment began to advance in line of skirmish but encountered none of the enemy. After firing a few shells into the Pas both were set alight and it appeared that once again the Maori had abandoned their positions in the face of the British advance.

On the 2nd October a field force of 950 men; from the 12th, 40th and 65th Regiments, the Naval Brigade, Royal Artillery and Engineers together with 150 native from friendly tribes; was assembled at New Plymouth for operations to the south on the Kahihi river.

Due to heavy rains which made the rivers un-fordable, the departure of the force was delayed until 9th October but once started the column made good progress with the men of the Naval Brigade dragging an 8" gun. The force camped for the night on the Tartaraimaka block and the next morning began their advance on the enemy positions and after covering difficult ground, crossing the Katikara river and numerous ravines, eventually made camp at the sea near the Mangakuio creek less than a mile from Kahihi.

The Maori occupied three nearby Pas at Orongomailhanghai, Mataiaio and Pukekakariki. After setting up his camp, General

Pratt sent out two parties of 100 men to reconnoitre the Pukekakariki Pa, one party advanced up the coast while the other proceeded along the Mangakuio creek. The path along the creek, crossed by numerous ravines and overgrown with dense brambles was deemed to be impractical for an attack, however, the route along the coast proved to be free of any obstructions and as a bonus, the Orongomailhanghai Pa, which had been covered by the bush, was discovered.

On the 11th October, a working party numbering about 400 men, carrying gabion baskets, advanced along the coast towards the Orongomailhanghai Pa and after drawing out the line of a trench established a defence with the gabions. While under the constant fire of the Maoris the British troops advanced their trenches towards the Pa but when they got to within striking distance, the Maori deserted the place and the British advanced on the Mataiaio Pa which had also been abandoned. The Pukekakariki Pa was occupied and then all three Pas were destroyed.

With news from Auckland that the Maoris were now congregating at the Waitara, the British proceeded to return to New Plymouth, which they reached on 13th October, rather than continue operations in the south.

On his arrival back at New Plymouth, General Pratt ordered the camp at Waitara to be reinforced and a stockade at the old Puketakauere to be established and garrisoned by 50 men with a month's supply of food, this was completed by the end of the month.

On the 6th November, General Pratt intended to establish another stockade at the old Mahoetahi Pa but on the 5th November he received the news that the Maori, men from the northern tribes, had reoccupied the Pa on the previous day. As the force was estimated to be between 1,600 and 2,000 they could not be left unmolested so General Pratt directed two columns to advance against them; a column of 620 men from New Plymouth under the command of the General and a column of 280 men from Waitara under the command of Colonel Mould.

General Pratt arrived at Mahoetahi, in advance of Colonel Mould who had been delayed but with his forces, including two 24 pounder howitzers, in place the General decided to attack. For once the Maori decide to face the British, rather than retreat, and suffered heavy losses which were increased by the arrival of Colonel Mould's force just as they began their retreat. After burying the dead, the British force built the intended stockade and Colonel Mould and his force was left to form a garrison while General Pratt and his force returned to New Plymouth.

When news of the victory, with over 100 Maori warriors killed, reached Auckland, a request was sent to General Pratt for 400 troops to reinforce Auckland, who feared a reprisal attack following the losses to the northern tribes. The requested troops arrived at Auckland, on board *HMS Niger* and *HMS Victoria* on the 13th October.

With his forces having been considerably reduced by the reinforcements sent to Auckland and a detachment of 200 men sent to Ngapuke-turua to construct a new stockade, General Pratt could do little in the way of operations against the Maori until the return of his men.

General Pratt was convinced that if a general uprising across all of the tribes of the North Island was to be prevented, his campaign in the Taranaki district would have to be successfully concluded before the start of the rainy season in April and to achieve this aim had been requesting a resupply of troops and ordnance for months. In this regard, matters took a turn for the better when on 1st December men from the 14th Regiment arrived from England and four days later on the 5th December, the troops sent to Auckland returned to New Plymouth.

In early December, intelligence was received that the Maori were constructing a new Pa at Matororikoiko between the Pa at Huirahgi and the British camp at Waitara. Torrential rains delayed operations until 28th December when a new field force of 1,320 men was assembled at the camp at Waitara in preparation for an attack on the Pukerangioria Pa. In the early morning of the 29th December, the force set out for Kairau where it was intended to establish a permanent post in preparation for an attack on the Matororikoiko Pa.

On reaching a position, about 800 yards from the Pa, the British force began the work of constructing a stockade, which continued unopposed until about 9 o'clock in the morning when the Maori began to fire on the works, keeping up a continuous fire until 7 o'clock in the evening. With the works suitably advanced, a force of about 450 men; from the 12th and 40th Regiments, with detachments of the Royal Artillery, Royal Engineers and Naval Brigade; were left to garrison the stockade while the remainder of the force returned to the camp at Waitara.

In the evening of the 30th December, the 65th Regiment relieved the men of the 40th in the garrison and on the morning of the 31st December, after finding the Pa to have been abandoned it was occupied by the British and destroyed while a new stockade was constructed.

The Maori retreated to the Pas at Huirahgi, Manutahi and Mataitawa in the middle of the forest and sent envoys to the south to encourage other tribes to concentrate at Waireka, threatening New Plymouth in the hope that the British would either have to split its forces or suspend operations at Waitara.

In early January 1861, following the arrival of more men from the 14th and 65th Regiments at Auckland, a detachment of about

200 men was despatched and joined the field force on the 15th January.

General Pratt continued his strategy of containing and disrupting the Maori by establishing stockades, this time numbered and called redoubts, placing his forces in a position of his choosing rather than making attacks against Pas in locations favourable to his enemy.

No. 1 redoubt was established at Kairau and then on the 14th January a smaller redoubt No. 2, only 26 yards square but capable of holding 100 men with one gun, was built 600 yards to the front of No. 1 and a day later No. 3 was constructed a further 500 yards ahead of No. 2, close to the edge of the bush. During the construction of No. 3 redoubt, the works were under constant enemy artillery fire from the forest followed by occasional volleys of musket fire. On the 19th and 20th January, troops were used to enlarge No. 3 redoubt which it was now planned to garrison with 450 men.

With the advance of the redoubts it was evident that there was disagreement in the ranks of the Maori chiefs, with most taking the view that they must take some decisive action and it was reported that they planned an attack on No. 3 redoubt on the night of the 21st January. The night of the 21st January passed without incident so on the next day the men began making their approach to the site for the location of the next redoubt and perhaps because of the reduction of the garrison the Maoris made a determined attack on No. 3 redoubt on the morning of the 23rd January. The garrison, commanded by Colonel Leslie, managed to keep the enemy at bay though they did try to scale the parapets. Colonel Wyatt, in command of No 1 redoubt sent men from the 12th and 65th Regiments to the aid of No. 3 redoubt and the combined force routed the Maori, inflicting heavy casualties.

Work continued on extending the line of redoubts, No. 4 a small redoubt for 50 men was completed on the 27th January and No. 5, for 100 men was completed on the 29th January. On the 2nd February, the first line of enemy rifle pits in the forest was reached and work on a large redoubt to accommodate 450 men with two 24 pounder and one 8" gun was started. This redoubt, No. 6 was completed the next day and garrisoned by men of the 65th Regiment and detachments from the Naval Brigade, Royal Artillery and Royal Engineers. Occupation of No. 6 redoubt forced the Maori to retire deeper into the forest and occupy positions at Te Area and Pukerangioria.

After clearing about five acres of trees to give the flank of the No. 6 redoubt a good field of fire, the British force continued their advance towards the new enemy position and at a point about 800 yards from their lines began to construct No. 7 redoubt. Because this redoubt was so close to the forest, it was essential that the work was completed before nightfall so that a garrison could be installed. Despite having a perimeter of 240 yards the work was completed on time and units from the other redoubts were used to form a temporary garrison. For the next night and day, work continued to raise the height of the parapet after which it was garrisoned by men from the 40th Regiment and some of the older redoubts; No. 2 to No. 5 were abandoned.

Trenches were now advanced towards the Te Area Pa but on the night of the 26th February the Maori managed to pull down 100 yards of the works, setting fire to the gabions. For the next two days the British repaired the damage and established No. 8 redoubt about 300 yards from the Pa with a garrison of 80 men to guard the works. A further attack on the works was made during the night of the 5th March, however, this was repulsed by the British forces and by the 11th March the entrenchment had reach to within 200 yards of the Pa.

Also on the 11th March, chief Tamahana the acknowledged leader of the Maori movement arrived at the Te Area Pa and sent a message to General Pratt requesting a truce while he consulted with other chiefs regarding a peace. Perhaps cynically, having just received new from Auckland that Armstrong guns and mortars had at last arrived and would be with him in a few days, General Pratt agreed to the request and hostilities were suspended until the afternoon of 14th March by which time the guns had arrived and were in position. Having received no acceptable terms from the Maoris, work was restarted on the 15th March and No. 7 redoubt was enlarged to hold the battery of artillery.

Colour Sergeant John Lucas – Victoria Cross No. 298

The last action of the war was fought on the afternoon of the 18th March 1861, Colour-Sergeant Lucas was acting as Sergeant to a party of skirmishers to the right of No. 7 redoubt, when at 4 o'clock his men were assailed by a heavy enemy fire from the bush to their left. Three men were soon wounded, two of them mortally and help was called for to carry them back to the redoubt, the reinforcements had just arrived when one of them was also wounded, together with Lieutenant Rees.

Although only 30 yards from the enemy line, Colour-Sergeant Lucas ran to the aid of his officer and sent him back to the rear with another soldier. Using the arms of the killed and wounded men the Colour-Sergeant provided covering fire until support under the command of Lieutenants Gibson and Whelan arrived.

For this action Colour-Sergeant Lucas was later awarded the Victoria Cross.

End of the War

On the same day, Mr McLean accompanied by some influential Nga-Puki chiefs arrived and at the request of Chief Tamahana, a truce was granted on the morning of the 19th March to discuss terms but although seeming to agree with Mr McLean's proposals they requested a delay until the next day. On the next morning all of the Maoris except their chiefs had disappeared and negotiations were delayed further until 27th March when the Governor arrived to take charge of the negotiations. However, with the war effectively concluded, on 31st March General Cameron arrived to assume command of the forces in New Zealand and General Pratt returned to resume his command of the forces in Australia.

The main outcome of the war was that the British Government increased the size of the garrison in the New Zealand colony so as to be in a better position to deal with any future trouble from the Maori tribes.

The fact that the Maori issues with the sale of their land were never resolved, ensured that trouble would rear its head again at some time in the future.

6

THE SECOND CHINA WAR (1856–60)

The second China War, is sometimes called the 2nd Anglo-China War, which is not quite accurate as France, Russia and even the USA were also involved in the conflict. The war is also known as the Second Opium War, which is again inaccurate; yes one of the objectives was to secure the lucrative Opium trade with China but it was also about the much wider objective of opening up China to tariff free trade between Europe and China. Finally the war is also known as the "Arrow War", in reference to the ship whose detainment by China was used as an excuse to start the war.

Origins of the War

The First China War (1839–42), which was concluded with the Treaty of Nanking[2] signed on 29th August 1842, granted trading concessions to Britain and opened up five ports.[3] However, despite this, it did not lead to the improved trade and diplomatic relations with China that Britain desired. It was the failure of this treaty that ultimately led to the Second China War.

The French and Americans were also looking to China as a place for the expansion of their overseas markets and their treaties, respectively; the Treaty of Huangpu (signed on 24th October 1844) and the Wangxia Treaty (signed on 4th July 1844); crucially contained clauses for renegotiation after an initial 12 year term.

In an effort to improve their superiority in China, Britain demanded that the Qing government renegotiate the Treaty of Nanking to reflect their *"most favoured nation"* status. The British demands included opening up all of China to trade from British companies, the legalisation of the opium trade, exemption from foreign import duties, the suppression of piracy, a British ambassador in Peking and that the English language version of all treaties would take precedence over the Chinese language versions.

2 The first of what the Chinese referred to as the "unequal treaties"
3 Hong Kong island was also ceded to Britain

Figure 10. China

The "Arrow" Incident

Within this tinderbox of negotiation, only a small incident would be required as the spark to ignite an escalation to outright war; this spark would prove to be the *"Arrow"* incident.

On the 8th October 1856, the merchant ship *Arrow*, a Hong Kong registered vessel with a Chinese crew, was boarded by a Chinese war ship, while anchored in the river off Canton. The boarders arrested 12 of the Chinese crew and hauled down the British colours, this action was observed by the British Viceroy who informed Mr Harry S. Parkes, the British Consul at Canton. Mr Parkes immediately proceeded to the *Arrow* and demanded that the crew be released, stating that if the Chinese had acted in ignorance then the matter could be closed, if not then the British would consider the incident to be an insult and a violation of their national rights.

The Chinese Officers refused to give up the men, stating that they had been authorised to capture Koo-lan, a pirate, who they had been informed was on board the *Arrow*. When the officers said that they would enforce their actions by force if necessary, Mr Parkes returned to his Consulate and wrote a letter of protest to Ye Mingchen, the Chinese Imperial Commissioner.

Ye Mingchen replied that some of the arrested men were notorious pirates but nine of the men had been returned to the *Arrow*; also, on the evidence of one of the crew, he disputed the fact that the vessel was British but was in fact Chinese. After further examination of the events and registration of the vessel, including an interview with the 21 year old Master of the *Arrow*, Thomas Kennedy from Belfast, who was not on board at the time of the incident, Mr Parkes issued an ultimatum to Ye Mingchen. Mr Parkes demanded an apology from the Imperial Commissioner and an assurance that in the future, the British flag would be respected and if an appropriate reply was not received within 48 hours then "*... the English naval authorities were to be called on and the dogs of war let loose*".

Figure II. Ye Mingchen

Ye Mingchen, replied within the two day deadline, however, he stated that having interviewed the men who had boarded the *Arrow*, no foreigner was on board and the Ensign was not flying but was found stowed away below decks. The Imperial Commissioner did concede that in the future, Chinese officers would not seize men from any foreign vessel, however, the British should not sell registrations to Chinese built and owned vessels as this confused matters.

Apart from the insult to the British flag, an underlying issue was the long outstanding "City Question", the detainees from the *Arrow* had been taken into the City of Canton where no foreigner was allowed. For some time the British had demanded the right of entry into Canton by her officials, so that they could have direct dialogue with the Chinese officials resident there.

With conflicting views on the facts of the incident and neither side willing to give way it was inevitable that matters would escalate into military conflict.

The War Begins

On the 23rd October 1856, British naval forces, under the command of Admiral Seymour, captured the Barrier Forts about five miles below Canton and also took the Blenheim and Macao Forts. On the 25th October, the British demanded entry into the City of Canton and when this was refused the British fleet began a bombardment of the city on the following day. On the 27th October, the British fire was concentrated on the Governor's Compound in the city, with a shell falling about every 10 minutes. By the 29th October, a breach had been made in the city walls via which troops entered the city, the flag of the United States of America was planted on the walls of Ye Mingchen's residence by James Keenan the US Consul; allied losses in the assault were 3 killed and 12 wounded.

Having demonstrated to the Chinese that he could enter their city, Admiral Seymore withdrew his men but then went on to capture the Rouge and Annunghoy forts giving the British total command of the river.

Up until now the American policy had been to keep out of the conflict and maintain a position of neutrality, the American Naval Commander Captain Andrew H. Foote had been furious when the American flag was raised on the walls at Canton and went to great pains to explain that this was entirely unauthorised and issued orders that the American neutrality was not to be compromised.

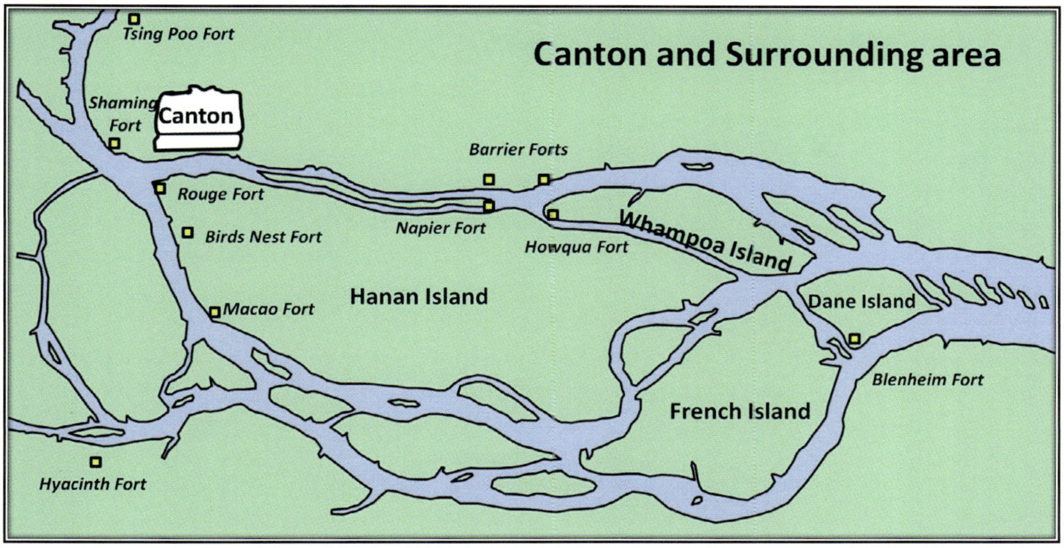

Figure 12. Canton and Surrounding Area

When Commodore Armstrong arrived at Hong Kong from Shanghai, he ordered Captain Foote to withdraw the American forces from Canton, to avoid any breach of American neutrality. While endeavouring to carry out this order, an American war ship was fired upon from one of the Barrier Forts and despite the American flag being waved, the fire continued until the war ship managed to retreat. American retribution was swift, Commodore Armstrong ordered Captain Foote to take his ship the *Portsmouth* together with the *Levant* and destroy the Barrier Forts. On the 16th November the ships began a bombardment of the forts and on the 20th November a storming party was landed but the fort was found to be deserted. On the next day further forts were captured and the final Barrier Fort was taken on the 22nd November.

To avoid further conflict with the Americans, Ye Mingchen wrote to Commodore Armstrong explaining that the attack on the American war ship had been a mistake and should not be the reason for the breakdown of good relations between their two countries. Happy to let sleeping dogs lie, Commodore Armstrong was content to accept the explanation and replied that in his eyes the matter was ended and the American ships fell back from Canton to the fort at Macao.

In December 1856, the year came to an end with the Chinese burning the foreign factories and warehouses in Canton to the ground.

The mail steamer *Thistle*, which operated between Hong Kong and Canton, was boarded by Chinese officials checking for armaments and 11 Europeans on board were killed and beheaded, so that the heads could be used to claim the bounty offered by Ye Mingchen. The *Thistle* was then set on fire.

Meanwhile, the Chinese were causing trouble in the British colony at Hong Kong where the Governor requested 5,000 troops from India; 500 troops were promised by the Governor of Singapore. Apart from trying to cause discontent amongst the population of Hong Kong, in January 1857 a direct assault on the foreigners in the colony was made when arsenic was put in their bread supply. Hundreds of people consumed the poisoned bread but fortunately, due to the high concentration of arsenic, it induced vomiting and although causing great discomfort no deaths occurred. The owner of the bakery, a Chinese named Alum, plus nine others were put on trial for this capital crime but were acquitted.

The British carried out minor naval engagements in the early part of 1857 and on 25th May Commodore Elliot mounted an attack up Escape Creek where his gunboats destroyed 16 junks.

After advancing further up the river the next day, the British arrived at Tang-Koon where they destroyed 12 large war junks. On the morning of 29th May, Admiral Sir Michael Seymour, commander-in-chief of the British naval forces, boarded the paddle steamer *Coromandel* and together with some gunboats sailed up the river past the Rouge Forts and attacked and captured the fort opposite Hyacinth Island. The Chinese abandoned the fort together with 72 junks which were destroyed. Another detachment of the British force led by Commodore Keppel, advance up the Fa-shan branch of the river and destroyed several more junks and a battery of six guns but after reaching the town of Fatshan, where the Chinese had retreated, he was recalled by Admiral Seymour.

Disquiet in England

Back in England news of the *Arrow* incident and the military response became a divisive issue and on 3rd March the British Government were narrowly defeated in a vote of confidence, in the House of Commons, regarding their handling of the situation. In response, the prime minister Lord Palmerston dissolved Parliament and called a General Election, following which he was re-elected with an increased majority. One of the most vocal government opponents was Benjamin Disraeli who wanted to outlaw the trade in opium and thought that the government's hostile position towards China was barbaric.

The British government issued requests to the representatives of France, the United States and Russia regarding the formation of an alliance against China. All parties sent high powered envoys to treat with the Chinese Emperor; W. B. Reed from the USA, Count Pouiatine from Russia, Baron Gros from France and the Earl of Elgin from Britain.

Lord Elgin takes control

Due to events taking place in India (the mutiny), Lord Elgin was delayed in his arrival in China and it was not until 12th December 1857 that he was able to send a letter to the Imperial Commissioner Ye Mingchen. In his letter Lord Elgin pointed out that all of the ports opened up to trade by the treaty of 1842 had flourished, with the exception of Canton where relations had been strained. He also stated that the Government of France was united with that of England in a demand for compensation following losses due to the recent hostilities following the insult to the British flag. He also demanded that China adhere to all of the terms of her treaties including the admission of British subjects to the city of Canton.

Ye Mingchen was given ten days to agree to the terms and if he did, the British would lift their blockade of the port and normal commerce would be allowed to resume, however, the British and French would occupy the island of Honam and the forts on the river until a treaty was signed. If the Chinese did not agree to these demands then the British and French forces would escalate their military operations. Commissioner Ye replied within two days but just reiterated his previous statements and after a further exchange of messages Lord Elgin formed the view that *"It is clear that there will be no peace till the two parties fight it out"*.

On the 20th December 1857, Lord Elgin issued a proclamation in the name of the naval and military authorities of the French and British forces, to the authorities and people of Canton stating that the Imperial Commissioner's reply to recent demands were deemed to be unsatisfactory and as peaceful negotiations had failed it was now necessary to extract agreement to the demands by the force of arms. The authorities were given 48 hours to evacuate the city, after which time it would be attacked.

In preparation for a possible attack, war ships had already steamed up the Canton river and occupied Honam island and established batteries at the Dutch Folly and French Folly.

Capture of Canton

On the 28th December 1857, after a heavy bombardment on the previous day, the assault on the city began; the French Naval Brigade together with the 59th Regiment of Foot quickly occupied the heights overlooking the Lin Fort and the country as far as Gough's Heights. After capturing a Buddhist temple, the 59th Regiment began to lay down a heavy fire on the Lin Fort and when the Chinese were seen to be abandoning the fort the French Naval Brigade rushed forward and captured it. A large Chinese force advanced from Fort Gough but was halted and

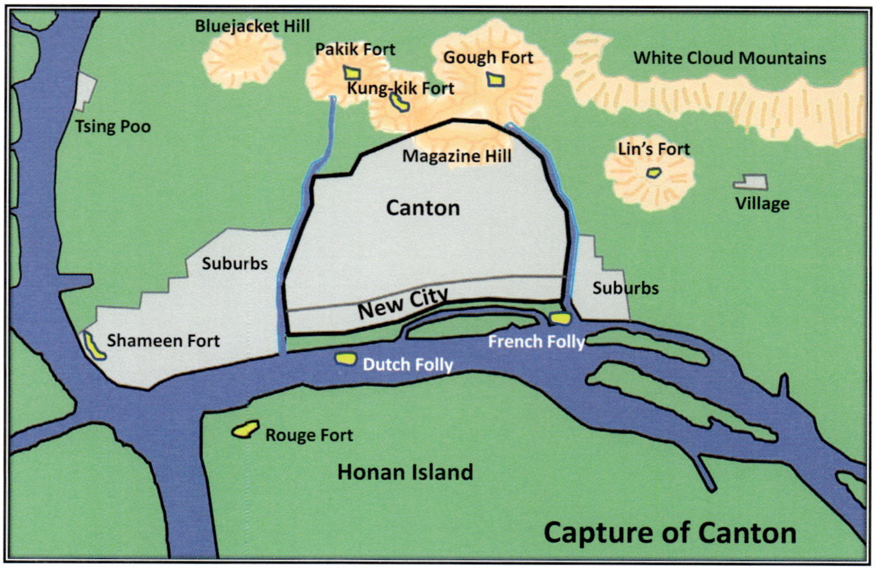

Figure 13. Capture of Canton

driven back by British artillery fire and operations were halted for the night.

Before daylight on the morning of 29th December, the French Naval Brigade and the 59th Regiment, now joined by the British Marines commanded by Colonel Lemon, were opposite the East Gate, waiting for the end of a naval bombardment before beginning their assault. Using ladders, the joint British and French force scaled the walls and soon captured the five story Pagoda and Magazine Hill which offered little resistance; the Chinese offered more resistance at the North Gate but this was also captured. On the morning of the 30th December, white flags of surrender could be seen to be flying across the city and when the allied forces advanced from the North to the West Gate, thousands of the population were seen to be escaping from the city.

Gough Fort and Bluejacket Fort were both blown up with gunpowder and for nearly a week, the victorious allies occupied the walls of the city without going into the streets below. On the 5th January 1858, the allies entered the city and after some searching found and arrested the Imperial Commissioner who was incarcerated on board *HMS Inflexible*, as a prisoner of state. It was decided that if Ye Mingchen was allowed to remain in the City then he would only become the focus for future dissent, he was therefore despatched into exile in Calcutta where he starved himself to death a year later.

Lord Elgin was concerned that if Kwangtung province was left without effective government then it could possibly fall prey to anarchy; to prevent this he proposed that Pih-kwei be retained as Governor but that a tribunal of officers would be established to deal with criminal cases involving foreigners and on the 9th January this was put into effect.

The blockade of the Canton river was lifted and commercial trade was allowed to resume. Under orders from England, Lord Elgin was ordered to move with his forces down to the mouth of the Pei-ho river.

Treaty of Tientsin

Having moved to the delta of the Pei-ho, Lord Elgin prepared to act in conjunction with representatives from France and the United States to treat with the Emperor of China and resolve all of the disputes between the nations. After several attempts to communicate with the Emperor, via his Prime Minister at Shanghai, which remained unanswered, Lord Elgin sent a final demand on the 24th April, for direct communication with Peking and set a six day deadline for an acceptance, otherwise the allies would take further military action.

The deadline passed without a response, however, as Lord Elgin was still awaiting the arrival of some of his gunboats, he started negotiations with Commissioner Tau on the 6th May, in order to buy some time. As a condition of the talks, Lord Elgin demanded that the forts at the mouth of the Pei-ho river should be surrendered to the allied forces.

On the morning of 20th May, when no response had been received from Commissioner Tau, the British and French fleets began a bombardment of the forts followed up by land assaults during which the forts on both sides of the river were captured. After the capture of the forts, a move was made up river to the town of Taku, where they were halted by a row of junks held in position by chains across the river, near to a sand bar.

After waiting for a couple of days, Lord Elgin now on board *HMS Slaney* crossed the sand bar at high tide and proceeded towards Tientsin where the French mission under Baron Gros joined the British delegation on board *HMS Slaney*. Mr Reed, the minister from America, together with Count Pouiatine the representative from Russia soon arrived on the scene on board the Russian ship *America*.

Now stationed on the outskirts of Tientsin, Lord Elgin once again sent a message to the Prime Minister of China requesting that the Imperial Government immediately send a representative to negotiate with him. With the allied forces now at the very gates of Peking, and probably fearing a similar fate to that inflicted on Canton, Kweiliang and Hwashana were appointed to treat with the foreigners. In early June serious negotiations were now underway regarding a new treaty and on the 9th of June, Kweiliang and Hwashana were joined by Keying, the chief negotiator of the 1842 treaty with Britain but on learning that the British were in possession of a letter in which he was praised for deceiving the foreigners, he returned to Peking in disgrace.[4]

On the 11th June Lord Elgin reported that negotiations were going well, with the Chinese prepared to concede to most of the British demands. On the 15th June, Lord Elgin received a message from Count Pouiatine that he had managed to conclude a treaty between Russia and China; a few days later a similar message was received from Mr Reed regarding an American treaty. The British treaty with China was finally signed on 26th June 1858 and on the next day the French signed their treaty. With the treaty signed and now awaiting ratification, Lord Elgin sailed to Japan to sign another treaty, believing that the war was at an end.

Phase two of the War

When Lord Elgin returned to China, to sign some of the commercial agreements resulting from the treaty of Tientsin, he

4 Keying later committed suicide by drinking poison.

received a communication from Commissioners Kweiliang and Hwashana, pleading that the treaty had been extorted by military force and that above all else the Chinese authorities feared the establishment of a permanent Embassy in Peking. They also implied that their lives were at stake if they could not overturn this element of the treaty. As a compromise, Lord Elgin suggested that if the Ambassador was officially received at Peking, at the time of the treaty ratification, then he would reside outside the city and only visit occasionally; this seemed to meet with Chinese approval.

After a trip up the Yangtze river to Nanking, Lord Elgin returned to Shanghai and wrote a letter of farewell to the Chinese Commissioners and announced that the British Minister to China, Mr F. Bruce (his brother) would arrive shortly for the ratification of the treaty. With his business now concluded Lord Elgin set sail from China on his return to England.

When Mr Bruce arrived at Hong Kong he relieved Sir John Bowring of his duties as Chief Superintendant of British Trade and began to transfer British affairs in China to Shanghai. Like the French, Britain was willing to wait for an opportune moment before forcing the issue of a permanent residence in Peking. Mr Bruce sent a message to Commissioner Kweiliang announcing that he was ready to exchange and ratify the Treaty of Tientsin and that he was about to depart for Tientsin by ship.

After reaching Shanghai on the evening of the 6th June 1859 and meeting up with the French Minister M de Bourboulon the next morning, Mr Bruce found three letters that had been sent by the Imperial Commissioners. These letters proposed that Mr Bruce should remain in Shanghai to discuss details regarding bringing the treaty into operation and conclude discussions not completed by Lord Elgin, rather than proceeding to the north. Mr Bruce replied to Kweiliang, stating that he was determined to proceed to Peking and that he refused to enter into any further discussions until after the treaty had been ratified. He also threatened *"evil consequences"* if he was not received in a manner befitting the dignity of his nation. The French Minister sent a letter in a similar vein.

Mr Bruce arrived at the mouth of the Pei-Ho river towards the middle of June and found that a fleet of British ships under the command of Admiral Hope had already arrived, with the intention of escorting him up river to Peking.

On the 16th June, Commander Commerell, with the interpreter Mr Mongan, left on board *HMS Fury*, escorted by two gunboats, to deliver a message that the British and French ministers had arrived. The progress of Commander Commerell was halted by a barrier across the river and an armed crowd on the bank would not let him land. After requesting to speak to the authorities, Commander Commerell was advised that no civil or military authorities were at that place but the leader said he was willing to take a message to Tientsin and bring back an answer.

Commander Commerell was sent up the river again, to say that the ministers had arrived and demanded that a passage be opened up within three days to allow them to proceed upriver to Tientsin. The reply was that a messenger had already been sent and that the river would be opened up at the required time. On the 21st June Mr Bruce and M de Bourboulon jointly requested Admiral Hope to clear the river so that they could proceed to Tientsin.

On the 24th June, Mr Ward, the Minister for the USA, approached the forts on board the steamer *Toeywan* and requested free passage up river. He was told that the passage to Tientsin via the Pei-Ho river was closed but Governor-General Hangfuh was waiting to receive him at Pehtang about ten miles further up the coast.

Mr Bruce received a letter from Governor-General Hangfuh on 25th June asking him to proceed to Peking via the overland route from Pehtang (this was the route traditionally used by bearers of tribune to the Emperor). The letter went on to say that the British Queen was not on the same level as the Emperor of China. This was a clear violation of the clause of equality in the treaty, so the letter was returned with the comment that Mr Bruce intended to travel to Peking by way of Tientsin.

As the tone of this last communication was completely at odds with the recent communications from the Imperial Commissioners, Mr Bruce concluded that hostile forces were now in control of Peking and that the only way forward was the employment of force.

Attack on the Taku Forts

Unfortunately, since the signing of the Tientsin treaty a year earlier, a great deal of work had been done to improve the defences of the forts at the mouth of the Pei-Ho river and formidable booms were now stretched across the river. As instructed, Admiral Hope had proceeded with a force to clear a passage up the river and after arriving on site on the 24th June had given notice that if a suitable reply had not been received by 8 o'clock in the evening then he would have to resort to force. During the night a British force commanded by Captain G. O. Willes, cut the cable of one boom and blew away two others with blasting powder but in the morning these had been rejoined.

Admiral Hope now decided that his best approach was to bombard the forts and silence their guns before launching an assault with landing parties. It took the morning of the 25th June for the Admiral to get his boats into place but at two o'clock in the afternoon, four British ships had pushed past the first barrier

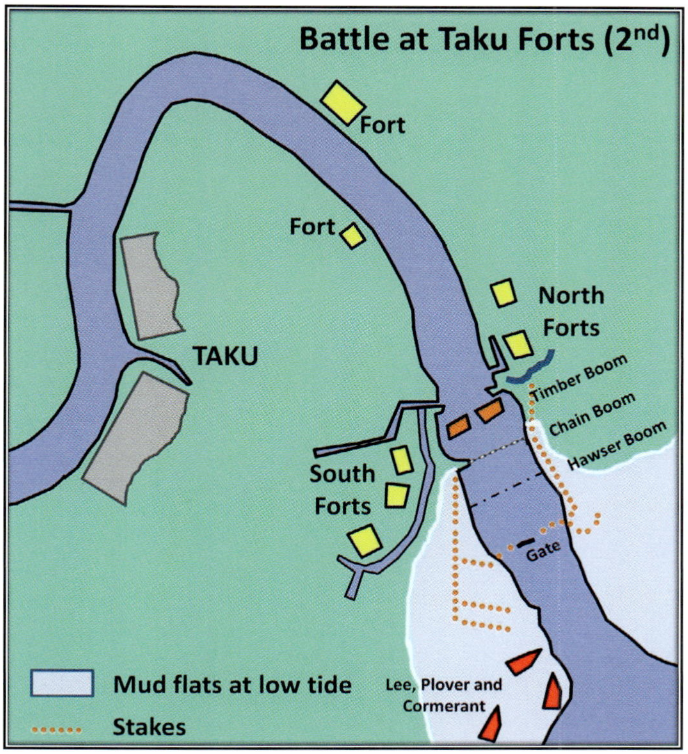

Figure 14. Battle of Taku Forts (2nd)

and were approaching the second when they came under devastating fire from 30 to 40 guns in the fort. By 3 o'clock the ships were so disabled that they had to withdraw.

Admiral Hope was forced to change his flagship from *HMS Plover* to *HMS Cormorant* and after being severely wounded handed over his command to Captain Shadwell. By 5:40 *HMS Kestrel* had been sunk and *HMS Lee* had been grounded to avoid a similar fate; at 6:30 fire from the north forts stopped and half an hour later only a few guns were firing from the south forts.

In light of the greatly reduced fire from the forts, a force of marines commanded by Captain Shadell together with a detachment of French seamen under the command of Commandant Tricault landed opposite the outer bastion of the south fort at 7:20 where they could be supported by their ships guns. The attempted assault was a complete disaster, the guns in the fort had not been silenced and their fire killed many of the men before they were even landed on the shore, only about 50 men managed to reach the walls of the fort but with only three scaling ladders, all of which soon broke, it was clear that the attack could proceed no further. Captain Shadwell, Captain Vansittart and Colonel Lemon had all been wounded and command of the enterprise had now fallen to Commander Commerell, who after a short discussion gave the order to retire.

During the night, the troops and the wounded were evacuated and before dawn all were back on board their ships. As the British and French ships retreated back down the river, *HMS Plover* was grounded within range of the fort's guns and *HMS Cormorant* also ran aground. As the tide had turned, a small flotilla of British gunboats was having difficulty in going up river to rescue the crews of the stricken vessels, including the badly wounded Admiral Hope. Although the USA had declared its neutrality in the conflict, Commodore Josiah Tattnall of the US navy flouted international law and towed the British boats up river to where British forces were able to rescue their comrades.

American Treaty Ratified

The American delegation led by Mr Ward, complied with the Chinese request to proceed to Peking via the overland route and towards the end of July they arrived at Pehtang. Escorted by Chinese officials and soldiers the American party travelled across country and arrived at the Pei-Ho river about 10 miles upstream from Tientsin, from where they travelled by river to Tungchow, the port of Peking. After arriving in Peking, Mr Ward had a meeting with the Imperial Commissioners Kweiliang and Hwashana on 30th July 1859 at which it was explained that the American Minister would be required to kowtow to the Emperor during the ratification ceremony. Mr Ward refused this condition and left Peking the next day, the treaty was finally ratified at Pehtang on 15th August 1859.

Final Phase of the War

News of the disaster at the mouth of the Pei-Ho river was met with much consternation in Britain and France but there was a determination to reverse this set back by sending a substantial military force to Peking to ensure ratification of the treaty of Tientsin.

In March 1860, while the allied forces were being assembled Mr Bruce sent an ultimatum to Pang Wan-Chang, the Senior Secretary of State. After reiterating the circumstances of the blocking of their passage to Tientsin and the subsequent attack on the ships of Admiral Hope, Mr Bruce stated that the British Government considered that the Chinese government was responsible for this outrage and demanded an immediate acceptance of the British terms. The demands included; an apology for the actions of the Chinese troops at Taku, permission for the British Minister to travel to Peking via the Pei-Ho river to ratify the treaty without delay and immediate compliance with all provisions of the treaty. Mr Bruce stated that the agreement made with Lord

Elgin, regarding the permanent residence of a British Minister in Peking was now null and void and the location of the British Minister was now to be totally at the discretion of the British Government, the Chinese Government would also be expected to pay compensation for their actions. If a positive response to the British demands was not received within 30 days then force would be used to ensure that the Emperor complied with these demands. The French government submitted similar demands.

The reply from China, just reiterated their previous position and complained about the intemperate language of the British Minister's communication. With this reply, it was obvious that matters would only be settled by military action and a large Anglo-French expeditionary force was assembled. Command of the expeditionary force was given to General Sir Hope Grant who was currently serving in India where several Sikh regiments enthusiastically volunteered to serve in China.

The French Emperor, Napoleon III also assembled a large force, under the command of the distinguished General Montauban.

Lord Elgin and Baron Gros were once again despatched to China as the senior representatives of their respective governments, their journey being somewhat marred when the steamer *Malarbar*, on which they were travelling, struck a rock in the harbour at Point de Galle in Ceylon and was totally wrecked. Baron Gros eventually arrived at Shanghai on the 28th June and Lord Elgin arrived the next day. The expeditionary force reached China on 21st April 1860 and the British and French forces immediately occupied Chusan.

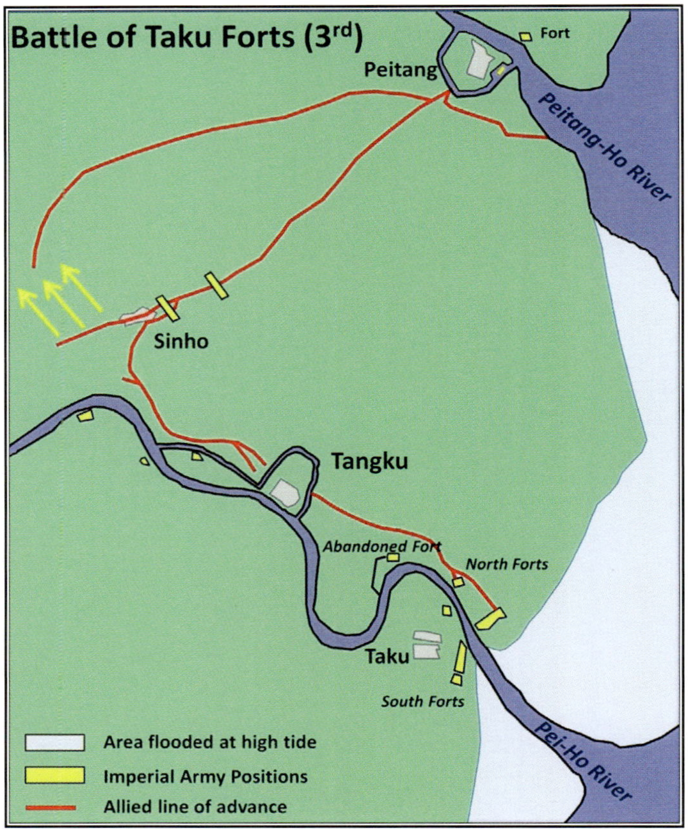

Figure 15. Battle of Taku Forts (3rd)

Battle of Shanghai

In May 1860, a strange situation developed at Shanghai where, while preparing to engage with China in war at Peking, they had to act as China's allies at Shanghai. For some time Taiping rebels had been waging a civil war against the Emperor but now that they were advancing towards Shanghai, the centre of British trade in China, Mr Bruce and M de Bourboulon decided that British and French forces must be used to protect the city against the rebels.

The Taiping rebels eventually mounted an attack against Shanghai on the 17th August but after an extended period of fighting were defeated and retreated from the area on the 31st August 1860.

Anglo-French Expeditionary Force

Lord Elgin on hearing that no response had arrived, to the demands made by Mr Bruce and M de Bourboulon in March, decided that he would wait until the Expeditionary forces had seized the Taku forts and opened up the way to Tientsin before he next communicated with the Emperor of China.

In late July the Anglo-French Expeditionary force of about 14,000 British and 7,000 French troops, was assembled off the coast at Pehtang with a fleet of 173 British and 33 French ships.

The British force comprised the Cavalry Brigade (1st Kings Dragoon Guards, Probyn's Horse, Fane's Horse and Stirling's Horse Artillery) commanded by General Pattle; the 1st Division commanded by General Sir John Mitchell with the 1st Brigade (Royal Scots Guards, 31st Regiment of Foot and the 15th Ludhiana Sikhs) commanded by General Staveley and the 2nd Brigade (2nd Regiment of Foot, 60th Kings Royal Rifles, 15th Punjab Native Infantry, one company of Royal Engineers and Desborough's artillery battery) commanded by General Sutton; the 2nd Division commanded by General Sir Robert Napier with the 3rd Brigade (3rd Regiment of Foot, 44th Regiment of Foot and the 8th Punjab Native Infantry) commanded by General Jephson and the 4th Brigade (67th Regiment of foot, 99th Regiment of Foot and the 19th Punjab Native Infantry) commanded by General Reeves.

On the 1st August 1860, the troops began to disembark at Pehtang, north of the Pei-Ho river, with the intention of attacking the Taku forts in the rear, i.e. from the landward side. The landing was virtually unopposed, with only a few Tartar cavalry watching on, and that night, after the fort at Pehtang was found to be deserted, was occupied by the allied troops on the next day.

Because of heavy rains, the allies did not leave Pehtang until 12th August and as the main force continued along the main road, a column led by Sir Robert Napier headed towards the town of Sinho where they were confronted by a large Tartar force. The British Cavalry and Artillery managed to disperse the Chinese who retired back within the defences of the town. Sir John Michel's division, supported by French artillery attacked the town and managed to push the Chinese out of their defences.

Over the next two days, the allied force advanced slowly towards Tangku, on the banks of the Pei-Ho, having to bridge many ditches and creeks as they made their way, destroying batteries and junks with artillery fire. On reaching Tangku, the allies managed to circumvent the defences, drive out the garrison and occupy the town without much difficulty, the main objective of the Taku forts was now in sight.

Taking of the Taku Forts

As mentioned earlier, the defences of the forts had been much improved since they were last captured by the British two years earlier in 1858; the walls had been repaired and extended and extra gun batteries had been installed within new emplacements. Externally the forts were ringed by deep water filled moats and the approaches were covered with sharp wooden stakes driven into the ground to slow down the advance of enemy infantry and cavalry. Both of the fort complexes consisted of a main fort and a detached secondary fort.

The allied Generals had a difference of opinion regarding the plan of attack against the Taku forts which were located on both the north and south banks of the river Pei-Ho. General Sir Hope Grant favoured continuing the advance on their present line and attacking the forts on the north bank, on the other hand the French General Montauban wanted the allies to cross the river and attack the town of Taku in preparation for taking the forts on the south bank. The British General considered the French plan to have a much greater risk, as the force would be exposed to fire from all of the forts while they crossed the river and when they landed their right flank would be exposed to the enemy cavalry. General Sir Hope Grant therefore insisted that the British plan be adopted and although he still remained unconvinced that this was the best approach, the French General agreed to support the plan with his forces.

In preparation for the attack, the siege guns and ammunition were brought forward from Pehtang and the admirals agreed that gunboats would advance up the river and cross the sand bar.

In the early morning of the 21st August 1860, the attack on the forts began with the ships sending down a barrage against the outer forts on the north and south banks. The siege guns concentrated their fire on the inner north fort which was to be the target for the first infantry attack. After a short time the allied artillery attack was beginning to tell and at 7 o'clock in the morning a huge explosion in the inner north fort indicated that a magazine had been hit. Soon afterwards a similar explosion was heard in the outer north fort.

Following the success of the artillery, the infantry storming parties now began to advance with the French to the right of the line and the British to the left with two Companies of the 44th Foot, one commanded by Captain Gregory, the other, "E" Company, by Lieutenant Rogers; and two Companies of the 67th Foot leading the way. They crossed marshy ground until they reached the last 200 yards which was covered by iron and wooden spikes, all the while under a constant musket fire from the fort walls.

Lieutenant Nathaniel Burslem – Victoria Cross No. 299
Private Thomas Lane – Victoria Cross No. 303

Only the moat now separated the storming parties from the walls of the fort. A group of about six men managed to swim across the moat and cut the ropes to the drawbridge. As the doors to the fort were locked and barred, the men found a small hole in the wall, next to the doors, which they began to enlarge.

Lieutenant Burslem ran across the bridge and despite having been hit in the chest, continued across to the hole where he assisted Private Lane who was trying to enlarge the hole with a piece of wood. A 12 pound shell was dropped from the walls onto the head of Private Lane, which concussed him but his helmet saved his life. As he continued to enlarge the hole, Private Lane was also wounded by a bayonet thrust at him through the hole. During the action Lieutenant Burslem received a further two wounds.

For their actions to help in gaining access to the fort, both Lieutenant Burslem and Private Lane were later awarded the Victoria Cross.

Lieutenant Edmund Lenon – Victoria Cross No. 300
Lieutenant Robert Rogers – Victoria Cross No. 301
Private John Leishman McDougall – Victoria Cross No. 304

Also at the forefront of the assault was Lieutenant Rogers who managed to cross the moat and reach the parapet wall, inspiring more men of the storming party to follow him. With vases of lime, stones and other objects being rained down on the men, Lieutenant Rogers tried to force his way through an embrasure but was driven back.

He ran to another embrasure but this was too high, however, Lieutenant Lenon who was also in the group came to his assistance, providing him with a step by pushing the point of his sword into the wall. Using the improvised step, Lieutenant Rogers leapt up and through the embrasure becoming the first man to enter the fort, he was closely followed by Private McDougall and then Lieutenant Lenon. Despite being seriously wounded in the side by a musket ball, Lieutenant Rogers continued to help men enter the fort by this route.

For their service in being the first men to enter the Taku fort, Lieutenants Rogers and Lenon, together with Private McDougall were all later awarded the Victoria Cross.

Ensign John Chaplin – Victoria Cross No. 302

Almost as soon as the assault began, Ensign Fraser, who was carrying the colours of the 67th Regiment, was severely wounded and fell to the ground. Ensign Chaplin immediately picked up the colours and with his sword in hand continued to push forward. As the order to advance was sounded, Ensign Chaplin rushed to the front with the colours but had not gone far before he was shot through the arm. Instead of going to the rear, the Ensign quickly bound up his wound and once again rushed to the head of the regiment, he wanted to plant his regiment's colours in the fort ahead of the French.

After crossing the bridge over the moat, Ensign Chaplin forced his way through a breach in the wall that had been made by the artillery, where he was wounded for a second time. Yet again the Ensign was urged to give up the colour and return to the rear to have his wounds attended to, however, as he was still ahead of the French officer carrying the French colours he carried on without delay. The inside of the fort was full of men fighting each other in a desperate struggle but aided by Private Lane, he managed to plant the colours on the high point (cavalier) within the fort where he was shot again in the leg. Despite bleeding profusely from his three wounds Ensign Chaplin remained with the colours until he was relieved after the fort was taken.

For his service at Fort Taku, Ensign Chaplin was later awarded the Victoria Cross.

Hospital Apprentice Andrew Fitzgibbon – Victoria Cross No. 305

Hospital Apprentice Fitzgibbon was attached to the 67th Regiment as a medical orderly and during the attack on the fort he had reached the walls when, Assistant Surgeon Ross directed him to go to the aid of a wounded dhoolie (stretcher) bearer. Leaving cover, Hospital Apprentice Fitzgibbon crossed open ground under heavy fire and bandaged up the dhoolie bearer's wounds. As he finished this task, he noticed a wounded artilleryman nearby and rushed to his aid.

After successfully treating the soldier, and just after placing his unused bandages back into his haversack, Hospital Apprentice Fitzgibbon was himself wounded by a musket ball which entered his forearm and lodged in his elbow. Now that he was incapacitated, he left the field of battle and sought treatment from Surgeon Lamprey.

For his deeds at the Taku Fort, Hospital Apprentice Fitzgibbon was later awarded the Victoria Cross.

Figure 16. Interior North Taku Fort

Almost simultaneous with the British entry into the fort, the French gained access on their side and now British and French troops were pouring into the fort. At 8:30 am, after an hour of fighting the detached northern fort was in allied hands and the fort guns were now turned on the other three forts.

Moves were made to bring forward fresh troops for a second assault, but as General Hope Grant expected, this was not necessary as, after a short bombardment, white flags of surrender appeared on these forts. The infantry now advanced on the northern outer main fort and entered by scaling the walls, without any resistance from the Chinese and took the garrison of 2,000 men prisoner. As evening approached, detachments were sent across the river by boat and occupied the south forts which had been abandoned by their garrisons.

For the scale of the operation the British casualties were relatively light, with 17 men and 19 officers killed and 165 men wounded.

The Route to Peking now open

With the Taku forts now in allied hands, the river route to Peking was now open and after the booms and iron stakes were removed from the river, a passage was opened up and on the 22nd August, gunboats were moored at Tangku. On the 24th August, Admiral Hope arrived at Tientsin where he informed the Viceroy, that he must consider the city to now be in British hands; marines occupied the East Gate and raised the British and French flags.

A few days later, Lord Elgin arrived at Tientsin and on the 29th August wrote to the Imperial Commissioners reaffirming the ultimatum sent in March by Mr Bruce and doubled the amount of compensation required from China that had been outlined in the 1858 treaty. On the 2nd September the Commissioners replied, with assurances that the 1858 treaty would be observed and all the points in the March ultimatum and Lord Elgin's letter of the 29th August were conceded in full.

A draft convention was drawn up and Mr Wade and Mr Parkes visited the assistant Commissioner Hang-ki on the 6th September to discuss the document. During the visit, news leaked out that there was some doubt regarding the powers of the Commissioners to negotiate with the allies. When Lord Elgin heard this news, after consultation with Baron Gros, he informed the Commissioners that because of this doubt, he was now going to advance to Tungchow and would not communicate with them again until he reached that place.

The allied force now advanced towards Tungchow, with little resistance, and after reaching Yangtsun on 10th September, Lord Elgin received a message from two higher Imperial Officers; Tsai, Prince of I, President of the Clan Court and a near relative of the Emperor and Muh-yin, President of the Board of War. Lord Elgin replied that he had already informed Chinese officials that he would not sign any treaty until he reached Tungchow and that this was still his intention.

On the next morning, just as he was about to continue his journey north, two mandarins arrived with another message from the Commissioners, stating that they could not understand the hostile advance of the allies and added a veiled threat with the information that troops of the Chinese Government held positions throughout the neighbourhood of Ho-se-woo. Lord Elgin ignored the message and moved on to Na-tsie-tsun about eight miles from Yangtsung, where yet another message, this time from the Princes, was waiting. The Princes hoped that Lord Elgin would halt at Ho-se-woo or Nanking and enter negotiations.

As General Sir Hope Grant, had informed Lord Elgin, that a delay in the advance was required, in order to bring forward heavy guns and stores, in case an attack on Tungchow was necessary, it was agreed to accede to this wish. Mr Wade and Mr Parkes were sent to have an interview with the Prince of I and Muh-yin at Tungchow, where they would also deliver a letter from Lord Elgin. After a meeting which lasted for over eight hours, the pair returned with a letter in which the Prince and Muh-yin agreed to conclude the convention and afterwards would exchange ratifications of the 1858 treaty at Peking.

What would prove to be important to future events was a paragraph in the letter, referring to the disposition of the allied forces during the negotiations; *"The Prince and his colleague, having accepted the above conditions without exception, have now to express an urgent wish that his Excellency the Ambassador will not bring up the main body of the British forces to Tung-chow, but will limit his escort to about 1,000 men: also that the former shall not occupy any position nearer than five Li (two miles) from the town of Chang-kia-wan"*. Mr Parkes was requested to return with a letter from Lord Elgin accepting these terms.

M de Bastard was given a letter from Baron Gros agreeing to the terms requested from the British and together with M l'Abbé Deluc acting as an interpreter, he left to deliver the message to the Prince at Tungchow. Mr Parkes set out with a letter of agreement from Lord Elgin, with an escort of five men from the King's Dragoon Guards and twenty men from Fane's Horse, under the command of Lieutenant Anderson. Mr Parkes was accompanied by Lord Elgin's private secretary, Mr Loch and General Sir Hope Grant also sent, Colonel Walker, the Quartermaster General and Mr Thompson from the Commissariat Department to discuss the sighting and provisioning of the camp, for the escort, during the negotiations at Tungchow. Mr de Normann, an attaché to Mr Bruce and Mr Bowlby a correspondent from the *Times* also accompanied the party.

Murder of British Delegation

On 18th September, the day after the British party had departed, the sound of heavy guns was heard in the distance and at noon, Lord Elgin received a letter from Mr Parkes at Tungchow stating that the Commissioners had raised objections to his letter, mainly in regard to the statement that he may deliver a letter from the British Queen to the Emperor. This letter was the last communication from Mr Parkes as a treacherous attack had been made against the British party.

Colonel Walker and some of the men had been able to cut their way out of the clutches of the Chinese army but Mr Parkes, Mr Loch, Captain Brabazon, Lieutenant Anderson, Mr de Normann, Mr Bowlby, a Dragoon Guard and 18 Sowars had been captured. The allied army which had slowly followed the British party were surprised to find Tartar cavalry drawn up to impede their way. Treachery was suspected and this was confirmed when Colonel Walker broke through to the British lines and reported the attack on Mr Parkes party.

Advance on Peking

An attack on the Chinese forces was immediately ordered, the French were directed to turn the left of their line while the British carried out a frontal assault, the result of which was a complete defeat of the Tartar force after which the allies occupied Chang-kia-wan. A message was now sent to the chief Mandarin of Tungchow, demanding that the British and French subjects be returned immediately, otherwise Peking would be attacked and taken.

On the 21st September, Tartar forces were attacked and defeated at their camps between Tungchow and Peking and the French won a great victory at the Palikao bridge less than three miles from Tungchow. General Sir Hope Grant now had to call a temporary halt to his advance while he waited for the arrival of reinforcements, supplies and ammunition.

On the 22nd September, a message was received from Prince Kung, the Emperor's brother announcing that the Prince of I and Muh-yin had been relieved as Imperial Commissioners, that he was taking over the negotiations and that he was sending Hang-ki and Lau-wei-wan for an interview and requested that hostilities be suspended. Lord Elgin replied that he would not halt hostilities or negotiate a peace until the missing men were returned; further messages were exchanged while the allied armies prepared for the final advance on Peking.

On the 6th October the allied armies entered and seized Yuan-ming-yuan (the Summer Palace), which was extensively looted. During the evening of 7th October, Prince Kung received a message from Thomas Wade, which said that unless the Chinese Government immediately returned the prisoners, the city of Peking would be stormed.

On the afternoon of the 8th October, eight men were observed making their way to the allied camp just outside the walls of the city; these were Mr Parkes, Mr Loch, M d'Escayrac de Lauture, a trooper from Probyn's Horse and four French soldiers. On 12th October a further nine prisoners were released; eight troopers of Fane's Horse and a French soldier, together with news that Lieutenant Anderson and Mr de Normann had died during their captivity. Later two Sikh troopers were returned, with twelve corpses, including those of Lieutenant Anderson, Mr de Normann and Mr Bowlby. It was believed that Captain Brabazon and M l'Abbé Deluc the French interpreter had been beheaded on the orders of a Chinese General. It was also apparent that many of the prisoners had been subjected to the most horrendous torture.

Allied forces enter Peking

On the 13th October, the Chinese were requested to surrender possession of the Anting Gate to Peking and when the Chinese tried to delay they were informed that if the gate was not given up immediately then Peking would be bombarded. The gate was surrendered and British and French flags were hoisted as it was occupied.

There was much demand for severe retribution for the Chinese mistreatment of the French and British peace envoys and various options were discussed, in the end it was agreed that a large indemnity should be paid to the British and French governments for distribution to those injured and the relatives of those killed. It was also agreed that the Emperor's Summer Palace would be burnt to the ground, as this would have a direct impact on the Emperor, rather than on the people of Peking. On the 18th October, the Summer Palace and all of the nearby Royal palaces were set on fire, the fires burned for two days.

The War Ends

At long last, on 24th October 1860, Lord Elgin with great pomp went to the Hall of Ceremonies in the "Forbidden City" and signed the convention, to which two clauses had been added; the legalisation of emigration from China and the cessation to Britain of Kowloon on a 99 year lease, the treaty of 1858 was also finally ratified. On the next day, the French signed their convention and their treaty with China was also ratified; the war with China was finally at an end.

7

THE TAIPING REBELLION, CHINA (1851–64)

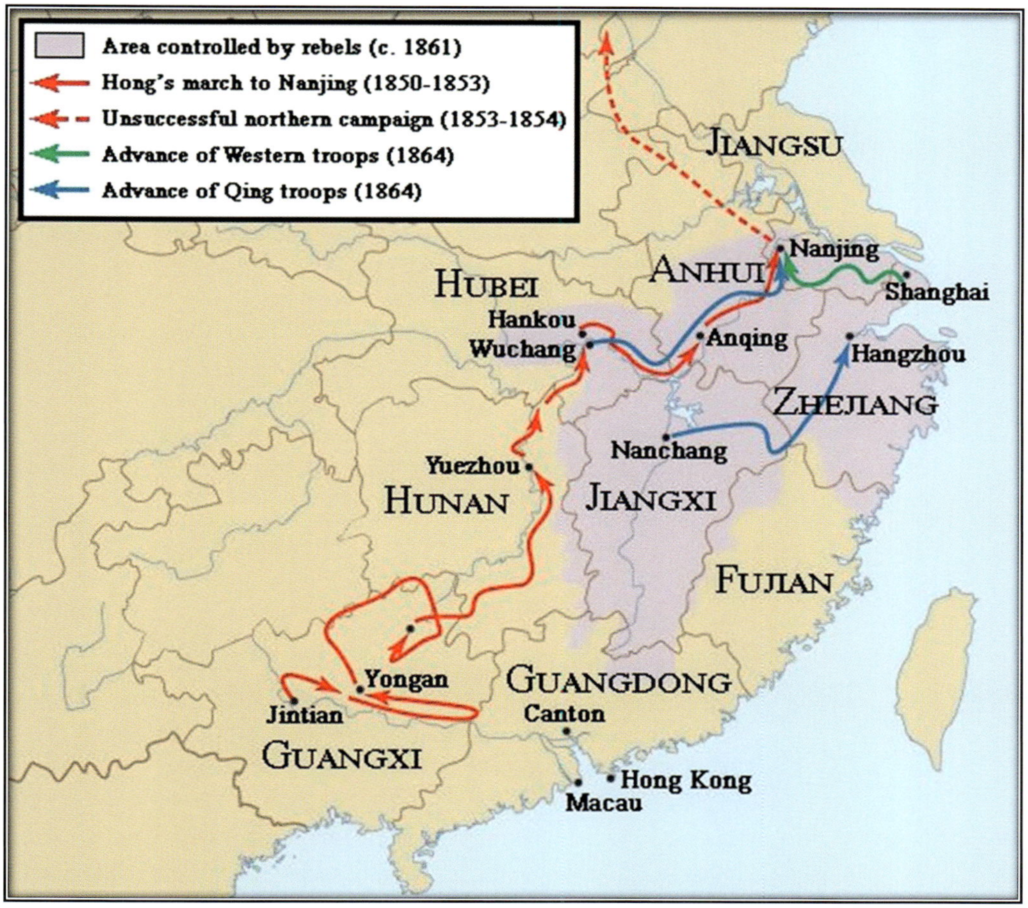

Figure 17. China 1860

The Taiping Rebellion was a civil war in China which lasted from December 1850 until August 1864 and involved forces of the Taiping "Heavenly Kingdom" who attempted to overthrow the established Manchu led Qing dynasty as the rulers of China. This was one of the bloodiest conflicts ever, with estimates of the dead being between 30 and 100 million people.

The "Heavenly Kingdom" movement was created by Hong Xiuquan who in 1837, while bed ridden, read a pamphlet from a Protestant Christian missionary and claimed to have had a vision in which he was the younger brother of Jesus Christ, sent to rid China of the hated[5] Qing government and spread Christianity. In 1843, Hong Xiuquan and Yang Xiuqing (who claimed to be able to act as the voice of God) together with other associates founded the God Worshipping Society with an American Baptist missionary, Isaac Jacob, acting as teacher and advisor.

5 Most of China was populated by Han Chinese who considered the Manchu Qing government as corrupt foreigners.

Figure 18. Hong Xiuquan

Start of the Civil War

The start of the civil war is generally accepted as being in December 1850 when a rebel army defeated Qing forces at Jintian in the Guangxi province. In early January 1851 Taiping forces repulsed Qing forces, who were attempting to enforce reprisals against the uprising.

For much of the rebellion, European forces considered this to be a purely internal Chinese affair and were not directly involved against the rebels. However, the initial successes of the Taiping rebels was largely due to the involvement of European forces against the Qing government during the second China War of 1856 to 1860 as this occupied and weakened the Qing military forces.

By 1853, the Taiping army was at its peak, estimated to number about 1 million men, and occupied Nanjing where they consolidated their forces.

In 1856 an internal power struggle between the Hong and Yang factions of the movement resulted in the death of Yang Xiuqing and his family.

During the second China War, the allied forces were under instructions to remain neutral in the civil war, however, it was inevitable that at some time there would be a clash between the allies and Taiping forces.

Lord Elgin's Mission up the Yangtze

A significant incident occurred towards the end of the first phase of the 2nd China War during Lord Elgin's diplomatic mission up the Yangtze river. On the 8th November 1858, Lord Elgin left Shanghai and proceeded by river towards Hangkow, the Expeditionary force observed that while the Imperial forces appeared to control the river, all of the important towns along both banks were occupied by the Taiping forces.

On the afternoon of the 20th November, as they were approaching Nanjing, the gunboat *Lee* was sent ahead to try and establish communications with the authorities and was under orders to raise a flag of truce if fired upon. Having already passed several Taiping occupied forts without trouble, the *Lee* was surprised when fired upon by a cannon in the Nanjing fort but as ordered raised the white flag. Despite flying the flag of truce, the *Lee* was subjected to seven more shots from the fort before the British ships were force to return fire. The British ships sailed past the fort continuing their fire and spent the evening anchored downstream of the city.

On the following morning they returned upstream and for an hour and a half bombarded the Nanjing forts again with little reply and in the evening anchored off the city of Tai-ping, having silenced some other forts on their way.

Lord Elgin continued and completed his mission without further incident, however, on his return to Shanghai, Mr Wade, the Chinese Secretary was despatched to Nanjing for an explanation as to why the flag of truce had been violated by the Taiping rebels, which apparently was as a result of some misunderstandings.

Lord Elgin's mission, however, gave the British a better understanding of the impact of the Taiping rebellion on the lands that they occupied. The cities of Hangkow, Hanyang and Wuchang had been devastated, were little more than ruins and were totally devoid of any commercial activity.

Heavenly Kingdom Expansion

In 1859, Hong Rengan, a cousin of Hong Xiuquan, was given considerable power within the movement and he developed plans to expand the boundaries of the Heavenly Kingdom's control.

Towards the end of 1859, the Imperial army tightened its siege of Nanjing (the self styled capital of the Heavenly Kingdom) which had been under some form of siege since it was occupied in 1853. However on the 3rd of March a strong Taiping army completely routed the besiegers and the Imperial army fled to the city of Soochow, which they destroyed and carried out a campaign of rape and pillage. Pursuing the Imperial army, the rebels occupied Hangchow on 19th March and Soochow on 24th May, where they were welcomed by the local population.

The rebel leadership now made the fateful decision to advance on Shanghai; they desired a sea port to improve their communications and to trade with the Europeans for arms. Knowing that the city was occupied by English and French forces, they believed that they would not intervene and so would be able to secure the city without much opposition. This miscalculation would eventually lead to the rebels losing the war and ultimately to the destruction of their movement.

Shanghai Threatened

It was true that the British and French troops were under orders not to get involved in the civil war, however, despite the war with China, the Europeans were still conducting a high level of trade for which Shanghai was the main hub. The merchants and officials, of Shanghai, would allow nothing to disrupt this lucrative trade.

British response to the threat

Mr Bruce the Minister, in his capacity as Superintendant of British Trade, issued a proclamation at Shanghai on 26th May 1860, to the effect that if Shanghai, as an open port, were to become the scene of attack and civil war *"commerce would receive a severe blow"*, therefore he would *"call upon the commanders of Her Majesty's naval and military authorities to take proper measures to prevent the inhabitants of Shanghai from being exposed to massacre and pillage … and to protect the city against any attack"*.

As soon as the threat was felt to be imminent, the gates of the walled city were placed under the control of Royal Marines and soldiers from the Indian army, the river was commanded by gunboats and the roads to the city were barricaded.

Merchant response to the threat

In may 1860, Takee (Yang Fang) and several other wealthy merchants at Shanghai, disturbed by the approach of the rebels, arranged with Woo, the city leader, for funds to enlist the help of foreigners to fight the rebels and defend the city. With funds available, Takee engaged the services of two Americans, Frederick Townsend Ward and Henry Andres Burgevine to enlist an army of mercenaries, and promised a large sum of money if the force could retake the city of Sungkiang about 18 miles from Shanghai, up the Whampoa river. "General" Ward, a filibuster of some note, having served with General William Walker in Central America, had arrived in Shanghai some time in 1859.

The "Ever Victorious Army"

Initially Ward recruited about 100 men, mainly sailors, to serve in what would later be known as the "Ever Victorious Army". In July 1860, Ward with his small force made an attack against Sungkiang but this was repulsed with some losses on each side.

Figure 19. Fredrick Townsend Ward

Not deterred, Ward augmented his force with a band of natives from Manila and lying up concealed during the day, they seized one of the city gates at sunset. The force managed to hold off repeated rebel attempts to dislodge them until the next morning, when Chinese Imperial troops arrived and using the secured gate managed to drive the rebels from the city.

"General" Ward received the reward for recapturing Sungkiang, and news of the success together with the high wages on offer attracted even more men to his army. With another reward on offer, "General" Ward with 280 of his own men and 10,000 Chinese troops under the command of General Li Adong and supported by 200 Chinese gunboats, prepared to mount an attack on Singpoo.

Learning from the Imperial Chinese, the Taiping rebels also employed Europeans and at Singpoo they were assisted by Mr Savage, an English sailor. When "General" Ward attacked Singpoo during the night on the 2nd August, his force managed to reach the city walls but were driven back with considerable losses and Ward himself was severely wounded in the jaw.

Ward returned to Shanghai, but despite his wound immediately returned to Singpoo having collected 100 fresh men (mostly Italians and Greeks) and two 18 pounder guns. These meagre reinforcements were to no avail as, the Taiping leader Chung-Wang arrived at Singpoo with a superior force and after surprising Ward's force, captured his boats and guns together with many muskets and drove him back to Sungkiang where he was besieged. With his rear now guarded, Chung-Wang now advanced with his force to join other elements of the rebel army on the outskirts of Shanghai.

Attack on Shanghai

On the 16th August 1860, as his forces approached Shanghai, the rebel leader Chung-Wang issued a communication to the British,

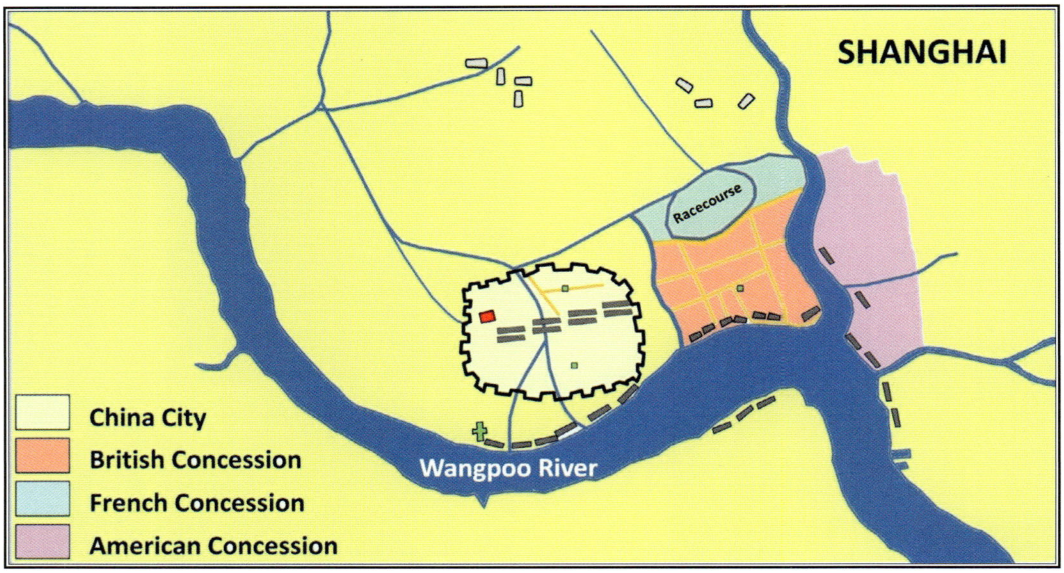

Figure 20. Shanghai

French and American ministers in the city, stating that his forces would soon be arriving and that they should raise yellow flags on their residences and commercial buildings which would then not be disturbed in any way.

After having driven the Imperial Army from their encampments just outside the walls, the rebels attacked the city on the 18th August 1860 but after facing heavy artillery and musket fire, they retired for the night out of the range of the allied guns.

During the night the rebels advanced on the French quarter of the town and the French forces, unwilling to allow their advance through the quarter with its crowded buildings and narrow streets set fire to the buildings to halt their progress.

The next day as the rebels tried to continue their advance they were driven from the city by artillery and musket fire. On the 20th August, the rebels change their line of attack towards the British quarter but rocket and artillery fire from the Marines eventually forced them to retreat. During the night, the gunboat *Pioneer* advanced up river and shelled the rebel encampments which had the effect of deterring further attempts against the city; the rebels broke camp and fell back on Sikawai.

Taiping retreat from Shanghai

After inflicting great amounts of injury on the local peasant population, on the 22nd August 1860, the rebel army left the vicinity of Shanghai. Bypassing Sungkiang, which was still occupied by "General" Ward and his men, the rebels capture Pinghoo and Kashing Fu causing the Imperial General Chang Yu-Liang to raise the siege at Kashing fu. By capturing the city of Shemen, the rebels managed to cut off some of General Chang's men, preventing them from retreating to Hangchow, the men surrendered and many of them joined the rebel cause. The rebel army now moved off to Soochow, where the population were suffering greatly from famine.

Rebel setbacks in the Yangtze river valley

With the British and French war with China now at an end, the Imperial War Commissioner, Tseng Kuo-fan redoubled the Imperial army's efforts against the rebels and started to press the siege at Nanking. The renewed efforts of the Imperialists forced Chung-Wang to return to Nanking and to protect the Taiping territories in the Yangtze river valley; Chen Kunshu was left in charge of the forces occupying Soochow. On his arrival at the Taiping capital, Nanking, Chung-Wang urged the various chiefs to increase their efforts to amass large supplies of food in the city to withstand a prolonged siege.

After ensuring the protection of the capital, Chung-Wang assembled his chiefs in October 1860 and resolved that their objectives for the coming year was the capture of Hangkow and the relief of Nanking. After suffering several defeats by the Imperial Army, Chung-Wang had to abandon his plans and in November 1861, the city of Nanking, which had been occupied by the Taiping rebels for three years, finally fell to Imperial Forces. On entering the city, the Imperial troops found thousand of the population lying dead in the streets having succumbed to starvation, the situation was so desperate that the population had resorted to cannibalism.

The Taiping from Soochow managed to capture Chapoo, however, when they made a move towards Ningbo, which was one of the consular ports, they were warned off by Captain Roderick Dew from *HMS Encounter*.

Neutrality Enforced

Now that the war with China was at an end, Admiral James Hope was able to turn his attention to the Taiping question namely the rebel effect on British trade, he also had to visit ports on the Yangtze which had been opened up to trade by the new treaty. In February 1861, the Admiral proceeded up the Yangtze to Nanking where he sent a message to the rebel leader Tian Wang, telling him that his forces should not approach within 30 miles of Shanghai. Tian Wang replied that his forces would leave Shanghai unmolested for one year.

Proceeding up the river, Admiral Hope reached Nanking which was still besieged by Imperial forces and then on past Kiukiang which was in ruins and on to Hangkow and having established a consulate at Kiukiang he did the same at Hangkow. On his return to Shanghai, the Admiral reported that the cities occupied by the Taiping were desolate and the people suffered great misery while the cities captured by the Imperialists showed confidence returning and trade being renewed.

At Shanghai, "General" Ward, during March and April 1861, was gathering a new force for a third attempt to capture Singpoo, and sent them to Sungkiang where Burgevine was entrenched with some Imperialist troops. Admiral Hope and the consuls, eager to enforce the British neutrality in the civil war, arrested Ward and some of his men on the 19th May and took him to Shanghai where he was tried as an American citizen illegally engaged in war. To avoid prosecution, Ward renounced his American citizenship and claimed Chinese nationality; he did, however, promise not to attempt to engage Europeans and Americans to fight on the side of the Imperialists.

New Chinese Leadership

On 21st August 1861, the Emperor Zianfeng died at his hunting lodge at Jehol at the age of 26 having served as Emperor for 10 years and was succeeded by his six year old son Ziachun, who would become Emperor Tongzhi. A regency council of eight men; Zaiyuan, Duanhua, Jungshou, Sushun, Muyin, Kuangyuan, Du Han and Jiao Youying was appointed to support the young emperor. The Chinese Supreme Council, the majority of whom were part of the anti-foreigner party, were opposed to the enforcement of the Treaty of Tientsin and the Peking Convention and Prince Sankolinsin still believed that the foreigners' demands could be resisted by military force.

When the Prince of Kung, the brother of the late Emperor and the person who had signed the Peking Convention was summoned to Jehol everyone expected his imminent demise, however, the Dowager Empress who led the Regency was a supporter who believed that the Prince understood the interests of the country better than her late husband's advisers. On the 2nd November, the Prince of Kung accompanied by the young Emperor, unexpectedly arrived at Peking and carried out a *coup d'ëtat* and overthrew the anti-Foreign party, the leaders of which were executed a few days later.

This new government consolidated friendly relationships with the Foreign Ministers and began working towards a long lasting peace in China, which required the destruction of the Taiping.

Operations around Shanghai and Ningbo in 1862

During 1861, after the arrangement between Tian Wang and the British authorities, Shanghai had been left at peace and the Taiping had concentrated their efforts on trying to take Hangkow and re-establish control in the Yangtze valley. However, the success of the Imperial troops was driving the Taiping out of the valley and closer to the Consular ports of Shanghai and Ningbo.

In the autumn of 1861 a Taiping army of about 100,000 men entered the rich province of Chekiang and occupied the city and port of Ningbo, as they left the Foreign settlement undisturbed, the allied forces maintained their position of neutrality, however, this did not prevent them from selling large amounts of arms and ammunition to the rebels.

On the 11th January 1862, Chung Wang moved down to Soochow and began to move his forces towards Shanghai. As they advanced, the Taiping burnt all before them driving hordes of distressed villagers into the security of Shanghai where they and the local merchants began to petition the Consoles for protection.

Admiral Hope and the French Admiral Protet decided to work together with "General" Ward who by now had 1,000 well trained Chinese troops at Sungkiang, and on 21st February attacked and captured the rebel headquarters which had been established at Kajow on the Pudong peninsula.

An Imperial decree on 16th March conferred the title of "Ever Victorious Army" on Ward's men in recognition of their efforts, and sent 9,000 troops from Nanking to join his ranks.

General C. W. Staveley replaced Sir John Michel, who was returning home, as commander of British forces in China and after consulting with Prince Kung and the British Minister at Peking determined to continue operations against the Taiping rebels. It was agreed to establish a 30 mile radius clear zone around Shanghai as a means of defending the city; this was subsequently approved by Sir Frederick Bruce, on the condition that any towns taken should be occupied by Imperial Chinese forces.

On the 4th April a combined force of British and French troops, together with the Ever Victorious Army, took Wong-kadza and two weeks later took Tsipoo, followed on the 27th April by Naizean and on the 1st May Kading.

After a time of peaceful coexistence, at Ningbo (the port south of Shanghai) the rebels became greedy and began to cast covetous eyes on the Foreign settlement. After shots were fired on the settlement and on his ship, the *HMS Ringdove*, Commander Craige informed Admiral Sir James Hope of the worsening situation. In response, the admiral despatched Captain Dew on board *HMS Encounter* to the area where he arrive off Ningbo on 24th April 1862. Soon after his arrival a large fleet of Imperial Army war junks, under the command of Apak, a former pirate, arrived on the scene and announced their intention of launching an attack on the city. Aided by a naval brigade led by Captain Dew, a combined British, French and Imperial Army force recaptured Ningbo and the rebels fled to Yuyow.

On the 6th May a new expedition led by Admirals Hope and Protet and General Staveley left Shanghai and took the cities of Singpoo, Najow and Cholin. At Najow, Admiral Protet was shot dead, causing the French marines and sailors to show no mercy to the Taiping defenders.

The small allied garrison left in Kading was joined by 5,000 Imperial troops from Nanking and Governor Sieh, agreed to an attack on the nearby town of Taitsan, however, hearing of this possible attack Chung Wang sent 10,000 handpicked Taiping troops from Soochow to reinforce Taitsan. An indecisive engagement was fought on the 15th May but on the next morning 2,000 of Chung Wang's men shaved their heads and pretended to defect to the Imperialist cause, this deception allowed the Taiping to inflict a terrible defeat on the Imperial Army and only about 2,000 of the original 7,000 men returned to Kading.

When Chung Wang began to follow up his success, the allied forces left Kading and returned to Shanghai and the Taiping force besieged Singpoo and Sungkiang which were held by General Ward's men. With limited forces at Singpoo, the position soon became desperate and on the 10th June 200 men of the 31st Regiment under the command of Colonel Spence and the Naval Brigade commanded by Admiral Hope launched an operation to relieve the town and evacuate the garrison. The operation was initially successful but a premature firing of the city by Ward's men alerted the rebels to the evacuation and the retreating garrison and relieving force were pursued and suffered heavy losses at the hands of the rebels.

Just as he was about to launch a concerted attack on Shanghai, Chung Wang received news that the Imperial Army was renewing their attacks on Nanking and that Tian Wang had ordered him to return with his forces to protect the capital. The Imperial army moved a force down the Yangtze from Nanking and occupied the two conical hills known as the Pillars near Wuhu while a further army of about 40,000 men established itself to the south west of Nanking near the Porcelain Tower Hill.

On arrival at Nanking, Tian Wang ordered Chung Wang to attack the Imperial army, who by now were occupying well entrenched and easily defendable positions. After wasting several weeks and loosing many men in this impossible task Chung Wang was censured for his failure, deprived of his noble rank and was despatched to Nganwhui to join the remnants of Ying Wang's force. The Taiping army were thus deprived of the skills of their most competent and successful leader.

During the summer months matters had remained quiet around Shanghai and the allied forces were allowed to complete their defensive works, however, rather than clearing the rebels from the vicinity of the city the allies only occupied Najow and Sungkiang.

On the 6th August, General Ward who now commanded a force of 5,000 men at Sungkiang, left the city with a force of 3,000 and retook Singpoo, leaving it to be garrisoned by Imperialist troops. On the 21st September 1862, during an attack on Tseki, General Ward was fatally wounded and Henry Burgevine assumed command of the Ever-Victorious Army.

The capture of Singpoo, triggered the Taiping forces at Soochow into action and in November the rebel forces, under Moh Wang, once again began to advance on Shanghai, driving the peasants before them. The force was repulsed by a force from the city commanded by Governor Lí and men of the Ever-Victorious Army commanded by Burgevine.

The Taiping forces continued to make attacks against the port of Ningbo, with some success capturing the walled suburb of Fenghua.

Able Seaman George Hinckley – Victoria Cross No. 306

It was on 9th October 1862 during an attack, by a naval brigade of men from *HMS Encounter* and *HMS Sphinx*, on the East Gate of the city that Able Seaman Hinckley performed the deeds for which he was later awarded the Victoria Cross.

Able Seaman Hinckley volunteered to go to the rescue of Mr Coker, the Masters Assistant of his ship *HMS Sphinx*, who was lying in the open severely wounded. Under continuous and heavy fire, Able Seaman Hinckley carried Mr Croker across 150 yards of open ground to the safety of a nearby joss house.

After returning to his position at the East Gate, Able Seaman Hinckley again volunteered to go to the assistance of Mr Bremer, an officer in the Ever Victorious Army, who had also been wounded during the advance and carried him to the safety of the joss house.

At about this time, the distrust between the Chinese and the Ever-Victorious Army was growing deeper, mainly due to the insulting behaviour of Burgevine. The Chinese merchants wanted General Charles William Dunbar Staveley, commander of the British troops, to intervene and take over command of the unit but he viewed the Ever-Victorious Army to be the responsibility of China, however, he did draw up a plan for how the army could be better organised with joint command by Foreign and Native officers.

In January 1863, after the army had not been paid for two months, when a force of 6,000 men was ordered to attack Nanking, Burgevine refused until the arrears had been paid. To force matters, Burgevine made a visit to the Mandarin banker Ta Kee, at Shanghai and in the course of an argument, Burgevine struck Ta Kee and made off with money that he found in his house.

General Staveley was again consulted by the Chinese who demanded that Burgevine be arrested; the General, however, informed Burgevine that he had been dismissed and that he should give up his command quietly, which he did. Captain Holland from the Royal Marines was put in temporary command of the force until Major Charles George Gordon was given command in March 1863.

General Gordon takes command of 'Ever Victorious' Army

In March 1863 Gordon proceeded to Sungkiang to take command of the force and without waiting to reorganize his troops he marched at once to the relief of Chansu, a town 40 miles north-west of Shanghai, which was invested by the rebels. The relief was successfully accomplished, and the operation established Gordon in the confidence of his troops. Gordon then reorganized his force, a matter of no small difficulty, and advanced against Quinsan, which was captured, though with considerable loss.

Gordon then marched through the country, seizing town after town from the rebels, until at length the great city of Suchow was invested by his army and a body of Chinese imperialist troops. The city was taken on 29 November 1863, and after its capture Gordon had a serious dispute with Li Hung Chang, as the latter had beheaded certain of the rebel leaders whose lives the former had promised to spare if they surrendered. This action, though not opposed to Chinese ethics, was so opposed to Gordon's ideas of honour, that he withdrew his force from Suchow, and remained inactive at Quinsan until February 1864.

Figure 21. Charles George "Chinese" Gordon

End of the Rebellion

Gordon then came to the conclusion that the subjugation of the rebels was more important than his dispute with Li, and visited the latter in order to arrange for further operations. After the meeting with Li Hung Chang the "Ever-Victorious Army" again advanced and took a number of towns from the rebels, ending with the capture of Chanchufu, the principal military position of the Taiping, in May 1864. After this decisive victory, Gordon returned to Quinsan and disbanded his force.

In June 1864 Tian Wang, the leader of the Taiping Rebellion, seeing his cause was hopeless, committed suicide, and the capture of Nanking by the imperialist troops shortly afterwards brought the Taiping revolt to a conclusion.

8

THE UMBEYLA CAMPAIGN, INDIA (1863)

Background

For many years, the North West Frontier area of India, which acted as buffer state between Afghanistan and the Punjab, had been an area of great lawlessness, with many of the local tribes acting as bandits on both sides of the border. It was not unusual for the British to wage punitive expeditions and sometimes wars against the Pathan hill tribes, however, these were usually quite minor affairs.

The root of the troubles which led to the Umbeyla campaign in 1863, began almost fifty years earlier when Sayyid Ahmed Shah Brelwi (originally from Bareilly in Oudh) returned from a pilgrimage to Mecca and began to preach war to the Yusafzai villages on the northern Peshawar border. In 1829, Brelwi and his followers captured Peshawar from the Sikhs but two years later were driven back into the hills and Brelwi was killed.

Despite the death of Brelwi, the Wahabi sect flourished and set up their base in and around the village of Sitana in a mountainous region to the west of the River Indus, about 75 miles north of Peshawar. For many years the sect, named the *"Hindustani Fanatics"* by the British, carried out campaigns of banditry on the Yusafzai plains, robbing and murdering peaceful merchants and traders.

In 1853, Colonel Frederick Mackeson led a force of irregulars, numbering about 2,000 men, against the sect but without much success. During, and after, the Indian Mutiny the sect expanded

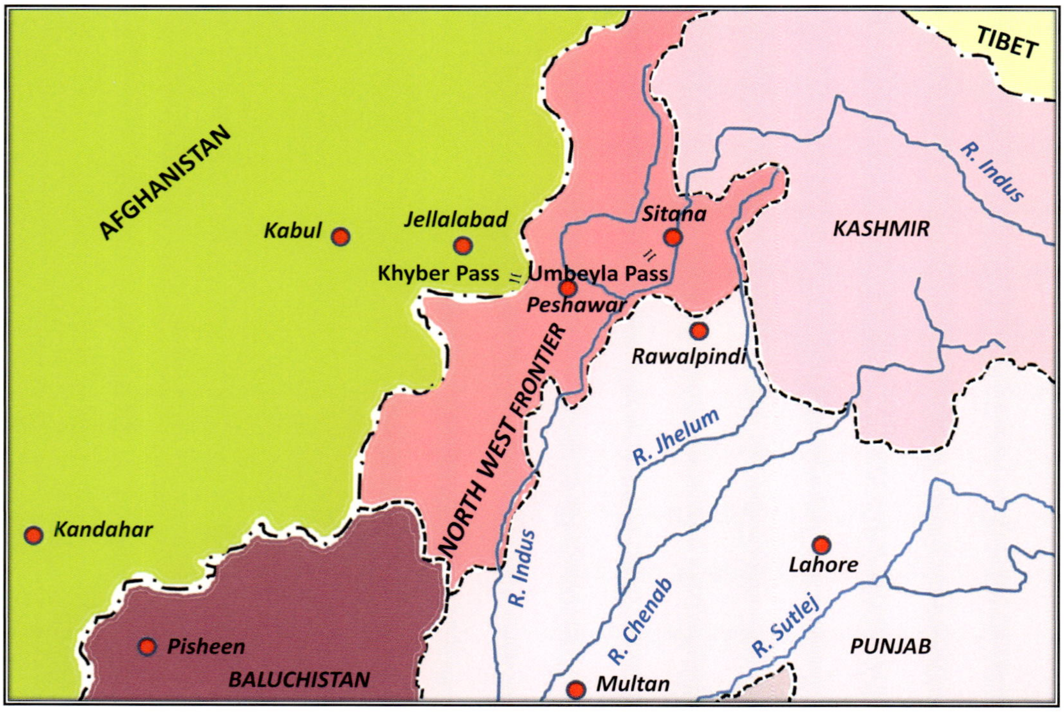

Figure 22. North West Frontier India

its ranks and its supply of arms and ammunition by welcoming many of the fleeing mutineers.

As the sect were still plying their trade of banditry, Sir Sydney Cotton led a larger expedition of 5,000 men against the *"Hindustani Fanatics"* in 1858. This expedition was more successful, with the sect being driven out of Sitana where their forts were destroyed. Unfortunately most of the fanatics escaped and set up a new base at the village of Malka on the north side of the Mahaban mountain.

For a short while, the fanatics were relatively quiet as they consolidated their position at Malka, however, by the summer of 1863 they were once again raiding the border area with increasingly larger groups of bandits. With these latest raids, Robert Montgomery, the governor of the Punjab, decided enough was enough and issued orders that the fanatics must be punished and their stronghold at Malka destroyed.

Sir Hugh Rose, the Commander-in-Chief, was against the campaign, however, his objections were overruled and he appointed Brigadier Neville Bowles Chamberlain[6] as commander of the expedition, who thought that a winter campaign in the mountains would be a stiff challenge.

The Umbeyla Campaign begins

Malka, the initial target for the expedition, was positioned in a very inaccessible location in a valley surrounded by high mountains; the Chumla valley was selected to be the base for the British operations which was within the heartland of the Bunerwal tribe. It was thought that the Bunerwal, who were themselves in dispute with the fanatics, would not try to impede the British columns.

An expeditionary force of about 5,600 men was assembled at Nowakilla on the Yusafzai plains, comprising men from 71st Highlanders, 101st Bengal Fusiliers, 32nd Bengal Native Infantry, 100 Ghurkhas, 4 regiments of Punjab infantry 100 men of Probyn's Horse, 100 men of the Guide Cavalry; supported by the Royal Artillery and the Peshawar Mountain guns.

The force was fully assembled by 12th October 1863 and five days later General Chamberlain arrived to take up his command. To reach the Chumla valley, the force would have to cross a range of mountains and had a choice of using the Durrun Pass, used by Sir Sydney Cotton during his 1858 expedition, or the Umbeyla Pass which was thought to be a less strenuous route.

In an attempt to persuade the local tribes, that the British would once again use the Durrun Pass, a small force commanded

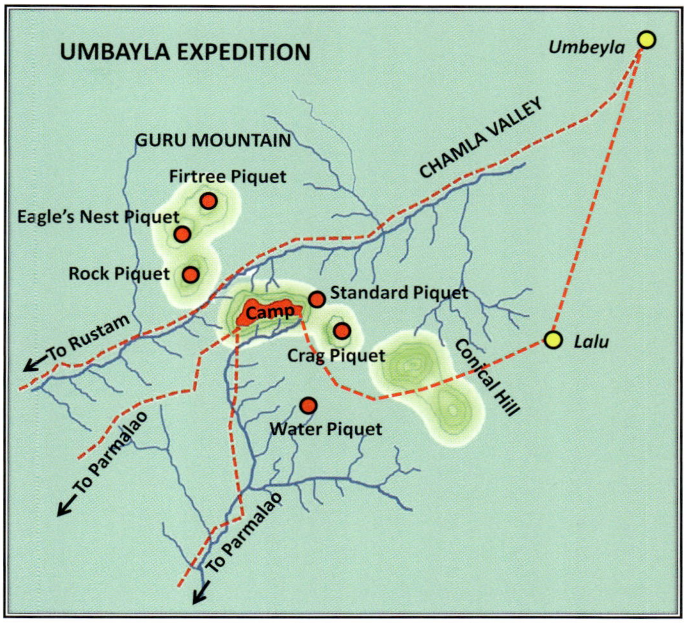

Figure 23. Umbeyla Campaign

by Major Keyes was sent to camp at the mouth of the pass. The Bunerwal tribesmen were quick to respond to this apparent threat to their territory, began to concentrate in large numbers in the Durrun Pass and construct a blockade.

On 19th October 1863, General Chamberlain broke camp at Nowakilla and after issuing orders for Major Keyes and his men to rejoin the force at Pernpouli, set off on a march to the Umbeyla Pass.

Rather belatedly, the General also issued a proclamation to the Bunerwal Tribe of the British intentions, to pass through their lands en-route to attack the *"Hindustani Fanatics"* and that they would be unmolested. The *"Hindustani Fanatics"* also sent messages to the Bunerwal, stating that the British would occupy their lands; in light of the British conquest of India it is not surprising that these were the messages that were believed. Having been consulted by the Bunerwal, the Akhund of Swat, a religious leader who held a tremendous influence with the Pathan tribes, supported resistance to the British invasion and from the near-by Guru Mountain made a call to arms to the surrounding tribes.

After an overnight march, the British forces had reached high ground above Roostum Bazaar and following a brief meal continued on to Surkhowa where they entered the mouth of the Umbeyla Pass. The pass was about nine miles long and by 22nd October, the British had reached a point two miles from the end of the pass where they established a camp to await the arrival of their artillery and the baggage column. While the camp was being formed, Colonel Probyn with a party of cavalry set out to

6 His nephew, Neville Francis Fitzgerald Chamberlain, an army major in India, invented the game of snooker in 1875.

reconnoitre the remainder of the route to the Chumla valley and after bypassing the village of Umbeyla proceeded as far as Kagah without meeting any resistance. On his journey, Colonel Probyn passed many Bunerwal tribesmen, however, these men stated they would remain peaceable unless the British tried to force the Boneyr Pass. On his return to the British camp, the mood of the tribesmen seems to have changed abruptly and after being fired upon, Colonel Probyn and his men had to charge the Bunerwal and force their way into the British camp.

Now encircled by large numbers of hostile tribesmen, the British force was unable to proceed further so General Chamberlain set about establishing defensive positions with Eagle's Nest, Fir Tree, Rock and Nest Piquets to the west of the camp and Water, Standard and Crag Piquets to the east; the tribesmen established a strong position on Conical Hill. The Royal Engineers began to connect the various posts and establish defensive breastworks to accommodate the mountain guns wherever possible but due to the rugged nature of the terrain this was a most difficult task.

On 26th October, the Bunerwal made an attack in force against the eastern side of the British camp, however, Colonel Keys and his men managed to drive them off back to the Conical Hill, capturing one of their standards in the process. During an attack on the western flank, with additional men from the Guru Mountain, the enemy had more success and after losing about half of their men the British were forced to abandon the Eagle's Nest Piquet.

Attacks on Crag Piquet

The key to the defence of the eastern flank of the British Camp, was a high rock hill known as the Crag Piquet, that commanded all of the lower defences; the route to this position was a precipitous narrow path leading to a small plateau with only a little area of flat ground upon which men could stand. Up until the night of 29th October Colonel Keyes had only utilised the Crag Piquet as an observation post manned by 12 men.

Lieutenant George Fosbery – Victoria Cross No. 307
Lieutenant Henry Pitcher – Victoria Cross No. 308

Just before dawn on the 30th October, the Bunerwal, realising the importance of the position, mounted an attack with about 250 men and managed to capture Crag Piquet, driving off the small garrison. The nine survivors from the piquet, only retreated as far as the base of the Crag and after calling for reinforcements continued to fire at the enemy who were trying to consolidate their position.

Colonel Keyes and his adjutant Lieutenant Pitcher answered the call for support and together with about 20 men attempted to drive the enemy from the Crag but were repulsed by superior numbers. By daybreak about 75 men were assembled under overhanging rocks about 20 yards from the summit and when it was light enough to distinguish friend from foe, Colonel Keyes ordered the men to fix bayonets and charge. The attack, which had to be made up steep paths in single file was made by three columns led by Colonel Keyes and Lieutenants Pitcher and Fosbury.

Lieutenant Fosbury was the first man to gain the summit and would have been closely followed by Lieutenant Pitcher, had he not been wounded by a boulder hurled down from the summit. After intense hand-to-hand fighting, during which Colonel Keyes was severely wounded, the British managed to drive the enemy from the Crag and down the side of the mountain.

For their part in the action Lieutenants Fosbury and Pitcher were both awarded the Victoria Cross.

Following the action on the 30th October, Crag Piquet was enlarged, the defences were strengthened and the garrison was increased to 160 men.

From 31st October to 5th November, apart from some desultory sniping against the British positions, the tribesmen were relatively quiet and made no significant attacks.

For some time it was obvious that the route along the Umbeyla defile was unsuitable for the resupply of the British camp and also for the evacuation of the sick and wounded. This was due to the fact that the enemy held the heights on both sides of the defile and together with the men stationed on Guru mountain were able to rain down a heavy fire on any convoys. To overcome this problem Colonel Taylor of the Royal Engineers began the construction of two alternative routes, utilising the road between the villages of Khanpur and Sherdara. When the road was completed on 8th November, the base of operations was moved from Rustam to Parmalao.

Meanwhile, in the Punjab, Governor Sir Robert Montgomery was alarmed by the events and delays in the Umbeyla Pass and wanted to withdraw the British troops. General Hugh Rose, although he had initially been against the expedition, was against a withdrawal because of the adverse impact on British prestige in the area and pressed for reinforcements instead. General Rose's view was accepted and he began to assemble a force at Nowshera.

On the morning of 13th November, Major Charles Brownlow and his men were relieved by Lieutenant Davidson and a detachment of the 1st Punjab Infantry, after having spent 48 hours of constant work, fighting the tribesmen and strengthening the defences at the Crag Piquet. Almost before the new men had settled into their posts, they faced an assault and were driven from the Crag. Lieutenants Pitcher and Young were sent to retake the Crag but were driven back by superior numbers and during the charge Lieutenant Pitcher was severely wounded

The enemy now pressed on their attack against Major Keyes and his men at the lower piquet but accurate fire from the Peshawar Mountain Battery slowed their progress, and allowed Colonel Alfred Wilde with three companies of the Guides Infantry to come to the rescue. General Chamberlain with the 101st Bengal Fusiliers also arrived to provide assistance. This combined force continued upwards and managed to once again recapture the Crag Piquet.

From the 14th to 17th November, no serious attacks were conducted by the enemy so during this quiet period, stores and ammunition were moved from the western piquets in preparation for the move to consolidate the British troops on the hills to the east of the camp. On the 18th November, the positions on the Guru mountain were abandoned and the troops moved to new positions in the camp or on the eastern heights. With the concentration of the British troops now to the east and with the completion of the new roads, the engineers constructed the Water Piquet to the east of the camp as a secure area for the storage of the expeditions water, which had to be transported from Parmalao.

On discovering that the British had abandoned their piquets on Guru mountain, the enemy thought that this was the start of a retreat and made a strong attack on the British camp. After heavy fighting which lasted until nightfall, the attacks were finally repulsed. Following this concerted attack was a period of calm, which allowed 166 wounded and 286 sick men to be evacuated to Parmalao; to conserve fodder, all but the most essential animals were also evacuated.

On the 20th November, the enemy captured the Crag Piquet for a third time, however, a force of men from the 71st Highlanders and 5th Ghurkhas, led by General Chamberlain manage to recapture the position in quick order but during the assault, General Chamberlain received his ninth and final wound.

During the fighting, Major H. R. James, the Commissioner of Peshawar, who was acting as political officer to the expedition, was conducting negotiations with some of the tribal leaders in order that they would withdraw their men from the conflict. After the retaking of Crag Piquet for the third time, on the 20th November, it appears that his efforts had been at least partly successful as it was reported that about half of the Buner tribes, about 2,000 men, had returned home. Unfortunately this reduction in the enemy force was soon compensated by new arrivals who numbered over 3,500 men.

On 30th November, General John Garvock arrived at the camp and took over command of the expedition, from General Chamberlain who, due to his wounds had relinquished his command.

General Garvock's tenure in command was only intended to be temporary, as General Rose expected to take over command when he arrived on the scene, and as such he was under orders not to launch any attack until General Rose's arrival.

In early December much needed reinforcements; in the form of the 7th Fusiliers, 3rd Sikhs, 93rd Highlanders and 23rd Punjab Infantry; arrived at the British camp, bringing the expeditionary force to a total of about 9,000 men.

On the 10th December, a deputation of chiefs from the Buner tribes arrived at the British camp for discussions with Major James, regarding ways in which the conflict could be ended. It was finally agreed that they would send a force, together with British officers as observers, to destroy the village of Malka and that they would expel all Hindustani Fanatics from their lands. Unfortunately, when this proposal was put to the Akhund of Swat, on the following day, he denounced all attempts to make a treaty with the British.

On the advice of Major James, General Garvock decided not to await the arrival of General Rose and on the morning of 15th December assembled a force of about 4,800 men at the foot of the Crag, in preparation for an attack on the village of Lalu. The first objective of the attack, was the enemy positions on the Conical Hills which were taken in great style. After scaling the heights, the force advanced the 1½ miles to the village of Lalu reaching the village in time to see the enemy fleeing their positions.

So far the fighting had mainly been the preserve of the Infantry, as little opportunity arose to deploy the cavalry in the confines of the Umbeyla Pass, however, now on the open ground of the Chamla valley, Colonel Probyn with his 400 men formed up with the infantry to attack the enemy who had taken up position in the village of Umbeyla. On the 16th December, Colonel Probyn used his men to great effect and after turning the enemy flanks, set fire to the village and allowed the infantry to route the enemy forces who fled in some disarray.

During these attacks, which cleared the path along the gorge to the Chamla valley and routed the enemy at Umbeyla, the enemy in the gorge decided to attack the British camp in strength but were repulsed with some ease.

True to their word, obtained during the discussions on 10th December, the Bunerwals took no part in the attacks of 15th and 16th December and on the 17th December their chief returned to the British camp ready to carry out the plan agreed on the 10th, despite the Akhund of Swat's objections.

On 19th December Colonel R. G. Taylor, escorted by the Corps of Guides, commanded by Lieutenant F. H. Jenkins and a body of men under the command of the Sudum chief Aziz Khan left Umbeyla and by evening had reached Kuria at the head of the Chamla valley. The force was accompanied by Colonel J. M. Adye, Colonel A. Taylor, Major F. S. Roberts VC, Major H. C. Johnstone, Major T. Wright and Lieutenant T. T. Carter, who were to act as observers.

After some delays due to heavy rain, the party reached Nagrai, in Amazai territory on 21st December, where the Amazai leaders were informed of the expeditions intentions and after some deliberations the Amazai added some of their men to the force. On 22nd December, the force reached Malka and finding it deserted it was burnt to the ground after which they returned to Kuria and by the following day had arrived back at the British camp in the Umbeyla Pass.

Having completed their mission, the British forces assembled at Nawa Kala on Christmas Day, in preparation for the return to their home bases, now that the expedition was over.

Although a success, the expedition took much longer than expected and the force suffered significant losses with 238 men killed (15 British Officers, 4 native Officers, 34 British and 185 native rank and file), a total of 670 men were wounded (21 British and 27 native Officers, 118 British and 504 native rank and file). The total losses of the enemy were estimated to be about 3,000.

9

WAIKATO-HAUHAU WAR, MAORI, NEW ZEALAND (1863–66)

Background

The treaty of Waitangi, signed on 6th February 1840, between representatives of the British Crown and various Maori chiefs from the North Island of New Zealand, gave the Crown the sole right to purchase Maori lands, if they chose to sell; while the Maori acknowledged the sovereignty of Queen Victoria.[7]

This led to Lieutenant Governor William Hobson declaring British sovereignty over the whole of New Zealand on 21st May 1840; the North Island by treaty and the South Island by discovery and on the 16th November 1840, New Zealand was constituted as a separate colony from the Australian New South Wales colony.

Between 1845 and 1872, 13 major conflicts were fought between British, Colonial forces and the Maori people of New Zealand; the majority of these conflicts were related to the British acquisition of Maori lands.

Following the coronation of the first Maori king, Potatau Te Wherowhero at Ngaruawahia in June 1858 the Maori of the North Island were for the first time united as one people. King Potatau and his followers, the Kingitanga, had the main objective of maintaining the Maori lands and preventing further sales of land to the British for use by European settlers. The heart of the Kingitanga movement was located in the Waikato region. King Potatau, set a boundary of the Mangatawhiri River to delineate his area of responsibility from that of the Governor. This was taken by many of the British to be a move towards Maori independence, however, it is not clear that this was the Maori intention.

When King Potatau, died from influenza on 25th June 1860, he was succeeded by his son Matutaera Tawhiao, who would reign for 35 years.

7 According to the British interpretation of the treaty.

Figure 24. Waikato War

Causes of the Waikato War

The British government interpreted the creation of a Maori King as a direct challenge to the authority of Queen Victoria and he was not recognised to be the leader of the Maori peoples. These concerns were compounded when some of the Waikato tribes provided assistance to the Taranaki tribes during the war of 1860–61; to the extent that both Governor Colonel Thomas Gore

Figure 25. Matutaera Tawhiao

Browne and his successor Sir George Grey considered an invasion of Waikato to stem this help.

The Taranaki War of 1860–61 ended in stalemate, with no answer to the Maori land issues but the focus of Government attention for new settlement lands now switched to the Waikato region.

With the increase in tensions, arising from the demands for more settlement lands it is understandable that mistrust grew between the settlers and the Maori and some of the settlers on the outskirts of Auckland began to fortify their farmhouses in response to rumours that the Maori were going to attack the city. It later transpired that the Maori had put together a plan of attack (for 1st September 1861), however, this was placed on hold when Sir George Grey replaced Browne as governor.

Many of the influential residents of Auckland openly promoted a military invasion of Waikato, on the grounds that this would at least neutralise the Kingitanga movement and open up the region to European settlement. Governor Grey, also came to the conclusion that a war was probably inevitable and began to make preparations for such an eventuality. Towards the end of 1861, Governor Grey ordered General Duncan Cameron, overall commander of the Imperial and Colonial forces in the colony, to extend the Great South Road from Drury down to the Waikato River.

Another vital preparation for war was the creation in July 1861 of the Commissariat Transport Corps who in addition to their responsibility for extending the Great South Road were also responsible for organising the transport logistics required by the army. As part of the Commissariat Department, under the command of Deputy Commissary General Humphrey Stanley Jones, which reported to the Treasury rather than the Army, the Commissariat Transport Corps utilised pack horses and river transport to move materials and troops to where they were required.

An armoured river fleet, the Waikato flotilla,[8] was assembled comprising nine river steamers which operated on the Waikato and Waipahu rivers between 1863 and 1870. Three of these vessels; the *Avon*, *Pioneer* and *Koheroa* served during the Waikato War where they towed four armoured barges and several other smaller barges. The flotilla enabled rapid movement of forces and supplies into the Waikato heartland, as well as supporting the shelling and outflanking of Maori positions.

Building on the lessons severely learned during the Crimean War, which had been a logistical nightmare, the Commissariat ensured that the Waikato Campaign would be one of the best prepared and organised operation undertaken by the British Army. Proof of their effectiveness was the fact that the sickness rate of the soldiers never rose above 5% while during the Crimean War only a decade earlier the rate was 14%.

In parallel to the road building, a chain of redoubts and stockades were built to the south of Auckland and along the lower Waikato River. By early 1863 the new road had been completed as far south as Havelock where a large redoubt (the Queen's Redoubt), capable of housing 450 men, was built less than a mile from the Mangatawhiri river, which the Maori considered to be their northern border.

As an indicator of the imminence of war, the Auckland Militia was called to arms on 22nd June and a few days later on 9th July the Maori in South Auckland were ordered to take an oath of allegiance to the Queen and to give up their arms or be banished across the Mangatawhiri.

On 11th July 1863, Governor Grey issued a statement that was a virtual declaration of war:

> *"Chiefs of Waikato,*
>
> *Europeans living quietly on their own lands in Waikato have been driven away; their property has been plundered; their wives and children have been taken from them. By the instigation of some of you, officers and soldiers were murdered at Taranaki. Others of you have since expressed approval of these murders. Crimes have been committed in other parts of the Island, and the criminals have been rescued or sheltered under the colour of your authority.*
>
> *You are now assembling in armed bands; you are constantly threatening to come down the river to ravage the Settlement of Auckland and to murder peaceable settlers. Some of you offered a safe passage through your territories to armed parties contemplating such outrages.*

8 New Zealand's first navy

The well-disposed among you are either unable or unwilling to prevent these evil acts.

I am therefore compelled, for the protection of all, to establish posts at several points on the Waikato River, and to take necessary measures for the future security of persons inhabiting that district. The lives and property of all well-disposed people living on the river will be protected, and armed and evil-disposed people will be stopped from passing down the river to rob and murder Europeans. I now call on all well-disposed natives to aid the Lieutenant-General to establish and maintain these posts, and to preserve peace and order.

Those who remain peaceably at their own villages in Waikato, or move into such districts as may be pointed out by the Government, will be protected in their persons, property, and land. Those who wage war against Her Majesty, or remain in arms, threatening the lives of-Her peaceable subjects, must take the consequences of their acts, and they must understand that they will forfeit the right to the possession of their lands guaranteed to them by the Treaty of Waitangi, which lands will be occupied by a population capable of protecting for the future the quiet and unoffending from the violence with which they are now so constantly threatened".

On the following day, a small force of British troops crossed the Mangatawhiri River and the Waikato Campaign was underway.

Invasion of the Waikato

On 12th July 1863, acting on the orders of General Cameron, Lieutenant Colonel Austen left the Queen's Redoubt at Pokeno with the 2nd battalion 14th Regiment of Foot and after crossing the Mangatawhiri River entered Waikato thus beginning the war.

The small British force established their position on the site of an old Maori Pa, on a hill overlooking the river. A few days later they were reinforced by detachments from the 12th and 70th

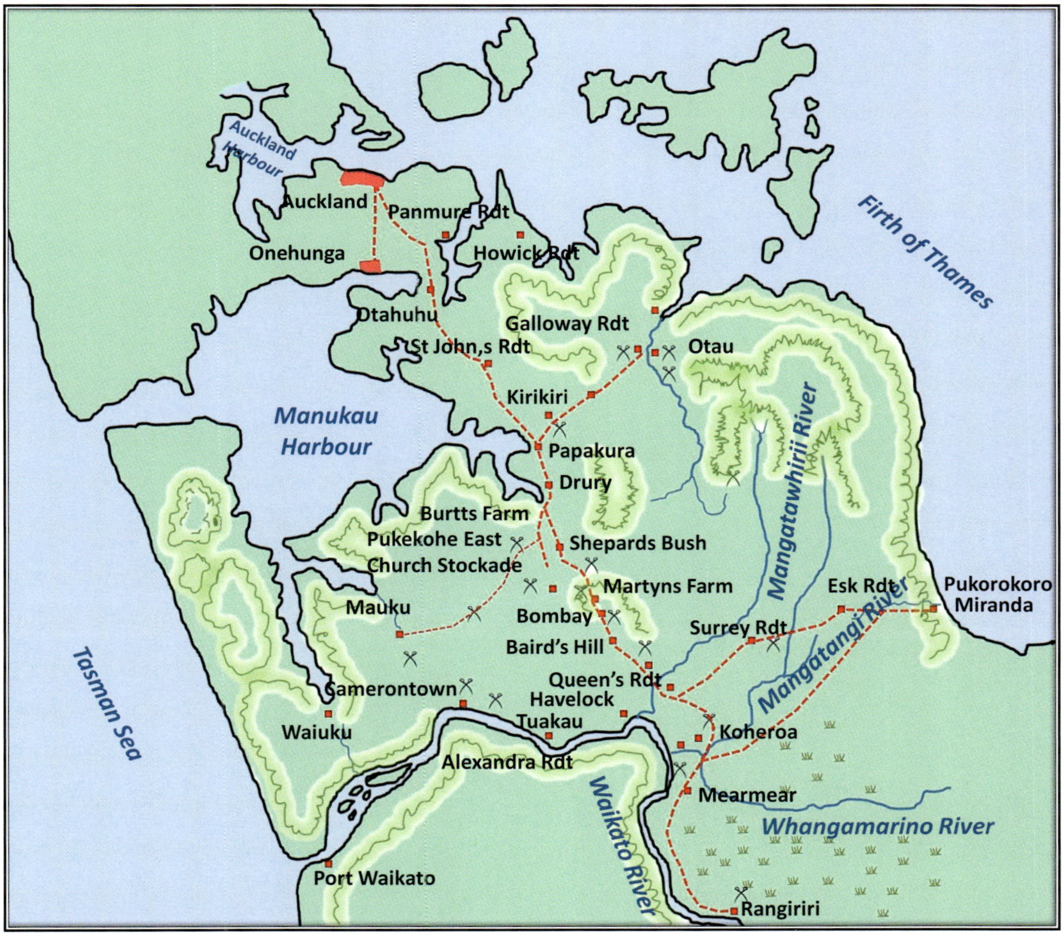

Figure 26. Invasion of Waikato

Regiments of Foot, bringing the strength up to about 500 men. To accommodate the larger force, three additional field works were established on the hill.

Expulsion of the Maori

In line with the terms of his dictate of 9th July, as the vast majority of the Maori had failed to sign the oath of allegiance, Governor Grey began the process of expelling the Maori from the lands to the south of Auckland. Maori settlements in the districts of Manukau, Papakura, Patumahoe, Tuakau and others were cleared, with the people being moved into the Waikato. The largest tribe to be evicted were the Ngati-Paoa, who had a large settlement at Tuakau on the north bank of the Waikato River.

The First Engagements

As was to be expected, after the British forces crossed into Waikato territory, the Maori tribes began to congregate in preparation to expel the invaders. Tribes from the upper Waikato, Ngati-Maniapoto, Ngati-Haua, Ngati-Raukawa and war parties from as far as Taranaki and the upper Whanganui began to assemble to the south of the Mangatawhiri River, ready to do battle with the British.

Battle of Koheroa Ridge

Before the concentration of Maori forces was complete, the first encounter of the war was precipitated by Te Huirama, a relative of King Tawhiao, who dug in with 200 to 300 of his men on the Koheroa ridge near Te Teoteo, overlooking the British camp on the south bank of the Mangatawhiri River.

In the afternoon of 17th July, men from the camp of the 14th Regiment observed the Maori activity and Lieutenant Colonel Austen immediately ordered his battalion to march on the Maori position, closely followed by detachments of the 12th and 70th Regiments. General Cameron, observing the activity from the Queen's Redoubt, formed up his own column which soon overtook Colonel Austen's men. Leading from the front, General Cameron spurred on the young men from the 14th Regiment who had hesitated before unexpected fire from advanced Maori rifle pits. Led by their officers, the men of the 14th charged the Maori entrenchments and at bayonet point drove them from their lines. The Maori retreated to the south falling back temporarily to each of their lines of defence, before they were driven to the heights above the Maramarua and Whangamarino rivers. The majority of the Maori survivors escaped down a gully, crossed the Whangamarino and made their way to Meremere.

The British casualties were slight with one killed and 12 wounded.[9] The Maori dead numbered 30, including their chief Te Huirama, many more were wounded. After the battle a British redoubt was established near the site of Te Teoteo, an old Maori Pa, which had a commanding view of the point where the Great South Road crosses the Whangamarino River; Lieutenant Pickard, with two field-guns was left to guard the post.

The second skirmish of the war also took place on 17th July and was the first of several guerrilla style attacks on British convoys and piquets along the Great South Road. A war party from the Ngati-Paoa tribe, led by chief Hori Ngakapa, laid an ambush on the forest road at the foot of the Pukewhau hill, near where a settler Mr Martin had his farm.

A convoy of six carts, escorted by 50 men of the 18th Royal Irish Regiment, under the command of Major Turner and Captain Ring, was moving along the road from the Queen's Redoubt towards Drury when the Maori, hidden in the bush at the edge of the road, let loose a volley of fire. This first volley, killed and wounded several of the British soldiers and the Maori attempted to cut off the rearguard of about 12 men, however, despite several of them being wounded they mounted a bayonet charge and managed to fight their way back to the main party.

Reunited the convoy continued their march towards Ramarama, pursued by the Maori who kept up a constant fire on the column from both sides of the road. A detachment of men of the 18th Regiment from Baird's Hill and other reinforcements from Drury arrived in time to drive off the attackers. The British had five men killed and eleven wounded, Maori casualties were slight.

Battle of Kirikiri

Kirikiri was a small settlement on the edge of the Hunua forest, where Mr Hay, one of the pioneering settlers had his farmhouse. While cutting timber in the nearby forest, a small party of settlers was attacked by a band of about 50 Maori raiders and one of the men, James Hunt, was shot and killed.

The remainder of the party managed to escape and took refuge in Mr Hay's farmhouse, from where the settlers managed to keep the Maori at bay with intense rifle fire. The settlers were soon reinforced by a small detachment of Militia, commanded by Captain Clare, who arrived from Papakura. Not long afterwards, Captain Ring arrived with 100 men of the 18th Regiment from the newly constructed Kirikiri Redoubt (later to be known as Ring's Redoubt). The newly arrived forces united and began to drive the Maori from the bush towards the hills where they took up position at a site previously established by Captain Ring.

9 One of the wounded was Colonel Austen, who was later fatally wounded at the Battle of Rangiriri.

The British forces managed to drive the Maori from this defensive position, which they then occupied, however, they were soon surrounded by the enemy and were in danger of having their flanks breached when Colonel Wyatt arrived with a force of men from the 65th Regiment, supported by Lieutenant Rait and men of the Mounted Artillery. Even though the Maori had also received reinforcements, the British forces managed to force the Maori to call off the engagement and they withdrew to the safety of the forest. This was the first engagement fought by men from the colonial Militia.

Following the Battle of Kirikiri, several minor actions took place; on 10th August action took place in the forests of the Hunua Ranges; on 25th August a Maori war party attacked contractors at Williamson's Clearing, who were clearing the forest from the edge of the Great South Road. On 2nd September an attack was made against the piquet at Pokeno and the Kakaramea Redoubt was attacked on 8th September.

Battle of Camerontown

Camerontown, named after General Cameron, was established on the north bank of the Waikato River as a half way storage depot for army stores being shipped up the river to the British field headquarters. The depot was managed by two European civilians and the Resident Magistrate of the Lower Waikato, Mr James Armitage, supervised the transport of the stores up river. The town was guarded by friendly Maori, who lived in a small Pa on a hill overlooking the depot; the Maori, using their canoes were also engaged in the transport of goods up river.

On 7th September 1863, Mr Armitage was at the mouth of the Waikato, supervising the transfer of the cargo of the barque *City of Melbourne* to a large flotilla of native canoes. Having completed this task and the despatch of the flotilla up river towards the Mangatawhiri, Mr Armitage was on his way back to Camerontown when he was ambushed by a group of about 100 hostile Maori. During the ensuing fire fight, Mr Armitage and two of his companions; Mr William Strand and Mr Heughan were all killed. On arriving at Camerontown, the Maori war party was engaged by the friendly Maori but after a brief skirmish they were driven off and the invading Maori managed to destroy a large quantity of commissariat stores.

Colour-Sergeant Edward McKenna – Victoria Cross No. 309
Lance-Corporal John Ryan – Victoria Cross No. 310

The noise of the skirmish at Camerontown alerted the troops at the nearby Alexandra Redoubt, which had been built in July 1863, and when Tuakau and his party of friendly Maori arrived at the redoubt with news of the death of Mr Armitage and the burning of the stores, Captain Swift of the 65th Regiment, who was in command, formed a column to intercept the invading Maori.

Together with Lieutenant Butler, the senior NCO Colour Sergeant McKenna and fifty of his men, Captain Swift set out for Camerontown and came across the war party in the bush near the town.

During the resulting battle, Captain Swift was mortally wounded and Lieutenant Butler was severely wounded, so as he lay dying the Captain ordered Colour Sergeant McKenna to take command of the column and to continue the fight.

Despite being heavily outnumbered, Colour Sergeant McKenna led his men with skill and courage and they managed to kill or wound between 20 and 30 of the enemy with the loss of only one man killed and another missing. During the heavy fire fight, Lance Corporal Ryan, together with Privates Bulford, Cole, Talbot and Thomas removed the mortally wounded Captain Swift from the field of action and guarded his body throughout the night.

For their actions during this battle, Colour Sergeant McKenna and Lance-Corporal Ryan were later awarded the Victoria Cross; tragically Lance-Corporal Ryan was later drowned in the river Waikato, while trying to save the life of a comrade. Privates Bulford, Cole, Talbot and Thomas were awarded the Distinguished Conduct Medal.

The Forest Rangers

Almost from the start of the war, after the British forces crossed the Mangatawhiri river and began their advance into the Waikato, Maori war parties who occupied the forest country of the Hunua and Wairoa ranges mounted guerrilla style attacks to the flanks and rear of the British army. These roving bands of Maori were able to raid the settler farmhouses and ambush convoys with little losses to themselves, before disappearing into the safety of the bush. At this time, neither the British army regulars or the city Militia had the skills or experience to pursue the Maori into the forest.

It soon became clear that a special force was required to take on the Maori on their own ground to counter this guerrilla warfare, clear the bush along the Great South Road and provide protection to the settlers and army convoys. In the first week of August 1863, the government published a notice in the Auckland Southern Cross newspaper, inviting young men with experience of the forest to join the ranks of the Corps of Forest Volunteers. After a large response from men of the settlement community and men from the declining gold fields of the Coromandel a company of 60 Forest Rangers was formed, under the command of Lieutenant William Jackson, a young settler from the Papakura district.

Towards the end of the year a second company of Forest Rangers was formed, under the command of Gustavus Ferdinand Von Tempsky who had served as 2nd in command to William Jackson.

The Forest Rangers were disbanded on 30th October 1867, after the end of hostilities.

Defence of the Pukekohe East Church Stockade

Pukekohe East was founded in 1859 by settlers who had arrived in New Zealand from Scotland and Cornwall. When the war started, all of the able bodied men were formed into a company of the Forest Rifle Volunteers, to defend their district. The families were sent to Drury or Auckland for safety.

Sergeant Perry was placed in command of the stockade, which had been built around the community church. Lieutenant D. H. Lusk, who was in charge of the defences between Waiuku and Pukekohe East encouraged the settlers to improve the defences of the stockade as he thought them to be inadequate and incomplete. After inspecting the stockade on 31st August, Lieutenant Lusk again found the defences to be incomplete and ordered the Volunteers to strengthen the log wall by piling up earth dug out from a trench at its foot.

On the evening of 13th September, four men from the stockade garrison (Privates Joseph Scott, Elijah Roose, William Hodge and a special constable from Drury) were returning to the stockade, having been away to feed stock at a nearby farm, when they came across Maori in the bush.

This large band of Maori were converging on the stockade, however, the four men from the Volunteers managed to break through them and joined their comrades within the stockade in time to help defend against the attack which began the next morning.

At the time of the attack, the stockade defences were still incomplete; the stockade wall was only five feet high, not seven feet and was not crowned by a row of iron spikes, as intended. Of more concern was the fact that the bush had not been cleared far enough from the walls to provide clear lines of fire; the stockade was almost surrounded by the Puriri forest and in some places this cover was only 40 yards from the walls.

There were only 17 people within the stockade to defend Pukekohe East against the Maori hoards; Sergeant Perry, Privates Joseph Scott, Elijah Roose, William Hodge, George Easton, James Easton and three generations of the McDonald family (Alexander McDonald, his son James and his grandson also called James) in addition to these eight members of the Volunteer Garrison were nine special constables. The young boy James, helped out by carrying cases of ammunition from the church and taking them to the riflemen. There were three other members of the garrison, however, they were absent at the time of the attack; Privates J. Comrie, J. B. Roose and T. Hawke. Comrie and Roose had been on leave, visiting their families and were returning from Drury when they saw the start of the Maori attack, they immediately turned their horses about and rode back to Drury for reinforcements.

When the Maori mounted their first charge, Sergeant Perry ordered his men to fix bayonets and soon the outer wall was bristling with bayonets on the end of rifles projecting through the loopholes.

For the next six hours, the small force kept up a withering fire against the Maori who also kept up a heavy fire while taking cover behind trees, logs and tree stumps; their charges against the stockade walls were ineffective due to the projecting bayonets. It was estimated that the Maori force numbered 200 or 300 warriors.

At about 1 o'clock in the afternoon, the first reinforcements arrived; after hearing the noise of rifle fire, Lieutenant Grierson and 32 men of the 70th Regiment of Foot arrived from their post at Ramarama. The new arrivals managed to force their way through the Maori lines and gain entry to the stockade to bolster the small force of defenders. Their arrival was most fortuitous, as the stockade garrison was almost out of ammunition and could not have held on for much longer.

Captain Moir, with a detachment of the 1st Waikato Militia and three ammunition carts arrived from Drury later in the afternoon and at about 4 o'clock Captain Inman and Captain Saltmarshe with a force of 150 men from the 18th Royal Irish and 65th Regiment arrived and engaged the Maori who were now only 40 yards from the stockade. After an intense fire fight, which lasted for about an hour, the Maori force was finally driven off.

British losses were three dead and eight wounded, not one of the stockade defenders was struck by a bullet, the only casualty was a slight wound caused by a flying wood splinter. It is not possible to accurately gauge the Maori casualties as both the dead and wounded were carried off into the bush by their comrades, however, the Maori dead were estimated to be between 30 and 40.

In recognition of his leadership in the defence of the stockade, Sergeant Perry was commissioned as an Ensign in the 2nd Regiment, Waikato Militia.

Battle of Burtt's Farm

The Battle of Burtt's farm is a good example of the resolve of the settlers who remained on their farms during the war.

Burtt's farm was a substantially built farmhouse at Paerata, midway between Pukekohe and Drury, that had been built by Mr James Burtt, an Auckland merchant, sometime around 1859. At the time of the Maori attack the farmhouse was occupied by Mr Watson (the farm manager) and his family; his wife who was ill in bed and his three sons and two daughters. Two workers, Mr Knight and Mr McLean were also at the farm.

At about 10 o'clock in the morning, Mr Watson, his son Robert a young lad aged 14 and the hired man Mr Knight were erecting some fencing a short distance from the house when they were fired upon by a band of about 20 Maori. This first volley mortally wounded Robert; Mr Watson and Mr Knight, who as usual were carrying their rifles, began to lay down fire on the Maori until their ammunition was exhausted.

Mr McLean assisted by John Watson, a lad of 18, were ploughing a nearby field when they heard the shots and started to run towards the house which they found to be surrounded by Maori warriors; ten of the Maori charged towards Mr McLean who bravely fired his rifle at them while John got the ammunition ready. Once the ammunition was expended both men ran down the hill to escape, John took off his boots so he could run faster and summon help. After a while John came across his brother William, who had been sent by his father for help and the pair arrived at Drury where they raised the alarm.

In the meantime, about 10 to 12 Maori were firing their guns into the farmhouse windows, however, one of Mr Watson's daughters managed to escape via the back door and run to the house of their nearest neighbour, Mr James Hamilton, who lived about half a mile away. Mr Hamilton and his employee Mr Goulan, who were both in the Militia, had heard the firing and with fixed bayonets, were already rushing to assist. From the cover of the bush, the two men sent down a fire on the Maori at the house and managed to drive them off into the bush. Imagining that they were being attacked by a much larger force the Maori retreated and melted away into the bush.

Soon afterwards a party of Mounted Artillery troopers, commanded by Lieutenant Rait arrived from Drury, closely followed by 40 infantrymen, however, by this time the Maori were nowhere to be seen. This small force escorted the occupants of the farm back to Drury, where Mr Watson's mortally wounded son Robert died in the military hospital. After the force had departed, the Maori returned and sacked the farmhouse and a few days afterwards, the body of Mr Hugh McLean was found in a nearby swamp, having been shot through the heart.

Burtt's farm now became the headquarters for a flying column commanded by Colonel Nixon and was also used as a base by Jackson's Forest Rangers.

Second Taranaki Campaign

In parallel with the events occurring in Waikato there was a resurgence of troubles in the Taranaki region further to the south.

Before the winter of 1861, most of the troops involved in the Taranaki War had been withdrawn to Auckland where many of them were employed on the extension of the Great South Road. On 11th May 1863, the government issued a proclamation announcing that they had abandoned efforts to purchase the Teira block of land (which had been the cause of the war) and renounced all claims to that land. Maori forces had occupied the Tataraimaka Block, which had been temporarily abandoned in 1860, and now claimed this land as their own by right of conquest. On 4th April 1863, Colonel Ware, with 300 officers and men from the 57th Regiment of Foot camped at Tataraimaka and built St George's redoubt at Bayley's farm near the Katikara river.

As the Taranaki tribe had previously informed the Governor and General Cameron that they would not give up Tataraimaka until the British gave up the Waitara, they viewed the building of a redoubt as an act of war and sent out messages to rally assistance from the other Maori tribes.

Battle of Allen's Hill

The principal engagement of the campaign in 1863, occurred on 2nd October at Allen's Hill (Hurford Road) on the south road about five miles from New Plymouth where a large band of Maori were entrenched threatening the St Georges redoubt.

Colonel Warre was in command of a large force of men from the 57th Regiment of Foot, with Captains Atkinson, Webster and Messenger commanding a force of about 90 Volunteers and Militia; Captain Mace was also involved with a mounted unit. Fierce fighting took place on Allen's Hill and in the fields around a farmhouse to the west of the hill.

Ensign John Thornton Down – Victoria Cross No. 311
Drummer Dudley Stagpoole – Victoria Cross No. 312

During the attack Drummer Stagpoole was part of an advanced group of soldiers approaching the Maori entrenchments when, while crossing a hedge or fence, they received a volley of fire and after several men were wounded they crossed back over the obstacle. Noticing that Private Henry Cain had been shot and was lying on the ground with the Maori rapidly advancing on him, Drummer Stagpoole handed his rifle to Sergeant Phelan, recrossed the fence, picked up the wounded man and handed him over to the British side of the fence. Drummer Stagpoole narrowly missed serious injury, when a bullet passed through his cap and grazed his scalp.

Soon afterwards the British force were forced to retire, however, in the process of their withdrawal Captain Shortt pointed towards a wounded man at some distance from the fence, close to the bush and stated *"we must have that man out of it."* Drummer Stagpoole, volunteered to get the man, in his own words *"I had been out once so I went back a second time."*

Accompanied by Ensign Down, Drummer Stagpoole went out to rescue Private Finn; trooper Rodreigues rode out to assist and Private Finn was carried to safety on his horse. As they reached safety, Drummer Stagpoole was again lucky to avoid serious injury when a bullet grazed his skull, leaving a scar. Unfortunately the two men who were saved, Private Henry Cain and Private Thomas Finn would later die as a result of their wounds.

Ensign Down and Drummer Stagpoole would later be awarded the Victoria Cross for their deeds.

Drummer Stagpoole was also awarded the Distinguished Conduct Medal for action a few days earlier, on 25th September when he again volunteered and brought in wounded men during an action near Kaipopako.

Maori Fortress at Meremere

The Maori established a huge hilltop fortress on the long narrow ridge of Meremere, which was protected by three artillery pieces; these were old ships guns which had been man handled to the site from the west coast. Without a ready supply of ammunition for these guns, they were loaded with a variety of strange projectiles ranging from nails to lengths of chain.

The fortress had been built in a very strategic position between a series of entrenchments at Paparata, designed to impede a British advance from the east and the advanced field base at Pukekawa which was intended to restrict advances from the west. The fortress at Meremere was the key to the position and the defence of the Waikato region and river.

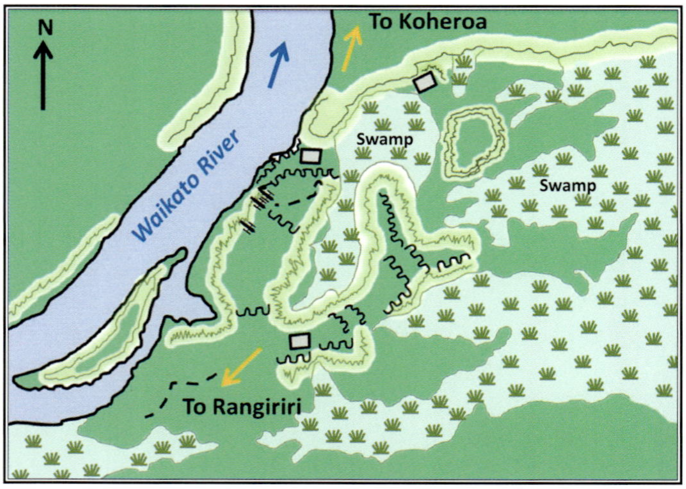

Figure 27. Maori Fortress Meremere

After a reconnaissance of the fortress, from the riverboat *Pioneer*, on 29th and 30th October by General Cameron, the General returned to the Queen's Redoubt and immediately began to organise an expedition to assault the Maori position.

A column of 600 men from the 40th and 65th Regiments of Foot, supported by two gun detachments of the Royal Artillery, marched to the British camp on the Mangatawhiri where they boarded the *Pioneer*. By daybreak on the 31st October the column, now accompanied by the *Avon* which was towing several smaller gunboats, had reached a position about eight miles above the fortress.

After the force landed on the right bank of the river they quickly established entrenchments on the high ground above the landing site and on the track between Rangiriri and Meremere. A small gunboat was left in the river to cut off Maori communication with the interior by river and the *Pioneer* and *Avon* returned to base towing the other small gunboats.

Realising the threat that this force presented to their fortress, the Maori mounted a strong attack at the landing site defences, on the next day, 1st November 1863, however, this was repulsed. Having been unable to dislodge the British landing force, the Maori decided to abandon the fortress at Meremere and retreated towards Paparata and the Thames. They were aided in their retreat due to the extensive flooding caused by the river Waikato being in spate.

When news of the Maori retreat reached General Cameron at the Queen's Redoubt he set off for Meremere collecting a force of about 250 men of the 12th and 14th Regiments of Foot from the Koheroa redoubts. Boarding the *Avon* and *Pioneer*, this force proceeded to Meremere where they found that the fortress had indeed been abandoned, with two of the three artillery pieces having been left behind.

The men from the 12th and 14th were left to garrison the position and they built a British redoubt on the heights.

Miranda Expedition

On 16th November 1863, Lieutenant-Colonel Carey left Auckland with a force of about 900 men bound for the Thames Gulf. The objective of the expedition was twofold; to occupy the Maori settlements on the west bank of the gulf, to stop them sending men and supplies to the tribes in Waikato and secondly to establish a line of redoubts from the sea to the Queen's Redoubt. The line of redoubts was required to help prevent the Maori attacking

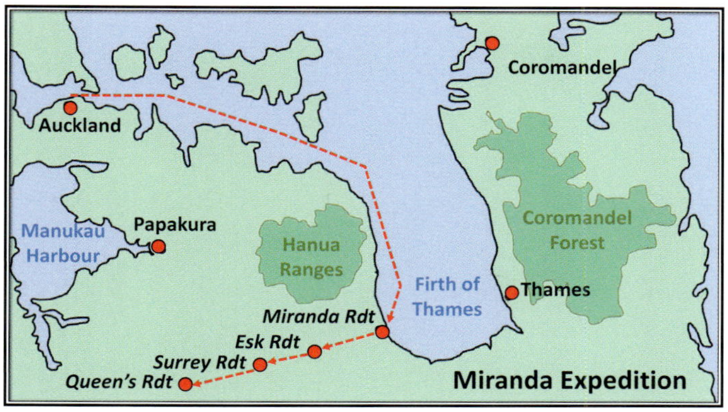

Figure 28. Miranda Expedition

the rear of the British army; from their base at Paparata raiding parties were able to cross the border at will and rove the Wairoa ranges.

Colonel Carey's force consisted of two companies of the Auckland Coastguards, commanded by Captain William C. Daldy; 60 men of the Colonial Defence Force Cavalry, commanded by Captain Walmsley; together with detachments from the 12th and 70th Regiments of Foot and the 1st Regiment of Waikato Militia. The warships *HMS Miranda* and *HMS Esk*, escorted a fleet of transports that included the steamships *Corio* and *Alexandra* which transported the men of the cavalry with their horses.

After a delay of eight days, due to bad weather, the fleet finally anchored off the Wakatiwai river, just north of Pukorokoro, where the landing site was named Miranda. The force of Coastguards landed at the Wakatiwai river and began to cut their way through the bush as they marched towards Pukorokoro about eight miles distant; on the outskirts of the town they came across a large force of Maori dug in on the beach. While getting his men into position, Captain Daldy, who by now had been joined by the rest of the British force, observed many of the Maori retreating towards Waitakaruru and the Piako swamp. With his men in position, Captain Daldy ordered an attack on Pukorokoro, however, in the face of the large British force the defenders also chose to withdraw and headed for the Piako swamp.

With the area cleared of the Maori, the British force constructed a redoubt to hold 120 men, which they named Miranda after the warship and then began to move westward where they established two further redoubts, the Esk and Surrey on the line between the coast and the Queen's Redoubt.

Battle of Rangiriri

Fifty six miles south of Auckland, on a hill overlooking the river Waikato, the Maori built a series of defensive works at Rangiriri. The works were not the traditional Maori Pa (a stockade) but rifle pits and a line of double trenches with a central parapet which stretched between the river and lake Kopuwera. These works represented a strong position from which the Maori could mount attacks against forces coming by river or down the Great South Road, which passed close to the defences.

After a reconnoitre of the Maori positions, from the river steamer *Pioneer*, on 18th November 1863, General Cameron decided on an attack using two forces, one to be landed from the river with the other force taking an overland route. The river force was transported by a flotilla, commanded by Commodore Sir William Wiseman, of the *Pioneer* and *Avon*, towing four armoured gunboats, filled with about 320 men from the 40th Regiment of Foot. The land force of about 850 men, marched along the river bank from Meremere and Takapau consisted of a Naval Brigade of 100 men from *HMS Curacoa* commanded by Lieutenant Alexander, men from 12th, 14th and 65th Regiments of Foot, supported by men from the Royal Artillery and Royal Engineers.

The land force assembled to the north front of the Rangiriri ridge at about 3 o'clock on the afternoon of 20th November; due

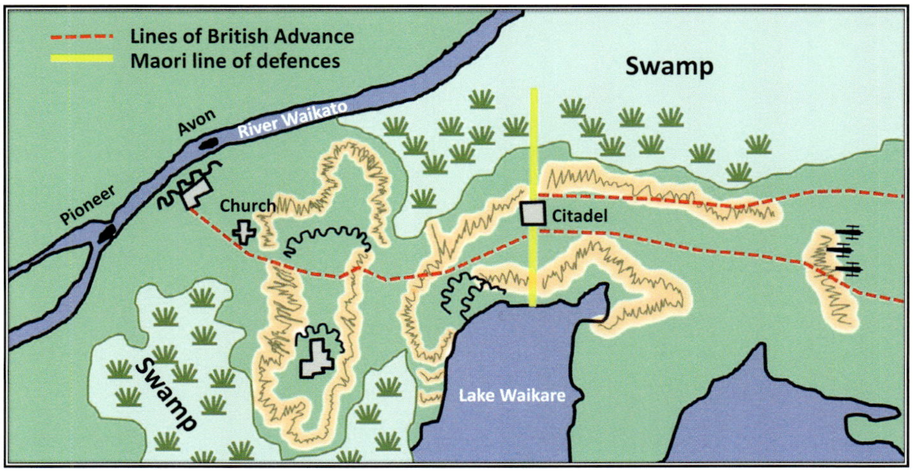

Figure 29. Battle of Rangiriri

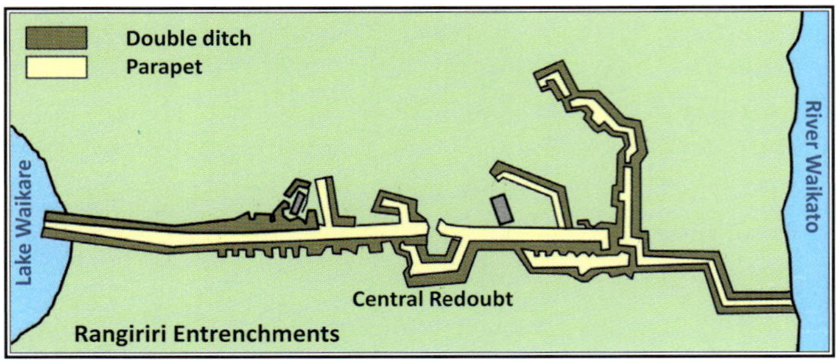

Figure 30. Rangiriri Entrenchments

to the strong river currents and a strong wind the river flotilla was delayed and could not anchor in their agreed positions.

The attack began with an artillery barrage which lasted for two hours and was supported by fire from the gunboats on the river. The solid Maori defences, which consisted of earthworks rather than palisades, suffered little damage, however, in the trenches the Maori suffered large numbers of casualties.

After the barrage, General Cameron ordered an assault on the trenches; a company of men from the 65th Regiment, under the command of Lieutenant Toker, supported by a detachment of Royal Engineers under the command of Captain Brooke, formed the storming party who advanced on the first line of trenches with scaling ladders and planks. The storming party was closely followed by three more companies from the 65th with men from the 14th in support.

The Maori defenders were quickly forced out of their first line of trenches, following a charge with fixed bayonets by the storming party, however, they lost several men. The Maori warriors fell back to their second line of trenches, which they held for only a few minutes before this line was also captured at bayonet point. The line of outer defences were now in British hands and the Maori fell back to their central citadel which was a rectangular redoubt with a high parapet, surrounded by a wide and very deep ditch.

The Maori, mainly those on the right flank, who could not reach the safety of their citadel, retreated to the lagoon and swamps to the rear of their position and were hotly pursued by men from the 65th.

In the late afternoon, the 40th Regiment were eventually landed from the steamers and they attacked and captured a line of entrenchments on the spur above their landing site. The Maori who retreated from these works, made their way through the swamps and crossed lake Waikare in their canoes and made their escape.

Men of the 14th and 65th, from the main British force, made an attack on the central citadel, however, this failed as their scaling ladders were too short to reach the top of the ramparts.

It was now late in the afternoon and General Cameron issued a most extraordinary order when a detachment of the Royal Artillery, armed only with revolvers and swords were ordered to storm the citadel.

Assistant Surgeon William Temple – Victoria Cross No. 313
Lieutenant Arthur Frederick Pickard – Victoria Cross No. 314

Captain Mercer led 36 of his men in the assault but after leaping into the wide trench only one or two men managed to reach the parapet, Sergeant-Major Hamilton reached the top and managed to fire a few shots from his revolver at the Maori before being forced back by a serious gunshot wound to his right arm.

Outside the trench, Captain Mercer fell mortally wounded having been shot in the mouth. Assistant Surgeon Temple and Lieutenant Pickard, both from the Royal Artillery, crossed to the front of the citadel, and in spite of the heavy Maori fire began to tend to the wounds of Captain Mercer and his men. Lieutenant Pickard crossed in front of the parapet several times bringing water to the wounded men.

For their brave actions both Assistant Surgeon Temple and Lieutenant Pickard were later awarded the Victoria Cross.

Despite the two previous unsuccessful attempts, General Cameron was determine to take the Maori redoubt and this time ordered an attack by men of the Naval Brigade. Captain Mayne, from *HMS Eclipse*, together with 90 men from the crews of *HMS Eclipse*, *HMS Curacoa* and *HMS Miranda*, armed with rifles and cutlasses made another frontal attack but after several attempts to scale the heights this attack also failed.

With darkness now falling, General Cameron was forced to halt operations for the night and his force surrounded the Maori citadel, ready to renew the combat in the morning. Despite being encircled, many of the Maori, including the leading warrior chief Te Wharepu, managed to escape through the cordon and headed south.

During the night, men from the Royal Engineers, commanded by Colonel Mould and Captain Brooke began a mine under the citadel parapet with the aim of blowing it up and making a breach in the defences, however, the fuses had been mislaid, so this had to be abandoned.

Soon after daybreak on the morning of 21st November, the Maori stopped firing and raised the white flag of surrender.[10] Mr

10 Some sources state that the Maori were duped by the British, saying that the white flag was a flag of truce not surrender, as they wished to parley with the British General. As the British forces entered the citadel under a flag of truce, their disarmament of the Maori was illegal. I have found no evidence to support this view.

Gundry, one of the staff interpreters, was sent forward and after some discussions with the principal Maori chiefs, they agreed to an unconditional surrender. The reason that the Maori had surrendered was that they had ran out of ammunition and after the British refused to supply them with gunpowder, so that they could continue the fight, they agreed to surrender. The captured Maori, 183 in number, were taken prisoner and escorted to the church near the river and soon afterwards boarded the *Pioneer*, to begin a journey into captivity in Auckland.[11]

Soon after the surrender of the Maori force at Rangiriri, another force of Maori, who had been on the way to reinforce the men in the citadel, arrived at Paetai on the south side of the Rangiriri river. As the main force had already surrendered, their leader told an interpreter that he was also prepared to surrender, however, his men refused to give up their arms and they moved off towards Ngaruawahia.

British losses during the battle, were significant with two officers killed and nine others wounded (four would later die from their wounds), 41 men were killed or died from their wounds and 72 were wounded. Maori dead were thought to number about 50, with many more having been wounded.

Advance on the Waipa

Following the success at the Battle of Rangiriri, General Cameron used the assembled troops to advance further into the heart of Maori country and by 8th December 1863 had reached Ngaruawahia, the capital of King Tawhiao. The British forces entered the town unopposed, as the Maori had abandoned their capital on observing General Cameron's advance.

After leaving Ngaruawahia, King Tawhiao led his men further south to the open lands of the delta that lay between the Waikato (Horotiu) and Waipa rivers. At Pikopiko (Puketoki) and Paterangi, in the foothills of the Pukekura Range the Maori established a formidable system of redoubts and entrenchments and towards their rear, at Rangiatea and Mangapukatea they constructed other formidable defences barring the way to Rangiaowhia. By the early months of 1864, the Maori had assembled a force of 2,000 warriors to garrison these redoubts.

General Cameron's plan was to drive the Maori out of the Upper Waikato region, which was heavily cultivated and provided most of their food. To prepare for the campaign, the Water Transport Corps shipped large numbers of men and vast amounts of stored down river; by the end of the year almost 3,000 troops had been assembled at the apex of the Waikato-Waipa delta. With his men assembling, General Cameron moved his headquarters forward to Tuhikaramea and by the end of January 1864 had move his HQ again, to Te Rore, about three miles from Paterangi where Colonel Waddy with 600 men took up an advanced position less than a mile from the Maori Pa.

11 After spending many months on the hulk *Marion*, in Auckland harbour, the prisoners managed to escape from Kawau island on the night of 11th September 1864.

Battle of Waiari

After a reconnaissance of the defensive works at Paterangi, it was decided that as they were more extensive and formidable than those at either Meremere of Rangiriri, the current British force was insufficient to mount any significant attack. As a result of this decision the fighting, for the moment, was limited to long range sniping with occasional shelling by the British guns, which due to the substantial nature of the works had little effect.

This hiatus was broken on 11th February 1864 by a brief but fierce skirmish that took place at Waiari on the Mangapiko River, about a mile south of the Paterangi defences.

Major Charles Heaphy – Victoria Cross No. 315

At a tight loop in Mangapiko, where the river doubled back on itself, there was an ancient Maori fortification (Waiari Pa) where three lines of high parapets with deep ditches crossed the narrow spit of land, these works could be reached by a primitive bridge, a log with a flattened upper side, as the river was less than 15 feet wide at this point. A short distance from this old fortress was a large pool that was used by Colonel Waddy's men as a bathing place.

Unknown to the British forces, Maori scouts from Paterangi, had reported back to their leaders that a route which passed close to this location could be used to come to the rear of Colonel Waddy's camp, placed in the lee of the hill where they were sheltered by firing from the Paterangi defences.

The Maori leaders agreed that this was a viable proposition so had planned a night attack where about 100 warriors would advance during the day to a point, near the bathing pool, and conceal themselves in the bush near the Mangapiko Creek, prior to launching a night time attack. When a large bathing party from the 40th Regiment came down to the creek with a small detachment of soldiers, acting as a covering party, the Maori could not resist breaking cover and firing at the British soldiers.

The soldiers were soon reinforced by about 200 men from the 40th and 50th Regiments, from their nearby camp, commanded by Colonel Sir Henry Havelock VC, together with Captain William Jackson of No. 1 company Forest Rangers and Captain Charles Heaphy of the Auckland Rifle Volunteers.

Maori reinforcements were also sent down from Paterangi and helped to threaten the British rear and flanks.

Captain Von Tempsky, with about half of the force of Forest Rangers, who was camped at Te Tore, about two miles away, immediately rushed to the scene with his men after hearing the firing. After reaching the action, Captain Von Tempsky and his men were directed by Colonel Havelock, towards the old Waiari Pa where many of the Maori had fled. After fierce hand to hand fighting, it took until nearly nightfall before the old Pa was finally cleared.

Near the start of the battle, Captain Heaphy was assisting a wounded soldier from the 40th Regiment, who had fallen into a hollow where many Maori were concealed. From a range of only a few feet, these Maori fired a volley at Captain Heaphy, wounding him in three places, five other musket balls pierced his cap and clothes. Despite his wounds, Captain Heaphy continued to tend to the wounded and directed other British soldiers to where the Maori were hiding and five of the party that had fired on him were shot dead.

As night began to fall, the Maori drifted away and Captain Von Tempsky with his Rangers helped to escort the men back to camp.

For his action Captain Heaphy was later awarded the Victoria Cross, the first colonial soldier to receive the award, following a Royal Warrant issued on 1st January 1867, which changed the original Victoria Cross warrant to include colonial forces in those eligible for the award.

During the battle five British soldiers were killed, however, Maori losses were believed to be 41. To guard against a further incursion across the Waiari a small redoubt was built and occupied.

Invasion of Rangiaowhia

With the summer well advanced, General Cameron decided to outflank the strong Maori defences at Paterangi and Rangiatea and make a surprise attack on the mission station of Te Awamutu, near Rangiaowhia, which was one of the Maori chief sources of food. After leaving a sizable garrison outside Paterangi, a force of about 1,000 men was assembled at Te Rore and under cover of darkness on the night of 20th February headed south.

The advance guard of the column was led by Captain Von Tempsky with his men of No 2 Company Forest Rangers supported by 100 men from the 65th regiment of foot commanded by Lieutenant Tabuteau. The advance guard was closely followed by the cavalry; with Colonel Nixon and the Colonial Defence Force Cavalry Corps and Rait's Mounted Artillery who were doing duty as cavalry. The main body of troops consisted of detachments from 50th, 65th and 70th Regiments of Foot with No 1 Company of the Forest Rangers acting as rear guard.

By daylight the column could see Reverend John Morgan's mission church at the Te Awamutu mission station, however, they pushed on a further three miles to the unfortified town of Rangiaowhia.

With Colonel Nixon's cavalry leading the way, the Forest Rangers and men of the 65th Regiment, soon reached the centre of the town with little opposition apart from some sporadic sniping from houses which bordered the road. At the north of the town, several Maori had taken shelter in the Roman Catholic church but as they had raised the white flag they were left unmolested. During the ride through the town, large amounts of food

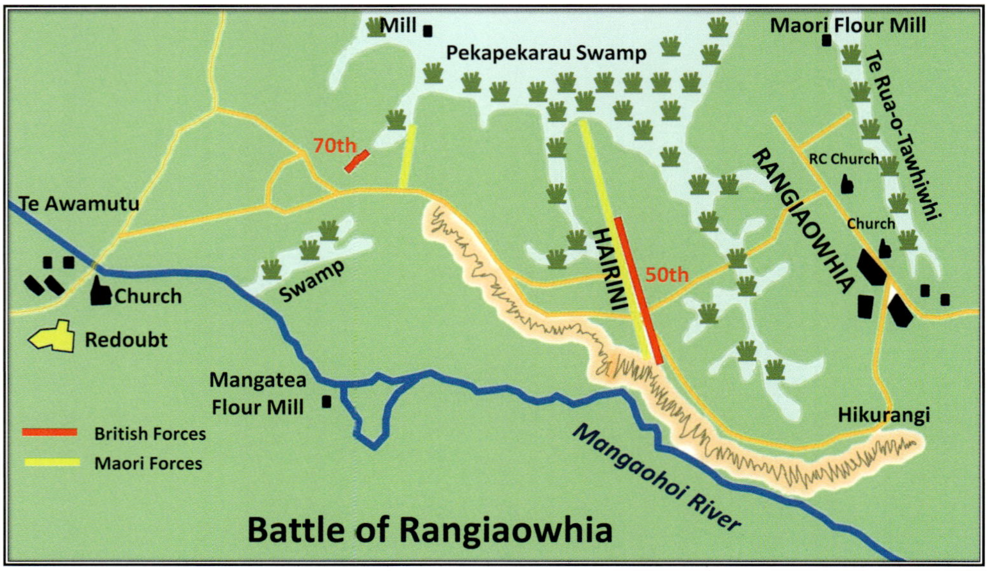

Figure 31. Rangiaowhia

bundled up and ready to be carted off to Paterangi were seen laid out in the streets.

The only significant resistance was at the south of the town, near the Anglican Church where a large band of Maori had taken refuge in the church and nearby houses. Colonel Nixon and his men dismounted and surrounded the church and houses and Lieutenant McDonnell and Ensign Mair (the interpreter) were sent forward to demand their surrender.

During the fire fight to dislodge the Maori, several British soldiers were killed, including Colonel Nixon who was shot through the chest. The position was finally taken when the houses were set on fire and the Maori, who were forced to leave their cover, were shot dead. Ten Maori had managed to hold off a force of about 100 British soldiers and managed to kill five before they were all killed. About a dozen houses were set on fire and the occupants fled north to the Roman Catholic church where they put up a short lived resistance before moving off into the swamps.

Battle of Hairini

When news of the occupation and destruction of Rangiaowhia reached the Maori leaders, they immediately evacuated their positions at Paterangi, Pikopiko and Rangiatea and headed off to protect their supply headquarters.

The British troops in camp at Te Awamutu had been reinforced by a large force from Te Rore, which included the 50th Regiment commanded by Colonel Weare with a detachment of Royal Artillery and a party from the Royal Navy with some guns.

On the morning of 22nd February, the Maori reached the Hairini Ridge, a high point mid way between the mission station at Te Awamutu and Rangiaowhia, where they had chosen to make a stand against the British forces. Building on an existing ditch, bank and some old fencing which was fencing in some of the cultivation, they quickly deepened the ditch and converted the bank into a strong parapet, with a rifle trench spanning the road.

When General Cameron was made aware of the Maori force, he immediately ordered an attack before they could strengthen their defences any further. Captain Pye VC and Captain Walmsley, with the Colonial Defence Force Cavalry led the advance on the Maori positions with the Forest Rangers at the head of the infantry corps. By early afternoon almost 1,000 British troops were advancing on the Hairini Ridge.

The British artillery was placed at about 500 yards from the defensive works and were soon putting down a barrage against the entrenchments, manned by 500 or 600 Maori.

With the artillery firing over their heads, the Forest Rangers, with the 50th and 65th Regiments in support, advanced to within 300 yards of the Maori line and lay down to release volleys of fire into the Maori ranks; the 70th Regiment were to the rear, having been held in reserve.

After a while, the order to charge was sounded and the Forest Rangers made for the Maori right flank while the 50th Regiment charged the centre with fixed bayonets. The ferocity of the British charge caused the Maori to break in confusion and take flight. Some raced to the shelter of the deep swamp to the north of the line, while others moved off towards Rangiaowhia.

General Cameron now deployed his cavalry, one of the few occasions during the Maori wars when they could be used with any possibility of success. One troop of the Colonial Defence Cavalry, commanded by Captain Walmsley attacked the right flank and managed to take the high ground overlooking the Mangaohoi river valley. Captain Pye VC, with the other troop charge the left flank where the Maori were fleeing to escape into the swamp, where several were cut down.

The Forest Rangers, with men from the 70th and 50th Regiments, now pressed on into Rangiaowhia where the fighting was ended.

Casualties during the battle were slight, two British were killed and 16 wounded, however, one of these would later die from his wounds. Maori casualties were about 20 killed with the same number wounded.

To secure the area, the British built a redoubt on the Hikurangi hill, that was garrisoned by a detachment from the 65th Regiment. Following their success at Rangiaowhia, General Cameron left garrisons at Te Rore and at Pikopiko and Paterangi, which had been abandoned by the Maori. The whole of the mid-Waikato and the fertile plain, between the Waipa and Horotiu rivers, down to the Mangapiko River was now under British occupation.

Lower Waikato Operations

Having now established control over the upper and mid Waikato regions, General Cameron now turned his attention to planning operations for the Lower Waikato; as part of his preparations the gunboats *Pioneer* and *Koheroa* steamed up the Horotiu river on 2nd March with a detachment from the 65th Regiment of Foot on board. The small flotilla anchored off the Maori village of Kirikiri-roa (this settlement later became the town of Hamilton) which had been abandoned by the inhabitants. On the next day the *Koheroa* ascended further up the river to Pukerimu, where the surveyors carried out a quick reconnaissance of the area.

Not long afterwards, redoubts were constructed to secure the area and were initially manned by detachments from the 18th and

70th Regiments of Foot, before later being garrisoned by men from the Waikato Militia. While preparations for further operations continued, a large British force was maintained at Te Awamutu which was now General Cameron's temporary headquarters.

Lieutenant Colonel John Carstairs McNeill – Victoria Cross No. 316

On 30th March 1864, Major McNeill from the 107th Regiment, Aide-de-Camp to General Cameron, was returning to his duties at Te Awamutu, escorted by Privates Gibson and Vosper from the Colonial Defence Force, when just after passing Ohanpu they came across a large body of Maori warriors.

Major McNeill, after sending Private Gibson back to Ohanpu to bring up infantry reinforcements, ascended a nearby hill with Private Vosper, to continue his observations of the Maori force. Soon after reaching the crest of the hill, they were suddenly attacked by a force of about 50 Maori who had been hidden in the dense ferns. The only way for the pair to escape with their lives was to about turn and ride off back down the hill, however, in the act of turning Private Vosper's horse fell and threw him. Seeing that Private Vosper was not by his side, Major McNeill turned back and observed the Private on the ground with Maori party descending upon him.

Without hesitation, Major McNeill galloped back to the dismounted Private and helped him remount, after which the pair managed to gallop off to safety.

For this brave action, which saved the life of Private Vosper, Major McNeil was later awarded the Victoria Cross.

After their defeats in the mid Waikato region, the Maori fled further south, towards the Pukekura Range and after spending a few days at Kihikihi, his home, chief Rewi Maniapoto and his men moved towards the Puniu River and established a base at Orakau. On 23rd February, a British force occupied Kihikihi, unopposed and established a redoubt and forward base.

Siege and Battle of Orakau

On 29th February, Colonel Waddy led a column from Te Awamutu to a point mid way between Kihikihi and Orakau, where a force of Maori had been observed constructing rifle pits and defences. The Forest Rangers, led by Captain Von Tempsky were leading the advance when they came across a newly built stake fence in front of a bank, beyond which were the expected trenches and rifle pits.

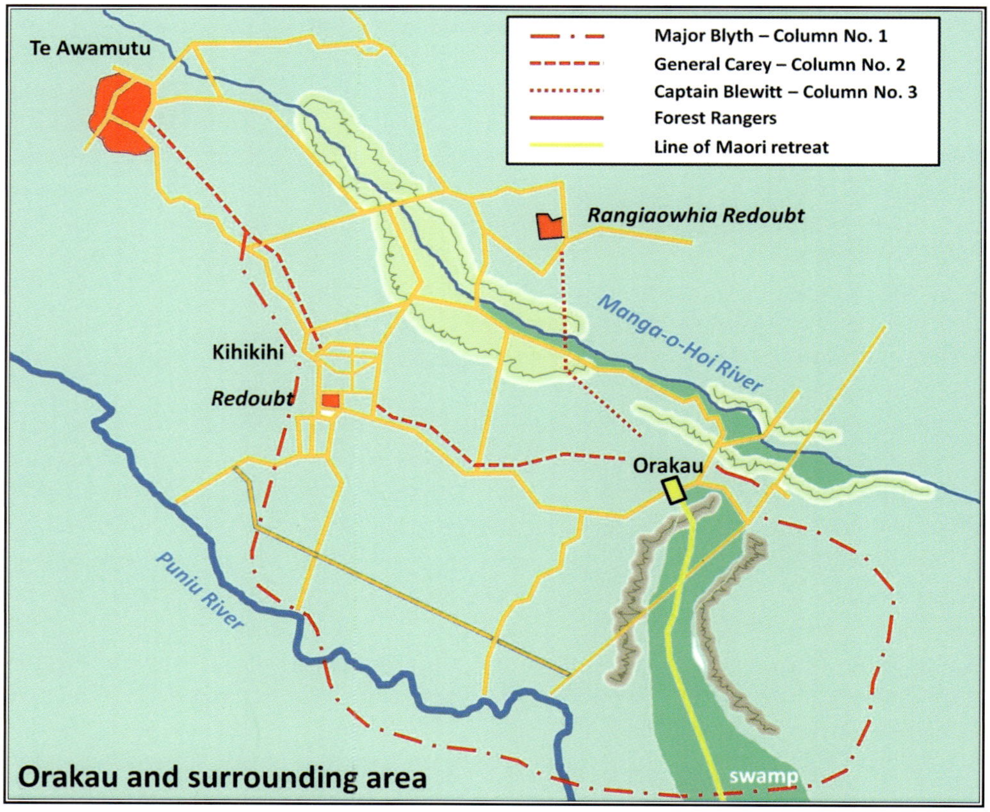

Figure 32. Orakau and surrounding area

With the advance of the British force, the Maori had abandoned their position and were seen to be retreating towards the village of Orakau; after destroying the fence and defensive works, the British advanced to Orakau but found that the village had also been abandoned, so returned to Te Awamutu.

Various Maori tribes had gathered at Wharepapa, a large village south of the Puniu River, where they held a conference to discuss the continuance of the war. The decision to continue with the war was unanimous and it was agreed that a new Pa would be constructed to the north of the Puniu River and after further discussions it was agreed that this should be built at Orakau. Chief Rewi Maniapoto, together with a force of just over 300 warriors, accompanied by about 20 women and some children, soon began the construction of a traditional Pa at Orakau.

On the morning of 30th March 1864, two surveyors Mr Gundry and Mr Wilkinson, working at Kihikihi observed the Maori construction efforts through their theodolite telescope and informed General Carey at his headquarters. General Cameron, who was stationed at Pukerimu, immediately organised an expedition and three columns were despatched against the Orakau Pa with the intention of surprising the Maori and surrounding their position.

Number one column, which left Te Awamutu at midnight on 30th March, was a body of 300 men commanded by Major Blyth of the 40th Regiment, and consisted of detachments from the 40th and 65th Regiment with about half of Captain Von Tempsky's company of Forest Rangers acting as the advance guard. Their role was to march to the west of Kihikihi, flanking the Whakatau-Ringaringa swamp crossing the Puniu river before recrossing the river near Waikeria to close on the rear of Orakau.

Number two column, the main force of about 600 men from various regiments, was commanded by General Carey and left Te Awamutu at daybreak on the 31st March. This force, with 19 men from the Forest Rangers, commanded by Lieutenant Roberts, forming the advance guard, marched to Kihikihi where they were joined by a detachment from the 65th Regiment and a company of the 1st Waikato Militia, before continuing on to Orakau.

The third column was a much smaller force, with men from the 65th Regiment and Waikato Militia, commanded by Captain Blewitt; they set out from the Rangiaowhia redoubt and guided by Sergeant Southee of the Forest Rangers, crossed the Manga-o-Hoi River and advanced on Orakau through the bush and swamps.

As Chief Rewi Maniapoto and his men had only spent two days and nights on the construction, the Pa was far from completed when the first British attack took place in the early hours of 31st March when men from the Forest Rangers, commanded by Lieutenant Roberts and 120 men from the 18th Royal Irish commanded by Captain Ring advanced on the Pa.

The British approach was spotted by the Maori, who were at their morning prayers, and Chief Rewi ordered the majority of his force to occupy the outer ditch, while about 40 of the older warriors took up position within the parapets.

Thinking that they were attacking a weak position, the British mounted a charge, however, the Maori held their fire until they were about 50 yards from their line, at which time they unleashed a volley from 200 guns. Several of the British troops were hit and Captain Ring fell mortally wounded, the signal to retire was soon sounded and the force withdrew in order to re-form.

Reinforced by a company of men from the 40th Regiment, the British mounted a second charge, however, this fared no better than the first and was repulsed by a second volley from the Maori guns. All of the Maori warriors now retreated, from the ditch, back to the cover of the Pa parapets.

Finding that the Orakau Pa was more formidable, than thought to be at first sight, General Carey withdrew his men and now that the columns commanded by Major Blyth and Captain Blewitt had reached their intended position, he decided to besiege the Pa and bombard it with his artillery.

The General placed his two six pounder Armstrong guns on the high point of the Karaponia Ridge and at a distance of about 350 yards they began to fire their shells into the Pa, but due to the strength of the earthworks they had little impact. General Carey, acting on the advice of Lieutenant Hurst of the 18th Regiment (who was serving as the Engineering Officer), now ordered the construction of a trench (sap) towards the Pa redoubt in preparation for undermining the Maori parapets.

Maori reinforcements arrived from Otihi, where they had been gathering but were kept to the northern side of the Manga-o-Hoi swamp by the Forest Rangers who had completed the encirclement of Orakau.

The British force rose to a strength of about 1,500 with the arrival, from Te Awamutu, of about 200 men from the 18th Regiment, under the command of Captain Inman.

With some sporadic firing from both sides, the siege continued for the rest of the day and throughout the night. On the next morning, a thick fog had descended, enveloping the Pa and concealing the combatants from each other. By this time, the Maori were running low on both ammunition and water and a proposal was made to abandon the Pa, under the cover of the fog but this was rejected and they agreed to continue the fight.

As the day progressed and the sun rose higher, the fog was burnt off and the firing recommenced. After a while, Chief Rewi led a charge against the British lines but this was repulsed and the Maori were forced back into the parapets of the Pa defences.

Further British reinforcements arrived on 1st April, the second day of the siege, including Captain Jackson with the 1st Company of the Forest Rangers who had been stationed at Ohaupo.

Work on advancing the trench towards the Pa continued, despite some sudden attacks by the Maori, and the British Artillery fired a few shells at the Maori reinforcements who were still being held at bay on the northern bank of the Manga-o-Hoi river.

During the very hot day, the Maori, especially the wounded, suffered greatly due to the lack of water and several warriors and women bravely crept through the British lines and returned with containers of precious water. There are several accounts that the British soldiers, after spotting this activity, ignored the Maori as they understood that the water was probably for the wounded.

Although they had some powder in reserve, the Maori were running very low on lead for their bullets, so began to fire small pieces of wood instead. During the second night of the siege, a proposal was made to abandon the Pa, under the cover of darkness, however, even though this had the support of Chief Rewi, this was once again rejected and it was agreed to continue the fight.

As morning approached Chief Rewi ordered his men to cook some potatoes so that they could eat, however, due to the lack of water they could not swallow the roasted potatoes. Judging the situation to be desperate, Chief Rewi managed to convince the other chiefs that they should make a breakout as the alternative was to be taken prisoner and he would rather die fighting, however, by now it was broad daylight.

By early afternoon, the sappers, who had been working all night, had advanced their trench to within a few yards of the Maori earthworks. Colonel Sir Henry Havelock arrived at the siege from Pukerimu with some men from the Colonial Defence Force Cavalry, leading some pack horses loaded with hand-grenades. Sergeant MacKay of the Royal Artillery, supported by covering fire by Captain Hereford and Lieutenant Harrison, managed to throw several of the grenades into the Pa from the head of the sappers trench.

General Cameron, who had arrived from Pukerimu at noon, ordered the Armstrong guns to be moved to the head of the trench and their fire managed to make a breach in the Maori defences, the grenades, artillery and rifle fire was now causing heavy casualties to those within the Pa and the Maori dead and wounded were lying everywhere.

Early in the afternoon, General Cameron who was impressed by the courage of the Maori defenders, decided to give them the opportunity to surrender and sent Mr Mair and Mr Mainwaring (the interpreters) to the head of the trench under cover of a white flag of truce. After some consultation with Chief Rewi and the other chiefs the offer of surrender was rejected by the Maori and even the offer to send out their women and children was refused.

With the refusal of surrender, the British fire intensified and at about 4 o'clock an attack was mounted by men from the Waikato Militia but this was repulsed. Soon after this abortive attack the Maori decided that it was time to break out and with the fittest warriors at the front and the women and children at the centre, surrounded by the other warriors, Chief Rewi led his men in a charge through the British lines. The main group of Maori, headed for the Manuka swamp between the Karaponia ridge and some, including Chief Rewi, managed to make their escape along the banks of the Puniu river, however, many were killed or wounded.

The Maori losses were estimated at 160 killed and 50 wounded, while British losses amounted to 17 killed with 51 wounded. The Battle of Orakau, was the final and decisive battle of the Waikato war and effectively brought the campaign to an end.

Tauranga Campaign

In January 1864, the Governor George Grey decided to despatch a military force to Tauranga on the east coast of the North Island,

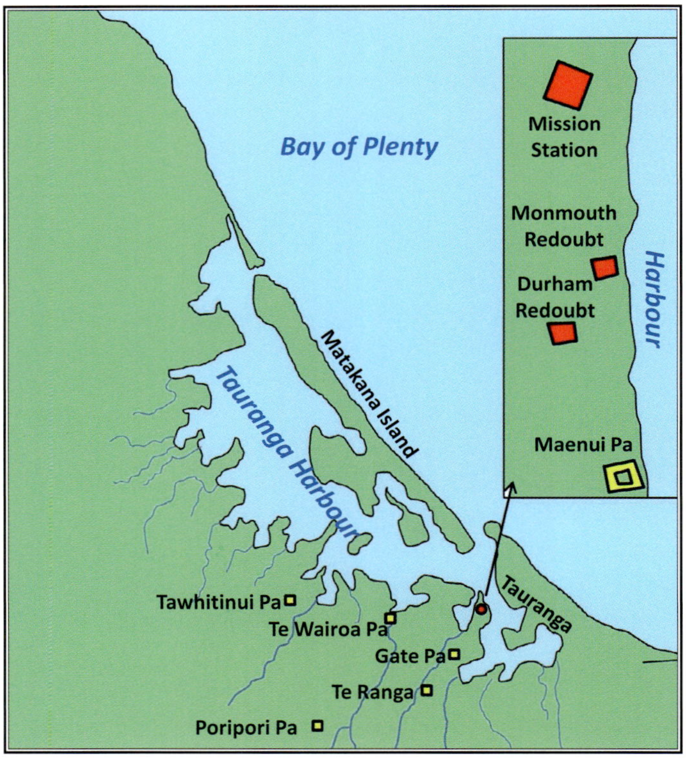

Figure 33. Tauranga Campaign

this was prompted by the knowledge that Tauranga was being used as a source of men and materials for the war in Waikato.

The force of about 700 men commanded by Colonel Greer, set sail from Auckland on board *HMS Miranda* commanded by Captain Jenkins and were landed at Te Papa, near the mission station at Tauranga harbour where they established the Monmouth Redoubt and Durham redoubt. Captain Jenkins, with *HMS Miranda*, remained on station off the Tauranga harbour, enforcing a blockade to prevent Tauranga being reinforced by tribes from along the east coast.

With news of the British invasion of their territory, many of the Tauranga tribesmen serving in the Waikato returned to help defend their homeland. The returning warriors, quickly helped to erect fortifications to withstand the British assault with a major Pa being constructed at Waoku, near the Waimapu River and overlooking the Bay of Plenty, on the site of an ancient fortification. Other positions were established at Kaimai, Poripori, Wairoa and Tawhiti-nui.

When the main stronghold at Waoku was completed, chief Rawiri Tuaia sent a letter to the British commander at Tauranga, challenging him to battle saying that he had built a Pa but had also built a road down to the harbour so that the British soldiers should not be too tired when they arrived to fight. When this challenge was ignored, the chief who was eager for the fighting to begin, decided to be more aggressive and moved his men to the fortified Pa at Poteriwhi on the Wairoa, closer to the British position, from where he sent another letter challenging the British to battle.

With no response to his second challenge, chief Rawiri Tuaia decided to move his position even closer to the British troops at Te Papa and in April 1864 they occupied a fortified position on the Puke-hinahina Ridge about two miles from Tauranga Landing. The fortification was at a spot where there was a gate in the boundary fence, to allow passage along the Tauranga to Rotarua road, so the Pa was generally known as the Gate Pa.

Following this move by the Maori, Colonel Greer issued a demand to chief Rawiri that they should cease hostilities and give up their arms. Rawiri replied to this demand with the retort that he would take breakfast with the Colonel in Te Papa, a threat that the Maori would soon attack the British camp.

On 21st April, General Cameron arrived from Auckland on board *HMS Esk* to take over command of the campaign and established his headquarters at Te Papa. By the 26th April a naval brigade of 429 sailors and marines from a flotilla of ships from the Australian Squadron, which included *HMS Harrier*, *HMS Curacoa*, *HMS Esk*, *HMS Falcon* and *HMS Miranda*, under the command of Commodore Sir William Wiseman, had been landed and the General now believed that he had sufficient men to mount an attack against the Gate Pa. One 110 pounder Armstrong gun and two 40 pounder Armstrong guns from *HMS Esk*, along with 12 other artillery guns, were also landed.

Battle of Gate Pa

During the 27th and 28th April, General Cameron moved his troops and guns forward to the Pukereia Hill, less than a mile from the Gate Pa. On the night of 28th April, following a feigned attack to the front, Colonel Greer with about 700 men from the 68th Regiment, moved across the swamp and took up positions to the rear of the Maori position, they were joined by a detachment of the Naval Brigade under the command of Lieutenant Hotham. These forces were deployed so that they would be able to cut off any retreat by the Maori.

In addition to the 700 men from the 68th Regiment; 420 men from the Naval Brigade, 50 Royal Artillery, 300 men from the

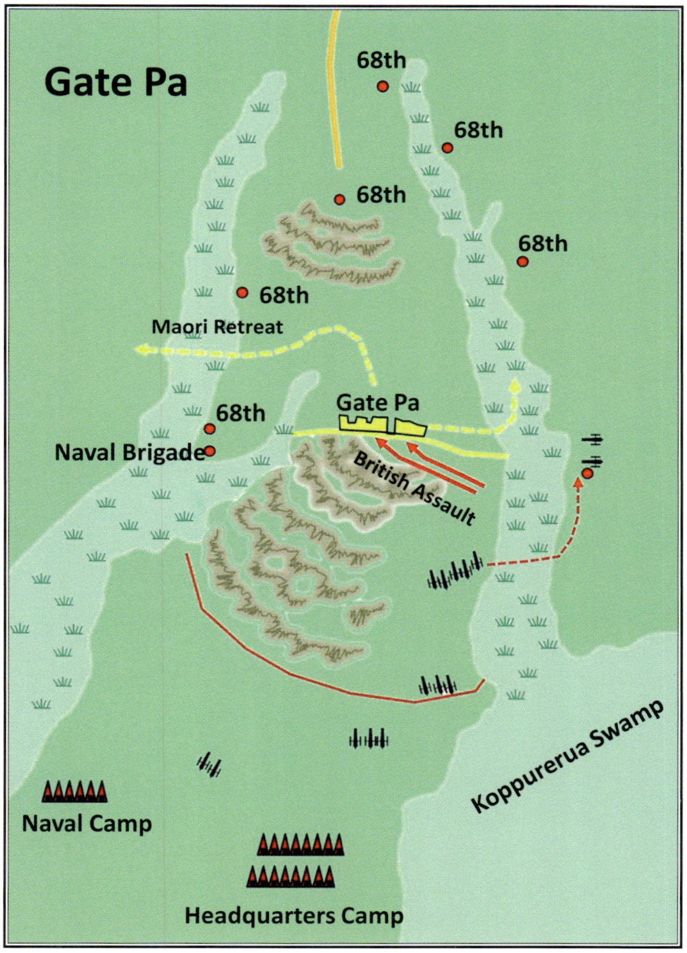

Figure 34. Battle of Gate Pa

43rd Regiment and 180 men from a moveable column which consisted of detachments from the 12th, 14th, 40th and 65th Regiments; a total of 1,650 men were to be employed in the attack.

Soon after daybreak on the morning of the 29th April, the guns and mortars on Pukereia Hill opened fire on the Pa entrenchments. The fire was directed mainly at the left angle of the main redoubt, with the aim of making a breach for the assault party. At about noon, a 6 pounder Armstrong gun was hauled across the Kopurererua swamp and placed on a hill to provide an enfilading fire.

After such an intense barrage, a breach was effected and by 4 o'clock in the afternoon this was considered to be large enough for a storming party to gain entry to the Pa. The storming party consisted of 150 sailors and marines under the command of Commander Hay from *HMS Harrier* and 150 men from the 43rd Regiment under the command of Colonel Booth. Men from the moveable column, under the command of Major Ryan, formed an extended line in front of the Pa to provide covering fire for the assault. The remainder of the Naval Brigade and the 43rd Regiment, about 300 men, were held in reserve.

A rocket was fired to signal the start of the attack and while the storming party advanced in a column, four abreast, the 68th Regiment, to the rear of the Pa, also advanced and began to lay down a heavy fire on the defenders.

Assistant Surgeon William George Nicholas Manley – Victoria Cross No. 317
Captain of the Foretop Samuel Mitchell – Victoria Cross No. 318

With Commander Hay and Colonel Booth leading the way, the storming party entered the breach and managed to push back the defenders, however, Colonel Booth and many of the other officers were disabled and fell wounded.

During the fierce hand to hand fighting of this initial assault, Commander Hay fell mortally wounded, Captain of the Foretop Mitchell, also from *HMS Harrier*, in the face of heavy fire carried his commander out of the Pa to relative safety; for this deed Captain of the Foretop Mitchell was later awarded the Victoria Cross.

On leaving the Pa, Mitchell met Assistant Surgeon William Manley, who had volunteered to join the storming party, and who began to treat Commander Hay's wounds after which he entered the Pa to see if he could treat more of the wounded. For his actions, Assistant Surgeon Manley was also awarded the Victoria Cross.

Some of the Maori, after being pushed back, tried to retreat from the rear of the Pa but were forced back into the entrenchments by the men of the 68th Regiment. These men now joined several of their comrades who had taken refuge in underground burrows during the British bombardment and began to mount a strong attack at the assault force. Confused by the complex layout of the Pa and this sudden influx of Maori into the fight, the British attack stuttered.

Seeing that the attack was faltering General Cameron ordered the reserve into the attack and Captain Hamiliton from *HMS Esk* led his men into the breach but was soon shot dead. With the arrival of the reserve, even more Maori poured into the fight and without many officers to rally the men they began a disorderly retreat. Assistant Surgeon Manley was one of the last to leave the Pa.

With the British retirement, the Maori left the cover of their Pa and began to fire on the retreating force but were soon forced to return after their ammunition was expended.

General Cameron managed to rally his men and as dusk was falling he decided against a further assault but instead ordered some earthworks to be constructed about 100 yards from the Pa, where they spent the night. After nightfall, the Maori decided that with their defence having been breached they should abandon the Pa and with the cover of darkness they made their way across the Kopurererua swamp, through the lines of the 68th Regiment. On the next morning, the British found the Pa to be deserted apart from the dead and wounded of both sides.

The British casualties during the battle were high with almost one third of the storming party being killed or wounded; ten officers were killed (or died from their wounds) and four were wounded; 21 NCOs or Privates were killed and 76 were wounded. The Maori losses were thought to be about 25 killed with several wounded; one of the Maori dead was chief Rawiri who was initially buried at Te Ranga but was later reinterred at the cemetery in Tauranga next to the grave of Colonel Booth.

There was a great outcry, both in New Zealand and England, that a force of some 1,700 soldiers and sailors could have been defeated by 200 Maori and General Cameron was roundly criticised.

Battle of Te Ranga

After the Battle of Gate Pa, a portion of the British force returned to Auckland on board the warships, only *HMS Harrier* remained on station at Tauranga. In May, Captain Pye, with troops from the Colonial Defence Force, took possession of an abandoned Maori position on the Wairoa stream.

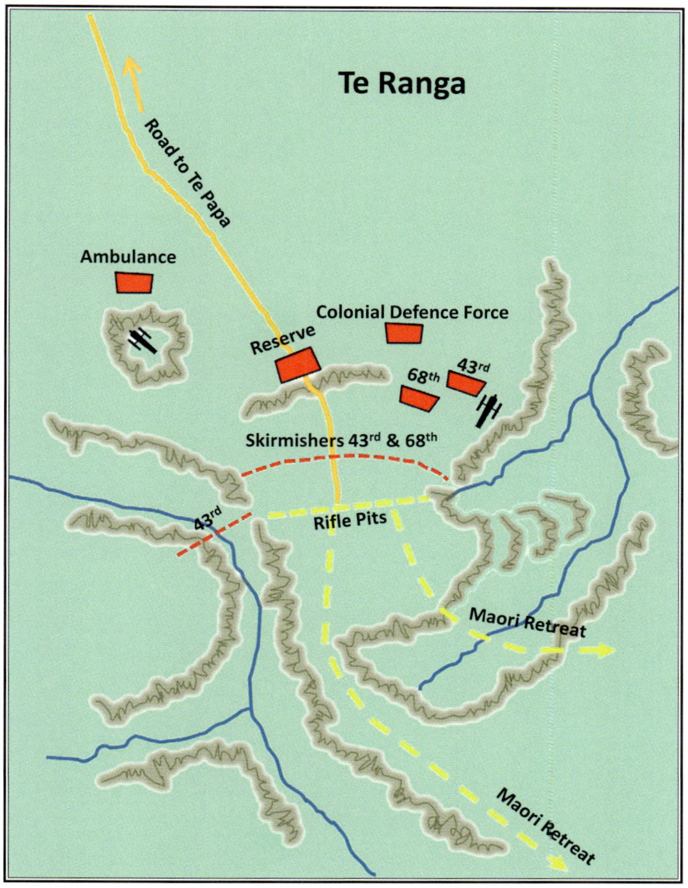

Figure 35. Battle of Te Ranga

On 20th June, the Maori, eager for another fight with the British, began to congregate at Te Ranga on the Puke-hinahina ridge where they began work on fortifications, about three miles inland from the Gate Pa. On the following day, Colonel Greer was leading a strong reconnoitring force of about 600 men along the ridge from the Gate Pa, when he came across the Maori at Te Ranga working hard to build their new Pa. The Colonel; with detachments from the 43rd Regiment commanded by Major Synge, the 68th Regiment under Major Shuttleworth and men from the 1st Waikato Militia under Captain Moore; decided to make an immediate attack before the Maori could complete their works.

After sending a message back to the British camp at the Gate Pa, for reinforcements and an Armstrong gun, Colonel Greer sent out a line of skirmishers to engage the Maori outposts. Detachments from the 43rd and 68th Regiments were sent out to both flanks, from where they maintained a heavy fire against the Maori in their trenches.

After about two hours, the Armstrong gun and reinforcements arrived and Colonel Greer ordered an assault; men from the 43rd and 68th Regiments, together with men from the 1st Waikato Militia led the charge with fixed bayonets and in short order cleared the Maori trenches.

Captain Frederick Smith – Victoria Cross No. 319

Captain Smith from the 43rd Regiment was leading the attack on the right flank when, despite having received two wounds, he jumped down into the Maori rifle pits and engaged in hand to hand fighting, thus setting a fine example to his men.

For this action, Captain Smith was later awarded the Victoria Cross.

Sergeant John Murray – Victoria Cross No. 320

During the attack, Sergeant Murray from the 68th Regiment, distinguished himself when, unassisted, he jumped into a rifle pit occupied by about 8 to 10 Maori and after killing or wounding them all, continued to advance up the enemy entrenchments.

During the desperate hand to hand fighting, the gallant Sergeant managed to kill a Maori who was about to kill a Corporal with his tomahawk.

For his action during the charge, Sergeant Murray was later awarded the Victoria Cross.

Despite putting up a brave resistance to the charge, the Maori line was broken and the survivors fled for the cover of the gullies and swamps to the rear of their position. The retreating Maori were chased for several miles by the Colonial Defence Force cavalry but because of the difficult nature of the ground the chase had to be abandoned.

The British casualties in this, the last battle of the campaign, were 13 privates killed with six officers and 33 NCOs and Privates wounded. The Maori losses were 120 killed, with many wounded; several of the wounded who were treated in the hospital at Te Papa, later died from their wounds.

The defeat at Te Ranga broke the resistance of the Maori and in July, they came to Te Papa, surrendered their arms and pledged peace to Governor Grey, bringing the Tauranga Campaign to an end.

Wanganui Campaign

Immediately after the new year in 1865, Governor Grey ordered General Cameron to the Wanganui district on the west coast of the north island, on a mission to take possession of the Waitotara

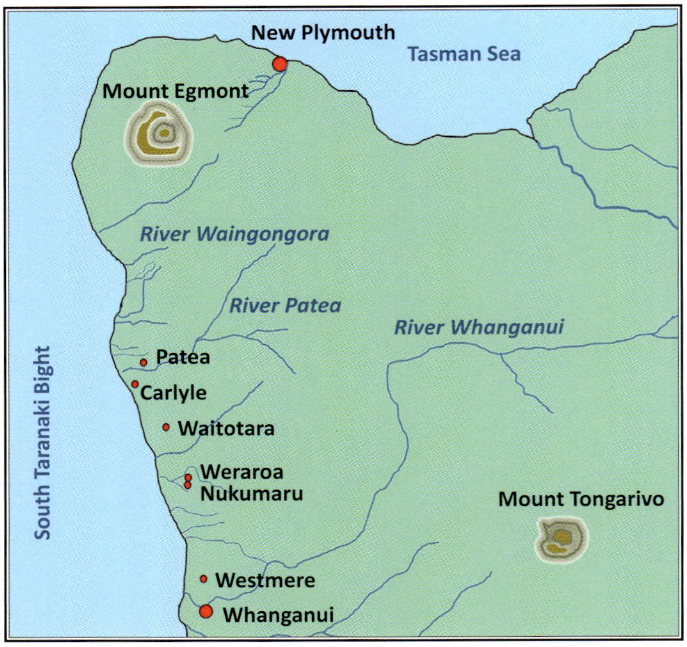

Figure 36. Wanganui Campaign

block of land, which had been purchased by the crown but had been reoccupied by the Maori.

The west coast tribes had concentrated their forces to the south of the Waitotara River and had built a fortified Pa on the summit of a hill at Weraroa. On the river plain below, several hundred Hauhau,[12] with their prophet Te Ua Haumene, were assembled at the village of Perekama.

With about 2,000 troops and two field guns, General Cameron marched into the Wanganui district and on 24th January established his first camp at Nukumaru in south Waitotara, on an open plain a short distance inland.

Battle of Nukumaru

Captain Hugh Shaw – Victoria Cross No. 321

After Colonel Waddy had established the camp, he sent out piquets; amongst these was a party of the Royal Irish, under the command of Captain Shaw who was ordered to take up a position about half a mile to the north of the camp.

Advancing in skirmishing order, Captain Shaw and his men approached a patch of bush which it was necessary to occupy. The party were within 30 yards of the bush, when suddenly a large number of Maori broke cover and began to lay down a heavy fire. Having just passed a ditch, with a fence in front, which would offer some cover, Captain Shaw ordered his men back to this position so that they could put up a defence against the Maori, who were now about 60 yards away.

After deploying his men, Captain Shaw did a headcount and discovered that one of his men was missing; he was lying wounded at a point midway between the British and Maori positions. To leave the man where he lay would have been to condemn him to certain death as at nightfall he was certain to be killed by the Maori.

Captain Shaw called for volunteers to go to the rescue of the wounded man and Privates Brandon, Brien, Kearnes and Clampitt came forward. With these men, Captain Shaw rushed across open ground, under heavy fire from the Maori, while his men laid down a covering fire. After reaching the wounded man, Captain Shaw lifted him onto his back and the party rushed back to the remainder of the piquet and the cover of the ditch; incredibly none of the party was hit by the Maori fire.

For this action, Captain Shaw was later awarded the Victoria Cross; the volunteers, Privates Brandon, Brien, Kearnes and Clampitt were each awarded the Distinguished Conduct Medal.

The British camp was also attacked by a large body of Maori, hidden in the bush on their right flank. After firing a volley, the Maori broke cover and charged into the camp where there was fierce hand to hand fighting before the Maori force was forced back into the bush by a charge of mounted troops, part of the military train, under the command of Major Witchell.

The British losses during the battle were 15 killed, including Lieutenant Johnson the Assistant Adjutant-General, and 32 wounded. It is believed that the Maori losses were even larger with 23 men killed.

On the following day, the Maori mounted an even more determined attack, with about 2,000 men who had been assembled at the Weraroa Pa, which drove in the piquets and caused further British loss of life.

Advance Along the Coast

After the battle, General Cameron moved his camp nearer to the sea, to what he thought was a more secure location and remained there until the night of 2nd February 1865. On the night of 2nd February, the General with half of his force, which now numbered 2,300 men, headed out on a march up the coast and in the early morning of 3rd February, crossed the Waitotara River on a raft of casks built by the Royal Engineers. While the troops camped on the level ground on the right bank, a redoubt to hold 150 men, was built on a cliff on the left bank and armed with two field-guns.

12 Followers of a religious sect, the Pai Marire, who espoused Christian and Maori virtues.

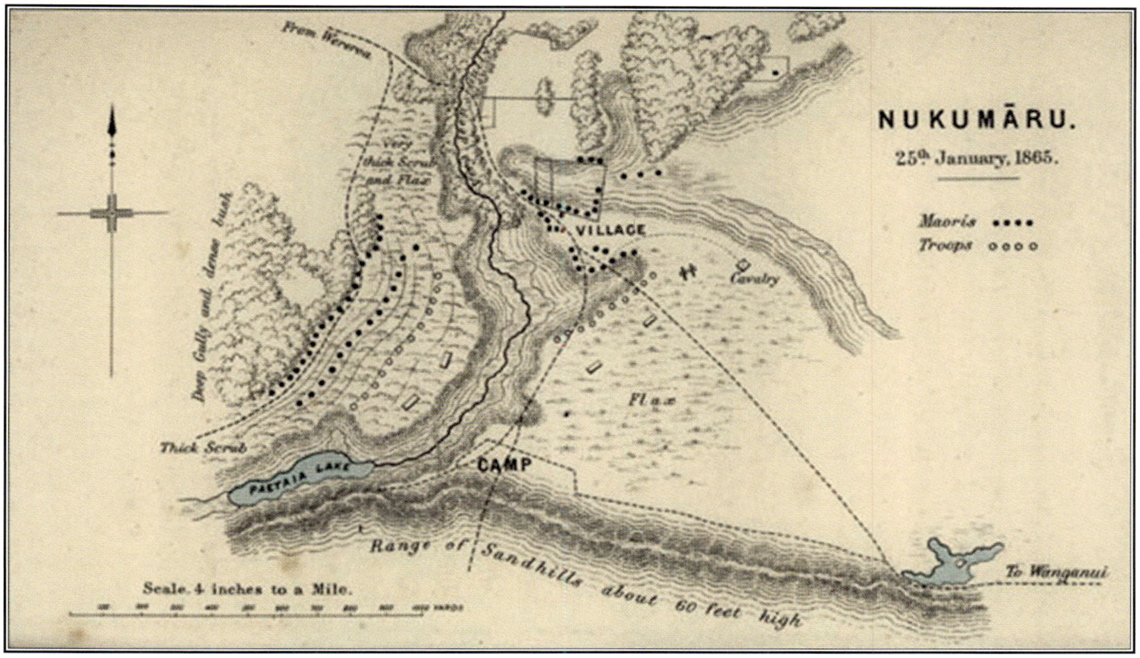

Figure 37. Battle of Nukumaru

On the night of 15th February, General Cameron once again carried out a night march up the coast and crossed the Patea River where another redoubt, this time to hold 200 men, was built on high ground on the right river bank. At a later date, with the erection of huts the redoubt was turned into a large supply depot with accommodation for 600 men.

The men who had been left at Nukumaru, marched up the coast and occupied the position at Waitotara, soon after it had been vacated by the General and his advanced column.

General Cameron and his force remained at Patea for about a week before recommencing their journey up the coast. During his march the General decided to bypass the Weraroa Pa, which was the Hauhau headquarters; following his bitter experience at the Gate Pa General Cameron considered that his force was insufficient to either besiege or attack such a well defended position.

When General Cameron communicated his decision to Governor George Grey, this led to an acrimonious exchange of letters as Governor Grey was of the opinion that occupation of the Weraroa Pa was the key to British control of the west coast.

General Cameron, who had been against the Campaign from the outset, as he believed it was a war of land plunder so that the Colonial Government could satisfy the settlers demands for more and more land[13] and that the campaign could not deliver a decisive blow that would make the Maori surrender disagreed with the Governor.

The General continued his journey north and on 15th March the column was attacked by a band of 200 warriors at Te Ngaio, having tendered his resignation to Governor Grey on 2nd February, this would be the General's last military action and by August he had left the colony.

The General reached the Waingongoro river on 31st March, where he established a large camp and redoubts between Hawera and Manaia. From this point onward the coastal route was not tenable, due to the lack of harbours for resupply and as the overland route to New Plymouth was deemed to be too hazardous, General Cameron decided to turn back south.

In June, Governor Grey, unhappy with General Cameron's refusal to attack the Weraroa Pa, decided to take matters into his own hands and leading a collection of colonial forces with Captain Thomas McDonnell attacked several villages near the Pa, taking several prisoners. After some shelling, the force made an attack on the Weraroa Pa but found it to be deserted. Unable to entice the British forces into an attack, the Pa had ceased to be of any value to the Maori cause so had been abandoned.

General Trevor Chute arrived at New Plymouth on 20th September, as a replacement for General Cameron, just as the British government began the withdrawal of troops from New Zealand. General Chute carried out several operations until late 1866, however, by this time most of the fighting was being undertaken by colonial forces – the wars over land ownership would continue until 1872.

13 The New Zealand Settlements Act of 1863, provided the basis by which Maori tribes involved in rebellion against the Government after 1st January 1863, could have their land confiscated. On 30th January 1865, Governor Grey issued a proclamation to seize nearly a million acres of land in the Taranaki-Wanganui district; a further 2 million acres of land had previously been seized in the Waikato and Bay of Plenty districts.

10

THE SHIMONOSEKI EXPEDITION, JAPAN (1864)

Background

For over 250 years, the Tokugawa shoguns had ruled the over 300 individual and uncooperative clans (Daimyos) of Japan in a peaceful but fragile alliance, however, by the early 1850s with the arrival of foreign traders wishing to establish commercial and diplomatic relations with the county this was in danger of breaking down. What had kept the alliance together was a universal commitment to the policy of isolationism to keep foreigners from their shores.

In 1853, the American president Millard Fillmore ordered an expedition to Japan to establish commercial and diplomatic relations between the two countries. Commodore Matthew Calbraith Perry, who had the authority to use force if necessary, was given command of the mission.

On 8th July 1853, Commodore Perry and his fleet of four warships; *Mississippi*, *Susquehanna*, *Plymouth* and *Saratoga*; arrived at Uraga at the entrance to Edo Bay and moved past the Japanese lines toward the capital at Edo. After making threats of violence, Commodore Perry was eventually allowed to land and presented a letter from President Fillmore, for the Japanese to consider.

Commodore Perry left Japan on 17th July 1853, with a promise that he would return to hear the Shogun's reply to the president's letter. Due to unforeseen events, it was not until 13th February 1854 that Perry was able to return to Japan (with a fleet of 10 warships) and after much discussion, during which the American again threatened violence, the location for talks was finally agreed to be the village of Yokohama.

Following three weeks of negotiations, the Convention of Kanagawa was signed on 31st March which allowed American access to the ports of Shimoda and Hakodate, they were also allowed to establish a consulate at Shimoda. It took some time for the treaty to be ratified by both governments and it finally came into effect on 30th September 1855. This treaty would later be used as the model for similar trade treaties with Japan by Russia, Britain and the Netherlands.

These treaties were not universally accepted by the clans of Japan and the Shogun came under intense pressure, especially from the Choshu and Satsuma clans, to return to the traditional policy of isolation.

Incidents leading up to the conflict

Several events, resulting in military action against Japan, set the precedents which resulted in the Shimonoseki conflict.

The Richardson Affair

On the morning of 14th September 1862, Shimazu Saburo, the uncle of the young Daimyo of Satsuma, was leaving Yedo on his way to Tokaido. As was the norm, Saburo travelled in a military column, while he and his officials were carried in norimono (litters) the accompanying force of 800 Samurai were mounted on horses. The column also had a large number of pack horses which carried the supplies and baggage of the party.

In the afternoon of the same day, a party of four Europeans, three men and one woman, left Yokohama on horseback for the village of Kowasaki, where they intended to visit a temple. One of the party was Mr Charles Richardson, a merchant of long standing in Shanghai, China who was on a visit to Japan, prior to his return to England. Either ignoring or ignorant of the long established etiquette of the road which gave precedence to military columns and required riders to dismount and stand at the road edge to let them pass, Mr Richardson and his party continued riding along the road, weaving their way through the oncoming column.

As the riders came alongside the litter carrying Shimazu Saburo, several of the Samurai guards, outraged at the action of the foreigners, who should have been dismounted at the roadside with heads bowed, in deference to the representative of the Daimyo, launched a savage attack against the party. During the

Figure 38. Map of Japan

attack, Mr Richardson suffered a mortal sword wound to his left side and fell dying at the roadside; the two other men were also severely wounded and the woman who had her hat knocked off by a sword, narrowly missing injury, managed to about turn and rode back to the village of Kanagawa which they had just passed.

In response to this outrage, the British Government issued demands to the Shogun for the capture and punishment of the assassin, the payment of £100,000 indemnity by the Shogunate with a further payment from the Daimyo of Satsuma. Despite these terms having been agreed by the Shogunate, the Daimyo of Satsuma ignored the demands and Admiral Kuper, with a fleet of seven warships was despatched to Kagoshima to enforce the demands. Admiral Kuper arrived off Kagoshima, a prosperous city of 180,000 inhabitants on 11th August 1863, and when his negotiations failed to reach a settlement he was left with no alternative but to take military action.

The guns of Admiral Kuper's fleet now began a heavy bombardment which destroyed the gun batteries that lined the shore, as well as most of the city. Three steamers which had recently been purchased by the Daimyo were also destroyed. Following this demonstration of military might, the Daimyo made the necessary payment, however, he was unable to identify and punish the Samurai who had killed Mr Richardson.

Shimonoseki Strait Incidents

Breaking with centuries of imperial tradition, Emperor Komei began to take an active role in matters of state and on 11th March and 11th April 1863 issued two proclamations, his "Order to expel barbarians", which set a deadline of 11th May by which this should be accomplished.

Acting in accordance with his Emperor's order, but in direct defiance of the Shogunate, Daimyo Mori Takachika, leader of the Choshu clan, ordered his men to fire without warning on all foreign ships trying to traverse the Shimonoseki Strait. The Shimonoseki Strait, less than half a mile long, was a treacherous but strategic waterway between the islands of Honshu and Kyushu that connected the Inland Sea with the Sea of Japan.

In line with Daimyo Takachika's orders, on 25th June 1863 the American steamer *SS Pembroke*, captained by Simon Cooper, was fired upon by two of Takachika's European built men of war, as she sailed between Yokohama and Nagasaki. The *SS Pembroke*, which suffered only minor damage and no casualties, managed to escape through the Bungo channel and reached Shanghai where the incident was reported to the American Consulate at Yokohama.

On the following day, while at anchor at the mouth of the strait, the French warship *Kien Chan* was fired upon by Japanese artillery from the hills above the town of Shimonoseki. The *Kien Chan* crew suffered four casualties and some damage was caused to her engine room before she escaped to the safety of the open ocean.

On 11th July, despite warnings from the *Kien Chan*, the heavily armed Dutch warship *Medusa* decided to sail through the strait. Her captain, Francois de Casembroot, thought that, because of his armament and his governments friendly relations with Japan, it would be safe to do so. This proved not to be the case and the *Medusa*, with the Dutch Consul General on board, was fired upon by Japanese ships and shore batteries. Captain Casembroot, managed to negotiate the strait, and returned the Japanese fire with good effect, however, he lost nine men killed or wounded in the process.

As expected, these unprovoked attacks could not go un-avenged and on the morning of 16th July 1863, Captain McDonald on board the American frigate *USS Wyoming* arrived off Shimonoseki to extract revenge for the attack on the *SS Pembroke*. Captain McDonald sailed the *USS Wyoming* into the strait and engaged a flotilla of Japanese warships, the *Daniel Webster*, *Lanrick* and *Lancefield* (which ironically had been purchased from the US Navy), sinking two of them and causing significant damage to the third. Unfortunately, *USS Wyoming* also suffered significant damage and four of the crew were killed and seven wounded (one of these would later die from his wounds).

A few days later two French warships, the *Tancrede* and *Dupleix*, under the command of Captain Benjamin Jaures, arrived at Shimonoseki to exact revenge for the attack on the *Kien Chan*.

After a bombardment had destroyed one of the shore batteries, 250 marines were landed and they destroyed what remained.

Battle of Shimonoseki

In addition to their revenge attacks, the treaty powers sought reparation from the Shogunate and eventually the US government received $12,000 for damages to the *SS Pembroke*. They also sought to negotiate a treaty which would guarantee free passage through the Shimonoseki Strait to give unfettered access to the Inland Sea but after nearly a year of discussions they were no closer to a conclusion.

On 11th July 1864, the US steamer *Monitor*, had entered the harbour at Nagato, to take on board coal and water when she was fired upon by Japanese artillery. This was the final outrage which prompted the Treaty powers to mount a multi-national offensive to open up the Shimonoseki Strait.

Sir Rutherford Alcock, the British Minister and leader of the diplomatic efforts, organized the expedition to subdue the Choshu clan and on 25th August 1864, the coalition of treaty powers signed a memorandum declaring the necessity to resort to force to achieve their objectives.

This was communicated to the naval commanders and four days later the allied squadrons put to sea to execute the plan; a flotilla of nine British, four Dutch and three French warships, together with 2,000 sailors, soldiers and marines was to be used as the attack force for the Shimonoseki Campaign; they were to be accompanied by a US chartered steamer *Ta-Kiang* as a token American show of support (due to the ongoing civil war a larger US commitment was not possible).

Sir Alcock's action was unofficial and not supported by the Foreign Office in London, however, due to the slow communications between London and Japan, he felt that he should act on his own initiative. Unknown to Sir Alcock, a despatch dated 26th July was already on its way and this prohibited the adoption of military measures in the interior of Japan and limited naval operations to defensive measures required for the protection of life and property of British subjects.

By the time that this despatch arrived, the Shimonoseki Campaign had already been concluded, however, Sir Alcock was subsequently called to account, but was able to justify his actions based upon the need to protect British trade with Japan.

The force of 17 ships, which was under the overall command of the British Admiral Sir Augustus Leopold Kuper, comprised the following vessels:

HMS Euryalus commanded by Captain Alexander, which acted as the Admiral's flagship; *HMS Tartar* under the command of Captain Hayes; *HMS Barrosa*, commanded by Captain Dowell; *HMS Conqueror*, commanded by Captain Luard; *HMS Leopard*, commanded by Captain Leekie; *HMS Argus*, under the command of Commander Moresby; *HMS Coquette*, under the command of

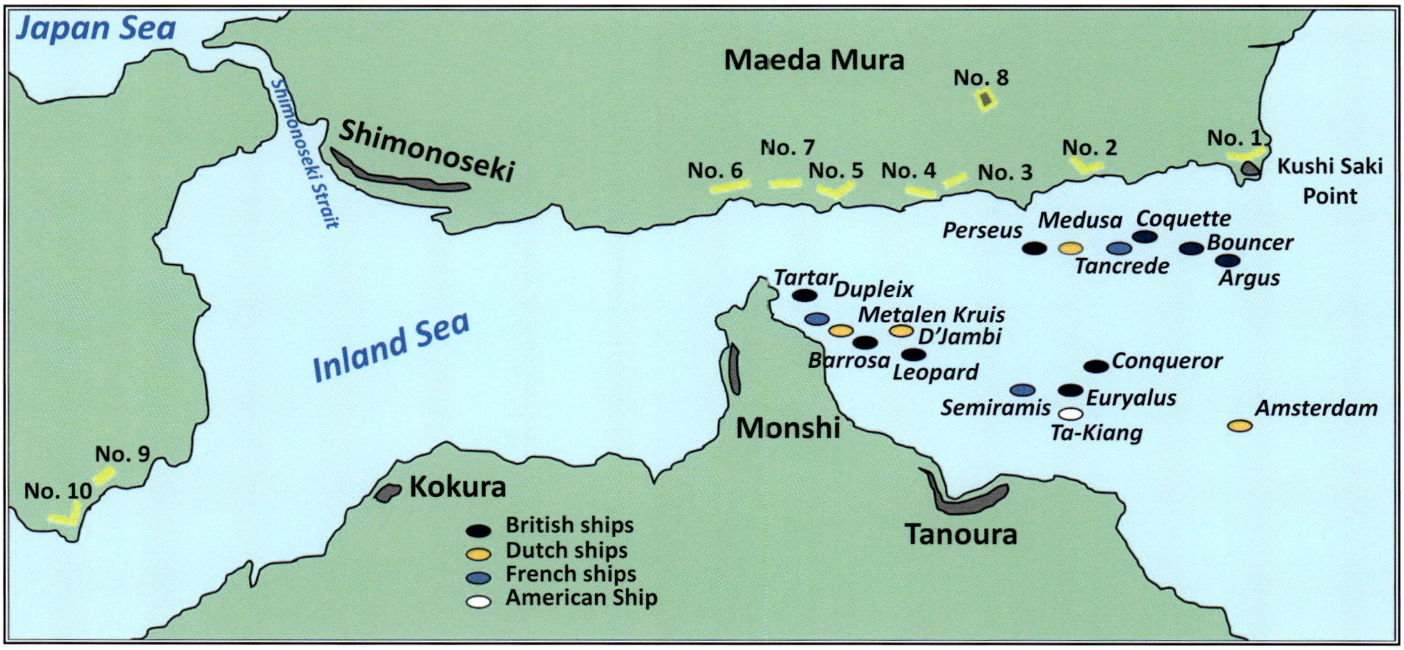

Figure 39. Battle of Shimonoseki

Commander Roe; *HMS Perseus*, under the command of Commander Kingston and the gunboat *HMS Bouncer*, commanded by Lieutenant Holder.

The Dutch Squadron consisted of: *Metalen Kruis*, under the command of Captain de Man; *D'Jambi*, under Captain van Rees; *Medusa*, under the command of Captain de Casembroot and the *Amsterdam*.

The French Squadron consisted of the warships, *Tancrede*, *Semiramis* and *Dupleix*, operating under the flag of Admiral Jaures.

The American chartered steamer, *Ta-Kiang*, was under the command of Lieutenant Pearson and was crewed with men from the US corvette *Jamestown*.

On 2nd September, the force began to assemble off the island of Himeshima and at 9 o'clock on the morning of 4th September, the fleet weighed anchor and set sail for the Shimonoseki Strait; with *HMS Euryalus* leading the way, the British Squadron took the centre with the French Squadron and the *Ta-Kiang* on their left and the Dutch Squadron on their right.

The fleet entered the Inland Sea, from the Sea of Japan, on the afternoon of 5th September and began to proceed into the Shimonoseki Strait: *HMS Barrosa*, *HMS Tartar* and *HMS Leopard*, together with *D'Jambi*, *Metal Kruis* and *Dupleix* moved along the southern coast and took up station in front of Tanoura; while *HMS Perseus*, *HMS Coquette* and *HMS Bouncer*, together with *Medusa* and *Tancred* (the light squadron) moved along the northern shore; *HMS Argus* and *Amsterdam* were held back, in reserve.

HMS Euryalus, *HMS Conqueror*, *Semiramis* and the *Ta-kiang* anchored out of range of the Japanese batteries at a distance of about 2,500 yards from Maeda Mura but within range of the British 110 pounder Armstrong guns.

HMS Euryalus began the bombardment at just after 4 o'clock in the afternoon, soon followed by the ships of the squadron off Tanoura and the light squadron soon silence the three gun battery on Kushi Saki Point. *HMS Conqueror*, the *Semiramis* and the *Ta-kiang* also took part in the shelling of the batteries. Having silenced the batteries at Kushi Saki Point, the light squadron began an enfilading fire on the No. 4, No. 7 and No. 9 batteries on the south shore.

After about an hour of fire, the principal batteries had been silenced and a signal was sent to the fleet to stop firing. Soon afterwards, a fire broke out amongst the buildings and batteries at Maeda Mura, which caused a magazine to explode. Captain Kingston, with some of his men from *HMS Perseus* together with Captain de Casembroot with some of his men from *Medusa*, landed at Maeda Mura and spiked 14 guns.

At the end of the first day of the conflict, the allied casualties were six men wounded, all of whom were on board *HMS Tartar* who had taken the brunt of the enemy fire.

In the early hours of the next morning, one of the batteries at Maeda Mura opened fire on the squadron off Tanoura but was soon silenced by return fire which also set on fire the barracks behind the battery. Two men were killed with a further two wounded on board the *Dupleix* and a first Lieutenant on board *HMS Tartar* was also wounded.

It was now decided to mount a land assault, the force to be deployed comprised: Captain Alexander with 200 men from *HMS Euryalus*; Colonel Suther commanding a battalion of 450 marines mainly from *HMS Conqueror* and *HMS Euryalus* but with detachments from some of the other British ships; the French had a landing party of 350 with a Dutch landing force of 200. In total the assault force, which was commanded by Captain Alexander, numbered about 1,900 men, 1,400 of whom were British forces.

At about 9 o'clock on the morning of 6th September, the assault force landed unopposed, opposite the main Maeda Mura batteries; each of the allied forces immediately moved off to their designated targets. Throughout the day, the assault forces only met limited opposition and managed to destroy most of the batteries that they came across; magazines were blown up, gun carriages set on fire, guns were spiked and many of the fortifications were pulled down.

Midshipman Duncan Gordon Boyes – Victoria Cross No. 322
Captain of the Afterguard Thomas Pride – Victoria Cross No. 323
Seaman William Henry Harrison Seeley – Victoria Cross No. 324

In the afternoon, at about 4 o'clock, it was decided that enough work had been done for the day and the French and Dutch elements of the assault force had begun their re-embarkation when suddenly the British force was fired upon by what appeared to be a large Japanese force.

Seaman Seeley, from *HMS Euryalus*, moved off in the direction of the firing, in order to ascertain the location of the enemy force, which he found to be concealed in the bush near to a stockade. Seaman Seeley returned to the British position and reported his findings to Lieutenant Edwards, the commander of company 3.

Lieutenant Edwards immediately organised an attack, and despite being wounded Seaman Seeley moved off with No. 3 company which was leading the assault. Also in the leading company was the 'colour party' carrying the Queen's colours into battle, as was the common practice. When one of the colour Sergeants was killed and the other, Petty Officer Pride was seriously wounded, Midshipman Boyes, who was only 17 years of age, stepped forward to carry the colours. Petty Officer Pride and Midshipman Boyes, continued to carry the colour at the head of the column until they were order to retire with the colours by a senior officer.

The Japanese force, retired into the nearby stockade and fierce hand to hand fighting was required before they were eventually expelled and seven of their guns were captured.

During this final assault Captain Alexander was wounded, and despite his wounds Seaman Seeley placed him on his back and carried him the half mile back to the safety of the main British force.

Petty Officer Pride, Midshipman Boyes and Seaman Seeley,[14] who were all members of the crew of *HMS Euryalus*, were later awarded the Victoria Cross for their actions.

After the stockade was captured, it was set on fire and the magazine was blown up; during the assault 7 marines were killed and 26 were wounded.

Over the next few days, further parties were landed on shore to complete the destruction of the batteries and no fewer than 62 heavy guns were captured and brought back to the ships. On 10th September the Daimyo of Choshu surrendered and signed an agreement not to erect any more batteries and to keep the Strait open to allied shipping; soon afterwards a similar agreement was reached with the Daimyo of Satsuma.

During the campaign, the allied losses were 12 killed and 60 wounded, the bulk of the casualties were part of the British force which lost 8 killed and 48 wounded.

14 Seaman Seeley was the first American citizen to be awarded the Victoria Cross

11

BHUTAN (DUAR) WAR, INDIA (1864–65)

Background

Located in the Himalaya mountains, Bhutan was a rugged country bordered by Tibet as well as the East India Company territories of Assam and Bengal. The country was almost inaccessible with only one major road from the Chumbi valley which crossed the country from west to east with all of the principal centres of population situated near to it. To the south of the country down to the Brahmaputra river was the disputed Duar plain region, where 18 gorges (Duars) ran up from the river plain via passes into the foothills of Bhutan.

Bhutan was ruled under a dual leadership system where the Dhurma Raja was the spiritual/religious leader and the Deb Raja looked after temporal affairs. The Deb Raja was supported in the administration of the country by Penlows who were regional governors and Jungpens who were each in charge of a fortress. The country had no unified army, however, each of the Penlows and Jungpens maintained their own retinue of armed men. Their arms were limited to old matchlock rifles, bows and arrows, swords and slingshots and many of the men wore chainmail armour.

Apart from two minor trade missions that occurred in the mid 1700s, there had been no interaction between Bhutan and Britain or the East India Company, however, following the end of the First Anglo – Burmese War during which Assam was ceded to British India in 1826, things were about to change.

Under the rule of Burma, the Assam princes had become very lax regarding border affairs and ownership of the Duars became blurred, with many of the Bhutan tribes assuming control of the area. When Assam passed into the ownership of the East India Company border transgressions were treated as banditry and were vigorously suppressed by Company troops.

With these border incursions still on the increase, Captain Pemberton was sent on a mission in 1837 to treat with the Bhutan government to bring these raids to an end, unfortunately the mission was unable to gain the assistance of the Bhutan government in achieving this objective. Despite further attempts at negotiation, border raids continued and in 1841 the seven Assam Duars were formally annexed by the East India Company who agreed an annual payment of 10,000 rupees to the local chiefs by way of compensation. These arrangements seemed to resolve matters for some time and it was not until 1863 that border matters once again became contentious.

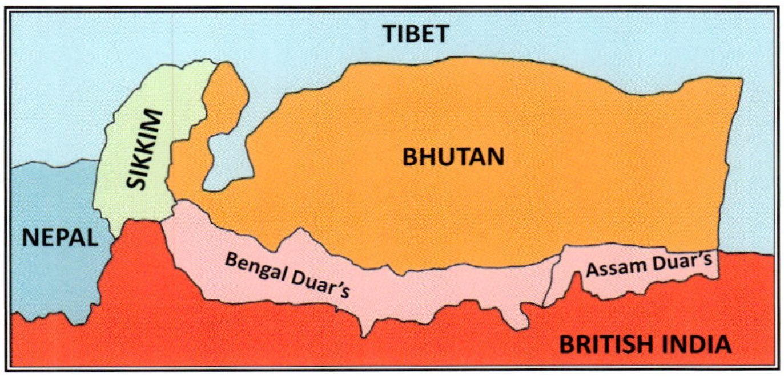

Figure 40. Location of Bhutan

Eden's Mission

Following several border disputes, regarding payment of dues and raids that by now were taking place in the Bengal Duars it was agreed that a British mission under the leadership of Ashley Eden (a much respected Company diplomat) would be sent to Bhutan to treat with the leadership and establish improved political relations. Mr Eden with his mission finally left Darjeeling on 4th January 1864 and after many delays and a very harsh journey eventually arrived at Poonakha, the Bhutan capital, on 15th March.

Following the conclusion of an internal power struggle, the Bhutan governing council was now manned by people hostile to Britain, and it was obvious from the start that Mr Eden's mission

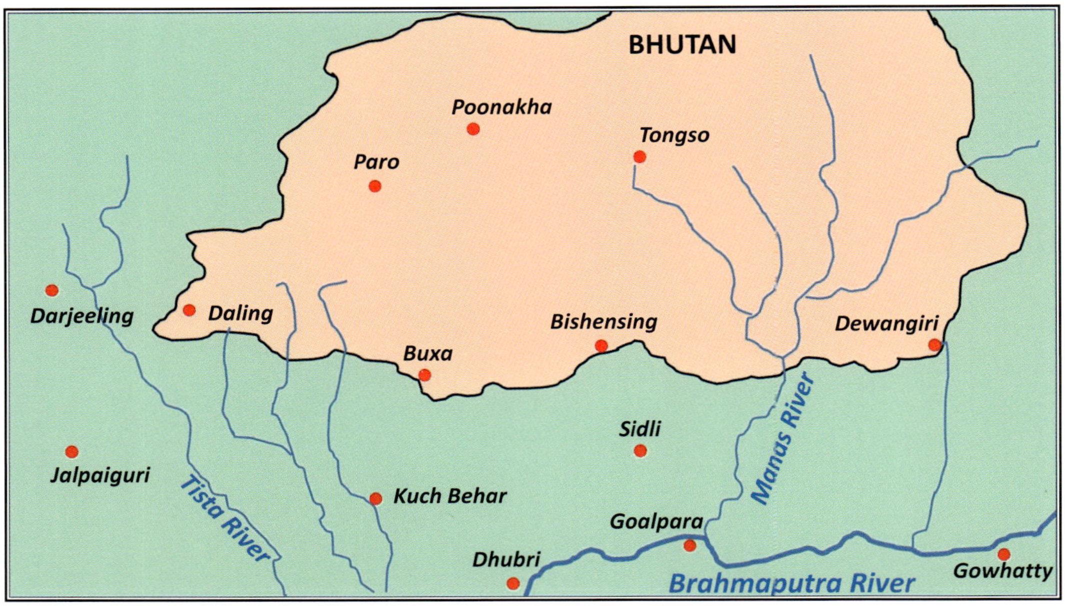

Figure 41. Bengal Duar Region

was doomed to failure. Mr Eden had his first meeting with the governing council on 17th March at which a minor dignitary, Cheeboo Lama, was assigned as the interface between the British mission and the Council. Over the next few days a draft treaty was produced and Cheeboo Lama gave this to the council for their consideration.

After several meetings with the council during which the British party and Mr Eden were subjected to constant harassment and humiliation, the Penlow of Tongso made the demand that the only treaty that he would sign was concerning the British return of the Assam Duars and failure to achieve this would result in war. With this turn of events, Mr Eden considered his mission to have failed and on 25th March began preparations to leave Bhutan.

Via Cheeboo Lama, Mr Eden was presented with a paper from the Penlow of Tongso which stated that the Indian Government must adjust the whole of the boundaries between the two counties, return the Assam Duars, pay compensation and deliver up all runaway slaves and political offenders who had taken up refuge within British territory. Under pain of imprisonment of himself and his mission, Mr Eden was forced to sign this "treaty" in order that he could return to India.

Immediately upon the return of the mission to Darjeeling, on 21st April, the British Government repudiated the "treaty" extracted from Mr Eden and as a punishment for the ill treatment that had been meted out: the Ambari Falakata region of Sikkim was annexed and the annual payments to Bhutan, in respect of the Assam Duars, were stopped for ever. The Bhutan government were also informed that if their demands, communicated by Mr Eden during his mission, were not complied with by 1st September 1864 then further measures would be adopted to enforce these demands.

Military Action in Bengal Duars

When the deadline passed, without any action by the Bhutan Government, military planning for operations against Bhutan began in earnest, the military authorities had been advised of this possibility on 24th August by the Indian Government.

Rather than invade Bhutan, it was agreed that the Bengal Duars were to be permanently annexed and the districts and forts to be occupied by British troops. This required the existing border to be advanced between twenty and thirty miles over a length of about 180 miles, from Daling in the west to Dewangiri in the east. In order to secure the area, the British forces would have to capture and occupy the forts and passes on the crest of the hills, which were currently occupied by Bhutan forces.

Early in the planning process, Sir Hugh Rose, Commander-in-Chief of British forces in India, decided that four sizable columns should be formed with their objectives being Dewangiri, Sidli, Buxa and Daling. General Mulcaster, commander of forces in Assam, was given overall command of operations and would also lead the right Brigade composed of two columns, while General Dunsford would command the left Brigade which was also composed of two columns.

The right or Dewangiri column which would start from Gowhatty, was assigned to the country between the Manas River and Bor Nadi (the Kamrup District). The right centre or Sidli column which would start from Goalpara was assigned to the Goalpara District between the Sankos and Manas Rivers.

The left centre or Buxa column, which was the strongest, would assemble at Kuch Behar and was assigned to the upper Kuch Behar district between the Jaldhaka and Sankos rivers. The left or Daling column would start from Jalpaiguri and was assigned to the country between the Jaldhaka and Tista rivers.

To guard against a possible attack against Darjeeling an additional force was to be established in the town, which could also act as a reserve to the main force if needed.

The above military plans were approved by the Governor General on 11th September and the necessary forces began to be assembled. On 22nd November 1864, with the military preparations almost complete, a proclamation issued by the Governor General at Fort William on 12th November, was displayed in many of the towns and villages of the Bengal Duars. The proclamation, outlined the British intention to occupy the region and the reasons why this was necessary and further declared that the local population and their goods would go unharmed as long as they did not resist the British forces.

It was originally intended that the campaign would begin with each of the four columns, simultaneously marching off towards their objectives, however, for a variety of reasons, the Dewangiri and Sidli columns were delayed and the start of the campaign fell on the shoulders of the Left Brigade when an advance party of the Daling column, under the command of Major Gough VC, crossed the Tista river near Jalpaiguri and entered the disputed territory on 28th November.

In quick succession, Major Gough's men had captured the Bhutan outposts at Gopalagan, Maynaguri and Domohani where they had encountered little or no opposition. By the 1st December, Major Gough's men had built a bridge of boats across the Tista River at Paharpur which was crossed by General Dunsford with the remainder of the Daling column which was reunited at Domohani on the following day. After resting for a day the column proceeded northward and by 5th December had reached Ambiokh, a village immediately below the fort at Daling. Although, the Jungpen initially indicated that he would surrender the fort, it soon became obvious that he taking strenuous actions for its defence.

Early in the morning of the 6th December, the British column began its advance on the fort, and their guns and mortars began a bombardment from the village of Ambiokh; during the ascent the column was assailed by the arrows and sling shots of the defenders and suffered two men killed and several wounded. To help with their passage two mortars were brought up, however, a powder cask exploded and tragically three officers and four men were killed, while several others were wounded.

After an Armstrong gun was brought up, a breach in the defences was soon effected and without much further effort the fort was occupied as the Bhutan force had evacuated their position.

After leaving a garrison at Daling, General Dunsford and his men moved on to the fort at Dhumsong, which surrendered without resistance and now having secured his initial objective of the Daling pass the General moved his force back down to the plain, so that he could move on his next objective of the Chumarchi Pass which was 30 miles further to the east. After some initial resistance, the fort at Chumarchi was captured on 1st January 1865 and after leaving a garrison force, the Daling column returned to camp at Tondu and General Dunsford moved off to join up with the Buxa column, which was operating even further to the east.

The Buxa column, under the command of Colonel Watson, which also entered the campaign on 28th, had a relatively easy time; finding that Chichacotta had been abandoned, the main column advanced unopposed and took possession of the fort at Buxa without opposition on 7th December. After leaving a garrison at Buxa, the force returned to the plain and advanced on the Balla Pass which they again occupied without opposition, thus completing their assigned objectives.

On 2nd December, the Dewangiri column, commanded by Colonel Campbell and accompanied by General Mulcaster, crossed the Brahmaputra River by steamer and troopship and proceeded towards the Daranga Pass which they reached on the 9th December. By the 12th December the force reached the fort at Dewangiri, which had been abandoned, and after leaving behind a garrison, returned to Kumrikatta and on 26th December moved off to join up with the Sidli column at Sidli.

After leaving a garrison at Sidli, the column moved off towards Bishensing some 42 miles distant, however, due to the difficult jungle terrain they were only able to advance at the rate of 3 or 4 miles a day, and finally reached the town on 8th January 1865. After leaving behind a garrison force, the column returned to their camp at Sidli.

With all four columns having achieved their objectives, the military command assumed that the annexation was now complete and in early February were on the verge of breaking up the Duar Field Force and withdrawing the British troops, leaving the garrison of the forts to men from the Bengal Police.

However, the Bhutan forces were planning counter attacks against the whole line of hill forts from Chumarchi to Dewangiri, even though ample warning of this intention was evident, for some inexplicable reason these warnings were ignored.

The Penlow of Tongso had even sent a letter to the British command at Dewangiri demanding that the town be evacuated within a week of the receipt of the letter, otherwise it would be attacked; unfortunately, as the message was written in Tibetan (which nobody at Dewangiri could read) it had to be sent to Darjeeling for translation.

On 30th January, a Bhutan force, led by the Penlow of Tongso, attacked Dewangiri and although they were repulsed with heavy losses, they managed to establish a stockade and take possession of the Daranga Pass cutting off the towns water supply and their communication with the plains below.

In the early hours of 5th February, with his water being very low, Colonel Campbell decided to evacuate his garrison of 250 men and retreated via the Lebra Pass down to the plains. Despite getting lost and having to abandon some of their guns (which were carried off by the enemy) the British force managed to get clear of the hills and reached the camp at Kumrikatta.

The Bhutan forces made several other attacks against the hill posts; at Bishensing on 25th January, Buxa on 4th February and Chumarchi on 5th February which were all repulsed. On 27th January an attack was made at Tazigong, the post at the head of the Balla Pass and after they were repulsed they erected a stockade in the pass in a similar fashion to the attack on Dewangiri; on 4th February a force led by Colonel Watson attempted to dislodge the Bhutan force but after two hours of fighting were forced to retire.

When news of these setbacks reached the powers that be in Calcutta, they took immediate action to rectify the situation. Reinforcements of 1,300 British Infantry, 2,000 Native Infantry and 100 artillerymen were made available to the Duar Field Force. General Tombs VC was sent to replace General Mulcaster as the commander of the Field Force (he would also command the Right Brigade) and General Dunsford, who was compelled to retire due to ill health, was replaced by General Tytler who would now command the Left Brigade.

Operations of Right Brigade

While the additional troops were being assembled, the right centre or Sidli column was ordered to make a strategic withdrawal from Bishensing and Sidli and concentrate their forces at Gauhati, which they reached on 10th March. By the 29th March, new forces had been assembled at Kumrikatta and preparations were well underway for the recapture of Dewangiri.

In a ploy to deceive the enemy regarding his real intentions, General Tombs formed a small post within the Shobankatta Pass and established a garrison under the command of Major Langmore. The major had instructions to carry out daily patrols and to feign building a road, with the intention of making the enemy believe that this would be the route used for the advance on Dewangiri. The deception was a total success and the Bhutan forces soon began to assemble at the head of the pass where they erected several stockades, leaving some of the other passes almost unguarded.

During the night of 31st March, Major Langmore, with the majority of his garrison returned to base, in preparation for the advance on Dewangiri but in order to continue the deception a few men were left behind and all of the tents were left standing.

On the afternoon of 1st April, Major Langmore and his men were part of the force commanded by Colonel Richardson which advanced towards Dewangiri via the Daranga Pass where they were later joined by General Tombs and the main force commanded by Colonel Hume. The enemy had been completely deceived and by 2nd April the British force had been established at a point only half a mile below Dewangiri, without the loss of a single man.

With his force in place General Tombs saw no need for any delays and on the morning of 3rd April,[15] after a brief artillery bombardment, pressed ahead with the attack to recapture Dewangiri.

Major William Spottiswoode Trevor – Victoria Cross No. 325
Lieutenant James Dundas – Victoria Cross No. 326

Following the artillery fire, volleys from the British Enfield rifles and a determined charge from the assault force, many of the enemy fled, however, about 150 took refuge in a large blockhouse from where they were determined to make a last stand.

It was for their actions in the capture of this blockhouse, that Major Trevor and Lieutenant Dundas would later be awarded the Victoria Cross. The action is best described in Major Trevor's own words, taken from a letter written soon after the events occurred "*... Here we are safe at last, covered in blood and glory. I have a broken head and something of a lump from a slight spear wound in the thigh ... In compensation for these little troubles I am informed that the General is going to recommend Dundas and myself for the Victoria Cross as being the first two to climb into the principal stockade. Garnault was the third and besides us some 4 Sepoys and a Bugler of the 55th were all in the place until resistance almost ceased. Dundas has a broken head, not as bad as mine, and an arrow wound in his side which luckily turned on a rib or it might have been disagreeable ... We had to scramble up a stockade 12 feet high, built in the form of a blockhouse, about 50 feet square, having two tiers of loop-holes, the upper accessible by means of a veranda all round, the centre being open. We killed*

15 The Victoria Cross citation for Major Trevor and Lieutenant Dundas, incorrectly gives the date as 30th April.

63 I believe inside and took some 25 wounded prisoners; a lot more who jumped over were shot or bayoneted outside. The attack was very successful so far as surrounding the place with troops went, but they hung fire about going in; the General was shouting at them to get in, in a frantic state of excitement, so the Engineers had to show them the way to do it. We plied our revolvers while they lasted and then got muskets and pistols etc. handed up. I counted 8 to my revolver, Garnault accounted for 8 in the same way and Dundas for 5 or 6. I was first in, Dundas second and Garnault third; who came afterwards I don't know. Just as our heads came level with the top Dundas got a clap on the head with a stone which sent him to the bottom again, knocking over Garnault in his fall. At the same time a fellow cut at me with his sword and another chucked a stone at me; I succeeded in guarding both with my sword but a man on the left hit me a whack on the head with a stone which brought a perfect deluge of blood and nearly blinded me. Just as I was going to get in again Dundas reappeared on the field and blew out my stoners brains. The others then gave ground enough to let us gain a footing, and we drove them out of the veranda before us with our revolvers. They kept charging with their swords by ones and twos, but went down like ninepins Once they tried a general charge by the beat of a drum, but we were then strongly established and they were shot down faster than they calculated. We have accounted for about 150 of the enemy dead and a lot of wounded prisoners. Our loss is 6 killed and about 50 wounded ...".

After the battle, the fleeing enemy were pursued to the top of the Shobankatta pass, but due to the heat of the day and lack of water the British force had to give up the chase, and many of them escaped unharmed.

Because Dewangiri was totally inhospitable in the rains, it was decided to evacuate the town after first having destroyed all of the fortifications; when this was complete, the Brigade moved back to their base at Kumrikatta where they arrived on 6th April.

Having achieved his objectives, General Tombs handed over command of the Right Brigade to Colonel Richardson on 23rd April.

Operations of Left Brigade

General Tytler took over the command of the Left Brigade from General Dunsford on 15th February 1865 and immediately began an inspection of the posts in his command, which included Darjeeling, Dhumsong, Daling, Ambari, Chumarchi, Buxa and Pandu; most of these positions suffered from the same problem, an inadequate water supply. Having completed his inspections, General Tytler decided to mount an attack on the Balla Pass, which was held by a large enemy force. A reconnaissance on 13th March, discovered that the enemy flank bordering the Torsa river, was lightly guarded so this was agreed to be the line of attack.

In the early hours of the 14th March, the attack was begun and quickly secured a ford and two bridges across the Torsa, when an advance party came under heavy fire from the Tazigong stockade, in the centre of their position it was returned in full by the British mortars and guns which deflected their attention from the flanking movement which managed to turn the position.

With their flank turned, the enemy position quickly fell and the British force now moved off to Buxa, where the enemy were well established in stockades, however, with the approach of the British, the Bhutan commander indicated his willingness to retire, if asked to do so. General Tytler replied with a message stating that if he wished to show his sincerity, then he should immediately abandon his position and set fire to the stockades. Soon afterwards, the stockades were seen to be burning and the British occupied Buxa without a shot having been fired.

On 24th March a move was made against Chumarchi, with General Tytler leading a force of troops from Ambari; after a few rounds from the British artillery the enemy abandoned their positions and the town was occupied unopposed. This action brought the fighting season to a close.

End of the War

With the start of the rainy season, military operations were on hold; General Tombs had returned to Gwalior and General Tytler was appointed to the command of all troops in the eastern districts of Bengal and the Duars. The government in India had decided that only two military posts would be maintained in the Bhutan foothills, at Daling and Buxa.

By the end of June 1865, it had been agreed that an expedition into Bhutan should be considered for the next campaign season and even though the Bhutan government were making overtures for peace, the planning for such an operation went ahead. On 4th October 1865, Colonel Richardson received orders to reoccupy Dewangiri, which was accomplished by 23rd October, in preparation for an advance on the Bhutan capital.

The expedition into Bhutan, in the end proved to be unnecessary as the Bhutan government finally agreed to the British terms and the war came to an official close with the signing of the treaty of Sinchula on 11th November 1865.

12

CANADA (1866)

The award of this Victoria Cross is unusual, in that the deed resulting in the award did not take place during a war. On the 10th August 1858, the Royal Warrant was amended to "Extend the Victoria Cross to Cases of Conspicuous Courage and Bravery Displayed under Danger but not before the Enemy". This was the first (of only six) awards to be made under this amendment, before it was scrapped in 1881.

In 1866, Private O'Hea was despatched to Canada with his regiment the 1st Battalion of the Prince Consort's Own Rifle Brigade. The regiment was sent to Canada as part of a force to quell a possible "Fenian Uprising"; following the end of the American Civil War in 1865 some soldiers of Irish descent, who had fought in the war, crossed into Canada intent on causing trouble to the British Government, in support of the movement for home rule of Ireland.

Private Timothy O'Hea – Victoria Cross No. 327

On 9th June 1866, Private O'Hea and three or four other men from his regiment, were acting as guards on a munitions shipment being despatch by rail from Quebec to Lake Erie. The munitions which consisted of 2,000 pounds of ammunition (including 95 barrels of gunpowder) were stored in their own separate box car which had been attached to a passenger train. The remainder of the train consisted of several converted box cars, that were locked, carrying 800 German immigrants as passengers.

In the late afternoon, while the train was stopped at Danville, in the Eastern Townships, Private O'Hea noticed that the munitions car was on fire and raised the alarm. The boxcar was disconnected from the rest of the train, however, before a decision regarding further action could be taken, Private O'Hea grabbed the keys to the boxcar from the Sergeant in command, opened up the car and began to tackle the fire on his own; apparently after the alarm was sounded the railwaymen and the soldiers from his regiment had all fled.

Entering the blazing boxcar, Private O'Hea proceeded to rip the burning covers off the cases of ammunition and hurl them outside, after which he made 19 trips to a nearby creek for buckets of water with which to douse the flames. His actions took almost an hour and during this time he was cheered on in his quest by the German immigrants who were unaware of their peril.

By evening the ammunition had been loaded on another boxcar, which was attached to the passenger train which then proceeded on its way.

For displaying great courage and putting his own life at risk, Private O'Hea had diverted a disaster which could have ended the lives of the 800 immigrants, an action for which he was later awarded the Victoria Cross.

To date this is the only Victoria Cross to have been awarded for action in Canada.

13

GAMBIA (1866)

Background

For centuries the west coast of Africa had been an important source of slaves for European and American traders, however, during the 19th century the more enlightened countries were switching their trade towards African agricultural and mineral products which were generally exchanged for European manufactured goods. Wanting to explore further inland, for trading opportunities, the French and British conducted missions along the Gambia river and eventually reached an amicable agreement where the British had control of a strip of land adjacent to each bank of the river, while the French would control the strip of land on either side of the British lands.

In 1807, an Act of Parliament abolished the slave trade throughout the British Empire and with the help of the Royal Navy, the garrison at Goree Island in Senegal made efforts to stop the mainly Spanish and American slave traders from operating in the Gambia River.

In 1816, Alexander Grant established a British capital on St Mary's Island at the mouth of the Gambia River, which he named Bathurst after the then reigning Secretary of State for War and the Colonies. As the cannons at Bathurst could not adequately

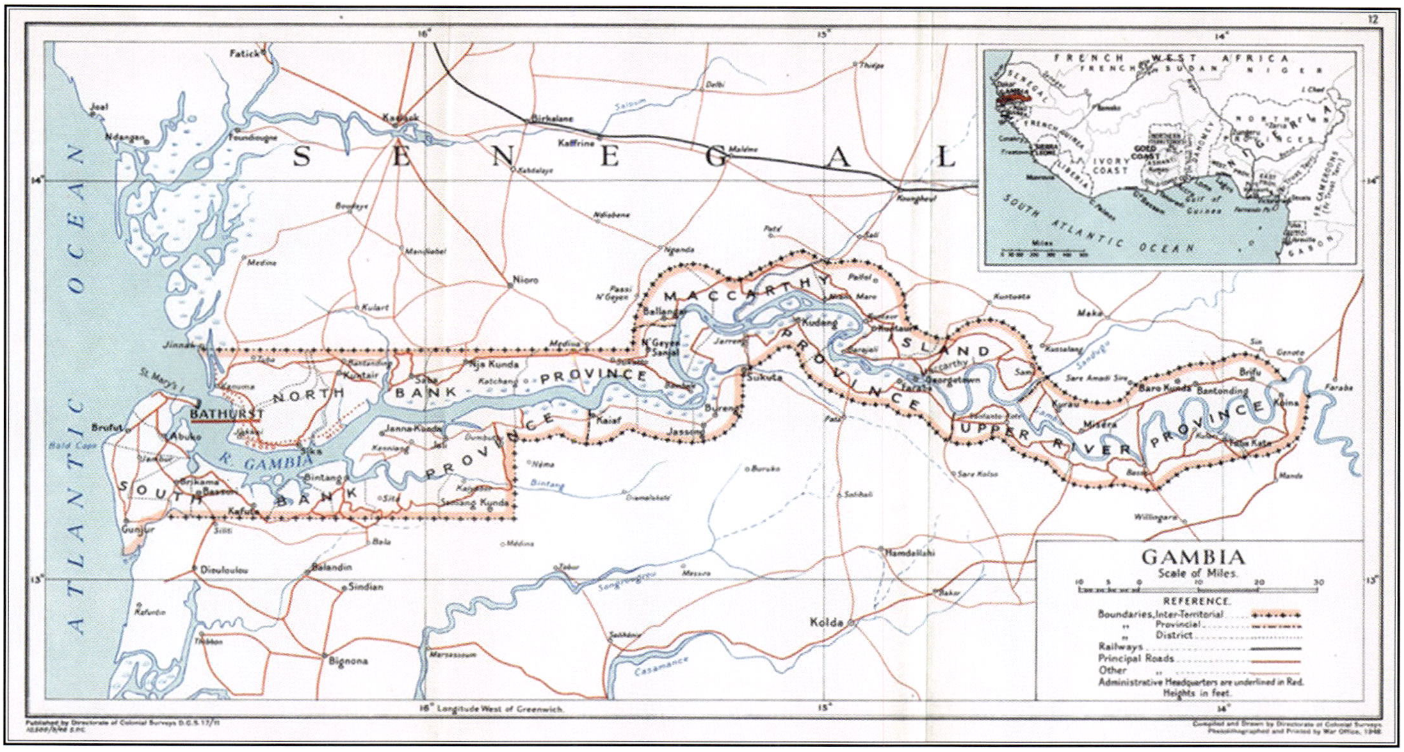

Image 42. Gambia

control the northern channel, a fort was built, at Barra Point in 1826 by Commodore Charles Bullen, on the northern river bank and armed with two guns from Bathurst.

Despite the British attempts to stop the slave trade on the river, some of the local people continued with this lucrative trade and British forces were often engaged in hostile disputes with traders. It soon became apparent that the British troops could not operate effectively in the severe climate of west Africa where malaria, blackwater fever (a serious complication arising from malaria)and dysentery were endemic; the levels of sickness and deaths amongst the troops led the coastline to be named "The White Man's Grave".

The solution implemented to resolve the problem was to deploy units from the West India Regiments in the Caribbean as the permanent garrisons for the forts and to deploy European troops, mainly naval landing parties, only for short duration campaigns. Some local tribesmen were also trained and employed by the crown as policemen or soldiers.

Soninke – Marabout Wars

In the 1850s Muslim fundamentalists from the Fula tribe, led by their religious leaders, the Marabouts, began to migrate into the Wolof and Mande kingdoms with the intent of transforming the mainly Mandinka tribesmen to their ideals. This led to a civil war that was to last for almost fifty years; during these conflicts Britain chose to remain neutral unless her commercial interests were threatened.

Battle of Tubabecolong

In the middle of 1866, one Marabout leader, Amar Faal, was creating severe difficulties for some tribal leaders who were dependent upon the British forces for protection so the British Governor of Gambia, Colonel George Abbas Koolie D'Arcy decided to intervene by attacking the Marabout and his followers at Tubabecolong where they occupied a stockade.

Private Samuel Hodge – Victoria Cross No. 328

Colonel D'Arcy, assembled an assault force of 270 officers and men from the 4th West Indian Regiment, who were part of the garrison at Bathurst and set sail up the Gambia river bound for Albreda, where they landed on 26th July 1866 and were subsequently joined by a force of 500 warriors from the Soninke tribe.

On the 30th June, with his force now numbering almost 900 men, Colonel D'Arcy decided to mount his attack on the town of Tubabecolong. After coming within range of the enemy stockade, the assault force began a bombardment of the stockade but the light guns and rockets accompanying the West Indian regiment were unable to break down the stout wooden walls.

Seeing that his artillery was ineffective, Colonel D'Arcy called for volunteers to assist him in effecting a manual breach of the walls. Two officers and fifteen men, including Private Hodge, stepped forward and after grabbing axes followed Colonel D'Arcy towards the stockade. The fire from the defenders was so intense that the two officers, Lieutenant Jenkins and Ensign Kelly, were killed almost immediately and 13 of the 15 men were wounded.

Colonel D'Arcy and Privates Boswell and Hodge, managed to reach the stockade and hacked a gap in the wall, large enough for a man to gain entry; at this point Private Boswell was shot dead, however, Colonel D'Arcy and Private Hodge managed to enter the stockade and Private Hodge was able to cut the fastenings to a gate in the wall before he was shot down.

Despite being severely wounded, Private Hodge helped Colonel D'Arcy keep the enemy at bay by handing him the rifles of fallen comrades; this allowed the remainder of the force to enter the stockade via the gate opened up by Private Hodge; Colonel D'Arcy continued to lead his men in the fierce hand to hand fighting that now followed until the Marabout followers were defeated.

For his action in the battle, Private Hodge was later awarded the Victoria Cross, on the recommendation of Colonel D'Arcy.

At the end of the battle the village of Tubabecolong and the stockade were burnt to the ground. It is believed that several hundred of the Marabout followers were killed; the British casualties were two officers and four men killed and about 60 wounded.

14

ANDAMAN ISLANDS EXPEDITION (1867)

Background

The Andaman and Nicobar islands are a group of over 200 islands scattered over a large area in the eastern part of the Bay of Bengal. Due to their location, the islands often provided a haven for ships escaping the storms of the region or a refuge for shipwrecked sailors.

Initially, foreigners landing on the islands were well treated by the natives, however, after hostile treatment by Arab slavers, European Merchantmen and finally by British Administrators, the situation radically changed to the point where foreigners were killed on sight and the islanders soon got a reputation for being cannibals.

Apart from some isolated ship wrecks, the islands were largely ignored by the British until 1789 when Captain Archibald Blair established a Penal colony at Port Blair on Chatham Island. Two years later Admiral Sir William Cornwallis transferred the penal colony to Great Andaman, where he also established a naval arsenal. In 1796, when it proved to be too costly it terms of both cash and lives; due to a variety of tropical diseases the majority of the guards and inmates died, within a matter of months; the colony was abandoned.

With a huge number of Indian soldiers being held prisoner, as a result of the Indian Mutiny, the British established another Penal colony near the first colony at Port Blair in 1857; until the nearby swamps were drained, deportation to this colony was seen as a death sentence.

In order to deal with the war like Jarawa tribe, who generally tried to kill all foreigners on sight, the British armed the Arioto coastal tribe who abused this new power by the slaughter of every Jarawa that they could find. Quite naturally, this just inflamed the Jarawa attitude to foreigners.

Assam Valley Incident

On 21st March 1867, the *Assam Valley* was sailing past the Andaman Islands when its Captain W. H. Manley decided to put

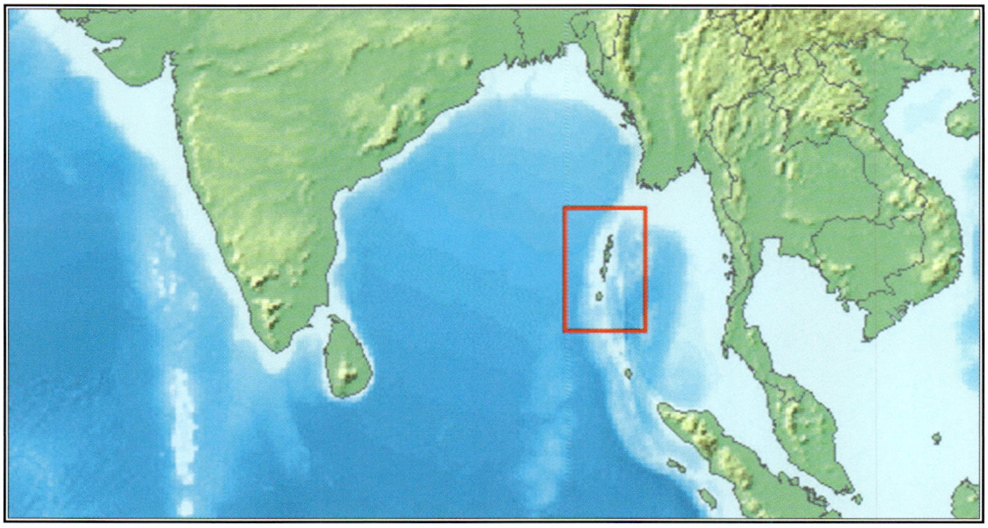

Figure 43. Andaman Islands

into the southern end of Lesser Andaman to obtain wood so that a damaged main topsail yard could be replaced. Captain Manley together with his 2nd Officer Edward Madden, the ship's carpenter and five of his crew boarded a ship's boat, together with their tools and set out for the shore.

The crew who remained on board, saw their Captain land and beach his boat before heading up the beach into the nearby jungle. About an hour later, Chief Officer George Bruford, who was on the poop deck with his telescope, spotted a number of natives milling about the beached boat, which they soon dragged away. Chief Officer Bruford waited in vain for two days for his Captain and crew to return, and as the shore party had taken all of the muskets and small arms he thought it unwise to send another party ashore so reluctantly set sail for his destination at Akyab where he arrived on 5th April.

Despite the delay it was still felt important to continue the search for the *Assam Valley*'s missing Captain and crew members, so a telegraph was immediately despatched to the Superintendant, Major B. Ford, at Port Blair ordering him to institute a search. On 16th April the steam surveying ship *HMS Sylvia*, was despatched from Port Blair to the Lesser Andaman in the hope of finding clues to the whereabouts of the crew. *HMS Sylvia* arrived off Little Andaman on 18th April, but due to a heavy swell could not put a party ashore, however, they did spot a sailor's cap and some rope on the beach.

Arracan Expedition

Due to having been unable to put a party ashore, the voyage by *HM Sylvia* was deemed to be insufficient and it was agreed that a further expedition was warranted. On 6th May the steamer *Arracan* set sail from Port Blair; on board the ship was a party of troops from the 2nd Battalion of the 24th Regiment of Foot, under the command of Lieutenant W. I. Much, together with Assistant Surgeon Campbell Mellis Douglas, seven men from the Naval Brigade and eight Indian Sappers.

Assistant Surgeon Campbell Douglas – Victoria Cross No. 329
Private David Bell – Victoria Cross No. 330
Private James Cooper – Victoria Cross No. 331
Private William Griffiths – Victoria Cross No. 332
Private Thomas Murphy – Victoria Cross No. 333

The *Arracan* arrived off the Lesser Andaman at dawn on 7th May and although the surf was very heavy two cutters were launched with Lieutenant Much commanding a party of men from the 24th accompanied by seven men from the Naval Brigade and five of the Indian Sappers, all distributed evenly between the two boats. The boat with Lieutenant Much on board, managed to break through the surf and after wading through five feet of water, the party of 17 managed to reach the beach.

The other boat stayed just off shore, moving parallel with the shore party's advance, in order to provide covering fire if necessary.

The shore party moved towards a large rock on the beach, which was believed to be the site of the massacre of the *Assam Valley* crew members, where they found a skull and a sailor's boot. Natives now appeared out of the jungle and began to let fly with their bows and arrows. The shore party managed to keep the natives at bay with fire from their muskets, however, after a time they began to run out of ammunition and Lieutenant Much issued the recall order. As they were making their way back to the original landing site, they discovered four partly buried bodies.

Since their landing, the ferocity of the surf had increased and when they attempted to depart, their boat floundered and sank in the surf but the party all managed to get back to the beach. Seeing the plight of the shore party rafts were launched from the *Arracan* and Assistant Surgeon Douglas, together with Privates Bell, Cooper, Griffiths and Murphy volunteered to man a gig to go to their rescue.

Lieutenant Much and some of the shore party managed to reach a raft, which had been loaded with replacement ammunition, but they were all swept off by the large waves. Without hesitation, Assistant Surgeon Douglas, who was a strong swimmer, dove into the water from the nearby gig and managed to save Lieutenant Much and Chief Officer Dunn from drowning, placing them back on the raft which was driven onshore. Unfortunately, after having struck his head on a rock, he could not save Lieutenant Glassford who was swept away and drowned.

Regaining the gig, Assistant Surgeon Douglas, with his gallant crew now tried to get through the surf to save the men on the beach; their first effort failed when the gig was swamped by a large wave that half filled the boat. The second attempt was more successful and Lieutenant Much and five of his men were plucked to safety and transferred to boats standing off outside the surf line. A third and final attempt managed to retrieve all of the remaining men and all were safely returned to the *Arracan*.

For saving the lives of the 17 men, Assistant Surgeon Douglas and Privates Bell, Cooper, Griffiths and Murphy were all later awarded the Victoria Cross.

With all of the shore party, except Lieutenant Glassford, having been recovered and the fate of the crew from the *Assam Valley* having been determined, the mission was ended and the *Arracan* returned to Port Blair.

15

ABYSSINIAN EXPEDITION (1867–68)

Background

For some time Abyssinia had been operating as a decentralized collection of regional states, governed by a number of Princes, who fought amongst themselves and periodically would appoint a titular Emperor to try and gain overall control of the country, however, they always failed to do so.

This was soon to change when Kassa Haile Giorgis, who was born during this "Era of the Princes" rose to power, with ambitions to re-establish a cohesive Abyssinian state. After managing to take control of the Dembiya region, Kassa came to the notice of Ras Ali II the warlord who controlled the capital of Gondar and had installed Yohannes III as emperor. To help maintain the current Emperor, and her son Ras Ali in power, the Empress arranged for Kassa to marry her granddaughter Tewabech Ali in 1848.

By 1852, Kassa had rebelled against Ras Ali and the Emperor; and over the next three years he defeated every army sent against him. After Kassa captured the Empress, Ras Ali fled and Kassa now turned his attentions towards Dejazmach Wube his sole remaining opponent, following his defeat he was crowned Emperor on 11th February 1855. On attaining the throne, Kassa took the title of Emperor Tewodros II (Theodore), based on a prophecy that a man named Tewodros would restore the Empire and rule for 40 years.

Initially Theodore's rule was well received, as he; stopped the cruel and barbaric customs of his predecessor, established the rule of law across the empire and abolished slavery. However, at around the time of his wife's death on 19th August 1858, he seemed to effect a personality change and succumbed to megalomania and paranoia which caused many of his subjects to rebel.

As a Coptic Christian, Theodore was proud of the fact that he was the only Christian leader in Africa, however, despite his former liberalism he now tried to unify the Empire under the Coptic faith and began this quest by ejecting the Roman Catholic missionaries. He also waged a war against the Galla people who were mainly Muslims, in an attempt to eradicate Islam from his realm. After several battles Theodore managed to capture

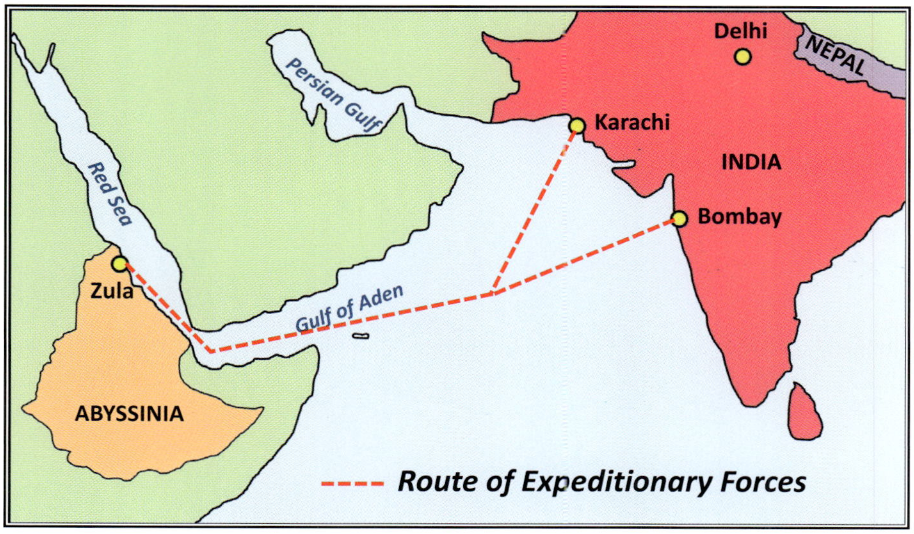

Figure 44. Abyssinia

the Galla capital at Magdala where he established a formidable fortress.

On 13th March 1860, while on a journey from Gondar to Massowah, the British Consul Mr Walter Plowden, a personal friend of the Emperor, was murdered by followers of the rebel leader Agew Niguse. Mr Plowden was buried in the Royal Enclosure at Gondar and the Emperor carried out devastating raids against Agew Niguse and other rebel leaders in retribution for the death of his friend. For his kindness to her Consul, Queen Victoria sent several presents to the Emperor, including a revolver inscribed (on a silver plate on the stock) with the inscription *"Presented to Theodore, Emperor of Abyssinia, by Victoria, Queen of Great Britain and Ireland, for his kindness to her servant Plowden, 1861"*. The presents were delivered to the Emperor by Captain Charles Cameron, who was to replace Mr Plowden as the British Consul, when he arrived at Gondar on 9th February 1862.

Emperor Theodore's letter to Queen Victoria

Having to wage almost constant war against the Empire's Muslims and other recalcitrant rebel forces while still wishing to make war with his tradition enemy, Egypt, Theodore was looking for help and expertise from the major European nations. In order to elicit this help, Theodore wrote letters to France, Russia and Austria which were mainly ignored. Following the urging of Consul Cameron to agree a treaty with Great Britain and to send an embassy to the Queen of England, Emperor Theodore also wrote a letter to Queen Victoria.

On his way to Massowah, Consul Cameron was held captive by a rebel leader for a short time, however, he managed to send the Emperor's letter onward via a native courier. The letter arrived in London in February 1863, and after having been read by the Foreign Minister, Earl Russell, was placed in a pending docket where it was ignored.

Theodore takes British prisoners

After his release by the rebels Captain Cameron spent time in Egypt on matters concerned with stopping the slave trade and afterwards spent time in the Sudan to investigate a new source for cotton, as the current supply to Britain was being disrupted by the American Civil war.

On his return to Abyssinia Captain Cameron had a meeting with Emperor Theodore, who was infuriated when he was told that he did not have a reply to the letter sent to Queen Victoria a year earlier, he was even more incensed when he learnt that

Figure 45. The Prisoners

the Captain had spent time in Egypt, the land of his enemy, and accused Britain of conspiring against him. Cameron was advised by the Emperor that he would be held in custody until a reply to his letter was received and in July 1863 he began a period of imprisonment, along with his companion Pietro.

Eventually, after three months of imprisonment, Captain Cameron received a letter from Lord Russell, however, this made no reference to the letter from the Emperor to Queen Victoria or his request for assistance. Maddened by what he viewed as a personal slight, the Emperor ordered Captain Cameron's servant to be beaten, he also ordered two of missionary Stern's servants to be beaten, this was so severe that they both died on the following day. Horrified at the sight of this cruel beating, missionary Stern raised his hand to his mouth, to stifle a cry; this action was interpreted by the Emperor as a threat against his person and under his orders the reverend Stern received a beating and joined Captain Cameron in his imprisonment. He was subsequently joined by his assistant Reverend Rosenthal and the reverend's wife and child. All of the captives were held in chains and were beaten on a regular basis.

Despite his imprisonment, Captain Cameron managed to get letters sent out from his prison; one letter that recounted his captivity and suffering at some length ended with the message *"There is no hope of my release unless a letter is sent as an answer to his Majesty's"* found its way on to the pages of the Times in London and the government were lambasted for their incompetent handling of the affair. The Foreign Minister immediately advised Queen Victoria to write to the Emperor, which she did. An Armenian, Mr Hormuzd J. Rassam, who had previously worked as secretary to Mr Layard MP and was currently working for Colonel Merewether, the political resident at Aden, offered his services to carry the letter to Emperor Theodore. This offer was gratefully accepted and Mr Rassam, with the title of Envoy Extraordinary, accompanied by Lieutenant Prideaux and Surgeon Blane set out for Abyssinia.

However, after reaching Massowah and following negative comments about Mr Rassam, during discussions in Parliament, Lord Russell felt compelled to recall Mr Rassam and dispatch Mr Palgrave instead, to effect the release of the prisoners. On receiving his recall Mr Rassam immediately set out for Suez where he sent a telegraph to the Consul General at Alexandria that Captain Cameron had been released. With this news, Mr Palgrave's mission was abandoned, however, he met up with Mr Rassam at Cairo and handed over presents which were to be delivered to the Emperor.

Mr Rassam once again set out for Abyssinia, and on 28th January 1866 arrived at Debra Tabor where he handed over the letter and presents to Theodore. Unfortunately, Theodore was not happy with the letter from Queen Victoria, considering it not to be sufficiently respectful and instead of releasing the prisoners Mr Rassam, Dr Blane and Lieutenant Prideaux were added to those already incarcerated.

War is declared

In the British general election of 1866, the Abyssinia dispute became an issue of some import and the Tory Party under Lord Derby and Benjamin Disraeli committed themselves to a rescue mission should they be elected. The Tory party won the election and after one more letter to Emperor Theodore, which was ignored, decided that all diplomatic avenues were closed so declared war on Abyssinia.

Having chosen to adopt military action, the British government decided that the required expeditionary force would be supplied from the British forces in India and appointed General Sir Robert Napier, the Commander-in-Chief of the Bombay army to command the expedition. After his appointment Queen Victoria sent a message to the General, via the new international telegraph system, that was simple yet explicit "Break the chains".

General Napier, a veteran of the Indian Mutiny and the war in China, was not enthusiastic about his mission, however, he saw the necessity of not being seen to yield to threats or force and in his own words stated that *"The expedition would be very expensive and troublesome ... Still, if these poor people are murdered, or detained, I suppose we must do something"*. During his time on the North West Frontier of India, General Napier adopted the motto of *"Never give way to barbarians"* for his troops, for his time in Abyssinia he adopted the Latinised form of Queen Victoria's message as his motto, *"Tu Fincula Frange"* – Break the Chains.

Military preparations

Having to prepare for a war over a terrain that was largely an unknown against an enemy whose strength and capabilities were also unknown was an incredible challenge; Bombay was soon chosen as the base for operations, it was intended that most of the troops would come from the Bombay Army. Colonel Phayre was assigned the task of determining where the expeditionary force should make land in Abyssinia and after some investigations it was decided that Massowah on the Red Sea would be the ideal landing site.

Initially, General Napier estimated that he would need about 12,000 troops and 3,000 native labourers. The men to be deployed would require arms and ammunition, the cavalry would need horses and the Artillery would need their guns. Food and other supplies to look after the needs of the men and the animals (i.e. medical treatment and accommodation) would also be required. A large fleet of ships would also be required to transport this vast amount of men and material from India to Abyssinia and a large number of mules, camels and oxen would be needed for the transport of goods within Abyssinia. From this short summary it is obvious that the logistics for the expedition would be complex and time consuming.

In addition to the usual war materials the following specialist equipment was prepared for use by the expedition: a telegraph system, suitable for use in the field was constructed; materials for the construction of a temporary harbour, with its own lighthouses; a mobile railway system; condensers capable of producing 120 gallons/hour of drinking water from sea water; the Enfield factory produced large numbers of the new Snider-Enfield breech loading rifles and mountain guns suitable for mule gun carriages were prepared by the Royal Gun Factories.

Figure 46. Route to Magdala

In addition to the above specialist equipment and the usual supplies and munitions, the expedition would eventually comprise: about 13,000 British and Indian soldiers which included five squadrons of cavalry, ten regiments of infantry, four batteries of field and horse artillery and 26,000 logistical support staff. On top of the horses used by the cavalry, the expeditionary force would march with 7,000 camels, 13,000 mules and donkeys, 7,000 bullocks and 44 Indian elephants.

A total of 280 ships would eventually be used to transport men and material to and from the theatre of war, 205 sailing ships and 75 steamers.

In addition to the merchant marine and land forces, the Royal Navy would also play an important role in the expedition: a squadron comprising *HMS Octavia*, *HMS Satellite*, *HMS Spiteful*, *HMS Star*, *HMS Dryad*, *HMS Nymphe*, *HMS Daphne* and *HMS Vigilant*, all under the command of Commodore L. G. Heath would operate from Annesley Bay; Officers and men from the ships would also form a Naval Brigade with a rocket battery and two artillery batteries, which would serve onshore with the Army.

In total, 62,000 people would be directly involved in the expedition together with 55,000 animals.

Military Operations

On 16th September 1867, an advanced party set sail from Bombay with the objective of finding a landing place on the shores of the Red Sea, owing to bad weather the party did not reach Massowah until 1st October. After deciding that the harbour at Massowah was unsuitable, the party landed at Malkatto in Annesley Bay and finally, on 4th October, Zula was selected as the disembarkation point for the expeditionary forces by Colonel W. L. Merewether.

A few weeks later on 7th October an advanced Brigade, comprising the HQ wing of the 3rd Light Cavalry, 10th Bombay Native Infantry and two companies of Native Sappers and Miners, set out from Bombay, with over six months of supplies, and arrived at Zula on 21st October to form the garrison. With the brigade were two influential war correspondent, one from the *Times* and one from the *Daily News*. The esteemed journalist Henry Morton Stanley,[16] representing the *New York Herald*, would arrive later with the main expeditionary force.

On 11th November 1867, the formal General Order was published directing the despatch of a force under the command of General Sir Robert Napier to Abyssinia.

16 Of "Dr. Livingstone I presume" fame.

Having established a bridgehead at Zula, work began on preparations for the landing of the main force and the supply vessels. Although well sheltered, the water in Annesley Bay was quite shallow and it was necessary to build two long jetties from the shore out into the deeper waters where the ships could approach. Work also started on the construction of the portable railway which was to be used to transport men and material to a point about 7 miles inland from Zula.

Soon after the advanced brigade landed, several transports arrived and discharged several thousand camels, mules and bullocks, however, having been landed without any handlers to manage them, the animals were allowed to roam free in search of pasture. Many of these animals wandered off into the bush and died from thirst or were stolen by the local population before the military command made arrangements to contain, water and feed them. The situation was greatly improved when the Sind Brigade, which had sailed from Karachi, was landed at Zula on 4th December as they arrived with steamers full of water. Soon afterwards the installation of the condensers was completed and desalinated water was now also piped into the camp.

Soon after the initial British landing, Emperor Theodore received the news that an invasion force was on the way and decided to move the hostages and his forces from the capital at Gondar to the substantial fortress at Magdala, believing this fortress to be impregnable, the Emperor did little to prevent the advance of the British forces.

On 4th November, now armed with the knowledge that the Emperor and the hostages were located at Magdala, the advanced brigade began the reconnaissance of a route to the fortress which was over 400 miles away, beginning with the route to Senafé which was about 63 miles away. The party managed to find a relatively easy route through the coastal ravines via the Komayli Pass, to Senafé which was on the coastal highlands and found the place to have an abundance of pasture and water. On their return to Zula, the party advised a move to Senafé as it was a much more hospitable place and by the 5th December the advanced Brigade had completed this move.

During the last week of December a further reconnaissance was made from Senafé to Adigrat, a distance of only 37 miles, however, due to the broken country it took three days to complete the march.

On 2nd January 1868, General Napier arrived at Annesley Bay on board *HMS Octavia*, however, due to illness did not land at Zula until 7th January. After a brief review of the situation, the General determined that the first priority was to establish a main expedition store at Senafé and instructed that the roadway, which had been constructed for transport by pack animals, be improved to allow for wheeled transport. He also sent orders that his main group of troopships, now at Aden having left Bombay on 21st December, should proceed to Zula post haste.

Prior to his arrival, General Napier had sent instructions that the advanced party should distribute a proclamation to the Abyssinian tribal leaders and the population at large. This outlined the reasons for the arrival of British forces, namely to rescue the hostages taken by Emperor Theodore, and that they had no intention of occupying any lands. It further stated that no person or property in Abyssinia would be harmed by the British force unless they tried to obstruct the British in their mission.

Having established a stores depot at Senafé, General Napier moved on to Adigrat, which he reached on 6th February and ordered a permanent entrenched post to be established as part of the defences required to protect his supply lines.

It was while at Adigrat, that the General received evidence of the success of his proclamation when the Abyssinian Prince Kassai entered the camp and stated that he would provide protection to the British route through his territory. With this auspicious start to his dealings with the Abyssinian leaders, the General proceeded to make treaties with each of the tribal leaders as he passed through their territory on his way to Magdala.

As the British Expeditionary force advanced towards Magdala, the Pioneers did everything they could to make a passable roadway but were hampered by frequent periods of heavy rain and the heavy equipment often had to be moved by block and tackle or elephants.

By the 2nd March, the column had reached Antalo where they established a major stores depot and rested for ten days before continuing on their journey south. As the advance continued, the column was steadily reducing in numbers as units were being left behind to guard depots and protect the supply line which stretched right back to the coast.

On the 24th March, the British force entered Didli from where they could see the fortress of Magdala on the far horizon which was only 25 miles distant, as the crow flies, however, because of the intervening mountains, a tortuous route of 60 miles through very inhospitable mountain country would be required to reach the fortress. Due to the deep ravines and precipices that would have to be negotiated the expedition could now only proceed at a very slow pace.

By the 4th April, the expeditionary forces were gathered on the Talanta plateau, from where the Abyssinian camp at Islamgie was visible.

On 5th April, General Napier sent a final message to Emperor Theodore by native messenger, demanding the immediate and unconditional surrender of the prisoners *"By command of the Queen of England I am approaching Magdala with my army, in order to recover from your hands Envoy Rassam, Consul Cameron,*

Dr. Blane, Lieutenant Prideaux, and the other Europeans now in your Majesty's power. I request your Majesty to send them to my camp as soon as it is sufficiently near to admit of their coming in safety." Although it was later confirmed that the message was delivered to the Emperor, General Napier received no reply.

By 9th April, the main British force had advanced to the brink of the Bashilo river valley, where they camped within sight of Theodore's army, who were camped on the other side of the river.

Battle of Arogi

On the 10th April, Good Friday, the second brigade advanced down the Arogi Ravine to the bed of the Bashilo river in preparation for an advance into Magdala along a road that had been constructed by the Emperor when he had moved to occupy the fortress. Soon after completing this move Abyssinian artillery fired on the British column and a force of about 6,000 Abyssinian troops descended the hills in a mass attack. The Naval Brigade opened up with their rocket battery and partially checked the enemy movement, however, some of the Abyssinian force continued to advance against the British column on the plateau while another force headed for the artillery and baggage, stationed at the head of the pass.

The 4th (Kings Own) regiment supported by a wing of the Baluchi regiment, a detachment of Royal Engineers and the Bombay Sappers advanced onto the Arogi plain where they opened fire and slowly drove the Abyssinian troops from the plain. The Abyssinians had some minor success against the British right flank on Fahla Hill when they emerged from a cactus grove, however, when they attempted to turn the flank they were soon repulsed. A sharp action was also fought at the point where the road to Magdala emerged from the Arogi valley.

When the "A" Battery of artillery managed to reach the plain from the valley floor, Emperor Theodore and some of his men charged down the hill but were met by a devastating fire from the battery. As this force continued to advance, they were met by a British force of Pioneers and a hand to hand contest between spear and bayonet ensued. The Abyssinians were driven off having suffered many casualties, however, they inflicted many spear wounds themselves.

On the left, where the Abyssinians were attacking the baggage train at the head of the defile, the enemy were held off by two companies of the Kings Own Regiment and with other British troops closing in the British Snider rifles inflicted severe casualties.

The battle which had started at 4 o'clock in the afternoon was over three hours later when, Emperor Theodore managed to withdraw his troops in good order back into the fortress at Magdala. At the end of the battle, which had been fought in almost constant heavy rain, the British troops set up camp at the foot of the Arogi Valley. British losses amounted to only 2 dead and 18 wounded, however, the Abyssinian losses were estimated at 700 killed and 1,200 wounded.

Battle of Magdala

By dawn on 11th April, the British forces were formed up ready to begin the final assault on the Magdala fortress, when a small party was seen to be advancing under a flag of truce. The party were bringing a proposal from the Emperor for negotiations with General Napier to end the conflict. The party was sent back to the Emperor with the message that the British terms had not changed, they required the unconditional surrender of the Emperor and his troops and the return of the hostages, however, a 24 hour period of truce was granted, in order for the Emperor to submit to these terms.

An uncomplimentary reply was sent by Theodore to General Napier, in which he refused to surrender himself or his troops, however, by sunset the eight European captives were set free and reached the British camp. On the following day, Theodore sent another message to General Napier, in which he apologised for the intemperate tone of his previous letter, this seemed to be the reason for extending the period of truce for a further 24 hours.

On 13th April, Easter Sunday, Theodore resolved to attempt an escape from Magdala, however, when many of his troops refused to accompany him and instead surrendered to the British, he abandoned this plan and returned to the fortress determined to make a last stand.

Private James Bergin – Victoria Cross No. 334
Private Michael Magner – Victoria Cross No. 335

With the period of truce now having expired, without the unconditional surrender of the Emperor, General Napier was now determined to take Magdala by force and launched his attack.

The assault was preceded by a bombardment from mortars, rocket batteries and artillery. The infantry then began to lay down covering fire for a party of Royal Engineers who were sent to blow up the gates to the fortress. The path to the gates led up a steep boulder strewn track which on one side was a perpendicular cliff face and on the other side a sheer drop. This perilous route led to the main gateway, known as the Koket-Bir, which was formed by thick wooden doors set into a 15 foot wide stone archway. Each side of the gateway was protected by a thorn and stake hedge. Further uphill along the path was a second fortified gate which gave entry to the final plateau with the fortress.

On reaching the gate, there was a pause in the advance as it was discovered that, incredibly the kegs of gun powder and the scaling ladders had been left behind by the Engineers and men had to be sent back to collect this essential material.

General Staveley, who was leading the advance, was not prepared to accept further delays so ordered the 33rd Regiment to continue with the attack.

Several officers and men from the 33rd, together with an officer from the Royal Engineers, separated themselves from the main force and managed to scale the cliff face. At the top the men were confronted by a wall and a thick thorny hedge, blocking their way. Private Bergin, who was a very tall man, used his bayonet to cut a hole in the hedge and then Drummer Magner climbed up on his shoulders and managed to crawl through the gap in the hedge. With Ensign Connor and Corporal Murphy pushing from below, Drummer Magner managed to haul Private Bergin through the gap.

While Private Bergin kept up a rapid fire on the defenders at the Koket-Bir, Drummer Magner managed to drag more men through the gap in the hedge. With sufficient men through the hedge, a charge with fixed bayonets was made against the Koket-Bir which was taken before it could be fully closed. The defenders now withdrew through the second gate which was also taken. With both gates now open, the main assault force had full entry to the fortress. Ensign Wynter, climbed up to the top of the second gate and raised the 33rd Regimental Colours, to show that access to the interior of the fortress was now secured.

For their part in this action Drummer Magner and Private Bergin were both awarded the Victoria Cross.

The main assault force now poured into the fort and just inside the second gate they found the body of Theodore, who had shot himself in the head with a pistol.[17] When the death of their Emperor became known, the Abyssinian forces quickly surrendered and the fortress now was firmly in British hands.

Having accomplished their mission to free the hostages, the fortress at Magdala was destroyed and on 19th April, General Napier and his troops began to retrace their steps and after leaving Abyssinia returned to their duties in India.

17 Although it has never been corroborated, it is generally believed that the pistol used was the one that he had received as a gift from Queen Victoria.

16

LUSHAI EXPEDITION, INDIA (1871–72)

Background

The Lushai Hills lie on the North East Frontier of British India and occupy an area about the size of Wales; to the north they are bordered by Manipur, to the east by the Chin Hills, to the west by the Chittagong Hills and to the south by the Arakan district of Burma. As the name suggests, the area consists of many hills which generally are in ranges that run north to south, the hills which are in size from 3,000 to 4,000 feet in height have steep slopes which are cut by many deep and treacherous ravines.

The area is populated by people of Mongolian origin and each village is ruled by a chief from one of the five royal Lushai families. The Lushai were generally a hostile people, prone to conducting raids against peoples all along their borders and they often resorted to fighting amongst themselves. In order to curb the activities of the Lushai raiding parties the British had carried out punitive expeditions in retribution for various outrages against British interests. Captain Blackwood carried out a successful expedition in 1844 and following another more extensive expedition in 1849, led by Major Lister, a period of relative peace was to exist for almost 12 years.

In January 1862, the peace was broken when three villages near Adampur were plundered and burnt to the ground. The Indian government, considered sending another expedition,

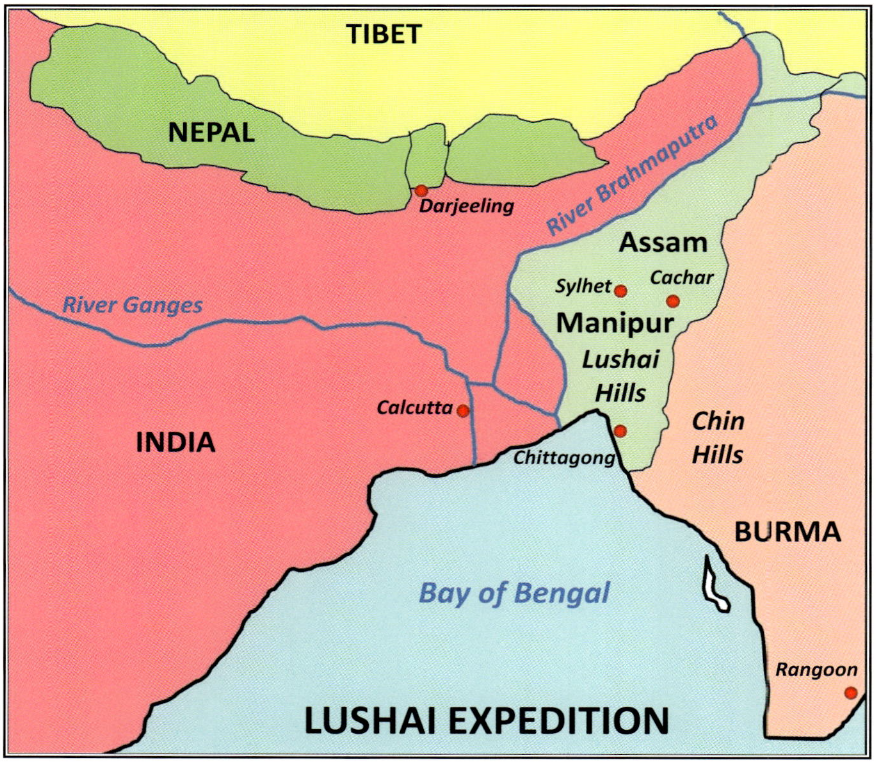

Figure 47. Map of Lushai

however, due to fear that this may cause the Lushai to attack the many tea plantations that had by now sprung up along their border a less aggressive approach was agreed. To resolve the situation, Captain Stewart, the Deputy Commissioner, began negotiations with Sukpial, one of the leading Lushai chiefs, regarding the return of captives. Unfortunately, these negotiations came to nothing and an expedition was approved, however, with the onset of the rainy season plans had to be abandoned, but eventually four captives were released. Captain Stewart was more successful with another Lushai chief, Vonpial, who for a small sum agreed to a treaty whereby he agreed to carry out no further raids.

Peace again reigned until the end of 1868, when some villages in Manipur and Hill Tippera were attacked, followed by raids against the tea plantations at Loharbund and Monier Khal in January 1869, thought to have been carried out by Sukpial and Vonpial. To avenge these attacks a large retaliatory expedition was mounted, however, as it was conducted outside of the normal campaign season, due to the bad weather this was a failure. The failure of this expedition, together with the talks of conciliation and concession which followed soon afterwards considerably diminished the British in the eyes of the Lushai, who now thought that the British were incapable of restraining their exploits.

In early 1871, various attacks were mounted by the Lushai against tea plantations in the Chittagong Hills, Hill Tippera and in Cachar. On 23rd January, Mr James Winchester, a local tea plantation manager, and his 6 year old daughter Mary were attending a party at the Alexandrapur plantation, which was owned by his friend George Seller. The party had been arranged as a farewell to Mary, who was returning to Britain to begin her formal education. The pair were strolling around the gardens when suddenly the plantation was attacked by Lushai warriors; Mr Winchester was killed and his six year old daughter Mary was carried off as a captive, as she was pulled from her dying fathers grasp Mary heard his last words *"Dear, only God knows your fate."*

Emboldened by these successful operations, the Lushai tribes carried out many more operations against tea plantations along their borders well into the month of March when the rainy season made further operations impracticable.

Military Operations

In July 1871, the Governor-General of India decided to send an expedition against the Lushai in retaliation for these latest attacks on the tea plantations, and to rescue the captured prisoners, including Mary Winchester. It was agreed that the force would consist of two columns; one starting from Cachar in the north, commanded by General G. Bourchier and the other starting from Chittagong in the south, commanded by General C. H. Brownlow. The Rajah of Manipur would also provide a contingent force to guard the southern borders.

By the instruction of the Governor-General, the expedition was not one of pure retaliation but British subjects held in captivity were to be released, permanent friendly relations were to be established with the tribes who were to be convinced that they had nothing to gain and everything to lose by adopting a hostile position towards the British government.

Cachar Column

The Cachar, or left, column was comprised of the following troops: 500 men from Punjab Native Infantry commanded by Colonel Stafford; 500 men from 42nd Assam Light Infantry under Colonel Rattray; 500 men from 44th Assam Light Infantry commanded by Colonel Hicks 100 police under Mr Daly. The infantry were supported by a half battery of the Peshawar Mountain Battery under Captain Blackwood and a company of Sappers and Miners under the command of Lieutenant Harvey. In addition to the military forces, the Commissariat Department provided a large contingent of porters and pack animals (including elephants) to carry the supplies and munitions.

Initially the main part of the column was assembled at the hill station at Silchar, however, Tipai Mukh, at the junction of the Tipai and Barak rivers, was to be the advanced base of operations and by 15th December 1871 the majority of the force was collected there.

The force then marched south through very difficult country, establishing camps at regular intervals. They were exposed to constant attacks, from an enemy that rarely showed themselves, by firing from the concealment of the jungle. By the 2nd of February 1872 the force had reached Sellam, the village and stronghold of chief Poiboi which after some stiff fighting was occupied. On 12th February a section of the column left Sellam to search for Chumpai, Lalboorah's chief village which they found on 17th February and occupied without opposition as it had been deserted. The tomb of Vonolel, the tribe's chief was found in the village and the village consisting of about 500 houses was burnt to the ground.

With the tribes of Vonpilal, Poiboi and Vonolel now having been subdued, the column proceeded to Chumsin, the village of Vonolel's widow where the General dictated the terms by which the remaining villages of Lalboorah could be saved from destruction: Free access for British forces to all Lalboorah's villages and transit through his lands; return of all hostages and arms that had been captured and a fine of two elephant tusks, a set of war gongs, a necklace, 10 goats, 10 pigs, 50 fowl and 24 maunds of rice; all to be delivered within 24 hours. The terms were agreed and with the exception of a small quantity of rice, the fine arrived the next morning.

Having completed his mission, General Bourchier and the column retraced their route and arrived back at Cachar on 10th March 1872.

Chittagong Column

The Chittagong or Right column, was commanded by General Charles Henry Brownlow and was comprised of: 500 men of the Punjab Native Infantry; 500 men of the 2nd Ghurkha regiment and 500 men of the 4th Ghurkha regiment. The infantry were supported by half of the Peshawar Mountain Battery and No.3 Company of the Sappers and Miners.

The column was initially assembled at Kassalong, with troops coming by steamer from Calcutta to Chittagong and then by river boat to the frontier; the 2nd Ghurkha regiment commanded by Colonel H. Macpherson VC were the first to arrive. An advanced camp was established at Demagree, near the village of a friendly Lushai Chief Rutton Poia, where a large stockade was built to house the Chittagong column as it assembled.

The objective of the column was to move against the Howlong tribe, who had been the main instigators of the attack on the Alexandrapur plantation and the abduction of Mary Winchester. Every effort was made to make peace with the tribal chiefs of the lands the column would have to pass through to reach the Howlong lands. Agreements were reached with chiefs Rutton Poia and Vanpoia, on the promise that they would be protected once the war was ended.

The main tribe now remaining between the British column and the Howlong was the Sylus, and it would be helpful to the cause to obtain a treaty with this tribe, however, it proved difficult to contact the leaders and engage them in a dialogue. Eventually, via a minor chief Lungura, who had been captured by a patrol, a message was sent to chief Vanlula. On 13th December, chief Lungura returned to the British camp with the message that five of the Sylus main chiefs, with their followers were assembled at the nearby village of chief Vanlula but that they would not treat with the British until they left their country. They also stated that if the column advanced any further, then they would attack. General Brownlow's response was to order an attack against chief Vanlula's village, to take place the next day.

Under the cover of an early morning mist, the 2nd Ghurkha regiment advanced in two parties; the right attack under Major MacIntyre was a distraction, while the main body led by Colonel Macpherson crested the hill and launched a charge, with fixed bayonets, into the heart of the village. Almost at once the Sylus broke ranks and fled and Vanlula set fire to the houses, scouts later determined that they had fled northwards. From possessions found in the burnt out buildings, it became apparent that the Sylus had been involved in the border raids against the tea plantations.

General Brownlow decided to use Vanlula's village as a depot for provisions and sent out patrols in all directions to scour the countryside for any hidden stores of grain or other foodstuff. Living off the countryside, would assist with the supply, as all supplies had to be transported to the columns from Calcutta via Chittagong.

The column continued their northward advance and on 21st December, Colonel Macpherson assaulted and captured the village of Lal Hlira and secured large quantities of grain. At the same time, Major MacIntyre burnt two villages, destroyed 56 granaries and captured some cattle.

On the 26th December the column moved forward and occupied the large village of chief Van Hnoya, without any opposition from the Sylus. Soon after entering the village, the nearby villages of Van Kunga and Van Hnuna were set on fire by their inhabitants before they fled ahead of the advancing British forces. By the end of December, the column had reached the great Towrang Tlang range, where the General hoped to observe or receive news regarding the progress of General Bourchier's column.

On 2nd January 1872, having reached the crest of the Towrang Tlang range, General Brownlow observed the village of Sylu Savung, about ten miles in the distance; this village was the largest of the Sylu villages and was the residence of Savunga, the head chief of the tribe. The strongly stockaded village of Lal Ngora, residence of Savunga's eldest son was also observed only eight miles away and far off on the horizon, the Howlong villages were now visible.

Major Donald MacIntyre – Victoria Cross No. 336

The General was determined to take the Lal Ngora village so on the next day, Captain Battye of the 2nd Ghurkha regiment, with two companies of his men, carried out a reconnaissance, reporting back that the village was occupied by a large force of men who seemed to be intent on a fight.

On the following day, the 4th January, the 2nd Ghurkha regiment, led by Major MacIntyre led the assault against the formidable stockade, which had walls about 8 to 9 feet in height. In the face of heavy fire from the defenders, Major MacIntyre was the first man to scale the walls and was soon followed by his men. Following fierce hand to hand fighting, the stockade was overrun and captured.

For his conduct during the assault, Major MacIntyre was later awarded the Victoria Cross.

Following the capture of the stockade, the village was burnt to the ground and a large quantity of grain was destroyed. British losses during the assault were slight, with one man killed and nine wounded (including Captain Battye who was slightly wounded).

That evening, after the attack, some Sylus tribesmen entered the camp for a parley and indicated that their chief Savunga wished to meet with the General with a peace offering of elephant tusks, the men were sent off with the message that chief Savunga could enter the British camp with complete safety, however, until he did so the advance would continue but if the tribe offered no resistance then their villages and crops would be spared.

The column rested during the next day, to see if Savunga would approach the camp for talks, however, when this did not happen, the advance to Savunga's village was continued on 6th January. On reaching a clearing on the approach to the village the British saw that it was filled with a large force of armed men, General Brownlow thought that this was an ideal opportunity to show the Lushai, the force of his artillery which had not been used so far in the campaign.

About 50 Ghurkhas were sent forward to form a skirmish line, while Colonel James Hills came up with his 7 pounder mountain guns. After initially firing some rounds over the heads of the Sylus, the battery began to direct their shot into the village with devastating effect and the tribesmen soon scattered into the jungle in all directions, abandoning the village. On the next day, the village was burnt to the ground, and once the flames had died down, was occupied by the British without further opposition on 11th January.

With all of the other Sylu villages having been destroyed by their inhabitants or occupied and destroyed by the British forces only the village of Lal Jika, residence of Savunga's youngest son, remained standing, it was therefore concluded that the Sylu people had been subdued and the force could now turn its attention to the Howlong villages.

Mindful of the Governor General's instructions to minimise the destruction to villages and crops, General Brownlow instructed his political officer, Colonel Lewin to try and negotiate a peaceful resolution with the Howlong tribe. On 13th January, with an escort of 50 Ghurkhas, Colonel Lewin approached the nearest Howlong village, which by now was within sight of the main column but as the party approached, the inhabitants set fire to their village and retired off to the north.

Having returned to Sylu Savung, Colonel Lewin reported the unmistakable declaration of hostility and the failure of his mission to treat with the Howlong. He proposed that the only way to peacefully approach Benkuia and Sangbunga, the two brothers who ruled the Howlong tribe was by an approach from their rear, which as it required a large detour would involve a long delay.

Reluctantly, General Brownlow agreed to this suggestion and chief Rutton Poia, who had accompanied the column, was sent off on this roundabout journey, as the head of a small deputation with the message that unless the Howlong unconditionally released all of their captives and gave the British free access to their territory, then they would be attacked. For the duration of the peace mission, General Brownlow and his troops took a well earned rest at Sylu Savung while they awaited the outcome of the mission.

On 21st January, General Brownlow decided to attack the only remaining Sylu village of Lal Jika, as no message of submission had been received, Colonel Hill's artillery were once again deployed and after the inhabitants fled, the village was occupied without lose.

After returning to the camp at Sylu Savung, news was received from Rutton Poia, that he had managed to effect the release of Mary Winchester and had delivered the child, who was unharmed, into the care of Colonel Tytler, in command of the 4th Ghurkhas at Demagree, and that she had been sent to Calcutta via Chittagong. Chief Rutton Poia also reported that he was continuing on his peace mission to the northern Howlong villages and requested that the British column abstain from hostilities while he completed his journey. Reluctantly the General agreed to wait a further week before continuing the northward advance.

At the end of the waiting period, on 12th February, General Brownlow decided to advance on the Howlong villages with a reduced force comprising; 300 men from the Ghurkha regiment supported by two mountain guns and half a company of Sappers. After reaching the border of the Howlong territory, the force set up camp for the night. In the morning a small party reconnoitring the route forward came across a village that had been burnt by the inhabitants on noticing the advance of the British force on the previous day. On the space that had previously been occupied by the village, stood a large body of Lushai who professed a desire for peace and that their chiefs were willing to release their prisoners The men were advised that they should get their chief to bring the captives to the British camp and settle the matter.

The exchange was reported to General Brownlow, who was pleased with the possible turn of events, however, the column still marched on to the village of Chongmama, which was about two days march from the villages of the Howlong tribal leaders, Benkuia and Sangbunga. In the jungles around Chongmama were many new houses that had been erected by the Sylus people, who had been burnt out of their own villages. The General ordered that these houses should be left untouched as he considered that the tribe had already suffered enough punishment.

On the following day, 15th February, one of two reconnaissance patrols discovered a body of armed men guarding a ford across a stream and the road to Benkuia's village. After reporting this to General Brownlow, Colonel Lewin was sent down to parley with the men, who were advised to get their chiefs to come to the British camp, where their safety was guaranteed.

In the evening, while asleep in his tent, Colonel Lewin was woken by a Lushai messenger who had crept into the camp unseen, the Colonel was asked to come down to the stream in the early morning to meet with the chiefs, however, he must come alone. As the Colonel knew that General Brownlow would probably not permit him to undertake such a dangerous mission, Lewin kept the matter to himself and in the early morning before the camp had risen he did as the messenger had asked.

At the Tuldung stream, Colonel Lewin was met by an escort of about ten Lushai warriors, and was taken to a small forest glade a short distance from the stream where the Howlong chiefs were waiting, along with a large force of their men. The two main chiefs, the brothers Sangbunga and Benkuia both came forwards and handed the Colonel a gun and a sword, the Colonel handed over a sword and dagger and after this ritual exchange of gifts discussions took place. The chiefs indicated that they desired peace and Colonel Lewin reiterated the terms that would make this possible: the return of all British prisoners; the granting of free and friendly access for the British to their villages now and in the future and finally to make a solemn oath that they would abstain from making future raids upon British territory. If they agreed to these terms then the British force would be withdrawn.

The chiefs indicated that they understood these terms, and after some deliberation they would provide their answer on the next day.

After returning to the British camp Colonel Lewin reported the events to General Brownlow, who was greatly satisfied with the result and left the Colonel to conclude matters with the Lushai when they reported back in the morning.

On the 18th February 1872, Colonel Lewin swore the blood and steel oath with the Howlong chiefs who presented a peace offering of elephant tusks, home spun cloth and other items for the government. On the following day, the first instalment of captives was sent to the camp with the promise that the other, who were scattered in distant villages, would be gathered up and delivered as soon as possible.

Over the next few days, representative from the Sylus tribe, came into the camp and conclude similar agreements and surrendered their prisoners.

Having achieved their objectives, the Chittagong column began their return journey to leave the country, arriving back at Chittagong on 24th February 1872.

Conclusion

With both columns having achieved their objectives and over 100 British prisoners having been released, including Mary Winchester, the campaign was brought to a close on 28th February 1872.

The success of the campaign should also be judged by the fact that relative peace would exist on the North East Frontier for 16 years until fresh border raids in 1888, required another expedition to be mounted in 1889.

Mary Winchester, was well treated during her time as a hostage, however, after just six days short of a year in captivity had lost some of her ability to speak English. Following her release, Mary was sent to Calcutta from where she was sent to Scotland to live with her grandparents at Elgin in Moray. She graduated from the Royal Moray College and after getting married moved to London, with her husband, where she worked as a headmistress for many years before her death in 1955 at the age of 90.

17

THIRD ASHANTI WAR (1873–74)

Background

Since the mid 16th century, Britain together with other European nations had conducted trade with the tribes on the West Coast of Africa setting up small trading posts along the coast as needed. By the beginning of the 19th century, things began to change as the small trading stations had now grown to sizable settlements, and forts had been erected to protect them; this development led to thoughts of colonisation by some of the European powers.

During this period, the Ashanti tribe had secured the supply of gold, slaves and other regional products required by the European traders. They also controlled the distribution of the European imports that they received in exchange for these goods. However, the Fanti tribe controlled the coastal region and enjoyed the lucrative position as middlemen between the European traders and the Ashanti tribesmen.

With this loss of revenue to the Fanti it was obvious that the Ashanti would try and eliminate the middlemen by securing the coastal areas and following a brief but decisive conflict in May 1806 they defeated the Fanti and achieved this objective and the Fanti lands were formally incorporated into the Ashanti Empire. Further minor campaigns were also fought in 1811 and 1814.

Soon after this political realignment of the region had started, the economic situation suffered a dramatic blow when in 1807, the British Government abolished the slave trade which accounted for about 90% of the wealth of the region. Despite the efforts of the "Company of Merchants Trading in Africa" lobbying for a postponement of the Abolition Act the Government stated that the act would be enforced with immediate effect.

In 1821, the "Company of Merchants Trading in Africa" was dissolved by an act of parliament and management of the forts on the "Gold Coast" was taken over by the government, controlled by the Governor-in-Chief at Sierra Leone. In 1823 trouble over control of the coastal regions once again came to the fore, resulting in the First Anglo-Ashanti War which only lasted for three years but took a further five years to be formally concluded with the signing of the Tripartite Treaty in 1831. This treaty gave the Ashanti free and open access to the coast so long as they were engaged on lawful activities. A minor campaign also took place in 1853 and although it was quickly resolved it resulted in the Ashanti deciding to trade only with the Dutch.

In 1850, the British purchased the forts and settlements managed by the Danish government and established a protectorate covering their possessions on the Gold Coast. In 1863, the Ashanti again carried out operations against the coastal states, now under British protection, to secure their passage to the sea routes. This conflict was resolved in 1864 but to the satisfaction of neither side and with trade now at an all time low, the British seriously considered abandoning the Gold Coast.

Following several Parliamentary investigations and enquiries into the administration of British possessions in West Africa, in 1867 it was finally decided to formally institute the British Gold Coast Colony and their territories were expanded in April 1872 when they purchased the Dutch possessions on the Gold Coast, ending a Dutch rule that had lasted for 274 years.

One of the Dutch possessions transferred to Britain was Fort Elmina, which under the treaty of Butre, between the Dutch and Ashanti people, signed in 1656, had been ceded to the Ashanti; and since this date the Dutch and Elmina people had been paying an annual tribute to the Ashanti for use of the land. With the transfer of Fort Elmina to Britain these arrangements were deemed by the British to be null and void, much to the anger of the Ashanti as this was their sole remaining access to the coast.

In January 1873, the Ashanti army crossed the River Pra and invaded the British 'Protectorate', however, believing that the coastal tribes were capable of handling the situation, it was some months before the seriousness of the situation was recognised, by the British, and they finally committed to a full scale war with the Ashanti.

At this time, Colonel Harley, the Gold Coast Administrator, was conducting negotiations for the release of European missionaries who had been captured on 12th June 1869 (the German

Mr Khune, the Swiss Mr Ramseyer with his wife and three children including a 10 month old infant)[18] and was completely surprised by the Ashanti invasion.

Mr Hennessey, the Administrator-in-Chief of the Sierra Leone colony, preferred to treat the invasion as a minor, local tribal affair, as to do otherwise would call into question his diplomatic management of the Gold Coast; it was primarily his attitude that delayed the British Government from treating the incident as a major problem.

In the short term Colonel Harley attempted to deal with four pressing problems; Firstly to assure the chiefs of the coastal tribes of British Policy to support the 'Protectorate'; secondly to ensure the protection of the forts scattered along the coastline; thirdly to encourage the local tribes to help themselves by disrupting and delaying the advance of the Ashanti invasion and lastly to find a solution to the problems of the people of Elmina and other settlements that had been under Dutch control such that they would align themselves with the British rather than the Ashanti.

To help with these matters Colonel Harley requested arms, ammunition and men from Sierra Leone from Mr Hennessey; which were all in short supply on the Gold Coast. In a continuation of his assertion that this was a minor local affair, Mr Hennessey was reluctant to send arms or troops, however, this changed on 7th March 1873, when Robert William Keate replaced him as Governor.

Governor Keate immediately despatched the requested arms and ammunition but delayed the sending of troops until after he had personally visited the Gold Coast and assessed the situation.

Governor Keate died on 17th March 1873, just ten days after his arrival at Cape Coast Castle, however, after only a short time in the colony he issued two despatches which had a great influence on future events. His first despatch was to London, which stated that this was the most serious incursion into the 'Protectorate' and suggested that the British Government were obliged to render the necessary assistance to repel all attacks against the tribes within the 'Protectorate'. The second despatch authorised the movement of 100 men of the West Indian Regiment to the Gold Coast, where they arrived at Cape Coast Castle on 20th March 1873.

With the arrival of Governor Keate's despatch, London was finally convinced of the serious nature of the invasion, however, they were still reluctant to commit further troops, believing that if suitably armed the local tribes could handle the situation. Large quantities of arms and ammunition were duly despatched, the first consignments arriving at Cape Coast Castle on 7th April 1873.

18 The missionaries were subsequently released, after a payment of ransom, however, the infant child died after only a few weeks into the captivity.

Unfortunately the arrival of almost unlimited arms and ammunition did little to improve the situation due to the complete disunity of the Fanti tribes who were unable to present a unified opposition to the Ashanti. This was further exacerbated by the Elmina people who were able to unify the western coastal tribes in support of the Ashanti.

When news of the worsening situation on the Gold Coast reached London, following successive victories by the Ashanti army and the alliance with the western tribes; Lord Kimberley, secretary of State for the Colonies, agreed with the War Office that the situation warranted the despatch of additional reinforcements. A further warship was despatched to the area with men of the Royal Marine Light Infantry and Royal Marine Artillery and large supplies of ammunition, rockets and a portable field gun. Four companies of the West Indian Regiment were also to be transferred from the West Indies to the Gold Coast with immediate effect.

HMS Barracouta, commanded by Captain Fremantle, arrived off the Cape Coast on 8th June and after the men and materials were off loaded on the following day, they were helping to secure the coastal forts.

After conducting a reconnaissance of Elmina, Captain Fremantle ordered Colonel Festing to mount a surprise attack against the town and following a naval bombardment of Elmina an attack was launched against a force of 2,000 Ashanti on 12th June with considerable success.

Preparations for War

With the need for a full scale military operation against the Ashanti having been finally established, on 13th August 1873 the government appointed General Sir Garnet Wolseley to the overall command of the expedition. General Wolseley, accepted the command on two conditions; that he would not be required to remain as Civil Governor once military operations had been concluded and that he would be given an adequate supply of European troops to carry out the task.

It was also planned to send a subsidiary expedition from Volta, under the command of Commander Glover, to attack the Ashanti capital Coomassie from the rear, acting as a diversion for the main expeditionary forces and perhaps obviate the need to send European troops.

After spending a short time familiarising himself with the intelligence regarding the Gold Coast territory, the Ashanti forces and dispositions and the local British forces and their dispositions; General Wolseley sent a memorandum outlining his proposals.

He proposed the involvement of two European battalions (each with 29 officers and 654 men) with the appropriate support services, which should be despatched to the Gold Coast in time to begin operations on the 1st December 1873.

The 2nd battalion of the 23rd Royal Welsh Fusiliers and the 1st battalion of the Rifle Brigade were brought up to strength and held in readiness for deployment, however, probably as a result of the high levels of sickness experienced by the Marines who were sent in June, it was decided not to despatch the troops until General Wolseley reported back on the prevailing conditions after his arrival on the Gold Coast.

In addition to arranging for the necessary men, General Wolseley also sought to equip his force with clothing suitable to the climate and the most up to date small arms.

The government also impressed on Wolseley that although it was agreed that the Ashanti needed to be taught a lesson, not to carry out hostilities against the British or their protected allies, it was also essential not to totally destroy the Ashanti hierarchy as a long lasting peace should also be negotiated.

First Ashanti Expedition

Having concluded his initial preparations, General Wolseley boarded the *SS Ambriz* at Liverpool on 12th September 1873 and set sail for the Gold Coast to launch the First Ashanti Expedition, also known as the third Anglo-Ashanti War. The General was accompanied by his staff officers, 27 Special Service Officers, Captain Strahan (the new Administrator for Largos, who left the ship at Sierra Leone) and special correspondents for the *Times* (Mr W. Reade) and the *Standard* (Mr G. A. Henty).

After arriving at Sierra Leone on 27th September, the General despatched Captain Furze and Lieutenant Saunders to Bathurst in Gambia to raise two native regiments from the Mandingoe and Jolliff tribes. Lieutenant Gordon was left at Sierra Leone to recruit native workers to support the Royal Engineers.

Road Building

Soon after completing their recruitment at Sierra Leone, the detachment of Royal Engineers arrived at Cape Coast Castle, where they set about the task of improving the single file track to Coomassie into a roadway suitable for troop movements. This roadway would have to cover a distance of about 160 miles and at the end of each day ten miles of road was complete and a stockade, with huts, was built to provide shelter and protection to the troops and workmen.

The majority of the stockades were just way stations, however, some were built larger and acted as store depots; the camp at the bridge across the Pra was stocked with 400 tons of food and over 1 million rounds of ammunition.

A total of 237 bridges were built to span the various rivers and streams, the majority of which used the local materials of trees, bamboo and creepers, however, the bridge across the River Pra, which needed to span over 60 yards, was made from prefabricated sections brought from Chatham.

Despite a daily dose of quinine, sickness claimed several of the European Engineers, however, the road including a telegraph line had been completed up to the River Pra by 24th January 1874.

General Wolseley's Arrival on the Cape Coast

Continuing her journey the *SS Ambriz* anchored off the Cape Coast on 2nd October and the next day, General Wolseley was received at government house where he was sworn in as Governor by Colonel Harley, the Administrator.

After making enquiries, the General discovered that he had fewer men at his disposal than originally supposed; the force at his disposal consisted of 700 men from the 2nd West India Regiment who were distributed between Cape Coast, Elmina, Secondee, Dixcove, Axim, Napoleon, Abbaye and Accroful. Of these troops, only 400 would be available for field duties while the remainder continued to provide protection to the coastal settlements.

In order to inspire confidence and to induce the Fanti into providing resources for their self protection, General Wolseley organised for a durbar to be held with the kings and chiefs of the Protectorate tribes. Prior to this taking place he held a levee with the military and naval officers and principal merchants.

With much pomp and ceremony, the durbar took place and after having been introduced to each of the chiefs, the General delivered his speech to a respectful and attentive audience. It was agreed that a second meeting would take place on 6th October where, having carried out their deliberations, the chiefs announced their willingness to comply with the Generals wishes and would collect their men but would appreciate it if the General would appoint some of his officers as special commissioners to aid them in this task.

Letters were sent to those chiefs who did not attend the durbar, requesting them to assemble with their men at Dunguah which was the designated assembly area. Some of the chiefs replied with various excuses for their not attending, however, the chief of Essaman sent the insolent reply *"Come and fetch me; white men no dare go bush"*. This challenge could not go unanswered, so General Wolseley planned a secret mission to go after the Essaman chief, using the press to spread rumours about a mission to go to the aid of Captain Glover at Addah, the force set out for Elmina instead.

On 14th October, the force left Elmina and entered the bush, heading for Essaman where after a brief yet fierce fire fight, the village was captured and burnt to the ground. This action, which dispelled the view of Ashanti invincibility in the bush, did much to increase moral and encouraged the Fanti to take up their arms.

General Wolseley's Ultimatum

Just prior to the attack on Essaman, General Wolseley sent out two important messages; one to Koffee Kalkalli, King of the Ashanti was an ultimatum, requiring the Ashanti to: withdraw to the north of the river Pra by 12th November, surrender all British prisoners and make a payment of compensation for the British losses. One of these letters was opened by Amanquatia, Commander-in-Chief of the Ashanti army, sent a reply pledging the peace of the Assin, Denkera, Akim and Wassaw peoples; after the defeat at Essaman he had also promised to retire the Ashanti army.

General Wolseley's Request for Troops

The second message, was to the Secretary of State for War, sent on 13th October, which requested the immediate despatch to the Gold Coast of the European troops being held in readiness (Two battalions of Infantry – 1,300 men, supported by a Royal Artillery detachment – 60 men, a Royal Engineers detachment – 40 men and Administrative services – 50 men) an overall total of 1,450 men. A second letter was despatched on 24th October, requesting a further battalion of infantry.

During this time, small detatchments for Russell's and Wood's native regiments, recruited in Sierra Leone were now arriving to augment the British forces.

Advance to the Pra River

On 25th October, with the news that Amanquatia had broken his camp at Mampon and was now retreating towards the Pra, heading for Dunguah; General Wolseley decided to move some of his men northward to strengthen his forces on the newly created road. While waiting for his European troops to arrive, the General could do little more than harass the retreating Ashanti army and strengthened his garrisons at Abrakrampa and Dunguah as staging posts.

On 4th November, the Ashanti made the long expected attack on Abrakrampa and although determined in nature the Ashanti were repulsed without difficulty due to the arrival of reinforcements from Dunguah.

On 8th November, General Wolseley returned to Cape Coast Castle where soon afterwards he contracted the fever, that had affected many of his officers and men; it was not until 21st November that the General was able to move back into government house and resume his duties.

Small British columns continued to follow and harass the retreating Ashanti until on 5th December it was reported that they had crossed the Pra river and on 22nd December the Ashanti army was disbanded at Coomassie; it is estimated that of the 40,000 warriors who embarked on the invasion only half that number had returned the others having perished due to the ravages of dysentery and small-pox as well as the combat. This effectively ended the first phase of the war.

Second Phase of Expedition

While awaiting the arrival of his European troops, General Wolseley continued to move stores and ammunition to his depots on the road to the River Pra and each of his camps were now strongly garrisoned with his local troops.

On 30th November the *SS Volta* arrived at Cape Coast Castle with a number of Special Service Officers, as replacements for those incapacitated by the malarial fever.

With the arrival of his troops now imminent, the General turned his attention to the problems of transportation; with no pack animals available all material had to be carried on the backs of men, however, the locally recruited porters were very unreliable and generally disappeared after completing only one journey. To resolve this problem, General Wolseley ordered that 3,000 of his Fanti troops be disarmed and employed as porters. On 10th December, he also informed the Fanti kings and chiefs at Dunguah, that unless they raised a force of 5,000 porters, he would not land his troops when they arrived.

The recruitment drive proved to be successful and on 22nd December a force of 6,000 carriers was placed under the control of Colonel Colley, who had arrived on board *HMS Sarmatian* only a few days earlier.

Arrival of the European Troops

On 9th December, *HMS Himalaya* arrived off the Cape Coast and landed: the 2nd Battalion Rifle Brigade with 30 officers and 652 men; the 28th Company of Royal Engineers with four officers and 68 men; Army Hospital Corps with two officers 26 men, 13 medial officers and two chaplains.

On 12th December, *HMS Tamar* anchored off the Cape Coast and landed: the 2nd Battalion 23rd Royal Welsh Fusiliers with 30 officers and 650 men; No 1 Battery 17th Brigade Royal Artillery with 3 officers and 61 men and 13 medical officers and two chaplains.

On 17th December, *HMS Sarmatian* arrived and disembarked: 42nd Highlanders with 30 officers and 652 men; Army Service Corps with one officer and 12 men; Army Hospital Corps with one clerk and 26 men; General Archibald Alison, appointed to the command of the European Brigade, together with Colonel Greaves, his chief of staff, 10 Special Service Officers and 15 medical officers were also on board.

On 29th December, the 1st West India Regiment with 24 officers and 554 men arrived from Jamaica.

Invasion of Ashanti Lands

With his European troops now having landed, General Wolseley completed his planning for the invasion of the Ashanti lands across the Pra River. The plan indicated a start date of 15th January 1874, by which time the depot at Prahsu was expected to be completed and fully stocked, and would involve several columns converging on the Ashanti capital, Coomassie; the campaign was expected to last no longer than 6 weeks, and so should be completed during the dry season.

On 24th December, the General received a despatch from Captain Glover, stating that he expected to cross the river Pra on 15th January with a force of 16,000, possibly 30,000 men.

On 27th December, General Wolseley began an inspection tour of the route along the road to the river Pra and after finding that all was in order, arrived at Prahsu on 2nd January 1874 which now had a garrison of 970 men. The majority of the garrison had been employed on clearing the bush and cutting down acres of palm trees, for poles and thatching to create huts to receive the 2,000 men of the European regiments and their support staff; this was scheduled to be completed by 15th January.

Not long after his arrival at Prahsu, two messengers from the Ashanti King Koffee Kalkalli arrived in camp with letters from the King, one of the letters indicated that a minor action at Faysowah, had been built up into a great Ashanti victory so in his reply the General gave a true account of affairs and stated the terms by which a lasting peace could be concluded. To reinforce the fact that he had the means to enforce his demands, if this proved to be necessary, the Naval Brigade, of over 270 officers and men, were paraded before the kings envoys and the effectiveness of a Gatling gun was demonstrated. On 12th January, a further emissary from the king, accompanied by Mr Khune, the German missionary entered the camp with a reply from King Kalkalli, to the effect that if the British wanted to avoid conflict then they should halt their advance at the river Pra. In reply the General reiterated his previous demands.

The first advance into Ashanti territory took place on 5th January 1874, when Major Russell's regiment of 500 men accompanied by the 170 scouts, commanded by Lieutenant Lord Gifford crossed the river Pra on a scouting mission in strength.

On 7th January, Lieutenant Gifford advanced to Ansah and then to the Foomoosu river without meeting any opposition and on 12th January occupied Accrofoomu. On 18th January Lieutenant Gifford advanced to Quisah which was then occupied by Major Russell's troops.

After experiencing continued problems with the porters, several men from the native contingents had to be pressed into service as carriers and this delay caused General Wolseley to change the date for the invasion of Ashanti territory from the 15th to 20th January 1874.

By 23rd January, General Wolseley and his troops had reached Moinsey where a further deputation from the Ashanti King arrived with the remaining white prisoners (Mr & Mrs Ramseyer and their two children and M Bonnet a French merchant). A letter from the King, promised to accept the General's terms, however, requested the British advance be halted so that they could carry out peaceful negotiations.

While distrusting the Ashanti King's message, believing it to be just delaying tactics so that he could assemble his forces for a final attack, the General did send a message to London stating that all the white prisoners had now been freed and that the King had accepted the British terms. He further stated that he would wait a few days at Fommanah, about 30 miles from Coomassie in order to conclude arrangements.

On the 24th January, General Wolseley sent a reply to the Ashanti King, stating that he intended to go to Coomassie and it was up to the King to decide if this would be as his friend or enemy. If it was to be as his friend then the King must send his mother, his heir and the heirs of four princes as hostages together with the Fanti prisoners and a portion of the indemnity. Until these demands were met, the General would continue his advance but at a slow pace.

By 27th January, Lieutenant Gifford had scouted as far as Insarfu, where information was received that the King of Adansi was at Borborassie with 1,000 men.

On 29th January, General Wolseley arrived at Detchiasu where he received a further two letters from King Koffee, reiterating his request for the British to stop their advance on his capital. The General swiftly replied that he had waited for four days at Fommanah but would not stop again until his terms were complied with.

During the night of 29th January Lieutenant Gifford scouted the Ashanti positions beyond Egginassie and found the enemy to be congregating in great force, obviously in preparation for an imminent attack.

On the following morning, with the possibility of an Ashanti attack, the General moved his forces off in four columns which formed a hollow square, to guard against flanking attacks by the enemy; the baggage and wounded were held in the centre of the square where they were offered some element of protection.

Battle of Amoaful

At daybreak on 31st January, the British force advanced from Insarfu, still in their square formation, and soon afterwards came across the Ashanti forces, where their centre position was dug in to the front of the village of Amoaful, surrounded by dense bush. The first action was at about 8 o'clock in the morning when Lieutenant Gifford and his scouts were fired upon while approaching the village of Egginassie, which they soon cleared.

As usual, the enemy adopted a horseshoe formation, attacking the British flanks from the cover of the bush.

Lance Sergeant Samuel McGaw – Victoria Cross No. 339

During the battle, Lance-Sergeant McGaw led his section through the bush in a most excellent manner and continued to do so throughout the day, despite having been badly wounded at the start of the engagement. For his exploits Lance-Sergeant McGraw would later be awarded the Victoria Cross.

Due to the excellent defensive positions chosen by the Ashanti, the battle was hard fought and took most of the morning; it was not until the British Artillery were brought to bear on the central Ashanti positions that their lines finally broke. With the Ashanti central ranks in disarray, the flanking attacks soon ceased and just before 2 o'clock in the afternoon, the British were in possession of Amoaful.

It is believed that the Ashanti lost between two and three thousand killed or wounded, Chief Amanquatia was one of those killed and the King of Mampon was wounded. The British losses were relatively light with four killed and 194 wounded.

On 1st February, the baggage and reserve of ammunition were brought forward to Amoaful from Insarfu without incident.

Lieutenant Edric Frederick Gifford – Victoria Cross No. 337

On the afternoon of 1st February, Lieutenant Gifford and his scouts carried the town of Becquah and held their position until the arrival of the Naval Brigade who consolidated the position.

For this and other actions during the campaign, Lieutenant Gifford was later awarded the Victoria Cross.

Following the Battle of Amoaful, the road to Coomassie was now clear and the General continued his advance on the Ashanti capital.

Battle of Ordashu

On 3rd February, General Wolseley received another two letters from the Ashanti King requesting that the British halt their advance; the General replied that as he had previously been deceived by the King, he would only halt his advance once the Kings mother and Prince Mensah were in his hands as hostages.

The British force continued their march towards the River Ordah, where the Engineers began to construct a bridge and on the morning of the 4th February, the force crossed the river and advanced on the village of Ordashu.

Lieutenant Mark Bell – Victoria Cross No. 340

Lieutenant Bell was in command of an unarmed party of Fanti workmen, clearing the bush, when the Ashanti warriors in the village opened fire on the British column. Lieutenant Bell continued to supervise the work of the party, now under heavy fire, and leading from the front encouraged them to complete their work.

For this act, Lieutenant Bell was later awarded the Victoria Cross.

Advancing along the road, under the cover of artillery, the Rifle Brigade entered the village and inflicted heavy losses on the enemy. Despite this set back, the Ashanti continued with their usual flanking attacks and managed to mount a counter attack against the village but after an attack on their rear and a frontal assault by artillery they were finally dispersed.

End of the War

Following the Battle of Ordashu, the British columns continued their advance to Coomassie which they entered unopposed by mid afternoon on the 4th February. The occupation of Coomassie was a strange event as the town contained hundreds of armed Ashanti warriors, however, these men were intent on carrying off their arms and ammunition rather than engaging in any fighting and not a shot was fired.

The royal palace was found to be deserted and no sign of the King or members of his household could be found, so the palace was destroyed by explosives and after a short rest the British forces began their journey to leave the country, having successfully concluded their mission.

The war was formally concluded with the treaty of Fomena which was signed on 14th March 1874.

Major Reginald Sartorius – Victoria Cross No. 338

Major Sartorius, of the 6th Bengal Cavalry, attached to the West African Housas, was part of Captain Glover's force which advanced along the river Volta on the right flank of the main British advance on Coomassie. On 17th January during an attack at Abogoo, Major Sartorius saved the life of Sergeant-Major Braimah Doctor, who was severely wounded, by moving him to safety while under heavy enemy fire.

As Captain Glover's column approached Coomassie and travelling through unknown country, Major Sartorius volunteered to try and make contact with the main British force led by General Wolseley. After riding over 50 miles through hostile country, with 25 of his men, the Major was successful in making contact with the main force.

For these two events, Major Sartorius was later awarded the Victoria Cross.

18

PERAK WAR, MALAYA (1875–76)

Perak is one of the small states on the Malay Peninsula adjoining the southern boundary of the Province of Wellesley, part of the British Colony of Penang. With a coast line of almost 100 miles and extending about 50 miles inland, the Perak river divides the central plain from north to south; the west of the country consists of fertile lands reaching down to the sea while on the east the country rises to the great central range of mountains, which form the spine of the Malay peninsula.

The northern region of Perak, known as Larut was rich in tin and during the 19th century was a major producer, rivalling the output of Britain, and as such was an important trading partner to British merchants.

Figure 49. Perak

Background

By 1826, the Crown Colony of the Straits Settlements, which included Penang, Malacca and Singapore had been established, however, due to the extensive operations in British India, little imperial interest had been shown in the remainder of the Malay peninsula.

Two events in the early 1870s prompted a change in the British position; since the death of Sultan Ali of Perak on 26th May 1871 leadership of the state of Perak was in dispute as there were three contenders for the position as Sultan; disputes between the two Chinese secret societies who controlled the tin mines which had been raging since 1861 once again erupted in 1871 with the Larut War.

Although these events were threatening the stability of the Straits Settlements and was disrupting the supply of tin, the British also saw this as an opportunity to expand its influence in the region and to strengthen its monopoly in tin.

In 1871, following the death of Sultan Ali, Raja Abdullah, as the heir apparent fully expected to succeed to the role of Sultan, however, for the spurious reason that Raja Abdullah had not attended the burial of the late Sultan, Raja Ismail was proclaimed as Sultan of Perak instead. Dissatisfied with the situation, Raja Abdullah contacted his friend, Tan Kim Chin in Singapore and together with an English merchant, William H. Read, they drafted a letter to Sir Andrew Clarke, the governor of the Straits Settlements, expressing his desire to place Perak under British protection with himself as Sultan.

Since 1861, two Chinese secret societies; the Ghee Hin, led by Chin Ah Yam and the Hai San, led by Chung Keng Quee; had been waging an almost constant battle for control of the tin mines in the Larut region of western Perak. This "Larut War" had a devastating effect on the production of tin and the commerce of local Chinese merchants; on 26th September 1872, Chung Keng Quee, together with 44 other Chinese leaders sent a petition to the British Government, requesting assistance in resolving the problems and disruption to trade.

In response to these petitions from Perak, on 20th September 1873, Lord Kimberley, the Secretary of State for the Colonies, decided to send Sir Andrew Clarke, Governor of the Straits Settlements, to Perak to investigate and report back on the situation.

In mid-January Sir Andrew Clarke and his deputation, on board the *SS Pluto*, arrived off the island of Pangkor on the coast of Perak and began a series of meetings with several influential Malay and Chinese leaders (including Raja Abdullah and Chung Keng Quee) regarding the perilous situation in the state of Perak. Governor Clarke exceeded his mandate to investigate and report back on the situation and instead on 20th January 1874 concluded the Pangkor Engagement which: acknowledged Raja Abdullah as the legitimate Sultan of Perak to replace Sultan Ismail who was awarded a pension; the Sultan would receive a British Resident, who would advise the Sultan on all matters except Malay customs and religion; a British Officer would be appointed to administer the district of Larut and Dinding and Pangkor Island would be ceded to Britain.

On the same day a Chinese Engagement was signed by 26 Chinese leaders to settle the tin mine disputes.

In 1873, Captain Tristram Speedy resigned his position as Superintendant of Police at Penang, in order to take up the new appointment of Chief of Police in the Larut district. After a recruitment mission to Lahore in India Captain Speedy returned with 110 mainly Sikh, ex-soldiers and on 23rd September 1873 formed the Perak Armed Police force which was deployed across the state to enforce the law and guard the tin mines.

Following on from the Pangkor Engagement, James Wheeler Woodford Birch was appointed as the first Resident to Perak on 4th November 1874 and general administration of the country was placed in British hands.

Almost immediately after his appointment as Sultan, Abdullah adopted a negative stance towards the British and many of the Malay chiefs and officials resented the appointment of a British Resident, who they feared would interfere with traditional customs such as debt slavery.

On 2nd November 1875, Resident Birch landed at the village of Pasir Salak, on the lower Perak river, in the performance of his administrative duties when he was challenged by the local leader, Maharaja Lela who was backed by a large group of armed Malays. Mr Birch instructed his interpreter to post proclamations, however, these were almost immediately torn down while the crowd responded with verbal abuse. On hearing of this, Mr Birch ordered the notices to be reposted before retiring to a screened off floating bath house, to bathe.

As the interpreter reposted the notices, he was attacked and mortally wounded, while another group of Malays surrounded the bath house and struck out at Mr Birch with their spears, forcing him into the river where he was killed by a sword wound to the head.

Although Mr Birch had been escorted by a 12 man party of well armed Sikhs under the command of Sub-Lieutenant Thomas Francis Abbott, Royal Navy (*HMS Thistle*), no precautions to protect Mr Birch had been taken and in fact at the time of the attack Sub-Lieutenant Abbott was on the other side of the river hunting game. After the attack, Sub-Lieutenant Abbott retreated down river to the nearby Residency Fort at Banda Bahru which he proceeded to defend with the garrison of 50 Sikhs and four seamen from *HMS Thistle*.

Mr Birch's body, was recovered from the river by a friendly Raja and on the evening of 6th November he was buried with full military honours at Banda Bahru. Mr Frank Swettenham, the senior Assistant Special Commissioner for Perak who had arrived at the fort on the previous day, sent an urgent request for military assistance to his superior in Penang.

Fearing a general uprising, William Jervois, who had succeeded Sir Andrew Clarke, as Governor of the Straits Settlements in May 1875, sent a telegraph to India requesting the urgent despatch of 1,500 troops to avenge the murder of the British Resident, signalling the start of the Perak War.

Perak War Begins

Following the request from Mr Frank Swettenham for reinforcements, Lieutenant-Colonel A. E. H. Anson, the Lieutenant Governor of Penang was quick to despatch a force of 60 men from the 10th Regiment of Foot, commanded by Captain W. Innes of the Royal Engineers, who was the Head of the Penang Public Works Department, accompanied by Lieutenants Thomas George Booth and Armstrong William Elliot. Superintendent Plunkett of the Penang Police with 25 of his men were also part of the reinforcements who arrived at Banda Bahru; on 6th November.

Failed Attack on Pasir Salak

On 7th November, the above force, accompanied by Mr Frank Swettenham and 20 of his scouts and intelligence agents advanced up river towards Pasir Salak where the murder of the

Resident had occurred. When they were about three miles from Pasir Salak, the force abandoned their boats and advanced on foot along the river bank.

Mr Swettenham, with his scouts, led the column, followed by an advanced guard of four men from the 10th Regiment led by Corporal Anderson. The advanced party was closely followed by Lieutenant Booth with 21 men; then Captain Innes and Sub-Lieutenant Abbott with his four seamen from *HMS Thistle* who were in charge of labourers carrying rockets; Superintendant Plunkett with his 25 policemen were next with Lieutenant Elliot and 25 men from the 10th Regiment forming the rearguard.

The force did not expect to meet any opposition until they reached Pasir Salak, however, after having marched for just over a mile, they came across a stockade in a corn field from which they were assailed by musket fire. The naval rocket team immediately came into action but their fire was ineffective with most of their rockets passing harmlessly over the top of the stockade. The Penang police and Mr Swettenham's Sikhs clustered behind a large tree and began to fire wildly, wounding several of the British soldiers in the process; as none of the officers could speak Urdu it was difficult to control this erratic behaviour.

Lieutenant Booth was severely wounded in the foot, so it was Lieutenant Elliot who ordered a charge against the stockade; the British managed to reach the ditch which surrounded the stockade but were unable to cross this defence. As the force was taking heavy casualties, it was decided to withdraw and return to Banda Bahru. During the attack four of the force were killed, including Captain Innes and Private Fay from the 10th Regiment of Foot, two officers and 9 men from the 10th Regiment were wounded.

Destruction of the Pasir Salak Stockade

After hearing that the Malay chiefs were planning to withdraw from Pasir Salak, the British at Banda Bahru decided to mount an attack to forestall any withdrawal.

The following force, under the command of Captain Whitla of the 10th Regiment, was assembled to carry out the attack: Royal Artillery, 20 men with a 12 pounder howitzer; 10th Regiment, 3 officers and 125 men; Royal Navy, 15 Royal Marines and 70 seamen from *HMS Thistle* and *HMS Fly* with two 12 pounder howitzers and two 24 pounder rocket tubes and Mr Swettenham and his local scouts and intelligence agents. Several of the transport boats were also fitted with mortars, rocket tubes and howitzers.

The expedition set out from Bandar Bahru, by river, on 14th November and due to good use of the boat mounted artillery were soon able to seize several of the enemy strongholds. On 16th November, in the face of a determined attack by the British forces, Pasir Salak was hastily evacuated and five guns were abandoned. The stockade and Maharajah Lela's house, together with other houses, were burnt to the ground before the force returned to Bandar Bahru. British casualties were slight with three people, including Mr Cope, the Reuters correspondent and Police Inspector Laggis, being wounded.

Advance to Kinta

On 10th November 1875, Major General Francis Colbourne, the commander of British troops in China, Hong Kong and the Straits Settlements, left Hong Kong to take up command of the Perak Field Force. Following his arrival at Banda Bahru in early December, the General worked with Captain Alexander Buller, of the Royal Navy, who was the senior officer of the Straits Division, on a plan to advance up the Perak river towards Kinta, with the intention of capturing the insurgent leaders who were making their escape by elephant.

On 8th December, the General loaded his force on a flotilla of 45 boats and began the journey towards Kinta. The force consisted of: Royal Artillery, 40 gunners with two guns; Infantry, 100 men from 1st Battalion 10th Regiment, commanded by Captain Whitla and 100 men from 80th Regiment, commanded by Major Charles Frederick Amiel and a company of the 1st Goorkha Regiment, commanded by Colonel P. Storey; a Naval Brigade of 70 men drawn from the crews of *HMS Modeste* and *HMS Ringdove* manned two guns and two rocket tubes. Mr Frank Swettenham, a fluent Malay speaker, acted as Intelligence Officer and was accompanied by his local scouts and agents.

Major Dunlop, Royal Artillery, Her Majesty's Commissioner for Perak, had organised the transport from friendly chiefs in Banda Bahru, obtaining sufficient river boats with Chinese crews. Four boats were converted to mount the naval guns and 24-pounder rockets, and flat-bottomed boats sent from Singapore were used to convey rations and stores.

Heading upriver against a strong current, the heavily loaded flotilla was only able to make slow progress, covering less than ten miles each day, however, by 13th December they had reached Blanja without encountering the enemy.

On arriving at Blanja, General Colbourne and Captain Buller, learned that the main rebel leaders, Maharajah Lela and Raja Ismail had recently left the village and were proceeding by road to Kinta so they decided to leave the river and continue their pursuit on foot. One officer and 50 men from the 10th Regiment were left at Blanja as a garrison and 22 men from the Naval Brigade were left behind to tend to the boats; while the rest of the column proceeded through the jungle towards Kinta.

Due to the swampy ground, wood had to be laid across the track at regular intervals to enable the passage of the guns. The column had only progressed about two miles, when the advanced guard commanded by Lieutenant Patton of the 10th Regiment, came across a defensive position blocking the track. Accurate fire from one of the rocket tubes and an artillery piece were instrumental in clearing the obstruction; during the action, Doctor Randell, the Principal Civil Medical Officer within the Straits Settlement was severely wounded by a shot through his thigh.

Later in the day, the force arrived at a defended but partially constructed stockade where rockets were used to disperse the defenders. By now it was obvious that the retreating enemy were not very far ahead of the British force and a concerted effort was made to catch up with them, however, when darkness fell they had to give up the attempt.

On the next day, the General rested his troops, while Malay and Chinese porters brought forward stores to replenish his supplies; the column resumed their march on the following day and arrived at the Papan tin mines late in the afternoon of 15th December.

With the aid of a friendly Raja, Mr Swettenham and his scouts reconnoitred Kinta and after having been caught up by the main force, an attack was made against the stockade and town on 17th December which was taken with little difficulty. After occupying the town, during which they seized nine cannon, the General learned that the men that they were chasing had retreated up the Kinta river by boat and were heading for Patani, in Lower Siam. On hearing this news, the General decided to call off the pursuit and after leaving small garrisons at Kinta and Blanja, set off by river with the rest of the column and returned to Banda Bahru.

Arrival of Reinforcements from India

Despite the speed with which the force was assembled and despatched, the reinforcements requested from India arrived in Malaya when most of the fighting was finished; the advanced party arrived at Penang on 27th November 1875.

The force, was commanded by General J. Ross and comprised: Colonel Talbot Ashley Cox in command of 600 men from 3rd Regiment; Colonel R. Sale Hill in command of 400 men from the 1st Goorkha Regiment; supported by 3rd–5th Royal Artillery, a field telegraph with 100 miles of wire, a superintendant and 10 signallers, a company of Madras Sappers and Miners and a Medical Officer.

The Indian troops were detailed to occupy the upper regions of the country and marched to Kuala Kangsa on the upper reaches of the Perak River, having established garrisons at Bukit Gantong and Campong Boyah. The presence of the British troops in the region, managed to keep the disaffected chiefs in check and prevent them from joining in with the disturbances lower down the river.

The Larut Field Force

At the turn of the year, General Colbourne appointed General Ross to the command of the Larut Field force, composed of men from the Indian contingent and men from a Naval Brigade, with the objective of destroying the opposition at Kota Lama, a very anti-British village on the upper Perak River near to Kuala Kangsa but on the opposite bank of the river.

The Naval Brigade, Commanded by Commander Edmund St John Garforth of *HMS Philomel*, consisted of 107 officers and men (marines and sailors) from *HMS Modeste* and *HMS Philomel*, had rafted up the Larut River before marching across country to arrive at Kuala Kangsa.

On 4th January 1876, General Ross launched his attack on Kota Lama with forces advancing along both banks of the Perak River; Colonel Cox commanded the force on the left bank of the river which consisted of: 12 men from the Royal Artillery with one 7 pounder gun; 10 men from 3rd Regiment; 25 men from the 1st Goorkha Regiment. This force was accompanied by William Edward Maxwell, the British Deputy Commissioner for the region.

On the right bank of the river, Captain G. Young from the 1st Goorkha Regiment, commanded a force comprising: 50 men from the 3rd Regiment and 20 men from the 1st Goorkha Regiment. This force was accompanied by Captain Speedy with some of his Sikh policemen.

To complete the attacking force, Commander Garforth led three boats containing 3 officers and 29 men from his naval brigade as well as General Ross and his staff.

Commander Garforth and his party landed their boats just above Kota Lama and after leaving nine sailors to guard the boats, set off towards the village with General Ross and his staff, expecting to meet up with Colonel Cox and his group, however, Colonel Cox and his men had already searched the river and were following tracks into the jungle.

General Ross led the party in a search of the village looking for arms, however, after searching for about an hour and a half they had found nothing apart from some women and children occupying some of the houses. At this time they were suddenly and unexpectedly attacked by a force of about 50 natives, who rushed at them from the jungle. They were mostly armed with spears, however, a few had muskets. The British party was so shocked by the attack that they were almost surrounded and had to fight a determined action to withdraw, during which three men were killed and another four were wounded.

Those killed were the Brigade Major, Major Henry Lumsden Hawkins, Seaman Gunner William G. Loam of *HMS Philomel* and Goorkha Jangbir Basnait who were all killed by spear wounds. The wounded were Surgeon Townsend, Private Jasper Ball of the Royal Marines (who would die of his wounds 18 hours later) and the Goorkha sepoys Jhagru Thapa and Karak Sing Tapah.

As swiftly as it had started, the attack was over and the natives returned to the jungle, leaving behind five of their own men dead.

Soon after the attack, Colonel Cox and his group emerged from the jungle without having fired a shot and proceeded to help burn the village to the ground, a 12 pounder cannon was spiked and thrown into the river and a quantity of spears and muskets and smaller cannons were taken back to Kuala Kangsa. Captain Young had searched the village on his side of the river, without encountering any opposition.

After leaving a garrison at Kuala Kangsa, General Ross and Commander Garforth withdrew their forces and returned to Banda Bahru.

The Malacca Field Force

While the main operations were taking place along the Perak and Larut rivers, to the north of the region the Malacca Field force was raised to combat hostilities much further to the south in the region of Sungei Ujong located between Malacca and Kuala Lumpur.

The mission of the field force, commanded by Colonel Edward Bertie Clay, was to support the rule of chief Dato Klana, who was friendly to the British, against opposition mounted by his rival Chief Tunku Antah.

Colonel Clay set sail from Penang, with his force of about 250 men from the 1st Goorkha regiment, on board the *SS Malda* on 6th December 1875 bound for Malacca which they reached two days later.

Colonel Clay's force was supported by a Naval Brigade commanded by Commander Francis Stirling from *HMS Thistle*.

Prior to the arrival of Colonel Clay's force, a smaller British force of men from the 10th Regiment, commanded by Lieutenant Henry Charles Hinxman had been operating in the region and despite some success on 7th December, when they capture and destroyed some stockades at Paroe, they had been pushed out of the Terrachi region by superior forces, leaving Chief Tunku Antah's men to occupy the strategic Bukit Putus pass which was the gateway to the Terrachi and Sri Mentanti regions.

Colonel Clay arrived at Malacca on 8th December 1875 and after leaving Captain Rankin, with a force of 100 men from the 1st Goorkha regiment to garrison the town, set sail for the mouth of the river Lukut, where they disembarked and headed for Rassa, the home of the British Resident, Captain Patrick James Murray.

At Rassa, a plan was formulated for the capture of the Bukit Putus pass which involved the use of two columns: Colonel Clay's column which consisted of: Royal Artillery, Lieutenant Rigg, commanding 22 men with a gun, mortar and rocket tubes; Royal Engineers, Lieutenant William North; Infantry, Lieutenants Henry Charles Hinxman and Charles Talbot Peyton commanding 41 men from the 10th Regiment of Foot; Captain G. N. Channer and Lieutenant G. P. Churchill commanding a detachment of the 1st Goorkha regiment and the Naval Brigade, Captain de Fontaine commanding an Arab contingent of 70 men. The objective of this column was to make a frontal attack on the Bukit Putus pass.

The second column, commanded by Colonel R. Sale Hill, comprised: a Naval Brigade from *HMS Thistle*, commanded by Commander Stirling with 30 seamen and marines armed with a rocket tube; Royal Artillery, Lieutenant Henriques commanding 10 men with one gun and Infantry, Captain C. Mercer commanding 120 men from the 1st Goorkha regiment. This column was to advance along the Moar River, through Langkap to attack the Bukit Putus pass from the rear.

Colonel Hill and his column left Rassa on 19th December, and after a difficult journey up the Moar Valley, during which he had to destroy many obstacles which had been placed on the track, until finally they reached Sri Mentanti and joined up with Colonel Clay's column on 23rd December, after the Bukit Putus pass had been taken.

Colonel Clay left Rassa on 18th December 1875 and after difficulties in obtaining sufficient porters his column reached the foot of the Bukit Putus Pass on the 20th December.

Captain George Channer – Victoria Cross No. 341

That afternoon Captain Channer and 50 Goorkhas, accompanied by Lieutenant North of the Royal Engineers, were sent to reconnoitre the stockade, a fort that controlled the entry to the pass. After three hours, Captain Channer sent a message back to Colonel Clay, by runner, to say that the jungle was so dense that reconnaissance of the fort was impossible from a safe distance. Colonel Clay replied by runner telling Captain Channer to get as close as he could to the fort and to estimate ranges for the guns and rockets.

With these instructions from Colonel Clay, Captain Channer with his men and Lieutenant North moved up a river bed until brought to a standstill by trees which had been felled to block this approach. Leaving some men to remove this obstacle, the Captain sent his men out on either side of the obstruction.

He moved off with the left party, 25 of his men and advanced through the jungle until he saw smoke from the enemy fires which he followed until he came to one of their stockades. The stockade was stoutly built from logs surrounded by a palisade topped with pointed bamboo stakes.

From the wall of the stockade, Captain Channer observed that the Malay defenders, were all participating in a communal meal and had not posted any sentries; content that he had not been observed Captain Channer and two of his Goorkhas leaped the palisade and advanced into the defenders, who numbered about 20 or 30 men, firing into the mass of men, killing several of them.

At the sound of the gunfire, Captain Channer's remaining Goorkhas entered the stockade and the defenders, believing that they had been surrounded, evacuated their position and moved off to two other stockades further up the pass. With his two parties now reunited, Captain Channer and his men laid down fire on the other two stockades and after about half an hour of unremitting fire by the British, the Malays abandoned these positions, leaving the way clear to the summit of the Bukit Putus pass.

For his action during this engagement, Captain Channer was later awarded the Victoria Cross, Balbir Gharti and Jitman Thapa, the two Goorkhas who accompanied him were both awarded the Order of Merit.

Following the capture of the stockades, Colonel Clay and his men advanced up the pass and managed to clear the remaining Malay positions without too much trouble.

Conclusion

The major actions of the war were concluded by the end of 1875 and the war was declared to be over in March 1876, by which time the recalcitrant Sultans and Chiefs had all accepted defeat. Three insurgent leaders were hanged and three others were banished from Malaya, or fled the country.

Towards the end of 1876, Maharaja Lela, Sultan Abdullah and Ngah Ibrahim had been captured and were tried at Matang on 14th–22nd December 1876. Having all been found guilty, Maharaja Lela and two of his supporters were hung on 20th January 1877, while Sultan Abdullah and Ngah Ibrahim were sent into exile in the Seychelles.

19

BALUCHISTAN, INDIA (1877)

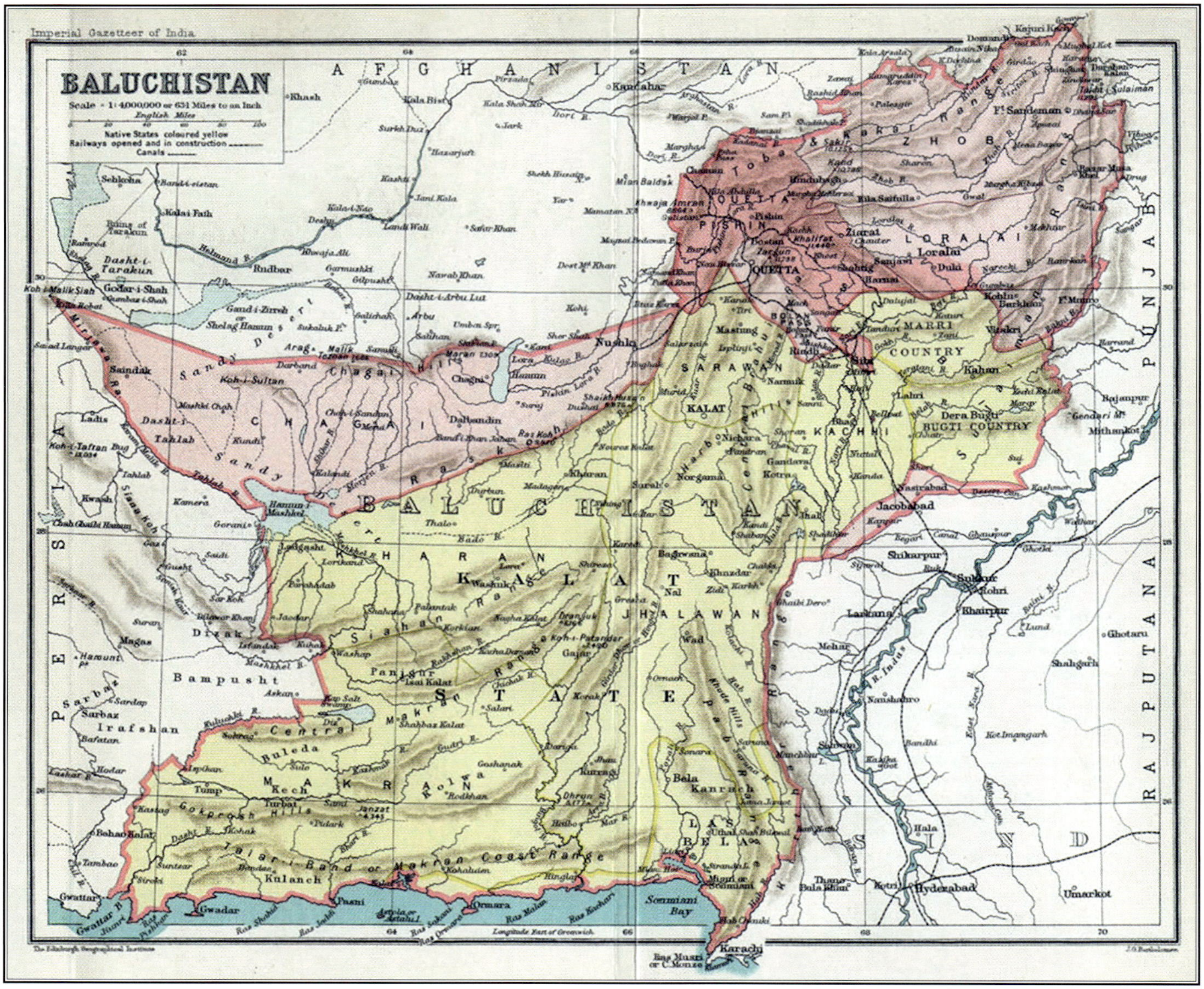

Figure 50. Baluchistan

Baluchistan was a region of princely states bordering the North West Frontier of British India. To help maintain stability in the area the East India Company established the Baluchistan Agency in 1877, following the treaty of Kalat which was signed at Jacobabad on 8th December 1876.

On 21st February 1877, Major Robert Groves Sandeman was appointed by Lord Lytton as the first Agent of the new agency where he was to introduce an innovative system of tribal pacification which was to last until 1947.

Captain Andrew Scott – Victoria Cross No. 342

Land had been acquired at Quetta for the construction of a new residency for the Agent and his escort of troops. Construction work, by the Royal Engineers, had begun when on 26th July 1877, the works were attacked by three Patan workers, who were dissatisfied with the increased British control.

During the attack, Lieutenant Hewson was killed and Lieutenant Kunhardt was wounded; Captain Scott who was on duty at the regimental parade ground rushed to assist when he became aware of the attack. On approaching the scene, Captain Scott found that Lieutenant Kunhardt was lying on the ground wounded and being protected by a sepoy from the regiment, he immediately bayoneted and killed two of the assailants and knocked the third to the ground, where he was killed by a sepoy.

For this action, which saved the life of Lieutenant Kunhardt, Captain Scott was later awarded the Victoria Cross.

The basis, under which the award of this Victoria Cross was made is unknown and unfortunately no documentation exists to help clarify matters.

At the time of the attack on the Royal Engineers at Quetta, the British forces were not at war in Baluchistan and to confuse matters further, the three assailants were employed as coolies by the Regiment.

Was this award made under the terms of the "not in the face of the enemy" clause or not? This remains an unanswered question.

20

CAPE FRONTIER WAR – 9TH (1877–78)

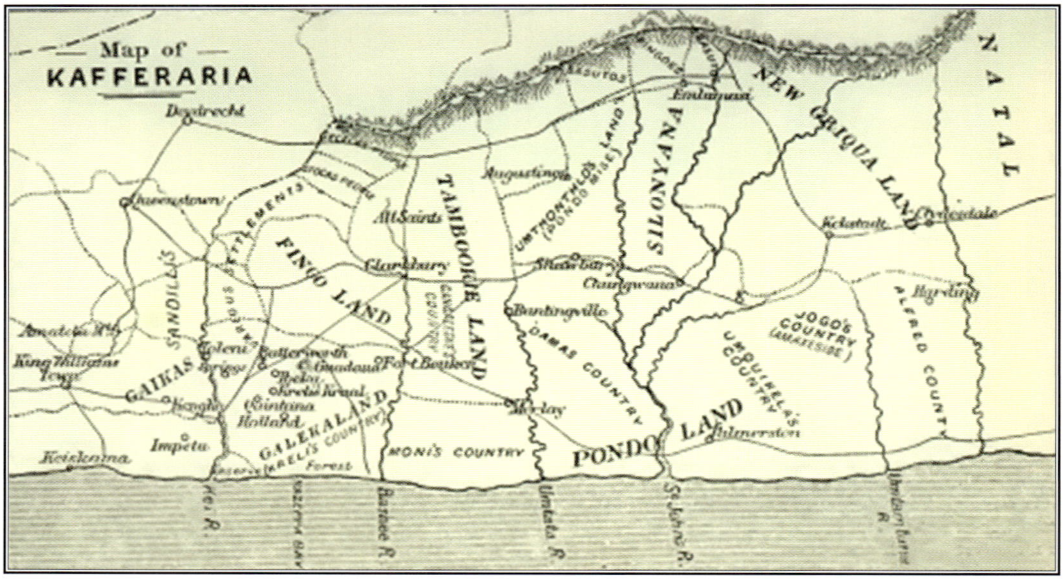

Figure 51. Kafferaria

The Cape Frontier Wars, Xhosa Wars or Kaffir Wars, also known as "Africa's 100 Years War" were a series of nine conflicts between the Xhosa tribes and European settlers on the eastern frontier of South Africa which occurred between 1779 and 1879. In common with many of the colonial wars, the conflicts mainly revolved around the desire for European settlers to acquire land.

The first two wars were fought between the Dutch and the Xhosa tribe, however, following the British takeover of the Cape colony, the remaining wars were conducted by the British. Following the Battle of Muizenberg in 1795, the Dutch lost their Cape colony to Britain, however, following the Peace of Amiens in 1802 the colony was returned to Dutch control. After the Battle of Blaauwberg in 1806, the British once again regained control of the Cape Colony and this was affirmed by the Anglo Dutch treaty of 1814.

The eighth war in 1850, known as "The Great Cattle-killing" because it resulted in the destruction of the Xhosa herds, severely reduced the tribe as a military power and peace was to reign on the frontier for the next 25 years.

In 1872, following extensive campaigning by the "Responsible Government" movement, the Cape of Good Hope colony achieved the status of self government and John Charles Molteno was appointed as the first Prime Minister on 1st December 1872.

In some ways the issues that led to the 9th or *"Wedding Party War"* were different to those of the previous wars as the whole of the country was in a state of transition. Due to the discovery of diamonds at Kimberley and gold in the Transvaal together with the demand for ostrich feathers by the fashion houses of Europe, the economy was undergoing a rapid growth and increasing numbers of natives were required to work in the mines, on the construction of railways and on the settlers farms.

The development of a new imperial policy regarding South Africa and the implications on the government of the Cape

Colony were disrupting the political status quo, threatening to further destabilise the area.

When Lord Carnarvon was appointed as the Secretary of State to the Colonies on 21st February 1874 he began to espouse the policy of confederation regarding the colonies in South Africa in a similar fashion to the policy that he successfully pursued in Canada, which resulted in the Canadian Confederation Act in 1867.

To assist him in the progression of this policy, on 31st March 1877, Lord Carnarvon appointed Sir Henry Bartle Edward Frere as the Governor of the Cape of Good Hope and High Commissioner for Southern Africa.

In September 1877, at the end of a Cape parliamentary session, which had done little to advance Lord Carnarvon's dream of confederation, the frustrated Governor Frere left Cape Town bound for the Eastern Province which was more sympathetic to his aims. The Eastern Province was the location of the native tribal lands and had borne the brunt of the violence of the previous Cape wars.

On reaching the region and conducting a tour of the Transkei, Governor Frere found the frontier districts to be in a restless state and in contradiction to the thoughts of the people of the Western Province, he felt that war was imminent.

Start of the War

Unknown to Governor Frere, the spark that would ignite the 9th and final Cape Frontier War, had already taken place.

On the 3rd August 1877, at a Kraal, on the Fingoland/Gcaleka border, owned by Quenquas another Fingo tribesman, Nchayechibi was holding a wedding feast when a fight broke out with some members of the Gcaleka clan of the Xhosa tribe. As was the custom, in addition to the invited guests, individuals who had loaned pots (generally used for brewing beer) to the organisers, were also permitted to attend. At some stage, presumably after copious amounts of beer had been consumed, a fight broke out between some of the Fingo guests and the Gcaleka attendees. It is believed that the dispute was over the rights of the Gcaleka to attend the party as their claim that they had loaned pots was disputed. During the ensuing fight a member of the Gcaleka party was killed before the remainder were ejected.

Ethnic tensions between the Fingo and Xhosa tribes had been fermenting for some time, since the last Frontier War, the Fingo tribe, who were supported by the British had prospered at the expense of the Xhosa who were eager to restore previously confiscated lands. The Fingo tribe had previously been slaves of the Gcaleka but were freed from their slavery by the British in 1835 and now occupied land from which the Gcaleka had been expelled 20 years earlier.

This incident, proved to be the spark that ignited an escalation of the conflict between the tribes; because of the circumstances of the incident the resulting war became known as the *"Wedding Feast War"*.

Initial Inter-Tribal Conflicts

On the day after the incident at the wedding feast a band of Gcaleka warriors attacked a Cape Colony police outpost that was manned by predominantly Fingo members of the force.

On the 6th August, Xhoxho, the son of the Gcaleka chief Mapassa, assembled a force and invaded Fingoland at four different points and carried off 150 head of cattle and 500 goats from several Fingo villages.

On the night of 9th August, Xhoxho again crossed the Gcuwa river with over 1,000 of his followers and at a point about four miles from the Butterworth Mission Station fought an action against Fingo tribesmen.

Another Gcaleka raid took place against the Fingos, on 24th August at Endochanga near Butterworth with losses on both sides.

With the rapidly increasing severity of these border disputes it was clear that a significant government response was urgently required if all out war was to be avoided. Unfortunately, Governor Frere and Prime Minister Molteno had different views on what form this response should take.

Prime Minister Molteno viewed the situation as a minor inter-tribal dispute, which should be handled by the Cape Colony Frontier Armed and Mounted Police. This force, commanded by Inspector Chalmers was a small, highly mobile, mounted mixed race commando unit recruited locally from Boer, Fingo, Khoi and frontier settlers.

Governor Frere, however, viewed the situation as being more serious as the Gcaleka had invaded Fingoland, which was British territory and attacked Fingo tribesmen, who were under British protection, he believed that Imperial troops should be deployed to resolve the conflict.

High level negotiations by the Cape of Good Hope Prime Minister, extracted a promise from Britain that imperial troops would stay put and would on no account cross the frontier.

Governor Frere left King Williams Town for the Transkei to hold talks with the dissident Xhosa chiefs, however, Sarhili ka Hintsa, also known as "Kreli", a Gcaleka who was the paramount Xhosa chief, refused to meet with Frere as an influential faction, within his clan who were intent on war refused to condone further concessions to the British. Angered by this rebuff, Governor Frere issued a warning to Sarhili that he would be held responsible for any further transgressions into Fingoland and returned to King Williams Town to prepare for war.

Conflicts with Colonial Forces

So far the conflicts had been inter-tribal, with fighting between the Fingo and Gcaleka tribes, however, when Inspector Chalmers and units of the Frontier Armed Mounted Police (FAMP), were moved to Butterworth to help quell the disturbances, Colonial forces were about to become involved in the fighting.

Battle of Gwadana

On 26th September 1877, the first action between the Gcaleka army and Colonial forces took place on the Government Reserve near Gwadana. While returning to the Idutywa reserve from the main police camp at Ibeka, Inspector Chalmers with about 180 members of the FAMP observed that a large part of the Gcaleka Army, thought to be between 3 and 4 thousand men had crossed the border and attacked a force of Fingo tribesmen.

With only a small force at his disposal, Inspector Chalmers sent a messenger to nearby Umpuluse, where Mr Ayliff was in command of about 1,000 Fingo troops. With the arrival of Mr Ayliff and his force of Fingos, Inspector Chalmers was now ready to do battle and after a short advance came across the Gcaleka army arranged in three divisions at the foot of the Gwadana Hill.

When the Gcaleka army began to advance on his position, Inspector Chalmers deployed his one and only artillery piece, a 7 pounder, and Sub-Inspector Cochrane the artillery officer opened fire on the enemy.

Unfortunately, after only firing ten rounds, the gun was disabled due to a broken carriage and to prevent it falling into enemy hands Inspector Chalmers ordered it to be removed from the field. This was carried out by Sub-Inspector Cochrane, Mr Maclean and 25 men acting as an escort.

At the sight of the gun leaving the field, the Fingos; who for the past two hours had been doing sterling work, firing volley after volley into the Gcaleka army from the summit of the Gwadana Hill which they had earlier ascended, panicked and thinking it was a general retreat left the field of battle.

Without the support of the Fingo troops, Inspector Chalmers had little alternative but to also leave the field and save his police troopers. During the retreat, six of the policemen were killed as was Inspector von Hohenau who was shot while trying to help a wounded man onto his horse.

Following the retreat, Inspector Chalmers managed to extract his men safely and by 27th September they were back on duty on the Idutywa Reserve, however, due to illness Inspector Chalmers was replaced by Charles Griffith, the Chief Magistrate of Basutoland and a former commander of the FAMP.

Battle of Ibeka

After his appointment as commander of the FAMP, Charles Griffith was quick to establish a fortified headquarters at Ibeka, on the outskirts of Butterworth where he established a garrison of 180 police troopers, 2,000 Fingo troops commanded by Captain Veldman Bikitsha, the largest landowner in Fingoland, and a small artillery unit comprising three 7 pounder guns and some Congreve rockets.

At first light on the morning of 29th September, emboldened by their success at Gwadana, Chief Kreli at the head of the Xhosa army, now numbering about 8,000 men, mounted an attack against the fort at Ibeka. Armed only with muzzle loading rifles and assegais, the Xhosa adopted their traditional horseshoe formation and advanced on the police fort.

Having been warned, by his scouts, of the approach of the Xhosa army Commandant Griffith was able to ensure that the fort was well prepared for an attack; shells and case shot had been placed next to the guns, cases of ammunition had been placed around the walls and barrels of water had been placed at convenient positions across the enclosure. The men even had time to partake of their breakfast.

At about 9:30 in the morning, after the arrival of 2,000 mounted men, Chief Kreli's men, commanded by his son Sigow, began to close on the fort, with the cavalry moving up a stony ridge on the left of the Colonials' position. After approaching to within 1,200 yards of the fort, the Xhosa sent out skirmishers, however, this move was countered by Captain Veldman and 500 of his men who occupied a walled enclosure and laid down heavy fire. The cavalry, approaching along the ridge were dispersed by rocket and artillery fire which caused many of their horses to bolt.

The Xhosa warriors made repeated attacks against the walls of the fort, often getting to within 50 yards of their objective, however, fire from the three artillery guns, rockets and the defenders Snider rifles caused considerable numbers of casualties and the attackers frequently retired to rest and reform. After many unsuccessful attempts, at about 5 o'clock they collected together for a final effort but as before they were mown down by the murderous fire of the defenders.

When this attacked faltered, Inspector Maclean with 50 of his policemen supported by a force of Fingos, left the safety of the fort and pursued the enemy who were also fired upon by the 7 pounder guns until they moved out of range.

Casualties amongst the defenders were relatively slight; the Europeans suffered only four or five men slightly wounded while the Fingo casualties were about 40 killed and 11 wounded. Three captured Gcaleka prisoners reported that their army had suffered serious losses with over 1,000 men having been killed or wounded.

On the morning after the battle, the Ibeka defenders, after having spent a miserable night due to heavy rains, observed Gcaleka forces congregating near the positions that they had occupied on the previous day. A party was advancing up the ridge with the intention of trying to turn the left flank of the position, however, when a force of Fingos was despatched to counter the threat they quickly retired. The main Gcaleka force continued to advance on the fort, however, were unable to get very close due to the barrage of artillery fire which kept them at bay.

At about 10 o'clock a heavy fog descended and when it lifted, about two hours later, the enemy were nowhere to be seen and the battle was finally over.

The Colonial War

Following the comprehensive defeat of the Gcaleka army at Ibeka, the dominance of the faction intent on war, within the tribe, was eliminated and Chief Kreli now sought to negotiate a peaceful settlement. Governor Frere, intent on the complete subjugation of Gcalekaland, so it could be included in a confederated South Africa was not disposed to negotiate and instead created a war council at King Williams Town, for the purpose of taking the war into Gcalekaland.

In addition to Governor Frere, the war council consisted of: Lieutenant-General Sir Arthur Augustus Thurlow Cunynghame, Commander in Chief of Imperial Forces in South Africa since 1874; John Xavier Merriman and Charles Brownlee, both colonial cabinet ministers who happened to be in the area, completed the council.

The council still had conflicting views regarding the use of Imperial troops in the conflict, however, a compromise agreement was finally reached whereby General Cunynghame was appointed to the command of all of the forces but Commandant Griffiths was given responsibility for the conduct of the war in the Transkei.

General Cunynghame appointed Colonel Richard Glyn with the 1st Battalion 24th Regiment of Foot to guard the supply lines to the Transkei, however, his troops were not permitted to cross the river Kei as only colonial forces were to be used in the fight against the Xhosa.

On the 5th October, Governor Frere issued a proclamation which deposed Chief Kreli and confiscated his lands which were now to be placed under the control of colonial officers, appointed by the Governor; Commander Griffith was appointed to this role. Soon after the proclamation was issued, Mapassa, one of Kreli's chiefs declared for the Government and as he was threatened by his brother Gcaleka chiefs, he was escorted with his followers, across the river Kei and allowed to settle at Impetu, near King Williams Town.

Following the defeat of the Gcaleka at Ibeka, Ngangelizwe, the Chief of the Thembu tribe brought his warriors into the war on the colonial side, considerably strengthening Commander Griffith's army. With his force now numbering about 8,000, Commander Griffith divided his men into three columns and on 9th October crossed the border and began the invasion of Gcalekaland.

After crossing into the Transkei, Commander Griffith ordered his columns to converge on Holela on the river Qora, where Kreli had his kraal which was known as the "Great Place". Arriving at Holela soon after sunrise, Griffith's force took the Gcaleka completely by surprise and after a few minutes of artillery fire had driven them from the kraal and chased them for some distance over the river Qora. Kreli's kraal, together with the kraals of other Gcaleka chiefs were burnt to the ground and all grain pits and stockades were emptied, with the grain, cattle and sheep all being confiscated.

The fast moving columns of colonial forces, advanced rapidly towards the coast driving the Gcaleka before them. They encountered very little opposition fighting minor engagements at Springs on 9th October and Lusizi on 22nd of October before forcing the Gcaleka across the river Bashee by the end of the month.

Having pushed chief Kreli and his warriors into the neutral territory of Bomvanaland, Commander Griffith considered the Gcaleka to be a spent force and with the bulk of his European volunteers being settlers who wished to return to their farms, he decided to call off the pursuit.

By the middle of November, Commander Griffith officially declared that the war was over and that the Gcaleka army had been *"entirely extinguished"* and on 19th November allowed his cavalry volunteers to return to their homes. Soon afterward, the main colonial force began their return home, driving the thousands of captured cattle, sheep and goats ahead of them. After leaving small garrisons at Fort Bowker, Springs and Toleni, commander Griffith arrived back at Ibeka on 29th November 1877, bringing the first phase of the war to an end.

Despite Commander Griffith's declaration, the war was far from over and would soon enter its bloodiest phase.

The Imperial War

Disposition of Imperial Troops

At the start of the conflict in the Eastern Cape, General Cunynghame, Commander in Chief of British forces in southern Africa, only had two battalions located in the Cape of Good Hope Colony; the 88th Regiment of Foot who were mainly based in Cape Town and the 1st Battalion of the 24th Regiment of Foot who were distributed in small units across Ciskei.

In addition to these troops, the General also had under his command; the 1st Battalion 13th Regiment of Foot in the Transvaal and the 80th Regiment with 5 companies of the 3rd Regiment in Natal, however, he was reluctant to deploy any of these troops to service in the Cape.

Disarming the Native Tribes

This phase of the war started with Governor Frere's plan to disarm the native nations, as a necessary prelude to the creation of a South African confederation following an invasion of Gcalekaland. The announcement of the Governor's plan to disarm "all Black peoples of the Cape" resulted in uproar amongst the Cape's many native soldiers and caused some of the Militia to desert. The Cape of Good Hope Prime Minister, Mr Molteno issued a furious protest to the British Government demanding that General Cunynghame be dismissed, that Governor Frere's racial disarmament policy be abandoned and that the Cape Colony be allowed to deploy its (predominantly Black) paramilitaries to re-establish order.

These demands were ignored by the British Government and General Cunynghame was released to unilaterally implement Governor Frere's policy.

As a convenient place to begin this task, the General chose to start with the clan of Chief Mapassa, who had deserted the Gcaleka cause and was now residing, with his people, on government land at Impetu which was only 40 miles from King Williams Town. The disarmament was planned to take place before Chief Mapassa and his people, who numbered about 4,500, were to be resettled in Gcalekaland in a region between the Qora and Shixini rivers.

Quite reasonably, Chief Mapassa was unhappy with this situation as he was being asked to relocate to an area within hostile Gcaleka without the means to defend himself. On hearing of the intention to disarm the Gcaleka at Impetu, a minor Chief Makinana (known as Mackinnon by the British) with about 60 warriors decided that he would not allow his men to be disarmed and fled to Draaibosch where he rejoined the Gcaleka army.

On 15th November, following discussions with Mr Brownlee, Chief Mapassa reluctantly surrendered his arms and subsequently, in early December, Chief Makinana also surrendered his arms to Inspector Chalmers.

Renewed Hostilities

Almost as soon as Commander Griffith began his return to Ibeka, the far from spent and defeated Gcaleka Army began to regroup and were soon recrossing the border, into their homeland, in large numbers intent on continuing the war.

Unaware of these events, on 1st December, soon after reaching Ibeka, Commander Griffith sent out a patrol consisting of 225 men under the command of Inspector Bourne, with instruction to patrol to the coast.

Battle of Umzitzani

On the morning of 2nd December Inspector Bourne, not expecting to encounter significant numbers of Gcaleka and being frustrated at being slowed down by his infantry, moved off with his mounted detachment, comprising 40 mounted FAMC and the Grahams Town Gun detachment, leaving instructions for the infantry to follow as quick as they could.

After a short time, Commandant Bayly of the Cape Town Artillery who was now leading the infantry, noticed that Inspector Bourne's small force was retreating in some disorder, being pursued by a large enemy force. Seeing that Inspector Bourne urgently required assistance, Commander Bayly, with his gun moved off to high ground near Holland's Shop where he began to lay down fire on the enemy force who were trying to cut off Inspector Bourne's retreat.

After the three sections of the patrol were finally reunited at Holland's Shop, they moved off to a more defensible position at the head of the small Umzitzani stream where they formed a laager, and from this hollow square began to lay down fire with their rifles and two artillery pieces.

In the late afternoon, just before darkness fell, the Gcaleka force made a last determined attack up the Umzitzani ravine, which was repulsed due to the constant fire put up by the patrol. The fighting continued up until 11 pm after which Commandant Bayly instructed the men to give three hearty cheers – it subsequently transpired that on hearing the cheers, the enemy assumed that the force had been reinforced so broke off and did not renew their attack.

Deployment of Imperial Forces

Following the Battle of Umzitzani, it was obvious that the Gcaleka army had not been defeated and were now congregating within Gcalekaland intent on continuing the war. With only limited forces at his disposal, Commander Griffith sent an urgent telegram to King Williams Town requesting reinforcements, however, Merriman had nothing to offer so proposed to Prime Minister Molteno that the colony should accept the offer of Imperial troops. Prime Minister Molteno refused to sanction the proposal and instead suggested that Gcalekaland be flooded with Fingo and Thembu warriors.

On 5th December, Griffith also wrote to General Cunynghame requesting 500 men and also suggesting that a force of marines, from *HMS Active*, should be landed at Mazeppa Bay.

At this stage, brushing aside the protests of Prime Minister Molteno, Governor Frere decided to step in and take control of the conduct of the war and on 6th December, he requested General Cunynghame to collect together the best force that he could muster and march across the river Kei and conquer Gcalekaland.

On 11th December, General Cunynghame appointed Colonel Glyn to the command of the Army of the Transkei, with the temporary rank of Brigadier General and replaced Commander Griffith as the colonial forces were also placed under his command.

Having already moved about half of the 88th Regiment (the Connaught Rangers) from Cape Town to King Williams Town, General Cunynghame now ordered the remainder of the regiment to the front line and moved men from the 1st Battalion of 24th Regiment to Ibeka, where the invasion force was to be assembled. Major Henry Pulleine of the 24th, who was an officer well respected by the colonials was given the task of raising a volunteer infantry unit, to operate under Imperial command, the resulting force was known as "Pulleine's Lambs". Another officer from the 24th, Lieutenant Frederick Carrington, was recalled from the Transvaal and asked to raise a volunteer cavalry unit which became the Frontier Light Horse.

On 10th December, *HMS Active* and *SS Florence*, left Cape Town with the remainder of the 88th Regiment on board and arrived at East London on 13th December, where at a meeting with Governor Frere and General Cunynghame, Commandant Sullivan agreed that a Naval Brigade of about 200 men together with about 50 men from the 88th would be landed at Mazeppa Bay. Due to bad weather, the Mazeppa Bay expedition was abandoned and on 13th December the full force was landed at East London.

The Naval Brigade, under the command of Commander H. T. Wright from *HMS Active*, consisted of 196 men (including 42 Marines), supported by six 12 pounder guns, two rocket tubes and a Gatling gun were accompanied by about 150 men from the 88th Regiment.

On 16th December, the force set out by train from East London by train and after arriving at the Kei Road began a march towards Draaibosch; on the road they received orders to send two guns and 100 men to Fort Cunynghame and after arriving at Draaibosch, where a detachment of the 88th was stationed, they continued on towards Komga. At Komga, where a detachment of the FAMP were stationed, the force left two guns and the Gatling gun, with 10 seamen to man them, to aid the defence of the town. Continuing their journey to the Kei river they marched past Pullen's Farm, where Lieutenant Edgar Anstey commanded a detachment of men from the 24th and Lieutenant Maurice Moore was in command of 50 men from the 88th, before passing through Toleni and arriving at Butterworth on 24th December.

Imperial Invasion of the Transkei

On 21st December, General Cunynghame left King Williams Town to be closer to the action and on Christmas day established his headquarters at Ibeka.

After Christmas, General Glyn considered that he had sufficient forces at his disposal so left Ibeka to begin the invasion of the Transkei. After crossing the river Kei, the General split his force into three columns and they advanced towards the coast and the border with Bomvanaland. The Imperial forces, consisting of large numbers of infantry, who campaigning in the intense midsummer heat were considerably less mobile than the colonial forces, had considerable difficulty in closing on the Gcaleka tribesmen who found it easy to slip past them.

After arriving at the river Bashee, General Glyn ordered a series of earthworks to be erected along the river bank, in a futile attempt to contain the enemy in Bomvanaland, however, these were easily circumvented by the Gcaleka warriors.

The Ngquika join the War

On 22nd December, Khiva, a most distinguished Gcaleka warrior, crossed the river Kei back into colonial territory, having evaded Imperial patrols and managed to reach the Ngquika reservation. After discussions with Sandile, himself a distinguished warrior and veteran of two previous wars and chief of the Ngquika clan of the Xhosa, Khiva managed to convince him to join the war with the Ngquika people.

Major Hans Moore – Victoria Cross No. 343

On 29th December 1877, Major Moore was proceeding from Komga, with a party of 32 men of the FAMP under the command of Sub-Inspector Mitchell, towards Draaibosch in an attempt to clear the road for the mail riders when he came across a force of about 100 Ngquika warriors who fired on his men. After dismounting and laying down a heavy fire, the FAMP patrol were able to drive the enemy off towards Kabousie.

After remounting and continuing their patrol, Major Moore spotted a larger force of Ngquika advancing on his position from Kabousie but after also spotting a force of about 40 men from the 88th regiment, commanded by Lieutenant Wood, who were escorting ammunition wagons from Draaibosch to Komga, he managed to join up with this force.

At about two miles from the ruins of Macdonald's canteen, the conjoined force was confronted by a body of 300 Ngquika warriors and once again Major Moore ordered the force to dismount and fire volleys into the advancing enemy, however, in the face of overwhelming numbers they were soon forced to remount and retire.

Seeing that the wounded Private Giese was unable to mount his horse and was at the mercy of the advancing enemy, Major Moore rode back alone into the enemy force and attempted to rescue the wounded Private. Major Moore continued his efforts until it was clear that Private Giese had been killed and then after killing two of the assailants and receiving an assegai wound to the arm he managed to extricate himself and rejoin his patrol which was now in full retreat.

For his efforts, Major Moore was later awarded the Victoria Cross.

It is thought that the action described above was one of the first involving the Ngquika, however, it was far from the last. By the end of the first week of the New Year, the tribe had destroyed most of the Fingo kraals in the area as well as the hotel at Draaibosch and a number of settlers farms.

The Ngquika force had managed to cut the supply line to the Transkei and were now besieging the forts on the colony side of the river Kei. The post at Mpetu, garrisoned by men from the 24th, under the command of Captain George Wardell became an overcrowded refuge for the districts displaced farmers. Captain Wardell sent urgent messages to the larger garrison at Komga, requesting artillery and supplies, however, Colonel Lambert who was himself cut off from King Williams Town, decided instead that Mpetu should be evacuated and the forces should be consolidated at Komga.

Murder of Colonial Officials

In early January 1878, three colonial officials; Mr R. G. Tainton, his brother J. H. Tainton and W. C. Brown, who were on a mission for the Colonial Government, were attacked by a small force of Gcaleka warriors near Berlin, about 12 miles from King Williams Town. Escorted by only a few native members of the FAMP, the officials tried to negotiate with the warriors, stating that they were on a peaceful mission and intended them no harm. Unfortunately, when their escort abandoned them, they had to resort to the use of arms but were overwhelmed and all three men were killed.

Some of the attackers were subsequently captured and hung, however, combined with the abandonment of the Kei Valley forts, the murder of the officials caused widespread panic on the frontier and considerable blame was heaped upon Governor Frere and General Cunynghame for the poor conduct of the war by the Imperial forces. Prime Minister Molteno, who had been most vociferous in his condemnation, transferred to King Williams Town with the intention of trying to oust the Governor.

Continued Operations in the Transkei

As it had become obvious that General Glyn's efforts to contain the Xhosa forces in Bomvanaland were ineffective and that a powerful enemy force was concentrating on the colony side of the river Kei, on 10th January 1878, General Cunynghame ordered General Glyn to return with his force to Ibeka.

On the morning of 13th January, after receiving intelligence that the Gcaleka were planning an attack against his right column, the Quintana column under the command of Major Owen, General Glyn ordered a forced march in order to unite his force with that of Major Owen who were camped at Nyumaxa. By mid afternoon, the Xhosa did attack the united force, however, largely due to the skilful deployment of the Fingo warriors by Captain Veldman Bikitsha the encounter was short lived and the Xhosa force withdrew at sunset.

After establishing his men at the camp in Ibeka, General Glyn decided to set up a forward base on high ground near Quintana, within easy striking distance of the Kei Valley under the command of Captain Russell Upcher.

Battle of Quintana

The force commanded by Captain Upcher, at Quintana (also known as Centane or Kentani), consisted of three companies of the 24th Regiment, 50 men of Carrington's Light Horse, 25 men of the Naval Brigade with a 24 pounder rocket tube, one troop of the FAMP, 11 men of the Police Artillery with a 9 pounder gun, 9 men of the Cape Town Artillery with a 7 pounder gun and 200 Fingos under the command of Allan Maclean.

On arrival at his new post, Captain Upcher lost no time in getting his men to erect suitable defences which involved the construction of strong earthworks, surrounded by trenches with rifle pits and artillery emplacements. It was just as well that Captain Upcher had taken precautions to defend his camp, as on the morning of 7th February, he was roused by his Fingo scouts with news that a large body of Xhosa warriors was advancing towards his position.

On reaching sight of the well defended camp, occupied by soldiers, the Xhosa force hesitated and then stopped to consider the situation. Captain Upcher ordered Captain Rainsforth with a detachment of infantry and Captain Carrington with a troop of his Frontier Light Horse to leave the defences and feign an attack with the intention of luring the Xhosa army into an attack.

After advancing a short distance, the small force fired off a few volleys before falling back to the camp. The ruse worked and the 3,000 Xhosa warriors immediately set off in pursuit, probably thinking that the small attack force were the only defenders as by this time Captain Upcher had his remaining men concealed in their trenches.

Once they were in range the British artillery opened fire causing many casualties, however, the Xhosa continued their attack without faltering, it was only when Captain Upcher's men assailed them with volley after volley of rifle fire from their trenches that the attack began to waver.

After two attempts to continue the advance, the Xhosa columns broke and began to retreat, closely followed by Captain Carrington and his cavalry who turned the retreat into full flight.

The Imperial casualties were slight with three Fingo killed and four wounded, Carrington's Horse had two wounded and one member of the FAMP was also wounded. On the other hand the Gcaleka lost about 300 killed with large numbers wounded.

As it was not yet 8 o'clock, when the battle ended, Captain Upcher ordered his men to be served their breakfast, they had only just started their meal when a new large force of Xhosa warriors were seen to be congregating on a ridge to the front of the camp.

Captain Francis Grenfell, one of General Cunynghame's aides, who was eager to repeat the ruse that had drawn the Gcaleka on to the waiting guns, persuade Captain Upcher to give him half a company of infantry and a troop of the FAMP for this purpose.

Unfortunately, this new band of warriors were Ngquika not Gcaleka, who deployed different tactics and were expert at isolating and destroying detached groups of men, and were soon stealthily beginning to surround Captain Grenfell's men. Now in great difficulties, Captain Grenfell and his men had to be extracted from this perilous position by Captain Carrington and his men who had just returned to camp after chasing down the retreating Gcaleka warriors.

With the unexpected arrival of reinforcements from Ibeka, the Ngquika warriors decided to retire and the battle was finally over.

Political Struggle

Since the start of the war, there had been a constant battle between Governor Frere and the Prime Minister of the Cape Colony Mr Molteno regarding the control and conduct of the war. With both men now at King Williams Town, face to face discussions now became very acrimonious.

Events reached a climax in January 1878, when Governor Frere asked Molteno to sign treasury warrants to pay for the landing of five companies of the 90th Light Infantry, the reinforcements

Figure 52. Governor Sir Henry Bartle Frere

Figure 53. Prime Minister Sir John Charles Molteno

he had applied for in defiance of Molteno's veto. When the Prime Minister refused to sign the warrants, Governor Frere appealed to the Colonial Office to formally dissolve the Cape of Good Hope government.

The Cape government were duly dismissed and with the Cape Colony now under his control Governor Frere appointed John Gordon Sprigg as the new Prime Minister, who took up his role on 6th February 1878.

Despite recent improvements in the conduct of the war and the arrival of much needed reinforcements in the form of men from the 90th Light Infantry and a large body of volunteer horse who arrived from Kimberley, a change in the command of the army was now about to take place.

Towards the end of February Lieutenant-General Cunynghame received a letter from the War Office at Whitehall, informing him of his promotion to the rank of full General. With this new rank, Cunynghame was too senior for his current command and was ordered to return to London upon the arrival of his replacement, Lieutenant-General Frederick Thesiger[19].

As General Thesiger was already approaching Cape Town, when General Cunynghame received his letter of promotion, the change of command took place on 4th March 1878 when he arrived at King Williams Town.

The Guerrilla War

After their severe defeat at the Battle of Quintana, the Gcaleka army were a spent force and would take no further part in the war, chief Kreli would formally surrender in June. Chief Sandile's Ngquika army, however, were relatively unscathed and had moved into the Amatola mountains to continue the war with a guerrilla campaign, which had served them well during previous wars.

On 9th March, having learned that the Ngquika force had evaded the colonial patrols and were now occupying their former strongholds in the Amatola mountains, General Thesiger gave command of the Amatola sector to Colonel Evelyn Wood VC, one of the special service officers who had accompanied him to South Africa. With the bulk of the army created by General Cunynghame still policing Gcalekaland, Colonel Wood only had some colonial commandos and the 2nd Battalion of the 24th Regiment (who were just arriving at East London) at his disposal.

Colonel Wood established his headquarters at Keiskammahoek and while waiting for the commando units of John Frost, Friedrich Schermbrucker and Edward Brabant, together with a contingent of Fingos from the Transkei to arrive, he formulated his plan for dealing with the Ngquika forces.

The bulk of the Ngquika warriors were reported to be hiding in the bush of a boulder strewn canyon known as the Buffalo Poort; Colonel Wood's plan was to ascend the highland plateau and converge on the canyon from three directions and push the enemy down to the plain below where a line of infantry would be waiting.

This first attack by Colonel Wood's men, which took place in heavy rain and mist, failed miserably as after being forced down the canyon the Ngquika warriors, used to this type of warfare, managed to easily slip past the waiting line of infantry and moving westward occupied another wilderness known as the Lotutu Bush.

General Thesiger now moved up five companies of men from the 90th Regiment, from Fort Beaumont, to place a cordon around the Lotutu Bush, however, when Colonel Wood moved in for his second offensive the Ngquika managed to break through the cordon under the cover of darkness and returned to their previous positions in the Buffalo Poort.

After four further offensives which met with similar lack of success, General Thesiger finally listened to the advice of his colonial commanders and adopted the tactics that they had been espousing for some weeks. The eastern part of the Amathole region was split into 11 military districts each of which contained a mounted garrison. When a party of Ngquika entered one district they were pursued by the mounted garrison until they passed into an adjoining district, at which time that districts garrison took over the chase. These tactics allowed for an uninterrupted pursuit and harassment by pursuers who always had fresh mounts and were never far from their supply bases.

Earthworks, manned by infantry, were also erected at all of the, by now well known, exits from the Buffalo Poort.

These changes in tactics slowly began to turn the campaign in General Thesiger's favour and coupled with the hardships of the winter months brought the Xhosa warriors to their knees and when chief Sandile was killed on 29th May, after a chance encounter in the Denge forest with a Fingo patrol led by Captain J. Lonsdale, the end of the war was in sight.

Chief Sandile's sons surrendered in July and with the pacification of Gcalekaland completed in August, the war was finally over

19 General Thesiger would become the 2nd Baron of Chelmsford upon the death of his father in October 1878.

21

AFGHAN WAR – 2ND (1878–80)

As part of what historians call the "Great Game", which was a power struggle (for control of central Asia) between the Russian and British empires between 1830 and 1895, Afghanistan was a source of contention between the two empires. Britain was seeking to make Afghanistan a British protectorate to act as a buffer state between Russia and British India while Russia proposed that Afghanistan should remain as a neutral independent state.

The Anglo-Afghan war of 1878 to 1880 was the second of three wars fought for control of the country. Following the end of the inconclusive first war which took place between 1839 and 1842 Britain had worked on fostering friendly relations with the Emir Amir Dost Mohammad who was ousted during the war but was reinstalled in 1843.

Following the death of Amir Dost Mohammad on 9th June 1863, he was succeeded by his son Shir Ali Khan but during 1866 he was ousted by his brother Mohammad Afzal Khan, however, after a period of internecine warfare Shir Ali Khan regained his position as Emir on 7th October 1868 which he held until his death on 21st February 1879.

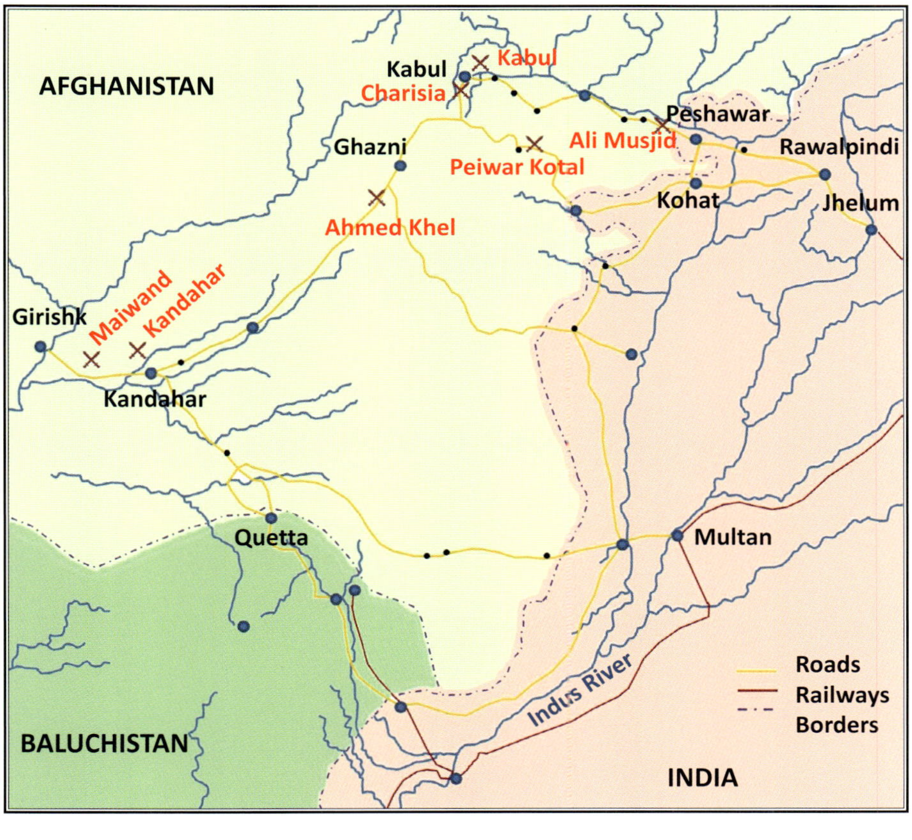

Figure 54. Afghanistan

Build-up to War

Following Russia's declaration of war against Turkey on 24th April 1877, tensions between Russia and Britain reached new heights and it was thought that war between the two empires was inevitable.

As a result of British refusal to support him during the war with his brother, Shir Ali Khan's relations with Britain were considerably less friendly than those of his father, however, he wished to maintain a strict neutrality in the deteriorating situation between Britain and Russia.

In spite of his wish to remain neutral, Shir Ali Khan had to bend to Russian pressure and allow them to establish a diplomatic Mission in Kabul, which was opened on 22nd July 1878. Britain was unhappy about this turn of events as they had been making requests for some years to establish a Mission which had been consistently denied. Believing that the granting of a Mission to Russia was tantamount to open hostility, on 14th August 1878 the British government in India sent a letter to Shir Ali Khan demanding permission to establish their own Mission in Kabul.

Before he received a reply to his letter, Lord Lytton the Viceroy of India despatched a Mission from Peshawar in September 1878, under the command of Sir Neville Chamberlain, which was accompanied by a strong military escort. On 21st September, an advanced party of the Mission, under the command of Major Cavagnari[20] arrived at Ali Masjid in the Khyber Pass and formally demanded passage to Kabul.

When this was refused by the Afghan officials, the Mission withdrew and returned to Peshawar; on hearing of the refusal, the government in India issued an ultimatum to the Emir and when the period of grace expired on 20th November, without any reply, war against Afghanistan was declared on the following day.

Preparations for War

Almost as soon as the government in India became aware of the Russian Mission in Kabul, in addition to making demands of the Afghan government for a British Mission they began the initial preparations for a war with Afghanistan. At the beginning of August, Sir Frederick Haines the Commander in Chief of troops in India was asked for his estimate of requirements for a campaign in Afghanistan to occupy the Kurram Valley and Kandahar. Sir Frederick provided his initial estimates on 10th August which involved: a Kurram Valley field force of just over 4,000 men; for Kandahar it was suggested that the garrison at Quetta which currently stood at 1,800 men should be strengthened to 5,000; a Kandahar column composed of two divisions should be raised with a total of almost 13,000 men and that the main column should be augmented with a reserve division comprising just over 6,000 men.

In addition to the estimate of forces required, Sir Frederick also made recommendations regarding preparations for the communications and supply chain to support the invasion.

On 23rd September, the day after he received news of the rebuff to Sir Neville Chamberlain, Lord Lytton gave his approval for the strength of the proposed Kurram Valley Field Force, he also sanctioned the despatch to Quetta of the suggested reinforcements and stated that he required the 1st Division of the Kandahar Column to be assembled and held in readiness to march by 1st November. Orders to implement these requirements were issued on the following day.

On 2nd October the Indian Government sanctioned an increase in the strength of the native regiments stationed to the north of the Narbudda river, each regiment would receive an additional 96 cavalry and an additional 200 infantry.

The government directed the Commander in Chief to prepare and assemble a field force on 4th October and ten days later on 14th October Sir Frederick, issued orders giving details for the staff and troops as follows: A column was to be assembled in the Kurram Valley under the command of Major-General F. S. Roberts VC; A division was to be assembled at Multan under the command of Lieutenant-General D. M. Stewart and Major-General M. A. S. Biddulph was to assume command of the forces at Quetta.

On 7th October, after Emir Shir Ali Khan had reinforced the Ali Masjid fortress at the head of the Khyber pass and along his border with Peshawar in British India, the Indian Government decided that troops allocated to the Kurram Field Force should be diverted to strengthen the Peshawar garrison. This change in the disposition of troops resulted in some changes to the intended invasion plans and Lord Lytton requested his Commander-in-Chief to formulate plans to assemble a force at Peshawar to advance on Kabul via the Khyber pass and Jalalabad.

On the same day Sir Frederick submitted the following proposals: a 1st Division would advance through the Khyber, capture Ali Masjid and eventually occupy Jalalabad; a 2nd Division in support of the 1st Division would be located in the Peshawar Valley; a 3rd Division, the Kurram Column would occupy the Kurram Valley and threaten Kabul and a 4th Division, the Rawalpindi Division would be held in reserve to support the other three divisions.

20 Sir Pierre Louis Napoleon Cavagnari

These proposals were not acted upon immediately, however, by 12th October the Peshawar garrison had been brought up to a strength of between 5,000 to 6,000; a Frontier Force moveable column under the command of Lieutenant-Colonel Jenkins was formed and a reserve division of 5,000 men was established at Hasan Abdal.

On 21st October, Sir Frederick submitted his proposals for the command and staffing of the force to be assembled at Peshawar and Hasan Abdal, which with some minor modifications was accepted by the Indian Government on 1st November.

The Peshawar Valley field force would be under the overall command of Lieutenant-General Sir Sam Browne VC and was comprised of: three infantry brigades, commanded by Brigadier-General H. T. Macpherson VC, Colonel J. A. Tytler VC, Colonel F. E. Appleyard and a reserve brigade commanded by Colonel; a cavalry brigade commanded by Colonel C. J. S. Gough VC; Artillery, commanded by Colonel W. J. Williams; Engineers, commanded by Colonel F. R. Maunsell; Medical department commanded by Surgeon-Major J. Gibbons and a Commissariat department commanded by Lieutenant-Colonel J. V. Hunt.

The Hasan Abdal Reserve force would be under the command of Major-General R. O. Bright, with an infantry brigade commanded by Brigadier-General J. Doran and a cavalry brigade commanded by Brigadier-General J. E. Michell supported by Artillery.

Having been ordered to have his forces ready to cross the border into Afghanistan on 21st November, the date after which the ultimatum would expire, the Commander in Chief issued the General Order detailing the final disposition of troops on 19th November 1878, which outlined the forces as follows: the Kurram Valley Column commanded by Major-General F. S. Roberts VC would have 116 officers, 6,549 men and 18 guns; the Multan Division (which would become the 1st Division of the Kandahar Column) commanded by Lieutenant-General D. M. Stewart would have 187 officers, 7,117 men and 60 guns; the Quetta Reinforcement (which would become the 2nd Division of the Kandahar Column) commanded by Major-General M. A. S. Biddulph would have 78 officers, 5,482 men and 18 guns; the Peshawar Valley Field Force commanded by Lieutenant-General Sir Sam Browne VC would have 325 officers, 15,854 men and 48 guns. This deployment consisted of nearly 36,000 officers and men with 144 guns.

The following forces were also subsequently sanctioned: on 27th November, the Kandahar Column, Reserve Division with 53 officers, 3,817 men and 24 guns and in December the Punjab Chiefs Contingent with 7 officers, 4,471 men and 13 guns was also sanctioned.

It was estimated that the Emir had a regular army of less than 20,000 men in the Kabul province and about 6,000 in Kandahar; a further 25,000 were located in the Herat and Turkestan provinces. He also had at his disposal over 300 artillery pieces, split between field guns and mountain guns, his troops were mainly armed with Enfield rifles and Tower muskets with only about 5,000 men (mainly in Kabul) armed with the more modern English Snider rifles. In addition to his regular army the Emir also had about 100,000 armed men forming an irregular army in the Kabul province.

During the lull between the repulse of the Mission and the declaration of war, Major Cavagnari spent his time with the Afridi and Shinwari tribes who occupied the Khyber and surrounding area and for a modest fee secured a right of free passage through their areas for the British troops. The tribesmen were also happy to provide intelligence regarding the Emir's troop movements and reinforcements.

The Afghan position at Ali Masjid was the subject of two recognisances, on 23rd October and on 16th November by General Browne. It was concluded that the Fort, with a garrison of 3,700 men, commanded a strong position at a point where the pass was very narrow, would cause great difficulties to a frontal attack up the defile. However, the position suffered from one major weakness in that it was surrounded by several higher peaks on the Rhotas ridge; General Browne's plan was to gain these heights, in order to fire down on the fort with his artillery and rifles.

Phase I of the War

Following the expiry of the Viceroy's ultimatum on 20th November, without any reply to the British demands, the government in India issued a declaration of war and ordered General Browne VC and the Peshawar Valley Field Force to begin the invasion of Afghanistan.

Peshawar Valley Field Force Operations

At 5:20 in the evening of 20th November 1878, the 2nd Infantry Brigade of the 1st Division, under the command of Brigadier-General J. A. Tytler VC, marched from their camp at Jamrud, crossed the border and commenced the campaign.

Early in the afternoon of 21st November, with his men exhausted after having marched in the heat of the day, General Tytler halted to await the arrival of his supplies but sent Colonel Jenkins with a party of Guides and the 1st Sikhs towards their objective of Kata Kushtia, a village which overlooked the Khyber

Pass. Soon after their arrival at the village in late afternoon, Colonel Jenkins observed a party of about 50 enemy cavalry making their way up the pass, and to demonstrate that their retreat was now cut off, he ordered his men to fire on the party. Despite being at a range of 500 yards, several of the enemy cavalry were hit and dismounted and the remainder rode off, some back towards Ali Masjid and others back up the Khyber pass. As darkness began to fall a larger body of cavalry with a small unit of infantry were seen to be coming from the direction of Ali Masjid, down the pass with the retreat from the fort apparently underway.

In the afternoon of 21st November, just over 8 hours since the departure of the 2nd Brigade, Brigadier-General H. T. Macpherson VC set out with the 1st Brigade from Jamrud, and after reaching the foot of the Tabai spur, leading to the Rhotas ridge he despatched a small force of about 250 men, under the command of Major Gordon to occupy the Tabai ridge. The General pushed on with the remainder of his force and gained the Sapri plateau from where he could mount an attack on the enemy defences on the Rhotas peak the next day.

On the morning of 21st November, Lieutenant-General Sir Sam Browne VC left the camp at Jamrud with the main column of the 1st Division. An advance party of signallers and engineers, under the command of Major H. P. Pearson, was sent ahead to the mouth of the Khyber pass where they set about improving the road and establishing a heliographic post on the Surkhai hill. The advanced guard continued along the Shadi Bagiar road into the Khyber pass until they reached Mackeson's Bridge where they moved off to the high ground and occupied the Shahgai ridge.

Having occupied the heights, the 1st and 2nd brigades completed their turning movements and were positioned on both of the enemy flanks. With the troops in position an artillery duel with the enemy forces at the Ali Masjid fort, was commenced, which continued for some time into the night.

At daybreak on 23rd November, the artillery fire was resumed by the 3rd Brigade, however, when no return fire ensued, the brigade advanced and found that the fort and entrenchments had been abandoned by the enemy. As many of their supplies were still in place and 24 artillery pieces were captured, it appears that the position was evacuated with much haste during the night. The majority of the force had escaped via the Bazar valley where they were harried by the Afridi tribesmen, however, some of the men tried to escape down the Khyber road where about 300 were captured by Colonel Jenkins and men of the 2nd Brigade.

Having successfully captured the fort at Ali Masjid and having cleared the enemy from the surrounding area, General Browne moved his forces to Dakka, after leaving a small garrison at the fort, where his men were able to rest for three weeks while all available transport was sent to Peshawar for much needed supplies.

During the halt, work continued on improving the roads and efforts were made by the cavalry to stem the looting in the Khyber pass being carried out by the Zakha Khel Afridis by establishing posts and escorting convoys.

On 30th November a messenger from Kabul entered the camp bearing a letter from the Emir which, although it declared that the Emir was willing to receive a Mission, fell far short of meeting the requirements outlined in the Governor's ultimatum.

At the beginning of December, with the aid of men from the Kuki Khel Afridis, a punitive raid was carried out against the Zakha Khel Afridis who were still raiding the British supply convoys. The 1st Brigade also moved off to Basawal in the search of supplies as these were becoming scarce in Dakka.

By the end of the first week of December, the reserve division under the command of General Maude had moved forward from Hasan Abdal and reached Peshawar which resulted in a redistribution of Brigade commands: a new Brigade, was formed under the command of Colonel Jenkins; the 4th Brigade was amalgamated with the 3rd Brigade under the command of Brigadier-General Appleyard would remain at Ali Masjid and Shahgai and now operate as part of General Maude's division; Brigadier-General W. B. Browne, who had commanded the 4th Brigade was ordered to Peshawar to await further orders.

On 10th December, General Sir Sam Browne VC, received approval from the Indian Government to continue his advance from Dakka to Jalalabad and after leaving General Tytler VC in command at Dakka, he set off with his 1st Division on 17th December and after having been joined by the 1st and 2nd Brigades arrived at Jalalabad on 20th December.

In order to cut off the enemy retreat via the Sissobi Pass, an expedition to the Bazar Valley was organised: under the overall command of Lieutenant-General Maude the expedition was composed of the 2nd Division of the Peshawar Field Force currently at Jamrud together with the 2nd Brigade of the 1st Division at Dakka, commanded by Brigadier Tytler VC. Both columns set out on 19th December and effected a junction at the village of Walai in the Bazar Valley on 21st December. On their way to the Bazar Valley neither force had encountered any opposition, however, when the people of the valley refused to submit to British command two villages and some towers were destroyed.

On the next morning it was decided that the forces would retire and General Maude's column managed to return to Ali Masjid without incident. General Tytler's Brigade, however, were attacked by tribesmen in the Sissobi Pass and suffered minor losses with one man killed and seven wounded, one of whom would later die from his wounds.

After their arrival at Jalalabad, General Browne received confirmation of the news that Emir Shir Ali had fled Kabul bound for Afghan Turkistan on 13th December, accompanied by the remaining members of the Russian Mission. It was reported that the Emir had lost all authority in Kabul and with his army weakened by desertions Sardar Yakub Khan had assumed command, however, the country between Jalalabad and Kabul was now in a state of anarchy.

Further news of the situation in Kabul reached the British camp in early January 1879; although things were quiet it was reported that one cavalry regiment had deserted en mass but the intention of Yakub Khan to continue the war was made clear when he issued orders for the Ghilzai tribal chiefs, together with their men to assemble at Jagdalak following which the chiefs were to proceed to Kabul for further orders. Fortunately, the Ghilzai ignored these orders and during January many of the chiefs actually submitted to the British command.

Due to bad weather, only limited operations were carried out during January; some minor raids were carried out against the Baizai clan of the Mohmand tribe in retaliation for their attacks on tribes friendly to the British forces.

On 24th January a more significant operation, a second expedition to the Bazar Valley, commenced. Lieutenant-General Maude set out with a column from Jamrud on 24th January; Brigadier-General Appleyard set out from Ali Masjid and on the same day Brigadier-General Tytler started from Basawal and by 27th January the three columns had joined forces and were camped on the plain at the Bazar Valley. With limited knowledge of the land ahead, General Maude ordered a reconnaissance in strength to the Bukar Pass and onwards towards the Bara Valley.

After reaching Halwai, the force came under heavy fire from Afridi tribesmen, however, having obtained a good idea of the approaches to the pass, the force returned to the British camp. On the following day, a detachment commanded by Colonel G. H. Thompson, returned to Halwai where they blew up the towers, once again the British force was attacked by the Afridi, this time with greater numbers, however, having completed their task the detachment returned to the British camp relatively unscathed.

General Maude now telegraphed army headquarters for further instructions and while he was waiting for a reply he received a message recalling the Basawal column as an attack on Jalalabad and Dakka was expected. He also received the news that the Zakha Khel clan of the Bara Valley had offered their submission and friendship to the British.

Lieutenant Reginald Hart – Victoria Cross No. 345

On 31st January 1879, while operating on convoy duty in the valley, Lieutenant Hart and the convoy was attacked by a force of unknown strength who mounted an assault against both flanks and also to their front from a river bed.

When a Sowar of the 13th Bengal Lancers was wounded by the force in the river bed, Lieutenant Hart ran across open ground in the face of heavy enemy fire to rescue him and after driving off some of the enemy he managed to bring the Sowar to safety, aided by some of the soldiers who had accompanied him.

For this selfless deed, Lieutenant Hart was later awarded the Victoria Cross.

On 3rd February, General Maude decided to retire from the Bazar valley and by the following day his forces were back in their previous locations at Jamrud, Ali Masjid and Basawal respectively.

At the end of January, intelligence was received at Jalalabad regarding the death of Emir Ali Khan at Mazar-i-Sharif, this was somewhat premature as he actually died on 21st February. General Browne also received a message from Peshawar that a large force of Mohmands and Utman Khels were assembling, intent on mounting an attack on Dakka or Jalalabad on 7th February, to be co-ordinated with an attack from forces arriving from Kabul.

In response to this possible attack, the General sent out reconnaissance parties in the direction of Gandamak and Kunar, he also improved his defences which included making repairs to the old British fort at Jalalabad which was renamed Fort Sale.

Probably as a result of the improvements to the defences, the planned enemy attack against Dakka or Jalalabad did not materialise, however, this did not stop the enemy forces from carrying out attacks against tribes in the area who were on friendly terms with the British. During February several operations were mounted to prevent these attacks.

On 24th February, Sir Frederick Haines the Commander in Chief of forces in India arrived at Jamrud from Peshawar on a tour of inspection during which he also visited Ali Masjid and Jalalabad before returning to Peshawar on 3rd March.

While at Jalalabad, Sir Frederick received the first of what would be several messages from Yakub Khan which confirmed the death of his father Emir Ali Khan and outlined his desire for a peace with the British. A subsequent letter advised that in line with the wishes of his father and the will of the people, he was now the Emir of Afghanistan and wished to negotiate a peace which would include allowing the British to establish a Mission in Kabul. He also agreed to meet with Major Cavagnari at Kabul to discuss matters further.

Despite the initial overtures towards peace, following a meeting with his general officers at Peshawar on 7th March, Sir Frederick issued orders to his commanders in Afghanistan to advance to more forward positions, in readiness for an assault on Kabul should this prove to be necessary.

Captain Edward Leach – Victoria Cross No. 346

Having just completed a survey of the country towards Mazina and Mahrez, on 15th March, Captain Leach, the Assistant Superintendent of Surveys, set out again from Barikao on a further survey towards Zarbacha. The survey party was escorted by 50 men from the Guides Cavalry, commanded by Lieutenant W. R. P. Hamilton and 100 men of the 45th Sikh Infantry commanded by Lieutenant F. M. Barclay.

On 17th March, the survey party accompanied by Lieutenant Hamilton with 40 of his Cavalry and Lieutenant Barclay with 40 of his Sikhs left their encampment at Zarbacha, heading for the village of Chilgazai where the headman Umra Khan was to guide them to a hill from where they could survey a large extent of the Safed Koh spurs.

After approaching to within half a mile of the summit of the hill, the cavalry were left behind, left in the charge of Jemandar Muhammad Sharif who had instructions to hold the position in the case of an attack but to send the horses to cover down a nearby ravine.

As they reached the crest of the hill, the survey party was fired upon by tribesmen in a group of villages, known as Maidanak, in the valley below and a number of armed Shinwari villagers were seen to be advancing on their position; Umra Khan went down to try and reassure the villagers, however, met with little success.

When a steady fire was rained down on the survey party they began to retreat towards the position of their cavalry but were rushed by a party of about fifty men. During the exchange of fire, Lieutenant Barclay was wounded in the shoulder by a musket ball and had to be carried by four of the men. The party continued their retreat but when they were in danger of being surrounded, Captain Leach ordered the men of the escort to fix bayonets and led a charge into the tribesmen, driving them back. After some determined hand to hand fighting, during which Captain Leach received a knife wound to his left arm and one of the Sikhs was killed, Captain Leach managed to lead the party back to the cavalry.

With the cavalry acting as a rearguard the survey party managed to reach the plain and without further trouble returned to their camp at Zarbacha.

For his part in the action, Captain Leach was later awarded the Victoria Cross. Unfortunately, the bullet which entered Lieutenant Barclay's shoulder also penetrated his lung and he died from his wounds at Landi Kotal on 1st April 1879.

To inflict punishment on the Shinwari tribe for this unprovoked attack, Brigadier-General Tytler VC was despatched with a force of 788 men, leaving Barikao after midnight on 21st March the force reached Maidanak at daybreak, where they were reinforced by a detachment of 434 men, under the command of Lieutenant-Colonel Ball-Acton who had been sent from Basawal.

Not wanting to instigate open hostilities with the Shinwari tribe, Major E. R. Conolly, the political officer who accompanied the force, was under instruction to obtain reparation without further bloodshed. The column penetrated the valley as far as Girdai where several village towers were destroyed in addition to those destroyed at Maidanak; fines were also levied against the villages and when the survey of the district was complete the force withdrew without encountering any opposition.

Three days earlier another outrage had occurred at Deh-Sarakh when a foraging party had been fired upon and when the party withdrew to Pesh Bolak, they were pursued by a force of between 300–400 Afridi tribesmen. On his return journey, Brigadier-General Tytler was ordered by General Sir Sam Browne to punish this new outrage.

In the early hours of 24th March, Brigadier-General Tytler, led a force of 150 cavalry and 500 infantry, supported by two guns, in an operation against Deh-Sarakh, following the surrender at Maidanak no opposition was expected. After the force reached the high ground at Pesh Bolak, General Tytler and the cavalry pressed on towards the village of Mausam, the chief instigator of the raid, and after noting three further villages situated about a mile away at the bottom of a slope, sent out a detachment of 11th Bengal Lancers under the command of Lieutenant H. R. Heath to cut off the enemy retreat to the rear of these villages.

Following the start of this manoeuvre, the British forces received fire from Mausam and the villages to the rear so a portion of the cavalry were dismounted and returned fire until the arrival of the infantry and artillery. When the guns had been unlimbered and commenced their fire against Mausam, at a range of 750 yards, a detachment of 13th Bengal Lancers, under the command of Captain D. Hamilton Thompson was sent to the west of Mausam.

Once the artillery fire began to take effect and in the face of the advancing British infantry the occupants of the fort at Mausam began to abandon their positions, initially unobserved by the retreating enemy Captain Thompson and his cavalry managed to approach and halt the retreat and mounted a charge into their midst causing many casualties.

The village of Mausam was now occupied, the towers blown up and the village was then set on fire, after abandoning Mausam the British forces moved to the village of Darwazai where they also destroyed the towers and set fire to the village. Having completed their destruction, the British force now began to slowly retire back towards Pesh Bolak but were followed by large numbers of the enemy. The British column halted frequently to allow the artillery to fire on the enemy masses, this continued until the column reached the walls of Pesh Bolak where after a time the enemy dispersed.

During this action, the enemy losses were considerable with over 160 men buried by the British on the following day, British casualties were slight with 2 killed and 12 wounded.

The operations outlined above were followed by more extensive operations a few days later; on 31st March General Browne received intelligence that Asmatullah Khan, the principal chief of the Ghilzai tribe had descended to the Kats Laghman, plains on the north bank of the Kabul river, with 1,500 of his followers and was inciting local tribes to take action against the British. In what appeared to be a co-ordinated action, men of the Khugiani tribe were also assembling on the Kabul road near to Futtehabad.

To counter these threats, General Browne immediately despatched two columns; Brigadier-General Macpherson was directed against the Ghilzai at Kats Laghman while Brigadier-General C. S. Gough moved against the Khugiani at Futtehabad.

General Macpherson split his force, sending a small detachment, under the command of Major Wood, comprising a squadron of 10th Hussars with a squadron of the 11th Bengal Lancers, to cross the Kabul river to the east of Jalalabad to mount a surprise attack on the Afghans at Kats Laghman while with the main element of his force he marched west along the south bank of the river to cut off a retreat to the south by the Afghan forces.

When the Cavalry reached the ford across the Kabul river, which was via a mid stream island (the river was almost a mile wide at this point) it was night but fairly light due to a nearly new moon. Leading the way, the squadron of 11th Lancers managed to cross the river safely, however, when crossing the second part of the ford, the squadron of 10th Hussars lost the path and floundered in fast flowing water which was about 6 feet deep. The bulk of the squadron was swept down river and subsequently it was discovered that one officer, one Farrier, three Sergeants and 42 men had been drowned.

When news of the disaster that had befallen the 10th Hussars reached the camp at Jalalabad, in addition to sending a strong detachment to render assistance to the missing men, another troop of Bengal Cavalry was sent to join up with the Force of Major Wood in order to help them complete their mission.

General Macpherson, with his column of infantry left Jalalabad, as planned on the morning of 31st March following the south bank of the Kabul river, however, due to severe flooding progress was slow and it was not until 2nd April that the force joined up with their cavalry who by now had discovered that Asmatullah Khan and his force of Ghilzai had already left the area.

At 1 o'clock in the morning of 2nd April Brigadier-General Gough left Jalalabad with his force: two squadrons of the 10th Hussars, two squadrons of Guides Cavalry, 400 men of 17th Regiment, 300 men of 27th Bengal Native Infantry, 300 men of 45th Bengal Infantry supported by 4 guns of the Royal Horse Artillery: and after arriving near Futtehabad before first light set up camp and sent out cavalry patrols. In the early afternoon, the patrols sent out towards Gandamak reported that large bodies of armed men were advancing on the camp from the direction of Khoja Khel.

While General Gough called his men to arms, Major W. Battye, with the Guides Cavalry were directed to advance along the Gandamak road and Colonel C. McPherson, with two troops of cavalry and 300 infantry was ordered to remain behind and protect the camp.

Battle of Futtehabad

General Gough, with three troops of Hussars and the four guns of the Royal Horse Artillery, quickly set off in pursuit of Major Battye and the Guides Cavalry while the 700 men of the infantry were ordered to advance as quickly as possible.

The British advance party soon came across a force of about 5,000 Khugiani tribesmen who occupied a well defended ridge near the village of Khoja.

Undeterred by the large enemy force that he faced, General Gough advanced with his small force of cavalry and Royal Horse Artillery to within 1,200 yards of the enemy position, from where the artillery began to lay down a heavy fire.

In response the enemy sent out skirmishers, however, just as his infantry arrived on the field and began to attack the enemy right flank, the General ordered his mounted troops and guns to retire and as expected were pursued by large numbers of Khugiani troops who had left their fortified positions.

As his infantry began to fire on the emerging Afghans, the General ordered his cavalry to about turn and charge the enemy.

Lieutenant Walter Hamilton – Victoria Cross No. 347

During the charge, Major Battye the Commanding Officer of the Guides Cavalry, who had previously been wounded in the arm, received a mortal wound to the chest. As the only surviving officer of his unit Lieutenant Hamilton assumed command of the Guides and after cheering them on to avenge the death of their Major continued to lead them in the charge.

During the pursuit of the retreating Afghans, Lieutenant Hamilton noticed that one of his men Sowar Dowlut Ram had been dismounted and become entangled with his horse and was

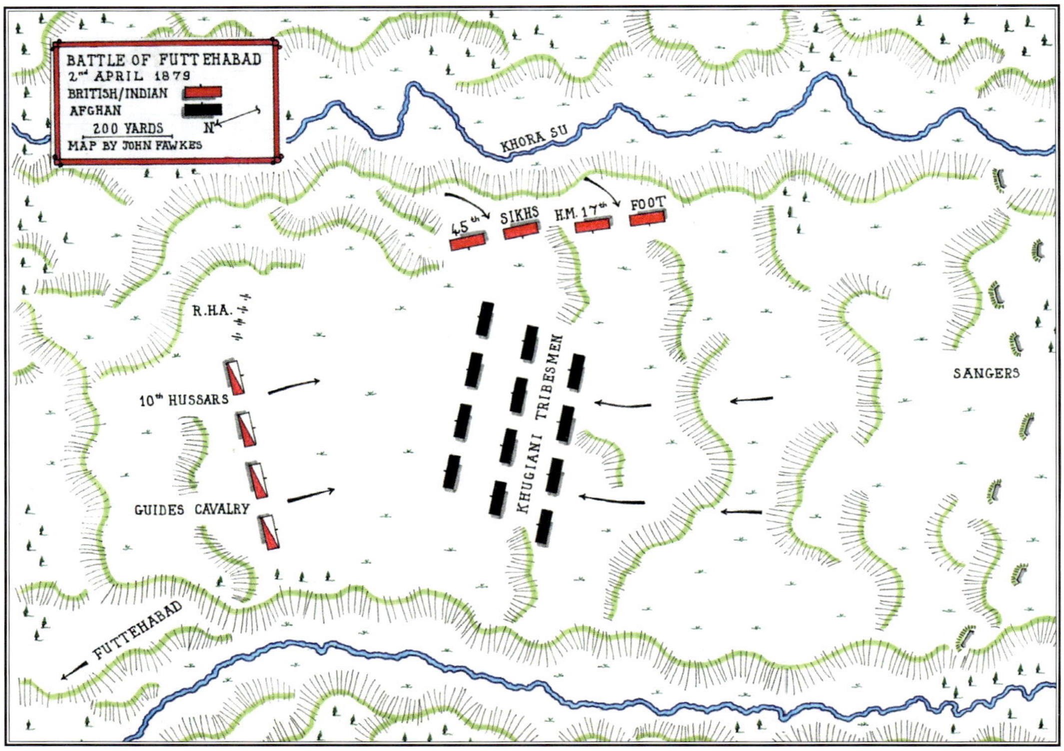

Figure 55. Battle of Futtehabad

being attacked by three of the enemy. Seeing his plight, Lieutenant Hamilton rushed to the side of Sowar Dowlut Ram, killed his three attackers and supported by some of his men carried him to safety.

For his part in this action and for saving the life of Sowar Dowlut Ram, Lieutenant Hamilton was later awarded the Victoria Cross.

The cavalry charges completely broke the spirit of the Afghan troops and the British infantry quickly occupied the enemy entrenched positions. With the Afghans now fleeing in all directions they were pursued by the Cavalry and any significant groups were fired upon by the artillery.

The Khugiani losses during the battle were 300 dead and about 900 wounded, the British losses were 6 killed and 40 wounded. Following the battle the village of Khoja was burnt to the ground and on 4th April General Gough continued the fight against Khugiani strongholds near Gandamak, several of which were also destroyed, these actions resulted in the complete submission of their chief Haidar Khan. With his objectives having been secured, General Gough and his troops returned to Jalalabad.

On the 8th April the government of India informed Sir Frederick that it would be politically expedient for troops to occupy Gandamak and on the following day the Commander-in-Chief conveyed these orders to General Sir Sam Browne.

The forward move to Gandamak was begun on 12th April when an advanced party of the General's divisional headquarters with a small column from the 1st Brigade left Jalalabad and arrived at Safed Sang on 14th April which was considered to be more suitable for occupation than Gandamak.

On 17th April, the troops at Futtehabad were ordered to proceed to Safed Sang and after leaving a garrison at Fort Sale, the remaining troops set off and arrived at Safed Sang on 20th April where they camped at higher and better ground on the Nimla plateau.

Following rumours that Mohmands were gathering with the intent of crossing the Kabul river and attacking Dakka or somewhere else on the British lines of supply, Lieutenant-Colonel O. Barnes, the commander at Dakka, set out with a small column to reconnoitre the area.

The party reached Kam Dakka without meeting any hostile tribesmen, however, it was reported that a large force of Mohmands were concentrating on the other side of the river. When this news was telegraphed to the divisional headquarters, the political officer Major Conolly recommended that two companies of the Mhairwara Battalion, stationed at Dakka, should be despatched to protect the inhabitants at Kam Dakka.

Accordingly, Captain O'Moore Creagh was despatched with 138 officers and men of the battalion on 21st April and arrived at Kam Dakka later in the day.

Captain O'Moore Creagh – Victoria Cross No. 348

On his arrival at the village, Captain Creagh was surprised to find that instead of being welcomed, his force was not allowed to enter the village as the villagers thought that their presence, rather than providing protection would bring down the wrath of their fellow tribesmen. On the following morning the villagers persisted in their position that they wished to remain neutral in what now seemed to be an imminent attack.

Having spent the night in a nearby cemetery, which he did the best he could to make defensible, Captain Creagh had just positioned his men when, at 5 o'clock in the morning the position was attacked by a force of about 1,500 men, including some from the village who had sided with the enemy.

After constructing some basic earthworks to protect his position, which by now was completely surrounded by the enemy, Captain Creagh and his men fought off several attacks by the use of bayonet charges. By 3 o'clock in the afternoon, when his ammunition was running low and the situation seemed to be desperate, Captain D. M. Strong with about 40 infantry and a troop of the 10th Bengal Lancers, commanded by Lieutenant C. E. Pollock arrived from Dakka and saved the day.

Charges by the cavalry managed to push back the enemy and with the aid of the infantry and Captain Creagh's men, who once again charged out from their entrenchments, managed to disperse the force and drive them back across the river. At this time further reinforcements, under the command of Major J. B. Dyce, consisting of a company of the 12th Regiment of Foot, supported by two guns of the Royal Artillery Mountain Battery, arrived and the fire from the guns force the enemy to make a full retreat. As it was deemed to be impracticable to maintain their existing position, Captain Creagh and the reinforcements who had come to his rescue managed to make a safe withdrawal.

For his service during this action, Captain Creagh was later awarded the Victoria Cross.

During the action at Kam Dakka, the British losses were 6 killed with 18 wounded, however, the enemy losses were believed to be 200 killed.

Pursuit of Peace

On 3rd May, General Sir Sam Browne sent a telegraph to Lord Lytton at Simla with the news that the new Emir Yakub Khan had left Kabul and was proceeding to Safed Sing to conduct peace negotiations. Improvements to the situation were further enhanced when on the same day Asmatullah Khan, chief of the Ghilzai tribe arrived in the British camp and submitted his tribes services to the General.

On 8th May, Emir Yakub Khan and his entourage arrived at the British camp in Gandamak and two days later began the peace negotiations which were concluded with the signing of the Treaty of Gandamak on 26th May 1879, which ended this first phase of the war. The treaty was ratified by Lord Lytton on 30th May at Simla and presented to the Emir at Gandamak on 6th June.

Having concluded arrangements with Major Cavagnari, for the reception of the British Mission to Kabul, the Emir left Gandamak on his return to Kabul on 7th June and on the following day, with Brigadier-General Tytler's brigade forming the rear guard, the Peshawar Valley Field Force began its withdrawal from Afghanistan.

Kurram Valley Field Force Operations

The movement of troops, who would form the Kurram Valley Field Force, began as early as 4th October 1878 and they soon began to assemble at a newly formed camp at Thal, near the border; a smaller force was also assembled at Kohat to provide protection to the lines of communication and supply.

The force, under the overall command of Major-General F. S. Roberts VC, consisted of: Artillery under the command of Lieutenant-Colonel A. H. Lindsay; Cavalry under the command of Colonel H. H. Gough VC; two brigades of infantry commanded by Colonel A. H. Cobbe and Colonel J. B. Thelwall and Sappers and Miners and engineers under the command of Lieutenant-Colonel E. Perkins. Major J. C. Auchinleck was appointed to the command of forces at Kohat.

Immediately after his appointment to the command of the force, General Roberts proceeded to Kohat where he organised the construction of defences, a main supply depot and a base hospital. At Thal he arranged for the construction of a forward supply depot and a trestle bridge across the Kurram river and in preparation for the advance, Captain F. S. Carr selected fords to be used to cross the river Kurram, one for the Infantry and another for the Cavalry.

In the afternoon of 20th November, General Roberts at last received his orders to advance into Afghanistan and in the early hours of the 21st November, he, together with his divisional staff accompanied the advanced party of 29th Punjab Infantry commanded by Colonel J. J. H. Gordon set out and crossed the border.

The remainder of the 1st Infantry Brigade, with field and horse artillery crossed the river immediately behind the advance force and advanced along the river bank to Khapianga where there was good camping ground and a fortified enclosure. The advance party, also moved towards Khapianga but by a more circuitous route, in the hope of intercepting the force that had occupied the village. After arriving at the village the place was found to be deserted, the garrison having departed on the previous evening.

With the 2nd Infantry Brigade having now crossed the border, General Roberts force slowly advanced in stages and have met no opposition were all concentrated at Fort Kurram, apart from a small force left at Khapianga, by 27th November. Two days earlier, the advanced party had reconnoitred towards Habib Kala where a large party of the Emir's forces, thought to number about 18,000 men had just retired and were seen to be retreating over the Peiwar Kotal.

On 28th November, after leaving a small garrison together with the sick and most of the baggage at Fort Kurram, the British force set out for Habib Kala in two columns with the intent of engaging the enemy. After arriving at Habib Kala, the General received intelligence that the Emir's troops had abandoned their guns at the foot of the Peiwar Kotal and were retreating in some disorder.

To ascertain the truth of the matter, a reconnaissance in force under the command of Colonel J. J. H. Gordon was despatched up the south east flank of the Peiwar and reported back that far from retiring in disorder and abandoning their guns, the enemy were in fact occupying very strong positions at the head of the pass protected by well placed artillery. In order to force the enemy to disclose their positions, Colonel Gordon pressed forward towards the Afghan rear guard where they came under heavy musket and artillery fire. At nightfall, Colonel Gordon ordered his men to retire and rejoin the main column at Habib Kala.

While the reconnaissance was taking place, General Roberts with a force of men from the 8th Regiment and 23rd Pioneers, advanced to Teri Mangal to locate a new site for the British camp, however, after receiving fire from Afghan artillery which had been located on a high ridge above Teri Mangal, the force retired about a mile to establish their camp at a more secure location. On the following day the remainder of the column was moved up to occupy this new camp.

It had now been determined that the enemy occupied a front of about four miles which stretched from the Spingawai Kotal along a ridge with successive peaks to Peiwar Kotal, initial observations indicated that the position at Spingawai Kotal was less well defended, which was confirmed by further reconnaissance patrols that took place over the next two days.

With his intelligence now having been gathered, General Roberts decided that he would lead a night attack against Spingawai Kotal, with the 2nd Brigade and after capturing this enemy position would proceed along the ridge and attack the defences at Peiwar Kotal. Once Spingawai Kotal had been captured Brigadier-General Cobbe would make a frontal attack on Peiwar Kotal with the 1st Brigade.

Battle of Peiwar Kotal

During the day on 1st December, patrols were sent out towards both flanks of the Peiwar position and gun batteries were established on the plain near the village of Teri, in an attempt to convince the Afghans that the main British attack would be against the Peiwar Kotal, preparations for the attack on Spingawai were kept secret, with orders for troop assembly only being issued at 4 o'clock in the afternoon.

At 10 o'clock in the evening, General Roberts quietly led his men from the camp, leaving their tents still erected and the camp fires burning. After advancing for a short time, two Pathans of the 29th Bengal Native Infantry fired their weapons in an attempt to warn the Afghans of the British advance, the men were disarmed and arrested.[21] Despite the going, which was heavier than expected, the force reached the foot of the Spingawai Kotal by 6 o'clock in the morning, just as the day was breaking.

The approach of the British force had so far been unobserved by the enemy, however, as the light improved, a barricade became visible at about 50 yards to their front and the sentries guarding this piquet fired off some shots to warn the rest of their comrades.

An advanced party of the 5th Ghurkha Regiment, led by Major Fitzhugh and Captain Cook, immediately rushed the barricade and the remainder of the regiment attacked around the flanks overwhelming the piquet and killing the occupants. The enemy guns on the heights now began to put down a fire on the advancing troops but caused little damage.

The 5th Ghurkhas with the 75th Highlanders, rapidly advanced up the steep slope and captured three enemy stockades in quick succession; the advance was ably supported by Captain J. A. Kelso, who despite the difficult ground had managed to bring two of his Mountain Battery guns near to the front of the column. When Captain Kelso was killed, Lieutenants Shirres and Osborne carried on his good work.

Captain John Cook – Victoria Cross No. 344

The next part of the action is best described in the words of Major Galbraith, Assistant Adjutant-General Kurram Column Field Force, who was accompanying the leading force;

21 Subsequently the men were found guilty by a court martial and one man was hung, the other being transported.

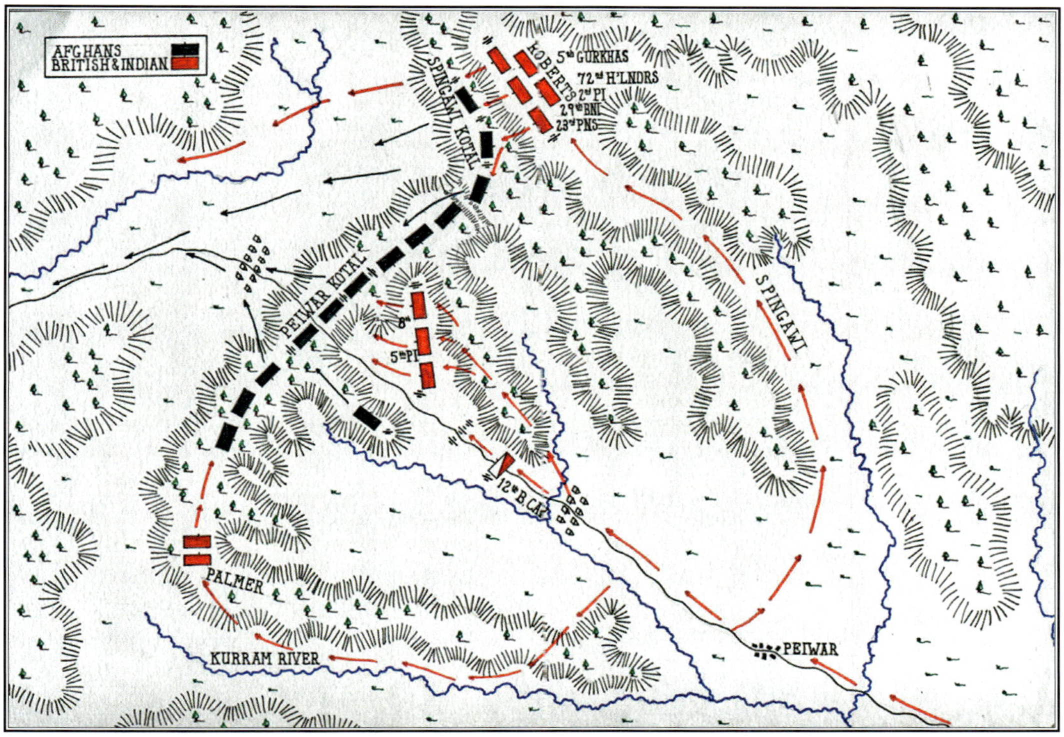

Figure 56. Battle of Peiwar Kotal

"On the morning of the 2nd December 1878, after our troops had stormed the second entrenchment above the 'Spin Gawai', the enemy attempted to rally in the woods at our right flank, and at the same moment about 150 to 200 men were observed moving down from a height on the left. The latter were at first supposed to be our own sepoys, and were thus enabled to approach unmolested within 50 yards of the entrenchment, when, their identity being established, Captain Cook opened fire with about 15 to 20 of his men. A very heavy fire was interchanged for two or three minutes, during which time he was reinforced by about 12 men of his own regiment and the 72nd Highlanders. Seeing that the enemy had a mountain gun with them, he charged out of the entrenchment with such impetuosity that the enemy broke and fled, leaving many of their men and three battery mules on the ground.

At the close of the mêlée I was on the left flank of the Goorkhas when a man rushed towards me from behind. I had seen him advancing but thought him a friendly sepoy, until he raised his rifle at about three yards from me, fortunately an intervening tree sheltered me for the moment, and gave me time to turn and discharge my pistol at him without effect. Captain Cook seeing my danger, with a shout distracted his attention to himself, and aiming a sword cut which the Duranee avoided, sprang upon him, and grasping his throat, grappled with him. They both fell upon the ground, the Duranee, a most powerful man, still endeavouring to use his rifle and seizing Captain Cook's arm in his teeth, until I was able to end the struggle by shooting him through the head. The whole affair was the work of a moment, but I feel convinced that but for Captain Cook's prompt endeavour to draw the man's fire upon himself, I should, in all probability, have been shot before I could have again discharged my pistol, several others of the enemy were at the time within a few yards of us."

For these actions Captain Cook was later awarded the Victoria Cross.

By 6:30 in the morning, all of the enemy entrenchments at the head of the Spingawai Kotal were in British hands and the line of the Afghan defence had been turned.

Meanwhile, on the south side of the Peiwar Kotal, a force of Field and Horse Artillery, supported by 100 men from the 28th Regiment of Foot, left camp at 5 o'clock in the morning and advanced to a position about a mile further up the Peiwar Valley. When dawn broke at about 6:15, Major Parry ordered his guns to fire on an enemy gun which had been placed on a crag commanding the lower reaches of the valley and when this was silenced, he turned his guns on the batteries at the head of the valley. For the next three or four hours an intense artillery duel was fought by the opposing forces until at about 11 o'clock in the morning the enemy guns were silenced.

While the artillery were doing their work to silence the enemy guns, the infantry detailed for the frontal attack on the Peiwar Kotal left camp at 6 o'clock and at a position slightly in front and to the right of the artillery took cover in the jungle. The men remained in the position until about 8 o'clock, when a signal was received from General Roberts, at the Spingawai Kotal, to make their advance.

A ridge, some 350 yards in advance of their position, was soon captured by men of the 28th Regiment commanded by Lieutenant-Colonel Tanner and men from the 5th Punjab Infantry led by Major McQueen. After this initial success the infantry of the 1st Brigade continued their advance from ridge to ridge, maintaining their cover whenever they could, until about noon by which time they were no more than 1,400 yards from the head of the pass. Now temporarily halted by a steep ravine across their path, the men kept up an intense fire against the masses of enemy on the opposite side of the ravine. Before the attack could be resumed, Brigadier-General Cobbe received a bullet wound to the thigh and was forced to resign his command to Colonel F. Barry-Drew of the 28th Regiment of Foot.

Meanwhile, after having gained the summit of the Spingawai and clearing the enemy defences, General Roberts called a short halt while his leading regiments were reformed and replenished their supply of ammunition. They then began the advance along the ridge towards the Peiwar Kotal and with the 29th Punjab Infantry leading the way, the men of the 2nd Brigade managed to advance for about one mile without meeting any opposition.

However, when the force reached a deep ravine they came under heavy fire from a large enemy force concealed in dense pine woods on the far side of the ravine. The left of the ravine was covered with deep gullies, occupied by large parties of the enemy, making an advance in this direction impossible, however, the 72nd Highlanders did engage with these men to keep them occupied. The 2nd Punjab Infantry and 23rd Pioneers made strenuous efforts to dislodge the enemy on the right of the ravine and despite the difficulties of the ground had some success but suffered heavy losses.

At about noon, the four guns of the Royal Artillery, which were carried by elephants, finally reached the British forward position and began to shell the enemy who were mainly concealed by the trees which covered the slopes. The fire of these guns was later augmented by three mountain guns which had managed to make their way through the dense woodland.

At this stage, the men of the 1st Brigade who were also halted in front of a deep ravine at the Peiwar Kotal, realised that the spur up which they were advancing did not in fact connect with the main Peiwar Ridge, however, via a slight detour it did connect with the men from the 2nd Brigade so they advanced in this direction instead.

With some of his men from both infantry brigades now joined, General Roberts decided that the frontal attack on the Peiwar Kotal had little chance of success so ordered the 2nd Punjab Infantry to maintain their hold on the hill which was the most advanced position that this force had reached.

The 29th Punjab Infantry were then ordered to occupy a hill overlooking the Spingawai where a field hospital was being erected and the remainder of the force under the command of Brigadier-General Thelwall was directed towards Zabardast Kala to threaten the Afghans line of retreat.

As soon as the movement of Brigadier-General Thelwell's troops was notice by the Afghans this spurred their movement to retreat. In turn, the slackening in fire as a result of the retreat precipitated a final advance by the British forces and by 2:30 in the afternoon they were in full possession of the Peiwar Kotal. The enemy who were now in full flight along the Ali Khel road were pursued by the cavalry led by Colonel Hugh Gough.

With the enemy retreat, General Roberts installed the 28th Regiment of Foot as a garrison at Peiwar Kotal while he and the rest of his force set up camp at Zabardast Kala.

The British losses during the battle were two officers and 18 men killed and five officers and 67 men wounded. Due to the heavily wooded nature of large parts of the battlefield it was impossible to estimate the enemy casualties, however, 70 dead were counted at the Spingawai defences.

After resting for four days, working parties were set to work preparing the positions for British occupation during the winter and after placing Brigadier-General Thelwall in command of a garrison at Peiwar Kotal, General Roberts with the main force moved off to Ali Khel on 6th December.

General Roberts and his forces eventually returned to Kurram where stores were being assembled for his forces to over winter. In early January 1879, following arrangements with Akram Khan, governor of the region, a force under the command of acting Brigadier-General Barry-Drew occupied the Khost Valley without opposition and established headquarters at Fort Matun. At the end of the first week of January, engagements were fought against hostile Mangal and Jadran tribes, in the south of the Khost Valley, to some extent these tribal raids were contained with the support of local tribal chiefs.

As the troops of the Khost Valley column were required by General Roberts, to complete his winter deployments for control of the Kurram Valley, occupation of the Khost Valley was abandoned and the troops returned to Kurram at the end of January.

During the winter months, General Roberts began preparation for an advance towards Kabul, at the start of the next campaigning season, however, in May, with talks taking place in the lead up to the Treaty of Gandamak, these were suspended and the General used the time to improve his knowledge of the upper Kurram Valley, in particular the passes that connected the district to Kabul.

On 23rd July, General Roberts left his command of the Kurram Field force and headed to Simla, bring the operations of this force, in the first phase of the war, to an end.

South Afghanistan Field Force Operations

British Mission to Kabul

Following the signing of the treaty of Gandamak, the Indian Government sent an official statement to the Secretary of State in London, which outlined the terms of the treaty. On the 4th August a vote in both Houses of Parliament outlined the thanks extended by the government to the Viceroy, Commander-in-Chief and the forces deployed during the war and on 7th August the Secretary of State officially replied to the Viceroy stating the government's acceptance and approval of the terms contained within the treaty.

After the treaty had been signed, Emir Yakub Khan returned to Kabul and Major Cavagnari proceeded to Simla to make a personal report to the Viceroy and agree the next steps to be taken by the Indian Government. The main agreement was that the British Resident should take up his appointment at Kabul without delay and Major Cavagnari himself was appointed to this important post.

As the Mission was to be established at the "special desire" of the Emir and would be located within the Emirs own stronghold in the city, close to his residency, it was thought that Major Cavagnari should be escorted by a small force.

After much discussion, it was agreed that the Major would be accompanied by: Mr Jenkins, who would act as his secretary; Dr A. H. Kelly, as medical officer, Lieutenant W. H. P. Hamilton[22] and an escort of 25 cavalry and 50 infantry from the Corps of Guides. On 6th July, the Major left Simla with his party and after reaching General Roberts headquarters at Kurram on 15th July was escorted by General Roberts and a small force to Karatiga in the Hazar Darakht defile where Sardar Khushdil Khan, the late Governor of Turkistan was waiting to escort the new Envoy to Kabul.

Envoy Cavagnari arrived at Kabul, with his staff and escort, on 24th July and established his Embassy in the Bala Hissar, about 250 yards from the Emir's palace. During the month of August, although the state of his nation was very unsettled and his authority did not extend far beyond the city walls, the Emir demonstrated great friendliness towards the Embassy, such that on 30th August Envoy Cavagnari wrote *"I personally believe that Yakub Khan will turn out to be a very good ally, and that we shall be able to keep him to his engagements".*

Two or three days after the British Mission arrived at Kabul, six regiments of Afghans, from Herat, also arrived at the city and after a further four days they marched through the city, shouting abuse at the Envoy and claiming that they would soon put an end to Cavagnari and the British Mission. After another few days the Herat soldiers received the pay that they were owed and then sent on forty days leave.

On the morning of 2nd September, three regiments, together with some of the people from the Bazaar began to advance on the British residency within the Bala Hissar and at about 8 o'clock they surrounded the Residency and an intense fire fight began. By now, almost 2,000 supporters of the Emir had surrounded his palace to provide protection and on several occasions the Emir directed some of these men to go to the Envoy's assistance but the pleas were ignored. At about 9 o'clock, Cavagnari together with the other three European officers within the Embassy led a charge at the head of a small force of about 25 men and managed to drive the Afghans away from some broken ground that they were holding. Three subsequent charges were made with the same limited success. At about 11 o'clock it was noticed that part of the Embassy was on fire, however, the defenders managed to keep up continuous rifle fire until about 9 o'clock in the evening when all became quiet and the attacking force dispersed, all of the Embassy occupants having been killed.

Phase 2 of the War

Late at night on the 4th September, Captain A. Conolly, the political officer at Ali Khel, received news of the attack on the British Residency in Kabul, and immediately forwarded this on to the Viceroy in Simla.

Although the full extent of the disaster was at this time unknown, after a meeting between the Viceroy and his Commander-in-Chief, on the following day, a telegraph was despatched to Brigadier-General Dunham Massy, temporarily in command of the Kurram Field Force while General Roberts was in Simla, ordering him to move the 23rd Pioneers, 5th Ghurkhas and the Mountain Train to the head of the Shutargardan pass and await further orders.

22 Who had just been awarded the Victoria Cross for action at the Battle of Futtehabad on 2nd April.

On the same day, following a request from Lord Lytton, Sir Frederick Haines submitted his suggestions for further operations against Afghanistan, should the news of the destruction of the British Mission at Kabul prove to be true.

Sir Frederick's plan was that Major-General Sir F. Roberts, with a brigade of cavalry and two brigades of infantry should advance on Kabul, via the Shutargardan Pass; Jalalabad should be occupied by another division, commanded by Major-General Bright and Kandahar should be reoccupied by troops commanded by Major General Sir D. Stewart, who would also threaten Ghazni, if necessary. A major force would also remain at the Shutargardan Pass to guard the communication and supply line through the Kurram Valley.

These plans were immediately approved and on 6th September, Sir Frederick Roberts left Simla to resume his command of the Kurram Valley Field Force. Before leaving Simla, Major-General Roberts sent a telegraph to Captain Conolly, the political officer at Ali Khel, instructing him to ensure that all of the headmen of the surrounding districts be available to meet with him when he arrived at the camp at Kurram.

After reaching Jhelum on 8th September, the Major-General sent a telegraph to Sir Peter Lumsden, Adjutant-General in India, stating that his main difficulty in the upcoming operations would be to maintain his long supply line and that he required strong garrisons to be maintained at Thal, Balesh Khel, Kurram Fort, Peiwar Kotal, Ali Khel, Shutargardan and Kushi and requested that one mountain battery, one British Infantry regiment, one native cavalry regiment and three native infantry regiments be moved up as soon as possible.

He further stated that these additional men would be required for the next three months or until the winter snows fell, at which time his supply and communications lines would be transferred to the Khyber pass route.

On 12th September, General Roberts arrived at Ali Khel, and had a meeting with many of the local chiefs who had been assembled by the political officer on his request. The meeting was very amicable and despite emissaries from Kabul trying to incite the local tribes against the British, the General felt that as long as a strong force was maintained in the area there would be no attempt at insurrection.

On 13th September, Brigadier-General Baker arrived at the Shutargardan Pass, to take up his command, just as the Sappers arrived to begin improvements to the roads to allow for the passage of horse artillery and the build-up of stores at the forward supply base.

General Roberts remained at Ali Khel while his main attack force of the 1st Division of the Kurram Field Force, now designated the Kabul Field Force, was assembled; this was proving to be a slow process due to the lack of sufficient transport and pack animals. On 17th September, General Roberts issued his plans to Army Headquarters; the initial step being for Brigadier-General Baker to advance from Shutargardan and occupy Kushi on or before 27th September.

Despite the tribal leaders on the Kushi side of the Shutargardan pass being inclined to friendship towards the British, having offered to aid them with supplies and transport when they made their advance, an attack by 200 to 300 Mangal and Ghilzai tribesmen on a telegraph party, marching between Sirkai Kotal and Karatiga, took place on 22nd September. When news that this force had also attacked a British force stationed in a blockhouse at Sirkai Kotal, General Baker despatched a detachment of the 72nd Highlanders to deal with the matter, however, on their arrival the tribesmen had dispersed.

On 24th September General Baker began his advance and by evening had occupied Kushi, thus securing the entrance to the Logar Valley.

In preparation for his joining up with the advance column of the Kabul Field Force, General Roberts handed over military command of all troops in Kurram to Brigadier-General T. E. Gordon on 26th September as well as political control of the district. On the next day, the General moved his divisional headquarters to Shutargardan and by the 28th September they were established at Kushi.

With his forces now assembling at Kushi, General Roberts was eager to push on towards Kabul, however, due to lack of adequate transport it became apparent on 1st October that this would have to be delayed for a few days and after arriving at Saiadabad on 4th October he set up camp and called a halt to await the arrival of supplies.

On 3rd October, General Roberts issued a proclamation to the people of Kabul, in which he stated that he was advancing at the head of a British army intent on taking possession of the city, hopefully peaceably, however, with force if necessary. He also advised that those not involved in the murders at the British Embassy or its plunder would not be harmed. As the British army did not make war against women or children he advised that they should be removed from the city out of harm's way. The General closed his proclamation with the statement that all armed persons found in or around the vicinity of Kabul would be considered as enemies of the British Government and would be treated accordingly.

By the 5th October, the main force, with the exception of a rear guard under the command of Brigadier-General Macpherson, which had been left at Saiadabad to protect the stores and ammunition, had reached Chaharasia about 11 miles from Kabul.

Immediately after arriving at Chaharasia, cavalry patrols were sent out along each of the three roads leading to Kabul, but despite receiving some sporadic fire they returned to camp without encountering any large concentrations of enemy forces.

At first light on the following morning, General Roberts once again sent out his cavalry patrols to locate and estimate the strength of the Afghan forces that would oppose his advance on Kabul.

General Roberts was also determined to capture the crest of the Sang-i-Nawishta Pass, which was about five miles from his camp, as this was his intended route forward to Kabul. With this objective in mind he despatched Lieutenant-Colonel A. A. Currie with a force of 450 men of the 23rd Pioneers, together with: 20 men of the 9th Lancers commanded by Captain H. W. Apperley, a squadron of 5th Punjab Cavalry commanded by Major F. Hammond; the 2nd Mountain Battery with two guns, commanded by Lieutenant C. A. Montanaro and 284 men of the 2nd Highlanders, commanded by Major G. S. White, to work on the road through the pass and make it fit for the passage of guns.

However, before the General could commence his advance on the Sang-i-Nawishta Pass, large masses of Afghan troops appeared on the crests of the hills on both side of the pass and at the head of the Chardeh Valley which was off to the left. Due to the deliberate and confident manner by which the Afghans took up their position, it was obvious that the bulk of these troops were regular soldiers from the Afghan army.

General Roberts determine that these Afghan forces would have to be dislodged from their positions before nightfall, as to allow them to establish a stronghold on the heights for even one night would encourage large numbers of men from the surrounding villages to join up with them.

What was already a difficult position for the British column was further compounded by the news that the road to their rear had been cut by an Afghan force and that the advance of General Macpherson's Brigade which was escorting the baggage would now be opposed. General Roberts sent a squadron of cavalry as reinforcements to assist the baggage column with news regarding the interposing enemy force and instruction for General Macpherson to try and reach Chaharasia before nightfall.

Battle of Chaharasia

The Afghan forces occupied the heights in an arc of almost three miles in length defended by at least 16 guns with their main position being located on an elevated ridge to the west of the Sang-i-Nawishta Pass, which was fronted by a series of undulating hills which provided many easily defensible positions.

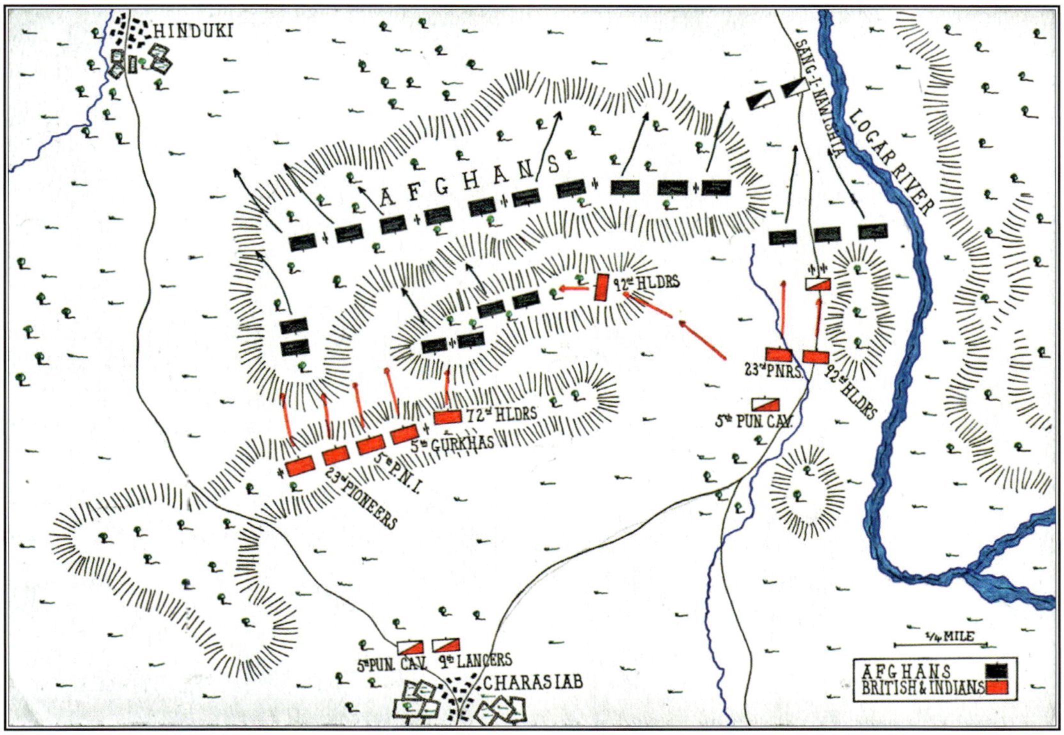

Figure 57. Battle of Chaharasia

General Roberts movements so far, had led the enemy to believe that he would make his main attack against the Sang-i-Nawishta Pass, which was to the left side of their position and had concentrated their forces in this area. However, General Roberts felt that to dislodge the enemy from these well defended position would entail unacceptable losses to his troops, so instead he instructed Brigadier-General Baker to mount an attack against the enemy right flank.

The force, commanded by Lieutenant-Colonel Currie, which had been sent out earlier to prepare the road up the pass and was already in place, between the British Camp and the main Afghan camp would be used to contain this position. However, when Colonel Currie and his 350 men of the 23rd Pioneers were assigned to General Bakers force, command of the remaining force was devolved to Major George White who was instructed to threaten the pass and prevent the enemy from occupying any part of the Chaharasia village.

General Baker assembled his men for the attack on the right flank in the wooded enclosure near to the villages of Chaharasia, concealed from the enemy, but when at about 11 o'clock he emerged into the open to begin his attack, he was immediately engaged by a large force from the Chardeh villages, supported by a force of Afghan regular soldiers.

A company of the 72nd Highlanders, commanded by Captain Brooke-Hunt managed to gain the heights of a spur to the extreme right of the enemy position but could advance no further until reinforced by two companies of the 5th Ghurkha regiment commanded by Captain Cook VC.

From their position on the spur, the small force supported the advance of the bulk of the 72nd Highlanders supported by two mountain guns, however, due to the stubborn resistance of the enemy and the difficulty of the ground the advance stalled. At this stage more men of the 5th Ghurkhas, commanded by Major FitzHugh and about 200 men from the 5th Punjab Infantry, commanded by Captain Hall rushed forward into the fray and after a very fierce fight, lasting about two hours, managed to secure the ridge at about 2 o'clock in the afternoon.

Having secured the ridge, the British forces continued to advance and forced the enemy to retreat further from their prepared positions as they fought towards the position at the Sang-i-Nawishta Pass.

Major George White – Victoria Cross No. 349

The advance of General Baker's troops on the Sang-i-Nawishta Pass was somewhat hampered by a strong enemy position on a hill to the south of the pass, which was preventing the General bringing his guns to bear on the main enemy defences.

At about half past 12 in the afternoon, despite being outnumbered by a factor of 8 to 1, Major White led a party of two companies of the 92nd Highlanders, commanded by Captain Cotton, to capture this strategic hill.

Moving up the hill from one steep ledge to the next, Major White and his men advanced to a position immediately to the front of the main enemy entrenchment, however, exhausted by their climb the men were beginning to falter so the Major grabbed a rifle and charged the enemy and managed to kill their leader. With the loss of their leader and confronted by a charge from the 92nd Highlanders the enemy abandoned their position and fled around the side of the hill, leaving Major White's men to occupy this strategic position.

Later in the afternoon, Major White and his men supported General Baker's final attack to capture the Sang-i-Nawishta Pass when he moved forward with his men and captured a defile with guns in front of it.

For his actions during the battle, Major White was later awarded the Victoria Cross.

Major White received a mention in his citation for a second event during the Battle of Kandahar when he led the final charge against a strong enemy position defended by two guns, and after driving the enemy off captured one of the guns.

Having now secured the main part of the ridge, General Baker's men and guns were able to rain down a heavy fire on the few remaining enemy positions which were quickly abandoned with the enemy retreating across the Kabul river.

For a short way the enemy were pursued by the British cavalry but the chase had to be abandoned due to the difficult ground after which the enemy were sent on their way with heavy British artillery fire. British losses during the battle were 18 killed and 70 wounded; enemy losses were thought to be over 300 killed with many more wounded.

Beni Hissar

On the day after the battle, General Roberts advanced with his force up the Sang-i-Nawishta Pass towards Beni Hissar where he intended to camp and rest his force, prior to making the final advance on Kabul. However, after learning that a large enemy force was assembling in the Asmai hills to the north west of Kabul, in the early morning of 8th October he despatched a force commanded by Brigadier-General Dunham Massy towards Deh Mazang, where they were thought to be camped. After dealing with this threat General Massy was ordered to maintain a position where he would be able to intercept any enemy retreat towards Turkistan.

Asmai Heights

General Massy left the camp at Beni Hissar, with his force of 720 cavalry troopers, at 1 o'clock in the morning and after heading north across the Siah Hills arrived at Sherpur which he found to have been abandoned by the enemy. From his position at Sherpur, the General could see the enemy entrenched in positions well guarded by guns on the Asmai Heights on the far side of the Kabul river.

As the enemy position was completely unassailable to his force of cavalry, General Massy sent a message by heliograph to General Roberts, detailing the disposition of the enemy troops and advising that an approach via the Chardeh plain was advisable.

On receiving this news, General Roberts determined that the enemy were intending to mount a final stand on the Asmai Heights and ordered General Baker to mount an attack against their position.

General Baker left the camp at Beni Hissar, with his advance force of just over 1,000 men, at 11 o'clock in the afternoon, and after his scouts found a suitable ridge, he found himself in a commanding position to the rear of the enemy position with a clear view into their camp. His force now began an artillery duel with the enemy while he waited for the arrival of his reinforcements, however, as these did not arrive until 5 o'clock, when darkness was falling, reluctantly he had to defer his attack until the next morning.

Having gained such a commanding position, General Baker was concerned that the enemy would use the cover of darkness to retreat via the Kohistan road and when this was communicated to General Roberts, a force under the command of Brigadier-General H. Gough was despatched to cut off this escape route. Still concerned that the enemy would escape during the night, General Baker sent forward a patrol in strength towards the enemy camp, which although it received sporadic fire, soon determined that the bulk of the Afghan forces had indeed dispersed to their villages.

General Baker immediately despatched a messenger to General Massy and his cavalry brigade at Deh Mazang who set out along the Ghazni road as far as the village of Kala Kazi (only 7 miles from Kabul) without finding any trace of the enemy. The party sent to the Kohistan road met with similar results, also finding no trace of the enemy.

With hardly a shot having been fired, the enemy entrenchments on the Asmai Heights were now in British hands and large numbers of baggage animals together with 21 guns had been captured.

Occupation of Kabul

With the Asmai Heights under British control Kabul was now open to occupation.

General Roberts now moved his camp from Beni Hissar to the Siah Sang, which was a low hill lying between Kabul and the confluence of the Kabul and Logar rivers and on the 10th October, after a visit, he ordered the 5th Punjab Cavalry to occupy Sherpur where a large quantity of stores and ordnance had been found.

On the next day, accompanied by a small escort General Roberts was able to enter the Bala Hissar and examine the destruction at the British Residency where Envoy Cavagnari and his party had been murdered.

After the ceremony to recognise the formal occupation of the Bala Hissar, General Roberts read out a proclamation to the assembled chiefs of Kabul that stated the city was now under martial law and rewards were on offer for the capture of any persons involved in the assault on the Residency and the massacre of its inmates; on the following day General Roberts entered Kabul at the head of his whole force.

The 67th Regiment of Foot and the 5th Ghurkha regiment were billeted in the Bala Hissar and Major-General J. Hills VC was nominated as Military Governor of Kabul, to be assisted by Nawab Sir Ghulam Hasan Khan.

On 16th October, the troops at Bala Hissar had to be relocated when an explosion within the great magazine of the fortress cause much damage and killed 22 men and severely wounded four others. Captain Shafto of the Royal Artillery who was one of those killed, was taking stock of the large quantities of war materials found within the magazine at the time of the explosion. Before the dust had even settled, the men of the Ghurkhas and the 67th ROF, were ordered to vacate their billets and set up camp outside the Bala Hissar. This proved to be a sensible precaution as two and a half hours after the first explosion a second more violent explosion occurred, no further loss of life was experienced by the troops, however, several residents were killed by falling stones which rained down up to 400 yards from the magazine. Despite the two large explosions, which had levelled a large part of the fort, an even greater danger threatened the city as the fires ignited by the explosions were close to engulfing the main magazine, where about 450 tons of gunpowder were stored. With a strong wind fanning the flames, the fire reached to within 90 yards of the main magazine before, after the winds had dropped, the fires were extinguished in the early morning.

With the dangers presented by the magazine at the Bala Hissar, General Roberts decided to utilise the brick built buildings at Sherpur as the winter accommodations for his Field Force; the camp at Siah Sang was broken up and by the 1st November, the main body of the force were in their new quarters.

Threat to Shutargardan

On 15th October, with news that a large force of Ghilzai tribesmen were being assembled to threaten Shutargardan, General Roberts despatched a force under the command of Brigadier-General Hugh Gough to go the assistance of Colonel Money and his garrison.

When General Gough and his column reached Shutargardan, Colonel Money and his men had already driven off the Ghilzai tribesmen, however, despite the removal of this threat it was decided to abandon the base as due to the onset of winter and imminent snows it had been decided to replace this supply route with the route via the Khyber Pass.

After despatching an ammunition convoy to Kabul, General Gough and his column, together with Colonel Money and his garrison also set off for Kabul and after picking up the men from Kushi, which was also abandoned, the force reached the new British camp at Sherpur on 4th November.

Abdication of Emir Yakub Khan

On the morning of 12th October, the day of the official occupation of the Bala Hissar, Emir Yakub Khan presented himself to General Roberts and informed him of his decision to resign from the Afghan throne, after this announcement the Emir with his retinue were sent back under guard to the British camp, while the General waited for instructions from Lord Lytton regarding his future.

On 26th October, General Roberts received news from the Indian Government that they had accepted the abdication of Emir Yakub Khan and two days later the General issued a proclamation advising that the Emir had abdicated of his own free will, leaving Afghanistan without a government.

Also, as a consequence of the outrage at the British Embassy, the British Government had been forced to occupy Kabul and other parts of the country by the force of arms. The chiefs and other figures of authority were commanded to continue in their roles and assist the British Forces in maintaining law and order and that following consultation with these persons of authority a declaration regarding the new permanent arrangements for governing the country would be made.

In December 1879, the Emir was sent to India, where he resided until his death, at Delhi, on 15th November 1923.

Khyber Supply Route

As early as September 1879, the Indian Government began the preparations for changing the communications and supply route, required to service General Roberts Kabul Field Force, from the Shutargardan Pass (which would be inaccessible during the winter months) to a route via the Khyber Pass. The new route was to be established simultaneously from both ends; to establish the route from India to the Khyber Pass, the Khyber Field Force was created while the route from Sherpur to the Khyber Pass would be established by the forces under General Roberts command.

Khyber Field Force

On 15th September, Major-General R. O. Bright arrived at Peshawar and was appointed to the command of the Khyber Field Force with responsibility for all troops from the Indus to the front line, involved in the Khyber communications and supply route. On the 20th and 21st September, Brigadier-Generals C. Gough VC and C. G. Arbuthnot also arrived in Peshawar and were given commands of the 1st and 2nd Brigades of the field force.

On 25th September, General Gough arrived at Landi Kotal and reported that the Emir had written to his officials forbidding them from opposing the advance of the British troops. On the 29th September, some of General Gough's force entered and occupied Dakka, without opposition, and the process of establishing supply way stations was begun. By 2nd October the force had reached Basawal and as soon as supplies and transport allowed they proceeded to Barikao and on 12th October occupied the fort at Jalalabad. By this time General Arbuthnot with the 2nd Brigade had reached Jamrud and on the 8th October General Bright arrived at Ali Masjid and on the following day established his divisional headquarters at Landi Kotal.

After arriving at Jalalabad, General Gough was ordered to despatch a force to Gandamak and occupy the town as soon as possible, to intercept any of the Afghan units broken up following the aftermath of the Battle of Chaharasia, however, this instruction was not immediately enacted due to the General's belief that this move reduced his force to unacceptable levels. On 14th October Colonel Jenkins, in command of a flying column consisting of the Guides, a wing of the 9th Regiment and the Hazara Mountain Battery, however, did advance as far as Futtehabad.

Following the arrival of about 1,000 camels at Jalalabad on 19th October, General Gough was able to continue the advance with his main force and was soon rejoined with his advance unit at Futtehabad where he was again forced to halt due to the news regarding the abdication of the Emir, it was thought that this news might incite the population of Jalalabad. On 23rd October, the General again resumed his advance and by 24th October his 1st Brigade had occupied Gandamak, however, once again the General was ordered to halt until communications were established with General Roberts's force.

On 26th October, General Gough received a message from General Roberts to the effect that during the first week of November, he expected to be able to despatch a strong brigade towards Gandamak to assist the General in his advance. After receiving this news General Bright decided that he would use his 1st Brigade as a moveable column and ordered General Gough to proceed towards Jagdalak, or further if necessary, to meet up with the brigade from Kabul.

A meeting or darbar was held at Jalalabad on 30th October between General Bright and the ex-Emir's Governor, during which the intentions of the British government were explained, assurances were also received that the Ghilzai chief had agreed not to oppose the British advance.

After receiving news that a brigade commanded by General Macpherson was about to leave Kabul, General Gough and his brigade set out for Jagdalak on 4th November and by the next day were in command of the Jagdalak Pass. On 6th November, after leaving a force under the command of Captain Stedman to garrison the Jagdalak fort, the remainder of the column advanced to Kata Sang where General Gough met up with General Macpherson and his advance guard. Having completed his mission to meet up with General Macpherson, General Gough began his return to Gandamak on the 7th November.

General Roberts's Force

In preparation for the change to the Khyber pass route for his supply and communication lines, General Roberts made a visit to Butkhak on 26th October to establish an outpost and construct the telegraph link with Sherpur.

On 1st November, Brigadier-General Macpherson was despatch to Butkhak, with a force from Siah Sang, in order to establish the new supply and communication route to Jalalabad via the Khyber Pass. Two routes from Butkhak eastwards via Lataband and Khurd-Kabul were evaluated and after this the Lataband route was chosen.

General Macpherson left Butkhak on 4th November, to join up with the force of General Gough, after advancing via the Khurd-Kabul pass and Tezin to Seh Baba, the Generals met on 6th November at Kata Sang.

Having confirmed that the Lataband Pass route was superior to that over the Khurd-Kabul Pass, General Macpherson arranged for a post to be established at Lataband Kotal by the 23rd Pioneers supported by Sappers, who immediately set about improving the road and extending the telegraph line. The new line of communications with India was completed on 19th November, however, the new route via the Khyber Pass was not used until the end of the month.

Activities around Kabul

With the winter quarters having been established at Sherpur, work began on dismantling the Bala Hissar and the destruction of the loose powder that was stored there. On 14th November, all time expired men, the wounded and those judged to be unfit for further active service left Kabul bound for India.

Since the middle of October a Military Commission had been sitting to enquire into the circumstances of the massacre of the Embassy and the events up to the Battle of Chaharasia. All of the Afghan prisoners taken in operations since Chaharasia were brought before the commission and every man proved to have been involved in the massacre was ordered to be executed. Of the 89 men tried in this manner, 49 were ultimately executed, however, with the exception of those involved in the massacre, a general amnesty was granted to all persons who had fought against the British since 3rd September.

With growing rumours of an uprising amongst the tribes surrounding Kabul, on 21st November General Roberts despatched a force under the command of General Baker into Maidan; the primary objective of this force was to assist in the collection of supplies which were being disrupted by the hostile local chiefs. After having sent back large quantities of forage to Kabul, General Baker and his force also returned to the city on 1st December and reported that the surrounding countryside now appeared to have quietened down. This situation was soon to change, however, as religious leaders across the country were inciting the people to rise up against the British and reoccupy their capital at Kabul.

With the possibility of Afghan forces converging on Kabul, General Macpherson with a force of three squadrons of cavalry and over 1,300 infantry, supported by artillery, left Sherpur on 8th December for a major road junction near Arghandi to prevent a junction between Kohistani and Wardak forces and if possible to push these forces back into the path of another brigade, commanded by General Baker, that was advancing from Chaharasia to block the Ghazni road near Beni Badam.

With new intelligence that a large Kohistani force was collecting at Karez Mir, only 10 miles from Kabul, on 10th December, General Macpherson was ordered to change his advance and after crossing the Kirskhana Pass and by maintaining an approach below the skyline arrived undetected at the Surkh Kotal. From his lofty position, General Macpherson was able to observe columns of the enemy moving in from the north and west to join a force of about 2,000 men congregated on the three small conical hills near Karez Mir across the plain to the front of his position.

Still unobserved, General Macpherson formed his men into three columns and after making a rapid descent from the pass mounted a devastating surprise attack on the enemy and captured their positions within an hour. With the arrival of the artillery, under the command of Captain Morgan, a heavy fire was put down against the retreating tribesmen who by now were a flying rabble, and inflicted heavy casualties. During the battle, the British force suffered 7 men wounded, two severely.

Battle of Kala Kazi

In the early hours of 11th December, General Massy with a squadron of 9th Lancers, left Sherpur bound for Kala Aushar, where he took command of the troops there and set off with the combined force which now included some artillery and men from the 14th Bengal Lancers. In accordance with his orders from General Roberts, General Massy slowly advanced along the Gandamak road towards Arghandi with the objective of preventing the enemy from entering the Chardeh Plain and to meet up with the force of General Macpherson.

Not knowing the exact location of General Macpherson's column, General Massy despatched a troop of the 9th Lancers, commanded by Captain J. J. Scott-Chisholme to look for the column, which reduced his force to 214 troopers and 4 artillery pieces.

In the hope of meeting up with General Macpherson's column, General Massy led his small force across country, rather than down the road, intending to meet up with the Ghazni road just beyond the village of Kala Kazi; Captain B. Gough was sent ahead with his troop acting as an advanced guard.

Soon afterwards, Captain Gough reported back that a large force of the enemy was congregated on either side of the Ghazni road, some three miles ahead. When further reports indicated that the enemy force was moving down the plain in the direction of Kala Kazi, despite his orders not to engage with the enemy until he had joined up with General Macpherson, General Massy decided to try and halt their advance until General Macpherson's force arrived.

The column halted and Major Smyth-Windham ordered his artillery to open fire on the advancing enemy force at a range of 2,900 yards. Although the enemy force was temporarily checked, it soon became evident that this was a major force, numbering about 10,000 men, and they intended to continue with their advance.

After moving a little closer to Kala Kazi, the artillery resumed their fire at a range of 2,500 yards but with the enemy attack developing towards the left of the British cavalry, General Massy moved his guns in this direction where they again resumed fire, now at a distance of 2,000 yards. Major Windham's artillery position was once again changed, this time to the right, on the river bank but even at a range of 1,700 yards the fire did not halt the steady enemy advance.

General Massy now ordered about 30 of his troopers to dismount and when the Afghans came within the range of their carbines they began to lay down a heavy fire but unfortunately this did little to deter the advance, so the cavalry and horse artillery slowly began to retire.

Reverend James Adams – Victoria Cross No. 351

At about this time, General Roberts arrived on the battlefield, accompanied by Reverend Adams who was serving as chaplain to the Kabul Field Force. The General, having left Sherpur to take up command of the united forces of Generals Massy and Macpherson, quickly evaluated the situation and ordered a full withdrawal and directed his efforts to saving the guns.

Two cavalry charges against the enemy were mounted in an attempt to gain time for the guns to get away but they only resulted in a brief respite.

While Major Windham was trying to cross a deep water filled ditch with his guns, the carriage of the leading gun broke, blocking the way for the other three guns; the lead gun was spiked and abandoned. Moving off towards the village of Bagwana, another attempt to cross the ditch and escape with the remaining three guns, also came to grief and the guns had to be abandoned.

While trying to cross this same ditch some men of the 9th Lancers also had difficulties and fell from their horses, what happened next is best described by the words of General Roberts *"Our Chaplain [Adams], who had accompanied me throughout the day, behaved in this particular place with conspicuous gallantry. Seeing a wounded man of the 9th Lancers staggering towards him, Adams dismounted and tried to lift the man onto his own charger. Unfortunately the mare, a very valuable animal, broke loose and was never seen again. Adams, however, managed to support the Lancer until he was able to make him over to some of his own comrades.*

"Adams rejoined me in time to assist two more of the 9th who were struggling under their horses at the bottom of the ditch. He was an unusually powerful man, and by sheer strength dragged the Lancers clear of their horses. The Afghans meanwhile had reached Bagwana, and were so close to the ditch that I thought my friend the padre could not possibly escape. I called out to him to look after himself, but he paid no attention to my warnings until he had pulled the almost exhausted Lancers to the top of the slippery bank."

For these actions and following the recommendation of General Robert, Reverend Adams was subsequently awarded the Victoria Cross.

Initially, the recommendation was rejected as Reverend Adams was a civilian working for the Bengal Ecclesiastical Establishment, however, his case resulted in a change to the Royal Warrant in order that the award could be made. Reverend Adams was the first clergyman and last of five civilians to be awarded the Victoria Cross.

As soon as General Roberts realised that a withdrawal was inevitable, he sent a message back to Sherpur with orders for 200 infantry to be sent immediately to the Deh Mazang gorge to prevent the enemy reaching the city.

General Roberts directed the retreat of General Massy's force, using the cavalry to slow down the enemy advance which gave the men of the 72nd Highlanders time to reach the gorge at Deh Mazang and bar the passage of the Afghan forces, allowing General Massy's men to pass through and reach Sherpur. Being unable to enter the city, the Afghans occupied Takht-i-Shah and some of the large walled villages in the Chardeh valley.

During the disastrous engagement at Kala Kazi the British force lost 4 officers and 23 men killed and 2 officers and 23 men wounded.

While the battle was in progress, General Macpherson advanced from Karez Mir and via the Surkh Pass reached the crossroads to Kabul and Arghandi where the sound of artillery fire could be heard coming from the direction of the Chardeh Valley. The General correctly assumed that General Massy's force must have engaged with the Afghans, so after leaving a small force to protect his baggage he set off with the remainder of his column towards Kala Kazi.

By the time that General Macpherson's force arrived on the scene the battle was over, however, his men did sterling work in breaking up and pursuing the enemy forces, driving them from the Chardeh plains. The force left with the baggage had to fight off a determined attack by the Afghans before managing to obtain the safety of the Deh Mazang gorge where the British forces were now congregating. During a gallant bayonet charge, which allowed the baggage train to make their escape Captain J. Cook VC and his brother Lieutenant W. Cook were both wounded.

Activities of General Baker's Brigade

On 9th December, General Baker left Sherpur with a force of 900 infantry supported by cavalry, artillery and a company of Sappers and Miners and after following a difficult road crossed the confluence of the Kabul and Logar rivers and reached the head of the Taitamur Pass.

After leaving the British camp at Chihildukhtaran on the morning of 11th December, Captain G. K. McCallum, with a force of about 300 infantry, acting as the rear guard and escort to the baggage train, was attacked by a large enemy force of about 3,000, however, after being reinforced by a further 100 infantry, a troop of cavalry and two mountain guns they managed to press through and rejoin the main column.

General Baker and his force moved forward, trying to meet up with General Macpherson's force but when his advanced cavalry unit met the Ghazni and Nirikh valley roads leading out of the Maidan Valley without meeting this force, General Baker decided to advance to Arghandi. On reaching the foot of the gorge leading to the Chardeh valley, the advanced guard found that a large enemy force was occupying the heights on either side of the gorge, blocking the road to Kabul. Deeming that it was essential to take control of the heights before dark, Major White led the 92nd Highlanders in a brave charge which captured the enemy positions.

After receiving orders from General Roberts, via heliograph, General Baker proceeded with his force to Deh Mazang, where he received further orders to return to Sherpur, where he arrived on the night of 12th December.

Meanwhile, back at Sherpur there had been a large build-up of enemy forces in the surrounding area, the local garrison was able to reinforce the outpost at Bala Hissar, however, this was threatened when the enemy occupied the Takht-i-Shah peak and began to advance along the saddle to the British position. Learning of the difficulties, General Roberts ordered General Macpherson to provide assistance. General Macpherson despatched a detachment of 560 men from his force, under the command of Colonel G. N. Money to mount an attack against the Afghans on 11th December. By mid afternoon, General Money's men had been able to dislodge the enemy from a mound to the front of their position, however, running out of ammunition and facing a force much larger than expected he decided to camp for the night and await reinforcements from General Baker's column which was now heading for Sherpur.

On the morning of 13th December, General Baker left Sherpur with a large force, heading for Beni Hissar with the intention of attacking the enemy at Takht-i-Shah.

Lieutenant William Henry Dick-Cunyngham – Victoria Cross No. 352

When Major White, commanding the advanced guard arrived on the plain below Bala Hissar, he observed large numbers of the enemy leaving Beni Hissar and rapidly advancing along the ridge towards the British position at Bala Hissar. It was immediately obvious to the Major, that if this advance was not checked then the British position could fall, so after directing his artillery against the enemy he led an attack up towards the centre of the ridge.

Lieutenant St John Forbes was leading the first party to reach the Afghans, however, in the fierce hand to hand fighting the Lieutenant and most of his men were killed. The advanced party was closely followed by another party of men from the 92nd Highlanders, led by Lieutenant W. H. Dick-Cunyngham who charged into the enemy, killing many and finally driving them from their positions, cutting the enemy line in two and gaining possession of the heights. The Afghans, were so staggered by this rapid and forceful assault that they retreated back towards Beni Hissar where they were pursued by Major Griffiths with a force of Sikhs.

For his conduct during this action, Lieutenant Dick-Cunyngham was later awarded the Victoria Cross.

With the danger to his flank now having been removed, General Baker advanced with his force against the Takht-i-Shah summit and helped by some men from Colonel Moneys force who advanced on the opposite side of the peak, the enemy were dislodged after some very determined fighting. The displaced Afghans fled southward towards Indaki, while large contingencies of their comrades began to occupy the Siah Sang heights and take up positions on either side of the road back to Sherpur.

In danger of being cut off from Sherpur, where the garrison had been much depleted, after delegating Colonel Money to hold the positions gained at Takht-i-Shah, General Baker and his force set off to return to Sherpur. On hearing that Major J. C. Stewart and his cavalry were having some success against the Afghans on the Siah Sang heights, General Baker despatched all of his cavalry to aid the Major and cut off the enemy retreat. Major Stewart's men were soon joined by the men sent by General Baker and not long afterwards by a further force of cavalry under the command of General Massy who now assumed command of the attack. By the end of the day, repeated cavalry charges had the desired effect and the Afghans were driven from the heights.

As the days operations had caused large numbers of enemy casualties, General Baker expected that the Afghans would suspend their operations for a few days while they regrouped, however, this was not to be the case and on the morning of 14th December large numbers of the enemy were seen to be advancing along the Kohistan road towards the crest of the Asmai Heights.

Having been thwarted in their operations from the south and the west, on the previous day, it soon became apparent that the Afghans were concentrating their forces in the north west with the intent of making a major attack from that direction. To counter the threat, General Baker decided to mount an attack against the enemy positions on the Asmai Heights and at 9 o'clock in the morning set out from Sherpur with a force of three squadrons of cavalry, 1,224 infantry and some artillery bound for the eastern slopes of the Asmai range.

After arriving at the foothills, General Baker's first objective was to capture some low hills immediately to his front so that he could place his artillery in a position to support the advance of his infantry. Supported by fire from the artillery on the plain, Colonel Clarke led an advanced party of 124 men and managed to capture and retain the conical hill, where the General was now able to place some of his guns. Taking the hill, which formed the northern boundary of the Alibad Kotal, also cut the enemy lines of communication, preventing them from receiving reinforcements.

Lance Corporal George Sellar – Victoria Cross No. 355

The main assault party, led by Colonel Brownlow, now advanced up the steepest part of the ridge to attack the enemy central positions and after fierce hand to hand fighting, the summit was finally reached. During this attack, Lance-Corporal Sellar was in the leading assault party and after pushing himself to the front became engaged in a desperate fight with an Afghan who sprang in front of him.

During this conflict Lance-Corporal Sellar was severely wounded, however, for his actions he was later awarded the Victoria Cross.

With the position having been turned, the enemy began to retreat to their left and many of their number were killed by intense fire from the British infantry and artillery. With the help of some troops sent by General Macpherson, the British troops proceeded along the ridge taking successive peaks until finally after some very heavy fighting the highest peak was at last in British hands, however, with most of the troops assigned to this part of the battle field, for a short time the conical hill was retaken by the enemy with the temporary loss of two guns.

While the main events were occurring on the Asmai Heights, the Afghans were seen to be congregating on Siah Sang, as they had done on the previous day, and were moving along the eastern flank towards Kohistan. To disperse this force, General Baker despatched a small force of cavalry, with two guns of the horse artillery, under the command of General Gough, however, due to their route being regularly intersected by deep water courses, progress with the guns was slow and by the time these obstacles had been passed the enemy had crossed the Kohistan road and being close to the hills pursuit was deemed to be hopeless.

Captain William Vousden – Victoria Cross No. 354

A party of the 5th Punjab Cavalry, commanded by Captain Vousden had better luck against the enemy. Quartered at the Kings Garden, about mid way between Sherpur and Kabul, Captain Vousden had been sent out by Colonel Williams to be on the lookout for any enemy that may be passing nearby. Just after noon, Captain Vousden, while out on reconnaissance with one troop of his men, observed a force of about 300 to 400 men moving along the left bank of the river and despite being heavily outnumbered he decided to mount an attack.

While the majority of his troop were stopped by heavy fire from Afghans taking cover behind some low stone walls, the Captain with 12 of his men charged into the enemy masses inflicting heavy losses, by his own hand Captain Vousden killed five of the enemy. By repeatedly charging to and fro between the enemy lines the small force managed to disperse the enemy, however, six of the party were wounded.

For his part in this action, Captain Vousden was later awarded the Victoria Cross.

For the last few days, the British operations had been directed towards the breakup of enemy concentrations on the hills around Kabul, in order to prevent the Afghans gaining the city and the stores of ammunition held at the Bala Hissar. General Roberts was reluctant to abandon Kabul and the Bala Hissar, however, being confronted by overwhelming numbers of Afghans, who were slowly establishing good positions the decision was made for all the British troops to fall back on Sherpur.

With the decision having been made, General Roberts issued his Generals with orders to fall back on Sherpur in an orderly fashion. General Macpherson's brigade was threatened with heavy enemy fire during their disengagement and retirement, however, the troops and baggage managed to withdraw with comparatively small losses.

Captain Arthur Hammond – Victoria Cross No. 353

The retirement of General Bakers brigade, down the eastern face of the Asmai Heights was also carried out under heavy enemy fire, the success being due in no small part to the actions of Captain Hammond and his men. Captain Hammond and some of his men from the Corps of Guides had occupied the crest of the ridge for some hours and as the men from the 72nd Highlanders and the rest of the Guides began their retreat he remained in position, faced by large numbers of Afghans who by now were swarming up the western side of the hills, to assist their departure.

With the Afghans only 30 yards from his position, Captain Hammond began to withdraw his own men and when during the retreat one of these was wounded he stopped and helped to carry him away.

For these actions, Captain Hammond was subsequently awarded the Victoria Cross.

General Baker's withdrawal was also accomplished with relatively few losses and by late afternoon his brigade was back within the cantonments at Sherpur. That night, Afghan forces occupied Kabul and the Bala Hissar.

Defence of Sherpur

Having assembled all of his troops in Sherpur, General Roberts had two initial objectives; to improve the town defences in order to fend off any attacks that the Afghans might make and to improve the comfort of the accommodation as Sherpur was now to be the winter quarters for his troops.

In the short term, General Roberts had no concerns regarding supplies as Sherpur had sufficient supplies to feed the men for about four months and feed for the animals for about six weeks. In addition there was an excellent water supply, an abundance of firewood and medical supplies together with sufficient ammunition for both guns and rifles to last for three to four months.

Soon after first arriving at Kabul, General Roberts had the foresight to convene a committee to investigate ways to defend Sherpur in the event of the cantonments being besieged. One of the recommendations, to construct six towers on the Bimaru heights, together with the digging of trenches and gun pits and positions for artillery had already been enacted, however, the trenches were now deepened and extended.

Although the perimeter of the defences at Sherpur was extensive, just over four miles in length, which would be difficult to man with only 7,000 active men; a large part of this was protected by a wall about 20 feet tall. Only one wall on the east of the enclosure was incomplete and only 7 feet tall, this was soon remedied and with the addition of an abattis and wire entanglements the defences were brought up to scratch.

General Roberts divided the defence of the town into five sections giving command of each section to; General Macpherson, Colonel Jenkins, General Hugh Gough, General Hills and Colonel Brownlow respectively. General Massy was appointed to the command of the centre of the cantonment and General Baker to the command of the reserve.

Since their occupation of the town on 14th December, the enemy had been fairly quiet as they concentrated their efforts on looting Kabul, so the British forces were able to direct most of their attention to improving the defences undisturbed.

On the afternoon of 16th December, General Roberts received the welcome news that Colonel Hudson, who was besieged at Lataband, had managed to successfully fend off an attack by the Afghans, however, as his food was due to run out in a few days the General organised two resupply missions by friendly Hazara tribesmen, one of which was successful.

On the 18th December, the General also received news from General Charles Gough who had been stationed at Gandamak with his brigade; General Gough reported that although he had been able to advance as far as Jagdalak, he did not consider his force to be strong enough to advance on Kabul.

As the 1,381 men under the command of General Gough were of excellent quality and included artillery and cavalry as well as infantry, General Roberts ordered General Gough to make every effort to reach Kabul and in order to supplement his forces he was initially directed to relieve Colonel Hudson and his troops at Lataband. A further message from Colonel Hudson was received on 21st December, stating that General Gough was expected to arrive on the following day, however, with depleted numbers of cavalry as some of these had been used by General Gough to reinforce some outposts. To rectify the cavalry issue, General Roberts despatched the 12th Bengal Cavalry to Lataband.

Battle of Sherpur

On 21st December, intelligence was received that the Afghans were planning an attack on the British positions, and the mullahs were making frantic appeals to the people to unite and exterminate the infidels. The night of 22nd December passed without incident, however, as dawn broke on the 23rd December signal fires were seen on the surrounding hills and as this was the last day of the holy month of Moharram it came as no surprise when heavy firing broke out.

Initially it was too dark to observe what was happening outside the walls, however, when star-shells were fired, a large enemy force was observed at about 1,000 yards away. With the improving light all of the British batteries opened fire, followed by volley after volley of rifle fire. Despite the withering fire, the Afghans mounted assault after assault, often reaching the abattis, however, each of these was repulsed with the enemy suffering heavy casualties.

At about 10 o'clock there was a short lull in the fighting, however, after about an hour it was renewed with increased vigour. Although the British fire was successful in repulsing each attack, fire from the walls would not drive the enemy from

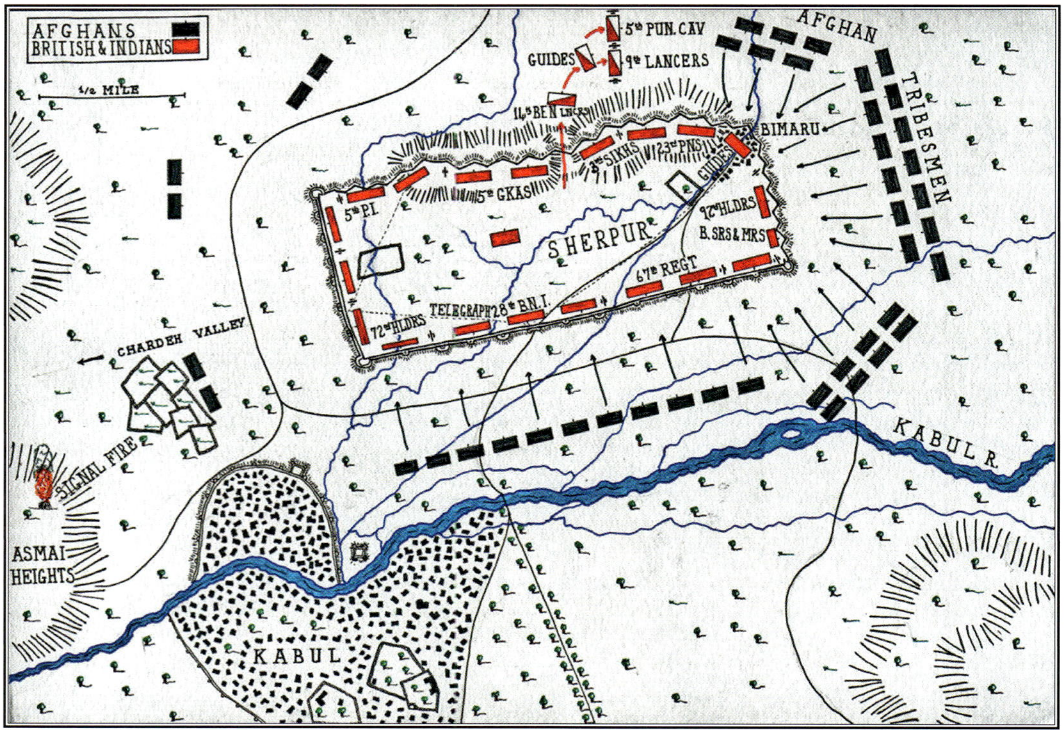

Figure 58. Battle of Sherpur

the field so General Roberts decided to go on the offensive and launch his own attack.

A force of the 5th Punjab Cavalry, under the command of Major Craster, supported by artillery commanded by Colonel Williams was directed against a large force assembled near the village of Kurja Kila with great success and the Afghans wavered and then broke. This British success seemed to reduce the enemy's resolve and by 1 o'clock they were in full flight, at which time General Massy and his cavalry were unleashed to give chase; by nightfall the area around Sherpur had been cleared of all enemy forces, so General Roberts took this opportunity to destroy some of the nearby villages which had been sheltering the enemy.

It was estimated that the Afghan forces employed in the attack were about 100,000; from the 15th December until the end of this first defence the British losses were 18 killed and 68 wounded, however, the enemy losses were estimated to be in excess of 3,000.

On the morning of 24th December, the fort of Mahomed Sharif was occupied and a force was sent out to escort General Charles Gough and his men into Sherpur.

Butkhak was reoccupied on 26th December and work was started on repairing the telegraph lines and re-establish communications with India; work also proceeded to allow the advance of troops from the Khyber Pass towards Kabul.

With Kabul now reoccupied, General Hills resumed his function as Military Governor of the city and General Roberts issued a proclamation, announcing a general amnesty for all but the enemy leaders, this did much to calm the local population.

On 29th December, communications were re-established with the Khyber and on the next day Seh Baba was occupied together with Lataband.

As a further defensive measure for Sherpur, all walls and enclosures within 1,000 yards of the cantonment, in the city and surrounding villages, were levelled to improve the British fields of fire and to deny cover to any attackers.

Kandahar Field Force

When news of the massacre of the Mission at Kabul reached the field force, they were in the process of withdrawing from Kandahar, in accordance with the terms of the treaty of Gandamak, and moving to Peshin. However, on 5th September, General Sir Donald Stewart in command of the field force, received orders to reverse this movement and concentrate all of his forces once again at Kandahar, this was accomplished within 10 days.

On 16th September, General Sir Frederick Haines, commander-in-chief of forces in India, informed the Indian government that a demonstration in strength from Kandahar towards Kalat-i-Ghilzai was needed and that he had issued General Sir Donald Stewart with orders to this effect.

General R. J. Hughes, with the 1,418 men of the 2nd Infantry Brigade, left Kandahar on 23rd September heading for Kalat-i-Ghilzai which they reached on 30th September without encountering any opposition. An advance of the brigade to Ghazni was considered, however, due to a lack of supplies and transport this was ruled out. An advance force under the command of General Hughes, did move forward to Ab-i-Tazi which was reached on 10th October.

With news that a force of Ghilzai warriors was congregating near Shahjui, on 24th October General Hughes sent out a strong patrol, under the command of Colonel Kennedy to reconnoitre the enemy positions.

After advancing for about ten miles, the fire of an enemy piquet was spotted on the road at a point about two miles from the village; the piquet was captured by a small force led by Captain J. H. Broome but not before some of the enemy managed to escape and give a warning to the main force at Shahjui. Captain Broome and his men advanced along the road and occupied an isolated mound on the plain in front of the village and with day now breaking, about 900 of the enemy left the village and advanced on the mound but halted when they saw Colonel Kennedy with the main British force.

The British artillery and infantry now began to fire on the enemy who were reluctant to engage in battle and began to move off to their left. A running fight now took place which continued over broken country for about six miles until the Afghans reached a high hill surrounded by broken ground, the site of a derelict fort, where they prepared to make a stand.

Captain Euston Sartorius – Victoria Cross No. 350

At this stage, Colonel Kennedy ordered Captain Sartorius, with men of the 59th Regiment of Foot, to seize the outworks at the foot of the hill and then work around and bring his fire on the enemy cavalry who were on the far side of the hill.

Captain Sartorius and his men captured the positions at the foot of the hill and after working around the hill were in sight of the enemy cavalry when two British shells, intended for the top of the hill fell short and exploded amongst his men. The Ghilzai horsemen chose this moment to launch an attack, however, they were distracted by Captain Broome and his cavalry, who after firing a volley began to slowly retire, followed by the enemy cavalry; during the ensuing hand to hand fighting the enemy cavalry were driven from the field, losing their standard and leaving their leader and 15 men dead on the ground. The enemy were now dispersing in all directions in some disarray, but due to the nature of the broken ground it was impractical to follow them.

A few of the Afghans still clung to what by now was a perilous position on the hilltop, so leading a party of 15 of his men up a narrow zigzag path Captain Sartorius moved off to capture the summit, while the remainder of his men laid down covering fire.

On reaching the crest of the hill, the seven enemy defenders fought valiantly, however, were all soon despatched. During the attack Captain Sartorius was wounded by sword cuts to both hands and one of his men was killed.

For his part in this action, Captain Sartorius was later awarded the Victoria Cross.

After the battle, Colonel Kennedy and his force rejoined the brigade at Shahjui and on 26th October, General Hughes and his brigade began the return march and after leaving a garrison at Kalat-i-Ghilzai arrived back at Kandahar on 8th November.

During December there was a great deal of discussion between the Viceroy and his Commander-in-Chief regarding the deployment of General Stewart and the Kandahar Field Force, the Viceroy wanted General Stewart to advance towards Kabul, to assist General Roberts. When asked for his plan of campaign, General Sir Frederick Haines replied that the movement to Kabul could not start before the end of March, due to the need to assemble troops to replace General Stewarts men at Kandahar and the need to assemble stores and transport for the move to Kabul.

In preparation for the upcoming operations, General Phayre and his staff together with the headquarters of the 1st Bombay Infantry arrived at Kandahar and took over command of the garrison. Detachments of the 1st Bombay Division continued to slowly arrive at Kandahar, however, the build-up was slower than expected and General Stewart, who had originally planned to leave on 15th March had to delay the departure until the end of the month.

On 29th March, General R. Barter left Kandahar with his brigade, closely followed on the 30th by the Field Force Headquarters and Cavalry and on 31st March, General Hughes left Mohmand with the 2nd Brigade. General Barter's brigade advanced via Tagak into the Khushk-i-Rud valley, while the remainder of the force advanced via Jaldak to Kalat-i-Ghilzai which was reached without incident on 6th–7th April 1880. On the 8th April, the Field Force continued their advance, moving along each bank of the river Tarnak, towards Shahjui which they reached on 11th April and then towards Mukur which was reached on the 14th April.

Throughout the journey large enemy forces were spotted by the scouts, marching on parallel paths to that of the column, however, no opposition was faced, apart from a few desultory shots fired at distance towards the British Force; which by 17th April had reached Jan Murad.

Battle of Ahmed Khel

On 18th April, the cavalry advanced guard reported that a force of between 8 to 10,000 Afghans was advancing on the flank of the British column. On the following day the column, which was 6 miles long, left Mashaki and on approaching a range of low hills, on either side of the road, the Afghans were noted to have taken up positions along the ridges on the left hand side of the road.

As they came to a position opposite that of the Afghans, the British field and horse artillery were deployed on the crests of a range of knolls on the right hand side of the road, however, before they could begin firing in earnest, the enemy who were spread out across a two mile front mounted an attack. While successive waves of enemy infantry poured against the British lines, their cavalry mounted an attack down two ravines to threaten the left flank and rear of the British position.

Despite the heavy fire of case and shrapnel into their midst, the Afghans continued their advance and General Stewart was forced to send his reserve into the battle lines. The deadly rifle fire from the increased British force now began to tell and after the artillery was deployed to the new position, the cavalry was also having considerable success. After an hour of fierce fighting, and with mounting losses the Afghans were forced back and the attack was soon turned into a rout with the force of about 15,000 men moving off into the hills.

The enemy losses were estimated to be about 3,000 killed or wounded while the British loss was limited to 17 killed and 68 wounded; after a rest of about two hours, during which the British recovered their wounded and buried their dead. the force moved off to Nani where they spent the night.

By 21st April, General Stewart and his men were camped outside Ghazni, which had been abandoned by the Afghan forces and on 23rd April an action was fought at the villages of Arzu and Shalez were a force of about 5,000 of the enemy had been concentrating. Enemy losses were estimated to be about 400 killed or wounded while the British losses were two killed and eight wounded.

On 28th April, in accordance with orders that he had just received from Simla, General Stewart handed over command of the Ghazni Field Force to Brigadier-General Hughes and proceeded to Kabul where he arrived on 2nd May and assumed command of all British forces in Afghanistan.

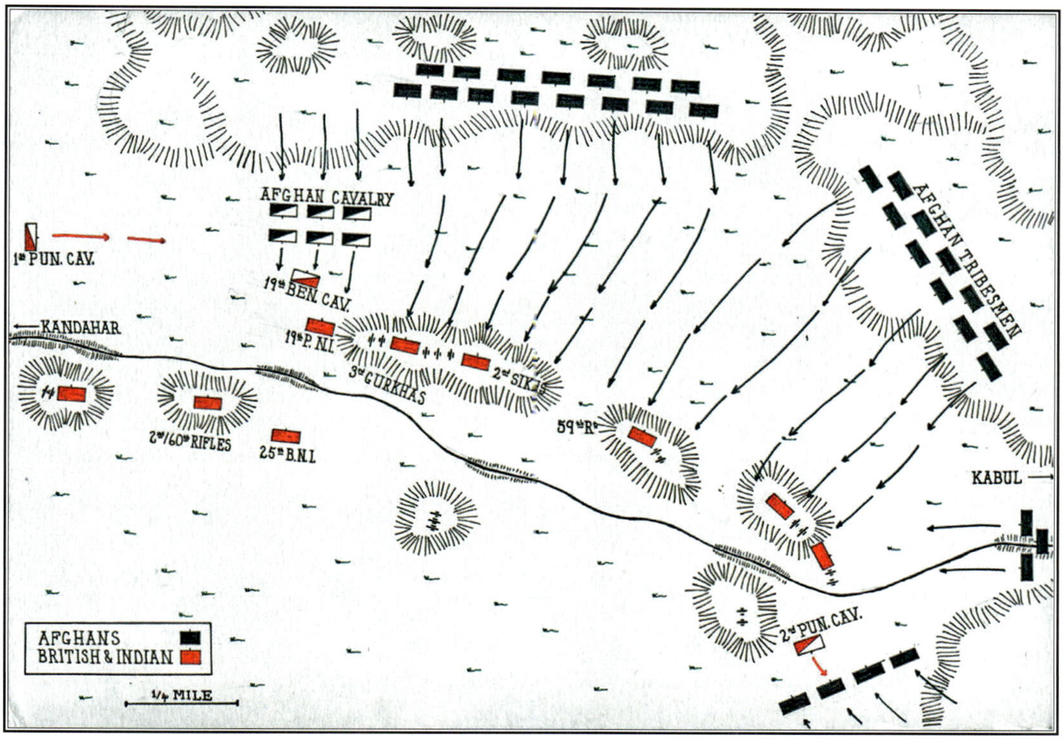

Figure 59. Battle of Ahmed Khel

Abdur Rahman Khan declared Emir

A durbar was held on 13th April 1880 to discuss the various candidates for the position as Emir of Afghanistan and after much campaigning and discussions with some of the main tribal leaders, Abdur Rahman Khan was confirmed as Emir at a further durbar held on 22nd July 1880. Abdur Rahman Khan would hold this position until his death on 1st October 1901.

Figure 60. Abdur Rahman Khan

Change of British Government

The general election of 1880 saw the Conservative government, led by Benjamin Disraeli (Lord Beaconsfield) replaced by a Liberal government and on 21st April 1880, William Ewart Gladstone was appointed as the new Prime Minister.

Following the change of government, Lord Lytton was replaced as the Viceroy of India by Lord Ripon and Lord Hartington was appointed as the Secretary of State for India.

Events at Kandahar

On 11th April 1880, Lieutenant-General Primrose arrived at Kandahar to take over command of the city from Brigadier-General Phayre who had been appointed to the command of the line of communications.

Sher Ali Khan was appointed as the Wali (governor) of Kandahar on 11th May.

When Abdur Rahman was proclaimed as the Emir of Afghanistan by Britain, his cousin Ayub Khan who was the brother of the former Emir, Yakub Khan, marched from Herat on 15th June, with 7,500 men and headed towards Kandahar to claim his throne.

On 4th July, Brigadier-General George Burrows, with a small force of about 2,500 British and Indian troops was despatched to intercept Ayub Khan's force and after reaching the river Helmand on 11th July established his camp on the river bank opposite Girishk. Wali Sher Ali Khan with 2,000 of his infantry were stationed at Girishk, however, with the arrival of General Burrows force they decided to mutiny and moved off to join Yakub Khan's force.

With the departure of Sher Ali Khan's men, General Burrows determined that his position on the open plain was now untenable and on 15th July he moved off with his men to Kushk-i-Nakhud, where supplies were plentiful and covered the roads from Girishk and Haidarabad (via the Malmand and Maiwand passes) to Kandahar.

On the afternoon of the 26th July 1880, General Burrows received news that the Afghan force was making for the Maiwand pass, only a few miles from his location and he decided that he would attack the advanced guard of the force on the following morning and take control of the pass.

Battle of Maiwand

At 4:30 on the morning of 27th July, the nearly 2,500 men of his command were called to parade by General Burrows in preparation for the advance on Maiwand. Just before daybreak, while the baggage was being loaded, an advance guard of cavalry was sent to scout the way ahead. Due to the lack of men to leave behind as a guard for his baggage, General Burrows was forced to advance encumbered by almost 2,000 pack animals carrying his baggage and stores.

Due to the heat of the day and lack of food and drink General Burrows force was further weakened, as illustrated by the words of Captain Mosley Mayne *"Even by nine in the morning the heat had become intense. It was to become hotter still, with the temperature reaching over 120 degrees in the shade, had there been any … We were marching along a wide flat valley, its sandy desert floor cut by dry watercourses and covered with flinty stones and scattered scrub. The shimmering haze, which had already given way to mirages, made it difficult to see clearly for more than about 1500 yards across the baking ground … The orders for our move to intercept the enemy at Maiwand had been given late the night before, much of which had been spent in packing up our camp at Khushk-i-Nakhud which was to be struck by 5.30 a.m. It was thus an already tired force that began marching north early that morning, the 27th July, few of whom had eaten since the previous evening."*

At about 10 o'clock in the morning, while advancing towards Maiwand, General Burrows force came across several large bodies of enemy cavalry and off in the distance large bodies of men advancing towards Maiwand. Unfortunately, this was not

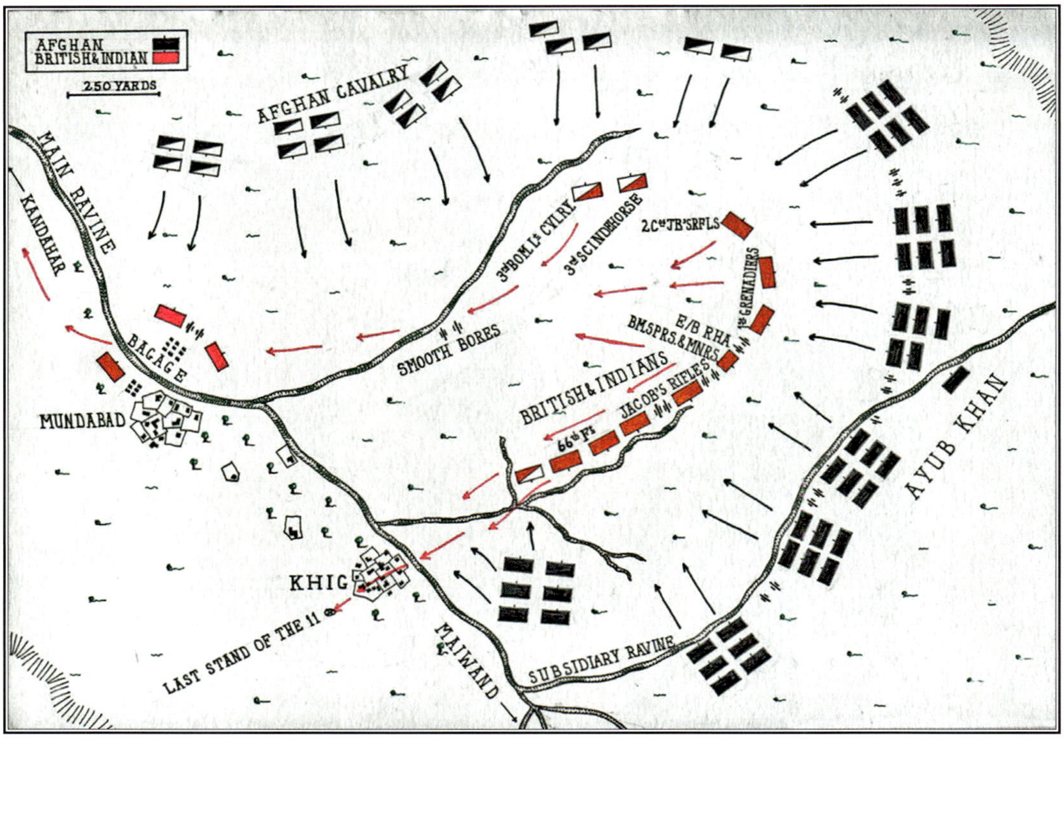

Figure 61. Battle of Maiwand

an advanced guard as expected but was in fact Ayub Khan's main force which numbered about 25,000 men (6,000 infantry, 4,000 cavalry and 15,000 irregular Ghazis) supported by five artillery batteries (36 guns).

After reaching the village of Mundabad, which was found to be unoccupied, General Burrows established a position in walled gardens, where he could leave his baggage and the sick, who by now numbered almost 100 men.

General Burrows moved his men to a point about 1,500 yards in advance of the Mundabad ravine and with the horse artillery at his centre placed the Grenadiers and field artillery on his left flank together with his cavalry, while the men of the 66th Regiment and Jacob's Rifles occupied the right flank.

The battle started with an artillery duel, however, with a larger number and range, the 36 guns of the Afghan army where having a greater effect than the 12 British guns, with most of the casualties being inflicted on the British cavalry. The bombardment lasted for two hours, until about noon, when a lull in the Afghan firing allowed their cavalry to mount an attack against the left flank while hordes of Ghazis attacked the right flank.

Despite their heavy losses, the superior numbers of the Afghan army enabled both flanks of the British position to be turned. At this point Captain John Slade, with his field artillery, withdrew from the action in order to replenish their expended ammunition, unfortunately many of the sepoys in the Indian native regiments, who had lost most of their European officers, took this as a sign to retreat and their line soon began to waver.

At about 2:30 in the afternoon, a concerted Afghan attack on Jacob's Rifles, who had lost almost a quarter of their number, including their only British officer, drove the men back into the ranks of the Grenadiers and began to roll up the left flank and began to threaten the guns of the horse artillery.

Sergeant Patrick Mullane – Victoria Cross No. 356

After firing a last volley of case shot into the Afghan hordes, Captain Slade, who had taken command of the horse artillery when Major Blackwood[23] was wounded, ordered the guns to be limbered up.

On the left, Lieutenant Maclaine's two guns were overrun and his gunners were engaged in vicious hand to hand fighting with the enemy, Sergeant Mullane rode up and managed to save one of the guns and while retiring under heavy fire he returned to pick up Driver Pickwell Istead[24] who was wounded and place him on the limber before charging through the Ghazis.

For this action Sergeant Mullane was later awarded the Victoria Cross; his citation also mentions several acts of bravery when during the retreat he volunteered to obtain water for the wounded.

On the right Lieutenant Osborne managed to limber up his two guns, but was killed while helping his gunners to hook up the guns.

Captain Slade, deployed the remaining four guns of the battery about 400 yards further back and attempted to cover the retreat but was eventually forced to retire to Mundabad, from where he continued to provide support to the retreating troops.

A vain attempt was made by the cavalry to give the infantry time to regroup, after their mauling by the enemy artillery, however, despite helping the retirement of the Grenadiers their charges were largely ineffective and they retired to Mundabad and joined the rearguard being formed by the horse artillery.

When the retiring Grenadiers and Rifles entered the dried up watercourse occupied by the 66th Regiment, the men of the 66th were forced out into the open and their commander Colonel Galbraith, had little option but to join in the general retreat and eventually reached the main ravine in front of Khig, to the east of Mundabad.

The 66th, now reduced to about 200 men, rallied around their colours and although surrounded and with their commanding officer Colonel Galbraith having been killed, they mounted a fierce resistance and retired slowly to a walled garden in Khig where a last stand was made. The men bravely fought to defend their colours until only 11 men remained standing, with their fate sealed these last 11 men left the walled garden and charged the Afghans, all being killed in the process.

In the face of such an overwhelming force, the British were forced to continue their retreat and began to make their way to Kandahar, the retreat was covered by E Battery / B Brigade of the Royal Horse Artillery commanded by Captain Slade and a detachment of Bombay Sappers and Miners commanded by Lieutenant Henn of the Royal Engineers.

Gunner James Collis – Victoria Cross No. 357

In the early stages of the artillery duel, the gun manned by Gunner Collis was struck by an Afghan shell which killed one gunner, Sergeant Wood and wounded Lieutenant Fowler and another gunner.

When the battle was lost Gunner Collis and E Battery provided covering fire, to allow the infantry to retreat, until their withdrawal was ordered. During the retreat of the Horse Artillery they were charged down by Afghan Cavalry and Gunner Collis received a sabre wound to the forehead, above his right eye, before he managed to shoot and kill his assailant.

23 Major Blackwood would be killed later in the day, during the last stand of the 66th regiment at Khig.

24 Sadly Driver Istead died soon after being placed on the limber.

When the pace of the retreat slowed down, Gunner Collis, despite being wounded himself, managed to place some of the wounded on his gun limber and with his carbine defended his charges against the enemy cavalry who were continuing to harry the battery.

Gunner Collis continued to tend the wounded throughout the day, stopping whenever possible to find water for the men.

It was on the second day of the retreat, while fetching water from a village well, that gunner Collis spotted a troop of Afghan Cavalry who threatened to overtake his gun and after urging his men to speed off he set about firing at the enemy from a pile of rocks. His fire was so accurate that it forced the Afghans to dismount in order to return his fire, allowing his gun carriage to make its escape.

Gunner Collis was himself rescued by the arrival of General Nuttall and a troop of Indian Cavalry who rode up and chased off the Afghans.

For this action, Gunner Collis was later awarded the Victoria Cross.

The last of General Burrows force finally reached Kandahar at 6 o'clock in the evening on 28th July, exhausted and having had no food since the evening of the 26th July.

The British force suffered a severe defeat at Maiwand with heavy losses, 21 officers and 948 men were killed and 8 officers and 169 men were wounded. Despite the heavy defeat, the British forces had inflicted significant losses on the enemy with 1,500 regulars and 4,000 Ghazis having been killed and about 1,500 men seriously wounded.

Siege of Kandahar

With the arrival of Ayub Khan's main force expected in a matter of hours, the garrison spent their time in preparing the city for defence; the cantonments were abandoned and the troops, baggage and sick and wounded were moved to the citadel within the city walls and the city gates were closed.

A large Durani population was resident in the city and as well as posing a security threat, they would also add to the drain on the limited supply of food and water; General Brooke proposed that the Afghans should be expelled and following orders from General Primrose, the entire Pathan population was sent out of the city on 29th/30th July.

With a garrison of just over 5,000 men, General Primrose assigned General Burrows to the Herat front, General Nuttall to the Kabul front, General Brooke to the Shikarpur front and Colonel Mainwaring (operating under his direct command) to the Eedgah front.

The advanced parties of Ayub Khan's force arrived outside Kandahar on 30th July and the main elements of the Afghan army arrived over the next few days. Instead of mounting the expected night assault on the city, Ayub Khan directed his men to occupy and fortify the villages and compounds that surrounded the city, from where he was able to keep up a constant but largely ineffective fire against the British garrison.

On 13th August, Colonel J. Hills VC, commander of the Royal Engineers, put forward a plan to disrupt the Afghan encirclement of the city by making an assault against one of the occupied villages. With some modifications the plan was accepted by General Primrose and on 15th August General Brooke was appointed to the command of a force of just over 1,500 men that was ordered to attack the village of Deh Khwaja on the following morning.

Battle of Deh Khwaja

At 4:45 on the morning of 16th August, the British artillery opened fire on the village and at 5 o'clock the first two columns of General Brookes force left the city via the Kabul Gate; a third column, forming the reserve remained at the Kabul Gate.

At 4:30, the British cavalry, under the command of General Nuttall, left the Eedgah Gate and moved to the south east of the village from where they would support the attack.

At about 5:30 the two British columns entered Deh Khwaja under heavy musket fire from the Afghans and at this stage, large numbers of the enemy were observed crossing the open ground to the south of the village; however, these were driven back when charged by a troop of cavalry commanded by Lieutenant Geoghegan. Unable to pursue the fleeing enemy, due to the broken ground, the cavalry returned to their position at the south of the village.

The British infantry were making good progress, clearing the village, however, as General Brooke determined that it would be impossible to hold the position, the order was issued for his force to retire. After a second cavalry charge to disperse a large Ghazi force approaching the village from Bala Karez, General Nuttall received orders for his cavalry to support the withdrawal of the British infantry from the village.

Lieutenant William Chase – Victoria Cross No. 358
Private Thomas Ashford – Victoria Cross No. 359

As soon as the British left the village it was immediately reoccupied by the Afghans who began to lay down a heavy fire on the retreating British columns, causing large numbers of casualties.

The 3rd Column, commanded by Colonel Heathcote had advanced to the centre in front of the village and were providing cover for the retreating British forces. It was during this action that Lieutenant Chase, assisted by Private Ashford went to the rescue of the wounded Private Massey who was taking refuge in a blockhouse.

Lieutenant Chase placed the wounded Private on his back and began the journey across 400 yards of open ground towards the safety of his company who were sheltering behind a wall. Under the heavy enemy fire directed against him, Lieutenant Chase had to fall to the ground on two occasions, while he fought for breath but eventually reached cover to the cheers of the men sheltered there.

During the dash across the open space, Lieutenant Chase was accompanied by Private Ashford, who provided assistance to the rescue.

For this action Lieutenant Chase and Private Ashford were both awarded the Victoria Cross.

During the disastrous retreat, General Brooke, who was supporting the wounded Captain Cruikshank who he had rescued from the village, was shot down and killed. By 7:30, the retreat was complete and the survivors were back within the relative security of the city walls. Although the operation had some limited success, having inflicted large numbers of enemy casualties including several notable chiefs the British force suffered high casualties with 106 men killed and 117 men wounded.

Relief of Kandahar

Following the Battle of Deh Khwaja, the Afghans continued their siege of Kandahar, however, the besieged men took heart in the news that a relieving force was being assembled at Quetta and that a strong force commanded by General Roberts was making its way to the city from Kabul.

When news of the siege at Kandahar reached the Viceroy in India, his commander in chief Sir Donald Stewart advised that a relieving force should be despatched from Kabul as soon as possible and on 8th August General Roberts left Kabul at the head of a force of almost 10,000 men to begin the long march to Kandahar.

After reaching Tirandaz on 26th August, General Roberts received a message from Kandahar to the effect that after hearing news of the approach of the General's force, Ayub Khan had raised the siege on 23rd August and had moved with his force to Mazra in the Arghandab Valley.

On 28th August, after arriving at Robat and having received the news that Ayub Khan was strengthening his position and intended to make a stand, General Roberts decided to call a halt at Robat in order to rest his men and animals before the final push to Kandahar. This halt was somewhat extended, due to the illness of General Roberts, however, after having covered the 280 miles from Kabul in just 20 days the additional rest was most welcome.

General Roberts and his men arrived at Kandahar on 31st August, having marched the 313 miles from Kabul under very trying circumstances due to the vagaries of the weather and on their arrival 940 sick were sent to the hospital in the citadel. The General established his camp in the old cantonments to the west of the city where there was a good supply of water and was a location within striking distance of Ayub Khan's camp.

A reconnaissance, determined that Ayub Khan had established a strong position on the Baba Wali Kotal, supported by three artillery pieces which would result in heavy losses if attacked directly. With this intelligence, General Roberts decided to turn the Afghan right flank to gain the rear of the Baba Wali range and make an attack against Ayub Khan's camp at Mazra.

Battle of Kandahar

On 1st September 1880, General Roberts outlined the following plan to his commanding officers; a feign attack by the 3rd Infantry brigade was to make a demonstration against the left of the enemy line on the Baba Wali Kotal, while the main attack by the 1st and 2nd Infantry brigades would be directed at the right of the enemy line near the village of Pir Paimal. The cavalry brigade, under the command of General Gough was held in readiness to advance to the Arghandab river to threaten the rear of Ayub Khan's camp and cut off his retreat towards Girishk and Khakrez.

By 9 o'clock, with all his forces in position, General Roberts launched the battle with an artillery barrage against the enemy position on the Baba Wali Kotal; as the enemy seemed to be preparing for a counter attack, rather than waiting for the British assault, it appears that General Roberts ruse had been successful. To continue the ruse, the 3rd infantry brigade remained in position facing the Baba Wali Kotal, prepared to deal with any counter attack that the enemy might mount.

Meanwhile, General Macpherson with the 1st brigade launched his attack against the village of Gundi Mulla Sahibdad, just short of Pir Paimal while General MacGregor and the 2nd brigade attacked the village of Abbasabad. The two villages were soon taken and the enemy fell back in some disorder to their positions at Pir Paimal which were soon turned, giving

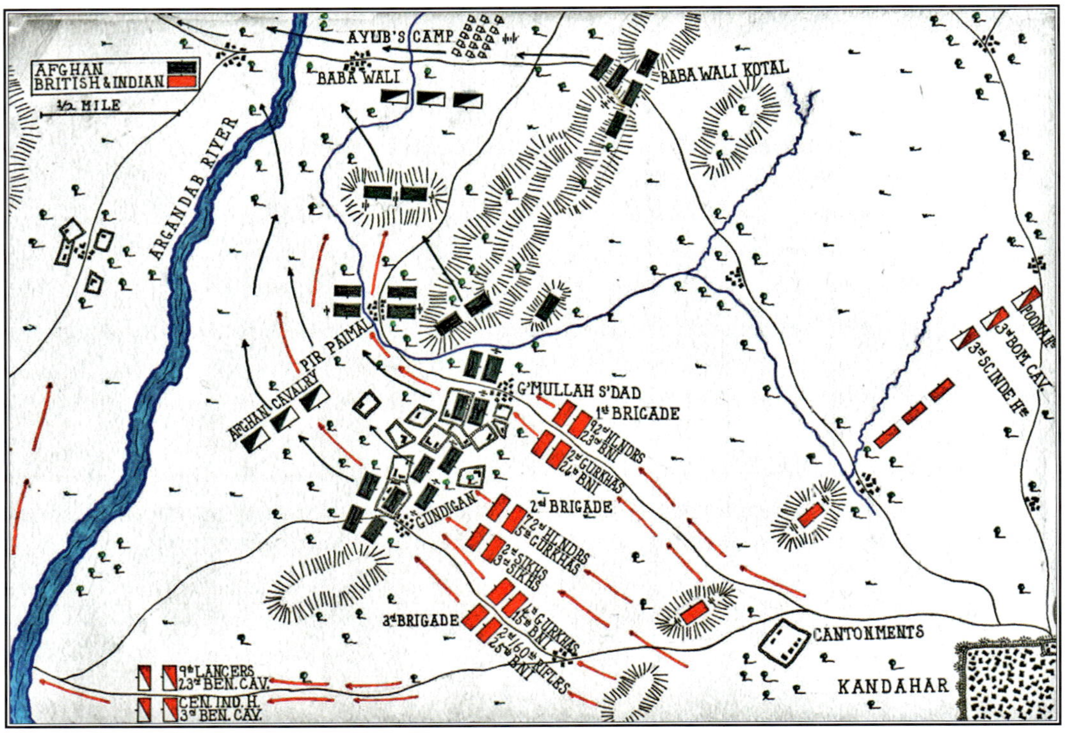

Figure 62. Battle of Kandahar

the British force access to the rear of the Baba Wali Kotal and a direct path to Mazra where Ayub Khan was entrenched in his camp.

The Afghans on the Baba Wali Kotal, turned their guns to face the British force and in the face of this increased artillery fire, it became clear that an attack on Mazra should be launched immediately to avoid becoming bogged down by the enemy fire. With fixed bayonets, the combined force of the 1st and 2nd infantry brigades charged into the defences around Mazra and after some fierce hand to hand fighting the enemy were driven from their positions and were soon in full flight.

Not realising the extent of his victory, and expecting the enemy to make a stand in fresh positions, General Ross ordered the men to halt and replenish their ammunition. After a short halt, the British brigades continued their advance and after reaching the camp of Ayub Khan, which had been abandoned, the scale of their victory became obvious as the enemy had moved off with such haste that they had left behind all of their artillery and vast amounts of ammunition.

British losses during the battle were 35 killed and 213 wounded, it was estimated that the enemy had about 1,200 killed and a large number of wounded.

After the battle the British troops returned to duties at Kandahar. Subsequently it became evident that Ayub Khan and a small number of his followers retreated to Herat, with the remainder scattering across the country.

End of the War

The Battle of Kandahar was the final event of note during the war, and with Ayub Khan and his followers now dispersed there was now no organised opposition and Abdur Rahman Khan was now the undisputed leader of all Afghanistan.

22

ZULU WAR (1879)

Background

Since 1685, the Dutch had operated a colony in southern Africa, however, in 1795 the British seized the Cape to prevent it falling into the hands of the French but in 1803 the British returned control of the Cape back to the Dutch. In 1805, the Cape again reverted to British control, when ceded by the French as a prize during the Napoleonic Wars. British sovereignty of the Cape was formally recognised by the Congress of Vienna in 1815, with the Dutch receiving a payment of £6 million.

Like the Dutch before them, the British had little interest in her South African colonies other than as a location for secure ports to resupply ships trading with their empire in India, however, in the 1820s significant numbers of settlers did arrive in the colony.

The Boer colony of Natalia was established on 12th October

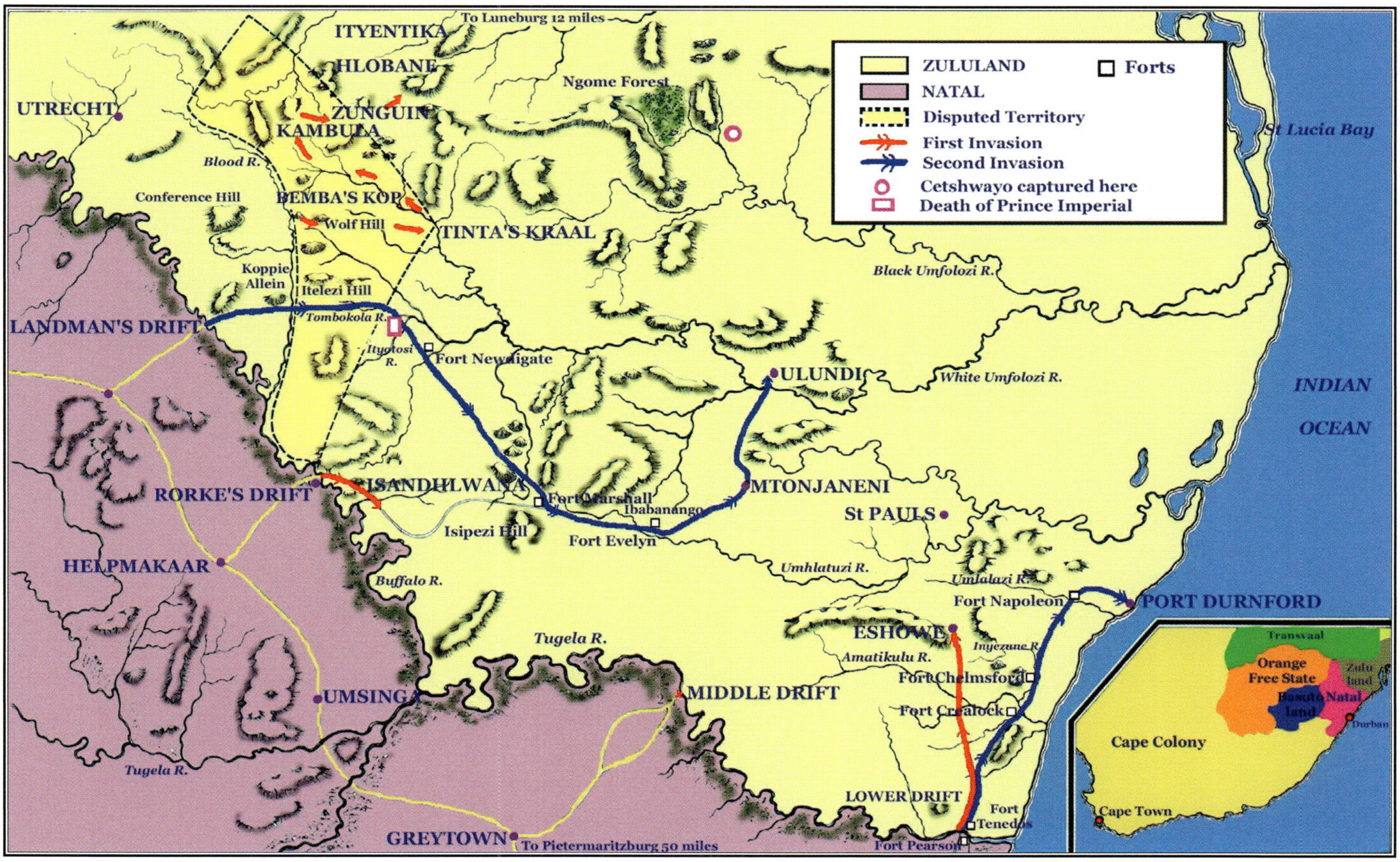

Figure 63. Zululand

1839, however, on 12th May 1843 the colony was annexed by Britain and renamed Natal.

Following the treaty of the Sand River Convention on 17th January 1852, the Boer colony of Transvaal was recognised by the British as an independent entity, to the north of the Vaal River, which was initially populated by about 40,000 Boer settlers. On 12th April 1877, due to the bankrupt state of the colony the British annexed the Transvaal.

The economy of the Cape was drastically reformed in 1867 following the discovery of diamonds, over the next few years the Cape produced more diamonds than India had in over 2,000 years and by the 1870s and '80s was responsible for 95% of the global diamond production. Operation of the diamond mines was dependent upon men from the native tribes, including the Zulu, for their labour and as an incentive, in addition to their wages, the workers were often given firearms by the mine owners.

For a number of years, the Zulu had been quiet on the Natal border and only some minor incursions occurred on their border with the Transvaal, however, a boundary dispute had the potential for trouble between the Zulu and Transvaal. A large tract of land on the west boundary of Zululand, between the Buffalo and Ponolo rivers, which had for many years been occupied by Transvaal settlers was claimed by the Zulu who had asked the Natal government to arbitrate on the matter.

Eventually on 7th March 1878, the Rorke's Drift Commission appointed to consider the matter sat for five weeks after which they decided that sovereignty rights remained with the Zulu king Cetywayo, however, the genuine settlers who had managed the lands were granted private rights and allowed to continue with their occupation of the land. This decision seemed to meet the needs of both parties.

The Build-up to War

On 31st March 1877, Lord Carnarvon, the Under-Secretary of State for the Colonies appointed Sir Henry Bartle Frere as High Commissioner for southern Africa. Frere was sent to Cape Town with the mission to implement Lord Carnarvon's vision of a British confederation of the states in southern Africa.

After a short time on the Cape, Commissioner Frere soon realised that the task of uniting the Boer republics, independent native states and British colonies into a single British confederation could not be advanced while a powerful Zulu kingdom existed on its borders.

Knowing that London would not sanction a war with the Zulu, being preoccupied with events in India and Europe, Commissioner Frere began looking for reasons to invade Zulu territory. To help in this matter, Frere turned to Sir Theophilus Shepstone, the recently appointed British Governor of Natal and the Transvaal. Governor Shepstone outlined the border incursions into the Transvaal by the Zulu, which were occurring on a regular basis as well as the increasing number of arms falling into Zulu hands as matters of concern.

Figure 64. Chief Cetywayo

On 28th July 1878, an incident occurred which was manipulated by Commissioner Frere into a cause for invasion; a wife of the Zulu chief Sihayo left him and escaped into Natal. On 28th July, a Zulu party, led by Mehlokazulu a son of chief Sihayo crossed into Natal, seized the woman and after returning to Zululand she was put to death in accordance with Zulu law. A week later, the party returned and seized another wife of Sihayo who had left her husband to take refuge in Natal, again upon the return to Zululand the woman was put to death.

A request was sent to chief Cetywayo to deliver the culprits responsible for the abductions, to be tried by a Natal court for their crimes, an apology and reparation was also requested. As no response had been made to the British requests, the High Commissioner Sir Henry Bartle Frere issued an ultimatum to the Zulu chief on 11th December 1878.

The ultimatum contained 13 demands, mainly relating to the handing over of persons and the payment of fines for a number of misdemeanours, however, it also demanded that Cetywayo should abandon the Zulu military system and disband his army; compliance with the demands was required by 31st December but this was later extended by ten days.

Confident that chief Cetywayo would be unable to accept the British demands, Commissioner Frere instructed General

Frederic Thesiger (Lord Chelmsford) to finalise preparations for the invasion of Zululand.

In preparation for the invasion, four columns were assembled near the river Tugela at the turn of the year, ready to enter Zululand at four different points. Number one (coastal) column, under the command of Colonel Pearson was formed on the Lower Tugela near Fort Pearson. Number two column, under the command of Colonel Durnford was located at Krantz Kop and would support the coastal column. Column three, commanded by Colonel Glyn was assembled at Helpmakaar and would be accompanied by General Thesiger. Column number four, commanded by Colonel Wood VC was based at Utrecht located on the Blood River near the disputed Transvaal border. A fifth column under the command of Colonel Rowlands VC (which had been operating against Sekukuni) was based at Middleburg on the Pongola River. The objective of the invasion force was to cross into Zululand, after the expiry of the ultimatum, and converge on Ulundi.

The War Begins

On the 11th January 1879, with the period of the ultimatum having expired without Cetywayo having met the demands of High Commissioner Frere, the commissioner issued a proclamation stating that he was invading Zululand to exact punishment on the Zulu chief for his incursions into British territory. However, he also stated that he had no quarrel with the Zulu people who would be unharmed unless they took up arms against the British forces.

With the expiry of the ultimatum deadline, Colonel Glyn and the No. 3 column crossed the Buffalo river into Zululand unopposed and moved off towards Rorke's Drift and then joined up with the No. 4 column under Colonel Wood, who were halted at Bemba's Kop.

On the 12th January the combined force of Colonels Glyn and Wood moved against the camp of chief Sihayo, where they captured about 500 cattle and destroyed the kraal by setting it on fire, during the fighting one of Sihayo's sons was killed.

Operations of Colonel Glyn's Column

Having spent some time in preparing the road ahead, which was in poor condition due to the rainy season, on 20th January Colonel Glyn moved with the bulk of his No. 3 column towards Isandhlwana where a camp was established to the east of Isandhlwana Hill; one company of the 1st battalion 24th Regiment of Foot was left behind at Rorke's Drift to form a garrison and guard the supplies.

Battle of Isandhlwana

After arriving at Isandhlwana, Colonel Glyn sent out a force under the command of Commandant Lonsdale and Major Dartnell to reconnoitre the way ahead towards Matyana and after the force reported back that a large force of Zulu warriors was congregating near to their position, General Thesiger decided to mount an attack on the following day.

At daybreak on 22nd January, General Thesiger and Colonel Glyn, together with half of the No. 3 column set out for Matyana after leaving Colonel Pulleine in charge of the remainder of the force which was to remain at the camp. Colonel Durnford, with the No. 2 column at Rorke's Drift, was ordered to move to the camp at Isandhlwana with his cavalry and rocket battery. Just outside the camp, Colonel Durnford was met by Lieutenant Chard, who was returning to Rorke's Drift after riding to the camp at Isandhlwana for orders, and was informed that the British troops were in column outside the camp and that Zulu warriors had been spotted on the crest of distant hills. Lieutenant Chard was concerned that several parties of Zulu were working around to the far left and *"was afraid that they might be going to make a dash at the Drift"*.

After arriving at the camp at about 9 o'clock in the morning Colonel Durnford was ordered by Colonel Pulleine to divide his force of 250 mounted troopers and 250 native infantry into three units which were despatched to positions on the left perimeter of the camp.

Out of sight of the British troops a large body of about 20,000 men from Cetywayo's Zulu army had been congregating near the British camp, initially there was no intention of mounting an attack, however, when the British force was split and a large number of the British troops moved off to Matyana, the opportunity that this presented could not be ignored.

Although significant numbers of Zulu had been seen on the distant hills, the British were ignorant of their strength which they initially supposed to be between 600–800, so Colonel Durnford despatched two of his troops of cavalry, to determine the enemy strength and movement. After reaching a point about five miles from the camp, they came across the whole Zulu army advancing towards Isandhlwana. The troop commanders, Captains Shepstone and Gardner, immediately ordered a retreat and returned to Isandhlwana where they warned Colonel Pulleine of the imminent threat.

Colonel Durnford with another two troops of his cavalry made an advance from the front of the camp and again at a

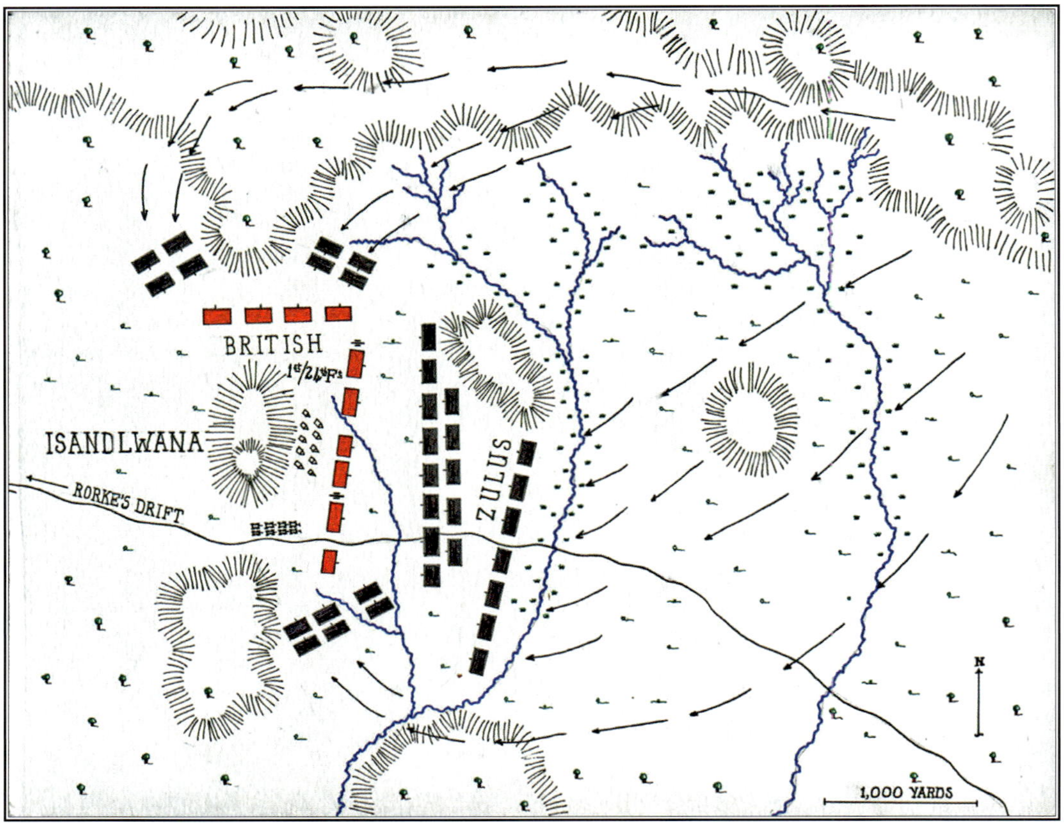

Figure 65. Battle of Isandhlwana

distance of about five miles came across a large body of Zulu warriors; the British cavalry slowly retired until they came across a gully, about 800 yards from the camp, where they decided to make a stand.

At about midday, the bulk of the Zulu army was in sight of the British camp and the artillery began to rain down case shot into their midst; for a time this seemed to have some effect and large numbers of the Zulu warriors took cover by lying on the ground.

This hesitation in the Zulu attack was short lived and they soon began to work their way to the rear of the British camp and had soon surrounded the British position.

Lieutenant Teignmouth Melvill – Victoria Cross No. 360
Lieutenant Nevill Coghill – Victoria Cross No. 361

When it became obvious that the camp would be overrun by Cetywayo's troops, Colonel Pulleine handed the battalions Queen's Colour to his adjutant Lieutenant Melvill with instructions to carry it to safety. In accordance with his orders, Lieutenant Melvill mounted his horse and rode off with the Colours and was soon joined by Lieutenant Coghill. As the Zulu had already cut the track leading back to Rorke's Drift, the only escape route was through a narrow gap to the south which led to the Buffalo River, the border between Zululand and Natal, which was some three miles distant. The pair hoped to cross over the river into Natal and proceed to the safety of Helpmakaar where there was a British garrison.

As they reached the river, dense bush and boulders rendered progress extremely hazardous and the way ahead down a steep gorge into the rushing waters of the river, which was in spate, only added to their difficulties. Lieutenant Melville, who was exhausted by his ride and hampered by the cased Colour and its colour-pike was dismounted and thrown into the river when his horse stumbled on the slippery decline.

Lieutenant Walter Higginson of the 1st battalion 3rd Regiment of the Native Contingent, who had also been dismounted, thrown in the river, and after trying to rescue Lieutenant Melville by grasping the Colour-pike, recounts what happened next; *"Coghill, who had got his horse over alright came riding back down the bank to help Melvill, and as he put his mount in close to us, some Zulus who were about twenty-five yards distant on the other bank commenced firing at us in the water. Almost the first shot killed Coghill's horse, and on his getting clear we started for the Natal bank and managed to get out alright, but when we had covered about a hundred yards up the steep bank we noticed two Zulus following us. When they got within thirty yards of us, Melvill and Coghill fired at them with their revolvers and killed them both. I myself was without arms of any kind, having lost my rifle in the river and did not possess a revolver. When we had gone a few yards further, Melvill said he could go no further and Coghill said the same. When they stopped I pushed on, and on reaching the top of the hill I found four Basutos in whose company I finally escaped by holding on to a horse's tail."*

Lieutenants Melville and Coghill, worn out by their exertions were unable to climb the last 30 yards to comparative safety and were killed by their Zulu pursuers at a place known as Fugitives Drift. For their attempt to save the battalion colours both men were later awarded the Victoria Cross.

Private Samuel Wassall – Victoria Cross No. 362

Private Wassall was another of the men who sought safety by retreating towards the Buffalo River, when the camp at Isandhlwana was overrun by the Zulu.

On reaching the river, Private Wassall saw a comrade, Private Westwood, floundering in the river struggling for his life as he was close to drowning. Without hesitation, he rode down the bank to the river where he dismounted and rescued Private Westwood from the raging torrent. After remounting his horse he dragged Private Westwood across the river to the Natal side, under a heavy fire from the Zulu warriors who were in pursuit.

For saving the life of Private Westwood, Private Wassall was later awarded the Victoria Cross.

Out of a total of 1,774 men involved in the Battle of Isandhlwana, 858 men from the Imperial forces were killed together with 471 native troops. Large amounts of stores, arms and ammunition were also captured by Cetywayo's men.

Defence of Rorke's Drift

Lieutenant John Chard – Victoria Cross No. 363
Lieutenant Gonville Bromhead – Victoria Cross No. 364
Surgeon James Reynolds – Victoria Cross No. 365
Assistant Commissary James Dalton – Victoria Cross No. 366
Corporal William Allen – Victoria Cross No. 367
Corporal Christian Ferdinand Schiess – Victoria Cross No. 368
Private Alfred Hook – Victoria Cross No. 369
Private William Jones – Victoria Cross No. 370
Private Robert Jones – Victoria Cross No. 371
Private John Williams – Victoria Cross No. 372
Private Frederick Hitch – Victoria Cross No. 373

Rorke's Drift, the former trading post of James Rorke an Irish Merchant, was a collection of a few buildings on the Natal side of the Buffalo River now being used as a mission station by the Swedish missionary Reverend Otto Witt.

In preparation for the invasion of Zululand, General Thesiger with Colonel Glyn and the no. 3 (central) column of the invasion force arrived at Rorke's Drift on the 9th January 1879 and after commandeering the mission station set about adapting the buildings for use as a commissariat stores and hospital.

When the ultimatum deadline expired on 11th January, the bulk of the invasion column crossed over the river and set up camp on the bank opposite to the mission station and as Rorke's Drift was an important staging post for supplies, company B of the 2nd battalion 24th Regiment of Foot, commanded by Lieutenant Bromhead, was detailed to remain behind and guard the station. Surgeon Reynolds was left in charge of the hospital, Reverend George Smith, the vicar of Estcourt in Natal acted as chaplain to the troops and three commissariat officers remained to look after the stores. Major Spalding of the 104th Regiment of foot, Deputy Assistant Adjutant General, was left in overall command of the post.

In early January General Thesiger sent a message to the Royal Engineers at Durban, with a request for an officer and a few good men with mining implements to join the No. 3 Column as soon as possible. As a result of this order, Lieutenant Chard with a Corporal, three Sappers, a driver and his batman set out with a wagon of implements as an advanced party to comply with the request.

The roads were so bad, that progress was very slow and it was not until the morning of 19th January that Lieutenant Chard and his party arrived at Rorke's Drift. There were two large pontoons being used, in addition to the ford (drift) to transport troops and materiel across the river, however, only one was in working order so the Sappers helped to get the other operational.

On the 20th January, Colonel Glyn with No. 3 Column left Rorke's Drift to set up camp near Isandhlwana and late in the evening of 21st January orders arrived for the recently arrived Royal Engineers to join the column at Isandhlwana. To assist with the defence of the mission station, Captain Stevenson, with 100 to 350 men of the 2nd/3rd Natal Native Contingent were ordered to remain at Rorke's Drift and Captain Thomas Rainforth in command of G Company of the 1st Battalion of the 24th Regiment of Foot, currently stationed at Helpmakaar was also ordered to move up to Rorke's Drift.

On the morning of 22nd January, the Royal Engineer contingent in their wagon left for Isandhlwana accompanied by Lieutenant Chard, who with the approval of Major Spalding was going to the camp for clarification of the orders regarding himself. With his orders clarified (to keep the pontoons in working order and improve the road between Rorke's Drift and

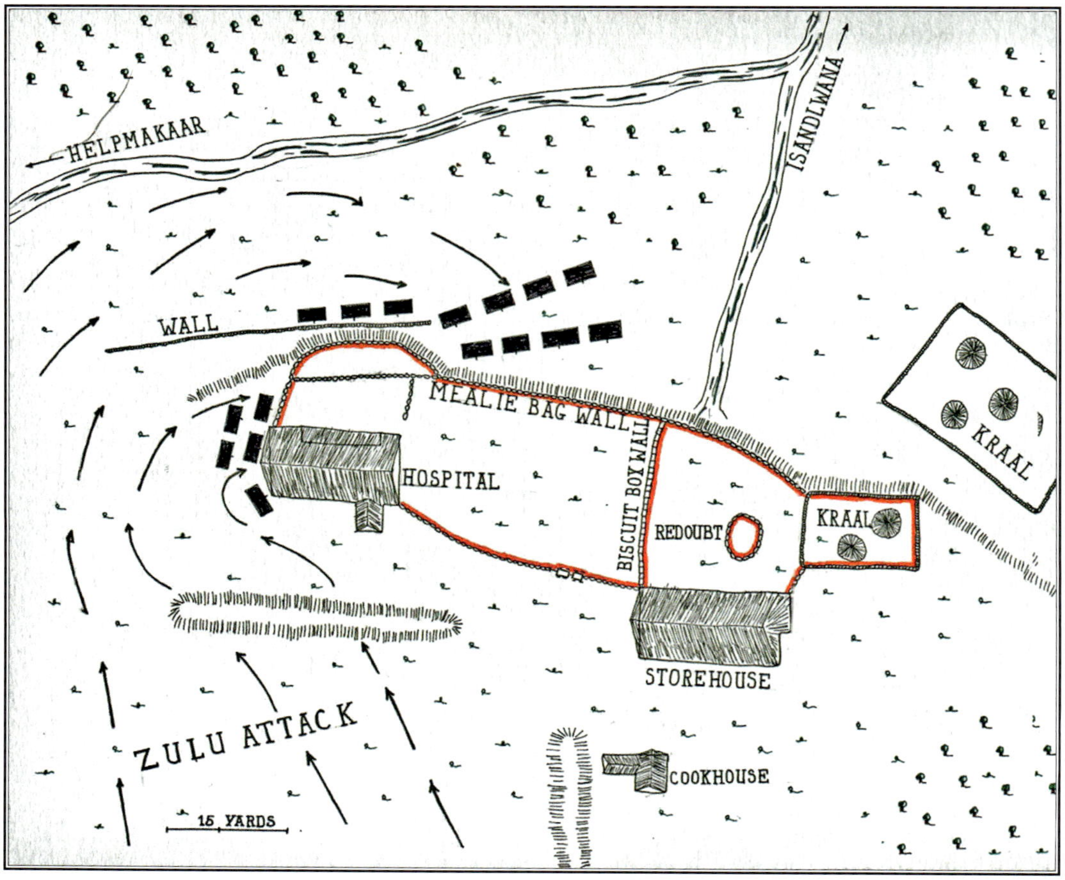

Figure 66. Battle of Rorke's Drift

Helpmakaar) Lieutenant Chard began his return to Rorke's Drift after becoming aware of the appearance of Zulu warriors on the distant hills and the possibility of an attack on the post at Rorke's Drift.

Lieutenant Chard arrived back at Rorke's Drift at around noon and reported to Major Spalding that a large force of Zulu appeared to be advancing on the mission station and that without the aid of Captain Rainforth's Company it would be impossible for him to effectively guard the pontoons and river crossing. Major Spalding stated that he would go to Helpmakaar to facilitate the departure of the reinforcements. At 2 o'clock in the afternoon, just as he was about to ride away Major Spalding asked Lieutenant Chard "*Which of you is senior, you or Bromhead?*" when Chard replied that he did not know, the Major went back to his tent and checked the army list and on his return stated "*I see you are senior, so you will be in charge, although of course nothing will happen, and I shall be back again this evening early*".

With news that Zulu forces may be making their way towards the mission station, Reverends Witt and Smith, together with Surgeon Reynolds mounted the summit of Oscarberg, a nearby hill and used their binoculars to look for any signs of an approaching army.

After taking lunch at his tent down by the river, at about 3:15, while writing a letter home, Lieutenant Chard observed two horsemen galloping to the drift from the direction of Isandhlwana. One of the men, Lieutenant Gerd Adendorff of the Natal Native Contingent reported that the Zulu had overrun the camp and that large numbers of the British force had been killed. His companion, Lieutenant Vaine rode off to take the news of the disaster to Helpmakaar.

Soon after hearing the disturbing information from Adendorff, Lieutenant Chard received an urgent message from Lieutenant Bromhead, who had just been informed of the disaster by a mounted infantryman carrying a note from Captain Allan Gardner, with the No. 3 column, which stated that the post should be strengthened and held at all costs.

After posting a Sergeant with six men to guard the pontoons, Chard returned to the mission station and had discussions with Lieutenant Bromhead and Assistant Commissary Dalton regarding the available options, to try and escape (thought to be too difficult due to having to escort wagons carrying the wounded) or to mount a defence of the mission station.

It was decided that the only viable option was to mount a defence, however, it was decided that it would be necessary to abandon the ford and concentrate their efforts on the mission station, accordingly at about 3:30 the guard left at the pontoons was recalled.

At about the same time, Lieutenant Alfred Henderson with about 100 troopers, from Colonel Durnford's column arrived and reported to Lieutenant Chard regarding orders. The force was ordered to move out in the expected direction of the Zulu advance and try to delay its progress before falling back to the mission station and helping out with its defence.

Work was immediately started to improve the defences of the mission station, the two main buildings, the hospital and storehouse were about forty yards apart and a wall of bags of maize were used to construct a roughly rectangular perimeter with the buildings forming the south east and south west corners.

As it was believed that the hospital could be defended, it was decided to leave the patients who were unable to bear arms within the building, which measure 18 feet by 60 feet sub-divided into several rooms, some with internal interconnecting doors and others only accessible via external doors. Although the hospital was under the command of Surgeon Reynolds, Lieutenant Bromhead detailed Privates Thomas Cole, Harry Hook, William Jones, John Williams and Joseph Williams to assist him in the defence of the hospital, the walls of which were loopholed and the windows and outside doors were barricaded by tables and mattresses.

At about 4 o'clock in the afternoon, Surgeon Reynolds and Reverends Smith and Witt came down off the hill with the news that they had seen a large body of Zulu, in three columns, advancing on the mission station. Mr Witt whose wife and three young children were at his house at Msinga, about 30 miles from Rorke's Drift, decided to move off and join his family; Lieutenant Thomas Purvis of the Natal Native contingent, who was ill in the hospital and only just capable of riding rode off with him.

At about 4:20 the sound of rifle fire could be heard from behind the Oscarberg hill and soon afterwards Lieutenant Alfred Henderson arrive at the drift with news that a large force of Zulu were approaching the mission station. He also stated that his 100 men would not follow his orders and had headed off towards Helpmakaar. Seeing Lieutenant Henderson and his 100 troopers leaving the station, Captain Stephenson and his men from the Natal Native Contingent, who had been helping to erect the maize bag walls, also deserted Rorke's Drift.

With only 156 men now at his disposal, 33 of whom were hospital patients, Lieutenant Chard realised that the line of defence, as constructed, was too large for the remaining men to man so immediately set the men to constructing an inner work from biscuit boxes. Of the 33 patients in the hospital the majority were suffering from illness caused by disease, only two men, Corporal Jessy Mayer and Corporal Frederick Schiess were suffering from combat wounds, both having been wounded in the leg during the storming of chief Sihayo's kraal on 12th January. A Zulu warrior, one of Sihayo's retainers who was captured during the same action, was also a patient in the hospital (he was killed during the action).

Figure 67. Rorke's Drift Hospital

Private Hitch, who had been making four kettles of tea for the men (he was serving as the hospital cook, was ordered by Lieutenant Bromhead to take station on the roof of the storehouse and maintain a lookout. At about 4:30 a body of about 500 to 600 Zulu, led by a chief riding a grey mare came around the south corner of the hill and began to slowly advance on the south wall. The first shot fired was reported to be by Private Hitch who allegedly shouted out *"Here they come! Black as hell and thick as grass."*, however, this cry is also attributed to Reverend Smith when he returned to the mission station after spotting the Zulu advance from the summit of the Oscarberg hill.

At a range of about 500 yards, the British opened fire on the advancing Zulu; the first casualty of the battle was the mounted Zulu chief who was shot by Private Dunbar; under the withering fire the Zulu scattered and moving to their left occupied the garden and orchard where there was plenty of cover and eventually encircled the mission defences. As evening set in, the Zulu used the failing light and cover from bushes and long grass to advance to within 5 yards of the hospital from where in groups of about 15 to 20 they launched repeated attacks against the corner of the hospital.

Surgeon Reynolds supervised preparations for the internal defence of the hospital, and throughout the action was accompanied by Dick, his fox terrier. In addition to caring for the patients within the hospital, Surgeon Reynolds also treated the wounded out in the open including Assistant Commissary Dalton who had been wounded in the shoulder and when the defenders in the hospital ran low on ammunition he went outside to the storehouse and obtained a supply which allowed the men to replenish their pouches. He also distributed ammunition to the men manning the walls.

Sergeant Joseph Windridge, acting as a store man for the commissariat stores was instrumental in preparing the storehouse for defence, forming loopholes and erecting barricades with the boxes and bags of stores. In this endeavour he was ably assisted by Lieutenant James Adendorff who remained in the storehouse to help with the defence.

After firing some long distance shots at the Zulu force, Private Hitch came down from the roof of the storehouse and joined Lieutenant Bromhead who had collected some men to charge, with fixed bayonets, the Zulu who were attacking the hospital. After a short time, the Zulu withdrew for a period before renewing their attack on the hospital, this time with more success, which required the occupants to smash their way through the walls to escape the warriors.

Private Robert Jones was stationed at a loophole in a room occupied by the patient Corporal Maher at the rear of the hospital. The room, which had its external door and window barricaded, adjoined the kitchen which extended out from the main line of the hospital rear wall. With the Zulu now swarming around the building, trying to gain access at several points and trying to set the thatched roof alight, Private Robert Jones moved Corporal Maher into the kitchen, when his ammunition became exhausted and joined Private William Jones (No. 593) who was caring for six other patients.

When they heard Zulu warriors trying to break in via the external door in the other room, they fixed bayonets and mounted a guard at the barricaded doorway. Trooper Henry Lugg of the Natal Mounted Police, firing from a loophole in the kitchen extension managed to shoot many of the assailants, however, with force of numbers they managed to break through the makeshift barrier at the door. Both of the Privates did sterling work with their bayonets, killing the Zulu as the pressed through the doorway, however, during the struggle Robert Jones received three Assegai wounds but when the action permitted they returned to the kitchen and helped the patients escape through a high window, which provided the only means of escape.

While Robert and William Jones were trying to keep the Zulu at bay, they were also trying to dress their last patient, Sergeant Maxfield who was delirious with fever, when a pick axe smashed through the wall behind them. This was Private John Williams (No. 1395) and Private Harry Hook, who had been quartered in the western end of the building who were helping eight of the surviving patients to escape. Private John Williams had been in another room with Private William Horrigan, Private Joseph Williams and four patients; when the men ran out of ammunition, the Zulu broke into the room and dragged Private Joseph Williams and two of the patients outside where they were killed. While the Zulu were thus occupied, Private John Williams and the remaining two patients used a pick axe to break through the wall while Private Horrigan defended their escape until he was killed. Once the ten new men were in the kitchen, Robert and William Jones took over the defence of the escape hole while Private Hook and Private Williams helped their patients to escape through the high window. The last patient through the window was Private John Connolly, who was in hospital with a broken leg, unfortunately he broke his leg again as he fell to the ground from the high window.

With the hospital roof now burning and Zulu warriors entering via the escape hole, Privates Hook, Williams and the two Joneses began to make their own escape through the window, however, Robert Jones turned back to make one last attempt to save Sergeant Maxfield but it was too late as he was lying on his bed being repeatedly stabbed by the Zulu. In addition to Sergeant Maxfield three other men were killed in the hospital

Private Robert Adams, Private James Jenkins and a soldier of the Natal Native Contingent.

Robert Jones, William Jones, John Williams and Harry Hook, together with 14 patients, were the last men to leave the hospital; Private Thomas Cole and Private Joseph Williams (No.1398) had both been killed while trying to save the hospital patients.

On leaving the hospital the men had to run through a gauntlet of Zulu for about 20 yards before reaching the safety of the storehouse; Lieutenant Bromhead with Privates Nichols, Chick, Fagan, Scanlon and Hitch and Corporal Schiess provided covering fire for their escape. During this action, Privates Nichols, Chick, Fagan and Scanlon were all killed and Corporal Schiess, who was wounded before the attack, was again wounded, this time in the foot. With only Private Hitch to assist him, Lieutenant Bromhead continued to defend the hospital corner but with the Zulu attacking from two sides this was an almost impossible endeavour. While Private Hitch was struggling with one Zulu another Zulu on the barricade shot him in the shoulder and when he fell to the ground he was about to be speared when Lieutenant Bromhead shot his assailant with his revolver.

After having to abandon the hospital building, Surgeon Reynolds with his patients, orderlies and some salvaged hospital supplies set up facilities within the storehouse where Surgeon Reynolds continued to operate by the light of the hospital fire. One of the men treated at this time was Private Hitch who had 36 pieces of shattered shoulder blade removed from his back before he was sewn up.

After only a few minutes, Private Hitch rejoined Lieutenant Bromhead who gave him his revolver in order to carry on the fight. When ammunition began to run low, Private Hitch, together with Corporal William Allen, who was also seriously wounded, helped to distribute the remaining ammunition to the men until finally overcome by exhaustion, loss of blood and thirst he collapsed and came to rest against the storehouse wall. Private Hitch was asked by Private George Deacon if he wanted him to end it all by shooting him, declining the offer Private Hitch responded "*... they have very nearly done for me and they can finish me right out when it comes to the last*". Soon after this Private Hitch succumbed to a feint from which he did not awake until after the battle was over.

Large numbers of the Zulu warriors took up positions as snipers on the slopes of the Oscarberg Hill and managed to rain down a heavy fire on the men defending the Maize bag walls and now facing fire from both their front and rear, Lieutenant Chard ordered the men to retreat to another redoubt that was being built with biscuit boxes near the storehouse building.

At about 6 o'clock in the evening, the British force including the wounded, now occupied the biscuit box redoubt and from the light of the burning hospital building were able to rain down heavy and accurate fire on the Zulu who mounted attack after attack.

By 10 o'clock, when the hospital fire had burnt itself out, the defenders had to resort to the use of the bayonet to prevent the Zulu attacks breaching their ramparts. At about midnight, after eight hours of unrelenting fighting, the Zulu attacks began to slacken and only a desultory fire was maintained until 4 o'clock in the morning when it stopped altogether and with the first light of the new day they could be seen retiring around the Oscarberg Hill.

Not sure if the battle was over, or if this was just a brief respite, Lieutenant Chard ordered the thatch to be removed from the storehouse roof and work was started to improve the defences. Patrols were sent out to try and determine the Zulu positions and when they returned, the Zulu warriors suddenly appeared on the hills lining the south west but without an obvious explanation, they continued to move off around the Oscarberg Hill without firing a further shot. It later transpired that the Zulu chose to retreat after observing the advance of General Thesiger's relief force, which arrived at Rorke's Drift at about 9 o'clock in the morning.

For their actions during the defence of Rorke's Drift Lieutenants Chard and Bromhead, Surgeon Reynolds, Assistant Commissary Dalton, Corporals Allen and Schiess and Privates Hook, Jones (R), Jones (W), Williams and Hitch were all awarded the Victoria Cross.

Of the defenders, 15 men were killed in the action and two would later die of the wounds that they received and ten men were wounded. During the fight, the defenders expended 21,000 rounds of ammunition.

The Zulu who attacked Rorke's Drift were a force numbering about 4,000, commanded by Dabulamanzi, a brother of chief Cetywayo. After the battle, 351 Zulu warriors were buried by the British soldiers, however, it is believed that at least 500 were killed with a further 500 wounded.

After arriving at Rorke's Drift, General Thesiger, very relieved that a further disaster had not fallen on the British troops under his command, sent Colonel Russell with a mounted escort to Helpmakaar to see if all was safe there. Before Colonel Russell could return, some officers from Major Bengough's battalion of the Natal Native Contingent arrived with the news that the road was clear and that no attack had been made on Helpmakaar. With this news, General Thesiger and his staff rode off to Pietermaritzburg via Helpmakaar where he arrived on 26th January.

British Reinforcements

Following the disaster at Isandhlwana, General Thesiger's invasion plans were in tatters; following their lamentable performance at Isandhlwana and later at Rorke's Drift, the native soldiers could no longer be trusted and although many deserted and just drifted away, many of the Native Contingent were disarmed and their units disbanded.

The General reported back to London, that if operations were to be continued against the Zulu then reinforcements were urgently required; three British Infantry regiments, two cavalry regiments, a company of Royal Engineers as well as 100 artillerymen were requested.

When news of the defeat at Isandhlwana, together with the request for reinforcements reached London on 11th February the request was immediately granted, however, some weeks would elapse before the arrival of the additional forces.

On 13th February, Frederick Stanley the Earl of Derby and Secretary of State for War sent a telegraph to General Thesiger with news that the following troops had been placed on immediate orders for despatch to Natal: Two regiments of cavalry, each with 648 men; two field batteries of artillery with 336 men; one company of Engineers; five infantry regiments from England, each with 806 men; the 57th Regiment from Ceylon; three companies of the Army Reserve Corps, with 140 men and the Army Hospital Corps, with 140 men. In addition to *HMS Shah* and *HMS Tamar*, which brought troops from St Helena and Ceylon respectively, 18 commercial steamers were employed to transport the men, their supplies and equipment.

The first ship to arrive was *HMS Shah*, which anchored off Port Natal on 6th March, having been dispatched by the St Helena Governor Hudson Ralph Janisch, *HMS Shah* disembarked a Naval Brigade of 392 men and a further 200 men from the St Helena garrison.

The next ship to arrive was, the troopship *HMS Tamar* that carried the men of the 57th Regiment from Ceylon. *SS Pretoria* was the first steamer to arrive from England, with 930 officers and men from the 71st Highlanders.

Operations of Colonel Pearson's Column

On 18th January, having crossed the Tugela River, Colonel Pearson in command of the No. 1 column began an advance towards Ekowe. The column of 1,200 men accompanied by over 130 wagons progressed slowly and although followed by large numbers of Zulu warriors the march was uneventful until 22nd January when the column reached the turning to Ekowe, which occupied the heights off to the left of the line of march.

After reaching the turning, the head of the column halted with the intention of taking breakfast when they were ambushed by a large force of Zulu warriors who managed to advance to within 150 yards of the British force before being held at bay by the artillery.

Once the extended wagon train had been moved forward, their escort was released to drive the Zulu from the bush and onto the open plain where the main body of mounted infantry was able to engage. After a battle which lasted for an hour and a half, the Zulu force of about 5,000 was comprehensively defeated with 300 of the enemy being killed. British losses were 12 killed and 11 wounded.

After the Zulu had fled the field, the column resumed its march and after an overnight camp reached Ekowe on the following morning. It was originally planned that the column would leave their surplus stores at Ekowe, with a small garrison as a guard while the main column pressed on towards Cetywayo's kraal at Ulundi, however, after news of the disaster at Isandhlwana arrived by messenger on 29th January this plan had to be changed.

Fearing an imminent attack by the whole of the Zulu army, Colonel Pearson was faced with a choice to withdraw his force back to the Tugela River or establish defences and hold his position at the British fort at Ekowe. After a short discussion it was decided to remain at Ekowe, however, in order to conserve their supplies the Cavalry were sent back, a surprising move that deprived the Colonel of the means to scout the enemy movements.

By 30th January, the garrison of nearly 1,700 men (including 340 non-combatants) were encamped within the fort and working hard to improve the defences. The church was converted into a hospital, the school and parsonage into storerooms and all other buildings were demolished. The fort defences were completed on 10th February with ditches 7 feet deep and 12 feet wide.

Although surrounded by a large Zulu army no attempt was made to dislodge the British force and the men settled into a rather relaxed routine. Supplies were such, that during the first month normal rations were issued before it became necessary to issue reduced rations, the supply of water was excellent and the men had sufficient ammunition to sustain a protracted siege.

Operations of Colonel Wood's Column

On 6th January, the No. 4 column, under the command of Colonel Wood VC, crossed the Blood River into Zulu territory and advanced on Bemba's Kop. Colonel Wood induced the Zulu chief Bemba to give up his arms and on 10th January he arrived at the British camp with 80 of his men and 1,000 head of cattle, sheep and goats, which were sent on to Utrecht.

On 11th January, Colonel Wood met with General Thesiger, on his way to Rorke's Drift with No. 1 column, and received instructions to move against the Zulu to his front and left flank before joining up with column No. 3 and advancing to Ingwe. After entering Zululand and finding operations more difficult than expected, on 16th January, General Thesiger instructed Colonel Wood *"to act altogether independently about the head waters of the White Umveloosi River"* and when Chief Seketwayo had either surrendered or been defeated to *"take up position covering Utrecht and the adjacent Transvaal border, wherever he considers his force can be most usefully employed"* and not to *"attempt to advance towards the Inhlazatye Mountain until an advance by the other three columns across the Umhlatoozi River has become possible"*.

Colonel Wood, with the No.4 column, advanced towards the Intemgeni River where they camped on 18th January and by 20th January set up camp at Chief Tinta's kraal, on the left bank of the Umveloosi River, where they proceeded to erect a stone fort. For the next few days, Colonel Wood's men carried out reconnaissance operations and were involved in various skirmishes with the Zulu, however, on 24th January when he received news of the massacre at Isandhlwana, he recalled his patrols and retired to the safety of the new Tinta Fort.

At the end of the month, Dutch farmers established a laager at Luneburg, under the command of Commandant Schermbrucker and Colonel Wood move his force to Kambula Hill where they created a strongly defended position.

The Zulu had abandoned the open countryside, taking to the mountains and broken country where rocks and caves provided them with secure positions.

On 1st February, Colonel Buller with a force of 140 irregular cavalry made an attack against the Zulu stronghold at the Amaqulisini kraal, a collection of about 250 huts in a basin surrounded by the summits of rugged hills. On approaching the kraal, it was found to be only occupied by a small force, which was quickly despatched, after which the kraal was burnt to the ground and 270 head of cattle captured before the force returned to Kambula Hill where a small fort had been erected.

Battle of Intombi Drift

Four companies of the 80th Regiment, part of Colonel Wood's column, were detailed to assist with the transport of supplies from Derby to Luneburg along a route which crossed several rivers, including the Intombi which was a tributary of the Pongola River.

On 7th March a company of the 80th, under the command of Captain David Moriarty, left Luneburg to go to the assistance of a convoy of 18 wagons full of ammunition, flour and maize which on its journey from Derby had become stranded at the Intombi River. When the convoy had arrived at the Intombi on 5th March, it was impossible to cross the drift with the heavy wagons due to flooding caused by heavy rains.

On his arrival at the Intombi Drift Captain Moriarty came upon Lieutenant Henry Harward, commander of the convoy escort, and some of his men camped on the Luneburg side of the river, while the 10 wagons and the remainder of the escort were still on the north side of the river, trapped by the fast flowing waters. Captain Moriarty and his 69 men managed to cross the river and join the men in the wagons, which had been drawn into the shape of an inverted V to form a Laager.

By the 11th March, the rains had stopped and the river level had fallen by about four feet, however, the flow of the river was still too strong to attempt a crossing with the wagons. The men settled down for the night, having posted only one man as a remote sentry, with the expectation that a river crossing would be possible on the following morning.

At about 3:30 in the morning, a single shot was heard near the camp and the men were turned out, however, as it was still dark and misty nothing to cause concern could be observed, so after about half an hour the men were returned to their beds, with the near sentries ordered to be extra vigilant. Unknown to the British force, the shot that they heard had been fired as a warning by the remote sentry before he was killed by an advancing party of about 4,000 Zulu.

Sergeant Anthony Booth – Victoria Cross No. 374

At about 5 o'clock in the morning, the mist began to clear and in the first light of the new day a sentry on the Luneburg side of the river observed a large body of Zulu warriors descending on the Laager on the opposite bank of the river. The sentry fired a warning shot, which raised Captain Moriarty and his men from their beds, however, they were immediately set upon by a vast number of Zulu warriors and were overwhelmed in a matter of minutes. Some of the British force attempted an escape by swimming the river but most were swept away and drowned.

The men on the Luneburg bank fired volley after volley into the Zulu hordes, however, due to their numbers this had little effect and when a party of about 200 Zulu were seen crossing the river upstream of their position in an attempt to outflank them, Lieutenant Harward decided that it was time for the surviving force to retreat back to Luneburg.

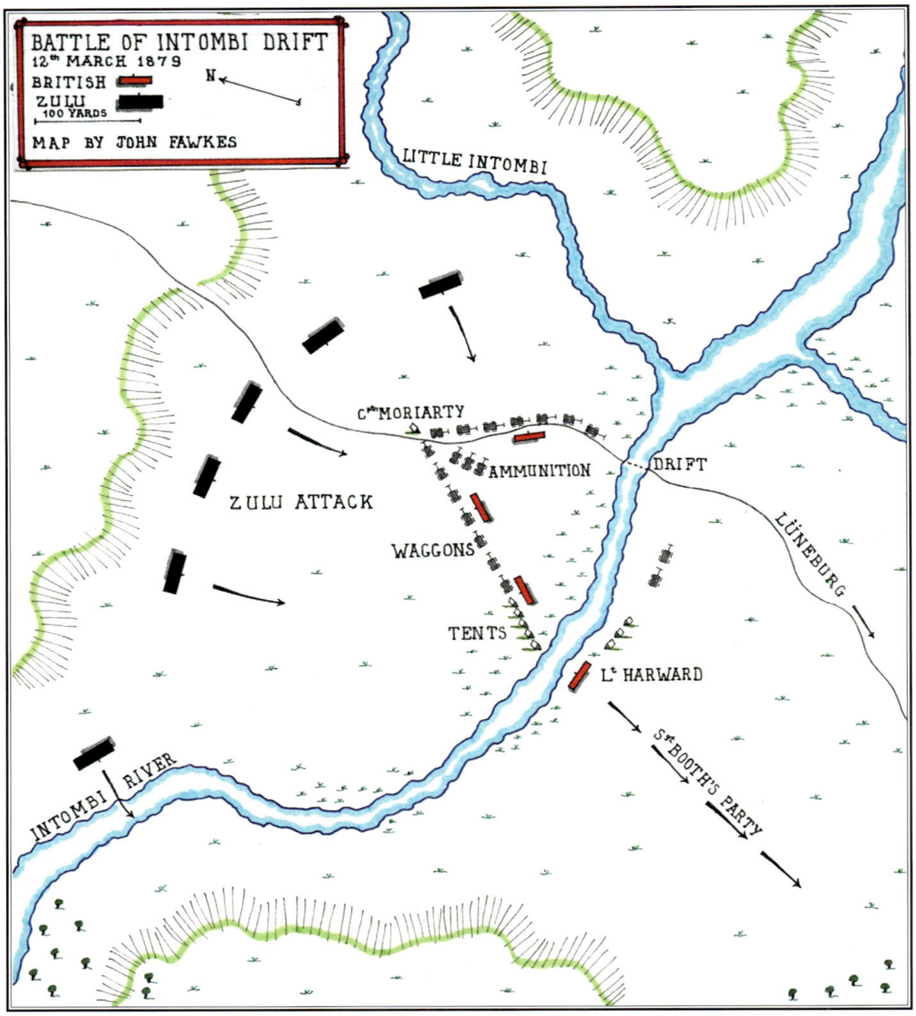

Figure 68. Battle of Intombi Drift

After leaving Sergeant Booth in charge of the small force, Lieutenant Harward saddled up his horse and rode off to Luneburg to raise the alarm and get reinforcements.

Sergeant Booth marshalled the 43 men now under his control and began a steady retreat back towards Luneburg, when the pursuing Zulu party got too close to his men, he ordered a halt and fired off a volley or two to good effect. The Zulu warriors continued to follow Sergeant Booth and his men for about three and a half miles before returning to the river.

For his actions during the retreat, Sergeant Booth was later awarded the Victoria Cross.

When the alarm was raised, a relief column was sent out from Luneburg and when they approached the river a large party of Zulu, estimated to be about 4,000 men were seen to be retiring along the crest of nearby hills.

Down at the river, Captain Moriarty with 41 of his men and 17 civilian drivers were found dead, having been stripped and disembowelled by the Zulu. A further 20 men from the 80th Regiment were missing, believed to have been swept away and drowned, over the next few days six of their bodies were recovered. The party brought into Luneburg by Sergeant Booth were the only survivors of the attack.

Lieutenant Harward was charged with deserting his men in the face of the enemy, however, at his subsequent court martial he was found to be not guilty.

During the rest of the month, things were relatively quiet for the British force at Kambula and on 16th March chief Uhamo and 958 of his people arrived at the camp to demonstrate their lack of support for chief Cetywayo's revolt against the British.

Battle of Hlobane

With intelligence that the Zulu were planning to make an attack on his force going to the relief of Ekowe, General Thesiger ordered Colonel Wood to mount an attack against Zulu forces that were occupying Hlobane mountain. The attack was intended to distract this Zulu force, so that they would be unable to take part in the attack on the relief column.

On 27th March, a force under the overall command of Colonel Wood left Kambula: Colonel Buller led a cavalry column of 400 men consisting of detachments from the Frontier Light Horse, Raaff's Corps, Weatherley's Rangers and Baker's

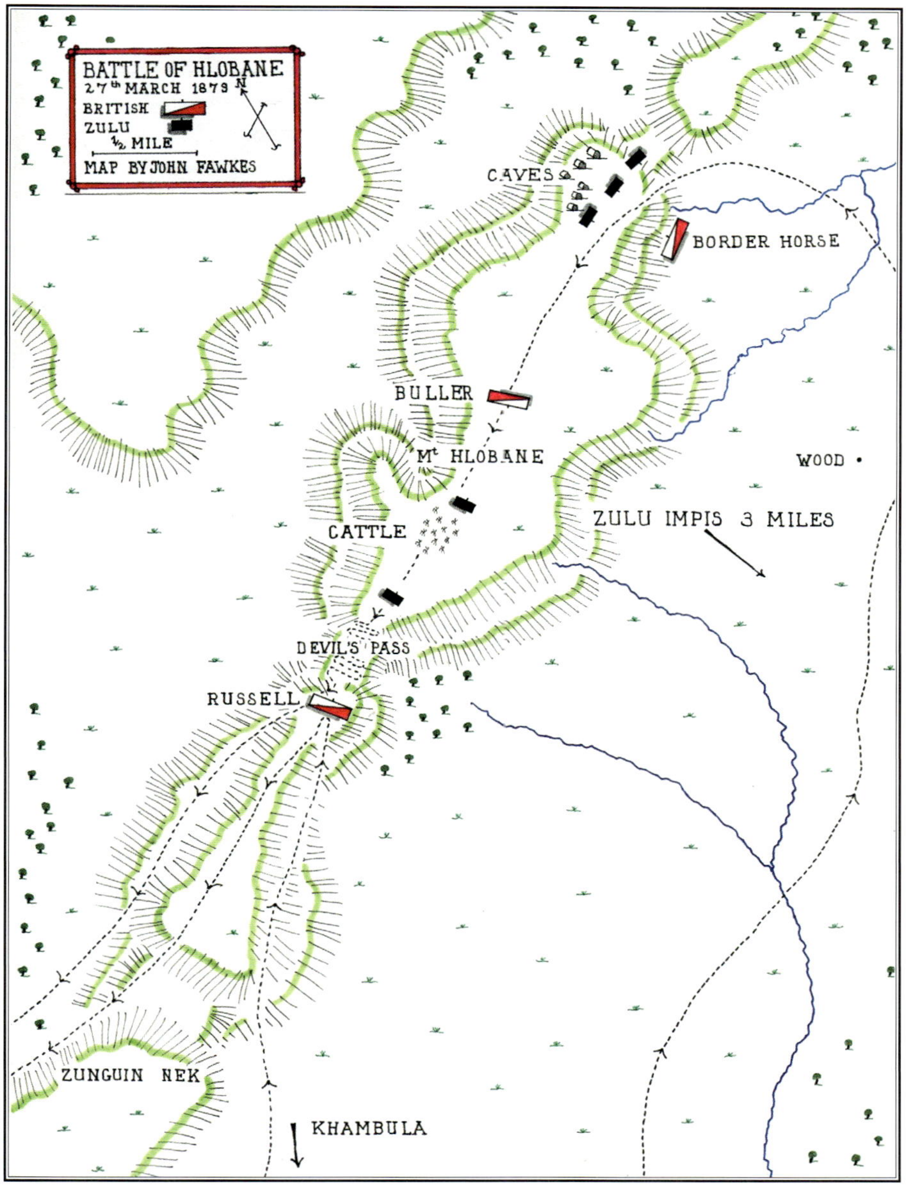

Figure 69. Battle of Hlobane

Horse, accompanied by Major Tremlett with rocket tubes and the burgher force. Major Leet and Lieutenant Williams led another column of men from the Native Contingent while a third column of mounted infantry made up from the Kaffrarian Mounted Rifles and Wood's Irregulars was led by Commandant Schermbrucker.

At about noon on the 28th March, Colonel Buller and his column reached the south side of the mountain and with Commandant Uys acting as their guide slowly moved to the eastern flank of the mountain. With Commandant Uys, Colonel Buller and Majors Leet and Tremlett leading the way, the British force began their ascent of the mountain and reached about 500 yards from the top before the Zulu opened up with fierce rifle fire, during which Lieutenant Williams was killed. After reaching a point about 100 feet from the summit, Colonel Wood had his horse shot out from under him and his interpreter, Mr Lloyd fell mortally wounded.

Lieutenant Henry Lysons – Victoria Cross No. 377
Private Edmund Fowler – Victoria Cross No. 378

A small band of Zulu, sheltering in a cave were causing many of the casualties to the British force, which due to the narrow nature of the path was required to advance in single file. In an attempt to dislodge the troublesome Zulus, Captain Campbell, Lieutenant Lysons and three men from the 90th Regiment vaulted a low wall and charged into the cave.

Captain Campbell was shot dead at the entrance to the cave, but undeterred Lieutenant Lysons and Private Fowler, who were close on his heels continued into the cave and cleared the Zulu from their stronghold.

For their actions during the assault Lieutenant Lysons and Private Fowler were both awarded the Victoria Cross.

After reaching the top of the mountain and silencing the enemy fire, Colonel Buller and Commandant Raaff rode to the western end of the summit and noticed that the Zulu had fortified the pass with stone walls. Having already spent about four hours on the summit Colonel Buller noticed a body of Zulu arriving on the northern extremity of the mountain and rode off with his men to attack them, however, before reaching these new arrivals it was noticed that large numbers of the enemy were trying to cut off the approaches to the only two passes by which it was possible to descend the mountain. At the same time two large columns were seen to be approaching the summit from the east and the south.

As there was a very real possibility of his force being cut off from their escape routes, Colonel Buller ordered his men to retreat down the steep and boulder strewn path that was the only exit now available.

During the descent, which after a time turned into a desperate flight Commander Uys and Colonel Weatherley were both killed.

Brevet Lieutenant Colonel Redvers Buller – Victoria Cross No. 375

During the perilous descent, many of the men lost their horses and had to attempt an escape on foot; Captain D'Arcy of the Frontier Light Horse was in such a position being closely pursued by the Zulu when Colonel Buller hoisted him on to the back of his horse. After he had caught his breath, Captain D'Arcy dismounted from Colonel Buller's horse but after becoming exhausted he was rescued for a second time by Lieutenant Blaine and again for a third time by Major Tremlett.

In a similar fashion, Colonel Buller also carried Lieutenant Everitt to safety.

Troopers Ashby and Gemmell were part of a small rearguard, who after every few yards stopped and fired into the chasing Zulu warriors were about to be swallowed up after one of their rifles failed, when Colonel Buller rode up and offered him a ride on his horse, due to his large size Trooper Ashby declined the offer so Colonel Buller stayed with the men and helped escort them to safety.

For his actions during the battle, Colonel Buller was later awarded the Victoria Cross.

Major William Leet – Victoria Cross No. 376

During the descent from the mountain, Major Leet rescued Lieutenant Smith of the Frontier Light Horse, whose horse had been shot out from under him, by giving him a ride on the back of his horse and carrying him to safety.

For this action Major Leet was awarded the Victoria Cross.

After completing their descent down the mountain, the British force managed to fight their way through the encircling Zulu warriors and reach the relative safety of the camp at Kambula.

During the battle, the British force had 96 men killed and suffered many wounded.

Battle of Kambula

Following on from their success on Hlobane Mountain, and advancing on Kambula with their full army, Colonel Wood expected a Zulu attack against his camp on the following day and set about preparing his defences accordingly. With a strength of only just over 2,000 men (88 of whom were sick in hospital) which included 121 men of the Royal Engineers and Royal Artillery, 1,238 infantry and 638 cavalry the British force was greatly outnumbered but were positioned within excellent defences.

At 11 o'clock on the next morning large numbers of Zulu warriors could be seen assembling in the distance and after hastily eating an early lunch, the tents were struck, the reserve of ammunition was distributed and the troops took up their battle stations.

At about 12:45 the right flank of the Zulu force circled the camp to the north, just out of artillery range and came to a halt in the north west. At about 1:30, Colonels Buller and Russell led a pre-emptive strike against the force on the right flank, with the intention of drawing the Zulu closer to camp and within the range of the British guns.

Lieutenant Edward Browne – Victoria Cross No. 379

After riding to within rifle range of the Zulu force, the British cavalry halted and fired off several volleys before retiring back towards Kambula closely followed by about 11,000 Zulu. During the retreat, Lieutenant Browne rode back towards the advancing Zulu to go to the aid of a trooper who was having trouble with his horse. With the Zulu less than 100 yards away, Lieutenant Browne's horse bolted while he was trying to get the wounded trooper on its back. By the time that he had his horse back under control and was able to mount the wounded trooper, the Zulu had advanced to within 30 yards, however, despite their heavy fire Lieutenant Browne was able to gallop off, saving the troopers life.

For this action Lieutenant Browne was later awarded the Victoria Cross.

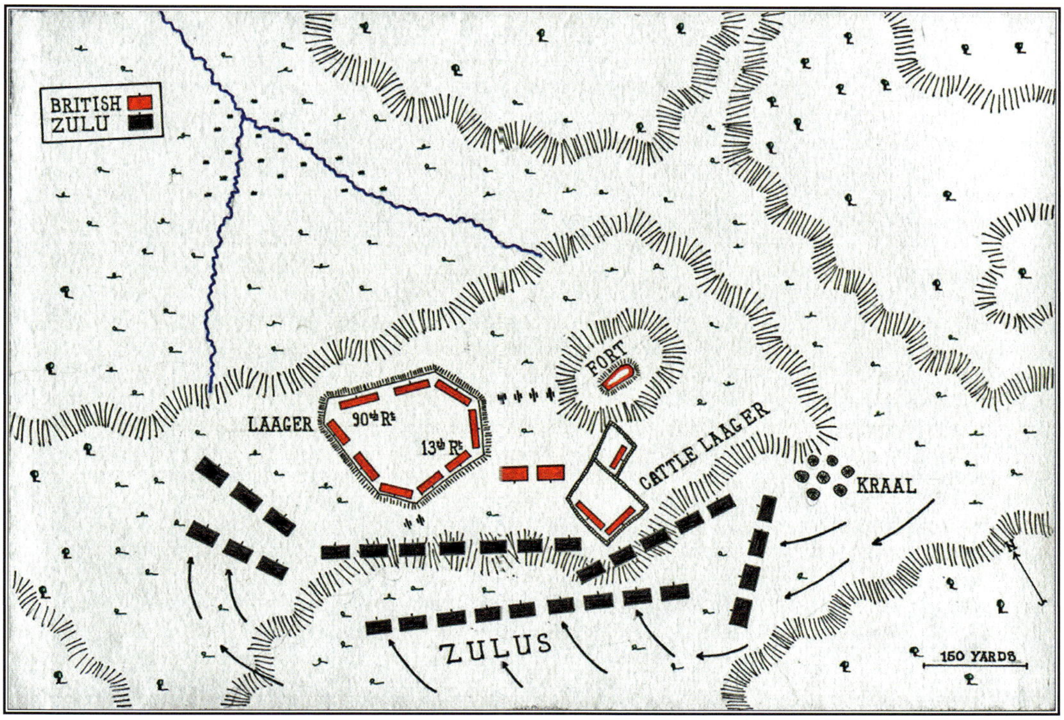

Figure 70. Battle of Kambula

As soon as the British cavalry had returned to Kambula and had cleared the lines of fire, the artillery opened up on the Zulu who were now within 300 yards of the defences. Under the barrage of British fire, the Zulu advance was checked but they swung right to attack the west side of the defences where they were again halted by the British fire.

After about half an hour, the Zulu right flank withdrew to the north east and at about 2:15 the Zulu left flank and centre emerged from a ravine and entered the fray. Some of the leading Zulu warriors managed to force their way into the cattle kraal where, hampered by the cattle, they engaged in hand to hand fighting; heavily outnumbered the British managed to extract themselves and pull back into the main defences.

The Zulu were now able to provide covering fire from their shelter behind the walls of the kraal and at about this time the Zulu right flank once again advanced, crossing the north face of the defences and putting pressure on the eastern side of the British position.

Although his force was now being attacked on two sides, Colonel Wood determined that the situation on his south face was critical and he ordered an attack in this direction. Major Hackett formed his men into a line and with fixed bayonets they charged across the open ground, forcing the Zulu warriors back into the ravine, however, after a while Major Hackett and his men came under heavy fire from a band of Zulu concealed within a refuse pit and were forced to retire. During the withdrawal of his troops, Major Hackett was mortally wounded by a shot to the head.

Following the withdrawal of Major Hackett's force, the Zulu once again emerged from the ravine and mounted another attack which was repulsed by repeated volleys of rifle fire. On the north side of the camp the Royal Artillery continued to fire their guns into the midst of the Zulu right flank and although they continued to launch attack after attack the effect of the guns was gradually reducing the impetus of their attacks.

At about 5 o'clock, sensing that the Zulu force was wavering, Colonel Wood decide to go on the offensive and the Zulu warriors were driven from the cattle kraal. As soon as the Zulu began to pull back, towards the east, Colonel Buller and his cavalry were ordered to pursue the retreating army and after harrying them for about seven miles, during which they caused many casualties, they returned to camp.

British losses during the battle were, 18 killed and 65 wounded (11 of the wounded would subsequently die as a result of their wounds), however, Zulu losses were about 1,000 killed and about the same number wounded.

Although it was not obvious at the time, the Zulu defeat at Kambula proved to be the turning point of the war; the shock of their defeat considerably weakened the Zulu resolve to continue the war and when their commander tried to get his regiment to return to Ulundi many of the Zulu were so demoralised that they simply returned to their homes.

Relief of Eshowe

With the situation at Kambula under control, General Thesiger now felt able to go to the relief of the forces besieged at Eshowe and on 29th March left Fort Tenedos with a force of nearly 6,500 men.

Colonel Law led the first division of the column with 3,140 men while Colonel Pemberton led the second division with 3,340 men; due to the swollen rivers and the large number of wagons which carried the column's supplies progress was slow but by 1st April the force was within sight of Eshowe.

Once again halted by a swollen river, the British constructed their camp at Gingindlovu, this was a substantial affair with a trench around the perimeter surmounted by a waist high earthen wall. While the defences were being constructed scouts were sent out to locate and determine the strength of any Zulu forces nearby. A Zulu force was located, however, due to darkness it was not possible to estimate their strength.

Battle of Gingindlovu

The night passed without incident and at 4 o'clock in the morning the troops were called to arms and as dawn was breaking scouts reported that a large Zulu force, in three columns, was advancing on the camp; by 6 o'clock the Zulu had encircled the British position. The enemy were able to take advantage of the good ground cover to advance to within 400 yards of the British defences without much trouble, however, heavy rifle fire and fire from the two Gatling guns managed to prevent a further advance.

After 90 minutes of this steady barrage it became evident that the British fire was having a considerable effect on the Zulu force so at about 7:30 General Thesiger ordered his cavalry to mount an attack. The cavalry managed to put the Zulu to flight and during a chase over a distance of four miles they inflicted heavy casualties on the retreating enemy force. The Zulu attempted to regroup on nearby hills, however, after further fire from the British artillery they were forced to disperse.

British losses during the battle were 11 men killed and 63 wounded, however, the Zulu losses were considerable, estimated at over 1,000 killed and wounded.

On the following day, the 3rd April, after leaving a garrison at Gingindlovu, General Thesiger and his men pushed forward to Eshowe and reached the beleaguered town at about midnight. As further operations were planned to take place along the coast road, Eshowe was abandoned on 5th April and the force, now

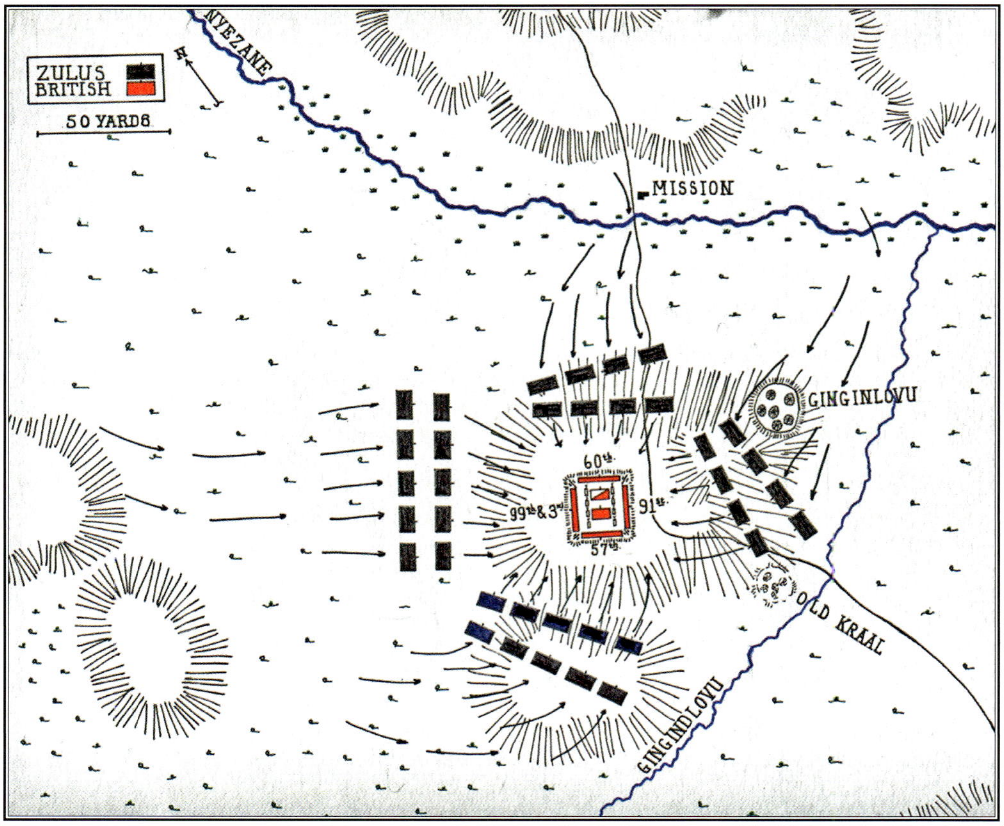

Figure 71. Battle of Gingindlovu

with Colonel Pearson's men moved off to Gingindlovu where a new camp was constructed. After leaving a small garrison at the new fort, the column moved off to the banks of the Tugela river on 7th April.

Second Invasion of Zululand

With the arrival of the requested reinforcements from England, by the end of April General Thesiger had at his disposal a force of just over 22,500 men: these were organised as follows; General Crealock was in command of the First Division with 9,215 men; General Newdigate with 10,238 men and a Flying Column of 3,092 men commanded by General Wood.

Although his troops were in place for a second invasion into Zululand by the middle of May, General Thesiger was beset by problems with supplies and transportation; unwilling to advance until his force was able to move off with two months supplies and with a further months supplies having been established at advanced depots there was a period of inactivity while these conditions were fulfilled.

It was during this period that chief Cetywayo, aware that the British were preparing for another invasion of his lands, sent envoys to General Thesiger to discuss peace but these were dismissed by the General who said that the time was for action not words and stated that Cetywayo should disband his army.

While awaiting the completion of preparations for his main assault force, General Thesiger wanted to use men from the Native Contingency to make raids into Zululand, however, Governor Lytton was opposed to this idea; the General resented the interference of Lord Lytton and this led to arguments between the pair which no doubt had an influence on the later decision to replace General Thesiger with Sir Garnet Wolseley.

On 28th May 1879, the Secretary of State for the Colonies, Sir Michael Hicks Beach, issued a despatch to General Thesiger which stated *"After full consideration of the condition of affairs in South Africa, her Majesty's Government have decided that the arrangements under which the chief civil and military authority in the neighbourhood of the seat of war is distributed among four different persons can no longer be deemed adequate to the requirements of the present juncture … Under these circumstances, her Majesty's Government have determined to place the chief military and civil command in the eastern portion of South Africa in the hands of one officer, and they have selected Lieutenant-General Sir Garnet Wolseley, G.C.M.G., for this duty. His high professional standing and his varied and distinguished services preclude any question as to the fitness of placing him for the time in supreme authority over the able men now commanding her Majesty's troops in South Africa and administering the Governments of Natal and the Transvaal, and it is equally beyond question that he will receive their most loyal and cordial support. Sir Garnet Wolseley will, in addition to his military command, be commissioned as Governor of Natal and of the Transvaal, and High Commissioner for Native and Foreign Affairs to the northward and eastward of those colonies. In the latter capacity he will assume for the time that portion of your functions which, at a crisis of such gravity as the present, could not be performed by any High Commissioner acting at a distance of more than 1000 miles from the scene of operations. You will, I am confident, be the first to recognize the necessity of the arrangement, and will readily assist Sir Garnet Wolseley, should you have returned to Cape Town by the time of his arrival there on his way to enter upon the duties of his office, with all the valuable information which your knowledge and experience enable you to afford."*

Although the appointment of Sir Garnet Wolseley was well received by many in South Africa, General Thesiger was now desperate to bring the war to a successful conclusion before the arrival of his successor.

To assist in the transportation issues, the gunboat *HMS Forester* was sent on a mission to find a suitable landing place on the Zululand coast. The mission was ultimately successful and resulted in Port Durnford being established as a place for landing supplies, this eliminated over 100 miles of transport by road; over 3,000 tons of stores were eventually landed at Port Durnford.

Forwarding the supplies and bridging the Tugela river was a task allocated to General Crealock and the 1st Division and was their sole occupation during May and well into June. The troops suffered from high levels of sickness but General Crealock did much to improve the sanitary arrangements and established an extensive hospital at Fort Pearson.

On the 18th June, the long awaited advance by the 1st Division commenced when General Crealock and his advanced force left Fort Pearson on the Lower Tugela and after marching via Fort Chelmsford reached the Umlalazi River on 22nd June and after bridging the river began work on Fort Napoleon on the left bank.

Sir Garnet Wolseley arrived at Durban on 27th June and soon afterwards proceeded to Pietermaritzburg from where he set sail for Port Durnford on board *HMS Shah*, however, being unable to land there, due to heavy surf, he was compelled to return to Durban and begin an overland journey to the front.

On 31st June, with the British forces now advancing on his capital, chief Cetywayo once again tried to strike a last minute peace deal, however, General Thesiger was not interested in any compromise as he wanted to win the war, to redeem himself after the disaster at Isandhlwana, before relinquishing his command to Sir Garnet Wolseley.

By the 1st July, General Wood with his Flying Column and General Newdigate with the 2nd Division had reached the southern bank of the White Umveloosi river, without encountering any opposition and were now within five miles of Ulundi.

On the 3rd July, Colonel Buller with the cavalry of the Flying Column crossed the river on a reconnaissance mission and about a mile from Ulundi they came across a body of about 5,000 Zulu warriors who had been concealed within the river bed.

When the Zulu fired on his column and began to move down his flanks, in order to cut off his retreat, Colonel Buller decided that it was time to retire with his force.

Captain William Beresford – Victoria Cross No. 380
Sergeant Edmund O'Toole – Victoria Cross No. 382

During the retirement, Captain Beresford went to the aid of Sergeant Fitzmaurice of the 24th Regiment, whose horse had fallen and rolled upon him. In the face of the advancing Zulu warriors, Captain Beresford, helped by Sergeant O'Toole, managed to mount the injured Sergeant behind him and continue with the retreat. Sergeant O'Toole, who was trying to keep the Zulu at bay by firing his carbine had to give up this endeavour in order to hold on to Sergeant Fitzmaurice who was having trouble maintaining his seat in the saddle due to extreme dizziness. The pair managed to keep the Sergeant in the saddle until they reached safety.

For their actions to save the life of Sergeant Fitzmaurice, Captain Beresford and Sergeant O'Toole were both awarded the Victoria Cross.

Captain Henry D'Arcy – Victoria Cross No. 381

During the retreat, Captain D'Arcy went to the rescue of Trooper Raubenheim of the Frontier Light Horse, who had fallen from his horse.

With the Zulu in close pursuit, Captain D'Arcy rode back to the Trooper and waited for him to mount up behind him, however, unfortunately Captain D'Arcy's horse dismounted them both and in the fall the Captain was injured. With no one nearby to provide help, despite his injury, Captain D'Arcy continued to try and help the stunned trooper to remount and only rode off when he was completely exhausted.

For his attempt to save the life of Trooper Raubenheim, Captain D'Arcy was awarded the Victoria Cross.

Major Baker, with his regiment of Light Horse, who had been left some way behind the advanced party, began to lay down covering fire for the retreat which combined with artillery fire from the British camp stemmed the Zulu advance and enabled Colonel Buller and his men to reach safety.

During the retreat the British force had two men killed and four wounded, unfortunately one of the dead was Trooper Raubenheim who Captain D'Arcy had tried to save.

Battle of Ulundi

On the 4th July, at about 6 o'clock in the morning General Thesiger began his move towards the Zulu capital at Ulundi; leading the advance party, Colonel Buller with the Light Cavalry from the Flying Column crossed the river Ulundi and occupied an area of high ground, that had been noted during the previous day's reconnoitre.

Soon afterwards, after leaving a garrison of about 1,000 men to guard the camp, the main body of the General's force also crossed the river and formed up on the high ground in a hollow square formation. With the ammunition carts and baggage in the centre the Flying column formed the front half of the square and the men of the 2nd Division formed the rear half; artillery was positioned such that it could be immediately brought into action and the cavalry provided cover to all sides of the square.

Not long after they had established their position, the British square was surrounded by large numbers of Zulu warriors. Some of the Zulu managed to reach within 30 to 40 yards of the rear face of the square, thanks to some cover, however, the main advance was checked at some distance by heavy artillery fire and volleys of rifle fire from the infantry.

After about half an hour of this unremitting fire, the Zulu advance began to waver and give way, at this point the British cavalry left the square by the rear face and advanced on the royal Nodwengo kraal. With the Zulu force in full flight they were chased into the kraal and a number who were heading for the safety of the hills were pursued until the steepness of the slopes prevented the cavalry from advancing any further.

By noon, after they had tended to their wounded, the British set fire to Ulundi and the nearby kraals and by 2 o'clock in the afternoon the force began their return march to the British camp across the river.

During the battle the British losses were 18 men killed and 85 wounded; the Zulu force, estimated to have been between 12,000 and 20,000 men experienced losses thought to be between 1,000 and 1,500 killed.

On 8th July, having *"... fully accomplished the object for which I advanced"* General Thesiger resigned his command of the army in South Africa.

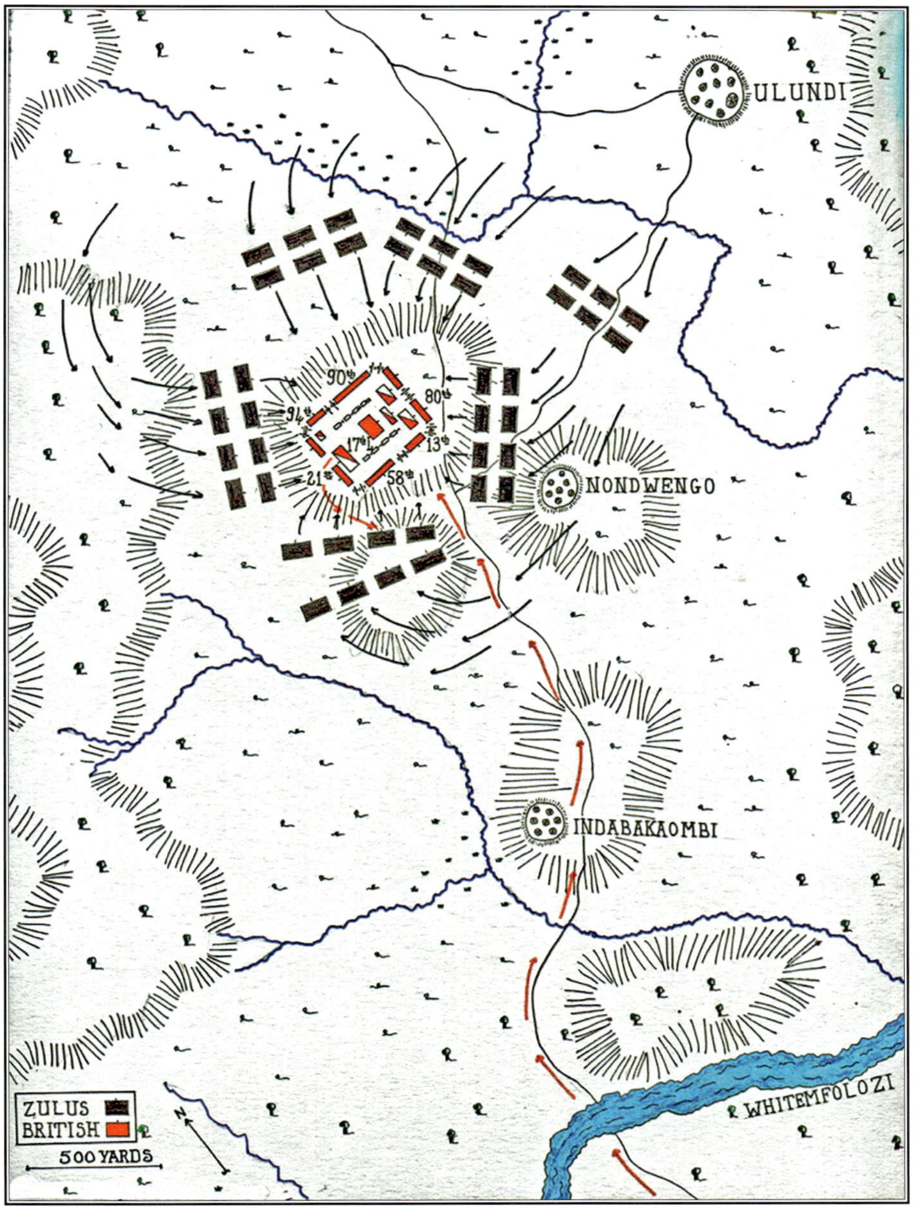

Figure 72. Battle of Ulundi

End of the War

With the destruction of Ulundi and the royal kraals and the dispersal of the Zulu army, the Battle of Ulundi effectively marks the end of the Anglo-Zulu war.

Sir Garnet Wolseley finally arrived at Port Durnford, the HQ of the 1st Division, on 7th July and immediately began the process of reducing the number of men involved in the conflict to *"... reduce the excessive rate of expenditure which has so far been maintained in connection with this war"*.

Arrangements were made to disband the Naval Brigade and dispense with the services of some of the colonial troops and all forms of reinforcement were stopped.

On the 15th July, General Thesiger met with Sir Garnet Wolseley at St Paul's where he formally handed over his command and on 17th July he began his journey to return to England.

On 14th August, Major Barrow, with a cavalry force left Ulundi with the mission to find and capture king Cetywayo but it was another patrol under the command of Major Marter, that managed to capture the king on 28th August and bring him to Ulundi on 31st August. On 4th September Cetywayo was taken to Port Durnford from where he was transported to Cape Town to await onward transport to London.

23

NAGA HILLS EXPEDITION (1879–80)

The Naga Hills occupy a long strip of mountainous land stretching from Jaipur to Cachar which forms the south east boundary of the Assam Valley in north east India. The area is occupied by six tribes of the Naga clan; the Aos, Lhotas, Angamis, Semas, Rengmas and Kacchas who collectively number about 100,000 people.

Background

The Honourable East India Company paid little regard to the area until 1835 when men from the Angamis tribe raided several villages in North Cachar, despite the increasing frequency of the raids the Company were reluctant to establish a permanent hill station in the area, preferring instead to control the insurgents by retaliatory expeditions; between 1839 and 1847 seven such expeditions were carried out by Company forces.

In 1847, it was thought that a Resident would be able to keep the Angamis in order and an Indian Police Officer, Bogchand Daroga, was sent to Samaguting, however, on a mission to Mozema where he was going to arrest some of the Naga raiders he was ambushed and together with 21 of his men was killed by the raiders.

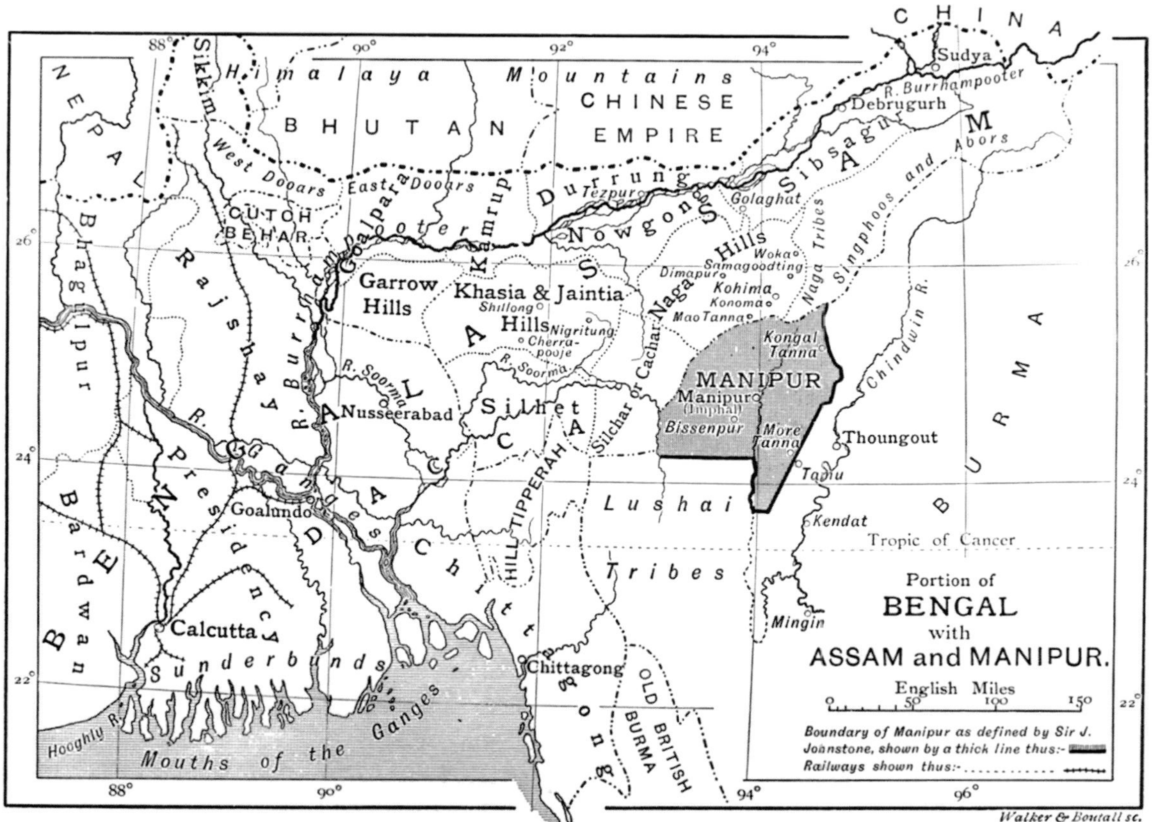

Figure 73. Naga Hills

The company response to this atrocity was to send a punitive expedition from Assam, under the command of Captain Vincent, however, when Naga tribesmen set fire to his stores this expedition failed. In 1849 another, stronger expedition, again led by Captain Vincent had more success and was able to inflict severe punishment on the Mozema and Khonoma villages.

In 1857, the Company decided on a non-intervention policy regarding the area and withdrew all of their troops, much to the delight of the Naga tribesmen who carried out 22 raids into British territory over the next year.

Over the next few years, the constant raiding finally resulted in another change in policy and Lieutenant Gregory, a Deputy Commissioner, was sent as Resident to Samaguting. The appointment had an almost immediate effect as when two new raids by the Angamis took place these were severely punished and raids across the border in Cachar and the plains ceased, with the Naga clan now concentrating their efforts on inter-tribal feuding.

Apart from the tribal feuding, the area was relatively quiet until 1874 when surveys of the Assam border were extended into the Naga Hills; these surveys prompted the Naga clan to once again resume their hostilities towards the British and one survey party, commanded by Lieutenant Holcombe was attacked and the Lieutenant together with the 80 men in his party were all killed.

In 1875, a punitive expedition under the command of Colonel Nuttall was organised and all of the villages involved in the outrage were destroyed and most of the plundered arms and equipment taken from the survey party was recovered.

For some months after this expedition the Naga were reasonably peaceful until December 1876 when another attack was mounted against a survey party, during which the Deputy Commissioner Captain Butler was killed; the village implicated in the attack was destroyed on the following day.

A raid into North Cachar, in 1877 resulted in another expedition led by Captain Brydon, which marched on the village of Mozema, where all of their stores were confiscated and a stockade was established.

At Mozema the Naga tribesmen were joined by fellow tribesmen from the villages of Khonoma and Jotsoma and as Captain Brydon felt that his force was too small to engage with this enlarged group he sent off for reinforcements and was subsequently joined by Lieutenant MacGregor with an additional 100 men.

When the reinforcements arrived, the men from Khonoma and Jotsoma began to enter into discussions regarding a peaceful settlement as they did not wish to have their stores confiscated like those at Mozema.

Unfortunately, Mr Carnegy, the Political Officer who was conducting the negotiations, was accidentally shot dead by a sentry when he wandered out of the stockade at Mozema and Captain Williamson, an inexperienced Assistant Political Officer, who had arrived with Lieutenant MacGregor continued with the negotiations. Being ignorant of the prevailing local situation, Captain Williamson was far too lenient with the Naga, letting them off scot free, so that when the British force returned to Samaguting some of the Naga were left with the belief that they could act with impunity.

The 1879 Expedition

In November 1878, Mr Guybon Henry Damant, who was now the Deputy Commissioner, moved the district headquarters to Kohima and was reasonably confident in the stability of the area as 16 Naga villages had tendered their submission, however, the resentment of the Naga was on the increase after finding that the establishment of a garrison at Kohima had not only put an end to their head hunting activities but also entailed the payment of a tribute.

In June 1879, there were signs of trouble brewing in the village of Khonoma, however, after they paid a fine during the following month this seemed to have dissipated. Later in the year, prior to a proposed tour of the Ao country, Mr Damant decided to visit Khonoma. Despite several warnings from one of his interpreters that the visit would be dangerous, Mr Damant set out for Khonoma with an escort of 86 men on 13th October.

After leaving half of his escort with the baggage at the foot of the hill leading the village, Mr Damant continued up the steep pathway up to the village gates, which were closed; as he stood before the gate he was shot dead and a volley was fired into his escort, who fled in some disorder. The Naga tribesmen charged out of the village and down the hill where they dispersed the troops, killing 35 and wounding 19 of the escort.

Siege of Kohima

As the survivors trickled back into Kohima with news of the attack at Khonoma, Captain Reid the commander of the 158 man garrison, hastily began to prepare the village for an attack; one of two stockades was abandoned in order to shorten the perimeter that needed to be defended and the garrison together with 240 non-combatants were moved into the other stockade.

Most of the command decisions were handled by Subedar Mema Ram and Jemandar Kurung Singh of the Field Police who took charge under Mr Cawley of the Civil Police as Captain Reid was ill throughout the siege. Mr Cawley sent messengers with news of the situation to Samaguting and Wokha, the Samaguting messengers were intercepted, however, a messenger did get through to Wokha and another reached Imphal.

The first Naga attacks took place on 16th October and for a time they cut off the defenders' water supply; the main supply via an external wooden aqueduct was destroyed and the defenders were prevented from using the two supplies from weak springs within the stockade by snipers, until these were dislodged.

A series of earthworks were erected by the Naga tribesmen, from where they attempted to set fire to the defenders' store houses, however, without much success.

On 19th October Mr Hinde, with 43 soldiers and 22 policemen arrived from Wokha and under the cover of darkness managed to enter the stockade without any losses.

Although several thousand Naga tribesmen were surrounding the village, only about 500 were armed with firearms, however, several attacks were mounted by this force and the unarmed men contributed by rolling boulders and logs down the hill and by throwing flaming missiles at the stockade rooftops.

The defenders were placed on quarter rations and after ten days only 45 men were fit enough to continue the fight; Mr Cawley was on the point of surrendering, subject to a condition that he was allowed safe passage to Samaguting, however, before this could be negotiated a messenger arrive with news that a relief force was close at hand.

Colonel J. Johnstone, the Political Agent for Manipur, arrived with a large force of over 2,000 men from Imphal and on 26th October they entered the village unopposed, the surrounding Naga tribesmen having faded away back to their villages.

Colonel Johnstone immediately began work to improve the Kohima defences, clearing away the Naga earthworks and cutting back the jungle away from the village defences. The Colonel wanted to mount an immediate attack against Khonoma but he was ordered to remain at Kohima as General Nation, commander of troops in Assam, had been given this task by the government.

General Nation raised a column of 1,135 troops at Piphima and was ordered by the Chief Commissioner of Assam to completely destroy Khonoma, prevent any rebuilding, execute all of the headmen of village implicated in the murder of Mr Damant, disarm the villages and extract a substantial reparation payment.

In advance of the attack on Khonoma, General Nation ordered attacks on some of the outlying villages; on 14th November Colonel Nuttall advanced on the village of Sachima but found it to have been deserted, however, after occupying the village he was immediately attacked by a large force of Naga tribesmen who had been hidden in the surrounding jungle. The attacks continued with some vigour until the main body of General Nation's column arrived on the following day. On the 16th November, Major Evans attacked and destroyed the village of Sephima.

General Nation and his force remained at Sachima until 22nd November, to await the arrival of mountain guns from Dimapur, and then after leaving behind a garrison, began the advance on Khonoma.

Battle of Khonoma

Arriving at the village, which was built along a hill side ridge, General Nation was surprised at the strength of the defences guarding the approaches, with stone walls and forts built on terraces.

The General decided to lead the main attack up the north spur of the hill, while a smaller force under the command of Lieutenant Ridgeway was directed to take up a position on the south spur, to intercept any retreating forces.

The British had seriously underestimated the quality and extent of the village defences as well as the number of Naga tribesmen guarding them.

Following an intense bombardment by artillery and rockets, the main attack was launched at 10 o'clock in the morning and despite casualties from the enemy fire managed to reach and occupy the first line of the defences, however, they were now faced by an inner line defended by a 12 foot high stockade which after two attempts they failed to take.

Lieutenant Richard Ridgeway – Victoria Cross No. 383

During the main attack, the enemy did make two attempts to escape to their rear, however, these were both driven back by the force at the south, commanded by Lieutenant Ridgeway.

In an attempt to breach the defences from the rear, Lieutenant Ridgeway led an attack against a barricade and after attempting to tear down some of the planking, to allow his men access to the enclosure, he received a serious gunshot wound to his left shoulder.

For his action during the assault, Lieutenant Ridgeway was later awarded the Victoria Cross.

With darkness falling, and both the frontal and rear assaults having failed, General Nation decided to maintain his positions and wait until the morning before renewing the attack. Unfortunately, due to a misunderstanding, some of the units guarding the rear of the enemy position were withdrawn during the night and in the morning it was discovered that the Naga had abandoned the village and fled to the Chaka spurs on the Japovo mountain.

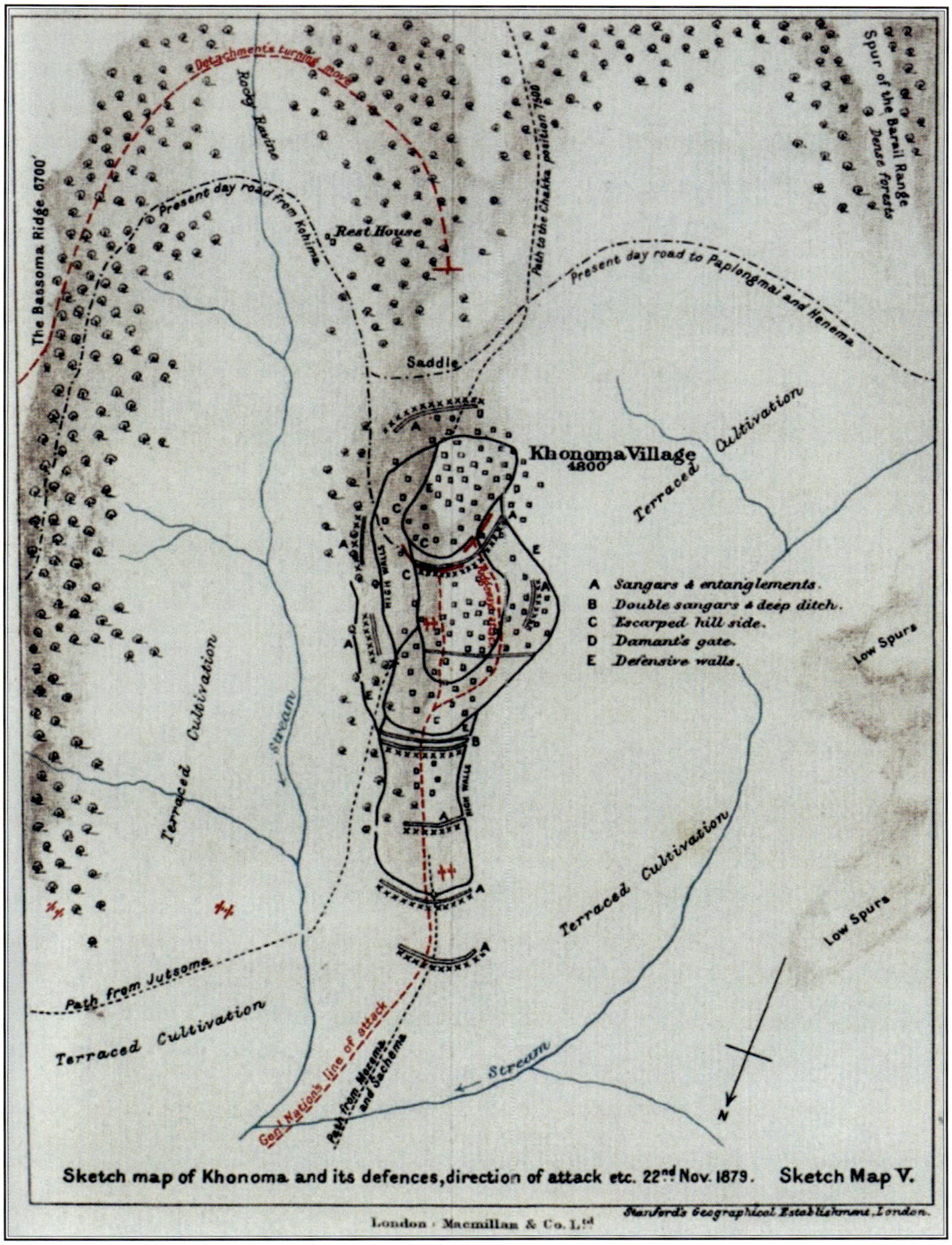

Figure 74. Battle of Khonoma

During the battle the British losses were 44 men killed or wounded while the Naga losses were twice that number.

End of the War

With the Naga tribesmen now occupying extensive and formidable defences on the Chaka spur, rather than mount an immediate attack, which would result in large losses, General Nation retired with his main force to Sachima to await reinforcements after leaving a garrison at Khonoma.

To contain the Naga and reduce their opportunity for reinforcements and resupply, the General attempted to blockage the Chaka position but this was largely ineffective.

All was relatively quiet until the middle of January 1880 when a group of 55 men from the Chaka position mounted a raid on the Baladhan tea estates, in North Cachar and killed Mr Blyth the estate manager and 16 of his workers before returning to Chaka with their plunder. The final action of the war was an attack by the Naga on the Nichuguard stockade.

By the middle of March, following the arrival of reinforcements, General Nation was able to enforce a more rigorous blockade and carry out reconnaissances in preparation for an assault.

This activity prompted the Naga to treat for peace and they finally submitted on 27th March. The Naga villages that had been involved in the war were punished by fines, confiscation of firearms and in some cases expulsion from their lands.

24

BASUTOLAND (1879–82)

The Basuto became an organised tribe in 1818 when Chief Moshesh unified remnants of various clans who had been scattered by Zulu and Matabele raids. When the Basuto lands came under threat from Boer Trekkers who were settling more and more of their territory, Chief Moshesh turned to the British for protection and eventually on 12th March 1868 Basutoland was annexed by the British Government.

Following the British annexation, the Boers of the Orange Free State signed the Aliwal treaty on 12th February 1869 which formalised the Basutoland / Orange Free State boundaries and returned the Boer conquered territory east of the Caledon River to Basutoland, however, much of the fertile land was retained by the Boer settlers. On August 10th 1871, the Cape Colony annexed Basutoland.

With the growth of the diamond mines at Kimberley, many Basuto workers left to work in the mines and obtain a cash salary; in addition to a salary, workers were also rewarded by the award of a gun with ammunition and the Basuto chiefs instructed their men to continue their work and not return until they had received this award.

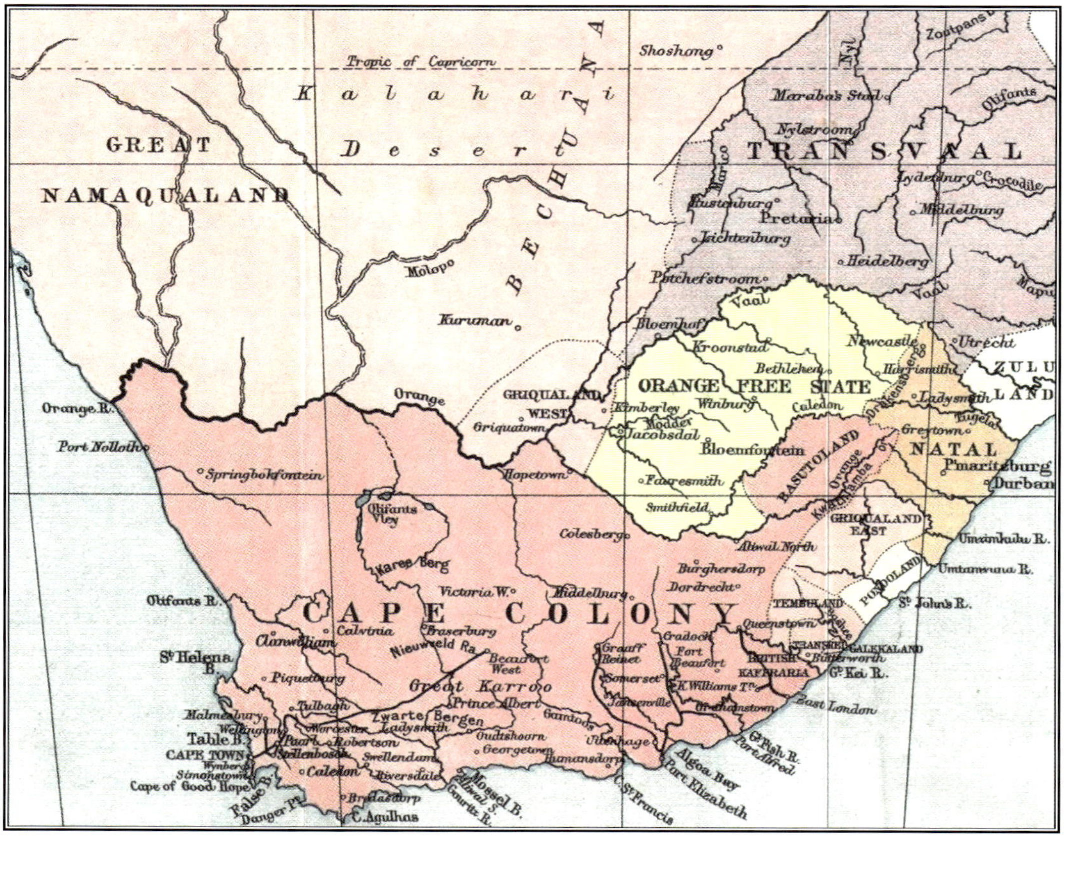

Figure 75. South Africa 1878

The actions that resulted in the award of the following Victoria Cross medals, are categorised in most books as Basutoland. While it is true that most of the actions were performed in Basutoland some were performed in the Transvaal and, they were awarded during three separate conflicts; The Morosi War, the Sekukuni War (Transvaal) and the Basuto Gun War.

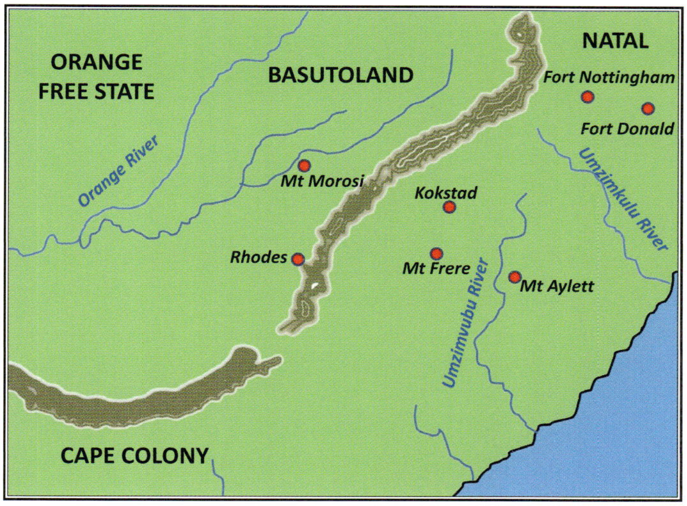

Figure 76. Morosi War

Morosi War

Background

Morosi was the chief of the Basuto BaPhuthi clan who occupied an area of south east Basutoland; renowned as cattle rustlers, the clan maintained a great deal of autonomy from the rest of the Basuto tribe but like the other clans, the men of the BaPhuthi had taken advantage of working in the diamond mines to secure firearms and ammunition.

For some time, the Cape Colony government had been looking for an excuse to invade Morosi lands and implement the provisions of the 1876 Peace Preservation Disarmament Act and disarm the BaPhuthi.

The pretext was provided by the actions of Doda, one of Morosi's sons who had persuaded some of the clan not to pay their "hut tax". The tax had been introduced when Basutoland was annexed, to pay for the administration costs. When the local magistrate, Mr John Austin, arrested some of the supposed ringleaders, Doda and some of his men rescued the defaulters from prison and moved off to his father's lands.

Battle of Morosi's Mountain

The first response to the outrage was for Mr Austin to send a troop of Cape Mounted Riflemen into Morosi territory, where the chief was asked to hand over his son or be considered as a rebel. The approach of the Cape Colony force was repulsed and the chief refused to hand over his son, however, he requested a week to respond to the government's offer of safe passage if he handed over the offenders.

During the week, Morosi with about 1,500 warriors along with their women and children moved to what became known as "Morosi's Mountain" which he had been fortifying for the past ten years. The mountain defences were formidable, with sheer drops on three sides and the only approach on the fourth side was up a steep slope reinforced with a series of strong walls between 8 and 12 feet high.

On 8th April, Colonel Griffith with about 900 men made the first attack against Morosi and his men, his force was comprised of about 200 men from the Cape colony regular and volunteer forces and 700 native levys including 100 Fingo warriors and 600 Basuto warriors who had been promised that their involvement would ensure that their arms would not be confiscated. Only about 550 of Colonel Griffith's men were on the mountain with the remainder guarding his lines of supply and communication.

The attack began with a barrage from two seven pounder mountain guns, however, these had little effect on the substantial stone walls of the defences. Despite the ineffective fire of his artillery Colonel Griffith ordered about 150 of his men to mount an attack but in the face of heavy rifle fire and being pelted by rocks the attack was soon pinned down so the Colonel threw his reserve forces into the attack but they were also pinned down.

Trooper Peter Brown – Victoria Cross No. 385

During the attack five of Griffith's men were killed and about 20 wounded. Hearing the cries from the wounded for water, Trooper Brown who was sheltering with his troop some 200 yards from the enemy defences, waiting for the order to resume the attack, rushed forward to give water to two wounded men sheltering in nearby rocks.

While giving water to the first man, Trooper Brown received a severe wound to his right leg and soon afterwards his right forearm was shattered by a rifle bullet.

For his actions Trooper Brown was awarded the Victoria Cross.

Sergeant Robert Scott – Victoria Cross No. 384

In an attempt to breach the enemy defences, Sergeant Scott and three of his men volunteered to use 7 pounder artillery shells as hand grenades against men sheltering behind the stone defences who were pouring down devastating fire on the Colonial troops.

After reaching the base of the enemy barricade, Sergeant Scott ordered his men to take shelter while he threw a time fused shell over the wall. On his second attempt at this dangerous act, due to a defect in the time fuse, the shell exploded almost as soon as it left his hand, blowing his right hand to pieces and wounding him severely in the leg.

Despite his wounds, Sergeant Scott ordered his men to wait until darkness before they retired, in order to avoid the worst of the enemy fire.

For this action, Sergeant Scott was later awarded the Victoria Cross.

After failing to capture Morosi's stronghold, Colonel Griffith's ordered his men to build their own defences and lay siege to the mountain; Morosi had foreseen this eventuality and had stocked his defences with large supplies of grain and had a large herd of cattle on the mountain.

On the 11th April, Colonel Brabant arrived on the mountain with a further 60 men as reinforcements and took over the command from Colonel Griffith's who returned to his administrative duties.

Patrols on 28th and 29th May managed to clear some of Morosi's men from caves where they had been hiding and in preparation for the next attack Colonel Brabant received a 12 pounder gun, which had been purchased from the Orange Free State.

Surgeon Major Edmund Baron Hartley – Victoria Cross No. 386

On 5 June 1879 a second attack was mounted against Morosi's defences which was again unsuccessful, the 12 pounder artillery piece proved to be just as ineffective as the 7 pounders.

During the attack Surgeon Hartley tended to the wounded while under heavy enemy fire and he carried one of the wounded, Corporal A. Jones of the Cape Mounted Riflemen to safety before returning to treat the wounds of other men injured during the assault.

For his actions Surgeon Hartley was later awarded the Victoria Cross.

During this failed assault five men were killed and a further nine wounded.

For the cold months of July, August and September only a small Colonial force was maintained on the mountain and due to the lack of grass the horses were withdrawn to the eastern Cape where it was slightly warmer.

On the 24th October, Colonel Zackary Bayly took over command of the Colonial forces and now with a force of just over 1,100 men began to prepare for what would prove to be the final attack. The most significant addition to his resources was an 8 inch, 30 year old, mortar that had been sent up from Cape Town. Unlike the 7 pounder and 12 pounder guns, the mortar was able to drop its shells just over the enemy defensive walls and after some practice, the gunners were able to drop their shells just over the walls where they would roll back and explode amid the defenders.

After four days of bombardment by the mortar, the final assault was carried out during the night of 19th – 20th November. Using scaling ladders, Bayly's men mounted a surprise attack up a fissure which became known as "Bourne's Crack" (after Captain Bourne who led this assault party) and reached the top of the mountain before Morosi's men could mount a challenge.

After despatching many of the defenders the storming party began to search for chief Morosi, who when he was found sheltering in a cave, was shot dead by Private Whitehead. Five of Chief Morosi's sons, with the exception of Doda, together with his wives were also killed plus about 200 of his men.

Doda with about 120 men escaped by jumping into the Orange River.

Sekukuni War

Background

Since the late 1700s, the Bapedi tribe had occupied lands in the Transvaal and prospered until the Matabele went on a rampage in the Transvaal during the mid 1820s and almost crushed their empire. After spending some years in the caves of the mountains to the north the tribe returned and established themselves at Phiring near Pokwani.

Again the Bapedi were at peace for some time until 1837 when the first party of Voortrekkers arrived in eastern Transvaal and began to settle the lands, which began a period of dispute between the Boers and the Bapedi peoples.

After Boer attacks in 1847 and 1852, Chief Sekwati considered that his stronghold at Phiring was no longer safe and in 1853 he moved his people to Thaba Mosega on the eastern slope of the Lulu Mountains where he established the heavily fortified village of Dsjate.

Constant friction between the Bapedi and the Boers continued for some years until 17th November 1857 when Chief Sekwati entered into an agreement with the Boers that established the Steelpoort River as the eastern boundary of Bapediland.

The tribe were again able to live in peace for several years and grew to a strength of about 70,000 people with an army of about 12,000 a third of which had firearms.

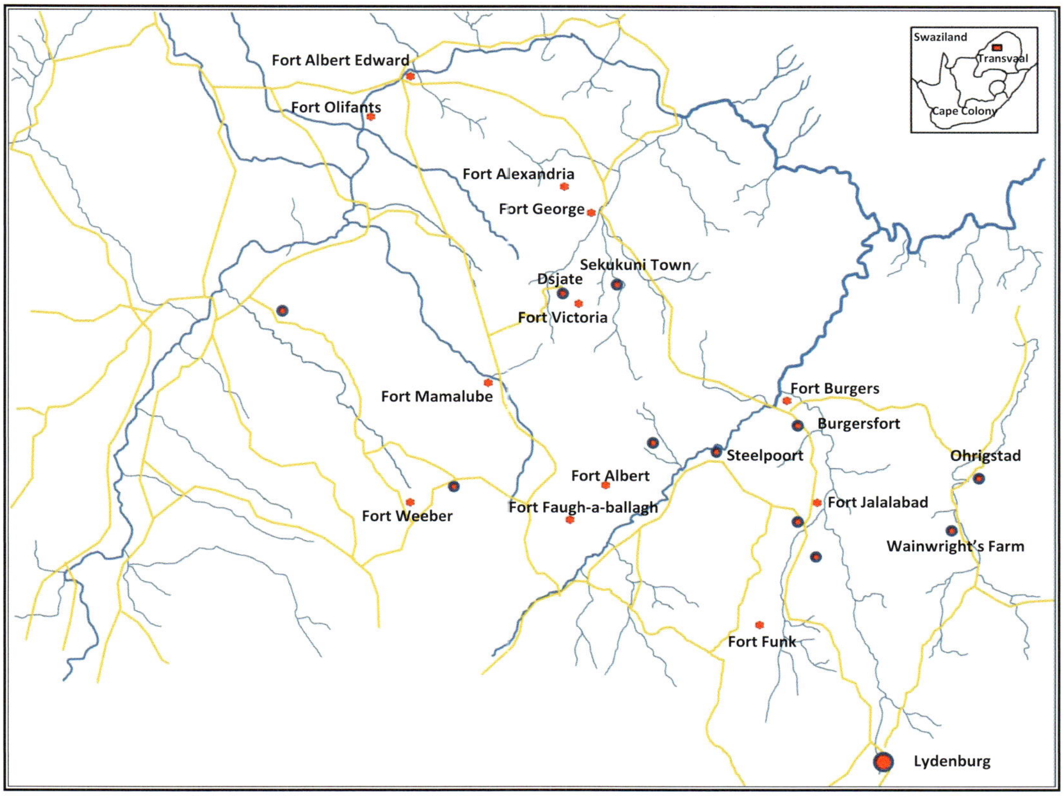

Figure 77. Sekukuni War

Figure 78. Chief Sekukuni

Chief Sekwati died on 20th September 1861 and was succeeded by his son Sekukuni who claimed the throne by force, overturning his half brother Mampuru, the rightful heir, who was forced to flee.

During the years after his succession, Sekukuni quietly collected a store of muskets and ammunition and with this armament his tribe were able to successfully fend off an assault by an army of Swazi in 1875.

Sekukuni considered Sekukuniland to be independent and not subject to the Transvaal Republic; this attitude led to friction between the parties one example being when Sekukuni refused to allow miners from the Pilgrims Rest goldfields to prospect on his side of the Steelpoort River.

War Begins

Matters came to a head when a Boer named Jancowitz was prevented from establishing a farm near Lydenburg where Johannes Drinkwanyane, brother of Sekukuni, had his village. As a result of this incident, the Volksraad declared war on Sekukuni on 16th May 1876.

By July 1876, the Boer leader President Burghers with a force of 2,000 of his own men and accompanied by a large force of Swazi were advancing up the Steelpoort River from Middelburg. The force was divided into an eastern section under the command of Commandant General Martinus Wessels Pretorius which had the objective of capturing Johannes Drinkwanyane's village before advancing on Sekukuni's stronghold; the western section, under the command of Commandant Nicolas Smit had the objective to clear the Olifants River area of hostile natives.

On 4th and 5th July 1876, the western section under Commandant Smit launched an attack on the Mathebes Kop, the initial assault was unsuccessful but when President Burgers arrived with reinforcements the position was taken.

The first clash between the eastern force and the Bapedi occurred at Magnet Heights on 8th July 1876, this was a resounding victory for the Boer who killed about 400 of the enemy with their losses limited to 9 killed.

On 13th July, the eastern force under Commandant Coetzee, supported by a large force of Swazi took up a position opposite Johannes Drinkwanyane's village on the Spekboom River. Without waiting for orders the Swazi launched a surprise attack on their own taking the village; during the fighting Johannes Drinkwanyane was mortally wounded. After the battle, the Swazi returned to Swaziland with the captured Bapedi cattle and the remnants of the Bapedi surrendered.

The two sections of President Burgher's force reunited and by 31st July 1876, after making an approach on Thaba Mosega from the east, were in position to mount an assault on Sekukuni's village. The plan was for a force commanded by Commander Jan Joubert to make an attack from the rear, while Commandant Smit and his force made a frontal attack, however, after being halted by large numbers of Bapedi warriors Joubert's force returned to camp. Unaware of Joubert's retirement, Smit continued with the frontal attack but without the support of Joubert was forced to withdraw after setting fire to some huts and also returned to the camp.

After this failed attack, many of the Boers decided to return to their homes and President Burgher decided to establish a line of forts and hold the line of the Steelpoort River. Fort Burghers was established at the junction of the Steelpoort and Spekboom rivers and another, Fort Weeber was built to the west of the Lulu Mountains.

On 29th September, Chief Sekukuni attacked Fort Burgers in order to recover cattle that had been looted from the Bapedi; the attack failed to capture the fort but the cattle were recovered.

By February 1877, the Boer policy of harassing the Bapedi and preventing them from sowing their crops, was having the desired effect and Sekukuni was forced to sue for peace. After agreeing to pay a fine of 2,000 cattle and settling the line of the border a treaty was ratified by the end of the month and peace was proclaimed.

For a time after the peace treaty the Transvaal settled into a period of restlessness and Sekukuni sent a message to Mr Theophilus Shepstone, who had recently been appointed by the Secretary of State for the Colonies to look into the affairs in the Transvaal and for protection from the Boers.

Mr Shepstone requested President Burgers to appoint a commission of enquiry which concluded that the peace treaty had little foundation as Sekukuni did not consider himself or his people to be subjects of the Transvaal Republic, however, he was thought to be agreeable to become a British subject.

Following the British annexation of the Transvaal on 12th April 1877, Sekukuni finally agreed to the conditions demanded by Mr Shepstone for the Bapedi to remain in the Transvaal, which included the requirement to pay the fine of 2,000 cattle. When the volunteer force was withdrawn from the forts in Sekukuniland, the pressure to obtain the cattle was reduced, which was just as well as due to the death of many of his cattle Sekukuni stated that it would take him many years to pay the fine.

Apart from some sporadic cattle thefts, things were reasonably quiet but by early January 1878 there were unmistakable signs that Chief Sekukuni was preparing for hostilities and had declared his intention to become the paramount chief of all the tribes. In February 1878 an attack was made against Pokwane, a minor chief friendly to the British. When Sekukuni was warned that attacks against friendly tribes was against the terms of the treaty, the chief replied that the British were afraid to fight and demanded that the British at Fort Burgers and in the Waterval area must leave his lands.

On 8th March, Fort Burgers was pillaged after it had been vacated and bands of Bapedi were roaming the countryside harassing the farmers east of the Lulu Mountains by stealing their cattle and burning their farmsteads.

With Imperial troops occupied elsewhere, defence of the Transvaal was carried out by a volunteer force raised by the Cape Colony government and a number of new forts were planned to be constructed on the plains between Fort Weeber and the Lulu Mountains; construction of Fort Mamalube was started on 27th April and in July Fort Faugh-a-ballagh was built near the Magnet Heights to command the pass to the Steelpoort Valley.

In August 1878, Colonel Hugh Rowlands VC was appointed to the command of the troops in the Transvaal and Imperial troops began to be deployed for use in operations against Sekukuni. After establishing his operational base at Fort Burgers, Colonel Rowlands started out on an expedition against Sekukuni's stronghold on 3rd October 1878, however, after a difficult journey and unable to find suitable supplies of water the expedition was force to return to Fort Burgers on 7th October.

At this stage, operations against Sekukuni were suspended when the imperial troops were withdrawn to Natal in preparation for the Anglo-Zulu war.

Following the end of the Zulu war, Sir Garnet Wolseley who had taken over command of the forces from General Thesiger (Lord Chelmsford) was determined to make a success of any continued operations against Sekukuni, however, before launching the campaign he gave the chief one last opportunity for a peaceful solution but this was scorned.

General Wolseley moved his headquarters to Middelburg in the middle of October 1879 and after assembling the Transvaal Field Force moved his advanced post to Fort Webber on 24th October. The force consisted of about 1,400 Imperial troops, 800 colonial troops and 10,000 native levies (including 8,000 Swazi warriors mainly armed with assegais).

There was a short delay while General Wolseley sorted out problems with the extended supply lines from Lydenburg and Middelburg but by 23rd November, he decided that sufficient supplies had been concentrated at Fort Albert Edward for the advance to commence.

On 24th November, after leaving a small garrison at Fort Albert Edward, General Wolseley and his main force advanced on Sekukuni's positions at Dsjate and managed to capture the kraal of chief Umkwane, one of his devoted followers later in the day.

On the following day, the British captured the Water Kop without any opposition as Sekukuni had called in all of his outlying detatchments to make his final stand at Dsjate. At the Water Kop the British created a fortification which was named Fort Alexandra.

In preparation for the upcoming battle, General Wolseley rode forward with a small escort to reconnoitre the battle area. After moving to within 250 yards of the "Fighting Koppie", the central fortress commanding Sekukuni's position, the General selected a camp site and the positions for his guns before moving off to Fort George to inform Major Bushman of his plans for the attack.

The plan was to attack the mountain first, and once the defenders on the mountain had been destroyed or driven off then following an artillery bombardment, the isolated "Fighting Koppie" fortress would be attacked from all sides. Major Bushman was ordered to have his men in position by 4:15 on the morning of 28th November.

The General's main force arrived at the new camp site in the early hours of the morning of 27th November, following a difficult journey through storms of hail and rain which had turned the roads to a sea of mud.

Battle of Sekukuni Town

Colonel Baker Russell divided the main British force into three columns; the right attack, which would begin the attack was commanded by Colonel Ferreira was assigned the objective of taking the main kraal; the left attack was commanded by Major Frederick Carrington, with the objective of taking Dsjate village and preventing reinforcement reaching Sekukuni and the central column, commanded by Colonel John Murray would act as reserve and restrict the fire from the "Fighting Koppie" which they would eventually storm.

Major Bushman and his force of Swazi warriors would ascend the mountain from the rear, during the night, and provide support to Colonel Ferreira and Major Carrington.

At about 2 o'clock in the morning the men were called to arms and in silence moved off to their designated positions, at 6 o'clock, as dawn was breaking, the start of the battle was signalled by artillery fire against the "Fighting Koppie".

Colonel Ferreira and his men launched their attack against the western side of Dsjate village and despite the heavy enemy fire managed to gain a position overlooking Sekukuni's Kraal. Major Carrington, attacked the eastern side of the village and met stern opposition from the Bapedi who occupied a line of rifle pits in front of the village. To counter this opposition, Major Carrington ordered his cavalry to dismount, join the infantry and mount a charge with fixed bayonets against the position, however, heavy fire from Bapedi warriors in caves above the position managed to halt their advance.

At about this time, Major Bushman and his force of 8,000 Swazi warriors swarmed down the mountain to attack the rear of the Bapedi positions which encouraged Major Carrington and his men to press ahead and join in the fierce hand to hand fighting.

Private Francis Fitzpatrick – Victoria Cross No. 387
Private Thomas Flawn – Victoria Cross No. 388

During the attack, Lieutenant C. J. Dewar of the King's Dragoon Guards fell, having been seriously wounded and was being carried to safety by six men of the Native Contingent, however, when they were attacked by a band of about 40 Bapedi warriors they dropped the Lieutenant and fled.

Privates Fitzpatrick an Flawn, seeing the plight of Lieutenant Dewar rushed to his aid and while one man carried him on his back, the other was firing his rifle to keep the enemy at bay. In this way the Lieutenant was brought to safety.

For this action Private Fitzpatrick and Private Flawn were later awarded the Victoria Cross.

At about 9:30, after three hours of fighting the town of about 3,000 huts had been captured and Colonel Russell now assembled his forces for the attack on the main enemy position, the "Fighting Koppie" which had been shelled by the artillery since the beginning of the battle.

When all of the forces were in position, two rockets were fired to signal the assault and with fixed bayonets the whole force mounted a charge against the Bapedi position. Initially the Bapedi laid down heavy fire from their prepared position but soon were force to retire to shelter in the many caves above their front line where fierce hand to hand fighting took place.

After about an hour of fighting, the position was under British control but many of the caves were still occupied by Bapedi warriors who refused to surrender; Royal Engineers set explosions at the mouth of these caves but these failed to dislodge the enemy.

With the enemy occupying the easily defended caves, Colonel Russell withdrew his men and placed a cordon around the Koppie with the objective of starving the Bapedi into submission; the remainder of the force returned to camp at about 1 o'clock in the afternoon.

During the night a thunderstorm broke with heavy rain and lightning and the Bapedi taking this as an opportunity to escape the clutches of the British cordon, charged the lines. During the confusion of the storm many of the Bapedi warriors, including chief Sekukuni managed to make their escape, however, the cordon was maintained as many were unable to escape and continued to refuse to surrender, several of these would subsequently die from thirst and starvation.

On 2nd December, Sekukuni was tracked down to a cave about nine miles from Fort Victoria and after a short siege and a promise from Major Clarke that his life would be spared he surrendered.

During the battle the Bapedi had suffered considerable losses, chief Sekukuni lost eight of his children and three of his brothers. The British losses were 13 killed and 35 wounded, however, the Swazi losses amounted to about 500 killed and a similar number wounded.

Immediately after the capture of chief Sekukuni, the Transvaal Field Force was disbanded and on 3rd December, General Wolseley set out, with his staff and the captured chief, for Pretoria where they arrived on 9th December 1879.

Basuto Gun War

Background

Following the problems of the Morosi War, the Cape Colony was eager to extend the provisions of the Peace Preservation Act of 1876 to Basutoland and took the annual visit of Prime Minister Sir Gordon Sprigg to Basutoland in October 1879 as an opportunity to discuss matters with the Basuto leaders.

At two meetings with some of the Basuto leaders; the major chiefs Letsia, Masupa and Molappo did not attend due to illness; Prime Minister Sprigg began by thanking them for helping the British in action against Morosi and then announced a doubling of the hut tax in order to pay for native education, road and bridge building and police protection to end cattle theft in the region. He also announced the intention to disarm the Basuto, in line with the terms of the Peace Preservation Act.

The majority of the leaders voiced little or no concern regarding the increased hut tax, however, all were opposed to disarmament feeling that it cast doubt over the loyalty of the Basotho, some of whom had fought on the side of the British in the wars against Morosi and also to a lesser extent against the Zulu.

Despite the feelings of the Basotho, Governor Frere was determined that disarmament should occur and on 22nd December

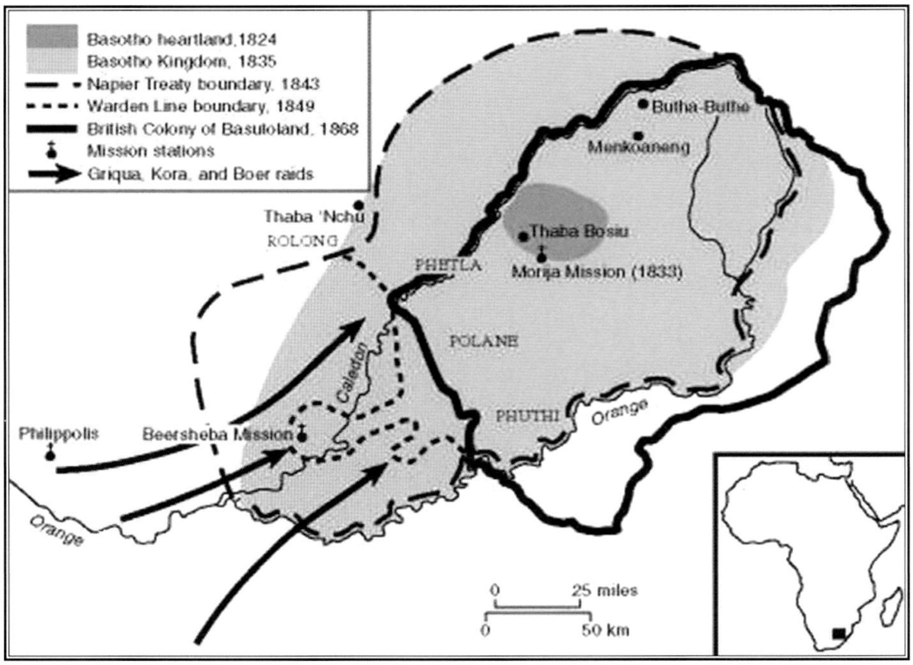

Figure 80. Basutoland

1879, Colonel Griffith (the chief magistrate) ordered the tribe to surrender their arms, for which they would receive a compensation payment, within a month but few of the natives complied with the order.

On 6th April 1880, the Cape Colony government issued a proclamation which applied the provisions of the Peace Preservation Act to Basutoland and extended the deadline for voluntary surrender of arms and payment of compensation to 21st May 1880. After this period the Basuto would only be able to carry arms if in the possession of a permit issued by the Chief Magistrate.

Chief Latsie, the paramount chief of the Basuto, sent a delegation to Cape Town to plead the Basuto case for the retention of their right to bear arms and his right to refer the matter to the Crown in London. The seven man delegation, led by the French missionary Pastor Cochet left for Cape Town on 29th April and after meetings with Prime Minister Sprigg and governor Frere were granted a further one month extension to the deadline for the surrender of their arms, which would allow the Cape parliament time to debate the issue. After three weeks of discussion in the Cape Parliament, despite some dissent the parliament decided to approve the application of the Peace Preservation Act to Basutoland.

The matter was also debated in the British parliament and again despite some dissent it was decided that there were no grounds for overturning a decision by the Cape Parliament.

Chief Latsie petitioned for a further extension to the deadline, so that his delegation would have time to return and make their report; as a consequence the deadline was changed from 21st June to 12th July.

Causes of War

In addition to the disarmament issues, land ownership was also a significant issue in the build-up to war; in 1880 a law was passed that recognised individual property rights in Basutoland. As a result of this new law each tribesman became the owner of the property upon which his house and kraal stood; this overturned the Basuto law where all land was communal and significantly reduced the power of the chiefs. The new law also permitted the Basuto to buy or sell land and opened up the opportunities for settlers to acquire land by purchase.

Civil War

As a result of the different positions adopted regarding the Gun Law, with the paramount chief favouring acceptance and other chiefs in favour of rejection a major split developed within the tribe and compounded by other clan and family quarrels this led to the outbreak of a civil war in June 1880.

The main agitators were Chief Latsie and his sons, on behalf of the loyalist faction and chiefs Masupa and Lerothodi on behalf of the rebel faction.

Basuto Rebellion

On 6th September 1880, Cape Colony forces crossed the border into Basutoland, ostensibly to provide protection to the loyalist faction to which, having mainly surrendered their arms, they were due, however, in reality it was mainly to stop the inter tribal conflict which was disrupting the operations of Cape Colony traders in Basutoland.

The initial action was by Chief Lerothodi and 600 of his cavalry when he attacked the advanced guard of the Cape Colony force near Mafetang; although they were driven off with some minor losses they mounted an attack on Mafetang on 21st September with a force of 7,000 men and afterwards besieged the town. Over the next few weeks the rebels, operating in small mobile units, mounted several small attacks against Cape Colony forces with some minor success.

On 10th October, Chief Masupa mounted an attack against Maseru which was driven back by the garrison and after besieging the town mounted a further unsuccessful attack on 25th October.

On 19th October, a force going to the relief of Maseru was ambushed at Kalabani Hill and although they suffered significant losses, the Colonial force did manage to reinforce Maseru.

In November, General Clarke was forced to suspend most operations against the rebels as he was required to send some of his troops home to deal with a rebellion in the Transkei.

With some aid from Natal, operations did continue with some limited success, however, the enemy strongholds were determined to be too well defended to warrant attacks and the colonial forces were concentrated around Mafetang.

Battle of Tweefontein

On 14th January 1881, on a misty and rainy day, Colonel Brabant left Mafetang with a force of 560 colonial troops, supported by a further 400 burgher volunteers from the Orange Free State, on a search and destroy mission towards Thaba Tsueu, a mountain about 10 miles from the town.

After reaching a wide marshy valley and the plateau leading to the village of Sepechele, Colonel Brabant ordered the burgher force to seize and burn the village of Radiamari on his right flank.

Having completed this task and disregarding their orders, the burgher force continued on to mount an attack against the village of Sepechele, which unknown to them was occupied by chief Maama with a force of about 3,000 rebels.

As they approached the village chief Maama's men suddenly emerged from the mist and attacked the burghers forcing them to retire towards the main colonial force.

Surgeon John Frederick McCrea – Victoria Cross No. 389

During the retreat the burgher force lost 16 men killed and 21 wounded; under heavy enemy fire Surgeon McCrea, accompanied by Captain Buxton, who were with the main column went out for some distance to go to the aid of the wounded.

After treating a burgher named Aircamp and having moved him to the shelter of a large anthill, Surgeon McCrea returned to his ambulance for a stretcher but on the way was severely wounded by a bullet to the right breast. Despite his wound, which he dressed himself, Surgeon McCrea continued to perform his duties at the ambulance and assisted in bringing several more wounded men to safety. He continued to attend to the wounded for the remainder of the day.

For his action Surgeon McCrea was later awarded the Victoria Cross.

As chief Maama's men approached the main column he was joined by chief Lerothodi with a force of a further 7,000 rebels, however, concentrated rifle fire forced the Basuto warriors to the flanks where they were contained.

After a fierce battle of about five hours, the Basuto were finally forced to withdraw due to intense artillery fire. After the battle the colonial force returned to their base at Mafetang.

End of the War

For some time, despite occasional actions, the war had developed into a stalemate with neither party able to inflict a decisive defeat on the other. This stalemate was exacerbated by the logistical difficulties being experienced by both sides.

In February 1881, the Basuto began to make overtures towards peace and on 18th February an armistice was agreed which lasted until 24th February.

Finally on 29th April a peace was agreed; under the terms of the treaty the Basuto accepted the Cape Colony rule of Basutoland and agreed to hand over 5,000 head of cattle as compensation for the war. The Basuto, however, were allowed to retain their arms, under licence and the rebel leaders all received an amnesty.

25

BOER WAR (1880–81)

The Boer War of 1880 to 1881 is known by several names; the First Boer War, the Transvaal War, the Transvaal rebellion, the First Anglo-Boer war and the first Freedom War. This war was fought by British Cape Colonisers and Boer colonisers of the Transvaal (South African Republic) from 16 December 1880 until 23 March 1881

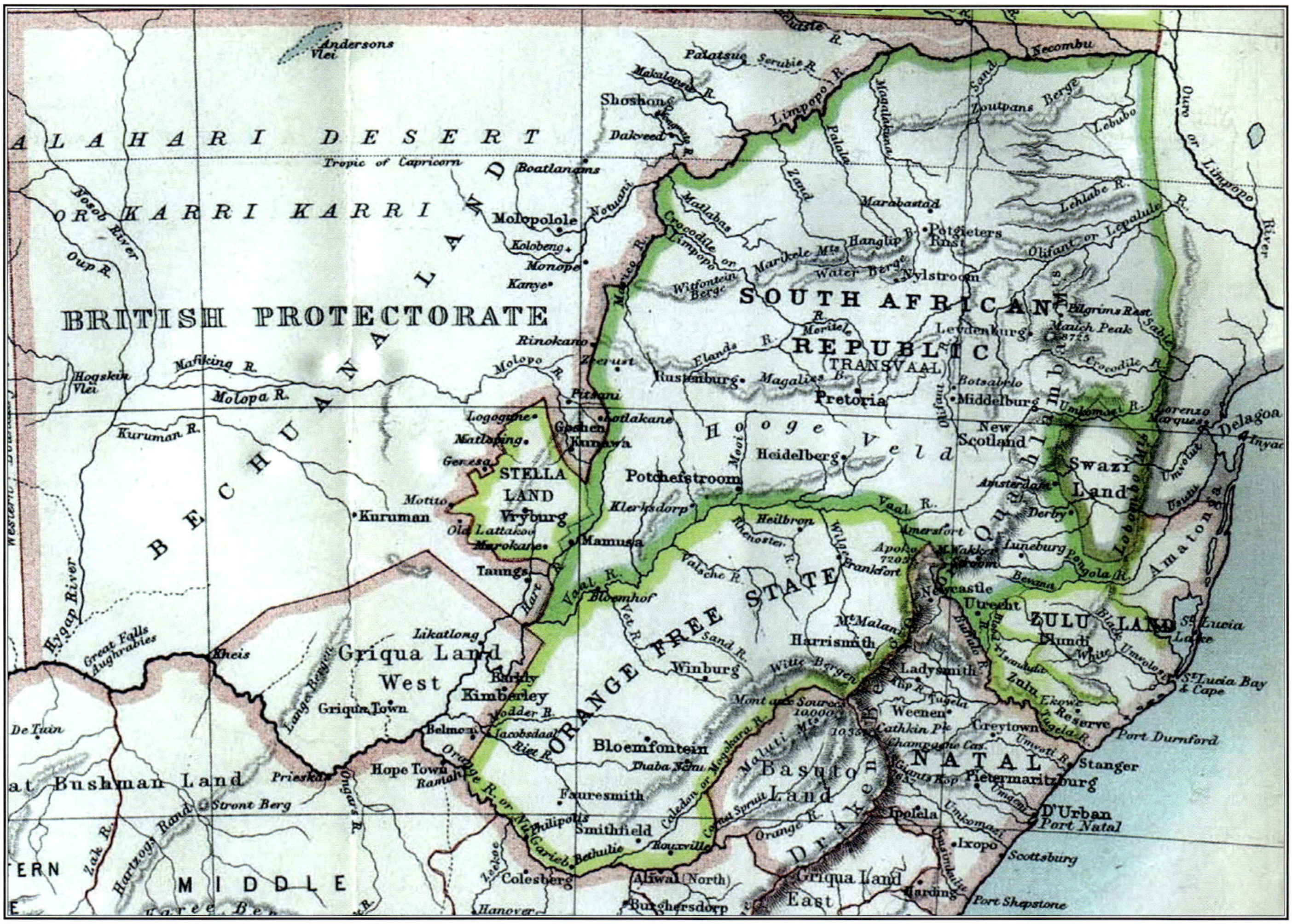

Figure 81. Transvaal and vicinity

Background

In 1833, the British Parliament passed the Slave Abolition Act which abolished slavery throughout the British Empire; this prompted many of the Dutch farmers (Boers) who had settled in the Cape Colony to migrate north eastward into the interior of Africa to escape British colonial rule. A large part of the Boer discontent was due to the level of compensation that they received from the British Government, for their freed slaves, which was thought to be a fraction of what they were worth.

During the "Great Trek" the Dutch settlers, known as Voortrekkers, established a colony on either side of the Vaal River in April 1837, known by the British as the Transvaal and the South African Republic by the Boers; also in 1837 the Boers established a colony on the Orange River which they named the Orange Free State and a further colony named Natalia was established on 12th October 1839.

Creating and maintaining these colonies was no easy task, as the land that they occupied had been appropriated from the native tribes such as the Matabele, Zulu and Bapedi and required military action to attain and defend their borders.

On 12th May 1843, the colony of Natalia was annexed by the British and renamed Natal, however, on 17th January 1852, following the Sands River Convention, the Transvaal was recognised by the British as an independent Boer Republic and on 24th February 1854 following the Orange River convention the Orange Free State was also recognised as an independent Boer Republic.

Causes of War

Expansion of the British Empire

Benjamin Disraeli, who was the British Prime Minister from 1868 until 1880, served at a time when the British Government was striving to expand the British Empire; this aim was actively supported by the 4th Earl of Carnarvon who served as Secretary of State for the Colonies during the Disraeli era.

The Earl of Carnarvon had a vision to establish a South African Confederation by joining together the British colonies, Independent Boer Republics and independent native groups in South Africa all under British rule. By 1876, Lord Carnarvon realised that it would not be possible to achieve his vision by peaceful means, however, as demonstrated by the 1879 Anglo-Zulu war he was prepared to use force.

To bring the Boer Republics into the fold, Lord Carnarvon expected that if he could "acquire" the Transvaal then the Orange Free State would soon follow.

Problems within the Transvaal government

The Transvaal population was almost universally disappointed with their leadership, including Mr T. F. Burgers who had been the president of the Republic since 1872. After wars with the Zulu and a war just started with the Bapedi led by chief Sekukuni, in the north east of the country, the administration was at the point of financial collapse, exacerbated by the fact that the Boer were unwilling to pay their taxes.

The perilous state of the Transvaal was a cause of concern to the British and Cape governments as a collapse could threaten the security of the whole area of South Africa.

The British annexation of the Transvaal

As a consequence of the concerns about the stability of the Transvaal, Lord Carnarvon sent Sir Theophilus Shepstone, a former Secretary of Native Affairs in Natal, to the Transvaal as a special commissioner.

After arriving in the Transvaal on 22nd January 1877, Shepstone had several discussions with Prime Minister Burgers, pointing out the dangers that would result from bankruptcy and the failure to deal with the Zulu and Bapedi insurgents.

By the end of January, Shepstone had told Burgers of the British intention to annex the Transvaal and provide the much needed resources and protection. Having been convinced of the necessity of annexation, Burgers did his best to convince the Transvaal government of this need but to no avail as they refused to see the urgency of the situation.

Boer opposition to British rule in the Transvaal

Lord Carnarvon, who was pursuing annexation as the first step to a confederation of South African states, was convinced that, due to their disillusion with their own government, the Transvaal people would welcome British rule, however, this was not the case.

Despite a petition with 3,000 signatures of the English speaking population who welcomed becoming part of the British Empire, the vast majority of the Boer population wished to retain their independence.

Build-up to War

On 12th April 1877, a proclamation announcing the annexation was read out in Church Square, Pretoria and the South African Republic became the Transvaal Colony. Paul Kruger and E. J. P. Jorissen, as representatives of the Transvaal government, made a visit to London to ensure that the British government were made aware of the Transvaal populations objections to the annexation. Despite taking a petition of objection, signed by 6,500 Boers, the British government was not swayed and insisted that the Transvaal would remain a British colony – although promises of some form of self government were made.

Failure to control raids of the Zulu against the colony and failure to conclude the situation with the Bapedi tribe resulted in the Colonial Office falling out of favour with Shepstone and on 4th March 1879 he was replaced as administrator of the colony by William Owen Lanyon. On 29th September 1879, Sir Garnet Wolseley was appointed as High Commissioner for South East Africa and governor of Natal and the Transvaal.

On 23rd April 1880, when W. E. Gladstone was elected to his second term of office as Prime Minister, replacing Disraeli, the Boers were hopeful that a change of government would result in a return to an independent Transvaal, however, Gladstone soon dispelled this hope when he stated that the British would remain in control of the colony.

On 24th April 1880, following the change in government, General Sir George Pomeroy Colley was appointed as High Commissioner and commander in chief for South East Africa and governor of Natal and the Transvaal, replacing Sir Garnet Wolseley.

Despite support from the Orange Free State and the Boers of the Cape Colony to the Transvaal independence cause, in October 1880 a Cape Colony newspaper correctly took the view that *"Passive resistance is now futile"*.

War Begins

Bezuidenhout Incident

The war was started by an incident in the district of Potchefstroom when the local administrator (landdrost) Mr A. M. Goetz issued a summons to Piet Bezuidenhout for non payment of £27 5s farm taxes. Mr Bezuidenhout was refusing to pay because he thought that the sum was £14 more than what was owed, however, after intense discussion with Mr Goetz he did offer to pay £13 5s on condition that the sum was put to one side for the coffers of a future republic. This cheeky offer was refused and Mr Bezuidenhout was taken to court where he won his case but refused to pay the £8 court costs.

To recover the court costs Mr Goetz confiscated Mr Bezuidenhout's wagon which was put up for auction at Potchefstroom on 11th November 1880. On the day of the auction a local Boer activist Mr P. A. Cronje, together with a commando of 100 armed men entered the town and seized the wagon which was then returned to Mr Bezuidenhout; the commando then set up camp on the outskirts of the town.

The new Transvaal Administrator, Mr Lanyon could not let such an act of defiance go unchallenged so ordered the local Special Constables to arrest the ringleaders. After the police were prevented from exercising their duty by Mr Cronje's armed followers, Mr Lanyon ordered Major Thornhill with companies of the 21st Regiment, into the town, however, the Boer commando were not intimidated and a standoff occurred.

Declaration of Independence

In light of the garrisons inability to deal with matters and seeing the political potential arising from the situation the Boer Volkskomitee brought forward a public meeting scheduled for 8th January 1881 to 8th December 1880. Mr Lanyon inflamed the situation when on 6th December, he published a notice in the government gazette to the effect that those attending the meeting would be charged with sedition.

On 8th December, about 5,000 Boer attended the meeting at Paardekraal which lasted until 15th December; between 9th and 11th December there was a meeting of the Volkskomitee and on 13th December the result of their deliberations were put to a mass meeting. It was decided to reconstitute the old Volksraad and in the absence of former president Burgers, who after annexation had retired to the Cape Colony, Paul Kruger resumed his position as vice president of the South African Republic. Former presidents Marthinus Wessel Pretorius and Piet Joubert were elected to joint leadership with Paul Kruger and an executive council was formed with J. P. Marié, W. E. Bok and E. J. P. Jorissen as members.

This revived republican government, issued a proclamation formally announcing the restoration of the Republic which they stated to be in a state of siege and under martial law and Piet Joubert was appointed as Commandant-General of the 7,000 mounted men of the Boer army.

On 14th December it was agreed to send a commando of about 400 men, under the command of Piet Cronje to Potchefstroom to compel the printer, J. P. Borrius, to run off copies of the proclamation; on 15th December, after cutting the telegraph wires, the Boers forced the printer to print their proclamation.

On the same day, the assembly at Paardekraal decided that as Pretoria was firmly in British hands, they needed a temporary capital and chose the small town of Heidelberg to fulfil this requirement. Members of the provisional government, with a commando of about 800 men arrived at Heidelberg on 16th December, where the British officials had no alternative but to surrender, and raise the republic flag.

On 17th December, Hendrik Schoeman handed a copy of the Boer Independence proclamation to administrator Lanyon with the demand that, while they did not want a war, they would fight if Lanyon did not hand over the administration of the Transvaal within 48 hours.

Lanyon took swift action against what he deemed to be a rebellion and on 18th December issued orders to Colonel Bellairs, commander of the imperial garrison "*... to vindicate the authority of Her Majesty's Government, and to put down insurrection wherever it may be found to exist*".

Potchefstroom – first shots fired

Unbeknown to Mr Lanyon, by the time that he issued orders to Colonel Bellairs, the first shots of the war had already been fired.

On 16th December some of Commandant Cronje's men, supervising the printing of the independence proclamation at Potchefstroom fired on some of Colonel Winsloe's troops who were occupying the fort outside the town, following which the British troops returned fire.

Major Clarke with 20 troops and 20 civilians who had occupied the Landdrost's office were besieged by Boers who occupied positions in surrounding houses but on the morning of 18th December, after Captain Falls and five of his men had been killed and the thatched roof set upon fire, the Major was forced to surrender his position.

Colonel Winsloe, who was besieged in the fort, managed to hold off the rebels for 95 days and only surrendered after an armistice was signed.

Poor disposition of Colonial troops

Whether by accident or design the Boer could not have chosen a better time to be involved in a conflict with the colonial forces; due to their involvement in the war in Basutoland, the Pretoria government could expect little help from Imperial troops. While the Boers could field some 7,000 soldiers, who as farmers were almost all excellent shots, there were only about 1,800 British soldiers in the Transvaal but these were stationed in towns across the region.

Towards the end of 1880, General Sir George Pomeroy Colley, who had his headquarters at Pietermaritzburg, ordered some troop movements in order to concentrate more of his troops at Pretoria but did not think it was necessary to obtain fresh troops from Natal or further afield.

Aware of the British intention to concentrate their forces, the new Boer government sent a force off in the direction of Middelburg and another towards Standerton and Wakkerstroom in an attempt to disrupt the British troop movements.

In addition to the main garrison at Pretoria the British also had garrisons at Potchefstroom, Rustenburg, Lydenburg, Marabastad, Standerton and Wakkerstroom; all of which were besieged by the Boers but all of which managed to avoid capture.

Battle of Bronkhorstspruit

On 27th November orders were issued for the HQ and two companies of the 94th Regiment to move from Lydenburg to Pretoria, however, due to transport difficulties, the column did not depart until 5th December. The column, under the command of Colonel P. R. Anstruther, which consisted of 9 officers, 239 men and three women with three children was accompanied by 34 wagons, including water carts, arrived at the Olifants River on the evening of 17th December.

It was while waiting to cross the river, which was in spate, that Colonel Anstruther received a message from Colonel Bellairs informing him to expect trouble and to take appropriate precautions; from this moment, each night the wagons were formed into a defensive laager and the men were ordered to sleep with their arms beside them.

On 20th December, after continuing on their journey, a body of about 150 Boer troops was noticed on a small ridge about half a mile away on the column's left flank; Colonel Anstruther immediately order the column, which was spread out along half a mile of road, to close up. As the order was being carried out, a man was seen to advance towards the head of the column under the cover of a white flag of truce.

The Boer messenger, Burgher de Beer, handed Colonel Anstruther a message from his commander, Commandant Frans Joubert, which enquired where the British force was headed, noting that although a declaration of Transvaal independence had been issued, a response from the British Government was still awaited and war had not been declared. Colonel Anstruther replied that "*I have my order to proceed with all possible despatch to Pretoria, and to Pretoria I am going, but tell the Commandant I have no wish to meet him in a hostile spirit*".

Although the details are unclear, it would seem that almost as soon as the Boer messenger began his return with the Colonel's reply, the Boer force which had now increased to about 250–300 men and had advanced to within 150 yards of the British column, unleashed heavy rifle fire into the troops.

The Boer firing lasted for about 15 minutes and during this time they had surrounded the British column and caused heavy casualties. In the face of these losses, Colonel Anstruther had no alternative but to surrender. British losses were 78 killed and a total of 157 casualties, the Colonel was one of the wounded with five wounds in the legs and thigh, he died on 26th December

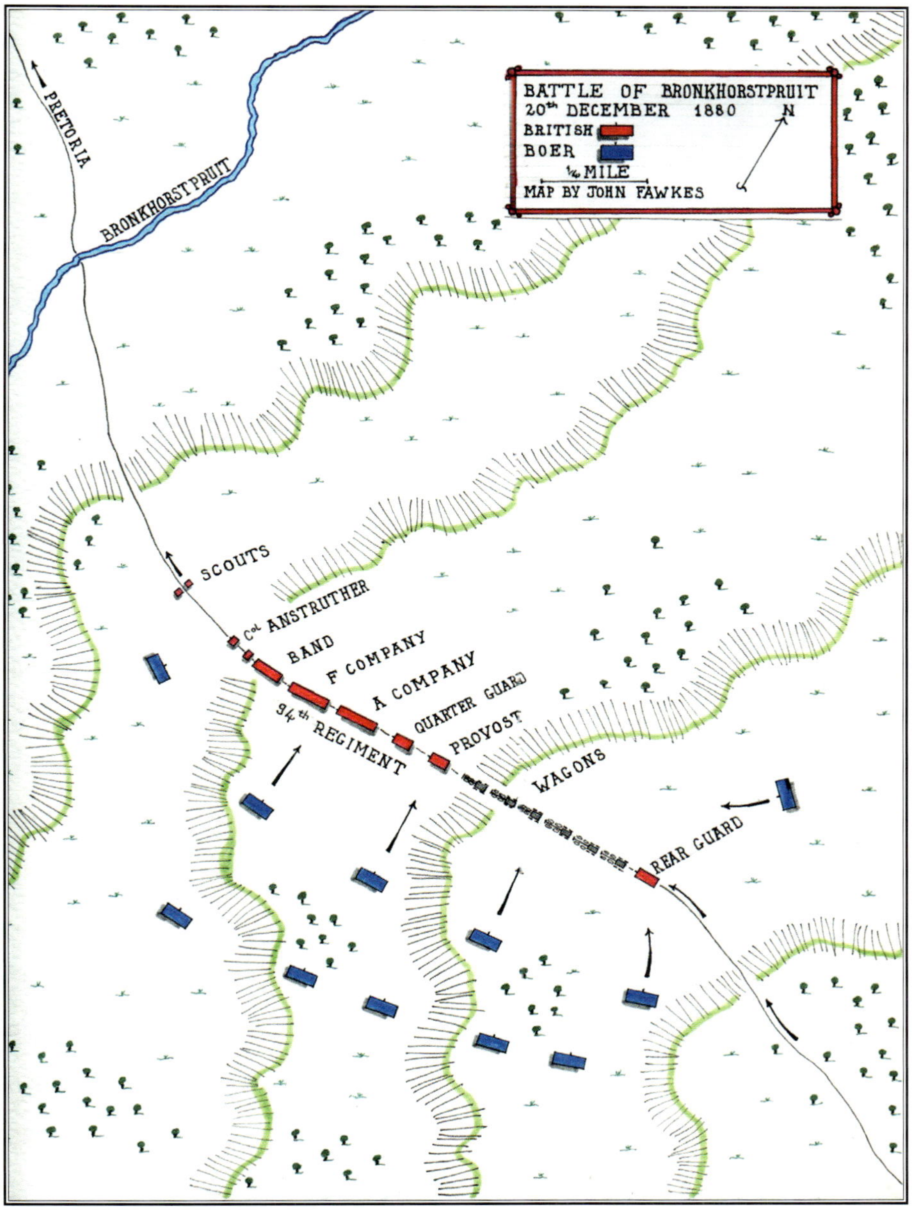

Figure 82. Battle of Bronkhorstspruit

after his leg was amputated. In comparison the Boer casualties were minor, with two killed and a further four wounded.

Commandant Joubert ordered his men to confiscate the British wagons but allowed them to remove tents and blankets so that a camp could be made for the wounded. Twenty unwounded British soldiers were allowed to remain behind to help bury the dead and care for the wounded but the remainder were taken prisoner. Conductor Egerton and Sergeant Bradley were allowed to go to Pretoria for medical assistance and after travelling through the night reached Pretoria and on 22nd December returned with medical help and supplies.

At the time, the Battle of Bronkhorstspruit was viewed as a despicable act by the Boer, described as the *"Bronkhorstspruit ambush"* or *"massacre of Bronkhorstspruit"*; the Times stated that it was no act of war but the *"... cold-blooded murder of British troops ... a deed worthy of savages."*

Dr Ward, together with the unwounded men left behind by the Boers, cared for the needs of the 101 British wounded until peace was declared when the men were brought to Maritzburg.

Battle of Elandsfontein

During the siege of Pretoria, with a need to cut grass and make hay for the horses the military authorities commandeered several mowing machines from the merchant stores in the town. On 11th January 1881, eager to obtain a good cut of grass, the first machine was taken too far down the valley, towards Elandsfontein, without a military escort, and was attacked by a party of Boer who captured the mowing machine, a wagon and some mules.

In an attempt to retrieve the mowing machine a reconnaissance in force was directed at a Boer laager on Elandsfontein farm, about 10 miles from Pretoria, on 16th January 1881.

The column of 470 men, 170 mounted and 300 infantry, under the command of Colonel George Frederick Gildea, left Pretoria at 4 o'clock in the morning; Lieutenant R. P. Littledale, of the Royal Engineers, with a small party of sappers was sent off in the opposite direction in order to create a diversion. At about 6 o'clock, when the main party was about half way to their destination the sappers set off several explosions in an attempt to draw Boer forces to their location.

After leaving 50 men of the Pretoria Rifles to hold a hill about three miles from their objective, the force moved towards Elandsfontein Ridge where they discovered that the Boer were established in strong positions defended by stone walls and a loopholed blockhouse.

A force of Carbineers was left about 2,000 yards from the ridge, to guard against the advance of any Boer reinforcements while the rest of the force moved to the end of the ridge where with good use of artillery they began to drive the enemy back along the ridge to their main blockhouse.

At this point Boer reinforcements began to arrive and the Boers on the ridge renewed their efforts; it soon became obvious that with the arrival of the large party of Boer reinforcements, a final assault on the ridge would probably result in a large loss of life so Colonel Gildea ordered a withdrawal.

Lance Corporal James Murray – Victoria Cross No. 390
Trooper John Danaher – Victoria Cross No. 391

During the withdrawal, that was generally carried out in an orderly fashion, Private Charles Byrne and Private Davis of the 21st Royal Scots Fusiliers, who had been on the extreme left of the skirmishing line failed to notice that their comrades had retired and when the Boers advanced they were both wounded.

Seeing the plight of the two wounded men, Lance Corporal Murray and Trooper Danaher rushed over 500 yards of open ground, exposed to the heavy Boer rifle fire, to rescue them. After joining the men it was immediately obvious that Private Byrne was beyond help and that his wound was mortal. The pair began to carry Private Davis to safety, however, when Lance Corporal Murray received a serious wound in the back he ordered Trooper Danaher to retire. Seeing that he was unable to help his comrades, after firing a few shots at the enemy, Trooper Danaher gathered up the rifles and returned to the British lines.

On the following day, under a flag of truce, Lance Corporal Murray and Private Davis together with the body of Private Byrne were returned to the British at Pretoria, unfortunately Private Davis died of his wounds five days later.

For their attempt to save the lives of Privates Byrne and Davis, Lance Corporal Murray and Trooper Danaher were subsequently award the Victoria Cross.

At about 11 o'clock the British column began their return to Pretoria, harassed by the Boers for most of the way; they eventually arrived back at the camp at about 3 O'clock in the afternoon.

Battle of Laing's Nek

One of the first military actions ordered by the new Transvaal Republic, after their proclamation of independence was issued, was to send a force to build and occupy defences at Laing's Nek, the mountain pass on the main road between Natal and the Transvaal, in order to stop British reinforcements from Natal reaching Pretoria.

On receipt of the news regarding the debacle at Bronkhorstspruit, Sir Owen Lanyon, the Administrator of the Transvaal declared martial law and sent despatches to General Sir George Pomeroy Colley, the Governor, High Commissioner and commander-in-chief of forces in South East Africa, to bring him up to date.

Despite being able to muster a force of only 1,400 men, General Colley, currently based at Pietermaritzburg, decided to mount an expedition to go to the relief of the British forces besieged in the Transvaal. After marshalling his troops at Newcastle, the General headed out for the Buffalo River and Laing's Nek on the road to Pretoria. After crossing the Buffalo River at 9:45 in the morning the force proceeded to Mount Prospect where they established a defended base camp on 26th January 1881.

Aware of General Colley's expedition from Pietermaritzburg, the Boer General Piet Joubert mustered as many of his forces as possible in the area of Laing's Nek, where he established three entrenched defended positions with about 2,000 men. On 27th January, General Colley carried out a reconnaissance of the Boer positions and determined that his first objective was to capture Engelbrecht's Kop on the Boer left flank.

At about 6 o'clock in the morning of 28th January, General Colley began his advance with men from the 58th Regiment leading the way and with cavalry, under the command of Major Brownlow, guarding his right flank to prevent Boar forces on what was later named Brownlow Hill, interfering with his main force.

After advancing to within 2,000 yards of the Boer positions, an artillery and rocket bombardment was commenced at about 9:15 but was halted at 10:00 o'clock when it seemed to be having little effect. At this stage the 58th Regiment began their advance, however, as their flanking guard of cavalry advanced too soon

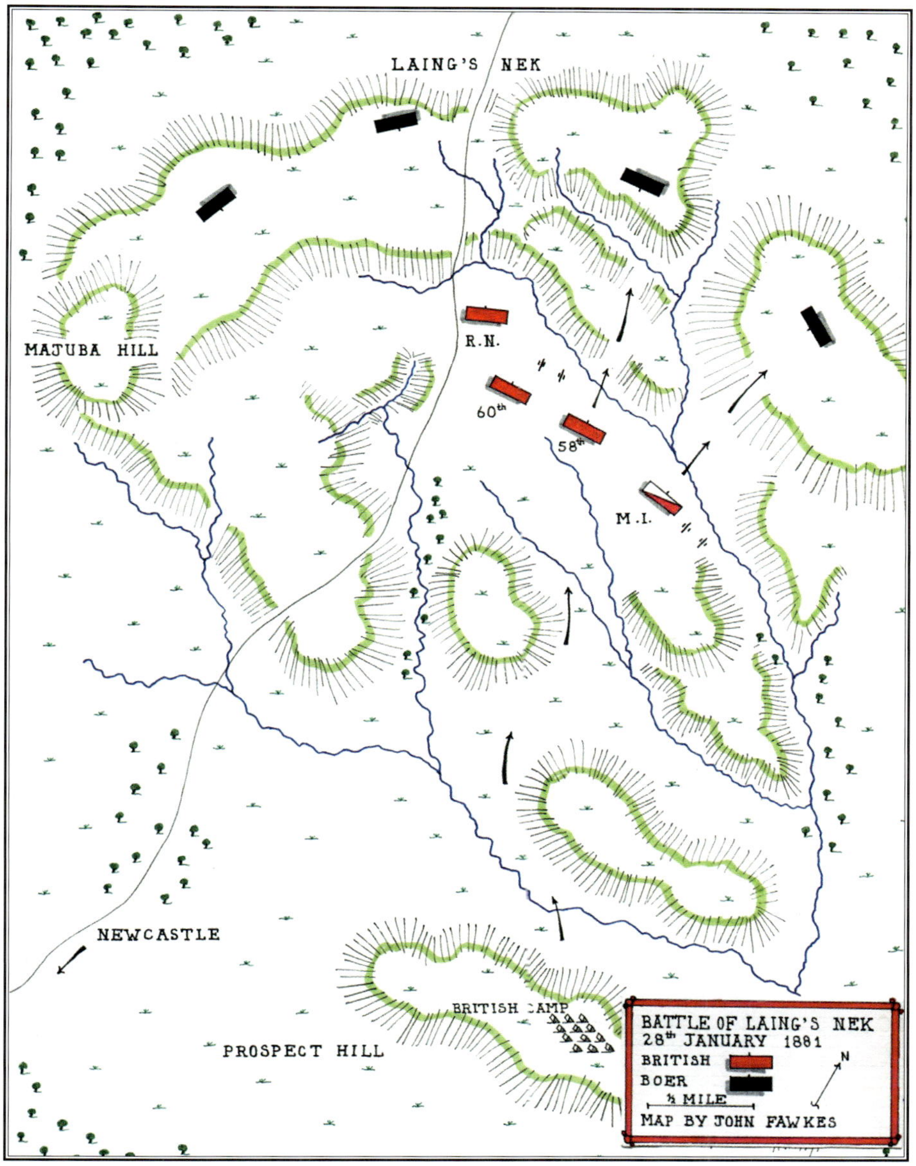

Figure 84. Battle of Laing's Nek

and too fast, they were able to provide the 58th with little protection.

Major Brownlow and his cavalry came at the Boers of Brownlow's Kop at the shortest but steepest approach to the enemy lines and by the time they reached the top the horses were all exhausted when they came under the heavy and accurate fire from the Boer rifles. Many of the leading men and horses were killed and thinking that all of their leaders were out of action, the remainder did an about turn and headed back to their start position.

Private John Doogan – Victoria Cross No. 393

During the cavalry charge, Major Brownlow had his horse shot out from under him and was dismounted amongst the Boer defenders. Seeing his plight, Private Doogan, the Major's batman, who was seriously wounded, rode up and insisted that the Major take is horse, during this exchange Private Doogan was once again wounded.

For this action, Private Doogan was later awarded the Victoria Cross.

Without the benefit of cavalry support, the 58th continued their advance and reached a point about 150 yards from the crest and the Boer positions before Colonel Deane, who was leading the attack, order the men to fix bayonets and mount a charge. Almost immediately, the Colonel had his horse shot out from under him but he continued to lead the charge on foot. From a range of only 150 yards, the Boer fire was devastating and Colonel Deane and most of his officers were either killed or seriously wounded. With the British troops suffering heavy casualties, Major Essex, one of the few surviving officers ordered a retreat.

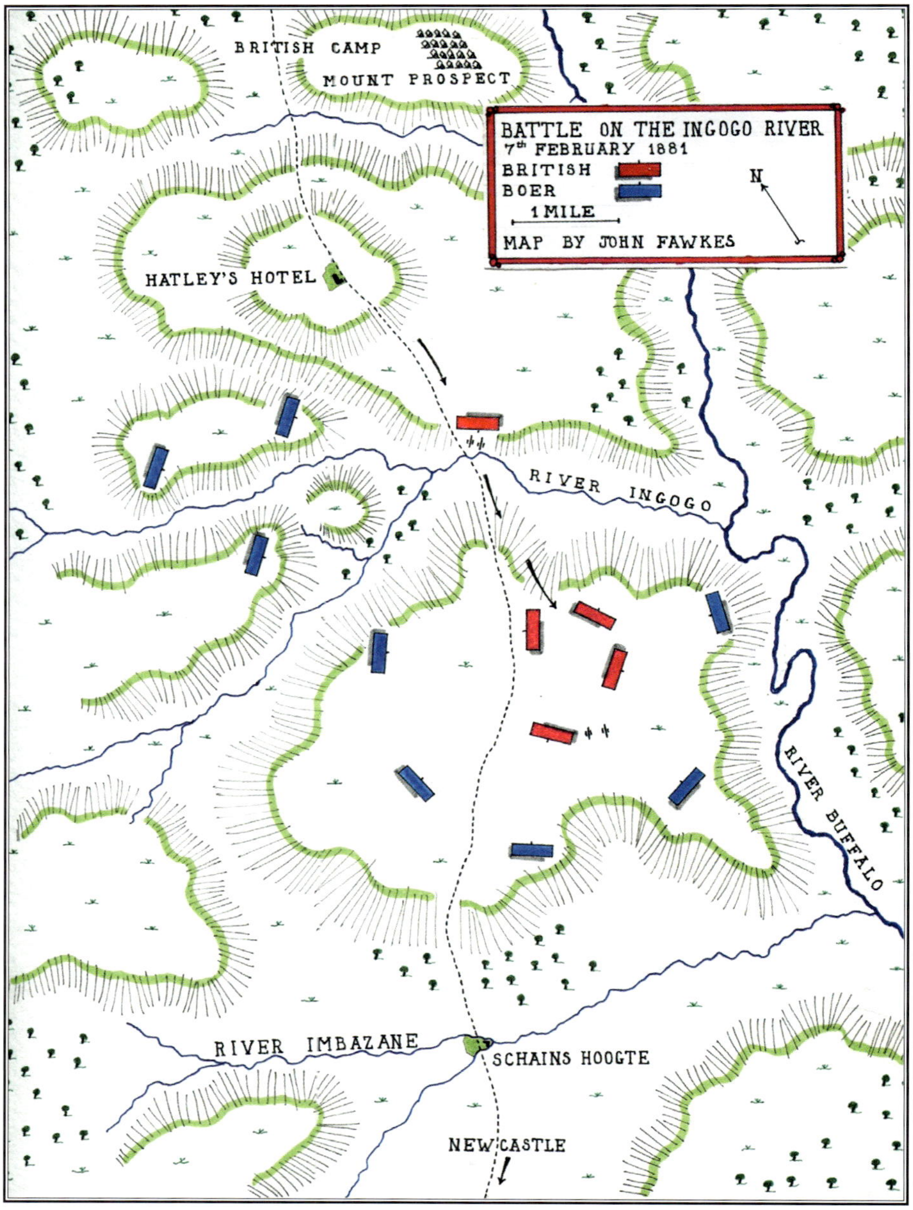

Figure 85. Battle of Ingogo (Schuinshoogte)

Lieutenant Alan Hill – Victoria Cross No. 392

During the retreat, Lieutenant Hill remained behind and tried to rescue Lieutenant Baillie who was lying on the ground severely wounded. Unable to lift the wounded Lieutenant up on to his saddle, Lieutenant Hill began to carry Lieutenant Baillie to safety in his arms, until he was once again wounded, this time fatally.

Lieutenant Hill returned twice more to the wounded and managed to bring two men to safety on his horse.

For this action, Lieutenant Hill was later awarded the Victoria Cross.

The total British casualties during the battle were 191, with 84 men having been killed; the Boer casualties were 24, with 14 having been killed.

After the battle, a truce was agreed so that both sides could tend to their wounded and bury the dead; following which the British returned to their camp at Mount Prospect.

The Battle of Laing's Nek is memorable in that it was the last occasion that regimental colours were carried into battle; the 58th regiment were led into battle with Lieutenant Baillie carrying the Regimental Colours and Lieutenant Hill carrying the Queen's colours, when Lieutenant Baillie was wounded, Lieutenant Hill handed both colours to the care of Sergeant Brigstock while he attempted to save Lieutenant Baillie's life.

Battle of Ingogo

For some days after the Battle of Laing's Nek things were reasonably quiet while General Colley and his force waited in the camp at Mount Prospect for reinforcements to arrive.

At first light on 8th February some ambulances and the mail left Mount Prospect for Newcastle, closely followed by General Colley with a strong escort. His plan was to escort the ambulances past the Ingogo River, where he would meet up with a convoy on the way from Newcastle which he would then escort back to Mount Prospect.

The force made good time and reached the banks of the Ingogo River, close to its confluence with the Harte River, without seeing any sign of Boer forces. After leaving a small force with two of his guns, to guard the position until his return, the General crossed the river at a double drift and began the long climb up the Schuinschoogte hill.

On reaching the plateau, the British force was fired upon by a Boer force of about 200 to 300 men who soon attempted to encircle the British. Due to the movement of the Boer force, the British artillery was ineffective and the gunners suffered heavy casualties from the Boer marksmen as they attempted to reload their guns. Major Brownlow, in command of a small cavalry unit of 38 troopers, attempted a charge at the Boers, however, accurate rifle fire aimed mainly at the horses soon brought this to a halt.

At about 5 o'clock in the evening a storm broke, with torrential rain but the fighting continued until darkness fell when both sides quit the battle field. Fearing a Boer ambush at the double drift, the General decided to cross the Ingogo, lower down but as the river was now in spate, several men were washed away and drowned.

From a force of just over 300 men, the British casualties were substantial, with 66 men killed and 67 wounded; with the 9 men who were drowned the total British casualties were 142. The Boer losses were relatively minor with 8 killed and 6 wounded, two of whom subsequently died from their wounds.

Battle of Wesselstroom

During the defence of besieged Wakkerstroom, a party of Boers made an attempt to cut off some natives, returning to the camp after having visited their kraals to the north west of the camp. Captain Saunders, seeing their plight, called for a party of mounted volunteers to go and cover their passage.

Private James Osborne – Victoria Cross No. 394

A Sergeant with 15 men of the 58th Regiment, accompanied by five mounted infantrymen (including Private Osborne) also left the camp to go to the aid of the mounted volunteers.

During the skirmish a group of Boer cavalry began to retire along a valley and were pursued by the five mounted infantry, however, after advancing about 150 yards they noticed that a further group of about 40 Boer horsemen were working around, trying to cut off their rear.

As the small British force tried to rejoin their comrades, two of their horses were wounded and one was killed; Private Mayes was dismounted and as he lay on the ground he was wounded in the leg.

Seeing the plight of Private Mayes, Private Osborne rode over to the wounded man and pulled him into cover behind his horse before picking him up and carrying him some 200 yards to safety.

For this action, Private Osborne was later awarded the Victoria Cross.

During the exchange, the British lost 6 men killed or wounded.

Battle of Majuba Mountain

Since January 1881, the British government in London had been having discussions with President Brand of the Orange Free State, regarding brokering a peace within the Transvaal and on 16th February Lord Kimberley, Secretary of State for the Colonies, authorised General Colley to agree to a suspension of hostilities if the Boers desisted from further armed opposition.

With the arrival of reinforcements at Mount Prospect, General Colley was more interested in a victory, to assuage his previous defeats, rather than a peace settlement at this stage. However, on 21st February the General wrote to Vice President Kruger that "*... I am to inform you that on the Boers now in arms against Her Majesty's authority ceasing armed opposition, Her Majesty's Government will be ready to appoint a Commission with large powers who may develop the scheme referred to in Lord Kimberley's telegram of the 8th inst. communicated to you through his Honour, President Brand. I am to add that upon this proposal being accepted within forty-eight hours, I have authority to agree to a suspension of hostilities on our part.*"

The letter was received by Commandant Smit, at Laing's Nek on 24th February, who immediately despatched it, by mounted messenger, to Kruger at Heidelberg where it arrived on 27th February.

It would appear that General Colley's letter to Vice President Kruger was more to appease his superiors rather than a serious attempt to bring a halt to hostilities as he began his preparations to occupy Mount Majuba on 26th February, after the expiry of his deadline but well before the time that he knew Kruger would be able to make his reply.

At about 9:30 in the evening, under the cover of darkness, General Colley and his force of just over 550 men set out from Mount Prospect and after climbing the south east slopes of the

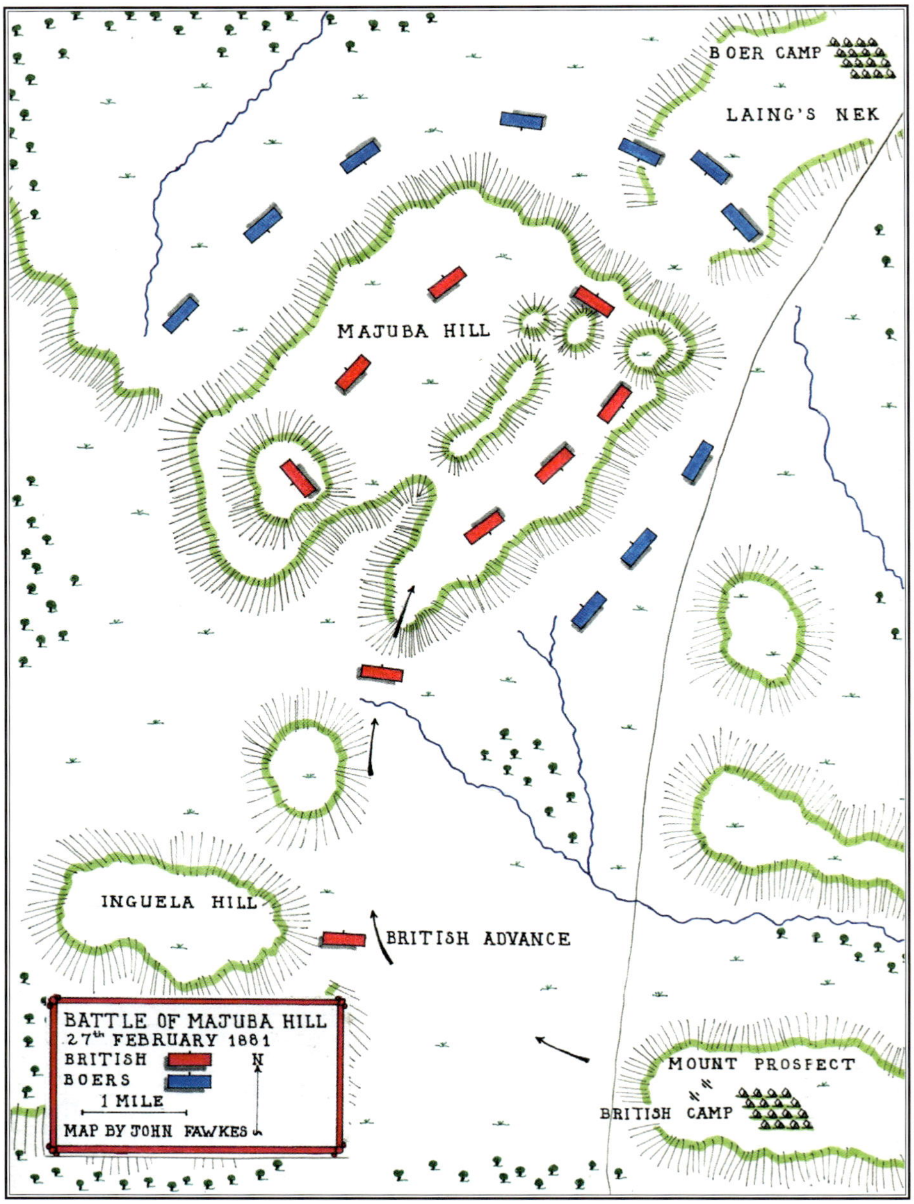

Figure 87. Battle of Majuba Mountain

Nkwelo Mountain, joined a connecting ridge and marched to the summit of Majuba Mountain. Having left some of his force on the slopes of Nkwelo Mountain, General Colley managed to reach the summit with about 375 exhausted men at about 3 o'clock in the morning.

Although a well was dug and a field hospital was established on the summit, due to the exhausted state of his men the General did not order the digging of an entrenchment, a decision that would lead to the downfall of the British position.

The British did nothing to hide their occupation of the hill, about 2,000 feet above the camp at Laing's Nek, from the Boers and at first light, when this was discovered, the Boer considered leaving Laing's Nek, however, when it was discovered that the British had no artillery, they decided to mount an attack instead.

With about 400 men the Boers began their advance at about 7 o'clock in the morning and using the concealment of hidden ground to cover their approach were close to the British positions by 11:30. With their lack of entrenchments, the British force were slowly picked off by the Boer marksmen and by 12:45 after they had retired to the final ridge General Colley was killed by a shot to the head.

Corporal Joseph Farmer – Victoria Cross No. 395

During the final Boer assault, Lance Corporal Farmer, with Senior Surgeon Sir Arthur Landon and another man of the Army Medical Corps were treating the wounded at the field hospital when Surgeon Landon and the private from the AMC were both wounded; the man that Lance Corporal Farmer was bandaging was also killed.

With the firing Boers still advancing, Lance Corporal Farmer jumped to his feet and waved his bandage, as a white flag, while shouting at the Boers that they were firing on wounded men.

The Boers continued their fire and Lance Corporal Farmer was wounded in the right wrist, making him drop his bandage. After retrieving the bandage with his left hand, the Lance Corporal rose again and continued to wave his flag of truce but was shot again, this time in the left arm near his elbow.

Despite his mortal wound, Surgeon Landon managed to give Lance Corporal Farmer a shot of morphine to lessen his pain.

For his action, Lance Corporal Farmer was later awarded the Victoria Cross.

Following the death of General Colley, the British began to surrender or retreat back down the mountain towards the camp at Mount Prospect.

The British losses during the battle were 92 men killed, 134 wounded and 59 men were taken prisoner. The Boer losses were one killed and five wounded.

War Ends

After the British defeat at Majuba and the death of General Colley, General Sir Evelyn Wood rushed to Mount Prospect and General Sir Frederick Roberts was appointed to replace General Colley.

On 5th March 1881, Sir Evelyn Wood and Piet Joubert agreed on an armistice and began peace negotiations at O'Neill's cottage, which lay mid way between the British and Boer lines. These negotiations were successfully concluded on 23rd March and the war came to an end.

The outcome of the negotiations was that a British Royal Commission would be appointed to draw up a statement regarding the status of the Transvaal and determine new borders. This agreement was ratified by the Pretoria Convention on 3rd August 1881.

The commission determined that the Transvaal would be an independent Boer Republic, however, with regard to foreign relations and treatment of the native tribes, approval of the British Government would be required and rule of the Transvaal was transferred to the Boers on 10th August.

26

ARABI REBELLION, EGYPT (1882)

The Arabi (or Urabi) rebellion in Egypt was initially an internal Egyptian affair until 1882 when the British became involved in what became known as the Anglo-Egyptian war 1882 or the Egyptian Expedition 1882.

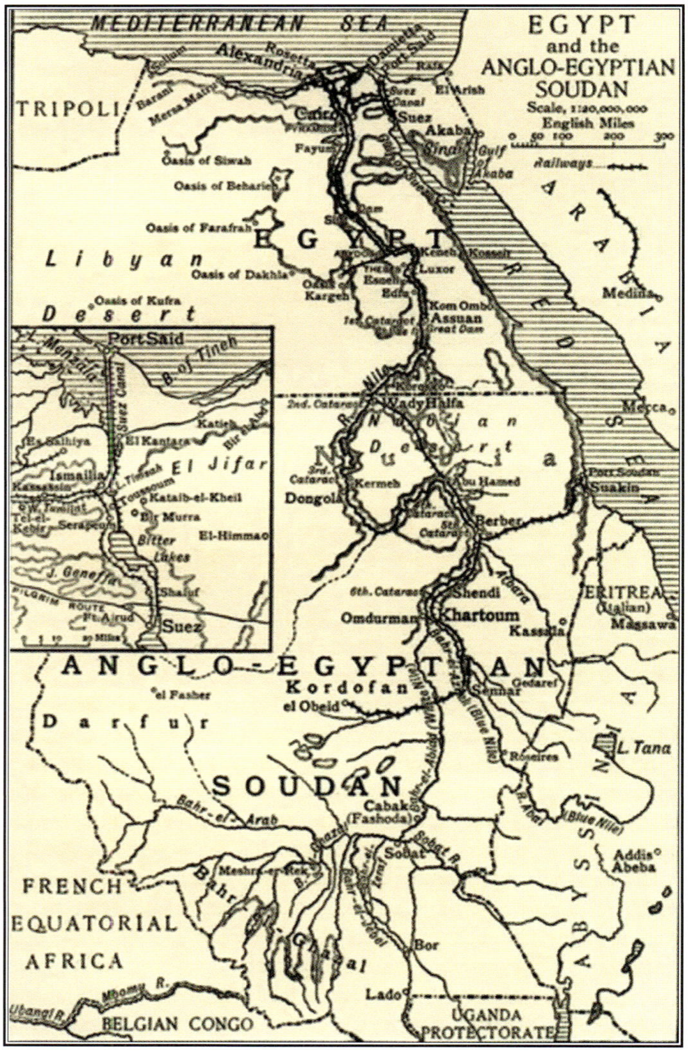

Figure 88. Anglo-Egyptian War

Background

Since 1517, Egypt had been a part of the Ottoman Empire, however, for many years Egypt had enjoyed a high level of autonomy under the Mamluks (feudal lords) and in 1805, Mehmet Ali was appointed as the governor (Wali) of Egypt by the Sublime Porte (Ottoman government).

Mehmet Ali spent the initial years of his reign in eradicating the power of the Mamluk feudal lords before expanding Egyptian territory to include Crete, Syria and Adana and in 1833 the Sublime Porte recognised his feudal sovereignty over Egypt and these new lands, however, after a war with Britain, Austria and Turkey, Egypt evacuated Syria, Arabia and Candia.

With the failing health of Mehmet Ali, he was succeeded as Wali by his son Ibrahim on 20th July 1848, however, Ibrahim's reign only lasted a few months as he died on 10th November 1848 and was succeeded by his nephew Abbas Helmi I until 13th July 1854 when Abbas was assassinated.

Following his death Abbas was succeeded by his uncle Muhammad Said, having granted Britain the rights to construct a railway between Cairo and Suez, Said on 15th November 1854 granted his old friend, the Frenchman Ferdinand de Lesseps, permission to construct a canal. Britain, who had always been in favour of an overland route (railway) rather than a canal, did everything in their power to delay the implementation of the canal scheme, however, ignoring the British objections Muhammad Said signed off the French plans for construction of the canal on 5th January 1856.

In 1858 Ferdinand de Lesseps launched the *Compagnie Universelle du Canal Maritime de Suez*, with capital of £8,000,000 over half of which was subscribed by French shareholders; in 1860 Muhammad Said purchased the remaining £3,500,000 of shares on behalf of the Egyptian government although consent for the scheme was not approved by the Sublime Porte until 1866.

Following the death of his father on 18th January 1863, Ismail succeeded to the position of Wali but was finally granted the higher title of Khedive on 8th June 1867 by Abdul-Aziz the Ottoman Sultan and a further decree in 1873 virtually confirmed the independence of Egypt.

Ismail was instrumental in developing cotton as a cash crop in the Nile valley and during a three year period exports rose from £4.5 million to £13 million, however, without the prudence of crop rotation the ground soon became exhausted and when the American Civil War came to a close, the USA once again dominated the cotton market.

In order to replace the lost cotton revenue, Ismail decided to cultivate sugar cane along the Nile Valley and after deciding to also refine the sugar crop he built 19 factories and refineries equipped with state of the art equipment from Europe. To support this manufacturing it was necessary to build railroads for access and canals for irrigation.

Construction of the Suez Canal which opened on 17th November 1869, was also a drain on Egypt's resources as the Khedive ordered the population to provide the required manpower to the detriment of agricultural production.

To fund these ventures and his own profligate expenses, Ismail was forced to obtain substantial loans from the major European banks and had to institute massive rises in taxation in order to make the necessary loan repayments.

By 1873, the outstanding loans amounted to nearly £59 million and the annual tax revenue was about £9 million, however, the treasury was almost exhausted forcing the Khedive to ask the British government for financial help. In December 1875, the British government purchased the Egyptian shares in the Suez canal for a sum of £4 million but this only stemmed the tide of financial ruin for a short time.

In November 1876, the English and French creditors sent a joint commission, consisting of Mr Goschen and M Joubert to Egypt with the task of finding a solution to the financial problems; this resulted in a consolidation of the debts into a new loan of nearly £85 million, with interest payments of £5.5 million and in 1878 a British and French comptroller were installed to manage Egyptian financial affairs.

With Egypt's financial affairs still at the point of collapse and the Khedive unwilling or unable to curb his vast expenditure Britain and France contacted the Ottoman Sultan with demands for the removal of Ismail and on 26th June 1879 he was deposed and replaced by his son Mehmet Tewfik. Disorder still prevailed until November 1879 when Britain and France re-established duel control of the country.

Figure 89. Ahmed Arabi Bey

Major Evelyn Baring (followed by Mr Colvin) and Monsieur de Blignieres were installed to manage Egypt's financial affairs and for the next two years almost governed the country while trying to implement reforms. The Liquidation Law of 1880 wrote off most of the debt prior to 1880 and following a bumper harvest and improved trade the financial climate slowly improved.

Despite the improving situation during 1881 there was a growing nationalist movement opposed to the foreign influence over their country and this was dominant in the army where native officers were being replaced with Turkish officers.

A leading figure within the dissenters in the army was Ahmed Arabi Bey, having been dismissed from the army for a slight misdemeanour, under the reign of Muhammad Said, Arabi entered Cairo university where he devoted himself to fanatical religious studies. When Ismail ascended to the throne, Arabi re-entered the army where he was active in the movement of discontent.

When Tewfik ascended to the throne, Arabi was promoted to the rank of Colonel and with his increased influence became one of the leaders of the disaffected troops. In February 1881, Arabi and the other colonels demanded the dismissal of Osman, the Circassian minister of war who favoured the Turks over the Egyptian officers; Arabi and two of the Colonels were arrested but were rescued from prison by Arabi's regiment.

For the next few months, the distrust between the military and the Khedive increased and on 9th September culminated in the "Insurrection of the Colonels" when Arabi submitted a document to the Khedive, calling for the dismissal of the military ministry, the drafting of a constitution and an increase in the strength of the army to 18,000 men. In the afternoon a force of 4,000 men, supported by 18 cannon, marched on the palace to await the Khedives answer; the Khedive gave way to the inevitable and on 14th September he formed a new ministry, led by Sherif Pasha.

On 4th January 1882, Arabi was appointed to the government as assistant minister of war by Prime Minister Sherif who also proposed to establish a constitutional government, however, this idea was vetoed by the British and French comptrollers on 7th January.

Arabi and the nationalists were incensed by the veto and issued an ultimatum to Sherif stating that he should either accept their constitutional demands or resign. Sherif decided to resign and Mahmud Barudi formed a new government, with Arabi as minister of war, the military faction were now leading the government. Arabi and six of his colonels were promoted to the rank of General, with the title of pasha.

In April 1882, Arabi claimed to have discovered an assassination plot against himself and the other Generals; fifty, mainly Circassian officers were arrested and after a court martial forty were found guilty and banished for life to the White Nile. The Khedive refused to sanction the sentence which he eventually commuted to exile from Egypt; this displeased the nationalist government.

Build-up to War

Having reconciled their differences, Britain and France gave notice that they were about to send a joint fleet to Alexandria to uphold the authority of the Khedive and on 20th May British and French squadrons appeared in the harbour at Alexandria. On 25th May British and French consuls demanded the dismissal of the ministry and the exile of Arabi; the ministers handed in their resignations, however, Arabi declared that he would continue as head of the army.

The fortifications at Alexandria were increased to improve the defence of the harbour as the Egyptians prepared to oppose by force any foreign intervention. The Ottoman Sultan declared that he would send a commissioner, Dervish Pasha, to Egypt to investigate matters and lend support to the Khedive.

After his arrival on 8th June, Dervish managed to form a new ministry, with Ragheb as president, that was supportive of the Khedive but Arabi remained in his position of Minister for War. The new ministry was powerless to quell the passions of the religious fanatics and the nationalist demands for independence.

An already tense situation was further inflamed by an anti Christian riot which broke out in Alexandria on 11th June and involved the police and some of Arabi's troops as well as the Arab population. Although many of the Europeans managed to flee the city, about 50 Europeans were killed during the massacre.

A conference was held at Constantinople on 23rd June, but as the Sublime Porte would not commit to any policy or action, nothing was accomplished, however, there were indications that the Ottoman Empire wished to restore its former powers over Egypt, much to the consternation of the British government.

On 6th July Admiral Sir Beauchamp Seymour, commander of the British fleet at Alexandria, protested to Tulba, the towns military governor, that if he did not cease working on improvements to the town fortifications then the British fleet would bombard the town.

Tulba protested that work had been stopped, however, the British noticed that works were continuing during the night time. In reply to this message, Admiral Seymour stated that unless the southern shore of the harbour was surrendered to the British by sunrise on 11th July, the bombardment would commence. Late in the afternoon of 10th July, all the ships except the British squadron left the harbour, taking with them refugees from many nations. Lack of support for armed intervention, by the French government, resulted in the French squadron also leaving the waters around Alexandria.

Battle of Alexandria

At 7 o'clock in the morning of 11th July, Admiral Seymour, on board his flagship *HMS Invincible*, signalled to *HMS Alexandria* to fire at the recently armed earthworks, known as the Hospital Battery and followed this with a general signal to the fleet to *"Attack the enemy's batteries"*.

The British fleet now began a steady fire against the forts that guarded the entrance to Alexandria harbour until about 10:30 at which time *HMS Sultan*, *HMS Superb* and *HMS Alexandria* anchored off the Light House Fort and with the assistance of *HMS Inflexible* managed to silence most of the guns in the forts on Ras-el-Tin, over the next two hours. Some heavy guns at Fort Ada managed to keep up a fire until at about 1:30 a shell from *HMS Superb* blew up their magazine, forcing the garrison to retreat.

Gunner Israel Harding – Victoria Cross No. 396

Despite the heavy British barrage, the shore batteries did have some success and as their aim improved they were able to land 25 shots on *HMS Alexandria*.

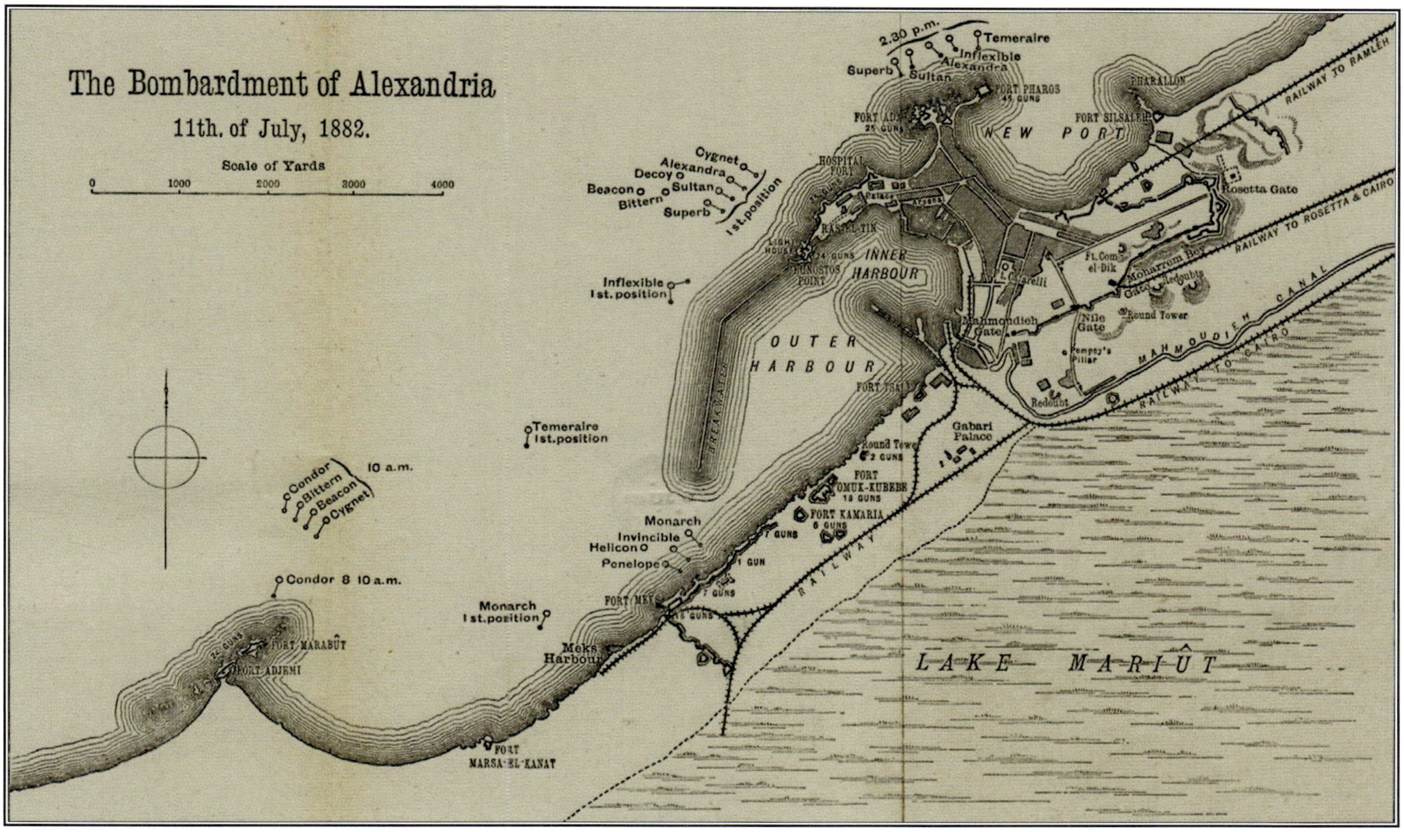

Figure 90. Bombardment of Alexandria

The events on board *HMS Alexandria* are best described by Gunner Harding's own words *"One fell close to the sheep-pen and killed all the poor animals. The next shell tore away our strong iron stanchions, bounded along between Captain Hotham and Staff Commander Hoskins, then tore a chunk out of the main mast and finally went overboard, little regretted. A third shell exploded in our steam launch, killing one man and maiming many others".*

"At this time I was passing through the main upper decks to inspect the supply of ammunition for the guns, when a huge shell from Fort Ada came plunging through Alexandra's port bulwark – just past the feet of commander Thomas, who was standing on the hammock netting. The projectile was deflected by an iron stanchion, and then entered the Commander's cabin, where it exploded with an appalling roar, tearing and destroying everything".

"I was then about to descend the ladder of the next deck leading to the after powder magazine, when another great shell pierced the ship's side and passed through the torpedo lieutenant's cabin. It then struck the strong iron combings of the engine-room, and bounded onto the deck among the blue-jackets, who instantly screamed 'A shell, A shell'".

"My own course of action was decided upon as quick as thought. I just picked up that shell, and flung it into a tub full of water. It was heavy, hot, and grimy. It is dreadful to think what would have happened had the shell exploded. Close at hand was the hatchway leading to the magazine which at that moment contained twenty-five tons of gun powder".

For this action Gunner Harding was subsequently awarded the Victoria Cross.

Following the attack on Fort Ada, *HMS Sultan*, *HMS Superb*, *HMS Alexandria* and *HMS Inflexible* who had now been joined by *HMS Temeraire* directed their fire at Fort Pharos and by 2:30 had silenced their guns.

The Hospital Battery, which had been the target of the first British shot, continued their fire throughout the day and it was not until about 5 o'clock that the enemy were forced to abandon their positions.

HMS Invincible, *HMS Penelope* and *HMS Monarch*, now operating inside the reefs, supported by *HMS Inflexible* and *HMS Temeraire*, operating in the Boghaz and Corvette Channels, after laying down fire for several hours managed to silence and partially destroy the batteries and lines at Mex and *HMS Monarch* destroyed the fort of Marsa-el-Khanat after exploding their magazine.

At about 2 o'clock in the afternoon, apparently not content with just causing damage with his ships guns, Admiral Seymour, having noticed that the gunners at the lower Mex battery had abandoned their guns, ordered a small party of volunteers into action on shore.

Under the command of Lieutenant Bradford from *HMS Invincible*, the 12 volunteers landed from their gun boats and destroyed two 10" guns with guncotton and spiked a further six guns before returning unharmed to their ship.

The bombardment, which had lasted for 10 and a half hours, was called off at 5:30 and the fleet anchored up for the night.

During the day, the British losses were six killed and 27 wounded; the enemy losses were thought to have been about 150 killed.

On the following morning, *HMS Temeraire* and *HMS Inflexible* resumed the barrage but after a few shots at Fort Pharos a white flag was raised at Fort Ras-el-Tin and Admiral Seymour sent Lieutenant Lambton to investigate. It transpired that the white flag was a ruse to delay the barrage and after the Admiral's demand to surrender the Boghaz channel batteries was ignored a shot was fired at the Mex Barracks batteries where another white flag was raised.

Lieutenant Morrison on board *HMS Helicon* was sent to the *Mahrussa*, the Khedive's yacht, which was moored in the harbour and found it to be deserted. In the afternoon, the Khedive, who had spent the duration of the previous days bombardment in his palace at Ramleh, sent a message to Admiral Seymour requesting his protection.

During the evening, Arabi had withdrawn from the city, with his forces, along the Mahmudieh canal, however, the local population were now engaged in a riot of destruction and during the ensuing massacre over 2,000 Europeans were killed.

On the 13th July, a party of marines was landed and on the following day, after more British ships had arrived, a larger force was landed and took possession of the entire city.

Declaration of War

On 15th July, a message was sent to the Sublime Porte requesting the Sultan to despatch troops to restore order in Egypt, however, with Arabi's contention that he was leading a rebellion to defend Moslem interests against the Christian invaders, the Sultan refused as he could not be seen to be acting against the interests of Islam.

The Khedive issued a proclamation denouncing Arabi as a rebel and dismissing him from the government, Arabi issued a counter proclamation, declaring Tewfik to be a traitor to his people and religion. With news of Tewfik's proclamation, Lord Dufferin, the British Ambassador at Constantinople, announced to the Constantinople conference that Britain was about to send an expedition to Egypt, to suppress the rebellion and restore the authority of the Khedive.

Following Lord Dufferin's announcement, the Sultan declared that he would also send an expedition to Egypt but refused to declare Arabi as a rebel. In preparation for a possible invasion of Egypt, the Sultan sent a force of 3,000 men to Suda Bay, ready to enter Egypt at a moment's notice.

On 21st July, General Sir Garnet Wolseley was ordered to Egypt and on 28th July the British parliament granted a sum of £2.3 million as expenses for the expedition.

War Begins

After the bombardment of Alexandria the city was occupied by a British force of sailors and marines and Arabi and his men withdrew to Kafr el Dawwar, where they began to construct a strongly defended camp with the intention of blocking the British route to Cairo.

General Sir Archibald Alison landed at Alexandria with the advanced elements of the British Expeditionary force; together with a battalion of marines and a large number of sailors from the fleet, the General was in command of over 3,750 men.

While establishing his base in the city, General Alison sent out patrols in all directions to ascertain the location and strength of enemy forces in the nearby vicinity; subsequently estimated to be about 15,000 men (four times the Alexandria garrison).

After the arrival on 24th July of reinforcements, numbering 1,108 men, General Alison moved his force to Ramleh where he established a fortified base.

Battle of Kafr el Dawwar

In response to rumours that the Egyptian forces were retreating, on the 5th August General Alison ordered a reconnaissance in strength towards the Egyptian position at Kafr el Dawwar, the advance was along the path of the Cairo railway line and the Mahmoudiyah Canal.

The British force was split into two wings, with the left wing following the canal where men progressed along both banks; 800 infantry on the east bank and 500 infantry with 80 mounted infantry on the west bank. The right wing following the line of the railway was made up of 1,000 marines supported by an armoured train manned by 200 sailors. In total the force comprised 2,600 men.

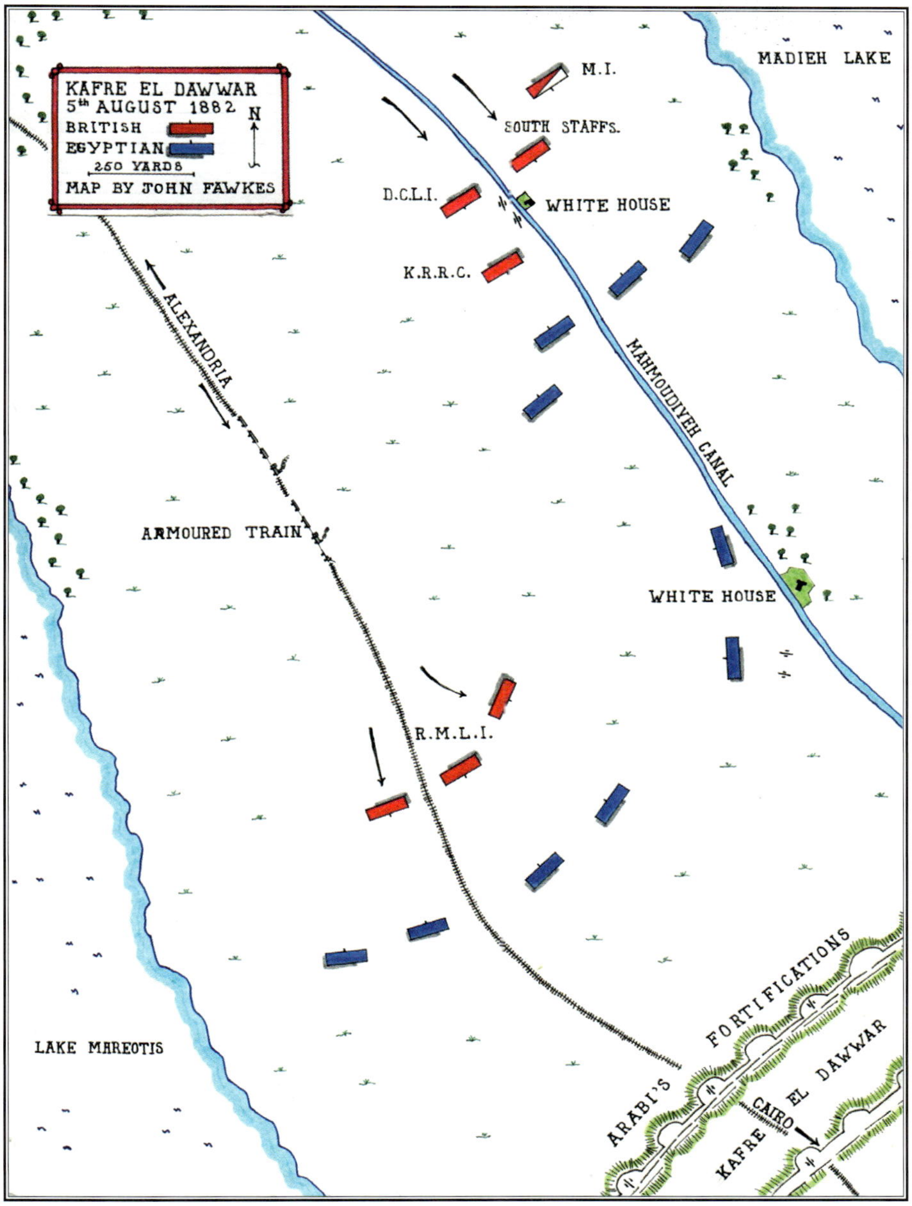

Figure 91. Battle of Kafr el Dawwar

Private Frederick Corbett – Victoria Cross No. 396

As the force advanced along the east bank of the canal, with the mounted infantry leading the way, Captain Parr with Lieutenants Pigott and Vyse accompanied by six troopers rode ahead of the main force to scout out the enemy positions.

The party chanced upon a large body of Egyptian infantry who immediately opened fire, mortally wounding Lieutenant Vyse, killing another man and wounding two more. The men dismounted and began to return fire, expecting reinforcements to arrive soon, they were unaware that a retreat had already been sounded and that they were now isolated.

Private Corbett tried to staunch the flow of blood from the wound to the thigh of Lieutenant Vyse, unfortunately as his femoral artery had been severed the Lieutenant bled to death after about 10 minutes.

Refusing to leave his officer, Private Corbett, despite the heavy enemy fire helped to carry away the body of Lieutenant Vyse.

For this action, Private Corbett was later awarded the Victoria Cross.

On the west bank of the canal, the men advanced in skirmishing order, firing the occasional shell into the Egyptian positions and after reaching to within 100 yards the order was given to charge with fixed bayonets; the charge caused the defenders to take flight, many of them throwing away their arms in the process.

At this point, Colonel Thackwell, commander of the left wing called a halt as he had been ordered to only advance as far as a white house on the canal bank, which marked the spot where the canal was closest to the railway; unfortunately, unknown to

Colonel Thackwell there was another white house on the canal bank and he was actually about one mile short of his objective.

With the armoured train leading the way and the marine force in a second train running behind, the right wing advanced until just after the Mahalla Junction where they came across a break in the railway line. After disembarking from the train and continuing their advance along the railway embankment, the marines and the armoured train came under heavy Egyptian artillery fire until the enemy guns were silenced by the British artillery.

As the marines drew ahead of the position of the halted left wing, their left flank came under fire from enemy soldiers posted on the canal banks but seeing that they were not supported by artillery, after firing a volley they mounted a charge with fixed bayonets driving the enemy back across the canal.

With the British force now in a diagonal line straddling both the canal and railway, General Alison who had accompanied the right wing, surveyed the Egyptian positions for about 45 minutes before, due to the failing light and the arrival of enemy reinforcements he ordered a general withdrawal and by 8 o'clock in the evening the battle was over.

During the battle, British losses were four killed and 27 wounded; Egyptian losses were subsequently discovered to be 79 men killed and about 120 wounded, an officer and 14 men were also taken prisoner.

Arrival of Expeditionary Force

General Wolseley, with a force of 35,000 men arrived in Egypt on 15th August 1882 at a time when Britain only held positions at Alexandria and Suez, while Arabi, with a force of 70,000 men held all of the Egyptian interior including Port Said and Ismailia.

In order to crush Arabi, General Wolseley decided that he would need to take Cairo, the route to which was either from Alexandria, through the delta or via the Suez Canal from Ismailia. The route via the delta was considered to be more difficult, however, use of the Suez canal would breach the neutrality of the canal zone. Operating on the principle that *"... the neutrality of any canal joining the waters of the Atlantic and Pacific oceans will be maintained, if at all, by the nation which can place and keep the strongest ships at each extremity."* decided to enter Cairo by way of Ismailia and the canal but this plan was kept secret.

General Wolseley left a division at Ramleh, under the command of General Sir Edward Hamley, to guard Alexandria; his force comprised two brigades, one commanded by General Sir Archibald Alison and the other by General Sir Evelyn Wood. Subsequently, on 29th August, General Hamley and General Alison with his brigade were ordered to join General Wolseley's main force, leaving just General Wood and his brigade to guard Alexandria.

On 18th August, plans for an attack on Abukir, where Arabi had a large concentration of his forces, were leaked to the press and on the next day troop transports moved eastward from Alexandria as if to attack Abukir. This attack, however, was a ruse and under the cover of darkness the transports headed for Port Said where they learned that thanks to the efforts of Admiral Seymour the whole of the Suez Canal was in British hands. On 21st August, General Wolseley and his troops met up with Sir Henry McPherson and his Indian contingent at Ismailia.

The next two days were spent preparing for the upcoming operations but during this time the Egyptians cut off the British water supply by damming the Sweet Water canal. On 24th August the British carried out a successful operation to remove the dam and on 26th August advanced to Kassassin, an important position on the canal and railway.

The British force was delayed at Kassassin for two weeks due to transport difficulties and the creation of hospital facilities. Arabi took this opportunity to gather his forces at Zagazig and Tel-el-Kebir and launched attacks against the British on 28th August and 9th September, both of which were repulsed.

Battle of Tel-El-Kebir

On 12th September, after extensive reconnaissance, General Wolseley decided to mount his own attack against Tel-el-Kebir which was strongly fortified and guarded by about 38,000 Egyptians with 59 siege guns.

As the only approach was across open desert, General Wolseley and his force of 11,000 infantry and 2,000 cavalry, supported by 60 field guns, left Kassassin at 1:30 in the morning of 13th September under the cover of darkness.

After maintaining excellent silent order, during their march, the British force managed to get to within 150 yards of the Egyptian lines before they were detected. At just before 5 o'clock in the morning, the British were finally spotted by the Egyptian forces manning the defences and they unleashed a murderous musket and artillery fire.

In response to the enemy fire, led by their mounted and dismounted officers, the British force charged the Egyptian line with fixed bayonets during which many of the officers and non-commissioned officers were mown down.

Lieutenant William Edwards – Victoria Cross No. 398

After reaching the centre of the enemy line, the battalion was confronted by a ditch which was 9 feet deep and 10 feet wide, however, a small party led by Lieutenant Goold managed to

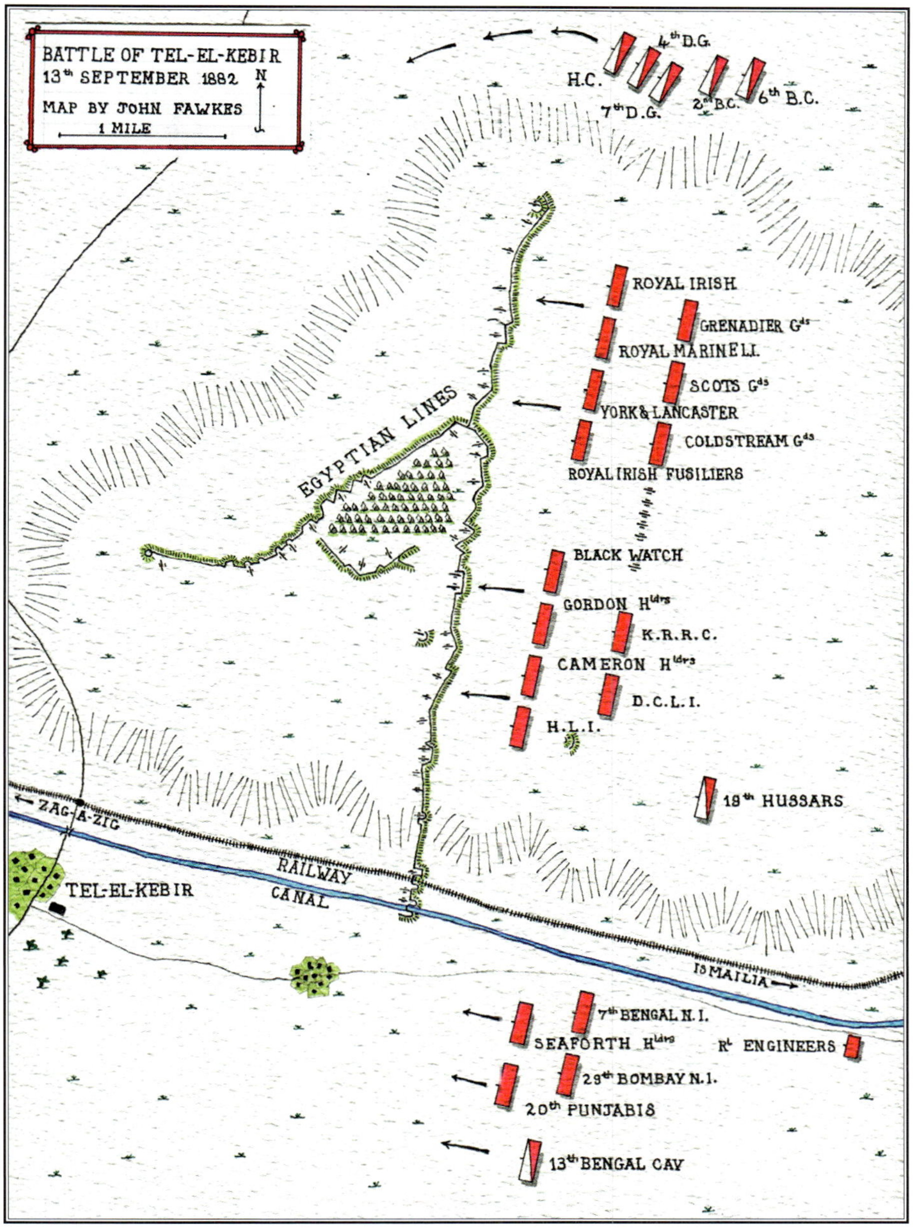

Figure 92. Battle of Tel-El-Kebir

reach the parapet on the far side of the ditch, from where they pulled up others to their position.

The men on the flanks of the British attack were more fortunate as the ditch to their front was shallower and Majors Wallace and Leigh on the right and Lieutenant Edwards on the left managed to lead their men into the entrenchments where they soon began to clear the enemy position.

For his actions during the battle Lieutenant Edwards was later awarded the Victoria Cross.

Almost as soon as the first shot was fired, Arabi and most of his officers fled the scene, galloping to Belbeis where they caught a train to Cairo; without any leadership it is not surprising that the rebel force was soon defeated and by 6:45 the British had command of Arabi's headquarters.

British losses during the battle were 57 killed, 380 wounded and 22 missing; the Egyptian force had about 2,000 killed.

End of the War

After what proved to be the decisive battle of the war, the enemy was pursued to Zagazig by General Sir H. Macpherson VC, with the Indian Contingent from the camp at Kassassin and the cavalry division led by General Lowe advanced to Belbeis which was captured on the evening of 13th September.

Anxious to avoid a rebel destruction of Cairo, General Lowe was ordered to advance to the city as fast as possible and after a march of 65 miles, in under two days, the British force arrived at the barracks of Abbassia, just outside the city in the early evening of 14th September.

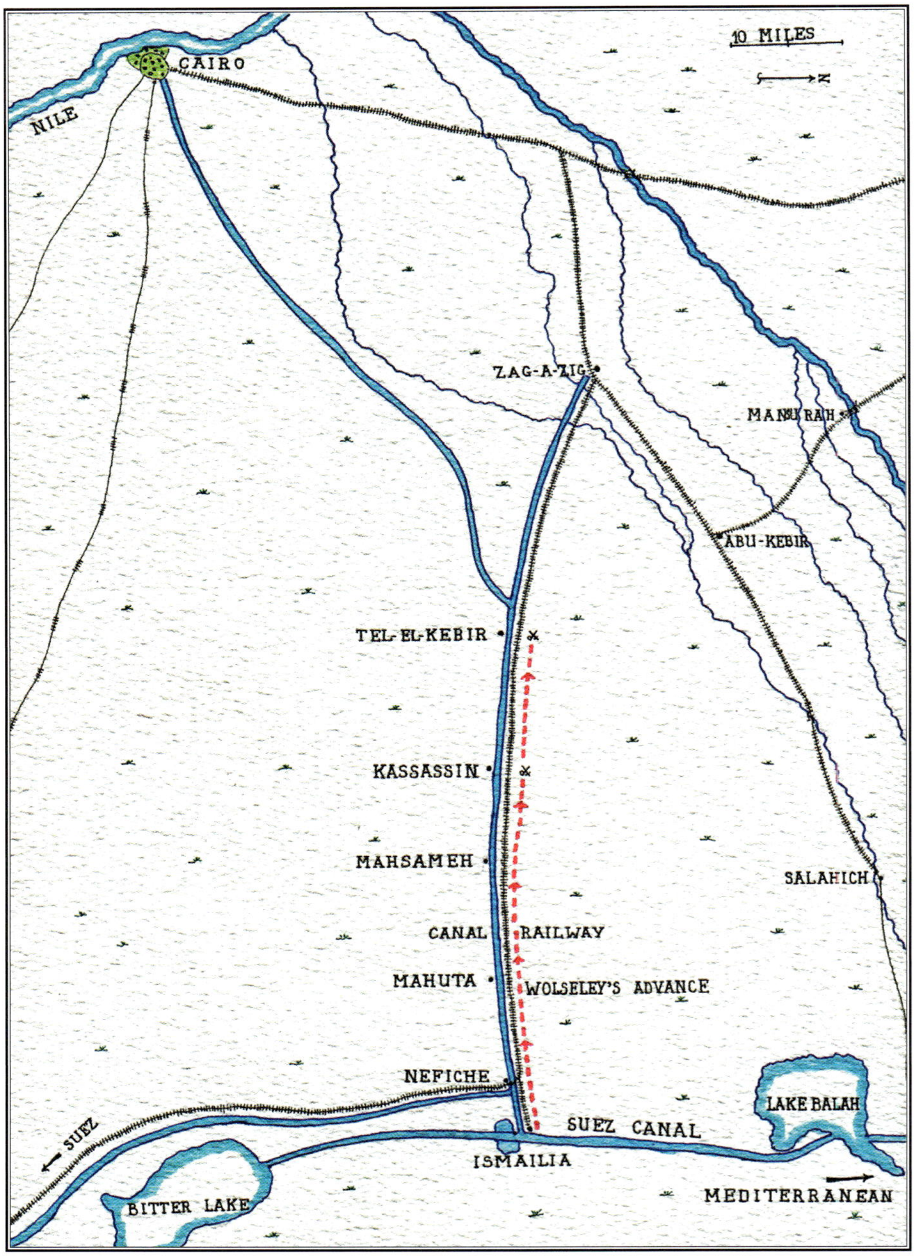

Figure 93. Tel-El-Kebir Campaign

Colonel H. Stewart, assistant adjutant general to the cavalry division, called upon the garrison of 10,000 men to surrender, which they did allowing the British to occupy the citadel.

A message was also sent into the city, calling on Arabi to surrender, which he did unconditionally. and on 15th September General Wolseley entered the city a day earlier than the date that he had predicted before he left England; the war was now at an end.

When news of the victory reached Lord Dufferin, who was still involved in negotiations at Constantinople regarding Turkish involvement in the war, he informed the Sublime Porte that their involvement was no longer required as the war had been concluded.

The French expected to take up their role in the share of control of Egypt, however, as they had not taken any part in the war this was refused by Britain.

27

SUDAN CAMPAIGN (1881-85)

The Sudan Campaign of 1881 to 1885 which was also known as the Mahdist Revolution, was followed by the Anglo-Sudan War leading to the formation of Anglo-Egyptian Sudan.

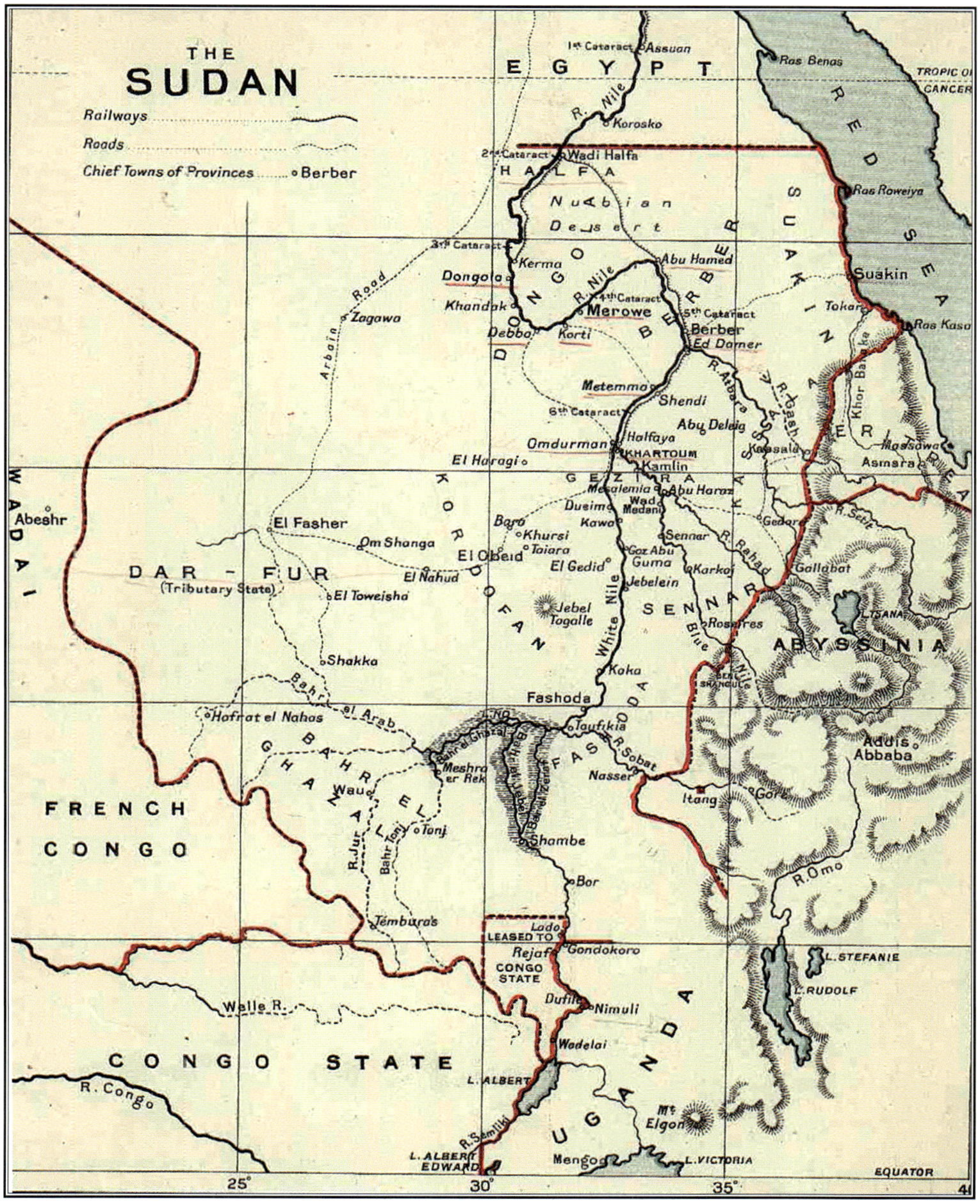

Figure 94. Sudan

Background

Sudan, on the southern border of Egypt had never had a formal unified government, the many war like tribes that occupied the country generally operated as independent entities involved in agriculture and the slave trade, which accounted for the majority of their revenue.

Although Christianity had been established in parts of the region since the 5th century, when the Egyptian Sultan Dhaber Bebars conquered the independent Christian Kingdom of Dongola in the 13th century the area became a region of fanatical Islamism.

In 1821 Mahomed Ali, the Khedive of Egypt sent his son Ismail on an expedition up the Nile during which the provinces of Dongola, Kordofan and Sennar were conquered and annexed and brought under Egyptian rule. The city of Khartoum was set up as the capital of Egyptian Sudan and military stations were established on the Blue and White Nile. Khartoum soon became the centre for the long established slave trade.

Although the Sudan had been annexed by Egypt, no attempt was made to establish any form of rule or government and during the reign of Abbas, Mohamed Ali's grandson, from 1848 until 1854 the country had lapsed into a deplorable condition; this situation continued when Abbas was succeeded by Said Pasha, although he did make a vain attempt to abolish the slave trade.

In 1869, when Sir Samuel Baker was appointed as Governor General of the Equatorial Provinces, with control of the country south of Gondokoro, he made strenuous efforts to eliminate the slave trade and although he dealt some heavy blows to the traders the trade continued to flourish.

In 1874, Sir Samuel Baker was replaced by Colonel Charles Gordon who regarded the abolition of the slave trade as his highest priority, in order fulfil this duty Colonel Gordon thought it essential that all of the provinces of the Sudan should be brought under firm rule so the provinces of Darfur and Harar were annexed.

On 4th August 1877, a convention between Britain and Egypt prohibited all public traffic in slaves; private trade was to be eradicated in Egypt by 1884 and in the Sudan by 1889.

In his quest against the slave trade, Colonel Gordon was assisted by Romolo Gessi, Governor General of the south Sudan province of Bahr el Ghazal and in one year from March 1878 to March 1879 they succeeded in capturing 63 slave caravans.

Efforts to suppress their slave trade was resisted by the major traders and in June 1878, Zobeir one of the principal traders instigated a revolt led by his son Suleiman; Gessi was instrumental in bringing the insurrection to an end and in July 1880, Suleiman and 11 other ringleaders were shot dead.

The Mahdi

The misery and poverty of the inhabitants of the Sudan, oppressed by Egyptian tax collectors and compounded by the discontent of the Baggara tribe, the great slave traders of the desert, who were in danger of losing their revenue, created an environment ready for rebellion. All that was needed was a leader capable of uniting all of the various factions in a common cause.

The leader who came to the fore was Mohamed Ahmed, a religious man from Dongola who, in August 1881, declared a Jihad (Holy War) against the Turks and advised that he was the Mahdi (guided one) or messiah, intent on consolidating the rule of Islam throughout Sudan.

The Mahdi Rebellion

Although it was nearly crushed at the outset, within a year the influence of the Mahdi had spread to all corners of Sudan. Several unsuccessful attempts were made by the forces of Rauf Pasha, the Governor General of Sudan to capture the Mahdi but he always managed to escape.

On the 9th December 1881, Rashid Bey Ayman, the Governor of Fashoda was defeated by Mahdi forces at the Battle of Jabal Qadir in the Nuba hills; during the battle the governor and 1,400 of his men were killed.

On 7th June 1882, Yussef Pasha with a force of 4,000 Egyptians was surprised and massacred at Mesat, near Jebel Gedir, which placed the whole of South Kordofan in rebel hands and

Figure 95. The Mahdi

at the beginning of 1883 the Mahdist forces captured Bara and then after a five month siege captured El Obeid and killed the governor Said Pasha.

In the province of Darfur, the governor Rudolf Anton Carl Freiherr von Slatin (Slatin Pasha) an Austrian, had some initial success against the Mahdist forces, however, at the Battle of Om Waragat in 1883, after losing 8,000 of his men during the first 20 minutes of the battle he was forced to surrender to the Mahdi.

Determined to stamp out the rebellion, the Egyptian Government appointed Hicks Pasha (Colonel William Hicks, formerly with the Indian Army) to command an army of 11,000 to accomplish this task. Setting out from Omdurman on 9th September 1883, Hicks and his force reached Kashgal, near El Obeid in Kordofan without any opposition where the Mahdi had assembled a force of about 40,000 men.

On 1st November, the two forces clashed and for four days, Hicks with his rabble army were engaged in an unequal struggle; on the 5th day Hicks and his force were led into some woods by a treacherous guide where they were ambushed and massacred by a large Mahdist force and in just over 15 minutes, with Hicks's men offering little resistance Hicks and most of his army were slaughtered, only 300 men managed to escape. In addition to Hicks, Alla-ed-deen Pasha, the Governor General of the Sudan, and Mr O'Donovan, the correspondent for the *Daily News* were also killed.

With this victory, during which he captured 36 mountain guns and large supplies of ammunition, the Mahdi was on the verge of total control of the Sudan.

In the east of the Sudan, while the Mahdi was consolidating his control along the Nile, his right hand man Osman Digna was harassing towns and villages around Suakin and on 6th November a force sent to relieve Tokar was cut to pieces by his men. During the fighting Captain Moncrieff, the British consol at Suakin, was killed.

In December an attempt was made to relieve Sinkat but this failed and 760 men out of the 800 men in the relieving force were killed.

The Egyptians, strongly influenced by the British Government, were most concerned about the safety of the Red Sea salt marshes and protection of the Suez Canal and appointed General Valentine Baker Pasha to raise troops to pacify the area; the Egyptian Army, created by Sir Evelyn Wood, had been raised on the understanding that they would be exempt from service in the Sudan. Gunboats were also despatched to defend the port at Suakin.

At the beginning of February 1884, General Baker left Suez with a force of about 3,500 men and headed for Suakin, from where he planned to relieve the inland besieged garrisons. On 3rd February, General Baker moved his force from Suakin to Trinkitat on the Red Sea coast near to Tokar where he established his camp.

Battle of El Teb (First)

On the 4th February, General Baker and his force set out for Tokar but after halting at El Teb, for a rest, they were attacked by a force of about 1,000 rebels. Despite their superior numbers and weaponry the ill disciplined Egyptian force were overcome by panic and after firing only one volley they fled; they were pursued by the rebel force who inflicted heavy casualties, killing 11 of the European officers.

General Baker, unable to rally his troops, retreated back to his camp at Trinkitat where he and the 700 survivors of the battle managed to defend themselves against the Mahdist forces.

Following the defeat of General Baker's relief force the garrison at Tokar surrendered to the rebel besiegers and on 8th February the garrison at Sinkat, under the command of Tewfik Bey, broke out and tried to march to safety at Suakin, however, they were all massacred.

Not long after his defeat, General Baker with his remaining troops left the camp at Trinkitat and returned to Suakin where he tried to bolster the defences of the town but the Egyptian soldiers were less than helpful in this endeavour, however, Admiral Hewitt landed a naval brigade of sailors and marines to supplement General Baker's men.

Battle of El Teb (Second)

In Britain, the defeat of General Baker incensed Lord Wolseley, who demanded the intervention of British troops in the Sudan; reluctantly the government agreed and several units, returning from India, were diverted to Suakin.

On 21st February, a force of 4,500 men, supported by 22 artillery pieces and 6 machine guns, under the command of General Sir Gerald Graham, left Suakin bound for El Teb, via Trinkitat and by 29th of February had reached the Mahdist positions on a hill near El Teb. The rebel positions consisted of entrenchments and rifle pits defended by artillery pieces, some of which had been captured at Tokar.

After a brief artillery duel, during which the rebel guns were silenced, the British force formed up in a square and advanced on the enemy positions. A squadron of 10th Hussars covered the front and left face of the square and a troop from the 19th Hussars covered the right face.

The remainder of the cavalry were formed up in three lines to the rear of the square, commanded by Colonels Wood, Barrow and Webster.

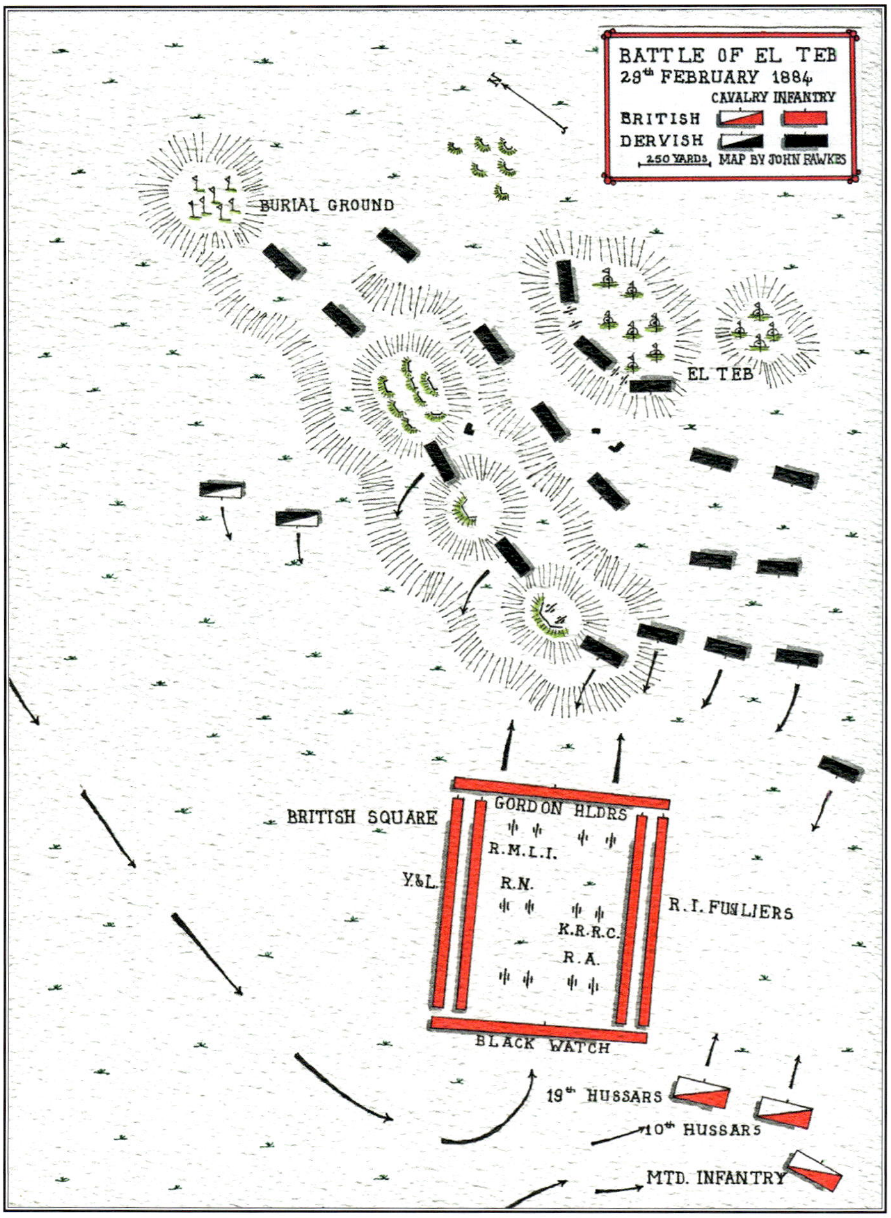

Figure 96. Battle of El Teb

The main part of the enemy defences was at the top of the hill, where the rebels had fortified a village, it was here that the Mahdist troops defended most stubbornly and the British had to clear their trenches at the point of a bayonet.

Captain Arthur Wilson – Victoria Cross No. 399

During the battle, Captain Wilson from *HMS Hecla*, who had attached himself to the right half-battery of the Naval Brigade, in place of a Lieutenant who was mortally wounded, was part of a detachment advancing with guns on an enemy battery.

As they approached the battery, the detachment was charged by some Mahdist warriors and Captain Wilson rushed to the front and engaged some of the enemy in single hand to hand combat in order to protect the men dragging the guns. He continued his efforts until some men from the 1st Battalion of the York and Lancaster Regiment came to his assistance.

The full story of Captain Wilson's exploits are best told in his own words: *"I had no business there, but as I had nothing to do here, and the place where the battle was expected to, and actually did, take place was within walking distance, I thought I would walk out at daylight this morning in time to march out with the troops.*

We had sent twenty-five men with Conybeare and Henderson and a Gardner gun to represent the ship in the Naval Brigade, but I had nothing to do with that, and simply went as a spectator. I am afraid you will say I had no business to go, but it would not do to miss such a good chance of learning one's trade, and it was a most enjoyable day. I would not have missed it for anything, and as I was free to go where I liked, I saw all the best of it.

We went out in square, with all the impediments, including myself, in the centre, the Naval Brigade with their machine guns occupying the two leading corners. We could see the enemy in the hills in the distance before we had left Fort Baker more than about a mile, but as we approached they all disappeared, and we saw nobody – nothing but two Krupp guns, which they had captured from Baker the other day, looking over a sort of parapet at us.

We marched steadily past them, as if we were going to leave them on the left, and still we saw no sign of the Arabs until we were nearly abreast of the battery and 900 or 1,000 yards from it, when they opened fire with their Krupp guns and with rifles. We marched steadily on without replying until we were right behind them, and had them between us and where we landed. Then we halted, and for some little time a sort of duel was kept up between the Royal Artillery with their 7-pounders and the Krupp guns in the fort, the naval machine guns occasionally joining also, but with no result of any importance on either side except occasionally a man or a horse being struck in the square; but most of the shots were kind enough to pass through without hurting anybody.

When we had had enough of that the General gave the order to advance, and the men marched at first very steadily without firing. At about 500 or 600 yards firing commenced, and then there was a frantic noise and shouting. Poor Lieutenant Royds of the Carysfort was shot through the body close to me and two or three men of the Naval Brigade, not, however, belonging to my own ship.

I went on with the 65th Regiment, who were making straight for the battery of Krupp guns which had been pounding us; when we got within twenty or thirty yards a lot of the men broke their ranks and rushed ahead to get into the battery. The first man, however, had scarcely put his head over the parapet than back they all came, with about twenty Arabs with their spears close after their heels. I stopped two or three and made them turn about, and one poor man said rather piteously, 'Don't stop me, sir, I am wounded,' and I saw he was wounded in the elbow.

The greater part of the Arabs were shot almost instantly, but the rest came on without the slightest sign of fear. One of them tried to run his spear into the soldier next to me, but missed him. I tried to run him through with my sword, but it broke, and while my attention was taken up with this man, another came up and cut me over the head with a sword. Thanks to my pith helmet it only made a nice clear cut through the scalp, and did not hurt the skull; in fact, I hardly felt it afterwards. But the blood ran all over my face and clothes, and as water is too scarce in the desert to be used for washing purposes, I looked rather an object, and all my friends kept thinking I must be badly hurt.

I picked up another sword, but got no other opportunity of using it, though the Arabs came on in the most plucky manner. They would lie hidden in ones and twos under the scrubby bushes on little sand hillocks until we were within a hundred yards of them or less, and then they would spring up and run straight at us with their spears, of course generally to be shot before they had come far.

They had any amount of rifles, and fired at us at long range, but they evidently thought the spear was the weapon for close quarters. They were certainly the most fearless creatures I have seen. One felt quite sorry such brave men should be killed, but there was no help for it. If they only learnt to use their rifles in the same fearless way they use their spears I don't think our men would have had much chance with them. I came back to the ship in the afternoon and convoyed poor Royds, who was very badly hit, and as it was dark before we got back and the last part of the way was knee-deep in stiff clayey mud, it was rather a job for the men to carry him. My head is done up with sticking-plaster and is all right. …"

For this action, Captain Wilson was later awarded the Victoria Cross.

As the British force cleared the enemy trenches, the Mahdi began to retreat across the plain to the rear of their positions and were pursued for some way by the British cavalry.

Quartermaster Sergeant William Marshall – Victoria Cross No. 400

After chasing off the main body of the retreating enemy, the cavalry had to return to deal with a large party of rebels who had been passed due to the broken ground.

The 10th Hussars and two squadrons of the 19th Hussars, commanded by Colonel Barrow, charged a large enemy party, made up of horsemen, men on camels and footmen and soon became involved in vicious hand to hand fighting. Thirty of the Mahdi cavalry charged one of the leading squadrons; enemy swordsmen and spearmen, taking advantage of the cover provided by scrub and the broken ground, hamstrung the British horses as they passed and then attacked the dismounted riders.

Captain Freeman of the 19th Hussars and several of his men were killed in this fashion, of all of the men dismounted from their horses, only Colonel Barrow escaped alive. After his horse was killed and he received a thrust from a spear that passed through his arm and penetrated his side, Colonel Barrow fell to the ground and was surrounded by the enemy.

Seeing his Colonel's plight, Quartermaster Sergeant Marshall, accompanied by Sergeant Fenton and Private Boseley rode to his assistance. The Colonel grabbed Quartermaster Sergeant Marshall's hand and was dragged to safety.

For this action Quartermaster Sergeant Marshall was later awarded the Victoria Cross.

The rebel force was finally dispersed when some of the British cavalry dismounted and fired volleys into their ranks.

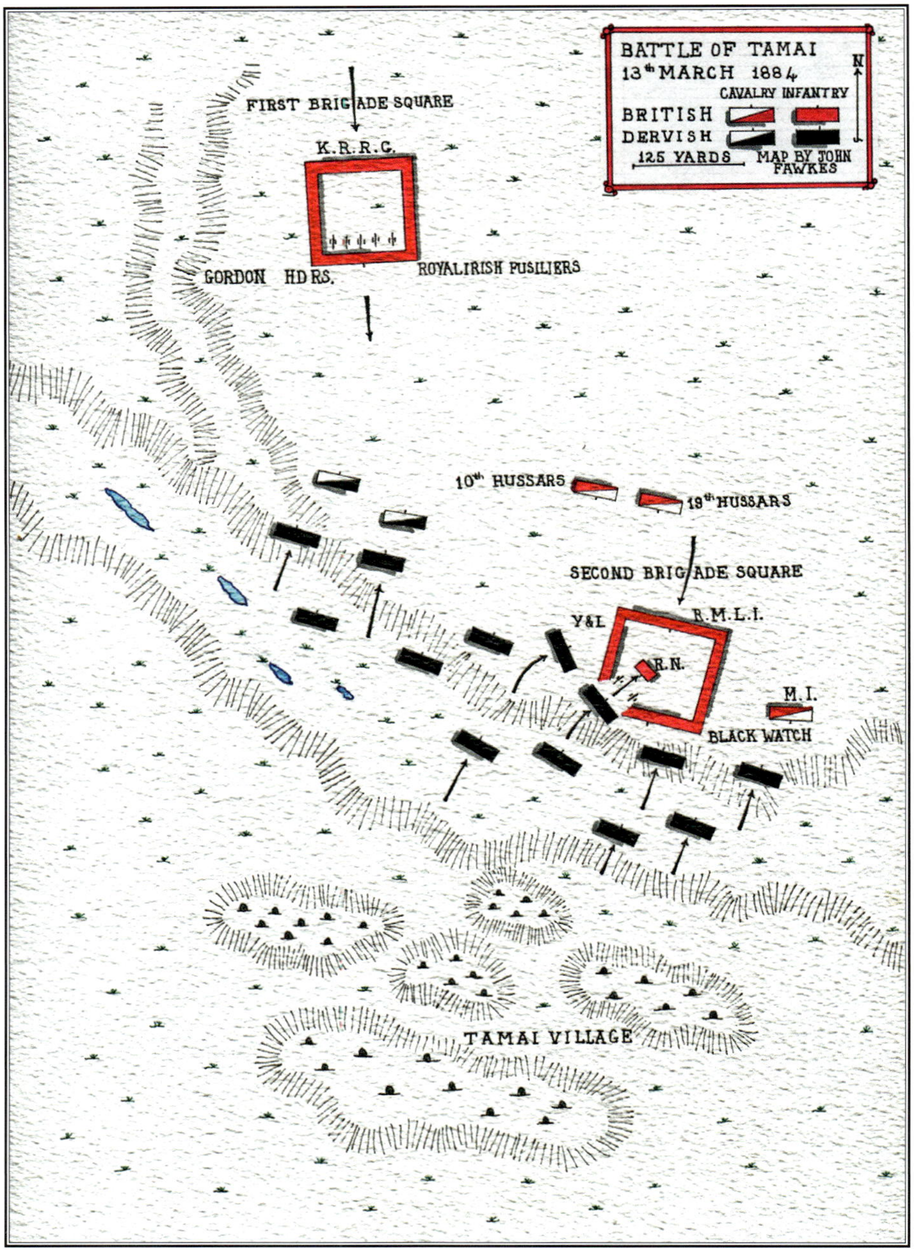

Figure 97. Battle of Tamai

The battle came to an end after three hours of desperate fighting during which about 2,000 of the Mahdist force were left dead on the field. The British losses were 30 men killed and 142 wounded, including General Baker who was wounded in the jaw.

Following the battle, General Graham and his men advanced on Tokar, which they captured without further opposition and most of the equipment lost by General Baker's force was recovered.

On the night of 12th March, General Graham and his force advanced and set up camp at Zariba, close to Osman Digna's camp at Tamai which was close to El Teb.

During the night, Mahdist riflemen approached the British camp and loosed off a few shots but to little effect.

Battle of Tamai

At dawn the British advanced and the battle was begun by artillery fire against the Mahdist skirmishers who were soon driven back.

In preparation for the main assault, the British force was formed up into two squares; one commanded by Colonel Davis, with General Graham in attendance and the other commanded by Colonel Buller.

When a scouting party discovered that the main enemy force was hidden in a nearby ravine, General Graham ordered the Black Watch to charge them but when they did so they left a large gap in the square which allowed the Mahdist force to rush in. With this serious turn of events, the integrity of the square was in danger as fierce hand to hand fighting broke out. The enemy advance on the square was slowed down by volleys from Colonel

Buller's square and some dismounted cavalry and when the Black Watch returned the rebels were expelled from the square which was then reformed.

The concentrated flanking fire from Colonel Buller's square and the cavalry had caused huge numbers of enemy casualties, causing them to retreat.

Lieutenant Percival Marling – Victoria Cross No. 401

During the battle, Lieutenant Marling rode to the rescue of the wounded Private Morley. The Lieutenant initially placed the Private in front of himself on the horse but due to his wounds Private Morley was unable to hang on and fell off almost immediately.

Lieutenant Marling now dismounted and placed Private Morley alone on his horse and through intense fire from the nearby enemy force, he led his horse and Private Morley for about 80 yards to comparative safety.

For this action, Lieutenant Marling was later awarded the Victoria Cross.

Private Thomas Edwards – Victoria Cross No. 402

Private Edwards, attached to the Naval Brigade as a Mule Driver, was part of a naval gun team commanded by Lieutenant Almack with responsibility for carrying the gun's ammunition on mules.

As the battle developed, the Mahdist threatened to overrun some of the British Guns, including Lieutenant Almack's gun which became separated from the main British force; when several of the gun team, including Lieutenant Almack were killed Private Edwards stepped up and took charge.

Despite having been wounded several times, Private Edwards managed to lead the remainder of the gun team back to the main force, saving the gun, ammunition and mules, as well as the rest of the team.

For this service, Private Edwards was later awarded the Victoria Cross.

After the British square was reformed, the British advance continued against the rebels in the ravine, who were driven out after suffering heavy casualties. In the face of stiff British opposition the enemy began to retreat and Osman Digna's camp was soon captured.

During this battle, the British force suffered their largest losses of the war with 82 men killed and over 100 wounded; enemy losses were estimated to be about 4,000 killed or wounded.

Following their victories at El Teb and Tamai, the British troops had accomplished their mission and, at least for the moment, the Red Sea Marshes were safe, so they returned to England.

Return of Gordon to Khartoum

In January 1884, Charles George Gordon now a Major General, who had returned to England from Egypt in 1880, was asked by the British Government to return to the Sudan and withdraw the beleaguered garrisons before they could fall to the Mahdi.

General Gordon was asked to do what he could to restore order and if possible to set up a native government at Khartoum, where the civil European and Egyptian population numbered about 11,000.

General Gordon arrived at Khartoum on 18th February 1884 and immediately grasped that the Sudan was now under the control of the Mahdi not the Khedive. In an attempt to calm down the situation, General Gordon appointed the Mahdi as the Sultan of Darfur, however, this honour was contemptuously declined.

Even though the British troops were now returning home to England, the rebellion was still spreading and on 20th March 1884, the Mahdist forces were firing into Khartoum and in May the station at Berber fell to the rebels leaving Debbeh as the last station to which the telegraph extended.

As each of the garrisons were forced to surrender the rebel grip on Khartoum was now tightened and the city was completely besieged; despite repeated requests to the British Government for assistance, General Gordon, Colonel Stewart and Mr Power were left to their own devices to resist the siege.

Regardless of the desperate situation in Khartoum, the Liberal government under prime minister Gladstone procrastinated until in August 1884 they succumbed to public pressure and ordered a relief expedition to go to the aid of General Gordon.

At the end of October, the rebels besieged Omdurman, on the opposite bank of the Nile to Khartoum; on 12th November, General Gordon sent a force to relieve Omdurman but despite being defeated in a vicious battle during which they experienced heavy losses the rebels were still able to retain their main positions and continue the siege. After building several forts on ground between Omdurman and Khartoum, the rebels were able to maintain a continuous fire on both towns.

During November, General Gordon sent a message to Sir Evelyn Baring, the British Consol in Egypt, stating that he could only hold out for a further 40 days. In December, after receiving a message from Faragallah Pasha, at Omdurman, that his supplies and ammunition were exhausted, General Gordon authorised the surrender of the town to the Mahdist forces.

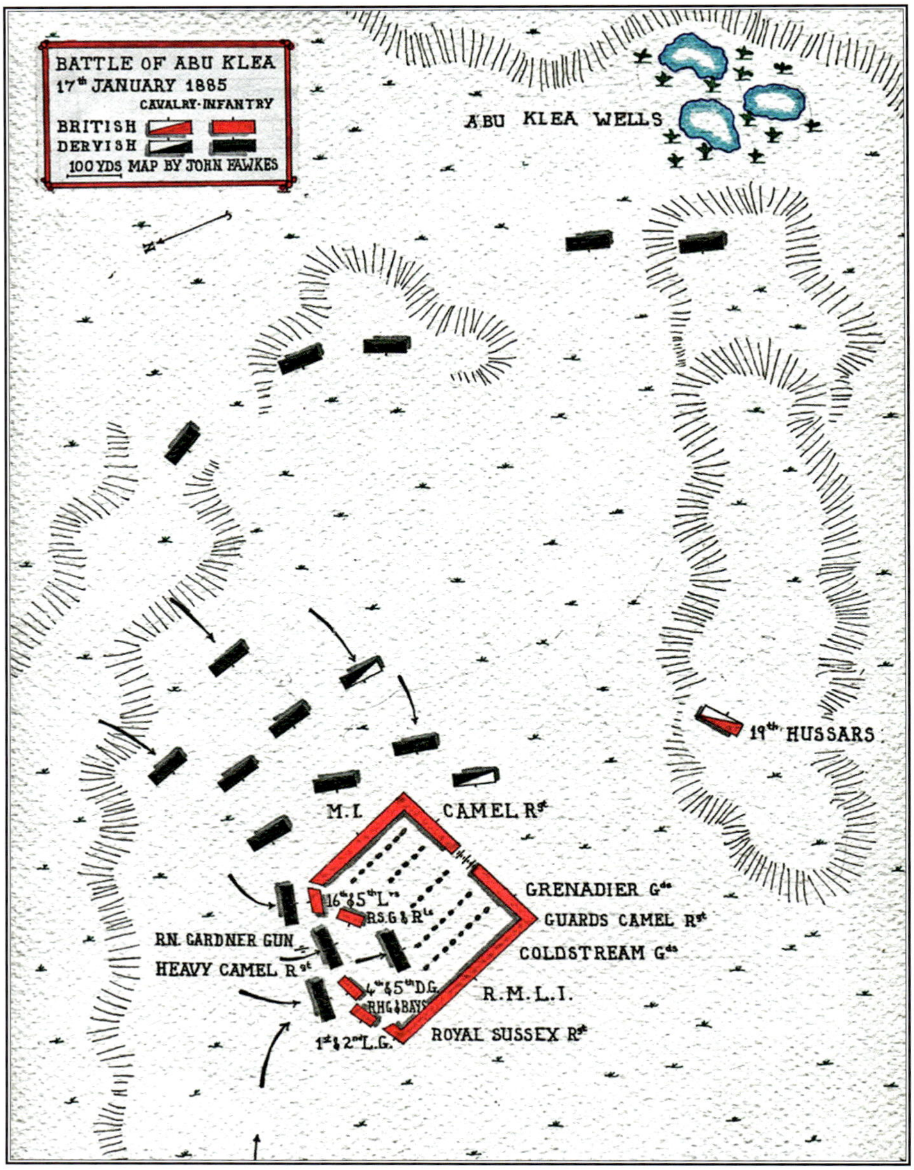

Figure 98. Battle of Abu Klea

With the fall of Omdurman and his supply line cut, the garrison at Khartoum were in dire straits, with people daily dying from disease and starvation.

Nile Campaign

At long last, towards the end of 1884 an expeditionary force of 14,000 men, under the command of General Wolseley landed in Egypt (the Nile Campaign) intent on going to the relief of General Gordon at Khartoum.

After advancing up the Nile in flat bottomed boats, General Wolseley established his forward base at Korti on 15th December 1884.

With further progress up the Nile expected to be very slow, General Gordon ordered General Sir Herbert Stewart to advance towards Khartoum by an overland route across the desert, while he continued with the remainder of his force up the Nile.

On 30th December 1884, General Stewart left Korti with a large force comprised of mainly the Camel Corps and mounted infantry and headed across the desert to Metemmeh, a distance of about 185 miles.

Battle of Abu Klea

General Stewart's desert column of 1,100 men had advanced about half way to their objective without encountering any opposition but just before sunset on 16th January 1885 they reached a salient overlooking the wadi at Abu Klea where a rebel force of about 10,000 men were guarding the wells.

With the day well advanced, General Stewart decided to establish a defensive position and allow his men to rest before pressing forward with an attack on the following day.

At first light on 17th January, General Stewart ordered his force to form a square, and with their camels in the centre they advanced across difficult undulating and broken ground towards the wadi.

The column, with their guns on the front face of the square and the machine guns of the naval brigade on the rear face, towards the left hand corner, advanced until they were suddenly charged by a large rebel force that had been concealed within the wadi.

The attack was directed at the rear left hand corner of the square and after halting to fend off the attack, Captain Beresford, the commander of the Naval Brigade ordered his Gardner machine gun out of the square to provide covering fire to the left flank and Colonel Frederick Gustavus Burnaby led the Camel Corps regiment out of the square to support the gun.

The machine gun jammed after firing about 70 rounds and as the crew tried to clear the jam, Lieutenants Alfred Piggott and Rudolph de Lisle were killed together with seven of the 40 man crew, a further 7 men from the crew were wounded. With a small gap left in the square a small group of the rebels rushed in but were prevented from advancing far due to the centre being occupied by the columns camels.

The troops in the rear ranks of the square, turned about and their fire chased the rebels from the square which was then closed up.

Gunner Alfred Smith – Victoria Cross No. 403

The British gun batteries were pushed to the edge of the square and each gun managed to fire off one round of case shot into the charging rebels before they became engaged in fierce hand to hand fighting.

When Lieutenant D. J. Guthrie was attacked by several of the Mahdi warriors and seriously wounded in the leg, Gunner Smith armed with a handspike from one of the guns rushed to his aid, deflected a spear thrust aimed at the Lieutenant and remained standing over him fighting off several assailants until the charge was repelled.

For this action, Gunner Smith was later awarded the Victoria Cross. Unfortunately Lieutenant Guthrie would later die as a result of his wounds.

Even though the battle was of short duration, lasting only about 15 minutes, the British losses were 74 killed and over 100 wounded; the rebel losses amounted to 1,100 killed.

On the day after the battle, the desert column pushed on towards Metemmeh and on 19th January 1885 were again attacked by the rebels near Abu Kru and during the Battle of El Gubat, despite another victory the commander of the force General Stewart was mortally wounded.

End of the Campaign

Following the death of General Stewart, General Sir Charles Wilson took over command of the Desert column and continued on towards Metemmeh which was reached on 21st January and found to be in the hands of the rebels.

At the river, General Wilson made contact with four of General Gordon's steamers who had sailed down the Nile from Khartoum with messages from Gordon. Abdul Hamid Bey, who commanded one of the steamers informed General Wilson that when he left Khartoum on 14th January, General Gordon informed him that unless he returned with British forces within ten days then all would be lost.

General Wilson and some of his staff boarded one of the steamers and on 24th January set off up the Nile and on 28th January arrived at Omdurman, opposite Khartoum, but due to fire from the batteries at Omdurman they were forced to retire. They did, however, receive the news that Khartoum had fallen to the rebels two days earlier and General Gordon was dead.

Aware of the rapidly approaching British forces, on the morning of 26th January the rebels made a last ditch attempt to take Khartoum and after forcing an entry they seized the town and slaughtered all of the European occupants.

With news of the fall of Khartoum and the death of General Gordon, the British relief mission was over and they withdrew from the Sudan, leaving the Mahdi to rule for the next 13 years.

The British public placed responsibility for the failure of the expedition at the door of Prime Minister Gladstone, for delaying the rescue mission for several months and in response to public pressure he resigned two months later.

28

KARENNI AND CHIN EXPEDITIONS, BURMA (1888–89)

Background

Situated as it was on the north east border of British India, it is not surprising that Burma attracted the attention of the Honourable East India Company (HEIC) and after Burma extended its territory by taking control of Assam, Manipur and Arakan the encroachment into British territory became unacceptable and resulted in the first Anglo-Burmese war in 1824. The war came to a successful conclusion for the HEIC and the provinces of Assam, Manipur and Arakan were absorbed into British India.

On 20th December 1852, following the conclusion of the second Anglo-Burmese war, the province of Pegu was annexed

Figure 99. Karenni – Burma

by the HEIC and renamed Lower Burma. The end of the war prompted an internal struggle for control of the kingdom and on 18th February 1853, Mindon Min was crowned as king, replacing his half brother Pagan Min. In 1857, King Mindon established Mandalay as his new capital.

Following the death of his father, Thibaw Min succeeded to the throne on 1st October 1878.

In the 1880s, British concerns regarding Burma increased when they saw Burma's relationships with the French, whose expansion into Indo China had reached the Burmese border, starting to develop and following the expiry of an ultimatum on 9th November 1885 the third and final Anglo-Burmese war was launched.

The war ended on 26th November 1885 when King Thibaw surrendered; King Thibaw was exiled to India and on 1st January 1886, the remainder of Burma (Upper Burma) was annexed by the British and the whole of Burma was now part of British India.

Despite Burma now being under British rule, increasing numbers of troops were required to maintain control in Upper Burma where the northern tribes continued to resist the British occupation. To quell the northern tribes, the British were required to mount several military expeditions against various tribes in Upper Burma.

Karenni Expedition

The Karenni people (also known as the Red Karen, Kayah or Kayahli) are a collection of tribes, originally of Mongolian/Tibetan descent who migrated to Burma and occupied an area in the north east of Lower Burma bordering the Shan States to their north and Thailand to the east.

The Karenni, together with other tribes like the Shan and Chin, had only loose feudal ties to the Burmese government and largely operated independent of Burma.

In 1875, in a treaty with Mindon Min, the British recognised Karenni independence when it was stated that both parties agreed that the area belonged to neither Burma nor Britain, consequently when the British completed their annexation of Burma the Karenni states were never fully incorporated into British Burma.

Following the complete annexation of Burma in 1886, the British maintained a garrison of Military Police in the village of Lwekaw, in the Karenni state of Kantarawadi, ruled by Chief Sawlapaw.

Unlike the Karenni states, which had a treaty of independence, the Shan states were incorporated into British territory following annexation.

In early 1888, when Karenni tribesmen occupied the Shan state of Mawkmai and expelled chief Hkun Hmon, a British force commanded by Colonel Sartorius was despatched to expel the Karenni.

After reaching Mawkmai on 16th May 1888, Colonel Sartorius found that the Karenni had abandoned the town so he occupied the town and reinstated Chief Hkun Hmon. After leaving Lieutenant Fowler, with 150 riflemen to garrison Mawkmai, Colonel Sartorius, with the remainder of his force returned to Fort Stedman. On 1st July 1888, Lieutenant Fowler moved his headquarters to Mongnai, after leaving 25 riflemen at Mawkmai.

Despite the assertions, in June by Chief Hkun Hmon, that the Karenni had left his territory, the Karenni once again attacked Mawkmai on 3rd July but were repulsed by the meagre 25 man garrison; after this activity, Lieutenant Fowler decided to move his headquarters back to Mawkmai.

When it became known that, rather than leaving the area, the Karenni had established an entrenched position less than a day's march from Mawkmai, Lieutenant Fowler launched an attack against their position and at the point of a bayonet drove the enemy from their entrenchments killing 60 of their number in the process.

In August 1888, after having referred the matter to the Indian Government in July, approval was granted to demand compensation from chief Sawlapaw for the damage that he had caused to Mawkmai and as security for his future good behaviour; approval was also granted to enforce these demands if they were not complied with.

In September 1888, as the Karenni chief showed no signs of complying with the British demands and refusing to meet with Mr A. H. Hildebrand, the Superintendant of the Shan states, Sir Charles Crosthwaite, the Chief Commissioner of Burma drafted an ultimatum to be issued in November if all attempts to persuade chief Sawlapaw to come to terms had failed.

This ultimatum required chief Sawlapaw to come to Fort Stedman and personally submit himself as a chief subordinate to the Queen Empress; he was also required to pay two lakhs of rupees as compensation, surrender 500 serviceable muskets and lastly to pay an annual tribute of 5,000 rupees to the British Government.

In October, when it seemed that chief Sawlapaw was having some misgivings, Mr Hildebrand in the hope of a peaceful conclusion, offered the chief some concessions; a reduction in the compensation and the number of muskets to be surrendered, the chief was also allowed to make his submission at Mawkmai rather than Fort Stedman.

Following an exchange of letters, Chief Sawlapaw suggested that he would meet Mr Hildebrand at Lwekaw on 17th December.

During the negotiations, preparations were made for the actions to be taken in the event that chief Sawlapaw failed to comply with the terms of the ultimatum. The plan was for two columns to mount attacks against the Karenni; the main force, which would mount an attack against Sawlon (the capital of Eastern Karenni) was assembled at Saga on 27th December; the second column, commanded by Colonel Harvey was to cover the districts of Lower Burma and prevent any retreat of the Karenni forces southwards.

In order to bring further pressure on the Karenni, who to a large extent depended on imported food, the British established a blockade and all exports from British territories to the Karenni were stopped.

On 10th December, Superintendant Hildebrand informed Sir Charles Crosthwaite, that there was no hope of a peaceful solution and Colonel Harvey was ordered to cover the border of the Salween district, however, on 17th December a large Karenni force attacked and burnt several border villages two days before his force arrived at Papun.

After receiving some additional men, Colonel Harvey moved his force to Bawlake on 26th December and soon afterwards attacked and occupied a Karenni stockade at Pazaung, where the Colonel established his headquarters and waited for the news that Sawlon had been occupied by the main column.

On 19th December, Superintendant Hildebrand received orders to proceed with the main column, commanded by General Henry Collett, to Sawlon where he was to obtain the submission of the East Karenni chief.

Having assembled his force at Saga, General Collett set out for Sawlon on 29th December, on a route which passed close to the village of Lwekaw. Despite the road being bordered by scrub jungle, offering ideal ambush cover, General Collett and his force reached the open plains on 1st January without encountering any resistance.

Battle of Lwekaw

While the British camp was being set up, a group of Beleuchi Scouts who were exploring some wooded ground near Lwekaw were fired upon and were soon joined by the Beleuchi Mounted Infantry, commanded by Lieutenant Tighe who drove the enemy from the woods.

Surgeon John Crimmin – Victoria Cross No. 404

On leaving the woods the enemy force of about 300 men, tried to attain the high ground but were forced down to the plain by the mounted infantry, where they broke up and began to retreat towards Lwekaw, about eight miles distance.

During the retreat, the enemy periodically halted and fired at their pursuers which provoked the British cavalry to charge; it was during one of these charges that Surgeon Crimmin went to the aid of one of the wounded, after which he joined the firing line and helped drive the enemy from small clumps of trees where they had been taking cover.

Later in the pursuit, while tending another wounded man, Surgeon Crimmin was attacked by a group of the enemy but with the use of his sword the surgeon managed to kill two of his attackers before fire from the troopers managed to drive the rest off.

For this action Surgeon Crimmin was later awarded the Victoria Cross.

To complete the rout, General Collett advanced with a portion of his force to Lwekaw, which he found to have been deserted.

On 2nd January, General Collett rested at Lwekaw in order for his remaining troops and baggage, in camp at Nga Kaing to join him. Progress was further slowed when on 3rd January it took all day for his force to cross the Balu river.

The General used this time to distribute a proclamation, which explained why the British force had entered Karenni territory and promised that peaceful inhabitants would not be harmed. With the advance of the British force, the majority of the peasant population had left their villages and fled to the hills, however, with the proclamation some of the elders returned and asked the General for a way of indicating that their villages were friendly; for this purpose flags made from red cloth were distributed.

General Collett and his force resumed their march towards Sawlon on 4th January which was reached, after encountering only minor resistance on 8th January; the town which they found to have been deserted was occupied by Colonel Sartorius with men from the Beleuchi regiment.

Election of Sawlawi

With the occupation of Sawlon, military operations came to an end and as the whereabouts of chief Sawlapaw was unknown, Superintendant Hildebrand issued a proclamation calling for him to meet with him before 18th January. On 17th January, a Karenni deputation met with Mr Hildebrand and requested an extension to the deadline and a written note of safe passage for chief Sawlapaw; both requests were granted and it was further stated that if the chief came in and fulfilled the conditions of the ultimatum then he would be confirmed in the position as head of the Karenni state.

It was eventually agreed that Sawlawi, a nephew of Sawlapaw and heir apparent, would meet with Mr Hildebrand on 25th

January, however, on that day a message arrived to say that he was on his way but was delayed due to exhaustion and would not arrive until the 28th January.

On the morning of 28th January, Sawlawi arrived at Sawlon with 29 Karenni chiefs and was duly elected as the chief of Eastern Karenni, in succession to Sawlapaw, and in this capacity he signed an agreement which fulfilled the requirements of the ultimatum.

On 30th January, General Collett and his troops left Karenni territory and marched back to Fort Stedman.

Chin Expedition

Along the west of the Upper Burma districts of Upper and Lower Chindwin, Pakokku and Minbu lies a region of wild hills, inhabited by a number of savage tribes collectively known as the Chins. In a mountainous region formed of high narrow ridges and deep valleys, which mainly run from north to south the Chins are split into numerous tribes with clans speaking many different dialects. With each village or small group of villages ruled by a headman, there is no centralised government, making it impossible to have negotiations with the Chin people as a whole.

For many years, the various tribes had carried out raids against villages on their borders, a practice that was ignored by the Burmese government, however, following the British annexation of the country this practice had to be eliminated.

In March 1887, Captain Raikes, the Deputy Commissioner of Upper Chindwin, met representatives of the Tashon tribes at Indin where he explained that the raiding must stop; these discussions seemed to have been successful as very few villages were raided for the next year.

British plans to open up the Chin territories by building roads from the Bengal border were a cause of much concern to most of the Chin tribes, so Captain Raikes arranged another meeting and on 3rd January 1888 met with Sonpek, the principal chief of the Tashon tribes. Although the meeting was courteous, Sonpek's concerns were not alleviated as Captain Raikes had no information regarding the routes that the road would take.

On 4th and 5th May 1888, a force of Tashon tribesmen descended on Indin and took the local chief prisoner, however, he was subsequently released and allowed to return to Indin on the understanding that he would join the resistance against the British. The chief, however, remained loyal to the British and sent messages to Mr Ross, the Deputy Commissioner asking for assistance.

With regional disturbances on the increase, Mr Ross authorised the movement of British troops into the area which managed to quell the disturbances and with the advent of the rainy season the Chins returned to their mountain retreats and the disturbances stopped altogether.

On 21st July 1888, Sir Charles Crosthwaite, Chief Commissioner of Burma, after voicing his opinion that there would be no peace in the area until the Chin tribes had been subdued, requested permission from the Indian Government to send an expedition against the Chins as soon as the dry season arrived.

The first step of the planned campaign was to permanently occupy, in force, the area below the Chin Hills and establish effective administrative control of the area.

The next step in the campaign was to mount an expedition into the Chin Hills; it was proposed to divide the expeditionary force into three columns; one to advance up the Kale Valley against the Siyin and Sagyilain tribes; a second column would simultaneously attack the Tashon country while a third column would move against the Yokwa Haka and Thatta Chins to prevent them from helping the Tashons. If possible a fourth column from Arakan or the Chittagong Hills would mount an attack against the rear of the Tashon positions.

In September 1888, while the Indian Government were still considering the Chief Commissioners proposals, the Tashons resumed their raiding and formed an alliance with the Haka tribe.

Convinced that these raids were a prelude to more serious border conflicts, the Government in India were once again asked to call for the immediate enlistment of a Military Police levy to protect the Chin Frontier. As a precaution against anticipated attacks, garrisons were established at Kalewa and Sihaung which were also used to prevent the Chins obtaining supplies from across the plains.

In October the Chief Commissioner received the news that the Indian Government had refused to sanction his proposals for expeditions against the Chin tribes. Following this refusal, the Chief Commissioner turned to General Sir George White, the military commander of Upper Burma for proposals on how to deal with the Chin insurgents.

It was agreed that a force of troops should be moved from Pakokku to Gangaw and along the line of the frontier subject to Chin raids; military posts were to be established at Tilin, Gangaw, Kan, Sihaung, Kambale and Indin. General Faunce, commander of the military district, was given command of these operations and Major Raikes was appointed as his political officer. The objective of the operations was to protect the frontier and capture and punish any raiding parties but due to the decision of the Indian Government they were forbidden to mount attacks against the Chin strongholds in the hills.

Before these arrangements could be completed, the Chin raids continued at a pace; on 14th October Homalin was attacked; on

17th October Chitpauk, in the Kabaw Valley was raided and 45 hostages taken; on 20th October Kambale was surrounded and six villagers captured; on 22nd October Kantha was attacked and 32 villagers were captured; on 29th October Kalemyo was attacked and 40 villagers were captured and on the same day Khampat was attacked and 27 villagers were captured.

These attacks and the capture of many villagers, who would be sold into slavery, prompted the Indian Government to reconsider their position and on 16th November the Chief Commissioner was given a free hand to address the situation, with the resources at his disposal.

On 14th November, General Faunce left Pakokku with a force of 356 infantry and 100 cavalry and as they proceeded along the frontier posts were established at Chaungu, Tilin, Gangaw, Kan, and Sihaung. In addition to the troops that accompanied General Faunce, a large force comprising 77 artillerymen, 58 Sappers and three companies of Ghurkhas, was sent by steamer to Kalewa and by the time that the General reached Kambale, where he established his headquarters, he had a force of 1,200 men under his command.

In addition to these troops, the General also had about 250 military police, who formed the garrisons at Indin and Kalewa, at his disposal.

With his forces in readiness, the biggest challenge to operations into the Chin hills was transportation and Captain Eyre was appointed to obtain the large number of coolies that would be required.

While these preparations were being made, the Chin bandits were assembling in large numbers and putting pressure on the military posts; in order to protect the post at Gangaw the garrison was supplemented by the garrison at Kan which was abandoned. The expanded garrison at Gangaw was attacked on a daily basis until 6th January 1889, when a relief force arrived.

During December, the Chin bandits continued their attacks against the frontier posts and General Faunce had to limit his operations to border patrols and defence and was forced to request reinforcements in order to carry out operations against the Chin strongholds.

On 26th December, General White who was at Mingin on the Chindwin river ordered a force of 200 men from Pakokku and Major Kingston with a force of 250 men from Alon to proceed at once to Gangaw; Colonel Macgregor, with a force of 150 Ghurkhas from Sihaung was also ordered to Gangaw. A force of 125 military police commanded by Lieutenant Philips was also despatched from Pakokku and met up with Major Kingston's column on 2nd January at Kyaw.

On 6th January the combined forces of Major Kingston and Lieutenant Philips attacked the Chin bandits who were surrounding Gangaw and inflicted heavy losses on the enemy. At the same time the force of Colonel Macgregor attacked the Chins to the south of Gangaw, driving them off, again inflicting heavy losses.

In December, General Faunce issued an ultimatum to the Chin tribes demanding that they free their captives, surrender some firearms and pay a fine and if these condition were not met then the General would destroy their villages and implement a severe blockade to prevent food supplies reaching the hills.

During December and January, General Faunce made preparations for these punitive missions, should they prove to be necessary and on 23rd January 1889, together with General White made a reconnaissance up to the summit of the Letha Range and onward into the Chin Hills. During the advance, sappers and coolies constructed a road and built rough stockades each night to protect the men and their stores.

The advance was obstructed by formidable Chin stockades, most of which were occupied but not strongly defended and the column was subjected to ambushes each day and night.

By 4th February the force had reached the village of Koset, which they occupied and after continuing to advance through the territory had occupied all of the villages within the territory of the Siyin by 5th March. A fortified post, named Fort White, was established at the Chin village of Toklaing and adopted as the headquarters of the Chin expeditionary force.

Clearly affected by the punishments that had been inflicted on the Siyin, representatives of the Kanhow tribe arrived at Fort White on 24th February, intent on avoiding the same damage being inflicted on their villages. The Kanhow representatives were advised that in order to prevent the destruction of their villages they must; surrender all of the prisoners, pay a fine of 1,000 rupees and pay a small annual tribute as a token of their submission, they were given ten days to consider and accept these terms.

On 6th March, the Kanhow representatives returned with six of their captives but failed to comply with the other conditions. In consequence on 8th March, General Faunce led operations against the Kanhow villages, during which many were destroyed and large stores of grain and other food supplies were captured; his mission accomplished the General and his men returned to Fort White on 20th March.

During April while negotiations were taking place with the Tashon tribe, the troops took a well earned rest.

Battle of Tartan

Following news that the Siyin tribe had built a new village at Tartan, which had been destroyed by earlier operations, General Symons and a force of about 150 men set out from Fort White to destroy the new village.

After arriving at Tartan on 4th May 1889, the force found that the village was strongly defended by two entrenched stockades occupied by the enemy.

Surgeon Ferdinand Le Quesne – Victoria Cross No. 405

At first it appeared as though the village had been abandoned, however, as Captain Mayne began deploying his forces for the final advance into the village his men were assailed by heavy fire from the two fortified stockades.

Lieutenant Michel leading the charge against one of the stockades was severely wounded and in the face of the heavy enemy fire his troops were forced to retire but managed to bring the Lieutenant out of the fray.

With Lieutenant Michel, still in a position exposed to the enemy fire, Private Crampion went to fetch Surgeon Le Quesne to treat his Lieutenant's wounds. Aided by the Private, Surgeon Le Quesne treated the Lieutenant's wounds and those of two of his men.

After about 10 minutes of working under the heavy enemy fire, Surgeon Le Quesne and the Private managed to move Lieutenant Michel to a place of safety outside the line of enemy fire.

While tending to the wounds of Lieutenant Michel, Surgeon Le Quesne had observed that Major Mayne, who was also wounded, was lying nearby and after moving the Lieutenant to safety he once again exposed himself to the enemy fire as he went to tend to the Major's wounds. During the treatment of Major Mayne's wounds Surgeon Le Quesne was himself seriously wounded.

For his actions, Surgeon Le Quesne was subsequently awarded the Victoria Cross, unfortunately Lieutenant Michel died from his wounds.

The words of Major Mayne, testify to the bravery of Surgeon Le Quesne *"The splendid coolness and gallantry displayed by Surgeon Le Quesne in attending to the wounded, he himself being exposed during the whole time to a very hot fire, under which several men dropped; this was more especially the case while attending to 2nd Lieutenant Michel, owing to his extremely exposed position. I consider that Surgeon Le Quesne's conduct is deserving of the highest possible recognition".*

With the British losses having reached four killed and eight wounded, Captain Westmoreland, who was now in command of the force called for a retirement and they returned to Fort White.

A few days later another force from Fort White arrived at Tartan and destroyed the village and two stockades, which by now had been abandoned.

Due to the onset of the rainy season, this was the last operation of the campaign. On the 6th May the Kanhow, submitted to demands, releasing their captives and paying the 1,000 rupee fine.

PART THREE

PORTRAITS OF VALOUR

John Augustus Wood
9th December 1856 (VC No. 112)

Figure 100. John Augustus Wood

Gazetted: 3rd August 1860 22409/2860

Rank and Unit: Captain – 20th Bengal Native Infantry

Citation

On the 9th of December, 1856, Captain Wood led the Grenadier Company, which formed the head of the assaulting column sent against Bushire.[25] *He was the first man on the parapet of the fort, where he was instantly attacked by a large number of the garrison, who suddenly sprang on him from a trench cut in the parapet itself.*

These men fired a volley at Captain Wood and the head of the storming party, when only a yard or two distant from that Officer; but, although Captain Wood was struck by no less than seven musket balls, he at once threw himself upon the enemy, passed his sword through the body of their leader, and, being closely followed by the men of his company, speedily overcame all opposition, and established himself in the place. Captain Wood's decision, energy, and determined valour, undoubtedly contributed in a high degree to the success of the attack.

His wounds compelled him to leave the force for a time; but, with the true spirit of a good soldier, he rejoined his regiment, and returned to his duty at Bushire before the wounds were properly healed.

Biography

John was born on 10th June 1818 at Fort William, Calcutta in India to father John Sulivan[26] a career army officer and mother Sophia Mary, he was baptised on the 17th July 1818.

Little is known of John's early life but he was probably educated in England.

On the 6th July 1839, at the age of 21, John was commissioned as an Ensign and joined the 20th Bombay Native Infantry on the 8th October 1839.

Almost immediately after joining his regiment, John was on active service as his regiment was part of the forces involved in the first Anglo-Afghan War (1839–1842).[27]

From 1840 until 1843, John served with a field force on operations in the province of Scinde and Afghanistan and in March 1841 he took part in the attack on the fort at Kujjuck.

As part of a force under the command of Brigadier-General Richards, John, as part of the Light Battalion, was involved in the advance on Kandahar and took part in the Battle of Hykulzye on 28th March 1842 and action against Akber Khan's army near Kandahar on 29th May 1842.

On the 31st March 1842, John received a promotion to the rank of Lieutenant.

John spent time with Colonel Wymer's force destroying the Afghan forts at Urghundaul, near Kandahar.

For his service during the war, John was awarded the Candahar, Ghuznee, Cabul Medal inscribed on the rear with Candahar.

Towards the end of the war, John was involved in operations for the subjugation of the Province of Scinde and took part in the final major battle of the war at Hyderabad on 24th March 1843.

For his service in this campaign, John was awarded the Scinde Medal annotated "Hyderabad 1843".

On the 17th December 1846, John was married to Louisa (née Liddiard) at Bath in Somerset, the couple would go on to have eight children (four sons and four daughters); however, only three would live long enough to outlive their father.

John Edmund Sulivan was born on 21st February 1853 but died on 11th April 1857, just after his fourth birthday; Melanie Marion was born on 10th May 1854; Owen Kippil Sulivan was born on 11th January 1856 but died on 11th March 1856 only three months old; Wilfred St Lawrence was born on 20th October 1860; Ethel Rose Marie was born on 9th September 1861 but died in January or February 1867 less than six years old; Cuthbert St Mark was born on 3rd September 1862 but died on 23rd August 1863 less than one year old; Cyril Fettercaison

25 The action actually took place at Rushire

26 John Sulivan would attain the rank of General and for a time served as Lieutenant of the Tower of London.

27 Sometimes referred to as "Auckland's Folly" after George Eden Lord Auckland, the Governor-General of India who ordered the conflict

was born on 24th February 1865 but died on 20th July 1866 just over one year old; Alice Monique was born on 20th May 1867.

On the 5th April 1856, John received a promotion to the rank of Captain.[28]

John was part of the expeditionary force of 5,600 men being assembled at Bombay, under the command of Major General Foster Stalker, to invade Persia after a declaration of war on 1st November 1856.

The force left Bombay on the 9th November 1856 and landed at Hallilah Bay, near Bushire, Persia's principal port, on the 7th December.

On the 9th of December 1856, John was involved in the storming of the fort at Reshire and it was during this attack that he performed the deeds for which he was later awarded the Victoria Cross.

During the assault, John was seriously wounded by seven musket rounds, which while not life threatening required medical treatment so he was evacuated back to Bombay.

Despite not having fully recovered from his wounds, John rejoined his regiment at Bushire in February 1857, where he spent the next eight months.

On the 28th September 1857, John and the regiment embarked on *HMS Melbourne* at Bushire for their return to Bombay where they landed on the 20th October 1857.

For his service during the war in Persia, John was awarded the India General Service Medal (1856) with clasp for Persia.

On the 19th January 1858, John received a brevet promotion to the rank of Major, in recognition for his services in Persia.[29]

On 27th May 1859, John was appointed as Brigade Major at the station at Mhow.

John was presented with his Victoria Cross medal at Dacca, India, in January 1861, this was the first Victoria Cross to be awarded to a man from a Native Indian Regiment.

On 25th June 1864, John received a brevet promotion to the rank of Lieutenant-Colonel.[30]

John received a substantive promotion to the rank of Major on 12th February 1865.[31]

On 12th September 1866, John was promoted to the rank of Lieutenant-Colonel.[32]

John was appointed to the position of Commandant of the 14th Bengal Native Infantry on 15th May 1867.

On 12th February 1870, having completed the qualifying period with the rank of Lieutenant-Colonel, John was promoted to the rank of Colonel[33] and having completed over 30 years of service was retired to pension on the same day.

Following a riding accident, John died on 23rd January 1878 from a "Concussion of the brain" and was buried in St Mary's Churchyard in Poona, his headstone named him as Augustus John Wood.

After having been in private hands until 2000, John's Victoria Cross Medal in now on display at the headquarters of the 2nd Battalion of the Raputana Rifles in New Delhi, India.

28 *London Gazette* 22698/217 – on 13th January 1863, following the formation of the Bengal Staff Corp as a result of the Royal Warrant of 16th January 1861, John was confirmed with the rank of Captain with effect from 5th April 1851.

29 *London Gazette* – 22406/2722 brevet Major from 24th July 1860, however, *London Gazette* – 22419/3259 was predated to 19th January 1858.

30 *London Gazette* – 23028/4987

31 *London Gazette* – 23012/4688

32 *London Gazette* – 23225/1475

33 *London Gazette* – 23683/5419

John Grant Malcolmson
8th February 1857 (VC No. 113)

Gazetted: 3rd August 1860 22409/2860

Rank and Unit: Lieutenant – 3rd Bengal Light Cavalry

Citation

On the occasion of an attack on the enemy on the 8th of February, 1857, led by Lieutenant-Colonel Forbes, C.B., Lieutenant Moore, the Adjutant of the Regiment, was, perhaps, the first of all by a horse's length. His horse leaped into the square, and instantly fell dead, crushing down his rider, and breaking his sword as he fell amid the broken ranks of the enemy. Lieutenant Moore speedily extricated himself, and attempted with his broken sword to force his way through the press; but he would assuredly have lost his life, had not the gallant young Lieutenant Malcolmson, observing his peril, fought his way to his dismounted comrade through a crowd of enemies to his rescue, and, giving him his stirrup, safely carried him through everything out of the throng.

The thoughtfulness for others, cool determination, devoted courage, and ready activity shewn in extreme danger by this young Officer, Lieutenant Malcolmson, appear to have been most admirable, and to be worthy of the highest honour.

Biography

John was born on 9th February 1835 at Muchrach, the family seat near Inverness to father James and mother Georgina Lily Cecelia (née Battye). He was baptised on 9th March 1835 at St James's in Westminster, London where the family were living.

John had a younger sister, Barbara Stark who was baptised at Forres, Moray in Scotland on 17th September 1848.

Little is known of John's early life until the start of his army career; on 28th August 1855 John received a commission as Ensign in the East India Company army and joined his regiment the 3rd Bombay Light Cavalry.

John was part of the expeditionary force of 5,600 men being assembled at Bombay, under the command of Major General Foster Stalker, to invade Persia after a declaration of war on 1st November 1856.

The force left Bombay on the 9th November 1856 and landed at Hallilah Bay, near Bushire, Persia's principal port, on the 7th December.

On the 9th December 1856, John was involved in the storming of the fort at Reshire and also the capture of the fort at Bushire on the following day.

Figure 101. John Grant Malcolmson

John received his promotion to the rank of Lieutenant on the same day as the Battle of Reshire, 9th December 1856.[34]

After the forts at Bushire and Reshire had been captured by the British, the enemy retreated towards the mountains followed by a force under the command of General Outram, as part of this force John took part in the Battle of Kooshab on the 8th February 1857. It was during this battle that John performed the deeds for which he would later be awarded the Victoria Cross.

For his service during the war in Persia, John was awarded the India General Service Medal (1856) with clasp for Persia.

After the war in Persia, John and his regiment were involved in the Indian Mutiny and as part of the Central India Field Force took part in the siege and capture of Rathghur in January 1858 and the capture of Kalpi in May 1858.

In February 1859, John acted as Orderly Officer with Brigadier Honner's column during the persuit of Tantia Topi.

For his service in the Indian Mutiny, John was awarded the Indian Mutiny Medal with clasp for Central India.

On the 9th November 1860, John was presented with his Victoria Cross Medal by Queen Victoria in a ceremony at Home Park, Windsor Castle.

On 25th July 1861, John married Annette Elizabeth (née Grimble) at Brighton. The couple would go on to have four children; James Grant born on 4th June 1862 in Byculla, India, Elsie Violet born in 1868, Annette Mary born in 1871 and Ivor Forbes born in 1873. Elsie, Annette and Ivor were all born in Paddington, London.

John retired from the army on 27th January 1865, with the honorary rank of Captain.

On the 25th May 1870, following the nomination of the Marquis of Normanby, John was appointed as a member of the

34 *London Gazette* – 22828/1368

Royal Victorian Order and Her Majesties Honourable Corp of Gentlemen at Arms (the Queen's bodyguard).[35]

At some stage after returning to England, John became involved with his wife's family business Grimble and Co which was a Manufacturer and Vendor of vinegar, acetic acid and glucose, based in St Pancras.

John was employed in the position of managing director when the company was dissolved on 31st December 1879.

John's wife Annette died at the family home 25 Selborne Road, Hove in Brighton on 16th November 1900 at the age of 59.

John died at his home 29 Bramham Gardens on 14th August 1902 and was buried in the family vault at Kensal Green Cemetery in London.

The location of John's Victoria Cross Medal is unknown, believed to be in the hands of a private collector.

Figure 101a. Grave of John Grant Malcolmson

35 *London Gazette* – 23619/2743

Arthur Thomas Moore
8th February 1857 (VC No. 114)

Gazetted: 3rd August 1860 22409/2860

Rank and Unit: Lieutenant – 3rd Bengal Light Cavalry

Citation

On the occasion of an attack on the enemy on the 8th of February, 1857, led by Lieutenant-Colonel Forbes, C.B., Lieutenant Moore, the Adjutant of the Regiment, was, perhaps, the first of all by a horse's length. His horse leaped into the square, and instantly fell dead, crushing down his rider, and breaking his sword as he fell amid the broken ranks of the enemy. Lieutenant Moore speedily extricated himself, and attempted with his broken sword to force his way through the press; but he would assuredly have lost his life, had not the gallant young Lieutenant Malcolmson, observing his peril, fought his way to his dismounted comrade through a crowd of enemies to his rescue, and, giving him his stirrup, safely carried him through everything out of the throng.

The thoughtfulness for others, cool determination, devoted courage, and ready activity shewn in extreme danger by this young Officer, Lieutenant Malcolmson, appear to have been most admirable, and to be worthy of the highest honour.

Biography

Arthur was born at Carlingford, Co Louth in Ireland on 20th September 1830 to father Edward Francis an army officer who served with the 45th Regiment of Foot.

Figure 102. Arthur Thomas Moore

After graduating from the East India Company College at Haileybury, Arthur was commissioned as a 2nd Lieutenant in the 3rd Bengal Light Cavalry on 29th July 1850.

Arthur was promoted to the rank of Lieutenant on 28 August 1855,[36] and was appointed Adjutant on the 7 August 1857 a position that he held until 1862.

Arthur saw his first active service during the Persian War when he was part of the expeditionary force of 5,600 men being assembled at Bombay, under the command of Major General Foster Stalker, to invade Persia after the declaration of war on 1st November 1856.

The force left Bombay on the 9th November 1856 and landed at Hallilah Bay, near Bushire, Persia's principal port, on the 7th December.

On the 9th December 1856, Arthur was involved in the storming of the fort at Reshire and also the capture of the fort at Bushire on the following day.

After the forts at Bushire and Reshire had been captured by the British, the enemy retreated towards the mountains followed by a force under the command of General Outram, as part of this force Arthur participated in the march to and from Boorzgoon and in the Battle of Kooshab on the 8th February 1857. It was during this battle that Arthur performed the deeds for which he would later be awarded the Victoria Cross.

For his service during the war in Persia, Arthur was awarded the India General Service Medal (1856) with clasp for Persia.

After the war in Persia, Arthur and his regiment were involved in the Indian Mutiny serving as part of the Central India Field Force under Sir Hugh Rose.

He took part in the siege and capture of Rathghur in January 1858, action at Baroda on 30th January, relief of Sangor on 3rd February, the siege and capture of Garakota on 12th February, the forcing of the Mudenpore Pass on 4th March, the siege and capture of Jhansi in April, the capture of Kalpi on 22nd May 1858, action at Morar on 16th June, capture of Gwalior on 18th June, the Battle of Jowra-Alipur and the action at Khow-Mohoni.

Arthur was twice mentioned in despatches first for his conduct at Rathghur *"... Lt. Moore of the 3rd Bombay Light Cavalry, who, on account of the few artillerymen, served a gun with effect, deserves also to be mentioned"* Major General Sir Hugh Rose 7th February 1858.

The second mention was for action on 4th September 1858 at Khow-Mohoni for *"gallantry in the capture of the enemy's guns in difficult ground"*.

For his service in the Indian Mutiny, Arthur was awarded the Indian Mutiny Medal with clasp for Central India.

36 *London Gazette* – 22828/1368

Following the mutiny, Arthur continued to serve as Adjutant to the regiment and was briefly placed second in command when the regiment adopted the silladar system.

Arthur was presented with his Victoria Cross medal by GOC Bombay, Lieutenant General Sir W. Mansfield, in India, on the 18th October 1861.

On the 19th July 1862, Arthur received a brevet promotion to the rank of Captain.[37] which was made substantive on 24th November 1864.[38]

Arthur was married to Annie (née Prentice) on the 9th June 1864 at Caledon Church in Co Tyrone, Ireland; the couple would go on to have six children; however, only two would outlive their father.

Anne Francis was born on 2nd May 1867 but died two weeks later on 17th May, Kathleen Frances was born on 18th October 1868 but died in 1889 at the age of 21, Arthur Henry Edward was born on 6th February 1870 but died in 1891 at the age of 21, Lenard Arthur was born on 4th August 1871 but died in 1891 at the age of 20, Nora Cecil was born on 23rd July 1873 and Aileen Edith was born on 24th November 1877.

From 1865, Arthur spent much of his time on Civil rather than Regimental duties and from 29th July 1870 was the Inspector in Chief, Cotton Frauds.

Arthur was promoted to the rank of Major in the Bombay Staff Corp on 29th July 1870[39] and on 29th July 1876 was advanced to Lieutenant-Colonel.[40]

On 29th July 1881, Arthur received a brevet promotion to the rank of Colonel;[41] however, this was subsequently antedated to be effective from 1st July 1881.[42]

Arthur was appointed as an Ordinary Member 3rd Class (Companion) of the Most Honourable Order of the Bath on 21st June 1887.[43]

On 20th September 1888, Arthur was transferred to the Unemployed Supernumerary List.[44]

On the 13th June 1891, Arthur was promoted to the rank of Major-General[45] and after over 40 years of service retired from the army; on his retirement Arthur returned to Ireland and took up residence in Dublin.

In 1902, Arthur was awarded the King Edward VII Coronation Medal.

37 *London Gazette* – 22952/1751
38 *Edinburgh Gazette* – 7578/1210
39 *London Gazette* – 23705/409
40 *London Gazette* – 24396/7059
41 *London Gazette* – 25026/5087
42 *London Gazette* – 25082/1066
43 *London Gazette* – 25773/213
44 *London Gazette* – 25864/5545
45 *London Gazette* – 26178/3532

Arthur died on 25th April 1913 at his home 18 Waterloo Road in Dublin from heart failure while suffering from influenza; he was buried in Mount Jerome Cemetery, Dublin.

Arthur's Victoria Cross medal is not on public display as it is held by a private collector.

Figure 102a. Grave of Arthur Thomas Moore

Charles Augustus Goodfellow
6th October 1859 (VC No. 296)

Gazetted: 16th April 1863 22727/2071

Rank and Unit: Lieutenant – Bombay Engineers

Citation

For gallant conduct at the attack on the Fort of Beyt, on the 6th of October, 1859. On that occasion, a soldier of the 28th Regiment was shot under the walls of the Fort. Lieutenant Goodfellow rushed, under the walls, under a sharp fire of matchlocks, and. bore off the body; of the soldier, who was then dead, but whom he at first supposed to be wounded only.

Biography

Charles was born in Poona, India on 27th November 1836 to father William Barclay a Captain in the Bengal Engineers and mother Henrietta Jane. He was baptised at Poona on 19th January 1837.

Charles was educated in England and in July 1853 entered the Honourable East India Company military college at Addiscombe, on his graduation he was commissioned as a 2nd Lieutenant in the Bengal Engineers on 8th June 1855.

On leaving Addiscombe, Charles was placed under the command of Lieutenant-Colonel Sandham at the Royal Engineers College Chatham, for field instruction in the art of Sapping and Mining. For the period of his instruction, from

Figure 103. Charles Augustus Goodfellow

22nd June 1855, he was assigned the local and temporary rank of Ensign.[46]

After the completion of his instruction at Chatham, Charles moved out to India and was appointed to serve with the Bombay Sappers and Miners on 16th March 1857.

On 17th December 1857 the Central India Field Force was established under the command of General Sir Hugh Rose, Charles and a detachment from the Bengal Sappers and Miners was assigned to the 1st Brigade, commanded by Brigadier C. S. Steuart which was assembled at Mhow.

Serving with the brigade, Charles commanded a company of Sappers and Miners and was involved in the siege and capture of Rahatghur from 24th to 28th January 1858, the capture of Garakota on 12th February 1858 and the siege and capture of Jhansi from 31st March to 3rd April 1858.

For his service at Jhansi, Charles received a mention in despatches.

Charles was promoted to the rank of Lieutenant on 27th April 1858.[47]

In early 1858, the Waghers, a tribe which inhabited Okhamandal, an isolated part of Kathiawar in western Gujarat, took the opportunity of the mutiny to stage their own uprising.

After an abortive attempt to subdue the uprising in April 1858, the Okhamandal Kathiawar Field Force was raised in September 1859, under the command of Colonel Donovan.

Charles and a company of Bombay Sappers and Miners was attached to the force and set sail from Bombay on 29th September 1859 for the rebel stronghold at Fort Byet.

It was during the storming of the fort on 6th October 1859, that Charles performed the deeds for which he would later be awarded the Victoria Cross.

The fort was successfully captured and the rebel leader Deva Chhabani was killed; however a large number of rebels escaped and established themselves in another fort at Dwarka.

After a naval bombardment, Fort Dwarka was taken on 31st October and the uprising was brought to an end.

For his service during the mutiny, Charles was awarded the Indian Mutiny Medal with clasp for Central India.

Charles was presented with his Victoria Cross Medal by Major-General Green, officer commanding of the Mhow Division, at Mhow in India.

On 2nd September 1864, Charles was promoted to the rank of 2nd Captain.[48]

Charles was married to Mary Agnes (née Cahill) on 12th December 1864 at Bombay.

46 *London Gazette* – 21733/2402

47 *London Gazette* – 22621/2241

48 *London Gazette* – 22903/4905

On 1st May 1865, Charles was appointed as Engineer 2nd Class in the Public Works Department at Dharwar.

Charles was appointed as Brigade Major of Engineers assigned to the force of Sir Robert Napier which was involved in the Abyssinian Expedition.

The force left Bombay on 21st December 1867 and arrived of the coast of Africa at Annesley Bay two weeks later.

After securing their beachhead, the force began their advance into the interior on 26th January 1868 and fought the Battle of Arogi on 9th April.

The decisive battle was fought at the capital Magdala on 15th April when the rebels were routed and the city was captured. On entering the city, soldiers discovered the body of King Theodore who had committed suicide by discharging a pistol in his mouth. Ironically the pistol had been a present from Queen Victoria.

For his service during the war, Charles was awarded the Abyssinian War Medal (1868–69), he also received a mention in dispatches.

At the end of the war, Charles returned to his job as Engineer in the Public Works Department at Dharwar.

Charles received a brevet promotion to the rank of Major on 15th August 1868.[49]

On 18th December 1869, Charles was promoted to Captain,[50] later antedated to 10th November 1869.[51]

Charles was promoted to the rank of Major on 5th July 1872.[52]

On 11th July 1877, Charles received a brevet promotion to the rank of Lieutenant-Colonel.[53]

In 1878, Charles was appointed as Executive Engineer 1st Grade at Dharwar.

Charles was promoted to the rank of Lieutenant-Colonel on 31st December 1878.[54]

On 11th July 1881, Charles was promoted to the rank of Colonel.[55]

In 1884, Charles moved to Kanara and in 1885 was appointed as superintending Engineer 3rd Class of the Southern District.

Having spent over five years as a Regimental Colonel, Charles was placed on the Indian Supernumerary List on 12th August 1886.[56]

In January 1887, Charles was appointed as superintending Engineer 2nd Class in the Southern District and in 1888 was appointed as Chief Engineer 1st Class of the Southern Division.

49 *London Gazette* – 23512/4512

50 *London Gazette* – 23590/1027

51 *London Gazette* – 23598/1736

52 *London Gazette* – 23876/3195

53 *London Gazette* – 24503/5235

54 *London Gazette* – 24671/347

55 *London Gazette* – 25000/3740

56 *London Gazette* – 25630/4785

Charles was moved from the Indian Supernumerary List and promoted to the rank of Major-General on 15th March 1889.[57]

On 1st April 1892, Charles was promoted to the rank of Lieutenant-General.[58]

By 1893, Charles was back in England living at "Seacroft", Pennington, Lymington in Hampshire and later moved to Avon View, Warwick Road in Leamington Spa in Warwickshire.

Charles was placed on the unemployed supernumerary list on 27th November 1896.[59]

On 2nd February 1898, like his father before him, Charles was appointed as the Colonel Commandant of the Royal Engineers.[60]

Charles was appointed as Honorary Colonel of the 3rd Bengal Sappers and Miners on 13th May 1904.[61]

Charles died at his home in Leamington Spa on 1st September 1915 at the age of 78 and was buried in the Leamington Spa Cemetery.

Charles's Victoria Cross Medal is on public display at the Royal Engineers Museum at Chatham.

Figure 103a. Grave of Charles Augustus Goodfellow

57 *London Gazette* – 25947/3351
58 *London Gazette* – 26277/2168
59 *London Gazette* – 26806/7617
60 *London Gazette* – 26943/1272
61 *London Gazette* – 27676/3089

William Odgers
28th March 1860 (VC No. 297)

Gazetted: 3rd August 1860 22409/2861

Rank and Unit: Leading Seaman – Naval Brigade *HMS Niger*

Citation

On the 28th of March, 1860, William Odgers displayed conspicuous gallantry at the Storming of a Pah during operations against Rebel Natives in New Zealand; having been the first to enter it under a heavy fire, and having assisted in hauling down the enemy's colours.

Biography

William was born at Falmouth on the 14th February 1834 to father William, a merchant seaman and mother Martha.

Initially educated at home by his mother, William completed his education at the Quaker charity school which he attended from the age of 6 or 7.

As he grew older William found work with the Cornish fishing fleets where he developed his love for the sea.

In 1848 when William was aged 14, his mother gave birth to a baby girl but died, from complications with the birth, three months later. Following the death of his mother, relatives from the mining districts took his new sister into their care but William being employed in the fishing fleet refused their help, he was never to see his father again.

On the 23rd August 1852, William joined the Royal Navy as a boy first class and was assigned to *HMS Vulture*, a 2nd class frigate.

Figure 104. William Odgers

William was promoted to the rank of Ordinary Seaman on 1st January 1854,[62] at which time he signed on for a 10 year Continuous Service Engagement.

On the 8th April, at the start of the Crimean War, William sailed with *HMS Vulture* as part of the Baltic fleet, with a role to disrupt Russian Merchant and Naval shipping.

During the early summer of 1854, the fleet was employed against towns and shipping in the Gulf of Bothnia and on 7th June *HMS Vulcan* was involved in the incident at Halkokari in the province of Kokkola in Finland.

William was one of 200 men, from *HMS Vulture* and *HMS Odin*, who were landed in the town from small boats, with the intention of destroying shipping materials.

As they landed, the British party was ambushed by men hidden on the dockside, for the next hour a fierce fight took place during which 52 men from *HMS Vulture* were either killed, wounded or missing. William managed to survive the ambush but the boat that he was on was badly damaged.

On the 9th August 1855, *HMS Vulture* was involved in the Battle of Sveaborg, the fortress at Helsinki which was a naval bombardment. The guns of the combined French and British fleets did significant damage over the two day bombardment and caused about 2,000 casualties, although the fortress remained intact.

Fire from the fortress caused few casualties to the fleet, however, the explosion of a projectile from a rocket tube on the pinnace of *HMS Vulture* seriously wounded nine men including William and his friend Henry Searle.

For his service during the campaign, William was awarded the Baltic Medal.

After having returned to England from the Baltic campaign, William left *HMS Vulture* on 2nd June 1856 and the next day joined *HMS Niger* which had just been recommissioned at Woolwich and set sail to join the China Squadron.

Following the first Anglo-Chinese war, tensions were still high and in October 1856 a minor incident sparked off the second Anglo-Chinese War.

By the time that *HMS Niger* arrived on station with the China Squadron open warfare was taking place on the Canton river. On the 7th November, *HMS Niger*, under the command of Captain Arthur Auckland Leopold Pedro Cochrane arrived at the Canton river and was involved in operations against Chinese war junks and fire ships up until the new year.

On the 1st June 1857, *HMS Niger* was involved in the Battle of Fatshan Creek during which Captain Cochrane was wounded and on the 28th December was involved in the bombardment of Canton.

Captain Cochrane's injuries finally caused him to be invalided home on the 8th September 1858 and Captain Peter Cracroft assumed command of *HMS Niger*.

For his service in the war, William was awarded the Second China War medal with clasps for Fatshan and Canton.

In March 1859, *HMS Niger* left the China station to become part of the Australian station.

At the start of the first Maori War in New Zealand, *HMS Niger* was involved in the transportation of supplies.

On 28th March 1860, having just returned to New Plymouth with supplies from Auckland, William was part of an impromptu naval brigade of 60 men, drawn together by Captain Cracroft from his men on *HMS Niger*, which attacked a Maori stockade the Kaipopo Pa near Omata.

It was during this action that William performed the deeds for which he would later be awarded the Victoria Cross. At the time, William was offered promotion to warrant rank, but declined.

On the 12th July 1860, William was promoted to Captain's Coxswain, a role that he had been performing since *HMS Niger* had left China.

For his service during the war, William was awarded the New Zealand Medal (1860–66).

After the war, William returned to England with his ship, which was paid off at Woolwich on 13th September 1861.

On the next day William was transferred to *HMS Cambridge*, a training ship initially moored at Plymouth but later moved to Torpoint, where he trained navy ratings in the use of navy guns.

During March 1862, William was married to Ann (née May) and the couple would go on to have a son John, who was born when they lived in Saltash, in Cornwall and son George Henry who was born on 8th March 1863 at Tamar Street in Saltash.

On the 23rd July 1862, William was presented with his Victoria Cross medal at Devonport by Admiral Sir H. Stewart the commander in chief Plymouth.

On 11th March 1863, William transferred to the Coastguard Service, where his experience was once again used to train new naval recruits.

During his four years with the service, William served as a boatman at Polruan and St Mawes and as Captain's Coxswain on the guard ship *HMS St George* at Portland.

On 28th February 1865, William's wife Ann died and was buried in St Stephen's Churchyard, Saltash; the only blot on William's service occurs at around this time when he was absent without leave for a short time, presumably caring for his ailing wife.

On 6th February 1867, William rejoined the Royal Navy and was assigned as Admiral's Coxswain on board *HMS Rodney* under

62 The move from 1st Class Boy to Ordinary Seaman was normally made when the recruit reached the age of maturity i.e. 18, so perhaps the Navy thought that William was born in 1836 rather than 1834 – it was not unusual in these times for people to be unaware of their actual birth date.

the command of Captain Algernon Heneage. *HMS Rodney* was to act as the flagship for Admiral Keppel at the China station.

On the 1st January 1868, *HMS Rodney* with her accompanying flotilla became the first foreign ships to enter the port of Kode in over 200 years.

A few days later, William was on board *HMS Rodney*'s steam launch carrying Admiral Keppel and a delegation across the mouth of the river at Osaka when the launch struck a sandbar.

As a result of the incident, William was taken ill and in July 1868 was returned to Plymouth on the troopship *HMS Tamar* and was discharged from service on *HMS Rodney* on 27th July 1868.

William was discharged from the navy on 14th August 1868 being judged to be unfit for further duties and continued living in Plymouth at lodgings in Buckwell Road, with Jane who was soon to become his second wife.

In January 1869, William was married in the Plymouth Registry Office, to Jane Stoddon (née Dunsford) in what was a bigamous marriage as his wife Jane was not divorced from her husband Isaac Stoddon. The couple would go on to have two children son Philip Llewellyn born at 1 Silver Street, Saltash on 31st January 1870 and a daughter Elizabeth Jane Dunsford, born at the 'Union Inn' in Saltash on 22nd June 1872.

At some stage, probably in 1870 to 1871, William became the landlord of the Union Inn at 121 Tamar Street in Saltash.

On 20th December 1873, at the age of 39, having suffered for some time from consumption, William died and was buried in St Stephen's Churchyard, Saltash, near to the grave of his first wife.

William's Victoria Cross medal, is on public display at the Sheesh Mahal Museum, Patiala, Punjab, India, as part of the Maharaja Yadavindra Singh collection.

Figure 104a. Grave of William Odgers

John Lucas
18th March 1861 (VC No. 298)

Gazetted: 19th July 1861 22531/2962

Rank and Unit: Colour-Sergeant No. 2607 – 40th Regiment of Foot

Citation

On the 18th of March, 1861, Colour-Serjeant Lucas acted as Serjeant of a party of the 40th Regiment, employed as skirmishers to the right of No. 7, Redoubt, and close to the Huirangi Bush, facing the left of the positions occupied by the natives.

At about 4 o'clock P.M., a very heavy and well-directed fire was suddenly opened upon them from the Bush, and the high ground on the left. Three men being wounded simultaneously, two of them mortally, assistance was called for in order to have them carried to the rear: a file was immediately sent, but had scarcely arrived, when one of them fell, and Lieutenant Rees was wounded at the same time.

Colour-Serjeant Lucas, under a very heavy fire from the rebels, who were not more than thirty yards distant, immediately ran up to the assistance of this Officer, and sent one man with him to the rear. He then took charge of the arms belonging to the killed and wounded men, and maintained his position until the arrival of supports under Lieutenants Gibson and Whelan.

Figure 105. John Lucas

Biography

John was born at Clashganny in the parish of Myshall, Co Carlow, Ireland some time in 1826, he was the eldest son of father also named John.

After working for some time as a carpenter, on the 6th January 1848 John enlisted in the British army at Dublin and was enrolled as Private No. 2607 in the 40th Regiment of Foot.

John was able to join up with his regiment almost immediately as they had been posted to service in Ireland in November 1847.

On the 5th February 1850, John was promoted to the rank of Corporal.

In June 1852, the regiment was drawn together at Cork from their various postings in Ireland, in preparation for an overseas posting to the Australian Colonies.

On 15th July 1852, the regiment, under the command of Lieutenant-Colonel T. J. Valiant, boarded *HMS Vulcan* and set sail for New South Wales, arriving at Hobson's Bay, Port Philip on the 19th October.

With a suspected case of small-pox on board, *HMS Vulcan* was held in quarantine until 1st November and the regiment did nor disembark until the 4th and 5th November, when they landed in Melbourne.

In early 1853, detachments from the regiment were sent to various locations such as Toorak, Ballarat and Geelong to help police the Bendigo and Mount Alexander goldfields in the colony of Victoria. These detachments were rotated on a regular basis throughout the year.

A force of 125, specially selected men were sworn in as constables and were mounted and equipped as light cavalry for escort duties protecting convoys from the goldfields to Victoria.

John received a promotion to the rank of Sergeant on 1st April 1854.

In November 1854, in response to increased civil disturbances by the miners, the detachment at Ballarat was significantly strengthened. The miners were protesting about the increase in Licence fees which had been increased to £3 in January 1852 and the increased efforts of the authorities to clamp down on defaulters.

The problems were also exacerbated by the burning of the Eureka Hotel on 7th October 1854 during which a Scottish miner James Scobie was killed, ten days later the prime suspect, James Bentley who owned the hotel was acquitted of the crime and later in the month several miners were arrested instead.

Tensions were further increased on 28th November when reinforcements arriving from Melbourne were attacked by the miners and a drummer boy, John Egan was allegedly killed.[63]

63 Drummer Egan actually continued his military service until he died in 1860.

At the beginning of December, two miners, Peter Lalor[64] and Henry Ross, began to organise a group of miners for an armed uprising and after erecting a stockade began to arm and train about 150 men.

At 3 o'clock in the afternoon of Sunday 3rd December, Captain John W. Thomas of the 40th Regiment in command of a force of 276 soldiers and police approached the "Eureka Stockade" and a short battle ensued during which 6 soldiers and 22 miners were killed.

About 120 miners were arrested but only 13 were brought to trial charged with high treason and all were acquitted.

Unfortunately it is not known whether John was involved in the events of the "Eureka Rebellion".

On 3rd July 1858, John was promoted to the rank of Colour Sergeant.

John was part of a large detachment of 280 men sent to Hobart in Tasmania on 30th December 1858, to relieve the 12th Regiment of Foot.

John re-enlisted for a further nine years of service on 7th January 1860 at Hobart in Tasmania.

On 23rd April 1860, John was part of a detachment 130 men sent from Tasmania to join colleagues from the regiment who had been despatched to New Zealand as reinforcements for the first Taranaki War which had started on the 17th March 1860.

Under the command of Captain Bowdler, the detachment landed at New Plymouth on 30th April and marched to the camp which had been established at the mouth of the Waitara River.

Still under the command of Captain Bowdler, John was part of the forces which attacked the Puketakauere Pas on 27th June 1860 and were repulsed by the Maoris.

During September 1860, John was involved in operations to clear the Pas in the Kairau plains and further operations in the vicinity of New Plymouth, until the end of the year.

On the 14th January 1861, John was part of a force sent to construct and occupy a redoubt near Huirangi, this was 26 yards square and designed to accommodate 100 men.

On the 11th February, John moved to a much larger redoubt that was to be permanently garrisoned by the 40th Regiment of Foot and it was near this redoubt on the 18th March 1861 that John performed the deeds for which he would later be awarded the Victoria Cross.

This proved to be the last major action in the war as on the next day the Maoris raised the white flag of surrender.

On 29th April, John and the regiment boarded ship at New Plymouth and set sail for Manukau Harbour where they landed

64 Peter Lalor escaped after the battle, was never charged and in later life became Speaker of the House in the Legislative Assembly of Victoria.

on 1st May and marched to the camp at Otahuhu where they were to be stationed for some months.

In late December the regiment were part of a force under the command of General Cameron which constructed a military road from Drury to Pokeno on the Waikato River and on its completion moved to winter quarters in Auckland where they arrived on 9th June 1862.

On 15th August 1862, John was promoted to the rank of Sergeant Major.

John was presented with his Victoria Cross Medal by Lieutenant-General Sir Duncan Cameron, the officer commanding troops in New Zealand, on 2nd October 1862 in front of a parade of all the troops in the area at Ellersle Racecourse in Auckland.

John with the regiment was also involved in some of the engagements in the 2nd Maori War, the invasion of Waikato which took place between 17th July 1863 and April 1864.

For his service during the Maori Wars, John was awarded the New Zealand Medal (1860–66).

In April 1866, the regiment was relieved by detachments of the 57th Regiment and moved to Otahuhu, in preparation for their return to England.

The regiment left Auckland in two detachment on 7th May, on board the *Mary Shepherd* and on the *Holmsdale* on 15th June arriving at Portsmouth on 10th August and 10th September respectively.

After a short stay at Portsmouth, the regiment boarded *HMS Orontes* on 13th April and were transported to Devonport where after arriving on the 16th April 1867, they occupied the Raglan barracks.

Having been stationed at Devonport for less than a year, John and the regiment boarded *HMS Simoom* for transportation back to Portsmouth, from where they travelled to the camp at Aldershot where they arrived on 12th November 1867.

On the 29th September 1868, the regiment once again boarded *HMS Simoom*. this time bound for Liverpool where they disembarked on 3rd October establishing commands at Ashton-under-Lyne and Whitehaven while headquarters were established at Carlisle Castle.

At his own request, John was discharged to pension from the army at Carlisle Castle on 12th January 1869 having completed 21 years of service.

On leaving the army, John was awarded the silver Long Service and Good Conduct Medal and returned to Ireland to live and work in Dublin.

After arriving in Dublin, John was employed as a Gatekeeper for the Parkgate Street entrance to Phoenix park in Dublin and lived in the 'Lodge' Parkgate Street.

On 29th February 1892, John died at his home aged 66 from the effects of influenza and was buried on the 4th March at St James's Churchyard, James Street, Dublin.

For decades his grave was lost, allegedly obliterated and the headstone destroyed by the IRA in the 1920s. The churchyard, which is now the Pearse Lyons Distillery, underwent some restoration work in 2017, during which fragments of the gravestone were rediscovered. After repair and restoration, the headstone was erected as close as possible to its original position.

John's Victoria Cross medal is on public display at the Lancashire Infantry Museum in the Fulwood barracks in Preston, Lancashire.

Figure 105a. Grave of John Lucas

Nathaniel Godolphin Burslem
21st August 1860 (VC No. 299)

Gazetted: 13th August 1861 22538/3363

Rank and Unit: Lieutenant – 67th Regiment of Foot

Citation

For "distinguished gallantry in swimming the Ditches of the North Taku Fort, and persevering in attempting during the assault, and before the entrance of the Fort had been effected by any one, to enlarge an opening in the Wall, through which they eventually entered, and, in doing so, were both severely wounded".

Figure 106. Nathaniel Godolphin Burslem

Biography

Nathaniel was born on 2nd February 1837 at Limerick in Ireland to father George James an officer in the 94th Regiment of Foot and mother Susan (née Vokes); he had a younger brother John Godolphin, born in1842, who was baptised in the British Chapel, Boulogne-sur-Mer, Pas-de-Calais in France on 25th March 1843.

Little is known of Nathaniel's early life until at the age of 18 he enlisted in the British army and joined the Land Transport Corps on 23rd November 1855 with the rank of Cornet.[65]

On the 20th February 1857, Nathaniel was transferred to the Military Train with the rank of Ensign.[66]

Nathaniel was promoted to the rank of Lieutenant on 28th May 1858[67] but this was later antedated to 26th February 1858.[68]

On 13th July 1858, Nathaniel was transferred to the 67th Regiment of Foot by way of exchange.[69]

Soon after joining his new regiment, Nathaniel was off on his first overseas posting to Barrackpore in India, towards the end of the Indian Mutiny.

Nathaniel was only in India for a short time before his regiment was sent to China to take part in the second phase of the second China War.

During the war, Nathaniel took part in the capture of the Taku forts on 21st August 1860 where he performed the deeds for which he would later be awarded the Victoria Cross; during the action he was wounded three times.

Nathaniel was also present at the capture and occupation of Peking, on 13th October 1860 which ended the war.

65 *London Gazette* – 21818/4371
66 *London Gazette* – 2970/614
67 *London Gazette* – 22145/2638
68 *London Gazette* – 22158/3136
69 *London Gazette* – 22161/3253

For his service in the war, Nathaniel was awarded the Second China War Medal with clasps for Taku Forts (1860) and Peking (1860).

After returning to England, Nathaniel was promoted to the rank of captain and placed on the unattached list on half pay on the 20th November 1860.[70]

Nathaniel was transferred from the unattached list on half pay to the 60th Regiment of Foot as Captain on 12th March 1861.[71]

Soon after joining his new regiment, Nathaniel was on the move again on board *SS Great Eastern* bound for service in Canada.

During his service in Canada, Nathaniel was involved with his regiment in the Trent Affair, during the first year of the American Civil War during which Britain came close to war with the new United States.

Nathaniel was presented with his Victoria Cross medal by General Sir W. Williams, the General Officer Commanding the forces in Canada at a ceremony in Montreal in September 1862.

On the 4th November 1864, Nathaniel left the army by way of the sale of his commission.[72]

After leaving the army, Nathaniel set sail for a life in New Zealand with his brother John after arriving in early 1865, the brother purchased some land on the North Island with the intention of growing flax.

Unfortunately, Nathaniel's life came to an early and tragic end on 14th July 1865 at the age of 28; while canoeing on the river Thames at Auckland with a friend, the canoe capsized and both men were drowned.

70 *London Gazette* – 22449/4304
71 *London Gazette* – 22488/1155
72 *London Gazette* – 22908/5207

Nathaniel's body was never recovered so he has no place of burial.

His Victoria Cross medal is on public display at the Royal Hampshire Regimental Museum in Winchester.

Edmund Henry Lenon

21st August 1860 (VC No. 300)

Gazetted: 13th August 1861 22538/3363

Rank and Unit: Lieutenant – 67th Regiment of Foot

Citation

For distinguished gallantry in swimming the Ditches, and entering the North Taku Fort by an embrasure during the assault. They were the first of the English established on the walls of the Fort, which they entered in the order in which their names are here recorded, each one being assisted by the others to mount the embrasure. (Rogers, McDougall and Lenon)

Biography

Edmund was born on 26th August 1838 at Mortlake in Surrey to father Thomas Bunbury a civil servant and mother Frances, he was baptised a few weeks later at Mortlake on 5th October 1838.

On the 15th June 1855, at the age of 17, Edmund enlisted in the army and was commissioned as an Ensign with the 67th Regiment of Foot.[73]

Edmund advanced his position within the regiment when he purchased a commission as Lieutenant on 14th November 1856.[74]

Figure 107. Edmund Henry Lenon

73 *London Gazette* – 21729/2307

74 *London Gazette* – 21940/3694

In 1858, Edmund was off on his first overseas posting to Barrackpore in India, towards the end of the Indian Mutiny but after a short time in India his regiment was despatched to China to take part in the second phase of the second China War.

During the war, Edmund took part in the capture of the Taku forts on 21st August 1860 where he performed the deeds for which he would later be awarded the Victoria Cross; during the action he was wounded in the arm.

Edmund was also present at the capture and occupation of Peking, on 13th October 1860 which ended the war.

For his service in the war, Edmund was awarded the Second China War Medal with clasps for Taku Forts (1860) and Peking (1860).

On 8th October 1861, Edmund again advanced his position within the regiment with the purchase of a commission of Captain.[75]

Edmund was married to Mary Margaret (née Margell) on 22nd October 1861 at East Knoyle in Wiltshire.

On the 19th August 1862, Edmund was presented with his Victoria Cross medal by General Sir George Brown, the General Officer Commanding forces in Ireland, at a ceremony held in the Great Hall of the Royal Hospital at Kilmainham in Ireland.

In 1864, Edmund and his regiment were sent from Shanghai to Japan to help protect the British Legation at Yedo and in 1865 started a year's deployment to the Cape Colony in South Africa where they served as part of the garrison.

During his service in South Africa, Edmund received a brevet promotion to the rank of Major on the 19th September 1865.[76]

On the 2nd January 1869, Edmund left the army after 14 years of service following the sale of his commission.[77]

After leaving the army, Edmund became active in the military Volunteers service and on the 16th November 1871 was appointed as Lieutenant-Colonel of the 1st Administrative Battalion of the Kent Rifle Volunteers.[78]

In June 1882, Edmund was appointed to the inaugural Executive Committee of the Volunteer Service Club in London, a gentlemen's club for present and former officers of the Volunteer Service.

On the 6th June 1883, Edmund was appointed as Honorary Colonel of the 2nd Volunteer Battalion, Queen's Own (Royal West Kent Regiment).[79]

Edmund resigned his commission as Lieutenant-Colonel with the 2nd Volunteer Battalion, Queen's Own (Royal West Kent Regiment) on 15th December 1883 and was appointed as Honorary Colonel of the Battalion.[80]

On the 18th August 1886, Edmund resigned from his appointment as Honorary Colonel of the 2nd Volunteer Battalion, Queen's Own (Royal West Kent Regiment) but retained his Honorary rank of Colonel and permission to wear the uniform of the battalion.[81]

Edmund died on 15th April 1893, at the age of 54, at St Thomas's Hospital, Lambeth in London and on 20th April 1893 was buried in an unmarked plot at Kensal Green Cemetery in London.

Edmunds Victoria Cross Medal is on public display at the Royal Hampshire Regimental Museum in Winchester. Sometime during 1886, Edmund pawned his Victoria Cross and China War medals and his pawn ticket is also on display in the museum.

Figure 107a. Grave of Edmund Henry Lenon

75 *London Gazette* – 22563/4456
76 *London Gazette* – 23015/4510
77 *London Gazette* – 23455/3
78 *London Gazette* – 23799/4904
79 *London Gazette* – 25239/2931
80 *London Gazette* – 25296/6441
81 *London Gazette* – 25617/4011

Robert Montresor Rogers
21st August 1860 (VC No. 301)

Gazetted: 13th August 1861 22538/3363

Rank and Unit: Lieutenant – 44th Regiment of Foot

Citation

> *For distinguished gallantry in swimming the Ditches, and entering the North Taku Fort by an embrasure during the assault. They were the first of the English established on the walls of the Fort, which they entered in the order in which their names are here recorded, each one being assisted by the others to mount the embrasure. (Rogers, McDougall and Lenon)*

Figure 108. Robert Montresor Rodgers

Biography

Robert was born on 4th September 1834, in Dublin, Ireland where his father James was a QC.

Having completed his education in Dublin, on 21st February 1855, at the age of 21, Robert enlisted in the British army and was commissioned as an Ensign in the 44th Regiment of Foot.[82]

Robert was promoted to the rank of Lieutenant on 3rd August 1855[83] and was part of the draft of reinforcements sent via Malta which joined the regiment in the Crimea on 27th August 1855.

Robert was only involved in the final days of the siege of Sevastopol which ended on 8th September 1855 when the Russians finally abandoned Sevastopol.

Hostilities were suspended in February 1856 and a peace treaty was signed in Paris on 29th March.

On 25th June 1856, Robert and the regiment boarded *HMS Colossus* at Balaklava and set sail for England, landing at Portsmouth on the 19th July.

For his service in the Crimea, Robert was awarded the Crimean War Medal with clasp for Sevastopol, he was also awarded the Turkish Crimea Medal.

The regiment spent at few days at the new camp at Aldershot before moving to Dover, where they arrived on the 4th August and on 25th September they moved to the camp at Shorncliffe.

With the mutiny still in progress in India, on 26th and 29th August 1857, the regiment were deployed to the sub-continent. The detachment despatched on the 26th was of three companies on board a sailing vessel and this arrived at Madras on the 12th January 1858, the second detachment of the HQ and seven companies left on board the steamer *Khersonese* arrived on the 28th November 1857.

During 1858 and 1859 the regiment remained at Fort St George in Madras until on the 31st January 1860, as part of an Anglo-French force they were deployed to the war in China.

After landing at Kowloon, the regiment headed to the north of China, landing at Talienwhan Bay, near the Gulf of Pecheli, where the troops were landed and employed in digging wells.

On the 24th July, the regiment re-embarked and sailed to the mouth of the river Peiho and then on the 30th July to the Pehtang river where they disembarked on the 6th August 1860.

The regiment, as part of the 2nd Division, commanded by General Sir Robert Napier, took part in attacks against the Tartar army at Sin-Ho on the 12th August and at Tangku on the 14th August 1860.

On the 19th August the regiment moved to an encampment near to the North Taku Forts and it was on the 21st August during the attack on the North Taku forts that Robert performed the deeds for which he would later be awarded the Victoria Cross.

During the action Robert received a severe gunshot wound to his right side.[84]

For his service during the war, Robert was awarded the China War medal 1857–60 with clasp for Taku Forts 1860.

On the 20th November 1860, Robert was promoted to the rank of Captain and placed on the unattached list at half pay.[85]

Robert was transferred from the unattached list on half pay to the 90th Regiment of Foot with the rank of Captain on 12th March 1861[86] and joined his regiment stationed at Allahabad in India.

82 *London Gazette* – 21666/703
83 *London Gazette* – 21756/2952
84 *London Gazette* – 22443/4083
85 *London Gazette* – 22449/4304
86 *London Gazette* – 22488/1155

On the 22nd December 1862, Robert was presented with his Victoria Cross medal by General Sir Hugh Rose, the General Officer Commanding troops in India, at a ceremony in Calcutta.

The regiment remained at Allahabad until December 1862 at which time it was moved by rail to Agra and then on to Meerut where they arrived on 31st December.

The regiment left Meerut for Lahore on 1st December 1863 and arrived at Meean Meer on the 6th January 1864 where, as the war on the North West Frontier had come to an end, they remained for a year.

After spending most of 1865 at Peshawar, the regiment moved to Nowshera on the 11th December 1865.

On the 15th January 1867, the regiment left Nowshera and arrived at their new station, Subathoo, on the 2nd March where despite the best efforts of the Medical staff, the lives of 50 men, women and children were lost to cholera.

In 1869, the regiment left India to return to England and were stationed at Edinburgh with detachments in Dundee.

On 6th June 1871, the regiment moved to Glasgow where they were quartered in the Gallowgate Barracks, however, detachments were also maintained at Stirling Castle, Ayr and Dundee.

On the 1st April 1873, Robert was promoted to the rank of Major.[87]

Home service continued until the end of 1877, with deployments in England and Ireland but by January 1878, the regiment was at the top of the list for deployment overseas.

The regiment suddenly received orders for an urgent deployment to the Cape Colonies, in response to rising difficulties during the Kaffir Wars.

On the 10th January, the first element of the deployment, commanded by James, left Southampton on board the *SS Danube* a further detachment left Southampton on board *SS Nubian* two days later.

After taking only a minor part in the ninth Kaffir War, the regiment was immediately involved in the Zulu War which started on 11th January 1879 and following the temporary promotion of his Commanding Officer to the rank of Brigadier, Robert was given command of the regiment for the duration of the war.

Robert commanded the regiment at the Battle of Kambula on 29th March and at the decisive Battle of Ulundi on 4th July 1879.

On 20th October, the regiment, still under the command of Robert, boarded *HMS Serapis* and left the Cape Colonies bound for India where they landed at Calcutta on 10th November 1879.

For his service during the war Robert was awarded the Zulu War Medal with clasp for 1879.

87 *London Gazette* – 23962/1713

In recognition of his service during the Zulu Campaign, Robert was awarded the brevet rank of Lieutenant-Colonel on 29th November 1879.[88]

On the 13th February 1880, Robert was promoted to the rank of Colonel.[89]

Robert received his South Africa Medal in April 1881 along with the rest of the Regiment at a grand medal ceremony and Trooping the Colour at Fort William, in Calcutta – the last time the Colours of the Perthshire Light Infantry were trooped.

On 1st July, 1881, the Perthshire Volunteers were reorganised under the Childers Reforms, and redesignated the 2nd Battalion, Scottish Rifles, consequently not requiring, as a Rifle Corps, any Colours.

Robert was moved onto the half pay list on 15th December 1884 after having served five years as a regimental Lieutenant-Colonel.[90]

Upon his return from India, in January 1885, Robert brought the old Colours with him, and in March 1885 presented them to be hung in St Mary's Church, Hamilton, Perthshire, by the Memorial Window to the Men of the Regiment who had fallen in South Africa

On 2nd July 1885, Robert was moved from the Half Pay List and appointed as Lieutenant-Colonel to the command of the 24th Regimental District (the South Wales Borderers).[91]

Having been appointed to the Army Staff, Robert was once again placed on Half Pay on 27th July 1885.[92]

On the 4th October 1885, Robert was appointed to the command of a Brigade of the Bengal Army with the rank of Brigadier-General,[93] with this appointment Robert moved to India as commander of the Bundlekhand District.

Robert was appointed as an Ordinary Member 3rd Class (Companion) of the Military Division of the Most Honourable Order of the Bath on 29th May 1886.[94]

On the 18th December 1889, Queen Victoria conferred the Honorary rank of Major-General, on Robert in recognition of his service to the army[95] at the time of his retirement from the army.

Robert was granted an annuity of £60 for Distinguished or Meritorious Service, by the War Office on 16th April 1890.

Robert died at his home in 4 Orchard Villas, Maidenhead on the 5th February 1895, at the age of 61 and was buried three days later at the All Saints Church, Boyne Hill in Maidenhead.

88 *London Gazette* – 24787/6940
89 *London Gazette* – 24811/684
90 *London Gazette* – 25423/5826
91 *London Gazette* – 25480/2754
92 *London Gazette* – 25517/4648
93 *London Gazette* – 25542/6193
94 *London Gazette* – 25592/2633
95 *London Gazette* – 26002/7282

Roberts Victoria Cross medal is on public display at the Imperial War museum in London, as part of the Lord Ashcroft collection.

Figure 108a. Grave of Robert Montresor Rogers

John Worthy Chaplin
21st August 1860 (VC No. 302)

Gazetted: 13th August 1861 22538/3363

Rank and Unit: Ensign – 67th Regiment of Foot

Citation

For distinguished gallantry at the North Taku Fort. This Officer was carrying the Queen's Colour of the Regiment, and first planted the Colours on the breach made by the storming party, assisted by Private Lane, of the 67th Regiment, and subsequently on the cavalier of the Fort, which he was the first to mount. In doing this, he was severely wounded.

Biography

John was born on 23rd July 1840 at Ewhurst Park, Ramsdell near Basingstoke in Hampshire, to father William James the MP for Salisbury and mother Elizabeth (née Alson) and was baptised at Ewhurst Park on 16th September 1840.

John was the youngest of three sons; with older brothers, Eustache St Pierre born in 1836 and Percy born in 1838.

From September 1853 until 1856, John was educated at Harrow school, like his brothers before him.

On the 13th April 1858, at the age of 18, John enlisted in the army and was commissioned as an Ensign in the 67th Regiment of Foot.[96]

Figure 109. John Worthy Chaplin

96 *London Gazette* – 22127/1867 & 22132/2095 (name correction)

In 1858, soon after his enlistment, John was off on his first overseas posting to Barrackpore in India, towards the end of the Indian Mutiny but after a short time in India his regiment was despatched to China to take part in the second phase of the second China War.

During the war, John took part in the capture of the Taku forts on 21st August 1860 where he performed the deeds for which he would later be awarded the Victoria Cross; during the action he was severely wounded, suffering from shell concussion and bullet wounds to his arm and thigh.[97]

John was also present at the capture and occupation of Peking, on 13th October 1860 which ended the war.

For his service in the war, John was awarded the Second China War Medal with clasps for Taku Forts (1860) and Peking (1860).

John was promoted to the rank of Lieutenant and transferred to the 100th Regiment of Foot on 20th November 1860[98] and joined his new regiment at Gibraltar where they formed the garrison.

In the Autumn of 1863, the regiment was relocated to Malta for further garrison duties. Initially the regiment was stationed at Fort Riscasoli and the at the St Elmo Barracks, known to the soldiers as the "Hell Hole" and finally under canvas near Fort Manoel.

On the 5th April 1864, John advanced his position within the regiment when he purchased the commission of Captain.[99]

John transferred to the 8th Hussars, by way of exchange, on 5th July 1864[100] and joined his regiment in York where two months earlier they had arrived from India.

In 1866, John was deployed with his regiment to Ireland and from 1869 until 1874, he served as an additional ADC to the Lord Lieutenant of Ireland.

On 22nd August 1871, John was married to Isabel (née Thompson) at the Bishopsthorpe Parish Church in Yorkshire; Isabel was the niece of the Archbishop of York. The couple would go on to have two children; Reginald Spencer born on 21st November 1871 who like his father would have a career in the army rising to the rank of Lieutenant-Colonel and Muriel Gladys born in 1884.

In 1875, John and the regiment returned to England initially based at Aldershot until a move to Hounslow in 1877.

John was promoted to the rank of Major on 15th September 1877.[101]

In December 1878, John and the regiment were posted to India arriving at Bombay in January 1879 from where they moved to Muttra for a most unhealthy posting due to the prevalence of cholera.

On the 14th November 1879, John was promoted to the rank of Lieutenant-Colonel.[102]

In December 1879, as commanding officer of the regiment, John was despatched to Afghanistan to reinforce Lord Roberts at Kabul.

After arriving in Peshawar in January 1880, the regiment was assigned to the Khyber Line Force in March helping to protect the lines of communication.

For his service during the 2nd Anglo-Afghan war John was awarded the Afghan Medal (1878–80).

In 1881, John and the regiment returned to India and were stationed at Rawalpindi.

John was promoted to the rank of Colonel on 14th November 1883[103] and retired on half pay[104] and returned to England.

On 21st June 1887, as part of the celebrations to recognise 50 years of the reign of Queen Victoria, John was appointed as an

Figure 109a. Grave of John Worthy Chaplin

97 *London Gazette* – 22443/4084
98 *London Gazette* – 22449/4304
99 *London Gazette* – 22841/1909
100 *London Gazette* – 22871/3380
101 *London Gazette* – 24507/5414

102 *London Gazette* – 24792/7415
103 *London Gazette* – 25287/5383
104 *London Gazette* – 25287/5382

Ordinary Member, 3rd Class (Companion) of the Military Division of the Most Honourable Order of the Bath.[105]

On the 14th November 1888, John moved from half pay onto retirement pay.[106]

In 1905/05 John was a founder and first president of the Kibworth Golf Club.

John died at his home, Park House in Market Harborough on 18th August 1920 at the age of 80 and was buried two days later in Kibworth Harcourt Parish Churchyard.

His Victoria Cross medal is on public display at the Royal Hampshire Regimental Museum in Winchester.

105 *London Gazette* – 25773/214 & 25712/3362

106 *London Gazette* – 25872/6009

Thomas Lane
21st August 1860 (VC No. 303)

Gazetted: 13th August 1861 22538/3363

Rank and Unit: Private No. 612 – 67th Regiment of Foot

Citation

For "distinguished gallantry in swimming the Ditches of the North Taku Fort, and persevering in attempting during the assault, and before the entrance of the Fort had been effected by any one, to enlarge an opening in the Wall, through which they eventually entered, and, in doing so, were both severely wounded".

Biography

Thomas was born in the city of Cork, Ireland in May 1836.

Like many of his contemporaries, Thomas joined the British army to escape the devastation of the potato famine and enlisted as private with the 47th Regiment of Foot, probably sometime in 1853.

Soon after his enlistment Thomas, with his regiment, was part of the Anglo-French expeditionary force that landed on the Crimean peninsula on 14th September 1853.

During the Crimean War, Thomas took part in the Battle of Alma on 30th September, the Battle of Inkerman on 5th November and the siege of Sevastopol up until the 8th September 1855 when the Russians evacuated the city. During his time in the Crimea, Thomas spent some time in the hospital at Scutari, where Florence Nightingale was a nurse.

Figure 110. Thomas Lane

For his service during the war, Thomas was awarded the Crimean War medal with clasps for Alma, Inkerman and Sevastopol; he was also awarded the Turkish Crimea medal.

Thomas remained in the Crimea until May 1856 when the regiment was posted to Malta and after spending a short time as the garrison at Gibraltar returned to England during 1857.

Soon after his return to England, Thomas was transferred to the 67th Regiment of foot and in 1858 was posted to Barrackpore in India, towards the end of the Indian Mutiny but after a short time in India his regiment was despatched to China to take part in the second phase of the second China War.

During the war, Thomas took part in the capture of the Taku forts on 21st August 1860 where he performed the deeds for which he would later be awarded the Victoria Cross.

Thomas was also present at the capture and occupation of Peking, on 13th October 1860 which ended the war.

For his service in the war, Thomas was awarded the Second China War Medal with clasps for Taku Forts (1860) and Peking (1860).

Thomas was presented with his Victoria Cross medal by Brigadier C. W. D. Staveley on 28th November 1862 while the regiment was stationed at Shanghai.

In 1864, Thomas and his regiment were sent from Shanghai to Japan to help protect the British Legation at Yedo and in 1865 started a year's deployment to the Cape Colony in South Africa where they served as part of the garrison until 1866, when they returned to Ireland.

At some stage prior to 1870, Thomas was discharged from the army; on 1st January 1870, he appeared as a witness for the defence in the trial of Timothy Sexton at the Cork Assizes who was charged with riot and an assault on the police and was described as a discharged soldier. Timothy Sexton was acquitted of the charges due to Thomas's evidence.

Thomas claims to have taken part in the Maori Wars in New Zealand, however, no evidence exists to support this claim. The records do show that for a time his Victoria Cross pension was paid via. the British Consulate in Boston in the USA and also in Auckland in New Zealand during the 1870s.

At some stage Thomas moved back to South Africa where he enlisted with Commander George Hamilton-Browne's 3rd Natal Native Contingent, serving as a Sergeant.

Thomas was involved in the Battle of Isandhlwana on 22nd January 1879, where the British were soundly defeated by the Zulu Impis.

Due to their poor performance in the battle, the 3rd Natal Native Contingent was disbanded a few days later at Rorke's Drift and the Officers and NCOs were formed into three troops of the Natal Horse; Thomas was a Sergeant in No. 2 Troop under the command of Captain J. W. Cooke.

In 1881, Thomas enlisted with the Landrey Light Horse and fought in the Basutoland Rebellion (Gun Wars).

On the 7th April 1881, while serving with the Landrey Light Horse, Thomas deserted his post at Ladybrand and took off with his horse, arms and equipment.

Thomas was caught by the authorities and tried by court martial for theft and desertion and on 27th July 1881 was convicted and sentenced to four months with hard labour for his crime.

Under the terms of clause 15 of the originating warrant, Thomas was removed from the roll of VC recipients for his "repeated acts of desertion and theft". His VC Pension was also cancelled as of 30th September 1881, one of only eight men to have suffered this dishonour.

Thomas was also in trouble with the civil authorities, serving time in the jail at Pretoria for tearing down the Transvaal flag, however, he soon recovered from this punishment as he later replaced a Boer, van Veen in the Staatsartillerie, a reserve unit of the South African army.

For a time, Thomas was employed as a warder at the Pretoria Jail and his wife was the matron, however, after he accused the chief warder of having designs on his wife he left this position.

For the last years of his life, Thomas served with the Cape Police at Kimberley until 13th April 1889 at the age of 52, he

Figure 110a. Grave of Thomas Lane

died in the Carnarvon Hospital in Kimberly from inflammation of the lungs.

On the following day, Thomas was buried in the Gladstone Cemetery, Kimberly; a new headstone was erected over his grave in 1991.

Following the forfeiture of his Victoria Cross, Thomas was supposed to return the medal to the War Office but there is no record that this occurred.

Thomas made an appeal to have his VC pension reinstated, but this also does not appear to have occurred, however, in February 1883 an order was received that Thomas's VC medal should be restored and in 1884 Captain J. Tennant of Landry's Horse wrote that he had forwarded a medal to Thomas. Mr Jones, later wrote to Captain Tennant, informing him that the medal was in his possession while he was attempting to track down Thomas.

Three Victoria Cross medals, supposedly belonging to Thomas have cropped up over the years, however, the two "authorised" medals are on public display at the Royal Hampshire Regimental Museum in Winchester.

John Leishman McDougall
21st August 1860 (VC No. 304)

Gazetted: 13th August 1861 22538/3363

Rank and Unit: Private No. 220 – 44th Regiment of Foot

Citation

For distinguished gallantry in swimming the Ditches, and entering the North Taku Fort by an embrasure during the assault. They were the first of the English established on the walls of the Fort, which they entered in the order in which their names are here recorded, each one being assisted by the others to mount the embrasure. (Rogers, McDougall and Lenon)

Biography

John was born in Edinburgh, Scotland during 1840 to father Robert and mother Mary (née Murdock), unfortunately very little is known of his life story.

It is likely that John enlisted in the army with the 44th Regiment of Foot, prior to August 1857 when the regiment was despatched to India, towards the end of the mutiny.

After arriving at Madras in late 1857 and early 1858, the regiment remained at Fort St George in Madras until on the 31st January 1860, when as part of an Anglo-French force they were deployed to the war in China.

After landing at Kowloon, the regiment headed to the north of China, landing at Talienwhan Bay, near the Gulf of Pecheli, where the troops were landed and employed in digging wells.

Figure 111. John Leishman McDougall

On the 24th July, the regiment re-embarked and sailed to the mouth of the river Peiho and then on the 30th July to the Pehtang river where they disembarked on the 6th August 1860.

The regiment, as part of the 2nd Division, commanded by General Sir Robert Napier, took part in attacks against the Tartar army at Sin-Ho on the 12th August and at Tangku on the 14th August 1860.

On the 19th August the regiment moved to an encampment near to the North Taku Forts and it was on the 21st August during the attack on the North Taku forts that John performed the deeds for which he would later be awarded the Victoria Cross.

For his service during the war, John was awarded the China War medal 1857–60 with clasp for Taku Forts 1860.

After the war, the regiment continued to serve in China, stationed at Shanghai, where they suffered great ill health due to the poor accommodation and climate.

On 15th November 1860, the regiment set sail for Hong Kong where they landed on the 27th November where they remained until September 1861 when they were ordered back to India.

After having been relieved by the 99th Regiment, the 44th set sail from Canton and after arriving at Bombay during December 1861, moved to Belgaum on the Malabar coast where they relieved the 83rd who were under orders to return to England.

In January 1862, the women and children of the regiment arrived from Madras, having been separated from their men for over four years.

On the 2nd October 1862, John was presented with his Victoria Cross medal by General Frank Adams, General Officer Commanding, at a garrison parade in Belgaum.

Figure III a. Grave of John Leishman McDougall

In November and December 1865, the regiment boarded the transports *Tweed* and *Dilawar* for the return to England. On the 15th March 1866, a fire broke out on board the *Dilawar*, in the spirit store which was only put out with much difficulty.

After landing in England at the end of March, the regiment moved to Dover where they formed the garrison until 8th March 1867 when they were moved to Aldershot and in January 1868 were deployed to Ireland.

John died in Edinburgh on 10th March 1869, at the age of 30 and was buried in an unmarked grave in the Old Calton Cemetery at Waterloo Place in Edinburgh.

In 1960, John's Victoria Cross medal was stolen from his relatives home in Scotland and has never been recovered. The thieves left behind the ribbon and suspension bar which are now on public display at the Essex Regimental Museum in Chelmsford, Essex.

Andrew Fitzgibbon
21st August 1860 (VC No. 305)

Gazetted: 13th August 1861 22538/3363

Rank and Unit: Hospital Apprentice – Indian Medical Establishment

Citation

For having behaved with great coolness and courage at the capture of the North Taku Fort, on the 21st of August, 1860. On the morning of that day he accompanied a wing of the 67th Regiment, when it took up a position within 500 yards of the Fort. Having quitted cover, he proceeded, under a very heavy fire, to attend to a Dhoolie-bearer, whose wound he had been directed to bind up; and, while the Regiment was advancing under the Enemy's fire, he ran across the open to attend to another wounded man, in doing which he was himself severely wounded.

Biography

Andrew was born at Petoragurh, Gujarat in India on 13th May 1845 to father William a Quartermaster-Sergeant in the Kumaon Battalion and Elizabeth (née Fitzgibbon – his cousin) and was baptised at Almorah on the 21st July 1845.

After having passed the appropriate examinations, Andrew was admitted as a Hospital Apprentice on the 5th July 1859 in the Bengal Subordinate Medical Department at Barrackpore.

The 67th Regiment of Foot arrived in Barrackpore on the 14th December 1858 but after less than a year at the station were despatched to China, Andrew departed with them, attached to the regiment as a medical orderly.

After spending the winter in Canton, the regiment occupied the island of Chusan and then on 30th July landed at Peh-Tang. On the 12th August, after all the stores were landed, the regiment occupied the village of Sin-Ho, the plan being to attack the Taku forts from the rear.

It was during the attack on the Taku north fort on 21st August 1860, that Andrew performed the deeds for which he would later be awarded the Victoria Cross.

At the time of the deed, Andrew was only 15 years and 100 days old, making him the youngest person (together with Thomas Flynn who was awarded the Victoria Cross on 28th November 1857 for deeds at Cawnpore during the Indian Mutiny – Thomas Flynn's exact birthday is unknown but it is generally accepted that he is joint youngest recipient of the Victoria Cross at 15 years three months old) to receive the award of the Victoria Cross.

During the deed, Andrew was himself severely wounded by a bullet to the elbow.

For his service in China, Andrew was awarded the China Medal (1857–60) with clasp for Taku Forts.

After returning to India in 1862, Andrew served in the Depot Hospital at Raneegunge and in 1863 saw service with B Battery of the 5th Royal Horse Artillery.

Andrew had further postings to Peshawar in 1864 and with the 20th Hussars in 1866.

On 2nd January 1867, Andrew was promoted to Assistant Apothecary 2nd Class.

Andrew was married to Mary Amelia (née Coleman) at St John's Church in Peshawar on 3rd May 1869; the couple would go on to have two children.

From 1870 until 1872 Andrew served at the Civil Dispensary in Mussoorie.

On the 2nd January 1872, having completed five years service as an Assistant Apothecary 2nd Class, Andrew was promoted to Assistant Apothecary 1st Class.

Andrew was promoted to the rank of Apothecary 1st Class on the 15th January 1877 and also appointed as an Uncovenanted & Subordinate Medical Officer.

As was quite common, Andrew also held the post of Civil Surgeon and was performing this role while serving at the Rest Hospital in Jumrood.

It was while serving at the Kotal Field Hospital at Lundi that Andrew's conduct began to deteriorate and on the 12th September 1879, the Adjutant General wrote that while Andrew had not been found to be drunk on duty, he was found to have drunk sufficient to make him unfit for his duties.

The letter was accompanied by statements from Surgeon Major J. Wallace and Dr L. H. Ker Innes, both of which stated that Andrew was *"addicted to intemperate habits"* and that it was unsafe to employ a medical subordinate of *"notoriously intemperate habits, on hospital duties where the lives of so many sick British soldiers are concerned"*.

Andrew seemed unwilling or unable to change his habits, in spite of being given the opportunity to do so and in light of this it was recommended that he be removed from military duties and he was dismissed from the service with effect from the 30th January 1880.

Although Andrew's length of service did not warrant a pension, a letter was written by the Finance Department on 26th February 1880, to the Secretary of State for India, requesting a Special Compassionate Allowance of 25 rupees per month in view of his gallant service; this was granted on 29th April 1880.

On the 7th March 1883, Andrew died from heat apoplexy (heat stroke) at Delhi and was buried later the same day in an unmarked grave in the Old Delhi Military Cemetery.

The whereabouts of Andrew's Victoria Cross and other medals is unknown, some believe that they were buried with him.

George Hinckley
9th October 1862 (VC No. 306)

Gazetted: 6th February 1863 22705/642

Rank and Unit: Able Seaman *HMS Sphinx* – Royal Navy – Naval Brigade

Citation

For volunteering, while under the East Gate of the city of Fung-wha, to carry to a joss house, a hundred and fifty yards distant, under a heavy and continuous fire of musketry, gingalls and stink-pots, Mr. Coker, Master's Assistant of the "Sphinx," who had been wounded in the advance to the gate; in which object Hinckley succeeded.

On his return to the gate, under a similar fire, he again volunteered, and succeeded in carrying to the joss-house Mr. Bremen, an officer of Ward's force, who had been also wounded in the advance on the gate; and he again returned to his post under the gate.

Biography

George was born on 22nd June 1819 at Liverpool in Lancashire, his father Joseph was a butcher.

Little is known of George's early life apart from the fact that shortly after his birth the family moved to Plymouth.

At some stage, George joined the Royal Navy, his first ship noted is *HMS Tortoise* a store ship at Chatham, however, as this employment was from 22nd February 1842 when he was 22 years old, it is likely that he joined the Navy at an earlier date.

From the 6th December 1844 until November 1846, *HMS Tortoise* was a store ship at the Ascension Islands, under the command of Commander Arthur Fleming Morrell.

There now appears to be a gap in George's service as he is next shown as serving on board *HMS Sphinx* from May 1860. *HMS Sphinx* was recommissioned on the 20th September 1859 and soon afterwards served on the China station under the command of Commander George Fiott Day VC until 1st January 1862, when command passed to Commander Theodore Morton Jones.

During his service with *HMS Sphinx*, George saw service in the Second China War and was involved in operations in the Gulf of Pecheli.

For his service in the war, George was awarded the Second China War medal.

After the war, George continued to serve with *HMS Sphinx* on the China Station and as part of the Naval Brigade took part in limited British operations in the Taiping Rebellion, where on

Figure 113. George Hinckley

the 9th October 1860 at Fung-wha he performed the deeds for which he would later be awarded the Victoria Cross.

In January 1862, George was promoted to Seaman 2nd Class but soon afterwards spent 28 days in prison at Hong Kong.

It would seem that George left *HMS Sphinx* at this point and was returned to England, where his next service was with *HMS Indus*, a guard ship of the steam reserve based at Devonport, commanded by Captain Astley Cooper Key, which served as the flagship of the Admiral Superintendant of the Devonport Dockyard Rear Admiral Thomas Sabine Pasley and then from 3rd July 1863 Rear-Admiral Thomas Matthew Charles Symons.

In January 1863, George was promoted to the rank of Leading Seaman and in July 1863 was promoted to Quartermaster and transferred to *HMS Royalist* on 5th November 1863, when the ship was commissioned at Devonport.

George was presented with his Victoria Cross medal by the Commander-in Chief at Plymouth, Admiral Sir Houston Stewart on 7th July 1863, at a ceremony at Mount Wise, Devonport.

George served on *HMS Royalist* on the North America and West Indies station, under the command of Commander Edwin John Pollard until the 8th July 1865 when he transferred to *HMS Canopus* on harbour service at Devonport.

George was married to Jane (née Oliver) on the 9th July 1865 at the parish church in Stoke Damerel in Plymouth; the couple would go on to have two children, Rosina Fanny Oliver born on 29th October 1867 and George Richard born on 18th February 1869, both children were baptised on 27th April 1876 at Devonport. The couple initially lived at Elm Cottage, Dittisham in Dartmouth.

From 1866 until 1867, George served on board *HMS Britannia*, a cadet training ship based in Dartmouth, commanded by Captain George Granville Randolph.

On the 25th October 1867, George served for a short time on *HMS Indus*, a stationary ship on Home Station at Dartmouth and soon afterwards retired from the Royal Navy after over 25 years of service.

On retiring from the Navy, George lived with his family at 5 Hood Street, Maurice Town in Dartmouth until 1877 when he moved to 15 Ross Street in Plymouth.

George also lived at 37 William Street in Plymouth but was living at 44 North Street, Plymouth when he died on 31st December 1904 at the age of 85 and was buried in Stonehouse and Devonport Cemetery on Ford Park Road in Plymouth.

The location of George's Victoria Cross medal is an interesting and complex story as there are several medals to consider.

In November 1863, George reported that he had lost his medal while attending a funeral in Plymouth, and on 23rd November 1863, the War Office informed the Admiralty, that subject to their approval a replacement would be provided.

Subsequently an official replacement was provided to George by the War Office, supplied as usual by Hancock's but George was required to pay £1 and four shillings for the replacement, £1 for the medal, 3 shillings for the engraving and 1 shilling for postage.

The controversy started even before George's death when in December 1900, Mr Samuel Mitchell was charged of receiving goods by false pretences, at Southwich Police Court when on 7th November 1900 he had obtained a gold watch and chain to the value of £5 12s 6d from Mr John Adams, while posing as Mr George Hinckley and leaving his Victoria Cross Medal as a deposit, the medal proved to be a fake.

George's Victoria Cross first surfaced when it was sold at auction on the 1st January 1925 for £43, and again on 19th July 1962 when it was bought by the respected medal dealer Baldwin's, who purchased the VC at a Glendining's auction for £440. The VC was engraved "GEORGE HINCKLEY, ABLE SEAMAN, 9TH, OCTR, 1862".

Almost immediately after the sale of Hinckley's VC at the Glendining auction of 19th July 1962, the Royal Naval Barracks in Portsmouth claimed that they held the original replacement Victoria Cross, which had been hanging in the Barrack Wardroom for at least forty years. The VC was engraved "G. HINCKLEY, OCT. 9TH. 1862" and was hung from a blue ribbon.

A director of Glendining's stated "we are satisfied that the medal we sold was genuine after being examined by Hancock's who gave it a clean bill of health". Glendining's suggested to the RN Barracks that they also submit their VC to Hancock's for verification, which they did, and after examination it was declared an "excellent copy", but was not genuine.

Following the 19th July sale, and to make matters even more confusing, a third Victoria Cross was taken into Glendining's office by an anonymous person claiming it was the original Hinckley VC.

After examination it was dismissed by Glendining's and Hancock's as a copy. This VC was engraved "GEO. HINCKLEY A.B., OCTOBER, 9TH, 1962.

The Glendining's Victoria Cross was next seen at a Sotheby's auction, held on the 10th November 1988, where it was described in the sale catalogue as "The official replacement 'Second China War' Victoria Cross", engraved as above to, "GEORGE HINCKLEY, ABLE SEAMAN, 9TH, OCTR, 1862". The Cross was sold to an anonymous buyer for £3,630.

It is known that a fourth George Hinckley Victoria Cross, which is in private hands, was acquired from an unknown source in 1991, the buyer believing it to be the replacement VC issued to Hinckley in November 1863.

The engraving on this particular VC, "AB GEO HINCKLEY, 9TH, OCT, 1862", is what might be expected of a Hancock's produced Cross. However, the provenance of this VC has not yet been proven.

Figure 113a: Grave of George Hinckley

George Vincent Fosbery

30th October 1863 (VC No. 307)

Gazetted: 7th July 1865 22988/3425

Rank and Unit: Lieutenant – 4th Bengal European Regiment

Citation

For the daring and gallant manner in which, on the 30th of October, 1863, acting as a Volunteer at the time, he led a party of his Regiment to re-capture the Crag Picquet, after its Garrison had been driven in by the Enemy, on which occasion sixty of them were killed in desperate hand to hand fighting.

From the nature of the approach to the top of the Crag amongst the large rocks, one or two men only could advance at one time; and "whilst I ascended one path," relates Lieutenant-Colonel Keyes C.B., commanding the 1st Punjab Infantry, "I directed Lieutenant Fosbery, of the late 4th European Regiment, to push up another at the head of a few men. He led this party with the greatest coolness and intrepidity, and was the first man to gain the top of the Crag on his side of the attack."

Subsequently, Lieutenant-Colonel Keyes being wounded, Lieutenant Fosbery assembled a party with which he pursued the routed enemy in the direction of the Lalloo ridge, inflicting on them further loss and confirming possession of the post.

Biography

George was born on 25th February 1832 at Stert, near Devises in Wiltshire to father Rev. Thomas Vincent and mother Emily Sarah (née Gooch), he was the eldest of seven sons and also had four sisters. George's brothers were William Thomas Exham, Henry Thomas, Leonard Arthur, Charles and Edward Henry, his sisters were Emily, Gertrude, Georgiana and Mary.

From 1846 until 1850, George was educated at Eaton and then studied at a military academy until the 20th January 1852 when he was commissioned as a Cornet in the East India Company Bengal Army and was initially placed on the unattached list.

On the 17th November 1852, soon after arriving in India, George was assigned to the 48th Regiment of Bengal Infantry.

George was transferred to the 3rd Regiment of Bengal Infantry on the 18th July 1856.

Soon after his regiment mutinied at Phillour on 26th May 1857, George was promoted to the rank of Lieutenant on 1st July 1857[107] and left on home leave.

107 *London Gazette* – 22828/1353

Figure 114. George Vincent Fosbery

On the 12th October 1858, George was married to Emmeline Georgiana (née Hall), the daughter of a Royal Navy Captain, at Wigmore in Herefordshire.

The couple would go on to have 10 children, many of whom emigrated to Canada. Percy George Wolfe Vincent was the oldest son baptised on 13th September 1859,Cecilia Mary was born on 15th October 1861 in Calcutta, Beatrice Caroline was born on 14th December 1862 in Calcutta, Maude Amelia was born on 13th January 1864 in Calcutta and Alice Emma was baptised at Reading on 29th July 1868.

Although George was absent, on home leave, in 1858 he was placed on the roster of the 4th Bengal European Regiment, along with the other officers from the mutinous 3rd Regiment of Bengal Infantry. The regiment was disbanded in 1861, but the roll was kept active until all of the officers had been reassigned.

On his return to India in 1861, George, while still on the roster of the 4th Bengal European Regiment was attached to the 104th Regiment of Foot (Bengal Fusiliers) and took part in the Umbeyla Campaign from October 1863.

It was while leading a detachment of men from the 71st and 101st Regiments on the assault on Craig Piquet on 30th October 1863, that George performed the deeds for which he would later be awarded the Victoria Cross. This unit used exploding bullets invented by George that were used for range finding to assist the artillery.

For his service during the campaign, George was awarded the India General Service medal with clasp for Umbeyla.

On the 20th January 1864, George received a brevet promotion to the rank of Captain and for a period of time until 1865 was adjutant to the Calcutta Volunteer Corps.

George was promoted to the rank of Captain on 12th September 1866[108] and a few days later on the 18th September he received a brevet promotion to the rank of Major[109] and soon afterwards went on home leave back to England.

During his time back in England, George spent his time working on his inventions and progressing several patents, most of which were to do with improvements to firearms and ammunition.

In 1870, after his return to duty in India, George was appointed to the 5th Bengal Native Light Infantry and on the 20th January 1872, after being promoted to the rank of Major[110] was appointed to the Bengal Army Staff Corps.

On the 14th April 1873, George was appointed as Wing Officer of the 35th Regiment of Bengal Native Infantry and on 20th February 1876 after receiving a brevet promotion to Lieutenant-Colonel was appointed to 2nd in command of the regiment.

George was promoted to the rank of Lieutenant-Colonel on the 20th January 1878[111] and a few months later on the 25th August 1878, after over 26 years of service he retired from the army[112] and returned to England.

Following his retirement from the army, George continued to pursue his interests in arms and ammunition and in addition to his inventions was a strong advocate for the modernisation of weapons used by the British army, being the first to encourage the adoption of machine guns.

Georges various patents and inventions now began to bear fruit and in 1885, Holland and Holland put into production a revolver based on his designs.

In 1890, Holland and Holland also started production of the "Paradox" gun designed by George. This was a hybrid shotgun, capable of firing standard buckshot the gun was also capable of firing a single ball round with some accuracy as the last six inches of the barrel was rifled. This gun was mainly used by big game hunters in Africa and India.

In 1895, George's design for a self cocking automatic revolver, was adopted by Webley and Scott and went into production in 1901 as the Webley-Fosbery pistol; during the First World War it was issued to airmen in the Royal Navy Air Service as their service revolver.

On the 25th June 1898, George was granted his own Armorial Bearings, independent of those previously used by his family and adopted the motto "Non Nobis Solum", not for ourselves alone.

108 *London Gazette* – 23266/3478
109 *London Gazette* – 23248/2641
110 *London Gazette* – 23889/3777
111 *London Gazette* – 24564/2069
112 *London Gazette* – 24625/5175

George died at his home, 38 Brock Street in Bath on 8th May 1907 at the age of 75 and was buried at St Mary's Cemetery on Horseshoe Road in Bath on 11th May 1907.

George's Victoria Cross medal is on public display at the Imperial War Museum, as part of the Lord Ashcroft collection.

Figure 114a. Grave of George Vincent Fosbery

Henry William Pitcher
30th October 1863 (VC No. 308)

Gazetted: 13th August 1861 22538/3363

Rank and Unit: Lieutenant – 1st Punjab Infantry Regiment

Citation

For the daring and gallant manner in which, in the course of the recent operations against the Frontier Tribes, on the 30th October, 1863, he led a party of his Regiment to re-capture the Crag Picket, after its garrison had been driven in by the enemy; on which occasion sixty of them were killed in desperate hand to hand fighting. From the nature of the approach to the top of the Crag amongst the large rocks, one or two men only could advance at one time; and "while I ascended one path," relates Major Keyes, commanding the 1st Punjab Infantry, "I directed Lieutenant Fosbery, of the late 4th " European Regiment, to push up another, at the head of a few men. He led this party with the greatest coolness and intrepidity, and was the first man to gain the top of the Crag, on his side of the attack. Lieutenant Pitcher, equally cool and daring, led a party of men up to the last rock, until he was knocked down and stunned by a large stone thrown from above, within a few yards of him.

Lieutenant Pitcher also displayed great gallantry in leading on a party of his Regiment to endeavour to recover the Crag Picket, when it again fell into the enemy's hands, on the 13th of November, as related in the following extract from Major Keyes's report of the 16th of that month; "The duty of leading the first charge devolved upon Lieutenant Pitcher, and I beg to bring to the special notice of the Brigadier-General Commanding, the admirable manner in which he performed this important duty, he was by many yards the foremost of his party, and the gallant bearing of this excellent young Officer was the admiration of all spectators. It is impossible to say too much, or to overrate his services on this occasion. Lieutenant Pitcher was severely wounded, and was obliged to be carried back."

Biography

Henry was born at Kamptee, Magpore, Madras on 20th December 1840, the second son of father Vincent an officer serving with the 6th Madras Light Cavalry and mother Rose Mary (née Le Geyt) the daughter of Vice Admiral George Le Geyt.

From 1848 until 8th August 1856, Henry was educated at Christ's Hospital School in Horsham.

Figure 115. Henry William Pitcher

Henry's older brother Duncan George also served in the army in India and rose to the rank of Colonel.

Henry was commissioned as an Ensign in the British army on the 26th July 1857 and joined his regiment, the 79th Highlanders in India, in time to take part in the efforts to subdue the mutiny.

During the mutiny, Henry served with his regiment throughout the Oudh Campaign and was involved in the taking of the Secundra Bagh, the siege and capture of Lucknow, the Battle of Rooya, the Battle of Allygunge, the capture of Bareilly, operations at Shahjehanpore, the capture of Rampore Kussia, the passage of the Gogra and operations on the Nepal frontier.

For his service during the mutiny, Henry was awarded the Indian Mutiny Medal with clasp for Lucknow.

On the 18th May 1858, Henry was promoted to the rank of Lieutenant with the 13th Punjab Native Infantry.[113]

Henry was transferred to the 1st Punjab Native Infantry on 15th March 1859 but was seconded as Acting Adjutant to the 3rd Punjab Native Infantry to serve in the expedition, led by Brigadier Chamberlain, against the Kabul Kheyl Wazirs in December 1859 to January 1860.

In February 1860, Henry was transferred on secondment to the 4th Punjab Native Infantry as Acting Adjutant and took part in the expedition against the Mahsood Waziris from April to May 1860.

For his service in these expeditions Henry was awarded the India General Service Medal with clasp for North West Frontier.

After his two secondments, Henry returned to his regiment the 1st Punjab Native Infantry and on 31st May 1861 was appointed as Adjutant to the regiment.

Henry was serving as Adjutant when the regiment took part in the Umbeyla Campaign in October 1863 and it was on the 30th November 1863, during the attack on Craig Piquet that he performed the deeds for which he would later be awarded the Victoria Cross, he was severely wounded during the action and was wounded for a second time on the 3rd November 1863.

For his service during the campaign, Henry was awarded the clasp for Umbeyla to add to his India General Service medal.

On the 30th January 1866, Henry was married to Emilie Selvia Augusta (née Chapman) at Bathwick Church in Bath.

While stationed at Kohat, as part of the garrison, Henry led the 1st Punjab Native Infantry as part of a force commanded by Colonel Charles Keyes in an attack against rebels in the Bizotee village of Gara, on 25th February 1869, who had been conducting operations against the British in the Kohat Pass.

On 26th July 1869, Henry was promoted to the rank of Captain[114] and was appointed as second in command of a wing of the regiment.

From April to December 1870, Henry was acting Commandant of the 1st Punjab Native Infantry and in February 1875 he was appointed as Officiating Commandant.

Henry was serving with the regiment when he died from sunstroke at Dehra Ghazi Khan on 5th July 1875 at the age of 34.

Henry was buried in the Dehra Ghazi Khan cemetery but due to flooding was later reinterred in the Dehra Ismail Khan Cemetery, the garrison cemetery at Kohat.

Henry's Victoria Cross medal is on public display at the Museum in Jersey.

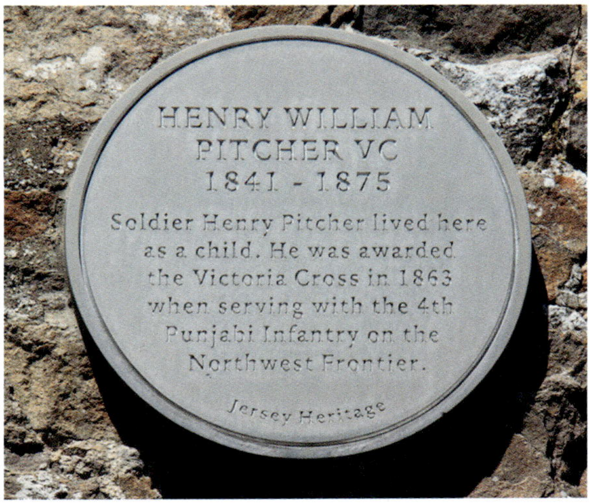

Figure 115a. Memorial Plaque to Henry William Pitcher

113 *London Gazette* – 22686/6161

114 *London Gazette* – 23582/595

Edward McKenna
7th September 1863 (VC No. 309)

Gazetted: 19th January 1864 22809/261

Rank and Unit: Colour-Sergeant No. 2194 – 65th Regiment of Foot

Citation

For gallant conduct at the engagement near Cameron-town, New Zealand, on the 7th of September, 1863, after both his officers, Captain Swift and Lieutenant Butler, had been shot, in charging through the position of an enemy heavily outnumbering him, and drawing off his small force, consisting of two Serjeants, one bugler, and thirty-five men, through a broken and rugged country, with the loss of but one man killed, and another missing. Lieutenant-General Cameron, C.B., Commanding Her Majesty's Forces in that colony, reports that, in Colour-Serjeant MacKenna, the detachment found a Commander whose coolness, intrepidity, and judgment, justified the confidence placed in him by the soldiers brought so suddenly under his command.

Figure 116. Edward McKenna

Biography

Edward was born at Leeds in Yorkshire on the 15th February 1827 and on the 12th January 1845, a month shy of his 18th birthday, he left his job as a wireworker and enlisted in the army at Leeds where he joined the 65th Regiment of Foot as Private No. 2194.

Just over a year after his enlistment, on the 18th May 1846, Edward left Woolwich on board the *Java*, bound for Hobart Town in Van Diemen's Land (Tasmania). Due to an outbreak of measles amongst the children at the Chatham depot, only un-married officers and soldiers were allowed to embark on the *Java*.

The *Java* was one of 10 ships used, between August 1845 and May 1846, to transport the regiment to Australia and then onward to New Zealand. On six of the ships the men of the regiment acted as guards for the convicts being transported to Hobart and Norfolk Island.

The *Java* arrived at Hobart Town on 5th October 1846, and 15 Officers and 624 NCOs and men of the 65th Regiment were disembarked (1 Sergeant and 6 Privates had died on the voyage).

Three days later the officers and men of the 65th reboarded the *Java* and set sail for Sydney, in Australia where they landed on the 13th October 1846.

Soon after arriving at Sydney, the regiment received news of disturbances in New Zealand and also orders to proceed to the colony forthwith.

The *Java* was rechartered and Edward and the regiment reboarded and set sail from Sydney on the 2nd November, landing 200 men at the Bay of Islands on the 19th November, to relieve a detachment of the 58th Regiment stationed at Wahapu, before continuing on the 22nd November, with the remainder of the men, landing at Auckland on the 30th November 1846.

For the first few years of their deployment in New Zealand, the regiment was distributed across the south of the Province of New Munster (North Island) and in 1850 were located in the Wellington area split between Wellington and nearby Porirua.

Edward was married to Elizabeth (née Gordon) on the 9th June 1853 at Wellington, it is believed that the couple went on to have 13 children.

In October 1858, in anticipation of the regiments departure from New Zealand, the regiment was moved to Auckland; however, the regiment remained in New Zealand and took part in the Taranaki War (1860–61) when they were based in Taranaki.

During the war, the regiment was involved in the majority of the major battles and engagements, including the Battle of Te Kohia on the 17th March 1860, the Battle of Waireka on 28th March, the Battle of Puketakauere on 26th June, the Battle of Mahoetahi on 6th November, the defence of No. 1 Redoubt at Matarikoriko on 31st December and the defence of No. 3 Redoubt at Huirangi on 23rd January 1861.

On the 1st March 1860, Edward was promoted to Corporal.

In April 1861, the regiment left Taranaki on board *HMS Niger* and *HMS Fawn*, bound for Auckland where for the next two years they were engaged in building the Great South Road in preparation for the invasion of Waikato.

Edward was promoted to Sergeant on 1st July 1862.

On the 15th May 1863, Edward was promoted to the rank of Colour-Sergeant.

In July 1863, the regiment was involved in the Waikato war were they occupied Tuakau on the 13th July and built the Alexandra Redoubt overlooking the Waikato river which was completed on the 28th July 1863.

It was on 7th September 1863, during the Battle of Cameron Town that Edward performed the deeds for which he would later be awarded the Victoria Cross.

Edward was commissioned as Ensign on the 8th September 1863.

During January 1864, the regiment were part of the main field force under the command of General Cameron which advanced up the Waipa river and on 26th January were based at the Tuhikaramea camp.

On the 21st February, the regiment was involved in the Battle of Rangiaowhia and at the Battle of Hairini on the next day.

Between the 30th March and 2nd April 1864, the regiment took part in the final battle of the war at Orakau Pa.

For his service during the 2nd and 3rd Maori wars, Edward was awarded the New Zealand War medal.

On the 18th June 1864, Edward was presented with his Victoria Cross medal by Lieutenant-General Sir D. A. Cameron, the General Officer Commanding the forces in New Zealand, at Te Awamutu camp.

Towards the end of 1865, the regiment were once again scheduled to return to England and wishing to remain in New Zealand, Edward sold his commission and left the army on 1st September 1865 after over 20 years of service.

On the 14th December 1865, Edward enlisted as an Ensign with the New Zealand Forest Rangers, a militia force established and commanded by Major William Jackson.

Edward served with the Forest Rangers for only a few months and retired on 31st March 1866.

After leaving the Forest Rangers, Edward obtained employment with the New Zealand Railways initially as a clerk but he soon rose to the position of Station Master and served in this capacity at Kaiapoi, Ashburton, Invercargill, Gore, Greatford and Halcombe.

In the early 1880s Edward became the Station Master at Palmerston North, which was his last position before he retired in 1903.

Edward was living at Palmerston North when he died on 8th June 1908 at the age of 81, he was buried two days later in the Terrace End Cemetery, Palmerston North.

Edward's Victoria Cross medal is on public display at the Auckland War Memorial Museum in New Zealand.

The medal is a replacement, as the original was stolen, which was provided to Edward at a cost of £1 and 4 shillings in May 1868, the original medal has never resurfaced.

Figure 116a. Grave of Edward McKenna

John Ryan
7th September 1863 (VC No. 310)

Gazetted: 19th January 1864 22809/261

Rank and Unit: Lance Corporal No. 261 – 65th Regiment of Foot

Citation

For gallant conduct at the engagement near Cameron-town above referred to. This Non-Commissioned Officer, with Privates Bulford and Talbot, of the same Regiment, who have been recommended for the Medal for distinguished conduct in the Field, for their behaviour on the same occasion, removed the body of the late Captain Swift from the Field of Action, after he had been mortally wounded, and remained with it all night in a bush surrounded by the enemy.

Biography

John was born some time during 1839 at Borrisoleigh in Co Tipperary, Ireland.

It is probable, like many of his countrymen, that John enlisted with the British army around the time of his 18th birthday in 1857.

John was enlisted in the 65th Regiment of Foot as Private No. 261, and would have joined his regiment at Wellington soon afterwards. The regiment had been on service in New Zealand since 1845.

In October 1858, the regiment was moved to Auckland and took part in the Taranaki War (1860–61) when they were based in Taranaki.

During the war, the regiment was involved in the majority of the major battles and engagements, including the Battle of Te Kohia on the 17th March 1860, the Battle of Waireka on 28th March, the Battle of Puketakauere on 26th June, the Battle of Mahoetahi on 6th November, the defence of No. 1 Redoubt at Matarikoriko on 31st December and the defence of No. 3 Redoubt at Huirangi on 23rd January 1861.

In April 1861, the regiment left Taranaki on board *HMS Niger* and *HMS Fawn*, bound for Auckland where for the next two years they were engaged in building the Great South Road in preparation for the invasion of Waikato.

At some stage John received a promotion to the rank of Lance-Corporal.

In July 1863, the regiment was involved in the Waikato war were they occupied Tuakau on the 13th July and built the Alexandra Redoubt overlooking the Waikato river which was completed on the 28th July 1863.

It was on 7th September 1863, during the Battle of Cameron Town that John performed the deeds for which he would later be awarded the Victoria Cross.

Tragically on 29th December 1863, John was drowned in the Waikato river near Tuakau, while trying to rescue a drunken comrade who had fallen in the river.

John was buried in an unmarked grave in the Alexandra Redoubt Commemorative Park Cemetery near Cameron Town.

John died before his Victoria Cross medal was available for presentation so it was sent by registered post to his mother in Ireland.

His Victoria Cross medal is now on public display at the York and Lancaster Regimental Museum in Rotherham, Yorkshire.

John Thornton Down
2nd October 1863 (VC No. 311)

Gazetted: 23rd September 1864 22896/4552

Rank and Unit: Ensign – 57th Regiment of Foot

Citation

For their conduct at Poutoko, on the 2nd October, in rescuing a wounded comrade from the rebel Maoris. They succeeded in bringing in the wounded man, who was lying at about fifty yards from the bush, although the enemy kept up a very heavy fire from the bush at short range, and also from behind fallen logs close at hand.

The man had been wounded during an engagement with the rebel natives, and Ensign Down, and Drummer Stagpoole, responded to the call of the Officer commanding the detachment of the Regiment for volunteers to "bring him in". The Medal for Distinguished Conduct in the Field has already been conferred on Drummer Stagpoole, for the energy and devotion which he displayed on the 25th September, 1863, at the affair near Kaipakopako, in having, though wounded in the head, twice volunteered and brought in wounded men.

Biography

John was born on 2nd March 1842 at Fulham in London to father also named John and mother Mary, he was baptised on the 10th June 1842.

After graduating as a gentleman cadet from the Royal Military College, John was commissioned as an Ensign with the 57th Regiment of Foot on 8th February 1861,[115] just before his 19th birthday.

His regiment had just arrived in New Zealand on 23rd January 1861 from Bombay in India and were based at Taranaki and Auckland, however, John did not join his regiment until 12th October 1861 when he arrived in New Zealand on board the transport ship *Northumberland.*

In December 1862, John was part of a detachment under the command of Major Logan stationed at Wanganui in Wellington Province.

From the 17th July 1863 until 31st March 1866, John and the regiment were involved in the invasion of Waikato, the 3rd Maori War.

It was during the defence of the Poutoko Redoubt on the 2nd October 1863 that John performed the deeds for which he would later be awarded the Victoria Cross.

115 *London Gazette* – 22478/515

Figure 118. John Thornton Down

For his service during the war, John received the New Zealand Medal (1860–66).

In 1864, the regiment was moved from Taranaki to Wanganui.

On the 13th March 1865, John was part of the force engaged in the Battle of Kakaramea.

John advanced his position within the regiment when he purchased a commission as Lieutenant on the 4th April 1865.[116]

Figure 118a. Grave of John Thornton Down

116 *London Gazette* – 22954/1883

John was presented with his Victoria Cross medal by Brigadier-General R. Waddy, at a general parade of the troops at Wanganui on the 7th February 1866.

John died from typhoid fever on 28th April 1866, aged 24, while at Camp Otahuhu near Auckland and was buried in the Otahuhu Old Cemetery in South Auckland, in an unmarked grave. A headstone was later erected by his regimental comrades.

The location of John's Victoria Cross medal is unknown.

Dudley Stagpoole
2nd October 1863 (VC No. 312)

Gazetted: 23rd September 1864 22896/4552

Rank and Unit: Drummer No. 2043 – 57th Regiment of Foot

Citation

For their conduct at Poutoko, on the 2nd October, in rescuing a wounded comrade from the rebel Maoris. They succeeded in bringing in the wounded man, who was lying at about fifty yards from the bush, although the enemy kept up a very heavy fire from the bush at short range, and also from behind fallen logs close at hand.

The man had been wounded during an engagement with the rebel natives, and Ensign Down, and Drummer Stagpoole, responded to the call of the Officer commanding the detachment of the Regiment for volunteers to "bring him in". The Medal for Distinguished Conduct in the Field has already been conferred on Drummer Stagpoole, for the energy and devotion which he displayed on the 25th September, 1863, at the affair near Kaipakopako, in having, though wounded in the head, twice volunteered and brought in wounded men.

Biography

Dudley was born some time during 1838, at Kilcummen, near Oughterard, Co Galway in Ireland, to father John and mother Nora (née O'Malley). He had two older brothers; Bartholomew born circa 1830 and Martin born circa 1833. All three brothers would serve in the 57th Regiment of Foot in the Crimea and New Zealand.

On the 15th May 1854, at the age of 16, Dudley enlisted as a Drummer with the 57th Regiment of Foot.

In July 1854, the regiment received orders to make ready for service in the east, however, a ship was not available until September and on the 12th of the month the regiment set sail from Corfu on board *SS Mauritius* arriving off the mouth of the river Alma on the 22nd September.

The regiment disembarked the next day and joined the Fourth Division under the command of General George Cathcart and on 27th September were camped on the hills above Sevastopol and on the 5th November were involved in the Battle of Inkerman.

During the siege of Sevastopol, the regiment was involved in the unsuccessful attacks on the Malakoff and Great Redan.

Having served for only 272 days in the Crimea, it is likely that Dudley arrived at Sevastopol on the 3rd September 1855 with

Figure 119. Dudley Stagpoole

a draft of men from the Reserve Depot at Malta so was only involved in the later stages of the siege of Sevastopol and the clear up operations at the end of the war.

For his service in the Crimea, Dudley was awarded the Crimea Medal with clasp for Sevastopol and the Turkish Crimea Medal.

On 28th May 1856, Dudley and the regiment boarded the steam transport *Etna* at Balaklava and set sail for Malta were on 2nd June they set up quarters in the Fort Verdala Barracks.

On the 11th May 1858, the regiment boarded *HMS Princess Royal* at the Calcara Warf in Malta and set sail for India via Alexandria.

On the 18th and 19th May the regiment was disembarked at Alexandria and made their way to Suez where they boarded the P&O steamer *Bengal* and the HEIC Steamer *Prince Arthur* and set sail for India where they landed at Bombay on 6th June 1858.

In December 1858, the regiment was moved by detachments to Malligaum for "Field Service" and then via Seerpore to Chopra where they stayed for six weeks before being deployed in detachments between Berhampoor and Tulloda to prevent incursions into Khaneish by Tantia Topi and his rebels who occupied the Satpoora Hills.

In January 1860, the deployed detachments rejoined the headquarters at Ahmednuggur near Poona and on the 14th February, following the departure of the 31st Regiment they occupied the Ghorpoorie Barracks.

On the 3rd November 1860, the regiment received orders to make ready for service in New Zealand and later in the month was despatched from Bombay in two detachments.

On 23rd November the right wing of the regiment boarded the transport *Star Queen* and were disembarked at Taranaki on the 23rd January 1861.

On 27th November, the Headquarters and left wing of the regiment boarded the transport *Castilian* and set sail for New Zealand and disembarked at Auckland on 26th January 1861 and set up camp in the Albert Barrack Square.

On the same day as their arrival at Auckland a detachment of 150 men marched to Onehunga where they boarded *HMS Cordelia* and were disembarked at Waitara on 28th January 1861.

On the 20th February the HQ and a detachment of 250 men boarded *HMS Niger* at Onehunga and were disembarked at Waitara on the following day.

From their camp at Waitara, Dudley and the regiment were involved in operations against the Maori rebels in the Taranaki War until the end of hostilities on 20th March 1861.

On the 4th March 1861, the Depot and families of the regiment left Poona by rail and arrived at Bombay the next day, on the 18th March they boarded *HMS Prince Arthur* bound for New Zealand and after arriving at Auckland on 31st May were disembarked at New Plymouth on the 4th June 1861.

Following the end of hostilities, the regiment remained in the Province of Taranaki, which was being governed under martial law, for the next two years.

On 24th March 1863, a detachment of 250 men from the regiment marched to Poutoko where they set up camp and built the St Patrick's Redoubt and in April a further detachment constructed the St George Redoubt.

From the 17th July 1863 until 31st March 1866, Dudley and the regiment were involved in the invasion of Waikato, the 3rd Maori War.

On the 25th September 1863, during an action at Kaipakopako, Dudley rescued two wounded soldiers and for his "energy and devotion" was awarded the Distinguished Conduct Medal.

It was only a week later on 2nd October 1863, in an action at Poutoko (Allen's Hill) near New Plymouth that Dudley performed the deeds for which he would later be awarded the Victoria Cross, during which he was slightly wounded.

In 1864, the regiment was moved from Taranaki to Wanganui and it was here in November that Dudley was presented with his Distinguished Conduct Medal.

On the 13th March 1865, Dudley was part of the force engaged in the Battle of Kakaramea.

Dudley was presented with his Victoria Cross medal by Brigadier-General R. Waddy, at a general parade of the troops at Wanganui on the 24th January 1866.

During March 1866, the regiment was concentrated at Wanganui in preparation for a move to Auckland where they were to occupy the Waikato district and on 18th April a detachment sailed on board the transport *Ahurire* arriving at Onehunga on the 22nd April 1866.

On the 7th October 1866, the regiment received orders to prepare for a return to England and in the early part of 1867, the regiment was concentrated at Auckland in readiness for such a move.

The right wing of the regiment set sail on board the transport *Maori* on 30th March 1867 and arrived at Liverpool on 31st July and were moved to Manchester by rail on the same day.

The Headquarters and Left wing of the regiment departed on board the transport *Electric* on the 12th April and after a journey of 15,850 miles arrived at Plymouth on 28th July; the regiment were disembarked at Liverpool on 6th August and were despatched to Manchester by rail on the same day.

Unlike Dudley, his brothers Bartholomew and Martin, chose to leave the regiment and settled in New Zealand.

During the Autumn of 1867, the regiment which was stationed in the Salford Barracks in Manchester were held in readiness to assist the civil authorities during the Fenian Riots.

Dudley was married to Elizabeth (née Sutton) in February 1868 at Salford in Lancashire, tragically Elizabeth died in December 1868 at Farnham, probably from complications during childbirth as their son John Bartholomew Dudley Stagpoole was born at around this time. John only survived a few months as he died in 1869.

On the 1st April 1868, the regiment was moved from Manchester to Aldershot until 22nd March 1869 when they moved to Devonport where they occupied the Raglan Barracks.

On 6th March 1870, Dudley was married to Mary Anne Discombe (née Gillard) at the Wesleyan Methodist Chapel, King Street in Plymouth, the couple would have four children: Ann Nora (known as Honora) born on 19th June 1871 at Stonehouse in Devon and baptised in Clare, Ireland on 3rd January 1872; John Bartley George born in 1873 at Woolwich; Mary Ellen Elizabeth (known as Elsie) born in 1877 at Woolwich and Charlotte Alice born circa 1880.

On 27th March 1870, Dudley was presented with the New Zealand Medal, for his service during the Maori wars.

On the 7th September 1871, the regiment received orders for their deployment to Ireland and on the 18th September they boarded *HMS Orontes* at Devonport and set sail, disembarking at Queenstown on 21st/22nd September and moved to Limerick and various outstations.

In early April 1873, the regiment was moved to the Curragh Camp until 31st May when the Depot Companies (including Dudley) moved to Kingston, boarded *HMS Simoom* and set sail for Woolwich.

For the remainder of his army service Dudley was stationed at Woolwich until he was discharged from the army, at his own request, on 16th May 1877, at the age of 39, after 21 years of service and was awarded the Long Service and Good Conduct medal.

On his retirement from the army Dudley spent the rest of his life in the Woolwich area of London, working at the Woolwich Arsenal and as a dockyard messenger.

Dudley's wife Mary died in 1883.

On 17th July 1902, Dudley was married for the third time to Marie (née Lee) at Woolwich the couple would have two children Dudley Michael born in 1902 at Woolwich and Michael Dudley born in 1905 at Edmonton.

Dudley died at his home at 24 Bowling Road in Ware on 1st August 1911 at the age of 73 and was buried four days later at Hendon Park Cemetery in London.

His Victoria Cross medal is on public display at the Princess of Wales's Royal Regiment museum in Dover Castle.

Figure 119a. Grave of Dudley Stagpoole

William Temple
20th November 1863 (VC No. 313)

Figure 120. William Temple

Gazetted: 23rd September 1864 22896/4552

Rank and Unit: Assistant Surgeon – Royal Artillery

Citation

For gallant conduct during the assault on the enemy's position at Rangiriri, in New Zealand, on the 20th of November last, in exposing their lives to imminent danger, in crossing the entrance of the Maori keep, at a point upon which the enemy had concentrated their fire, with a view to render assistance to the wounded, and, more especially to the late Captain Mercer, of the Royal Artillery.

Lieutenant Pickard, it is stated, crossed, and re-crossed the parapet, to procure water for the wounded, when none of the men could be induced to perform this service, the space over which he traversed being exposed to a cross fire; and testimony is borne to the calmness displayed by him, and Assistant-Surgeon Temple, under the trying circumstances in which they were placed.

Biography

William was born on 7th November 1833, at Monaghan, Co Monaghan in Ireland to father William who was a doctor and mother Anne (née Rooskey).

William was educated at the Reverend John Bleckley's Private School in Monaghan before attending Trinity College in Dublin where he qualified as a doctor.

At the age of 25, William joined the army on 1st November 1858 and was commissioned as an Assistant Surgeon with the 46th Regiment of Foot.[117]

On the 11th January 1859, William was transferred to the Royal Artillery Regiment as an Assistant Surgeon.[118]

On 20th November 1860, William began what would be an almost six year overseas deployment to New Zealand arriving for the final moments of the Taranaki War (1860–61) which ended on the 18th March 1861.

William was married to Anne Theodosia (née Mould) on 21st October 1862 at St Paul's Church in Auckland, the couple would go on to have ten children (6 daughters and 4 sons).

Annie Georgina was born on 18th August 1863 at Auckland, Beatrice Frances was born on 19th May 1865 in Auckland, Elizabeth Alice born on 6th August 1866 in Ireland, Mabel Eva born during 1868 at Woolwich, Ethel Kate born during 1870 at Woolwich and baptised on 21st October 1870, William Arthur Mould born on 14th June 1872 at Woolwich, un-named son born 26 June 1874 at Umbeyla in India (presumably died at a very early age), Reginald Cecil born on 13th August 1877 in Cashmere, Bertram Henry born on 14th August 1877 in Cashmere, Frank Valiant born on 17 August 1879 at Southsea and Eleanor born some time in 1880 in Southsea.

William next saw action during the Waikato Invasion which took place between 17th July 1863 and April 1864.

It was during the Battle of Rangiriri on 20th November 1863 that William performed the deeds for which he would later be awarded the Victoria Cross.

William also took part in the Battle of Rangiaowhia on 21st February 1864.

For his service during the Maori wars, William was awarded the New Zealand Medal.

On 31st December 1864, William was presented with his Victoria Cross medal in Auckland by General D. A. Cameron, General Officer Commanding the forces in New Zealand.

On 19th April 1866, William returned to England from New Zealand and on 26th June 1867 was transferred as an Assistant Surgeon to the Staff of the Army Medical Department.[119]

William was promoted to the rank of Surgeon on 1st November 1868 on the Staff of the Army Medical Department.

On 18th October 1873, William was promoted to the rank of Surgeon-Major[120] and posted to Portsmouth where he served in charge of the Station Hospital at Portsea, until 26th June 1877

117 *London Gazette* – 22202/4909

118 *London Gazette* – 22217/77

119 *London Gazette* – 23267/3542

120 *London Gazette* – 24026/4616

when he returned to a position of the Staff of the Army Medical Department.

From 1884 William served in India and with the rank of Lieutenant-Colonel performed the role of Secretary to the Surgeon-General of the Indian Army Medical Services.

On the 10th April 1885, William was promoted to the rank of Brigade Surgeon.[121]

In recognition of his service in India, William was appointed as Honorary Surgeon to His Excellency the Viceroy of India, a position that he held until his retirement.

On the 7th November 1889, after 31 years of service, William now aged 56 retired from the army[122] and returned to England.

William's wife Anne died at the family home, 7 South Parade in Southsea on 9th January 1914 at the age of 70 and was buried in the Highland Road Cemetery, Eastney in Southsea.

On 13th February 1919, after a long illness which included pneumonia and a kidney haemorrhage, William died at his home 4 Madeira Park in Tunbridge Wells and was buried on 18th February 1919 in the same grave as his wife at Highland Road Cemetery.

William's Victoria Cross medal is in private hands, within his family.

Figure 120a. Grave of William Temple

121 *London Gazette* – 25471/2279
122 *London Gazette* – 25994/6137

Arthur Frederick Pickard
20th November 1863 (VC No. 314)

Gazetted: 23rd September 1864 22896/4552

Rank and Unit: Lieutenant – Royal Artillery

Citation

For gallant conduct during the assault on the enemy's position at Rangiriri, in New Zealand, on the 20th of November last, in exposing their lives to imminent danger, in crossing the entrance of the Maori keep, at a point upon which the enemy had concentrated their fire, with a view to render assistance to the wounded, and, more especially to the late Captain Mercer, of the Royal Artillery.

Lieutenant Pickard, it is stated, crossed, and re-crossed the parapet, to procure water for the wounded, when none of the men could be induced to perform this service, the space over which he traversed being exposed to a cross fire; and testimony is borne to the calmness displayed by him, and Assistant-Surgeon Temple, under the trying circumstances in which they were placed.

Biography

Arthur was born on 12th April 1841 at Forest Hill in Northamptonshire, the 3rd son to father Henry William and mother Elizabeth, he was baptised at Worksop on 6th May 1841.

On 7th August 1855, at the age of 14 Arthur was enrolled as a Gentleman Cadet in the Royal Military Academy and on his graduation was commissioned on 22nd June 1858 as a Lieutenant in the Royal Regiment of Artillery.[123]

Towards the end of the first Taranaki War (1860–61) in New Zealand, Arthur with 'C' Battery of the 4th Brigade Royal Artillery, commanded by Captain Henry Mercer was despatched to New Zealand with a force of reinforcements. The Battery was equipped with six Armstrong Rifled Breech-Loading 12 pounder guns, which it was hoped would be more successful against the Maori stockades that the smooth barrelled guns used so far.

Arthur and the battery arrived at Auckland on board the transport *Norwood* on 3rd March 1861 and over the next week off loaded their guns, ammunition and stores.

On 12th March half the battery plus the mortars were embarked on the steamer *Victoria* bound for Taranaki, where operations against Maoris entrenched at Te Arei had been dragging on for some weeks.

123 *London Gazette* – 22162/3286

Figure 121. Arthur Frederick Pickard

Arthur briefly saw action at No. 7 Redoubt, before the war was ended with a truce on 19th March 1861.

During his time in New Zealand Arthur was also involved in the 3rd Maori War (1863–64), the Invasion of Waikato, taking part in the Taranaki, Waikato and Tauranga campaigns.

Arthur took part in the Battle of Katikara on 4th June 1863 and it was at the Battle of Rangiriri on 20th November 1863 that he performed the deeds for which he would later be awarded the Victoria Cross.

During the Tauranga campaign Arthur was involved in the defeat at the Battle of Gate Pa on 28th–29th April 1864 and the Battle of Te Ranga on 21st June 1864.

For his service during the wars in New Zealand, Arthur was awarded the New Zealand medal (1860–66).

Arthur was presented with his Victoria Cross medal by Major-General Ridley on 13th April 1865 at a parade at the Royal Barracks in Dublin, Ireland.

On the 1st May 1871, Arthur was appointed as an Equerry to His Royal Highness Prince Arthur the Duke of Connaught.[124]

Arthur was promoted to the rank of 2nd Captain on 28th September 1871[125] and was promoted to the rank of Captain on 5th July 1872.

On the 6th January 1872, Arthur received a brevet promotion to the rank of Major.[126]

Arthur was appointed as a Groom in Waiting to Queen Victoria on 21st December 1877.[127]

On the 8th February 1878, Arthur received a brevet promotion to the rank of Lieutenant-Colonel.[128]

Arthur was appointed as an Extra Equerry to Queen Victoria on 5th July 1878.[129]

On the 8th October 1878, Arthur was appointed as Assistant Keeper of the Privy Purse and Assistant Private Secretary to Queen Victoria.[130]

Arthur was promoted to the rank of Major on 16th October 1878.[131]

On the 15th March 1879, Arthur was appointed as an Ordinary Member 3rd Class (Companion) of the Civil Division of the Most Honourable Order of the Bath.[132]

At some stage Arthur was appointed as a Commander of the Order of Saint Stanislaus by the Russian government and as a Knight of the Order of Leopold by the Austrian government.

On the 1st March 1880, at the age of 38, Arthur died from tuberculosis at Cannes in France and was buried on the 4th March at the Cimitiere Protestant du Grand-jus in Cannes.

Arthur's Victoria Cross Medal is on public display at the Imperial War Museum in London as part of the Lord Ashcroft collection.

124 *London Gazette* – 23733/2122
125 *London Gazette* – 23783/4200
126 *London Gazette* – 23815/40
127 *London Gazette* – 24536/7457
128 *London Gazette* – 24591/3557
129 *London Gazette* – 24602/3968
130 *London Gazette* – 24632/5513
131 *London Gazette* – 24633/5560
132 *London Gazette* – 24697/2240

Charles Heaphy
11th February 1864 (VC No. 315)

Gazetted: 8th February 1867 23217/696

Rank and Unit: Major – Auckland Militia, New Zealand Military Forces

Citation

For his gallant conduct at the skirmish on the banks of the Mangapiko River, in New Zealand, on the 11th of February, 1864, in assisting a wounded soldier of the 40th Regiment, who had fallen into a hollow among the thickest of the concealed Maoris. Whilst doing so, he became the target for a volley at a few feet distant. Five balls pierced his clothes and cap, and he was wounded in "three places. Although hurt, he continued to aid the wounded until the end of the day. Major Heaphy was at the time in charge of a party of soldiers of the 40th and 50th Regiments, under the orders of Lieutenant-Colonel Sir Henry Marshman Havelock, Bart., C.B., V.C., the Senior Officer on the spot, who had moved rapidly down to the place where the troops were hotly engaged and pressed.

Biography

Charles was born during 1821 at St John's Wood in London, the youngest of five children to father Thomas who was an artist and the founder and first president of the Society of British Artists his mother was Mary (née Stephenson) who died soon after his birth.

Charles, along with his brother Thomas junior (born in 1813) and his two sisters Mary Ann and Elizabeth, became an accomplished artist like his father, with his skills and style being honed by informal tuition within the family circle.

He accompanied his father on a painting tour of Italy during 1831 and 1832 and soon after his father died on 23rd October 1835 he left the family home and took up employment as a draughtsman with the London and Birmingham Railway company.

From 1837, Charles attended the Royal Academy where he studied for two years, until his sponsor, a prominent publisher, brought him to the attention of the New Zealand Company.[133]

On the 6th May 1839, Charles entered the service of the New Zealand Company as a draughtsman and was immediately assigned to an expedition to the developing colony.

133 Set up in London in 1825, the company was engaged in the colonisation of New Zealand.

Figure 122. Charles Heaphy

The expedition, which was commanded by Colonel William Wakefield, set sail from Plymouth on board the merchant ship *Tory* commanded by Captain Edward Chaffers, on 9th May 1839 and landed at Ship Cove in Queen Charlotte Sound on the 18th August 1839.

By the end of the year Charles had completed some of his best known works which included landscapes and portraits of some of the leading Maori chiefs after the *Tory* proceeded to the Kaipara and Hokianga districts.

For a time Charles was based at Port Nicholson (Wellington)[134] where he was employed as an assistant surveyor and in April 1840 he took part in an expedition to the Chatham Islands during which he was wounded in a skirmish with the Maoris.

On his return, Charles joined another expedition of exploration which followed the west coast of the North Island to Ngamotu in Taranaki.

During these expeditions, Charles completed more of his best known artistic works, including the 'View in the valley of the Nairne' and 'Mt. Egmont, from the southward'.

In September 1841, a second colonising expedition arrived in Wellington and Charles was assigned to the party as draughtsman where he recorded the founding of the settlement at Nelson, on the South Island, with his watercolours.

Following company approval of plans for further exploration of the South Island, Charles returned to Nelson in December 1842, hoping to be employed as a company surveyor.

134 Wellington was named after Arthur Wellesley, the first Duke of Wellington (1769–1852), in 1840 by the directors of the New Zealand Company. The settlement was originally planned to be called Britannia.

For a time Charles tried to establish a farm on some land near Motueka with Frederick Moore but after this failed enterprise consumed all of his money, he was forced to seek paid employment.

He was engaged by William Fox, the company agent at Nelson, to explore the hinterland and in November 1843 began a series of journeys of exploration.

In February 1846, Charles accompanied William Fox, Thomas Brunner and Kehu a Maori guide on an expedition down the Buller River through the Rotoiti and Rotoroa districts to the Maruia River near Murchison.

On the 17th March, again guided by Kehu, Charles and Brunner carried out an expedition to identify and map a coastal route from Massacre Bay to the West Coast, in the hope of finding suitable land for farming.

After a journey of 65 days, the expedition reached the Arahura River at Hokitika where they rested at the Mawhera Pa until 8th June when they began their return journey during which they were the first Europeans to visit the Poutini Ngai Tahu settlements at Mawhera, Taramakau and Arahura, and identified Mount Cook as New Zealand's highest mountain.

Arriving back at Nelson on 18th August 1846 after a harrowing 6 months of exploration, their report concluded, that "It was unfavourable for settlement, and that for the most part its rivers were unfit for vessels to enter."

Having abandoned his farm in 1845, Charles had little prospect of supporting himself in Nelson so applied for a position with the colonial government in Auckland and in August 1848 took up the post of draughtsman in the Survey Office.

On the 30th October 1851, Charles was married to Catherine Letitia (née Churton) in Auckland, the couple would have no children of their own but after a time they took in a boy and a girl from the Churton family.

While retaining his position with the Survey Office, Charles served as gold commissioner at Coromandel from November 1852 until June 1853 and later in 1853 served as secretary to Governor George Gray on a voyage to the New Hebrides and Norfolk Island.

Charles was district surveyor to the Auckland government from February 1854 until March 1857 and was based at Matakana.

After briefly serving with Donald McLean, surveying blocks of land in Coromandel, Charles was appointed as provincial surveyor to the Auckland government in September 1859 and during 1859 assisted Ferdinand Hochstetter in his surveys of the economic geology of Auckland province.

In 1859, Charles joined the City Company of the Auckland Volunteer Militia as a Private with the Auckland Rifle Volunteers.

Having been an enthusiastic supporter of the war in Taranaki, Charles was involved with the survey work for the construction of the military road south from Auckland and following the outbreak of the Waikato Campaign in the 2nd Maori war was commissioned as a Lieutenant in the 3rd (Parnell) company of the Auckland Rifle Volunteers in August 1863 and was soon promoted to the rank of Captain.

In July 1863, Charles was in camp at Papatoetoe, in command of about 100 locally raised troops, but because of his knowledge of the local topography, in January 1864 he was attached to a flying column of British forces commanded by General Duncan Cameron as "Military Surveyor and Guide to the Forces", with the rank of Major.

It was with this force, while leading a party of men from the 40th and 50th Regiments of Foot in an action on the Mangapiko River, near the Paterangi Pa on the 11th February 1864, that Charles performed the deeds for which he would later be awarded the Victoria Cross. During the action Charles was wounded by three bullets and a further four bullets pierced his clothing.

Initially the recommendation for the award of the Victoria Cross was refused, as Colonial Forces were not covered by the originating warrant that determined eligibility for the award, however, following intensive lobbying on 1st January 1867 the warrant was amended to include men of the colonial forces and Charles was the first man to be awarded the Victoria Cross under the terms of this amendment.

For his service during the war, Charles was awarded the New Zealand Medal (1860–66).

Charles retired from the army in March 1864 and from January 1864 until December 1865 worked as chief surveyor to the central government, involved in the survey of the confiscated lands in Waikato, leading to the establishment of several military settlements notably at Hamilton and Cambridge.

After this, Charles once again was appointed as the Provincial Surveyor for Auckland.

Charles was presented with his Victoria Cross Medal by General Sir T. Chute, the General Officer Commanding troops in New Zealand, on 11th May 1867 at a parade in Auckland.

In June 1867, Charles was elected unopposed as Member of the House of Representatives for Parnell, a position that he held until October 1869.

During 1868 and 1869, Charles invested heavily and managed a gold mining company near Thames but failed to make any money.

After resigning from the General Assembly in October 1869, Charles was appointed to the post of Commissioner of Native Reserves by Donald McLean the Minister of Native Affairs and Colonial Defence, as a reward for his political support.

Charles was later appointed as the Government Insurance Commissioner and in 1878 was appointed as a judge in the Native Land Court.

Suffering from crippling rheumatism in later life, Charles retired from all his appointments in June 1881 and with his wife set sail for Australia where he hoped that the warmer climate would be better for his health.

Charles and his wife settled at Ann Street in Toowang, a suburb of Brisbane in Queensland and it was here on the 3rd August 1881 that he died from tuberculosis at the age of 60 and was buried in Toowong Cemetery. In 1961, the New Zealand government installed a plaque over his grave.

Charles's Victoria Cross medal is on public display at the Auckland Museum in New Zealand.

Figure 122a. Grave of Charles Heaphy

John Carstairs McNeill
30th March 1864 (VC No. 316)

Gazetted: 16th August 1864 22885/4027

Rank and Unit: Lieutenant-Colonel – 107th Bengal Infantry Regiment

Citation

For the valour and presence of mind which he displayed in New Zealand, on the 30th of March, 1864, which is thus described by Private Vosper, of the Colonial Defence Force.

Private Vosper states that he was sent on that day with Private Gibson, of the same Force, as an escort to Major (now Lieutenant-Colonel) McNeill, Aide-de-Camp to Lieutenant-General Sir Duncan Cameron. Lieutenant-Colonel McNeill was proceeding to Te Awamutu on duty at the time. On returning from that place, and about a mile on this side of Ohanpu, this Officer, having seen a body of the enemy in front, sent Private Gibson back to bring up Infantry from Ohanpu, and he and Private Vosper proceeded leisurely to the top of a rise to watch the enemy. Suddenly they were attacked by about 50 natives, who were concealed in the fern close at hand. Their only chance of escape was by riding for their lives, and as they turned to gallop, Private Vosper's horse fell and threw him. The natives thereupon rushed forward to seize him, but Lieutenant-Colonel McNeill, on perceiving that Private Vosper was not following him, returned, caught his horse, and helped him to mount. The natives were firing sharply at them, and were so near that, according to Private Vosper's statement, it was only by galloping as hard as they could that they escaped. He says that he owes his life entirely to Lieutenant-Colonel McNeill's assistance, for he could not have caught his horse alone, and in a few minutes must have been killed.

Biography

John was born on 29th March 1831 at Colonsay House in Argyllshire to father Alexander and mother Ann Elizabeth (née Carstairs). John was the oldest of six children with sister Cecil Anne born on 24th June 1832, brother Alexander born on 24th July 1834, sister Helen baptised on 15th March 1838, brother Malcolm baptised on 15th November 1839 and sister Hester Mary baptised on 12th June 1844.

John was educated at St Andrews and afterwards from 1849 until 1850 attended the Honourable East India Company military college at Addiscombe.

Figure 123. John Carstairs McNeill

After graduating from Addiscombe, John was commissioned as an Ensign in the Bengal Army on 9th December 1850 and was assigned to the 12th Bengal Native Infantry regiment.

On the 18th August 1855, John was promoted to the rank of Lieutenant.

After his regiment mutinied at Jhansi on the 5th June 1857 at the start of the Indian Mutiny, John served as Aide-de-Camp to Sir Edward Lugard and was involved in the siege and capture of Lucknow, during the campaign he received two mentions in despatches.

During the mutiny, John was also involved in the Battle of Jaunpore, the relief of Azimghur and various operations at Jugdespore.

For his service during the mutiny, John was awarded the Indian Mutiny Medal with clasp for Lucknow.

On the 31st August 1860, John was promoted to the rank of Captain[135] and on the 8th October 1861 received a brevet promotion to the rank of Major[136] now with the 107th Bengal Light Infantry Regiment.

In 1861, John was sent to New Zealand, where he served as Aide-de-Camp to General Sir Duncan Cameron and took part in the Battle of Katikara on 4th June 1863, the Battle of Rangiriri on 20th November 1863 and the Battle of Gate Pa on 28th April 1864.

On the 1st March 1864, John received a brevet promotion to the rank of Lieutenant-Colonel.[137]

It was during an action near Owapu on 31st March 1864, that John performed the deeds for which he would later be awarded the Victoria Cross.

135 *London Gazette* – 22667/4683
136 *London Gazette* – 22554/3982
137 *London Gazette* – 22826/1257

For his service during the war, John was mentioned in despatches on five occasions and was awarded the New Zealand Medal (1860–66).

John was presented with his Victoria Cross medal by Sir George Gray, the governor of New Zealand at a ceremony in Auckland on 6th December 1864.

On his return to England, John transferred to the 48th Regiment of Foot on 20th February 1866 by way of exchange.[138]

John advanced his position in the army when on 12th June 1867 he purchased the commission of Major and was transferred to the half pay list.[139]

During the winter of 1866–67, John was in command of the Tipperary Flying Column, deployed in Ireland to help quell the Fenian disturbances which culminated in an attempted rebellion in March 1867. He received the thanks of Lord Strathnairn in General Orders, for his services during the revolt.

In early 1869, John accompanied Sir John Young, Lord Lisgar, as his Military Secretary, to Canada where on 2nd February 1869 Lord Lisgar took up his position as the 2nd Governor-General of Canada; the dominion of Canada had been formed on 1st July 1867.

John would hold this position until 25th June 1872, when Lord Lisgar was replaced as Governor-General and returned to England.

On the 1st December 1869, the Canadian Government purchased Rupert's Land (the Red River Colony) from the Hudson Bay Company and installed the English speaking William McDougall as governor.

The French speaking Métis, the main inhabitants of the colony objected to the appointment and their leader Louis Riel established a provisional government.

The Méti government arrested opponents to their rule and on 4th March 1870 executed Thomas Scott, who had been tried and convicted of the attempted murder of Louis Riel.

Following discussions between the Canadian Government and the renegade provincial government, the Manitoba Act received the Royal Ascent on 12th May 1870 and the colony was incorporated into the dominion of Canada as the state of Manitoba.

In May 1870, Colonel Garnet Wolseley was appointed to the command of an expedition (the Red River Expedition) to proceed to the colony and enforce the Federal authority, John served on the staff of this expedition.

Refused permission to cross United States land, the expedition followed a difficult route down the Dawson road, which had been mapped three years earlier, and arrived at Winnipeg in August and on the 24th August occupied Fort Garry on the Red

138 *London Gazette* – 23073/974
139 *London Gazette* – 23262/3302

River, unopposed; Louis Riel and his forces had departed the day before their arrival. Unable to obtain an amnesty for his actions, Louis Reil fled to exile in the United States.

For his service during the expedition, John was awarded the Canada General Service Medal (1866–70) with clasp for Red River 1870.

On the 22nd December 1870, John was appointed as an Ordinary Member, Third Class (Companion) of the Most Distinguished Order of St Michael and St George.[140]

John, having completed the qualifying period as a Lieutenant-Colonel was promoted to the rank of Colonel on 25th April 1872.[141]

In 1873, John took part in the Ashanti Expedition, this was prompted by an invasion of the Gold Coast and an attack on the Port of Elmira which had been acquired, together with the rest of the Dutch Gold Coast, in 1871.

When a force under the command of Lord Wolseley was despatched to the Gold Coast on 13th August 1873, John was appointed as Chief of Staff and second in command of the expedition.

After arriving at Cape Coast Castle on 2nd October 1873, John was placed in command of a force of 180 marines and sailors, 200 men of the West India Regiment and 126 Hussars which progressed by sea to Elmira. After operations at Amkwana, John was seriously wounded on 13th October, during an attack on the village of Essamen and was forced to return to England.

On the 23rd December 1873, John was appointed as a member of the Legislative Council of the Gold Coast settlement.[142]

For his service during the 3rd Anglo-Ashanti (Sargenti) War,[143] which was ended by the treaty of Fomena on 14th March 1874, John was awarded the Ashanti Medal (1873–74).

On 31st March 1874, John was appointed as an Ordinary Member, 3rd Class (Companion) of the Military Division of the Most Honourable Order of the Bath.[144]

Sometime in 1874, John was appointed as Aide-de-Camp to HRH Prince George the Duke of Cambridge, Commander-in-Chief of the British Army.

John was appointed as an Equerry in Ordinary to Queen Victoria on 1st August 1874.[145]

On 17th August 1880, John was appointed as an Ordinary Member 2nd Class (Knight Commander) of the Most Distinguished Order of St Michael and St George.[146]

140 *London Gazette* – 23690/5873
141 *London Gazette* – 23855/2198
142 *London Gazette* – 24047/6075
143 Herbert Morton Stanley of "Dr. Livingstone I Presume" fame was one of the correspondents covering the war.
144 *London Gazette* – 24082/1921
145 *London Gazette* – 24121/3965
146 *London Gazette* – 24874/4509

John next saw active service during the Anglo-Egyptian War of 1882 which was launched to subdue the nationalist uprising against the Khedive Tewfik Pasha by Arabi Pasha (Ahmed 'Urabi).

General Garnet Wolseley was appointed to the command of a land force, with General HRH Prince Albert, the Duke of Connaught in charge of the 1st Brigade. John served on the Duke's staff during the war and was involved in the Battle of Tel-el-Kebir on 13th September 1882 and the capture of Cairo on the next day which brought the war to a close.

For his service during the war, John was awarded the Egypt Medal with clasp for Tel-el-Kebir, the Order of the Medjidieh (2nd Class) and the Khedive's Star (1882).

John was promoted to the rank of Major-General on 1st October 1882.[147]

On 24th November 1882, John was appointed as an Extra Member 2nd Class (Knight Commander) of the Military Division of the Most Honourable Order of the Bath.[148]

John next saw active service in 1885 when in command of the 2nd Infantry Brigade of the Suakin Expeditionary Force commanded by General Sir Gerald Graham VC, he took part in the Mahdist War in the Sudan.

On the 2nd March 1885, John commanded the British troops at the Battle of Tofrek where he only just managed to avoid a massacre, he received some criticism for his command but was subsequently exonerated by an enquiry.

For his service during the war, John received the clasps for Suakin 1885 and Tofrek, to add to his Egypt Medal.

John was awarded the Queen Victoria Jubilee Medal (1887) to celebrate the Queen's Golden Jubilee and was also awarded the clasp for 1897 to celebrate the Diamond Jubilee.

On the 7th June 1890, after 40 years of service, John retired from the army.[149]

In addition to his military and royal duties, John had also served as Justice of the Peace for the County of Argyllshire and Deputy Lieutenant for the County of Argyllshire and for Forfar.

In 1898, following the death of Sir Lyndoch Gardiner, John was appointed as Bath King of Arms, one of the six officers of the Order of the Bath.

On the 2nd February 1901, John was appointed as an Ordinary Member 1st Class (Knight Grand Cross) of the Most Distinguished Order of St Michael and St George.[150]

147 *London Gazette* – 25168/5109
148 *London Gazette* – 25175/6250
149 *London Gazette* – 26064/3519
150 *London Gazette* – 27285/1145

John was appointed as an Extra Equerry to King Edward VII on 22nd February 1901.[151]

In addition to his numerous decorations, at some stage John was appointed as a Grand Cross of the Order of the Red Eagle and a Grand Cross of the Order of the Crown by the Prussian Government.

In recognition of the coronation of the new king, John was awarded the King Edward VII Coronation Medal (1902).

In 1877 on the death of his uncle Sir John McNeill, one time ambassador to the Persian Court, John inherited the estate of Colonsay and Oronsay and during their summer cruise in 1902 he was honoured by a visit by the King and Queen to his island home.

After a short illness, John died on 25th May 1904 at his residence in Colour Court, St James's Palace at the age of 73 and was buried in the family vault at Oronsay Priory on the island of Colonsay.

John's Victoria Cross Medal is on public display at the Imperial War Museum in London as part of the Lord Ashcroft collection.

151 *London Gazette* – 27288/1349

William George Nicholas Manley
29th April 1864 (VC No. 317)

Gazetted: 23rd September 1864 22896/4552

Rank and Unit: Assistant Surgeon – Royal Artillery

Citation

For his conduct during the assault on the Rebel Pah, near Tauranga, New Zealand, on the 29th of April last, in most nobly risking his own life, according to the testimony of Commodore Sir William Wiseman, Bart., C.B., in his endeavour to save that of the late Commander Hay, of the Royal Navy, and others. Having volunteered to accompany the storming party into the Pah, he attended on that Officer when he was carried away, mortally wounded, and then volunteered to return, in order to see if he could find any more wounded. It is stated that he was one of the last Officers to leave the Pah.

Biography

William was born in Dublin, Ireland on 17th December 1831, the second son of father Reverend William Nicholas and mother Elizabeth (née Brown).

After being educated at the Blackheath Preparatory School William studied Medicine and in 1852 became a member of the Royal College of Surgeons in England.

Following a period as a temporary assistant surgeon, William was commissioned as an Assistant Surgeon attached to the Royal

Figure 124. William George Nicholas Manley

Regiment of Artillery Ordnance Medical Department on 3rd March 1855.[152]

Almost immediately after joining the army, William saw active service, serving during the Crimean War from 11th June 1855 where he was present during the siege and capture of Sevastopol.

For his service during the war, William was awarded the Crimea Medal with clasp for Sevastopol and the Turkish Crimean Medal.

William next saw active service in New Zealand during the Maori War between 1864 and 1867, it was during an attack on the Gate Pa, near Tauranga on 26th April 1864 that he performed the deeds for which he would later be awarded the Victoria Cross.

During the war, William was involved in the expedition of General Trevor Chute, the campaign which brought the war to an end and took part in the attack and capture of the Okotukoo, Putahi and Waikohou Pas. During the campaign, William was wounded on two occasions and received a mention in despatches.

William was presented with his Victoria Cross Medal on 31st December 1864 at Auckland by General Sir D. A. Cameron, General Officer Commanding the troops in New Zealand.

On 21st July 1865, while artillery was being off-loaded from a boat on the river Waitotara, a gunner fell into the river and would have drowned had it not been for the prompt action of William who jumped in and saved him. For this action William was later awarded the Royal Humane Society Bronze Medal.

For his service during the war, William was awarded the New Zealand Medal (1860–66).

On the 20th October 1865, in recognition of his service in New Zealand, William was promoted to the rank of Surgeon on the Army Medical Staff[153] and a few weeks later on 7th November 1865 was transferred to the 12th Regiment of Foot.[154]

William was married to Maria Elizabeth (née Darton) on 9th February 1869 at Sheerness, the couple would go on to have 8 children; William George Henry born at Woolwich on 23rd December 1869, Reginald Harwood born at Woolwich on 9th December 1870, Lilian Frances born at Woolwich circa 1872, Georgina Frances Ethel born in March 1873, Edgar Norman born at Woolwich on 27th July 1874, George Errington Drummond born at Woolwich on 9th January 1876, John Charles Medland born at Cheltenham on 2nd March 1883 and Edward Lovell born at Cheltenham on 29th June 1886.

During the Franco-Prussian War (19th July 1870 – 10th May 1871), William was placed in command of the "B" division of the British Ambulance Corps which was attached to the 22nd Division of the Prussian army and marched with the division for about 300 miles during the severe winter.

William was involved in actions at Chateauneuf and Bretoncelle on 18th and 21st November and the battles of Orleans and Cravant on the 10th December 1870.

He was also present at the siege of Paris and when the armistice of Versailles was agreed with Emperor Bismarck and on 28th January 1871 he entered the city with supplies for the French hospitals.

For his part in the war, tending to the wounded of the Prussian 22nd Division, William on the recommendation of Crown Prince Friedrich was awarded the Iron Cross 2nd Class by Emperor Bismarck; possibly the only person to be a recipient of both the Victoria Cross and the Iron Cross.

William was also awarded; the War Commemorative Medal 1870–71 (Steel War Medal for non-combative) by Kaiser William I and the Bavarian Merit Cross for Sanitatswesen 1870–71.

For his service to the French wounded, after the siege of Paris, William was awarded the Croix de la Societe Francaise de Secours aux Blesses (1870) giving him the distinction of having been awarded medals by both sides involved in the war.

On the 1st March 1873, William was promoted to the rank of Surgeon-Major.

William lodged Patent No. 4472, covering improvements to ambulance wheeled litters on 22nd December 1875.[155]

In 1877, William purchased 1 Hatherley Place in Cheltenham, where his wife and family would live during his lengthy periods of overseas service.

During the second Anglo-Afghan War (1878–1880), William served as part of the Quetta Field Force commanded by General Sir Michael Anthony Biddulph and was present during the siege and occupation of Kandahar (19th May – 1st September 1880).

On 23rd June 1880, William was promoted to the rank of Brigade Surgeon (Brigade-Major).[156]

For his service during the war, William was awarded the Afghanistan Medal (1878–80) and received the thanks of the Viceroy of India. After the war, William served for a period of time in Bengal.

On 1st August 1882, William was appointed to the local rank of Deputy Surgeon-General while serving with the forces in Egypt.[157]

In 1882, William served as the principal medical officer of the 2nd Brigade, commanded by General Sir Edward Bruce Hamley, part of the British force commanded by Lord Wolseley in the Anglo-Egyptian war (July – September 1882) and was present at

152 *London Gazette* – 21679/1142
153 *London Gazette* – 23027/4943
154 *London Gazette* – 23034/5192
155 *London Gazette* – 24286/260
156 *London Gazette* – 24876/4627
157 *London Gazette* – 25134/3581

the decisive Battle of Tel el Kebir which took place on 13th September 1882 and was mentioned in despatches for his actions.

For his service during the war, William was awarded; the Egypt Medal (1882–89) with clasp for Tel el Kebir, the Khedive's Star (1882) and the Order of Osmanieh (3rd Class) from Turkey.[158]

On the 18th October 1882, William was promoted to the rank of Deputy Surgeon-General.[159]

After 39 years of service, William retired from the Army on 28th June 1884 with the honorary rank of Surgeon-General[160] and on his retirement moved to 3 Lansdown Terrace in Cheltenham.

On 26th May 1894, William was appointed as an Ordinary Member 3rd Class (Companion), Military Division, of the Most Honourable Order of the Bath[161] – it is reputed (but not confirmed) that he was subsequently offered an appointment as a Knight Commander of the Bath, which he politely declined saying that he could not afford the life style required of a Knight.

In 1896, William was granted a distinguished Service Pension and at some stage was appointed as a Knight of Grace of the Most Venerable Order of Saint John of Jerusalem in England.

On the 16th November 1901, William died from diabetes at his home in Lansdown Terrace, Cheltenham at the age of 69 and was buried four days later in the Cheltenham Cemetery.

William's Victoria Medal is on loan to the Royal Artillery Museum in Woolwich, London where it is on public display.

Figure 124a. Grave of William George Nicholas Manley

158 *London Gazette* – 25169/5172
159 *London Gazette* – 25169/5174
160 *London Gazette* – 25370/2797
161 *London Gazette* – 26516/3116

Samuel Mitchell
29th April 1864 (VC No. 318)

Gazetted: 26th July 1864 22879/3711

Rank and Unit: Captain of the Foretop – Royal Navy *HMS Harrier*

Citation

For his gallant conduct at the attack at Te Papa, Tauranga, on the 29th of April last, in entering the Pah with Commander Hay, and when that Officer was mortally wounded, bringing him out, although ordered by Commander Hay to leave him, and seek his own safety. This man was at the time Captain of the Fore-top of the "Harrier," doing duty as Captain's Coxswain; and Commodore Sir William Wiseman brings his name to special notice for this act of gallantry.

Biography

Samuel was born in Apsley Guise near Woburn in Bedfordshire in 1841 to father William a mat maker who would later become a Methodist lay preacher and mother Eleanor (née Field); he was christened at the nearby village of Husborne Crawley on 8th September 1841.

Samuel had five sisters; Susan, Mercy, Lydia, Martha and Esther as well as an older brother, John.

In August 1857, just before his 16th birthday, Samuel enlisted in the Royal Navy and on 19th August 1857 was assigned as a Boy 2nd Class to the naval receiving ship *HMS Crocodile* which was moored near to the Tower of London.

Figure 125. Samuel Mitchell

Samuel was transferred to *HMS Vigilant* in January 1858 and from September saw uneventful service on the Mediterranean station under the command of Commander William Armytage, until 22nd December 1859, during this deployment he was promoted to Boy 1st Class.

On 22nd December 1859, Samuel was sent to the naval gunnery school training ship *HMS Excellent* based at Portsmouth, where until 14th December 1860 he received training as a gunner and became an Ordinary Seaman.

After completing his training as a gunner, Samuel joined *HMS Harrier* in December 1860 and soon afterwards departed for service on the Australia Station, under the command of Commander Malcolm McGregor.

In January 1861 Samuel was promoted to Able Bodied Seaman and in October of the same year to Leading Seaman. During 1861, *HMS Harrier* patrolled New Zealand Waters and for most of 1862 was placed at the disposal of the New Zealand governor Sir George Grey to transport him around the New Zealand coast.

On 24th June 1862, Commander Francis William Sullivan was appointed to the command of *HMS Harrier* until 9th November 1863 when he was replaced by Commander Edward Hay and soon afterwards in February 1864, Samuel was promoted to 2nd Captain of the Foretop and served as the Captain's Coxswain.

On 7th February 1863 *HMS Harrier* was involved in the rescue of survivors from *HMS Orpheus*, the flagship of Commodore William Farquharson Burnett of the Australian Station and captained by Commander Robert Heron Burton, which had gone aground on a sand spit at the entrance to Manukau Harbour, New Zealand. In going to her rescue *HMS Harrier*, was also grounded and had to be refloated later.

Of the 256 crew of *HMS Orpheus*, 189 including Commodore Burnett and Commander Burton lost their lives and only 69 men were saved.[162]

During the Maori War, men from *HMS Harrier* took part in the Waikato campaign, manning a flotilla of ships operating on the Waikato River.

Operations included a reconnaissance of Paparoa and Haurake in August 1863, moving soldiers to support a raid at Cameron Town in September 1863 and as part of a Naval Brigade taking part in the assault on the Rangiriri Pa in November 1863.

It was on 29th April 1864, during an attack on the Gate Panear Tauranga that Samuel performed the deeds for which he would later be awarded the Victoria Cross, as part of a naval Brigade led by Commander Edward Hay, Captain of *HMS Harrier*.

During the attack, Commander Hay was mortally wounded and died on the next day; Commander William Henry Francis was appointed as his replacement to command *HMS Harrier*.

On the 21st September 1864, Samuel was promoted to the rank of Boson's Mate and three days later on the 24th September was presented with his Victoria Cross medal by Sir John Young, the governor of New South Wales at Hyde Park in Sydney.

For his service during the war, Samuel was awarded the New Zealand Medal.

Samuel left Sydney on 20th October 1864 when *HMS Harrier* began its return journey back to England, making its way via Auckland in New Zealand and Cape Horn she arrived at Portsmouth on 31st March 1865 where the crew were paid off.

On leaving *HMS Harrier*, Samuel was transferred to *HMS Duke of Wellington*, used for harbour duties in Portsmouth, in preparation for his discharge from the Navy and on 1st May 1865, after eight years of service he received a free discharge from the Royal Navy.

After leaving the Royal Navy, Samuel spent some time in England and visited Commander Hay's mother, who presented him with a silver plated revolver in thanks for trying to save the life of her son.

With news of the gold rush on the west coast of New Zealand appearing at around this time, at some stage Samuel set sail for Australia, with the intention of moving to New Zealand and making his fortune.

After spending some time in Sydney, Samuel moved to New Zealand, arriving on the west coast of the South Island towards the end of 1868 and set to work in the gold fields.

On 21st May 1870, Samuel was married to Agnes (née Ross?) in the Registrar's Office at Ross near Hokitika, the couple would go on to have 11 children; Ellen, Esther, Ada, Ruby, Isabella, Edith, Samuel, Stewart, John, William and Frank.

Having little success as a gold miner, at some stage Samuel and Agnes purchased land near the Mikonui River, about 21 miles to the south of Hokitika, where they developed a farm.

Under the terms of the Naval and Military Settlers' and Volunteers' Land Act 1891, Samuel made a claim and was granted a thirty pound certificate for the purchase of land in the district of Westland, it is not known if this grant was utilised.

Samuel was tragically drowned on 16th March 1894 at the age of 52, while trying to cross the swollen river Mikonui near his farm. His body was found three days later, down the coast, by a local farmer William Green who coincidentally was a former sailor who had also taken part in the attack on the Gate Pa.

Samuel was buried in the Ross township cemetery, in a grave later to be shared with his wife Agnes who died in 1918.

162 The sinking of *HMS Orpheus* is still one of the greatest maritime disasters in New Zealand history.

Samuel's Victoria Cross medal is held by the West Coast Historical Museum in Hokitika, New Zealand, however, it is only a replica that is on public display.

How the medal arrived at the museum is an interesting story.

When Samuel left Sydney to move to New Zealand, he left his sea chest, which contained his medals with a family called Goodman, who ran the boarding house where he was staying until he settled in New Zealand.

Once settled, Samuel tried to contact the Goodmans but when he received no reply he put the matter in the hands of the police and was later informed that they had returned to England and could not be traced.

The whereabouts of Samuel's Victoria Cross was unknown until 1909, when it came up for action at Glendining's in London and was purchased for £50 by Colonel Frederick Gascoigne of Lotherton Hall, Aberford, Yorkshire, to add to his collection.

When Agnes became aware of the sale, which was reported in the New Zealand press, she contacted the commissioner of police at Wellington and obtained details of the purchaser.

For the next 19 years, Agnes, and on her death her daughter Edith, endeavoured to recover the medal using the services of; their local Member of Parliament, the New Zealand Minister of Defence, the New Zealand Governor-General, the New Zealand High Commissioner in London, the Christchurch Returned Soldiers Association, the British Empire Service League in London and, as Samuel had been a Mason, the United Grand Lodge of Ancient Free and Accepted Masons of England.

Figure 125a. Grave of Samuel Mitchell

In 1912, contact was made with Colonel Gascoign, by the New Zealand government, who stated that he wanted a replacement navy Victoria Cross and the sum of £70 to return the medal but the Admiralty advised that a duplicate medal could not be issued as the location of the original was known.

Matters changed in 1927, when the Duke of York (the future King George VI) visited Hokitika and the local Member of Parliament brought the situation to his attention; on his return to London the Duke caused enquiries to be made.

In June 1828, Edith wrote again to Colonel Gascoigne and this time received a more positive reply, the Colonel stated that he had sold his medal collection to his son Alvary, however, he was sure that he would sell it to Edith for £70.

Edith raised the £70 by a public fundraising campaign and forwarded the money to the High Commissioner in London and in August 1828 she received Samuel's Victoria Cross medal in the mail.

Edith retained the medal until her death when the medal was gifted to the museum.

Frederick Augustus Smith
21st June 1864 (VC No. 319)

Figure 126. Frederick Augustus Smith

Gazetted: 4th November 1864 22908/5187

Rank and Unit: Captain – 43rd Regiment of Foot

Citation

For his distinguished conduct during the engagement at Tauranga, on the 21st of June. He is stated to have led on his Company in the most gallant manner at the attack on the Maoris position, and, although wounded previously to reaching the Rifle Pits, to have jumped down into them, where he commenced a hand to hand encounter with the Enemy, thereby giving his men great encouragement, and setting them a fine example.

Biography

Frederick was born on 18th November 1826 at Dublin in Ireland, unfortunately little is known of his family or early life.

On the 1st June 1849, Frederick joined the British Army with the purchase of a commission as Ensign in the 1st Regiment of Foot.[163]

Frederick advanced his position within the regiment by the purchase of a commission as Lieutenant on 30th April 1852.[164]

In March 1854, Fredrick and the regiment set sail from Portsmouth for Gallipoli and then on to Varna where they arrived on 24th June 1854.

As part of the 1st Brigade of the 3rd Division, commanded by Sir Richard England, the regiment was part of the British Expeditionary Force which landed on the Crimean peninsula at Calamite Bay on 14th September 1854.

On 20th September, soon after landing, the regiment was involved in the Battle of Alma before taking up positions on the heights above Sevastopol on 28th September.

Frederick and the regiment took part in the Battle of Inkerman on 5th November 1854.

On the 30th March 1855, Frederick again advanced his position within the regiment when he purchased a commission as Captain.[165]

The regiment was involved in the siege of Sevastopol and the eventual capture of the city on 9th September 1855.

In April 1856, the regiment left the Crimea and on their return to England were stationed at the new camp at Aldershot.

For his service during the war, Frederick was awarded the Crimea Medal with clasps for Alma, Inkerman and Sevastopol and the Turkish Crimea Medal.

In 1857, Frederick and the regiment were deployed to India where they were stationed in the Madras presidency.

From 16th November 1858 until the 16th March the regiment served with the Berar Field Force commanded by Brigadier Hill.

On the 9th April 1861, Frederick transferred to the 43rd Regiment of Foot by way of exchange.[166]

In September 1863, Frederick and his new regiment were sent from India to New Zealand as reinforcements for the troops engaged in the Maori wars.

The regiment was involved in the battle at the Gate Pa on 28th April 1864 where they lost nine officers and 32 men killed in the action.

It was during action at Tauranga on 21st June 1864, that Frederick performed the deeds for which he was later awarded the Victoria Cross; during the action he was seriously wounded.

On 21st March 1865, Frederick was awarded a brevet promotion to the rank of Major.[167]

For his service during the war, Frederick received a mention in despatches and was awarded the New Zealand Medal (1860–66).

Frederick's Victoria Cross medal was sent to him by registered post on 31st January 1865.

On the 27th March 1866, after the end of the war, Frederick and the regiment set sail from Auckland and arrived at Plymouth on 4th July 1866 and soon afterwards were deployed to service on the Channel Islands.

Frederick was promoted to the rank of Major, without purchase, on 28th October 1868.[168]

163 *London Gazette* – 20983/1793
164 *London Gazette* – 21314/1211
165 *London Gazette* – 21686/1277
166 *London Gazette* – 22500/1494
167 *London Gazette* – 22950/1619
168 *London Gazette* – 23435/5598

In 1869, the regiment was deployed to Ireland where they remained until 1872 when they were once again deployed to the Madras presidency in India.

On 31st August 1874, Frederick received a brevet promotion to the rank of Lieutenant-Colonel.[169]

After 29 years of service, Frederick retired from the army on 2nd February 1878[170] and was awarded a step in rank to Colonel.[171]

On leaving the army, Frederick returned to Ireland and it was at his home in Brierly, Duleek in County Meath, that he died at the age of 61 on 22nd July 1887 and was buried in St Cianán's Churchyard in Brierly in an unmarked grave.

Frederick's Victoria Cross medal is on public display at the Imperial War Museum in London as part of the Lord Ashcroft collection.

169 *London Gazette* – 24146/5155
170 *London Gazette* – 24548/523
171 *London Gazette* – 24570/2452

John Murray
21st June 1864 (VC No. 320)

Gazetted: 4th November 1864 22908/5187

Rank and Unit: Sergeant No. 2918 – 68th Regiment of Foot

Citation

For his distinguished conduct during the engagement at Tauranga, on the 21st of June, when the Enemy's position was being stormed, in running up to a Rifle Pit containing from eight to ten of the enemy, and, without any assistance, killing or wounding every one of them. He is stated to have afterwards proceeded up the works, fighting desperately, and still continuing to bayonet the Enemy.

Biography

John was born in Whigsborough near Birr in Kings County, Ireland in February 1837 or possibly 1831, very little is known of his family or early life.

Like many of his countrymen, John enlisted in the British army to avoid a life of poverty in Ireland at this time. On the 5th February 1852, John joined the 68th Regiment of Foot as Private No. 2918.

John joined his regiment in Malta, where they were performing garrison duties and within two years was promoted to the rank of Corporal.

In April 1854, John and the regiment were despatched to the Crimea and as part of General Sir George Cathcart's division landed on the Crimean peninsula on 14th September 1854.

Figure 127. John Murray

A few days after landing, the regiment was involved in the Battle of Alma on 20th September 1854 and on 25th October the Battle of Balaklava.

On the 5th November 1854, John and the regiment were involved in the Battle of Inkerman, following which they served in the trenches during the siege of Sevastopol until the city was captured on 28th September 1855.

For his service during the war, John was awarded the Crimea Medal with clasps for Alma, Balaklava, Inkerman and Sevastopol, he also received the Turkish Crimea Medal.

At the end of the war, John and the regiment were posted to the Ionian Islands where they served as the garrison at Corfu.

After a brief return to England, the regiment was despatched to India in 1857 as the crisis of the Mutiny was escalating, however, soon after their arrival they were sent to Burma where they formed the garrison at Rangoon.

At some time during 1860, John was promoted to the rank of Sergeant.

Towards the end of 1863, after five uneventful years in Burma, the regiment was despatched to New Zealand as reinforcements for the Maori Wars, landing at Auckland in January 1864.

On 29th April 1864, the regiment was involved in the battle at the Gate Pa and it was on 21st June 1864 during the action at Te Ranga that John performed the deeds for which he would later be awarded the Victoria Cross.

For his service during the war, John was awarded the New Zealand Medal (1860–66).

John was presented with his Victoria Cross medal by General Richard Waddy on 5th December 1865 at Wanganui in New Zealand.

At the end of the war in 1866, the regiment returned to England where they served at Aldershot and Manchester before being deployed to Ireland in 1869, where they were stationed at Templemore and Cork.

Figure 127a. Memorial to John Murray

In 1872, the regiment was once again deployed overseas, to India where they were stationed at Poona, however, with his service reaching its end, John transferred to the 2nd North Durham Militia at Gilesgate, Durham City instead of going to India.

In February 1873, after 21 years of service, John was discharged to pension, awarded the Army Long Service and Good Conduct medal and returned to Ireland.

At some stage John was married, as at his death on 7th November 1911, while living at his sister's house in Derrinlough near Birr, it was noted that he was a widower. John was buried in the English Cemetery at Derrinlough in an unmarked grave.

John's Victoria Cross medal is on public display at the Durham Light Infantry Museum in Durham City.

Hugh Shaw

24th January 1865 (VC No. 321)

Gazetted: 28th November 1865 23044/6005

Rank and Unit: Captain – 18th Regiment of Foot

Citation

For his gallant conduct at the skirmish near Nukumaru, in New Zealand, on the 24th of January last, in proceeding, under a heavy fire, with four Privates of the Regiment, who volunteered to accompany, him, to within 30 yards of the bush occupied by the Rebels, in order to carry off a comrade who was badly wounded. On the afternoon of that day, Captain Shaw was ordered to occupy a position about half a mile from the Camp. He advanced in skirmishing order, and, when about 30-yards from the bush, he deemed it prudent to retire to a palisade about 60 yards from the bush, as two of his party had been wounded. Finding that one of them was unable to move, he called for volunteers to advance to the front to carry the man to the rear, and the four Privates referred to accompanied him, under a heavy fire, to the place where the wounded man was lying, and they succeeded in bringing him to the rear.

Figure 128. Hugh Shaw

Biography

Hugh was born at St Mary's in Madras, India on 4th February 1839 to father James who was the Principal Inspector-General in the Medical Department in Madras and mother Anne Amelia (née Stuart) his father's third wife.

Hugh was the oldest of seven children with four brothers; John Hay born on 22nd September 1840, Elphinstone born on 28th September 1841, James Charles born on 3rd October 1843 and William Sissmore born circa 1845; and two sisters Anne Amelia born circa 1842 and Maitland Coutland born circa 1847.

Hugh completed his education at the Military Academy Sandhurst and on graduation was commissioned as an Ensign with the 18th Regiment of Foot on 11th May 1855.[172]

Hugh joined the regiment soon after its return from service in India and would have been in barracks at Chatham or Canterbury, in October 1855 some companies were ordered to Windsor as part of the garrison.

After being brought up to strength with 400 men from the 94th Regiment and 150 men from the 51st Regiment, the regiment which now numbered nearly 850 men set sail from Portsmouth on board the steamship *Magdalene* on the 8th December 1854 and arrived at the Crimea by the end of the year.

Hugh was not with this first draft of men but he arrived in the trenches at Sevastopol before September 1855 and was present at the fall of the city on 9th September 1855.

For his service during the war, Hugh was awarded the Crimea Medal with clasp for Sevastopol and the Turkish Crimea Medal.

After the fall of Sevastopol, Hugh and the regiment were involved in the destruction of the docks at Sevastopol and on 20th June 1856, after boarding *HMS Majestic*, they finally left the Crimea.

The regiment arrived at Portsmouth on 18th July 1856 and after arriving at Farnborough by train they marched to their new camp at Aldershot where Queen Victoria was waiting to welcome them home.

Four day later the regiment was deployed to Ireland where they were stationed in Dublin.

On 9th January 1857, it appears that Hugh purchased the commission of Lieutenant;[173] however, it is also recorded that he was promoted to Lieutenant without purchase on 25th September 1857[174] and it is this date that is used in Hart's Army List.

For a time the regiment was on notice for deployment to the Cape Colonies, however, when news of the mutiny of the Bengal army reached England the order was cancelled but it was some months until the regiment was deployed to India.

On 24th September 1857 an advanced party was despatched followed two months later by the remainder of the Regiment, including Hugh, which arrived at Bombay in early February 1858.

172 *London Gazette* – 21710/1826

173 *London Gazette* – 21957/105

174 *London Gazette* – 22043/3195

The regiment hoped that they had arrived in time to take an active part in the campaigns, however, to their great disappointment they were ordered to Poona, a hot-bed of sedition which they managed to keep under control and prevent an outright revolt.

By April 1858, matters were very much under control and the regiment was deployed in small detachments across western India where they helped maintain civil law and order.

For his service during the Mutiny, Hugh was awarded the India Mutiny Medal (1857–58) without clasps.

In January 1859, the majority of the regiment were brought back together and spent the next few months trying to control bands of bandits in the Juana District until 21st June 1859 when the regiment arrived on station at Hyderabad.

Hugh was appointed as Adjutant to the 18th Regiment of Foot on 29th November 1859.[175]

On 25th March 1858, a second battalion of the regiment was raised at Enniskillen, the nucleus of which was formed by 100 veterans transferred from the 1st Battalion.

It is not known if Hugh was part of the initial formation of the 2nd Battalion, however, by early 1863, when the battalion was considered to be fit for active service, following training in England and the Channel Islands, he was part of their number.

On 2nd April 1863, a detachment of the 2nd Battalion, under the command of Lieutenant-Colonel Chapman set sail from Plymouth, on board the transport *Elizabeth Anne Bright*, for New Zealand arriving at Auckland on 4th July 1863.

A second detachment, under the command of Colonel G. J. Carey, set sail on 12th April on board the transport *Norwood* and arrived at Auckland on 25th July 1863.

After landing the regiment were sent to the camp at Otahuhu, to the south of Auckland, where General Cameron was concentrating his troops in readiness for a campaign against the Maori rebels.

At the camp, the Battalion was kitted out with their campaigning gear and then moved off to Drury, where a detachment of 200 men under the command of Captain Inman were left to form the garrison while the remainder occupied the Queen's Redoubt on the banks of the Waikato river.

Until the end of 1863, the regiment were involved in maintaining the line of communications from the Queens Redoubt to Auckland and conducted several operations against the Maori rebels in the Wairoa District.

Following the capture of Ngaruawahia, the regional capital, on 9th December 1863,the regiment's responsibility was extended to cover communications between this town and the Queen's Redoubt and detachments formed the garrisons in a chain of redoubts established between the Waikato river and the mouth of the Thames river.

At the end of March 1864, the regiment were involved in a decisive action against the Maori at Orakau, after which the enemy retired back into the mountains.

On 2nd April 1864, Hugh was promoted to the rank of Captain.[176]

The regiment formed the garrison at Ngaruawahia for three months and were then moved to Otahuhu camp where they were part of the Auckland garrison until the end of the year.

At the beginning of 1865, the regiment was sent to the Taranaki (New Plymouth) district as reinforcements to help protect the settlements.

On 2nd January 1865, a detachment of 500 men (including Hugh), under the command of Major J. H. Rocke, boarded *HMS Falcon* and *HMS Eclipse* and set sail for Wanganui where they joined a force commanded by Colonel Waddy.

It was on 24th January 1865, just after the force had set up camp near the village of Nukumaru, that Hugh performed the deeds for which he would later be awarded the Victoria Cross.

After the battle, the regiment was moved to Patea where they remained for the next few months, with detachments taking part in actions at Weraroa on 20th July and the Putahi Pa on 5th January 1866.

In October 1866, the regiment were involved in one of the last major actions of the war when on the 19th of the month they were involved in the capture of Papoia.

It is believed that Hugh was presented with his Victoria Cross medal some time during 1866, while serving in New Zealand.

For his service during the war, Hugh was awarded the New Zealand Medal (1860–66).

After the war the regiment remained in New Zealand until January 1870 when they were sent to Australia, with detachments being established at Sydney, Melbourne, Adelaide and Hobart.

In August 1870, the regiment were at last ordered home and after sailing from Sydney and Melbourne, they arrived back in Plymouth by the end of the year and were quartered at Devonport.

It would appear that before the 2nd Battalion left New Zealand for Australia, Hugh was transferred back to the 1st Battalion, possibly due to the army reorganisation following the introduction of the Cardwell reforms, and probably joined the Battalion in Ireland in late 1869 or early 1870.

Hugh was married to Emily Grace (née Sheffield) at the Holy Trinity Church in Bedford on 21st June 1870, the couple would

175 *London Gazette* – 22330/4480

176 *London Gazette* – 22879/3715

go on to have three daughters; Nina Jane born circa 1871 in Malta, Dolores Evangeline and Mabel Annie.

On 18th January 1872, Hugh was part of a force of the 1st Battalion, commanded by Lieutenant-Colonel G. H. Pocklinton despatched as a garrison to Malta.

Before the regiment completed its tour at Malta, Hugh returned to Ireland when he was appointed to the Staff position as Adjutant to the North Tipperary Militia with the rank of Captain on 12th June 1873.[177]

On the 1st October 1877, Hugh received a brevet promotion to the rank of Major.[178]

Hugh was promoted to the rank of Major on 22nd May 1878.[179]

On 9th November 1878, upon the expiry of his term of office, Hugh was replaced as Adjutant of the North Tipperary Militia and was returned to his regiment.[180]

It was probably early in 1879, that Hugh joined the 1st Battalion of the regiment who were in India and from March 1880 were the garrison at Peshawar.

On 2nd May 1880, the regiment arrived at Landi Kotal in Afghanistan, where as part of the Khyber Line force they guarded the lines of communication and escorted convoys through the Khyber Pass during the 2nd Anglo-Afghan war.

From their arrival in May until August, Hugh served as the Station Staff Officer at Landi Kotal and then as Brigade-Major of the 1st Section of the Khyber Line Force.

On 18th March 1881, after the end of the war, the regiment returned to India and for his part in the war, Hugh was awarded the Afghanistan Medal (1878–80).

Hugh was promoted to the rank of Lieutenant-Colonel on 14th September 1881.[181]

On 22nd May 1883, Hugh was appointed to the command of the 1st Battalion of the 18th Regiment of Foot, now renamed as the Royal Irish.[182]

In August 1884, while the 1st Battalion were stationed at Meerut they received orders for a deployment to Egypt and on the 29th August set sail from Bombay and arrived at Cairo three weeks later.

On 12th November 1884, Hugh led his battalion of nearly 750 officers and men by train to Assiut, the farthest point up the Nile reached by the railway and after a journey of 230 miles reached the town the next day.

177 *London Gazette* – 23992/3075
178 *London Gazette* – 24508/5463
179 *London Gazette* – 24599/3834
180 *London Gazette* – 24640/5938
181 *London Gazette* – 25074/708
182 *London Gazette* – 25247/3378

The battalion was towed up the Nile on barges and by 27th January 1885, after a very strenuous journey had reached Korti.

For completing the journey up the Nile to Debbeh, in a shorter time than any other regiment, they received a cheque for £100 from Lord Wolseley as a reward.

By the time that the regiment reached Korti, the situation for General Gordon, besieged at Khartoum was dire and the latest message to Lord Wolseley stated that he felt that he could only hold out for a matter of days, rather than weeks.

As the Nile was the only route to place a large force and their supplies within striking distance of Khartoum and this would take several weeks, Lord Wolseley was forced to change his plans and decided to divide his force.

The major part of the force would continue up river under the command of General Earle, while the Camel Corps and other troops, commanded by General Sir Herbert Stewart would take a more direct route across the Bayuda desert.

On 28th January 1885, Hugh and the regiment were order to follow in the footsteps of the Camel Corps and cross the desert to Gakdul.

Just before they reached Gakdul on 6th February, the regiment received the news that Khartoum had fallen and by 12th February had reached Abu Klea where they met up with the Camel Corps column.

On 23rd February, the regiment acted as the rearguard when the force at Abu Klea was ordered to fall back to Korti which was reached on 14th March.

On reaching Koti, the regiment was assigned to the movable column commanded by General Brackenbury and spent several months camped at the village of Kurot.

Lord Wolseley received an order on 11th May to withdraw the British forces from the Sudan and return to Egypt.

For his service during the war, Hugh received a mention in despatches and was awarded the Egypt Medal (1882–89) with clasp for The Nile (1884–85) and the Khedive's Star (1882 – Egypt).

Hugh was appointed as an Ordinary Member 3rd Class (Companion) of the Military Division of the Most Honourable Order of the Bath[183] on 25th August 1885.

On 24th August 1885, the regiment boarded *SS Stirling Castle* at Alexandria and set sail for home, arriving at Portsmouth on 9th September and were stationed at Devonport.

On 14th September 1885, Hugh was promoted to the rank of Colonel.[184]

183 *London Gazette* – 25505/4050
184 *London Gazette* – 25512/4389

Having completed four years in command of a battalion, Hugh was placed on retirement pay on 22nd May 1887 and was given the honorary rank of Major-General.[185]

On his retirement, Hugh set up home at "St Lanner", 5 Victoria Grove in Southsea and it was here on 25th August 1904, at the age of 65, that he died and was buried four days later at Highland Road Cemetery in Eastney.

Hugh's Victoria Cross medal is on public display at the National Army Museum in Chelsea, London.

Figure 128a. Grave of Hugh Shaw

185 *London Gazette* – 25702/2792

Duncan Gordon Boyes

6th September 1864 (VC No. 322)

Gazetted: 21st April 1865 22960/2130

Rank and Unit: Midshipman – Royal Navy – *HMS Euryalus*

Citation

For the conspicuous gallantry which, according to the testimony of Captain Alexander, C.B., at that time Flag Captain to Vice-Admiral Sir Augustus Kuper, K.C.B., Mr. Boyes displayed on the occasion of the capture of the enemy's stockade. He carried a Colour with the leading Company, kept it in advance of all, in the face of the thickest fire, his Colour-Serjeants having fallen, one mortally, the other dangerously, wounded; and he was only detained from proceeding yet further by the orders of his superior Officer. The Colour he carried was six times pierced by musket balls.

Thomas Pride, Captain of the After-guard, the survivor of the two Colour-Serjeants who supported Mr. Boyes in the gallant rush which he made in advance of the attack, is also recommended for the Victoria Cross for his conduct on this occasion.

Biography

Duncan was born on 5th November 1846, at 3 Paragon Buildings in Cheltenham, Gloucestershire to father John and mother Sabina.

Duncan was the youngest of six children, with two older sisters; Louisa Mary[186] born 1834 and Isabella born 1841, and three older brothers; George Thomas Henry[187] born in 1842, John Edward[188] born in 1844 and Francis Campbell born in 1845.

Between February 1858 and June 1860, Duncan was educated at Cheltenham College, following which he attended the North Grove House Academy as preparation for his career in the navy.

The 1861 census reports that Duncan was still residing at the family home in Cheltenham and was studying as a naval cadet.

It is probable that Duncan joined the Royal Navy sometime in January 1862 and joined *HMS Euryalus* as a midshipman when she was recommissioned, after a refit at Plymouth, on 24th January 1862.

186 On 10th January 1860, Louisa was married to Thomas James Young VC, who received his award for deeds at Lucknow on 16th November 1857.

187 George would also join the Royal Navy and rise to the rank of Rear-Admiral.

188 John persued a career in the army with the Gordon Highlanders and would attain the rank of Major-General.

Figure 129. Duncan Gordon Boyes

Setting sail for the East Indies station, under the command of Captain Alexander, *HMS Euryalus* arrived at Hong Kong on 12th August 1862 but quickly moved off to Japan where she arrived off Yokahama on 11th September 1862. *HMS Euryalus* returned to Hong Kong on 15th November 1862.

During the Anglo-Satsuma war, *HMS Euryalus* was the flag ship for Vice-Admiral Augustus Kuper and from the 15th to 17th August 1863 was involved in the bombardment of Kagoshima.

It was on the 6th September 1864, during the Shimonoseki Campaign, that Duncan performed the deeds that would later result in the award of the Victoria Cross.

After his time on the East India Station, Duncan returned to England with *HMS Euryalus*, probably sometime during early 1865.

On 22nd September 1865, Duncan was presented with his Victoria Cross medal by Admiral Sir Michael Seymour, GCB the Commander-in-Chief, Portsmouth at a ceremony on Southsea Common; two previous Navy Victoria Cross recipients, Hugh Talbot Burgoyne and John Commerell attended the ceremony.

On 9th February 1867, Duncan was charged, together with Midshipman Marcus McCausland, at a Courts Martial on board *HMS Cadmus* at Bermuda with disobeying a standing order of the Commander in Chief.

After having previously been refused entrance at the main gate of the naval yard, because they did not have a pass, the pair broke into the yard at some time after 11 o'clock in the evening.

Both men admitted the offence and pleaded guilty and were dismissed from the service.

Duncan was devastated by the disgrace of his dismissal and suffered from severe bouts of depression, not helped when he began to drink heavily.

In an attempt to improve his health, Duncan emigrated to New Zealand to work on his brother Francis's sheep station at Kawarau Falls in Otago Province.

Unfortunately, the move to New Zealand did little to improve Duncan's health and after suffering a complete nervous breakdown, he took his own life on 26th January 1869 when he threw himself out of a first floor window in a building at Dunedin. His death certificate gave the cause of death as delirium tremens.

Duncan was buried in the Southern Cemetery in Dunedin, however, on 4th May 1954 the Dunedin Returned Servicemen's Association arranged for his remains to be disinterred and reburied in the Servicemen's section of the Anderson's Bay Cemetery.

Duncan's Victoria Cross medal is on public display at the Imperial War Museum in London, as part of the Lord Ashcroft Collection.

Duncan is one of only 17 recipients of the Victoria Cross who did not receive a campaign medal.

Figure 129a. Grave of Duncan Gordon Boyes

Thomas Pride
6th September 1864 (VC No. 323)

Gazetted: 21st April 1865 22960/2130

Rank and Unit: Captain of the After-Guard – Royal Navy – *HMS Euryalus*

Citation

For the conspicuous gallantry which, according to the testimony of Captain Alexander, C.B., at that time Flag Captain to Vice-Admiral Sir Augustus Kuper, K.C.B., Mr. Boyes displayed on the occasion of the capture of the enemy's stockade. He carried a Colour with the leading Company, kept it in advance of all, in the face of the thickest fire, his Colour-Serjeants having fallen, one mortally, the other dangerously, wounded; and he was only detained from proceeding yet further by the orders of his superior Officer. The Colour he carried was six times pierced by musket balls.

Thomas Pride, Captain of the After-guard, the survivor of the two Colour-Serjeants who supported Mr. Boyes in the gallant rush which he made in advance of the attack, is also recommended for the Victoria Cross for his conduct on this occasion.

Biography

Thomas was born on 29th March 1835 at Wool in Dorset to father Robert, an agricultural labourer and mother Ann (née King) who was born in America. He was the second of seven children, with an older sister Mary Ann born in 1834, a brother Charles born in 1839, a sister Eliza born in 1841, a sister Isabella born in 1844, a brother George born in 1847 and a brother William born in 1850.

On 17th February 1854, Thomas left his job as an agricultural labourer and joined the Royal Navy where he was initially assigned to the training ship *HMS Illustrious* based at Portsmouth.

It is likely that Thomas joined *HMS Chesapeake*, after he had completed his initial training, on or around 27th September 1855 when the ship was launched at Chatham Dockyard.

As part of the crew of *HMS Chesapeake*, Thomas saw service on the East India and China station, initially under the command of Commodore Rudle Burges Watson and then, for a short time at the end of 1858, under the command of Commodore Harry Edmond Edgell.

During this period, Thomas spent time at Hong Kong, Shanghai, Kintang and the Gulf of Pecheli.

Figure 130. Thomas Pride

On the 16th February 1859, *HMS Chesapeake*, became the flagship of Rear-Admiral James Hope Commander in Chief of the East Indies and China station, and Captain George Ommaney Willes took over command of the ship.

HMS Chesapeake took part in the later stages of the 2nd Anglo-Chinese War in 1860; Thomas was awarded the 2nd China War Medal (1857–60) for his service during the war.

On 16th April 1861, *HMS Chesapeake* became the flagship of Rear-Admiral Lewis Tobias Jones and was commanded by Captain Rochford Maguire.

On 23rd May 1861, *HMS Chesapeake* set sail for England arriving at Sheerness on the 17th October 1861, where the crew were paid off.

Less than a month after arriving back in England, Thomas was married to Mary Eliza (née Croombes) at St Mary's church in Wareham in Dorset, on 11th November 1861.

The couple would go on to have four children; Flora born in 1862 at Wareham and baptised on 5th November 1862, Albert McCollock born in 1866 at Sandford, Walter Charles born in 1868 at Sandford and Alice Louisa born in 1871 at Christchurch in Hampshire and baptised on 27th October 1872.

After being discharged from *HMS Chesapeake*, Thomas joined *HMS Euryalus* when she was recommissioned, after a refit at Plymouth, on 24th January 1862.

Setting sail for the East Indies station, under the command of Captain Alexander, *HMS Euryalus* arrived at Hong Kong on 12th August 1862 but quickly moved off to Japan where she arrived off Yokahama on 11th September 1862. *HMS Euryalus* returned to Hong Kong on 15th November 1862.

During the Anglo-Satsuma war, *HMS Euryalus* was the flag ship for Vice-Admiral Augustus Kuper and from the 15th to 17th August 1863 was involved in the bombardment of Kagoshima.

It was on the 6th September 1864, during the Shimonoseki Campaign, that Thomas performed the deeds that would later result in the award of the Victoria Cross, however, he was seriously wounded during the action and was transferred to the Hospital Ship *Melville* at Hong Kong during January 1865 in preparation for his return to England.

On 22nd September 1865, Thomas was presented with his Victoria Cross medal by Admiral Sir Michael Seymour, GCB the Commander-in-Chief, Portsmouth at a ceremony on Southsea Common; two previous Navy Victoria Cross recipients, Hugh Talbot Burgoyne and John Commerell attended the ceremony.

In January 1866, Thomas was discharged from the Navy to pension, probably due to being unfit for further service due to his wounds, and moved to Sandford in Wareham where his two sons were born.

In 1870. Thomas moved his family to Purewell, Christchurch in Hampshire where he shared a house with his Brother-in-Law George Coombs, a tailor and his wife Maryann.

At some stage, before 1881, Thomas found employment as a Toll Collector and took up residence in the Toll Gate House on Bournemouth Road at Parkstone in Dorset.

After his children had all grown up and left home, Thomas and his wife returned to Wareham where they lived on St Johns Road in Lady St Mary's.

It was while living in Wareham, that Thomas died on 16th July 1893, having just entered his 58th year; he was buried five days later in the All Saints Churchyard at Branksome Park in Dorset.

Thomas's Victoria Cross medal is on public display at the National Maritime Museum in Greenwich, London.

Figure 130a. Grave of Thomas Pride

William Henry Harrison Seeley
6th September 1864 (VC No. 324)

Gazetted: 21st April 1865 22960/2130

Rank and Unit: Ordinary Seaman – Royal Navy – *HMS Euryalus*

Citation

For the intelligence and daring which, according, to the testimony of Lieutenant Edwards, Commanding the Third Company, he exhibited in ascertaining the enemy's position, and for continuing to retain his position in front, during the advance, after he had been wounded in the arm.

Biography

William was born on 1st May 1840 at Topsham in Sagadhoe County, Maine in the United States of America to father Dayton and mother Lucy (née Johnstone). William was the oldest of five children with sister Boadicea (Bessie?) born in 1842, brother Alden born in 1843, sister Mary born in 1846 and brother Charles born in 1849.

Little is known about William's early life but at some stage he pursued a career as a merchant seaman.

Sometime in early 1860, William set sail from Boston on the British owned merchant ship *Salem*, bound for the far east.

On 4th July 1860, William was on board the *Salem* at anchor in Hong Kong and when his request to go ashore, to celebrate Independence Day, was refused he jumped ship and went ashore to celebrate.

Figure 131. William Henry Harrison Seeley

After a few days on shore, and unable to return to the *Salem*, William enlisted in the Royal Navy and joined *HMS Imperieuse* on the 17th July, even though at the time it was illegal for an American citizen to join the British armed forces.

HMS Imperieuse, commanded by Captain Rochford Maguire was the flagship of Rear-Admiral Lewis Tobias Jones, Commander in Chief of the East Indies and China station.

For the next two years, William saw service on board *HMS Imperieuse* off the north China coast and Japan until with *HMS Imperieuse* scheduled to leave Hong Kong for England on 20th November 1862 he transferred to *HMS Euryalus* on the 17th November 1862.

During the Anglo-Satsuma war, *HMS Euryalus* was the flag ship for Vice-Admiral Augustus Kuper and from the 15th to 17th August 1863 was involved in the bombardment of Kagoshima.

It was on the 6th September 1864, during the Shimonoseki Campaign, that William performed the deeds that would later result in the award of the Victoria Cross, however, he was seriously wounded during the action by a grape shot wound to his right shoulder.

William remained with *HMS Euryalus* until paid off at Portsmouth in September 1865 when she returned to England.

On 22nd September 1865, Thomas was presented with his Victoria Cross medal by Admiral Sir Michael Seymour, GCB the Commander-in-Chief, Portsmouth at a ceremony on Southsea Common; two previous Navy Victoria Cross recipients, Hugh Talbot Burgoyne and John Commerell attended the ceremony. William was the first of five American citizens to be awarded the Victoria Cross.

Soon after his return to England, William was discharged from the Royal Navy to pension, probably being judged to be unfit for further service due to his wounded arm; it is recorded that on 1st December 1865 he was in receipt of pension at Oxford.

After his discharge from the Royal Navy, William remained in England for some years and probably did not return to America until sometime after 1868.

In 1873, it is noted that he was in receipt of his pension at Chicago and by 1875 had returned to Maine and was receiving his pension in Boston.

At some stage, William was married and had a son and daughter.

On 1st October 1900, William was married for a second time (at the age of 60) to Mary Silver (née Moore), a widow, at Sharon in Massachusetts.

It was while living with his son, at 26 Barrows Street, Dedham in Massachusetts, that William died on 1st October 1914 from a cerebral haemorrhage, at the age of 74.

William was buried on 4th October 1914 at the Evergreen Cemetery on Washington Street in Stoughton in a grave next to his sister Bessie's grave – a memorial stone was placed to mark his grave on 27th May 2009.

The whereabouts of William's Victoria Cross medal is unknown, last known to be in the hands of a granddaughter in 1943.

In a rare interview for a newspaper report in 1904, William stated that his Victoria Cross had been stolen on two occasions.

The first time it was stolen while he was in the Lord Howe Tavern in London in 1868, it was returned to William three months later after it had been sent anonymously to the War Office in Whitehall.

On the second occasion the medal was stolen by a shipmate at Boston in 1889, miraculously it was recovered 18 months later when William spotted a Victoria Cross medal on display in a curiosity shop in London. When he entered the shop to view the medal he was surprise to find that it was his medal and after providing proof of ownership to the police it was returned to him.

Figure 131a. Grave of William Henry Harrison Seeley

William Spottiswoode Trevor
2nd April 1865[189] (VC No. 325)

Gazetted: 31st December 1867 23338/7107

Rank and Unit: Major – Bengal Engineers

Citation

For their gallant conduct at the attack on the Block-house at Dewangiri, in Bhutan, on the 30th of April, 1865. Major-General Tombs, C.B., V.C., the Officer in command at the time, reports that a party of the enemy, from 180 to 200 in number, had barricaded themselves in the Block-house in question, which they continued to defend after the rest of the position had been carried, and the main body was in retreat.

The Block-house, which was loop-holed, was the key of the enemy's position. Seeing no Officer of the storming party near him, and being anxious that the place should be taken immediately, as any protracted resistance might have caused the main body of the Bhooteas to rally, the British force having been fighting in a broiling sun on very steep and difficult ground for upwards of three hours, the General in command ordered these two Officers to show the way into the Block-house.

They had to climb up a wall which was 4 feet high, and then to enter a house, occupied by some 200 desperate men, head foremost through an opening not more than two feet wide between the top of the wall and the roof of the Block-house. Major-General Tombs states that on speaking to the Sikh soldiers around him, and telling them in Hindustani to swarm up the wall, none of them responded to the call, until these two Officers had shewn them the way, when they followed with the greatest alacrity. Both of them were wounded.

Biography

William was born on 9th October 1831 at Calcutta in India to father Robert Salusbury, a Captain in the 3rd Bengal Cavalry and mother Mary (née Spottiswoode).

The second of eight children, William had an older brother John Salusbury born on 30th August 1830 in Cawnpore; three younger brothers, Salusbury Thomas born on 18th September 1834 at Sultanpore, Edward Walter born on 27th February 1838

Figure 132. William Spottiswoode Trevor

at Karnal and Arthur Charles born on 6th April 1841 at Jellahabad; three younger sisters, Mary Mildred born on 27th February 1833 at Dacca, Frances Elizabeth born on 26th October 1835 in Bengal and Jessie Macnaughten born on 16th July 1842 in Kabul.

At the beginning of the first Anglo-Afghan, in 1839, William's father Robert was assigned to the forces of Shuja Shah Durrani, the tribal chief that Britain was trying to install as leader of Afghanistan to replace Dost Mohammed.

On the 30th June 1839, the capital Kabul was taken unopposed after Dost Mohammed and his forces fled the city and Shuja Shah Durrani was installed on the throne. Dost Mohammed later surrendered to British forces and was exiled to India in late 1840.

William Hay Macnaghten was appointed as envoy to the new Shah and Captain Robert Trevor served as one of his political officers.

William's father moved his wife and family to Kabul and all was well until rebel forces began to be assembled by Dost Mohammed's son Akber Khan and on 23rd November 1841 these forces lay siege to Kabul.

On 23rd December 1841, William's father, together with Captain George St Patrick Lawrence and Captain Kenneth Mackenzie, attended a meeting between Akber Khan and Sir William Hay Macnaghten, supposedly to discuss the terms of a treaty.

William's father and Sir William Hay Macnaghten were murdered and Captains Lawrence and Mackenzie together with about 100 of the British soldiers wives and children (including William, his mother and brothers and sisters) were captured and held hostage.

On 1st January 1842, General William Elphinstone signed a treaty with Akber Khan which allowed him to lead the British garrison at Kabul, together with civilians (except those held hostage) to safety.

189 The *London Gazette* incorrectly gives the date of the action as 30th April 1865.

The March out of Afghanistan began on 6th January, however, the treachery of Akber Khan was once again evident and despite the treaty the British force was attacked in the passes leading out of Afghanistan. The men were slaughtered with only one officer, one NCO and seven men of the 44th regiment of foot being captured; Doctor William Brydon managed to make his way to safety.

On 15th September 1842, Kabul was relieved by British forces commanded by Major-General George Pollock and William and the other hostages were released after an incarceration of almost nine months.

William's youngest sister Jessie was born during the period of imprisonment but died at Ferozepore on 16th December 1842, soon after their release.

With her husband now dead, William's mother left India, returned to the UK and took up residence in Scotland with her family.

After completing his education at Edinburgh Academy, William joined the East India Company military seminary at Addiscombe in 1848.

On graduating from Addiscombe, William was awarded a commission as Ensign in the Bengal Engineers on 28th December 1849[190] and attended a course of instruction in the art of Sapping and Mining at the Royal Engineers college at Chatham under the tutelage of Colonel Sir Frederick Smith.

While attending Chatham, William spent some months on special duties at the Great Exhibition of 1851.

On the 5th February 1852, William joined his unit in India just in time to join the Expeditionary Force which left in March to take part in the 2nd Anglo-Burmese War (5th April to 20th December 1852).

William soon saw action, being involved in the attack and capture of the White House Piquet stockade near Rangoon on 12th April 1852. For his part in the action, during which he was severely wounded, William received a mention in despatches.

Bt the Autumn, William was sufficiently recovered from his wounds to join the force commanded by Sir John Cheape operating in the Donabew district during which he was involved in several actions around Prome culminating in an attack on Kym Kazim on 19th March 1853 during which he was again wounded.

For his part in this action William received the thanks of the Indian Government in a notification dated 22nd April 1853.

For his part in the war, William was awarded the India General Service Medal (1854–95) with clasp for Pegu.

On the 1st August 1854, William received a promotion to the rank of Lieutenant.

190 *London Gazette* – 21054/3944

After the war, William served with the Public Works Department in Burma where he was employed on the Pegu survey and a survey of the Bassein River, with a view to the construction of a sanatorium at the river mouth.

In October 1857, William was transferred to Bengal, appointed as Executive Engineer of the Darjeeling Division where he served with the Darjeeling Field Force during the Indian Mutiny and was involved in the attack on the 75th Bengal Native Infantry mutineers from Dacca at Cherabandar on 12th December 1857.

For his service during the mutiny, William was awarded the Indian Mutiny Medal (1857–58), without clasps.

On his return to Darjeeling, William was involved in the construction of new barracks at Senchal.

On the 19th June 1858, William was married to Eliza Ann (née Fisher) at Darjeeling, the couple would go on to have two children; Lylee Grace born in Dinapore on 3rd March 1860 and Florence Mary born at Fort William, Calcutta on 17th March 1862.

William was promoted to the rank of 2nd Captain on 27th August 1858.[191]

Until April 1861, when he was appointed as Garrison Engineer at Fort William in Calcutta, William was employed in the construction of the Ganges Darjeeling Road.

During his time at Fort William, William converted a tract of waste land on the banks of the river Hooghly into a pleasure resort, known as the Eden Gardens.

In February 1862, William was appointed as Superintending Engineer of the northern circle, during which time he oversaw the completion of the Ganges Darjeeling Road.

William was appointed as Controller of Accounts for the Public Works Department in Bengal in May 1863, where he made improvements to the methods of book keeping.

In September 1864, William was appointed to the command of the Bengal Sappers and Miners attached to the Duar Field Force, under the command of General Dunsford, and took part in the Bhutan (Duar) war which was declared on 12th November 1864.

William was attached to the Bhutan Field Force as field engineer under General Tombs in February 1865, it was with this force, in an attack on Dewangiri on 2nd April, that he performed the deeds for which he would later be awarded the Victoria Cross.

Suffering from illness at the time and having been wounded five times during the action, William was treated at Gauhati before being returned to England on sick leave.

For his part in the war, William was awarded the clasp for Bhutan to add to his India General Service Medal (1854–95).

191 *London Gazette* – 22621/2238

On 15th May 1866, William received a brevet promotion to the rank of Major.

William returned to India in 1867, after 20 months on sick leave, and was appointed as Superintending Engineer of the Bengal Presidency.

On 23rd March 1868, William was presented with his Victoria Cross Medal by General Fordyce, commander of the Bengal Presidency Division at the Maidan at Fort William in Calcutta.

In 1870, William returned to England on a two year furlough and on his return to India in 1872 was appointed as Superintending Engineer of Military Works.

William was promoted to the rank of Major on 5th July 1872.[192]

In January 1873, William was appointed as Chief Engineer for Central India and for three months up to April 1874 officiated as Inspector General.

William was appointed as Special Chief Engineer Famine Relief Works, North of the Ganges, in April 1874 and on completion of the works in April 1875 received the thanks of the Indian Government for his efforts.

On the 11th August 1874, William received a brevet promotion to the rank of Lieutenant-Colonel.[193]

In December 1875, William was appointed as the Chief Engineer to Burma and on 10th March 1876 was promoted to the rank of Lieutenant-Colonel.

For a time between 1878 to 1879, William was on furlough in England but on his return he took up his role as Chief Engineer in Burma.

William received a brevet promotion to the rank of Colonel on 19th August 1879.

In 1880, William was appointed as the Director General of the Railways in India (succeeding his older brother Major-General John Salusbury Trevor).

On the 20th February 1882, William was appointed as Secretary to the Government of India, for the Public Works Department.

William was promoted to the rank of Colonel on 16th September 1886[194] (subsequently antedated to 8th September).[195]

On 20th February 1887,[196] after 37 years of service, William was granted leave to retire with pension and an extra annuity, he was also given the honorary rank of Major-General.[197]

After leaving the Army, William returned to England and on the 2nd November 1907 died at his home in 11 Queen's Mansions, Victoria Street in London at the age of 76.

William was buried in Kensal Green Cemetery in London.

William's Victoria Cross Medal is on public display at the Royal Engineers Museum in Gillingham, Kent.

Figure 132a. Grave of William Spottiswoode Trevor

192 *London Gazette* – 23876/3194
193 *London Gazette* – 24123/4072
194 *London Gazette* – 25631/4835
195 *London Gazette* – 25657/6435
196 William was not placed on the Supernumerary Unemployed List until 27th February 1887.
197 *London Gazette* – 25688/1915

James Dundas
2nd April 1865[198] (VC No. 326)

Gazetted: 31st December 1867 23338/7107

Rank and Unit: Lieutenant – Bengal Engineers

Citation

For their gallant conduct at the attack on the Block-house at Dewangiri, in Bhutan, on the 30th of April, 1865. Major-General Tombs, C.B., V.C., the Officer in command at the time, reports that a party of the enemy, from 180 to 200 in number, had barricaded themselves in the Block-house in question, which they continued to defend after the rest of the position had been carried, and the main body was in retreat.

The Block-house, which was loop-holed, was the key of the enemy's position. Seeing no Officer of the storming party near him, and being anxious that the place should be taken immediately, as any protracted resistance might have caused the main body of the Bhooteas to rally, the British force having been fighting in a broiling sun on very steep and difficult ground for upwards of three hours, the General in command ordered these two Officers to show the way into the Block-house.

They had to climb up a wall which was 4 feet high, and then to enter a house, occupied by some 200 desperate men, head foremost through an opening not more than two feet wide between the top of the wall and the roof of the Block-house. Major-General Tombs states that on speaking to the Sikh soldiers around him, and telling them in Hindoostani to swarm up the wall, none of them responded to the call, until these two Officers had shewn them the way, when they followed with the greatest alacrity. Both of them were wounded.

Biography

James and his twin brother Colin Mackenzie were born on 12th September 1842 at Edinburgh to father George, Lord Manour a law lord of the Edinburgh High Court, and mother Elizabeth (née Mackenzie). One of nine children, James (apart from his twin) had three brothers; George Ralph born in 1845, William John born on 16th March 1849 and David born on 8th June 1854. He also had four sisters; Elizabeth Christian born in 1842, Mary Frances born in 1846, Helen Anne born in 1848 and Katherine Louisa born in 1849.

Figure 133. James Dundas

James was educated at Edinburgh Academy and between 1855 and 1857 attended Trinity College in Glenalmond.

In August 1858, just before his 16th birthday, James became a cadet at the East India Company Military Seminary at Addiscombe and following his graduation was commissioned as a Lieutenant in the Bengal Engineers on the 8th June 1860.

After completing a course for Sappers and Miners at the Royal Engineering College at Chatham, James set sail for India in March 1862 and initially served with the Bengal Sappers and Miners at Roorkee before being transferred to the Public Works Department as an Executive Engineer.

In September 1864, James was attached to the Duar Field Force, under the command of General Dunsford, and took part in the Bhutan (Duar) war which was declared on 12th November 1864.

It was while attached to the Bhutan Field Force, in an attack on Dewangiri on 2nd April, that James performed the deeds for which he would later be awarded the Victoria Cross. During the action, James was wounded by an arrow to the chest and a rock thrown at his head.

For his part in the war, James was awarded the India General Service Medal (1854–95) with clasp for Bhutan.

After the war was over, James returned to his role as Executive Engineer with the Public Works Department.

On 23rd March 1868, James was presented with his Victoria Cross Medal by General Fordyce, commander of the Bengal Presidency Division at the Maidan at Fort William in Calcutta.

In 1870, James was on leave in England and on his return in 1871 he was appointed as a personal assistant to General Sir Alexander Taylor in the Public Works Department.

198 *London Gazette* – incorrectly states the date as 30th April 1865.

On the 3rd August 1872, James received a promotion to the rank of Captain.[199]

When his uncle Sir David died without issue in 1877, James inherited the Ochertyre Estate near Stirling and took a short leave in England to manage his affairs.

On his return to India, James continued in his role as personal assistant to General Taylor.

In the summer of 1878, while serving at Simla, James saved the life of a native Indian. At a house in the Simla bazaar a house fire had caused the roof to collapse and bury a man so that he was unable to escape the fire. James who was passing at the time, attempted to enter the house but was driven back by flames and smoke. His calls for assistance were answered by an Artillery Officer and the pair this time managed to drag the man to safety, during the rescue James was badly burned on the hands and arms.

In the spring of 1879, James was appointed to the Secretariat of the Indian Government but served for only a short period as he took up a position with the Kurram Valley Field Force commanded by General Roberts going to fight in the 2nd Anglo-Afghan War.

The field force was attacked by Afghan troops near Sherpur on 23rd December 1879 but the attack was fought off by the British troops and in the afternoon, James was instructed to blow up an abandoned fort nearby.

Figure 133a. Grave of James Dundas

Together with Lieutenant Nugent of the Royal Engineers, James laid a mine to destroy the fort, however, a defective fuse caused a premature explosion that killed both men before they were able to get clear.

James was buried on the next day at the Seah Singh Cemetery near Sherpur.

For his service in the war, James was awarded the Afghanistan Medal (1878–80) with clasps for Charisa and Kabul.

James' Victoria Cross Medal is on public display at the Imperial War Museum in London as part of the Lord Ashcroft collection.

199 *London Gazette* – 23882/3441

Timothy O'Hea
9th June 1866 (VC No. 327)

Gazetted: 1st January 1867 23204/22

Rank and Unit: Private – 1st Battalion, Rifle Brigade (Prince Consort's Own)

Citation

For his courageous conduct on the occasion of a Fire which occurred in a Railway Car containing ammunition, between Quebec and Montreal, on the 9th of June last.

The Serjeant in charge of the Escort states that, when at Danville Station, on the Grand Trunk Railway, the alarm was given that the Car was on fire; it was immediately disconnected, and, whilst considering what was best to be done, Private O'Hea took the keys from his hand, rushed to the Car, opened it, and called out for water and a ladder.

It is stated that it was due to his example that the fire was suppressed.

Biography

Timothy was born some time during 1846 in the village of Schull near Bantry in Co Cork, Ireland, nothing is known regarding his parents or early life.

Soon after reaching his 18th birthday, Timothy joined the British army on 6th November 1863, enlisting as a Private in the 1st Battalion, the Rifle Brigade (Prince Consort's Own).

In 1864, Timothy was sent with his regiment to Canada to assist with the quelling of the Fenian Riots, arriving at Montreal on 7th September 1864.

It was at Danville in Quebec, on 9th June 1866, while escorting an ammunition train, that Timothy performed the deeds for which he would later be awarded the Victoria Cross. The award was made under the provisions of the 10th August 1858 amendment to the original warrant which allowed awards to be made for deeds not within the face of the enemy.

Timothy was presented with his Victoria Cross Medal on 26th April 1867, while still serving in Canada; to date this is the only Victoria Cross to have been presented for deeds which occurred on Canadian soil.

On 15th October 1867, Timothy was invalided back to England and left the army soon afterwards.

Sometime around 1872, Timothy emigrated to New Zealand and for a short time served with the Otago Mounted Constabulary, taking part in the last Maori War.

Figure 134. Timothy O'Hea

In June 1874, Timothy moved to Sydney in Australia, two days after his arrival he joined an expedition led by Andrew Hume, who had just been released from prison for horse stealing.

The expedition was intended to substantiate claims that a survivor, of an expedition led by Frederich Wilhelm Ludwig Leichhardt to the Swan river, was living with aboriginals in north west Australia.

Frederick Eccleston Du Faur, who was financing the expedition arranged for Timothy to join the team at Maitland.

The expedition slowly made its way towards south west Queensland and at Mungindi were joined by an ex-British soldier Lewis Thompson. They were later delayed for about six weeks at Thagomindhah station, while they waited for the owner Vincent James Dowling to return.

Growing impatient, the expedition left the station on 1st November and proceeding towards Cooper's Creek camped at Graham's Creek.

The next morning, after breaking camp, the expedition set out, inexplicably failing to replenish the large water bags that they carried, little knowing that this was the last water that they would see for several days.

After three days marching in the bush, without finding water, it was decided to return to Graham's Creek.

On the 6th November, Timothy collapsed through lack of water and after leaving Andrew Hume to care for him, Lewis Thompson set out on his own to find water, eventually staggering into the station at Nockatunga.

A search party later recovered Andrew Hume's body, Timothy's body was recovered some time later by aboriginals.

Timothy's date of death is assumed to be 6th November, when last seen by Lewis Thompson.

It is stated that Timothy was buried in an unmarked grave at the Nockatunga station in Queensland, however, this has never been confirmed.

Timothy's Victoria Cross Medal is on public display at the Royal Green Jackets Museum, Winchester, when he departed on the expedition he had left his medal with F. E. Du Faur's brother-in-law and after languishing in the Art Gallery of New South Wales for many years was eventually donated to the regimental museum.

Figure 134a. Memorial to Timothy O'Hea

Samuel Hodge
30th June 1866 (VC No. 328)

Gazetted: 4th January 1867 23205/84

Rank and Unit: Private No. 268 – 4th Battalion West India Regiment

Citation

For his bravery at the storming and capture of the stockaded town of Tubabecolong, in the kingdom of Barra, River Gambia, on the evening of the 30th of June last. Colonel D'Arcy, of the Gambia Volunteers, states that this man and another, who was afterwards killed, pioneers in the 4th West India Regiment, answered his call for volunteers, with axes in hand, to hew down, the stockade.

Colonel D'Arcy having effected an entrance, Private Hodge followed him through the town, opening with his axe two gates from the inside, which were barricaded, so allowing the supports to enter, who carried the place from east to west at the point of the bayonet.

On issuing to the glacis through the west gate, Private Hodge was presented by Colonel D'Arcy to his comrades, as the bravest soldier in their regiment, a fact which they acknowledged with loud acclamations.

Biography

Samuel was born some time during 1840 on Tortola, the largest of the Virgin Islands in the West Indies, unfortunately very little is known of his life story.

Samuel initially enlisted in the 3rd Battalion West India Regiment, in 1861 he was station with this unit at the Barbados and Jamaica station.

At some stage, Samuel was transferred to the 4th Battalion and was shipped, with his regiment, to form the garrison at Bathurst in Gambia, West Africa.

It was common during the 19th century to use West Indian troops in Africa as white troops suffered badly from malaria, blackwater fever and dysentery; Africa was widely known as "the white man's grave".

In 1866, Samuel was part of an expeditionary force, led by Lieutenant-Colonel George Abbas Kooli D'Arcy commanding officer of the 3rd Battalion and Governor of the Gambia, sent against the rebel leader Amar Faal at his capital Tubabecolong.

It was on the 30th June 1866, during an attack on the town, that Samuel performed the deeds for which he was later awarded the Victoria Cross. During the action he was seriously wounded.

Samuel was rotated back to the Caribbean, with his regiment and was based on British Honduras.

On 24th June 1867, Samuel was promoted to the rank of Lance Corporal and was presented with his Victoria Cross Medal by Brigadier-General Robert Hartley, while still serving on British Honduras.

Sadly, Samuel never fully recovered from his wounds and on 14th January 1868 he died as a result of a fever and was buried in an unmarked grave in the Belize City Military Cemetery.

The location of Samuel's Victoria Cross medal is unknown, believed to be in the hands of his family.

Figure 135a. Grave of Samuel Hodge

Campbell Mellis Douglas
7th May 1867 (VC No. 329)

Gazetted: 17th December 1867 23333/6878

Rank and Unit: Assistant Surgeon – 2nd Battalion, 24th Regiment of Foot

Citation

For the very gallant and daring manner in which, on the 7th of May, 1867, they risked their lives in manning a boat and proceeding through a dangerous surf to the rescue of some of their comrades, who formed part of an expedition which had been sent to the Island of Little Andaman, by order of the Chief Commissioner of British Burmah, with the view of ascertaining the fate of the Commander and seven of the crew of the ship "Assam Valley," who had landed there, and were supposed to have been murdered by the natives.

The officer who commanded the troops on the occasion reports: "About an hour later in the day Dr. Douglas, 2nd Battalion, 24th Regiment, and the four Privates referred to, gallantly manning the second gig, made their way through the surf almost to the shore, but finding their boat was half filled with water, they retired.

A second attempt made by Dr. Douglas and party proved successful, five of us being safely passed through the surf to the boats outside. A third and last trip got the whole of the party left on shore safe to the boats. It is stated that Dr. Douglas accomplished these trips through the surf to the shore by no ordinary exertion. He stood in the bows of the boat, and worked her in an intrepid and seamanlike manner, cool to a degree, as if what he was then doing was an ordinary act of every-day life. The four Privates behaved in an equally cool and collected manner, rowing through the roughest surf when the slightest hesitation or want of pluck on the part of any one of them would have been attended by the gravest results. It is reported that seventeen officers and men were thus saved from, what must otherwise have been a fearful risk, if not certainty of death.

Biography

Campbell was born on 5th August 1840 at Grosse Isle, Quebec City in Canada to father Dr. George Mellis and mother Charlotte Saxton (née Campbell). His father was the superintendant of the Grosse Isle Quarantine Station, on an island in the St Lawrence, which was the main immigration centre for British North America.

Figure 136. Campbell Mellis Douglas

Campbell was one of seven children, including; Archibald Lucius born on 8th February 1842 in Quebec who would go on to become an Admiral in the British Royal Navy, Justin, Charles Stuart and Agnes.

After attending St John's College and Laval University in Quebec, Campbell completed his education at Edinburgh University where he graduated as an MD in 1861; he would later become a Fellow of the Royal College of Surgeons.

On leaving University, Campbell attended the Army Medical School at Chatham and on graduation was commissioned as an Assistant Surgeon on the Army Medical Staff on 1st October 1862.[200]

On the 22nd May 1863, Campbell was transferred to the 24th Regiment of Foot as an Assistant Surgeon.[201]

Soon after his transfer, Campbell joined his regiment on the island of Mauritius where they had been serving as the garrison since 23rd May 1860.

Between the 5th and 6th October 1865 Campbell and the regiment boarded the ships *HMS Devonport* and *HMS Star of India* at Port Louis and set sail for British Burma where they landed at Rangoon between the 2nd and 10th December 1865.

At some stage, Campbell was sent as part of a detachment to Port Blair on Grand Andaman, a new penal colony was being constructed on nearby Ross Island.

Campbell was appointed as medical officer to an expedition led by Lieutenant W. T. Much that was sent to investigate the fate of the Captain and crew of the *Assam Valley* said to have been murdered on Little Andaman Island by natives.

200 *London Gazette* – 22724/1939
201 *London Gazette* – 22738/2687

The expedition set sail from Port Blair on 6th May 1867 and reached Little Andaman Island the next day, it was on this day, while rescuing some of the party, that Campbell performed the deeds for which he was later awarded the Victoria Cross. For this action Campbell was also awarded the Royal Humane Society Silver Medal.

It is believed that the award of the Victoria Cross to Campbell is unique, in that he is the only Army officer to have received the award for bravery at sea.

At some stage, the Andaman Island detachment returned to Rangoon in Burma and it was here on 16th April 1868 that Campbell was presented with his Victoria Cross medal by Major-General Robert Nicholas Faunce, GOC of British forces in Burma.

On the 31st December 1868 and 1st January 1869, the regiment departed in wings for Madras on their way to Secunderabad, where they arrived on 16th February 1869.

While serving at Secunderabad, Campbell was transferred to a position on the Army Medical staff as an Assistant Surgeon on 1st November 1871[202] and returned to England.

On the 31st August 1872, Campbell was transferred to the Royal Artillery as an Assistant Surgeon[203] and was posted to Halifax, Nova Scotia in his native Canada.

Campbell was promoted to the rank of Surgeon on 1st March 1873.

On 10th August 1874, Campbell married Eleanor Annie McMaster (née Burmeister) the widow of Surgeon Valentine Mumbee McMaster VC, who was awarded his Victoria Cross for deeds at Lucknow on 25th September 1857.

In addition to a son Bryce from her former marriage, the couple would have three children; George Mellis born at Halifax on 9th December 1875, son Lionel and daughter Muriel Constance.

On the 28th April 1876, Campbell was promoted to the rank of Surgeon Major.[204]

In addition to his Army career, Campbell pursued his other interests publishing books on both medical matters and his passion for canoeing. In 1880 he was granted a patent in Canada for his design for a collapsible canoe.

At some time in 1881, Campbell was assigned to further duties in India and was stationed in Bengal.

On the 1st October 1882, after 20 years of service, Campbell was retired to pension with the honorary rank of Brigade Surgeon[205] and returned to Canada where for a time he took up private practice at Lakefield in Ontario.

202 *London Gazette* – 23790/4428
203 *London Gazette* – 23891/3845
204 *London Gazette* – 24331/3244
205 *London Gazette* – 25159/4734

In early 1883, Campbell gave the first St John's Ambulance First Aid training course at Quebec city.

In 1885, Campbell was recruited as a medical officer with the rank of Lieutenant-Colonel to take charge of No.1 Field Hospital during the North West Rebellion (2nd Riel Rebellion) in Canada. The rebellion of the Métis people, led by Louis Riel was about establishing an autonomous French speaking state within British Canada.

Hospital staff and supplies, for the field hospital, were transported by rail to Saskatchewan Landing on the South Saskatchewan River, where the steamer *Northcote* was waiting to ship them downstream to Saskatoon.

When the *Northcote* seemed slow in returning from one of her trips downstream, Campbell decided to investigate what the problem was.

On the journey to Saskatchewan Landing, Campbell had brought with him a 12 foot collapsible canoe of his own design, which he used to paddle down the river to find the *Northcote*. It was not long before he came across the steamer stranded on a sandbar and seeing that matters were in hand to refloat the vessel he continued on to Saskatoon to join his field hospital.

Campbell arrived at Saskatoon in time to help treat the wounded from the Battle of Fish Creek which had taken place on 3rd May and remained at his station to help treat the wounded from the Battle of Batoche on 14th May, which was the last action of the rebellion.

For his service during the rebellion, Campbell was awarded the North West Canada (1885) Medal.

In 1889, Campbell canoed from New York to Boston.

Campbell returned to England in 1894 and took up residence at Dunmow in Essex and in June 1895, he crossed the English Channel in his collapsible canoe, which he had named "Saskatoon".

Figure 136a. Grave of Campbell Mellis Douglas

In his retirement, Campbell served as Depot Medical Officer for Berwick on Tweed until 1897 and then Depot Medical Officer for Perth until 1902.

It is likely that after retiring from his post at Perth, he went to live with his daughter at "Birdwood" in Horrington near Wells in Somerset. It was while living with his daughter that Campbell died at the age of 69 on 31st December 1909 and was buried on 4th January 1910 at Wells Cemetery.

Campbell's Victoria Cross medal is on public display at the Canadian War Museum in Ottawa, Ontario, Canada.

David Bell

7th May 1867 (VC No. 330)

Figure 137. David Bell

Gazetted: 17th December 1867 23333/6878

Rank and Unit: Private No. 330 – 2nd Battalion, 24th Regiment of Foot

Citation

For the very gallant and daring manner in which, on the 7th of May, 1867, they risked their lives in manning a boat and proceeding through a dangerous surf to the rescue of some of their comrades, who formed part of an expedition which had been sent to the Island of Little Andaman, by order of the Chief Commissioner of British Burmah, with the view of ascertaining the fate of the Commander and seven of the crew of the ship "Assam Valley," who had landed there, and were supposed to have been murdered by the natives.

The officer who commanded the troops on the occasion reports: "About an hour later in the day Dr. Douglas, 2nd Battalion, 24th Regiment, and the four Privates referred to, gallantly manning the second gig, made their way through the surf almost to the shore, but finding their boat was half filled with water, they retired.

A second attempt made by Dr. Douglas and party proved successful, five of us being safely passed through the surf to the boats outside. A third and last trip got the whole of the party left on shore safe to the boats. It is stated that Dr. Douglas accomplished these trips through the surf to the shore by no ordinary exertion. He stood in the bows of the boat, and worked her in an intrepid and seamanlike manner, cool to a degree, as if what he was then doing was an ordinary act of every-day life. The four Privates behaved in an equally cool and collected manner, rowing through the roughest surf when the slightest hesitation or want of pluck on the part of any one of them would have been attended by the gravest results. It is reported that seventeen officers and men were thus saved from, what must otherwise have been a fearful risk, if not certainty of death.

Biography

David was born some time in 1845[206] in Co Down, Ireland.

On 19th April 1860, David joined the army at Lisburn in Ireland and was enlisted as Private No. 330 in the 2nd Battalion of the 24th Regiment of Foot.

Soon after his enlistment, David joined his regiment on the island of Mauritius where they had been serving as the garrison since 23rd May 1860, having left Cork in Ireland on 13th March.

Between the 5th and 6th October 1865 David and the regiment boarded the ships *HMS Devonport* and *HMS Star of India* at Port Louis and set sail for British Burma where they landed at Rangoon between the 2nd and 10th December 1865.

At some stage, David was sent as part of a detachment to Port Blair on Grand Andaman, a new penal colony was being constructed on nearby Ross Island.

David was assigned to an expedition led by Lieutenant W. T. Much that was sent to investigate the fate of the Captain and crew of the *Assam Valley* said to have been murdered on Little Andaman Island by natives.

The expedition set sail from Port Blair on 6th May 1867 and reached Little Andaman Island the next day, it was on this day, while rescuing some of the party, that David performed the deeds for which he was later awarded the Victoria Cross.

At some stage, the Andaman Island detachment returned to Rangoon in Burma and it was here on 16th April 1868 that David was presented with his Victoria Cross medal by Major-General Robert Nicholas Faunce, GOC of British forces in Burma.

On the 31st December 1868 and 1st January 1869, the regiment departed in wings for Madras on their way to Secunderabad, where they arrived on 16th February 1869.

David and the regiment left Secunderabad on 14th November 1872 and began their journey to return home to England. On the 2nd & 3rd December the regiment boarded the Indian troopship *Euphrates* at Bombay and set sail for England, arriving at Portsmouth on 26th January 1873.

206 His army papers give a birth year of 1842, probably to reflect the minimum enlistment age of 18

After landing at Portsmouth, the regiment proceeded to Warley in Essex and it was here on 26th May 1873 that David was discharged from the army after 13 years of service.

Following his time in the army, David worked for some time as a labourer in a cement factory and then as a skilled labourer in No.8 Machine Shop at the Chatham Dockyard.

At some stage David was married and his wife Ann died at the age of 83 on 27th October 1944.

On 7th March 1920, David died at his home; 2 Unity Gardens, Gardiner Street in Gillingham, Kent; from senile decay, at the age of 75. He was buried on 12th March 1920 at Woodlands Road Cemetery in Gillingham.

David's Victoria Cross medal is on public display at the South Wales Borderers Museum in Powys, Wales.

Figure 137a. Grave of David Bell

James Cooper

7th May 1867 (VC No. 331)

Gazetted: 17th December 1867 23333/6878

Rank and Unit: Private No. 496 – 2nd Battalion, 24th Regiment of Foot

Citation

For the very gallant and daring manner in which, on the 7th of May, 1867, they risked their lives in manning a boat and proceeding through a dangerous surf to the rescue of some of their comrades, who formed part of an expedition which had been sent to the Island of Little Andaman, by order of the Chief Commissioner of British Burmah, with the view of ascertaining the fate of the Commander and seven of the crew of the ship "Assam Valley," who had landed there, and were supposed to have been murdered by the natives.

The officer who commanded the troops on the occasion reports: "About an hour later in the day Dr. Douglas, 2nd Battalion, 24th Regiment, and the four Privates referred to, gallantly manning the second gig, made their way through the surf almost to the shore, but finding their boat was half filled with water, they retired.

A second attempt made by Dr. Douglas and party proved successful, five of us being safely passed through the surf to the boats outside. A third and last trip got the whole of the party left on shore safe to the boats. It is stated that Dr. Douglas accomplished these trips through the surf to the shore by no ordinary exertion. He stood in the bows of the boat, and worked her in an intrepid and seamanlike manner, cool to a degree, as if what he was then doing was an ordinary act of every-day life. The four Privates behaved in an equally cool and collected manner, rowing through the roughest surf when the slightest hesitation or want of pluck on the part of any one of them would have been attended by the gravest results. It is reported that seventeen officers and men were thus saved from, what must otherwise have been a fearful risk, if not certainty of death.

Biography

James was born in September 1840 at Birmingham to father William, a jeweller and mother Elizabeth a Stay Maker.

On 12th November 1858, James, left his job as a jeweller and joined the army at Birmingham, he was enlisted as Private No.496 in the 2nd Battalion of the 24th Regiment of Foot which had been raised at Sheffield on 3rd June 1858.

Figure 138. James Cooper

In June 1859, James was moved with his regiment to Aldershot and then on 21st February 1860 boarded *HMS Urgent* and set sail for service in Cork, Ireland.

On the 13th March 1860, the regiment set sail for the island of Mauritius where they arrived on 23rd May 1860 to serve as the garrison.

Between the 5th and 6th October 1865 James and the regiment boarded the ships *HMS Devonport* and *HMS Star of India* at Port Louis and set sail for British Burma where they landed at Rangoon between the 2nd and 10th December 1865.

At some stage, James was sent as part of a detachment to Port Blair on Grand Andaman, a new penal colony was being constructed on nearby Ross Island.

James was assigned to an expedition led by Lieutenant W. T. Much that was sent to investigate the fate of the Captain and crew of the *Assam Valley* said to have been murdered on Little Andaman Island by natives.

The expedition set sail from Port Blair on 6th May 1867 and reached Little Andaman Island the next day, it was on this day, while rescuing some of the party, that James performed the deeds for which he was later awarded the Victoria Cross.

At some stage, the Andaman Island detachment returned to Rangoon in Burma and it was here on 16th April 1868 that James was presented with his Victoria Cross medal by Major-General Robert Nicholas Faunce, GOC of British forces in Burma.

On 4th September 1868, at Rangoon, James requested his discharge from the army, having completed his first period of limited engagement.

After having completed over ten years of service, James was discharged from the army at Sheffield on 31st December 1868.

On leaving the army James returned to work as a jeweller in Birmingham and in November 1871 was living at Berners Street in Birmingham.

On the 19th November 1871, James was married to Maria (née Hampton) at St Giles's Church in Birmingham and the couple moved to Aston's Buildings on Wheeler Street in Birmingham.

In 1876, James was living at Back Court, 4 New John Street in Birmingham.

On the 13th April 1878, James was recalled to service in the army and served with the 2nd Battalion of the 6th Regiment of Foot until 1st August 1878 when he was transferred to the reserves.

James was discharged from the reserves on 14th May 1881.

On 9th August 1889, at the age of 49, James died at his home; 43 Court Farm Street in Birmingham and was buried in an unmarked common grave at Warestone Lane Cemetery, Warestone, Hockley in Birmingham.

James's Victoria Cross medal is on display at the Royal Warwickshire (TA) Regiment, TA Centre, Barrows Lane, Sheldon, Birmingham, West Midlands, England.

Figure 138a. Memorial to James Cooper

William Griffiths
7th May 1867 (VC No. 332)

Gazetted: 17th December 1867 23333/6878

Rank and Unit: Private No. 1056 – 2nd Battalion, 24th Regiment of Foot

Citation

For the very gallant and daring manner in which, on the 7th of May, 1867, they risked their lives in manning a boat and proceeding through a dangerous surf to the rescue of some of their comrades, who formed part of an expedition which had been sent to the Island of Little Andaman, by order of the Chief Commissioner of British Burmah, with the view of ascertaining the fate of the Commander and seven of the crew of the ship "Assam Valley," who had landed there, and were supposed to have been murdered by the natives.

The officer who commanded the troops on the occasion reports: "About an hour later in the day Dr. Douglas, 2nd Battalion, 24th Regiment, and the four Privates referred to, gallantly manning the second gig, made their way through the surf almost to the shore, but finding their boat was half filled with water, they retired.

A second attempt made by Dr. Douglas and party proved successful, five of us being safely passed through the surf to the boats outside. A third and last trip got the whole of the party left on shore safe to the boats. It is stated that Dr. Douglas accomplished these trips through the surf to the shore by no ordinary exertion. He stood in the bows of the boat, and worked her in an intrepid and seamanlike manner, cool to a degree, as if what he was then doing was an ordinary act of every-day life. The four Privates behaved in an equally cool and collected manner, rowing through the roughest surf when the slightest hesitation or want of pluck on the part of any one of them would have been attended by the gravest results. It is reported that seventeen officers and men were thus saved from, what must otherwise have been a fearful risk, if not certainty of death.

Biography

William was born some time during 1841 at Co Rosscommon in Ireland.

On 11th April 1859, William left his job as a collier and joined the army at Warwick, where he was enlisted as Private No. 1056 in the 2nd Battalion of the 24th Regiment of Foot.

In June 1859, William was moved with his regiment to Aldershot and then on 21st February 1860 boarded *HMS Urgent* and set sail for service in Cork, Ireland.

On the 13th March 1860, the regiment set sail for the island of Mauritius where they arrived on 23rd May 1860 to serve as the garrison.

Between the 5th and 6th October 1865 James and the regiment boarded the ships *HMS Devonport* and *HMS Star of India* at Port Louis and set sail for British Burma where they landed at Rangoon between the 2nd and 10th December 1865.

At some stage, William was sent as part of a detachment to Port Blair on Grand Andaman, a new penal colony was being constructed on nearby Ross Island.

William was assigned to an expedition led by Lieutenant W. T. Much that was sent to investigate the fate of the Captain and crew of the *Assam Valley* said to have been murdered on Little Andaman Island by natives.

The expedition set sail from Port Blair on 6th May 1867 and reached Little Andaman Island the next day, it was on this day, while rescuing some of the party, that William performed the deeds for which he was later awarded the Victoria Cross.

At some stage, the Andaman Island detachment returned to Rangoon in Burma and it was here on 16th April 1868 that William was presented with his Victoria Cross medal by Major-General Robert Nicholas Faunce, GOC of British forces in Burma.

On the 31st December 1868 and 1st January 1869, the regiment departed in wings for Madras on their way to Secunderabad, where they arrived on 16th February 1869.

William and the regiment left Secunderabad on 14th November 1872 and began their journey to return home to England. On the 2nd & 3rd December the regiment boarded the Indian troopship *Euphrates* at Bombay and set sail for England, arriving at Portsmouth on 26th January 1873.

After landing at Portsmouth, the regiment proceeded to Warley in Essex where they were stationed until December 1873 when they moved to Aldershot.

In August 1875, William and the battalion were moved to the Citadel at Dover and on 28th January 1878 they received orders to prepare for deployment to the Cape Colony, to take part in the Zulu Wars.

The regiment set sail from Plymouth on 2nd February 1878, on board *HMS Himalaya*, bound for South Africa and arrived off Simon's Bay on 28th February.

After spending some days to make repairs and take on coal, *HMS Himalaya* continued her journey on 6th March and the regiment was disembarked at East London on 11th March, from where they were despatched to King William's Town.

In August 1878, the regiment was sent to Natal and for the next three months were stationed at Pietermaritzburg where they were refitted and drilled.

As war with the Zulu chief Cetywayo now seemed inevitable, in October 1878, William and the battalion were moved to Pott's Spruit a farm near the abandoned frontier post of Fort Buckingham on the river Tugela.

The first battle of the war, a minor affair, took place on 12th January 1879 at Sirayo's Kraal, however, it was at the Battle of Isandhlwana on 22nd January 1879, where the British suffered a heavy defeat, that William was killed in action at the age of 37.

William was buried in one of the many mass graves, marked by cairns, that were dug on the battlefield, the exact location of his grave is unknown.

For his service during the Zulu Wars, William was awarded the South Africa Medal (77–79) with clasp for 1877–8–9.

William's Victoria Cross medal is on public display at the South Wales Borderers Museum in Powys, Wales.

Figure 139a. William Griffiths – Location of burial site at Isandhlwana

Thomas Murphy
7th May 1867 (VC No. 333)

Gazetted: 17th December 1867 23333/6878

Rank and Unit: Private No. 1052 – 2nd Battalion, 24th Regiment of Foot

Citation

For the very gallant and daring manner in which, on the 7th of May, 1867, they risked their lives in manning a boat and proceeding through a dangerous surf to the rescue of some of their comrades, who formed part of an expedition which had been sent to the Island of Little Andaman, by order of the Chief Commissioner of British Burmah, with the view of ascertaining the fate of the Commander and seven of the crew of the ship "Assam Valley," who had landed there, and were supposed to have been murdered by the natives.

The officer who commanded the troops on the occasion reports: "About an hour later in the day Dr. Douglas, 2nd Battalion, 24th Regiment, and the four Privates referred to, gallantly manning the second gig, made their way through the surf almost to the shore, but finding their boat was half filled with water, they retired.

A second attempt made by Dr. Douglas and party proved successful, five of us being safely passed through the surf to the boats outside. A third and last trip got the whole of the party left on shore safe to the boats. It is stated that

Figure 140. Thomas Murphy

Dr. Douglas accomplished these trips through the surf to the shore by no ordinary exertion. He stood in the bows of the boat, and worked her in an intrepid and seamanlike manner, cool to a degree, as if what he was then doing was an ordinary act of every-day life. The four Privates behaved in an equally cool and collected manner, rowing through the roughest surf when the slightest hesitation or want of pluck on the part of any one of them would have been attended by the gravest results. It is reported that seventeen officers and men were thus saved from, what must otherwise have been a fearful risk, if not certainty of death.

Biography

Thomas was born some time in 1831 at Dublin in Ireland.

Based solely upon his regimental number, I have assumed that Thomas's career in the army, initially mirrored that of Private William Griffith.

Thomas probably joined the army in April 1859, and was enlisted as Private No. 1052 in the 2nd Battalion of the 24th Regiment of Foot.

In June 1859, Thomas was moved with his regiment to Aldershot and then on 21st February 1860 boarded *HMS Urgent* and set sail for service in Cork, Ireland.

On the 13th March 1860, the regiment set sail for the island of Mauritius where they arrived on 23rd May 1860 to serve as the garrison.

Between the 5th and 6th October 1865 James and the regiment boarded the ships *HMS Devonport* and *HMS Star of India* at Port Louis and set sail for British Burma where they landed at Rangoon between the 2nd and 10th December 1865.

At some stage, Thomas was sent as part of a detachment to Port Blair on Grand Andaman, a new penal colony was being constructed on nearby Ross Island.

Thomas was assigned to an expedition led by Lieutenant W. T. Much that was sent to investigate the fate of the Captain and crew of the *Assam Valley* said to have been murdered on Little Andaman Island by natives.

The expedition set sail from Port Blair on 6th May 1867 and reached Little Andaman Island the next day, it was on this day, while rescuing some of the party, that Thomas performed the deeds for which he was later awarded the Victoria Cross.

At some stage, the Andaman Island detachment returned to Rangoon in Burma and it was here on 16th April 1868 that Thomas was presented with his Victoria Cross medal by Major-General Robert Nicholas Faunce, GOC of British forces in Burma.

On the 31st December 1868 and 1st January 1869, the regiment departed in wings for Madras on their way to Secunderabad, where they arrived on 16th February 1869.

Thomas and the regiment left Secunderabad on 14th November 1872 and began their journey to return home to England. On the 2nd & 3rd December the regiment boarded the Indian troopship *Euphrates* at Bombay and set sail for England, arriving at Portsmouth on 26th January 1873.

After landing at Portsmouth, the regiment proceeded to Warley in Essex where they were stationed until December 1873 when they moved to Aldershot.

As there is no record that Thomas was awarded the South Africa Medal (1877–79) it is unlikely that he sailed with his regiment to the Cape Colony in February 1878 but was discharged from the army at about this time.

At some stage, like many of his countrymen, Thomas emigrated to the United States of America and at the age of 60 died on 22nd March 1900 while living in Philadelphia. He was buried on 28th March 1902 (it is speculated that his body was donated to medical research hence the delay in his burial) at Laurel Hill Cemetery in Philadelphia.

The location of Thomas's Victoria Cross medal is unknown.

James Bergin
13th April 1868 (VC No. 334)

Gazetted: 28th July 1868 23405/4187

Rank and Unit: Private No. 949 – 33rd Regiment of Foot

Citation

For their conspicuous gallantry in the assault of Magdala on the 13th of April last. Lieutenant-General Lord Napier reports that, whilst the head of the column of attack was checked by the obstacles at the gate, a small stream of Officers and men of the 33rd Regiment, and an Officer of Engineers, breaking away from the main approach to Magdala, and climbing up a cliff, reached the defences, and forced their way over the wall, and through the strong and thorny fence, thus turning the defenders of the gateway. The first two men to enter, and the first in Magdala, were Drummer Magner and Private Bergin, of the 33rd Regiment.

Biography

James was born on 29th June 1845 at Killbricken in Queen's County, Ireland.

At the age of 17, James joined the British army and was enlisted as a Private in the 10th Regiment of Foot at some time during 1862.

Soon after joining the army, James transferred to the 108th Regiment of Foot, which had been incorporated into the British Army from the 108th Madras Infantry after the East India Company armies were disbanded, and joined his new regiment in India.

At some time, probably in October or November 1867, James was one of the volunteers who transferred to the 33rd Regiment of Foot to become part of the force being assembled for the expedition to Abyssinia.

The force set sail from Bombay on 24th December 1867 and was landed at Zula by mid January 1868.

On the 26th January 1868, the expeditionary force began an overland trek of over 400 miles to the Abyssinian capital Magdala where they arrived in early April.

After a brief siege, an attack on Magdala was launched on 13th April 1868 and it was during this battle that James performed the deeds for which he was later awarded the Victoria Cross.

For his service during the expedition, James was awarded the Abyssinian War Medal (1867–68).

After the war, James returned with his regiment to India and it was at Belgaum in April 1869, that James was presented with his Victoria Cross Medal by Brigadier-General James Domville.

Figure 141. James Bergin

At some stage, James transferred to the 78th Highlanders and it was with this regiment that he took part in the 2nd Anglo-Afghan war for which he was awarded the Afghanistan Medal (1878–80).

After the war, James returned to India and it was at Poona on 1st December 1880 that he died from a fever at the age of 35 and was buried in an unmarked grave in St Patrick's graveyard in Poona.

James's Victoria Cross medal is on public display at the Duke of Wellington's Regimental Museum in Halifax, West Yorkshire in England.

Michael Magner (aka Barry)
13th April 1868 (VC No. 335)

Figure 142. Michael Magner

Gazetted: 28th July 1868 23405/4187

Rank and Unit: Drummer No. 3691 – 33rd Regiment of Foot

Citation

For their conspicuous gallantry in the assault of Magdala on the 13th of April last. Lieutenant-General Lord Napier reports that, whilst the head of the column of attack was checked by the obstacles at the gate, a small stream of Officers and men of the 33rd Regiment, and an Officer of Engineers, breaking away from the main approach to Magdala, and climbing up a cliff, reached the defences, and forced their way over the wall, and through the strong and thorny fence, thus turning the defenders of the gateway. The first two men to enter, and the first in Magdala, were Drummer Magner and Private Bergin, of the 33rd Regiment.

Biography

Michael Magner Barry, was born on 21st June 1840 in Co Fermanagh in Ireland to father Edward and mother Margaret (née Magner).

His father Edward is said to have been killed in a duel in Paris, after which Margaret returned with Michael to Cork in Ireland to live with one of Edwards brothers.

Michael was sent to boarding school, but at the age of 14 ran away and sometime in 1854[207] enlisted as a drummer boy in the 33rd Regiment of Foot, using his mother's maiden name Magner as his surname.

In 1857, the regiment were deployed to India by way of Mauritius and it was while serving in India that the regiment was assigned to the expeditionary force sent to Abyssinia.

The force set sail from Bombay on 24th December 1867 and was landed at Zula by mid January 1868.

On the 26th January 1868, the expeditionary force began an overland trek of over 400 miles to the Abyssinian capital Magdala where they arrived in early April.

After a brief siege, an attack on Magdala was launched on 13th April 1868 and it was during this battle that Michael performed the deeds for which he was later awarded the Victoria Cross.

For his service during the expedition, Michael was awarded the Abyssinian War Medal (1867–68).

Soon after the war ended, Michael and the regiment returned to England and on 4th November 1868 he was presented with his Victoria Cross Medal by Lieutenant-General Sir G. Buller VC at a ceremony in Portsmouth.

In 1873, Michael was married to Margaret (née Carroll) in Colchester; a daughter Mary was born in Colchester some time in 1874 and a son Michael was born in Tasmania during 1887.

In 1873, Michael returned to Ireland with the regiment and in 1875 was once again deployed to India.

It was on 23rd March 1880, while serving in India, that Michael was discharged to pension after over 21 years of service, having completed his second term of engagement.

On leaving the army, Michael returned to England and in 1881 was living at Golden Acre in Colchester with his wife and daughter.

In 1886, Michael emigrated to Tasmania and it was while living at Launceston that his son Michael was born.

In 1894, Michael moved with his family to Melbourne in Australia and was having a hard time supporting his family, as it was reported in the press in 1894 that he was begging on the streets.

On 6th February 1897, Michael died from tuberculosis at the City General Hospital in Melbourne and was buried in the Melbourne General Cemetery.

Michael's Victoria Cross medal is on public display at the Museum of Victoria, Carlton Gardens, Melbourne in Australia.

207 It is more likely that he joined the army in 1856, when the regiment were in Ireland, if he joined in 1854 then he would have served in the Crimea but there is no record that he was awarded the campaign medal.

Donald MacIntyre
4th January 1872 (VC No. 336)

Figure 143. Donald MacIntyre

Gazetted: 27th September 1872N23902/4489

Rank and Unit: Major – Bengal Staff Corp.

Citation

For his gallant conduct at the storming of the stockaded village of Lalgnoora on the 4th January, 1872.

Colonel Macpherson, C.B., V.C., Commanding the 2nd Goorkha Regiment, in which Lieutenant-Colonel Macintyre was serving at the time as second in command, reports that this Officer, who led the assault, was the first to reach the stockade (on this side from 8 to 9 feet high); and that to climb over and disappear among the flames and smoke of the burning village, was the work of a very short time. The stockade, he adds, was successfully stormed by this Officer under fire, the heaviest the Looshais delivered that day.

Biography

Donald was born on 12th September 1831 at Kincraig House, Kincraig to father Donald and mother Margaret (née MacKenzie). Donald was the youngest of five children with three older sisters, Colina Maxwell born on 17th November 1820 in London, Charlotte Ann born on 19th November 1824 in London and Mary Isobella[208] born on 7th September 1829 in London. He also had an older brother John Mackenzie born in London on 22nd September 1827 who would go on to achieve the rank of Lieutenant-General in the Royal Artillery.

Donald was educated at private schools in England and abroad and in 1848 enrolled in the East India Company Military Seminary at Addiscombe.

On graduating from Addiscombe, Donald was commissioned as an Ensign in the 66th Light Infantry (Goorkha) Regiment of the Bengal Army on 14th June 1850.

Soon after his arrival in India, Donald was involved with his regiment in expeditions led by General Sir Colin Campbell against hill tribes on the Peshawar frontier and saw action at the Battle of Ishkakot on 18th May 1852.

Donald joined an expedition against the Boree Afrids in November 1853 and in 1856 was part of the Kuram Field Force, commanded by Sir Neville Chamberlain in Afghanistan.

208 Mary would marry General James Travers VC, who was awarded the Victoria Cross for deeds during the Indian Mutiny in July 1857.

On 23rd November 1856, Donald was promoted to the rank of Lieutenant.[209]

During the Indian Mutiny, Donald was responsible for raising a new Goorkha Regiment (the 4th) on 6th August 1857 which was deployed on the Kale Kumaon frontier to keep the Rohilcund rebels in check.

For his service during the mutiny, Donald was awarded the India Mutiny medal without clasp.

On the 2nd November 1858, Donald transferred to the Sirmoor Rifle Regiment and on 12th March 1859 was appointed as the officiating adjutant.

Donald was appointed as 2nd in charge of the regiment on 2nd May 1860.

On 14th June 1862, Donald was promoted to the rank of Captain.[210]

In 1864, Donald served with the Doab Field Force in the Peshawar Valley and in 1868 took part in the 2nd Black Mountain Expedition.

For his service during many of the expeditions and operations on the Indian North West Frontier, Donald was awarded the India General Service Medal (1854–95) with clasp for North West Frontier.

On the 14th June 1870, Donald was promoted to the rank of Major.[211]

Donald served during the Lushai Expedition (1871–72) and it was on 4th January 1872, during the storming of a stockade at Lalgnoora that he performed the deeds for which he would later be awarded the Victoria Cross.

209 *London Gazette* – 22686/6159
210 *London Gazette* – 22686/6163
211 *London Gazette* – 23705/488

For his service during the expedition, Donald received several mention in despatches and was awarded the clasp for Lushai to add to his India General Service Medal.

On the 11th September 1872, Donald received a brevet promotion to the rank of Lieutenant-Colonel[212] and on the 6th April 1876 was appointed to the command of the 2nd (Prince of Wales Own) Ghurkha Regiment.

Donald received a brevet promotion to the rank of Colonel on 1st October 1877.[213]

Following the Cyprus Convention, signed on 4th June 1878, the Ottoman Empire ceded the island of Cyprus to Britain and Donald led his regiment as part of the force of Sir Garnet Wolseley that was sent to occupy the island.

Donald led his regiment during the 2nd Anglo-Afghan War (1878–79) and as part of the Peshawar Field Force commanded by Lieutenant-General Francis Maude VC, took part in the Zakha Khel Expeditions in the Bazar Valley.

For his service during the war, Donald was awarded the Afghanistan Medal (1878–80).

After over 30 years of service, Donald was retired to pension with the honorary rank of brevet Major-General on 24th December 1880.[214]

Following his retirement, Donald took up residence at the family home MacKenzie Lodge, Fortrose in Scotland.

Figure 143a. Grave of Donald MacIntyre

In 1882, Donald was married to Angelica Alison (née Patteson) in Forfar, the couple would have three sons; Donald born on 9th November 1885, Francis Hector born on 23rd April 1889 and Ian Agnew born on 24th August 1893.

In his retirement, Donald, who was an avid traveller and sportsman, wrote an account of his experiences in a book "Hindu Koh, Wanderings and Wild Sports on and beyond the Himalayas" which was published in 1889.

Donald was also a Fellow of the Royal Geographical Society and served as a Justice of the Peace for Ross-shire.

Donald died at his home MacKenzie Lodge in Fortrose at the age of 72 and was buried in the family plot in the nearby Rose Markie Churchyard.

His Victoria Cross Medal is on public display at the Ghurkha Museum in Winchester.

212 *London Gazette* – 23895/3971
213 *London Gazette* – 24942/853
214 *London Gazette* – 24950/1200

Edric Frederick Gifford
No Date of Action[215] (VC No. 337)

Gazetted: 31st March 1874 24082/1921

Rank and Unit: Lieutenant – 2nd Battalion, 24th Regiment of Foot

Citation

For his gallant conduct during the operations, and especially at the taking of Becquah. The Officer commanding the Expeditionary Force reports that Lord Gifford was in charge of the Scouts after the Army crossed the Prah, and that it is no exaggeration to say that since the Adansi Hills were passed, he daily carried his life in his hand in the performance of his most dangerous duties. He hung upon the rear of the enemy, discovering their position, and ferreting out their intentions. With no other white man with him, he captured numerous prisoners; but Sir Garnet Wolseley brings Him forward for this mark of Royal favour most especially for his conduct at the taking of Becquah, into which place he penetrated with his scouts before the troops carried it, when his gallantry and courage were most conspicuous.

Biography

Edric was born on 5th July 1849 at Ampney Park near Cirencester in Hampshire, the eldest son of Lord Robert Francis the 2nd Baron of Gifford and Lady Frederica Charlotte (née Fitzhardinge).

Born into what would become a large family, Edric had three older sisters; Eva born in 1846, Harriet Ella born in 1847 and Emily born in 1848; he also had three younger sisters, Eleanore born in 1852, Elspeth Fitzhardinge born in 1856 and Edith Charlotte born in 1863. Edric also had four younger brothers; Edward Robert born on 8th November 1853, Edgar Berkeley born on 8th March 1857, Maurice Raymond born on 5th May 1859 and Elton Vivian born on 14th April 1861.

Edric was educated at Harrow School between April 1863 and July 1867 and on 17th April 1869, just before his 20th birthday, he began his career in the army when he purchased a commission as Ensign in the 83rd Regiment of Foot.[216]

Soon after his enlistment, Edric would have joined his regiment at Gibraltar, where they had been serving as the garrison since 1867.

215 Citation does not give a date of the action; however "the taking of Becquah" occured on 1st February 1874.

216 *London Gazette* – 23489/2296

Figure 144. Edric Frederick Gifford

On the 11th March 1870, the regiment boarded the troopship *Tamar* and set sail for Alexandria, after a march to Suez the regiment boarded the troopship *Euphrates* and on 25th March set sail for India.

After arriving at Bombay on 8th April, the regiment proceeded to Poona where they were quartered in the Wanourie Barracks.

On the 30th November 1870, Edric advanced his position within the regiment when he purchased a commission as Lieutenant.[217]

Following the death of his father on 13th May 1872, Edric succeeded him as 3rd Baron of Gifford of St Leonards in the county of Devon and Lord of the Manor of Bosham.

Edric transferred, by way of exchange, to the 24th Regiment of Foot, currently stationed in England, on 26th February 1873.[218]

On the 13th August 1873, General Sir Garnet J. Wolseley was appointed to the command of an expedition to the Gold Coast, the Ashanti Expedition. Edric together with several other officers[219] of the regiment volunteered for special service to accompany the General in was would be known as the 3rd Ashanti (Sargenti) War.

Lord Gifford accompanied Sir Garnet Wolseley to the Gold Coast in September 1873 on special service. Trained the Winnebah Company of Russell's Regiment, and commanded it during the repulse of the Ashanti army at Abrakrampa on the 5th and 6th November 1873.

After arriving at Cape Coast Castle on 27th September, Edric was initially involved in the training of the Winnebah Company from Major Baker Creed Russell's regiment, which he

217 *London Gazette* – 23683/5418

218 *London Gazette* – 23952/784

219 Including Captain C. J. Bromhead who would be awarded a Victoria Cross at Rorke's Drift

commanded during the Battle of Abrakrampa on 5th and 6th November 1873.

For a short period, Edric performed the role of Adjutant to Russell's regiment, but then was given command of a scouting party.

It was with this scouting party that Edric led a force involved in the capture and destruction of Adubiassie, the capture of Egginassii and the Battle of Amoaful on 31st January 1874.

It was during the capture of Becquah on 1st February that Edric performed the deeds for which he was later awarded the Victoria Cross being slightly wounded during the action.

Edric was also involved in the final actions of the war which included the Battle of Ordahsu on 4th February and the capture of the Ashanti capital Coomassie on 6th February 1874.

From the 8th February to 4th March 1874, Edric served as Aide-de-Camp to General Wolseley.

Edric was promoted to the rank of Captain on 1st April 1874 and was transferred to the unattached list on half pay.[220]

For his service during the war, Edric received several mentions in despatches and was awarded the Ashantee Medal (1873–74) with clasp for Coomassie.

After the war ended, with the signing of the treaty of Fomena on 14th March 1874, Edric rejoined his regiment who were now serving in South Africa, after a short visit to England.

Edric was presented with his Victoria Cross Medal on 30th March 1874, by Queen Victoria at a ceremony held in Windsor Great Park.

From 22nd February 1875 to 20th October 1875, Edric served as Aide-de-Camp to General Wolseley in his capacity of General Officer Commanding in Natal.

On the 31st May 1876, Edric was appointed as Captain to the 57th Regiment of Foot.[221]

Following the Cyprus Convention, signed on 4th June 1878, the Ottoman Empire ceded the island of Cyprus to Britain and on 12th July 1878, Sir Garnet Wolseley was appointed as High Commissioner to the island; from 10th August until 11th January 1879, Ederic served as his Aide-de-Camp.

On 2nd April 1879, Edric arrived back in South Africa with two companies of the 57th Regiment to take part in the later part of the Zulu War. Serving with the 2nd Squadron, Mounted Infantry, Edric was involved in the search and capture of the Zulu Chief Cetywayo.

From 7th July 1879 until May 1880, Edric again served as Aide-de-Camp to General Wolseley who was now in the role of High Commissioner of Natal and GOC of troops in South Africa.

220 *London Gazette* – 24082/1924
221 *London Gazette* – 24331/3244

At the end of the war, Edric was sent back to England with the despatches and for his service during the war he was awarded the South Africa Medal (1877 – 79) with clasp for 1879.

Edric was married to Sophia Catherine (née Street) on 22nd April 1880 in London.

On the 24th July 1880, Edric received a brevet promotion to the rank of Major.[222]

From 2nd November 1880 until 21st January 1883, Edric served as the Colonial Secretary for Western Australia and was appointed to the Legislative council.

On the 14th March 1881, Edric was formally seconded from the army to his post as Colonial Secretary[223] and soon afterwards retired from the army after 12 years of service by sale of his commission on 1st July 1881.

After disputes with the Chief Justice, Sir Henry Wrenfordsley and the Governor Sir William Robinson, Edric was transferred from his role in Western Australia and appointed as Colonial Secretary for Gibraltar, a position which he held until 1887.

Edric had several commercial interests in South Africa, and in 1889 was one of the directors when the British South Africa Company was founded. He was also chairman of the Bechuanaland Exploration Company and had interests in several other mineral and metals companies.

Edric died at his home, Old Park in Chichester, on 5th June 1911 at the age of 61 and was buried three days later in the Fairfield Road Cemetery in Bosham, Sussex.

Figure 144a.
Grave of Edrick Frederick Gifford

222 *London Gazette* – 24866/4090
223 *London Gazette* – 25067/381

Edrick's Victoria Cross medal is not on public display, as it is believed to be in the hands of the family; his nephew John Fitzhardinge Paul Butler was also a recipient of the Victoria Cross for deeds performed on 17th November 1914 in Nigeria.

Reginald William Sartorius
17th January 1874 (VC No. 338)

Gazetted: 31st March 1874 24145/5113

Rank and Unit: Major – 6th Bengal Cavalry

Citation

For having during the attack on Abogoo, on the 17th January last, removed from under a heavy fire Serjeant-Major Braimah Doctor, a Housaa Non-Commissioned Officer, who was mortally wounded, and placed him under cover.

Biography

Reginald was born on 8th May 1841 at Sintra in Portugal the 2nd child of father George Rose, Admiral of the Fleet and mother Sophia (née Lamb).

One of six children, Reginald had an older brother George Conrad born on 2nd April 1840 and a younger brother Euston Henry born on 6th June 1844.[224] He also had three younger sisters; Rose born in 1846, Emily born in 1849 and Kate born in 1850.

In 1855, while his family remained in Portugal, Reginald and his younger brother Euston were sent as boarders to the Victoria College on the island of Jersey to complete their education.

Figure 145. Reginald William Sartorius

224 Euston was also awarded a Victoria Cross for service in Afghanistan on 24th October 1879, making them one of only four sets of brothers to receive the award.

Reginald began his career in the army on 20th January 1858 when at the age of 17 he was commissioned as an Ensign in the Bengal Army attached to the 72nd Bengal Native Infantry Regiment.

After joining his regiment in India, Reginald saw action in the final stages of the Indian Mutiny being involved in the Relief of Azimghur on 6th April 1858 and operations in the Goruckpore District.

For his service during the mutiny, Reginald was awarded the Indian Mutiny Medal (1857–58) without clasp.

On the 18th May 1858, Reginald was promoted to the rank of Lieutenant.[225]

Reginald was on home leave from 1862 to 1864 and when he returned to India he was attached to the 5th Bengal Cavalry Regiment and took part in the Bhutan (Duar) war (1864–65).

For his service during the war, Reginald was awarded the India General Service Medal (1854–95) with clasp for Bhutan.

In 1866, Reginald was attached to the 14th Bengal Cavalry (Lancers) Regiment until 20th August 1867 when he was appointed to the 6th Bengal Cavalry Regiment.

On 1st November 1868, Reginald was promoted to the rank of Captain[226] and assumed command of a squadron within the regiment.

Reginald was again on home leave during 1873 and on his return was sent with the Ashanti expeditionary force to the Gold Coast, where he was attached to the West African Hausa troops, commanded by Captain John Hawley Glover.

It was on 17th January 1874, during an attack on Abogoo that Reginald performed the deeds for which he would later be awarded the Victoria Cross.

Reginald was also involved in the final actions of the war which included the Battle of Ordahsu on 4th February and the capture of the Ashanti capital Coomassie on 6th February 1874.

For his service during the war, Reginald received two mentions in despatches and was awarded the Ashantee Medal (1873–74) with clasp for Coomassie.

Reginald was presented with his Victoria Cross Medal on 30th March 1874, by Queen Victoria at a ceremony held in Windsor Great Park.

Reginald received a brevet promotion to the rank of Major on 1st April 1874.[227]

On the 8th May 1874, Reginald was appointed as an ordinary member 3rd class (Companion) of the Most Distinguished Order of St Michael and St George.[228]

225 *London Gazette* – 22828/1354
226 *London Gazette* – 23540/5246
227 *London Gazette* – 24105/3050
228 *London Gazette* – 24093/2445

During 1875 and 1876, Reginald served on the staff during the Prince of Wales visit to India and returned to the 6th Bengal Cavalry Regiment on 1st April 1877.

Reginald was married to Agnes Maria (née Kemp) at Simla in India on 3rd October 1877, the couple would have two children; Hazel who was born at Rawal Pindi on 16th January 1880 but died on 28th February 1880 and Kenneth, also born at Rawal Pindi on 22nd July 1882.

On 12th September 1878, Reginald was promoted to the rank of Lieutenant-Colonel.[229]

From late 1878 until 1880, Reginald was involved with his regiment in the 2nd Anglo-Afghan war for which he was awarded the Afghanistan Medal (1878–80).

At the end of the war, Reginald returned to England on home leave, returning to India some time during 1882.

On 18th September 1885, Reginald was appointed as second in command of the 17th Bengal Cavalry Regiment when the regiment was reformed after having been disbanded in 1882.

Reginald received a brevet promotion to the rank of Colonel on 27th February 1886.[230]

In 1890, Reginald was once again on home leave in England and on 12th September 1890 was promoted to the rank of Colonel.[231]

Reginald received his final promotion to the rank of Major-General on 15th April 1895[232] before being placed on the unemployed supernumerary list on 12th September 1897,[233] after 39 years of service.

Figure ` 145a. Grave of Reginald William Sartorius

229 *London Gazette* – 24653/6989
230 *London Gazette* – 25596/2801
231 *London Gazette* – 26106/6025
232 *London Gazette* – 26624/2776
233 *London Gazette* – 26895/5322

After leaving the army, Reginald returned to England and lived at Hurtwood, Holmbury St Mary in Surrey.

A keen yachtsman and a member of the Royal Yacht Squadron, Reginald died suddenly on 8th August 1907 at Cowes on the Isle of Wight while visiting his younger brother Euston.

He was buried in St Mary's Churchyard, South Baddesley, Lyminton in Hampshire in a grave alongside his parents.

Reginald's Victoria Cross medal is on public display at the National Army Museum in Chelsea, London.

Samuel McGaw
21st January 1874 (VC No. 339)

Gazetted: 31st March 1874 24082/1921

Rank and Unit: Lance Sergeant No. 141 – 42nd Regiment of Foot

Citation

For having at the battle of Amoaful led his Section through the bush in the most excellent manner, continuing to do so throughout the whole day, although badly wounded early in the engagement.

Biography

Samuel was born in 1837, baptised on 10th September 1837, in Kirkmichael Village in Ayrshire in Scotland, the eldest son of father William and mother Sarah (née Thomson). Samuel had four brothers, one of whom died in infancy, and three sisters.

Sometime after 1853, the family moved to Kilmarnock where Samuel's father was employed as a labourer in the local railway works.

On 15th August 1857, at the age of 20, Samuel left his job as a mason and joined the army at Glasgow, where he was enlisted as Private No. 141 in the 42nd Regiment of Foot.

On the day before, Samuel enlisted, his regiment had set sail from Portsmouth bound for India as part of the forces sent to suppress the mutiny which had broken out.

Figure 146. Samuel McGaw

It is supposed that Samuel joined his regiment in India sometime in early 1858, in which case he would have taken part in the Siege and Capture of Lucknow in March 1858, the attack on Fort Rooya on 15th April 1858, the Battle of Bareilly on 5th May 1858 and the Battle of Sissaya Ghaut on 15th January 1859.

For his service during the mutiny, Samuel was awarded the Indian Mutiny Medal,[234] probably with clasp for Lucknow.

After the end of the mutiny, Samuel and the regiment continued to serve in India for several years and during this time he was promoted and demoted on several occasions, in 1861 while stationed at Agra he had the rank of Corporal and later rose to the rank of Sergeant, however, in 1865 he was reduced in rank back to Private.

On 20th February 1867, while stationed at Peshawar and having completed his initial engagement he re-engaged for a further term of service.

After having served nine years in India, Samuel set sail on 12th January 1868 with his regiment on their return to Scotland.

Soon after arriving at Edinburgh, Samuel was promoted to Corporal but three months later in June 1868 had again been reduced to Private.

At the end of 1868, Samuel and the regiment were moved to Aldershot.

On 21st December 1870, Samuel was married to Ann Stalker (née Clarkson) a widow at Kilmarnock in Scotland.

In 1872, Samuel was once again promoted to the rank of Corporal and in the following year was promoted to the rank of Lance-Sergeant.

Following the outbreak of hostilities on the Gold Coast, on 3rd December 1873 Samuel set sail from Portsmouth as part of the reinforcements to take part in the 3rd Ashanti War.

After arriving off the Gold Coast just before Christmas, the regiment were despatched towards Coomassie, the Ashanti capital, early in the new year and it was during the Battle of Amoaful on 21st January 1874, despite being seriously wounded, that Samuel performed the deeds for which he would later be awarded the Victoria Cross.

For his service during the war, Samuel was awarded the Ashanti Medal (1873–74) with clasp for Coomassie.

Having spent less than four months on the Gold Coast, on 27th February 1874, Samuel and the regiment set sail for home and arrived back at Portsmouth on 23rd March 1874, where they were stationed for the next eight months.

Samuel was presented with his Victoria Cross Medal by Queen Victoria on 20th April 1874 at Osborne House on the Isle of Wight.

234 The name Samuel McGaw does not appear on the Indian Mutiny Medal Rolls, however a Samuel Mcgan with the same regimental number does appear so this entry is likely to be a mis-spelling.

On 14th November 1874, Samuel and the regiment were despatched to Malta where they were to form the garrison.

Following the Cyprus Convention, signed on 4th June 1878, the Ottoman Empire ceded the island of Cyprus to Britain and on 12th July 1878, Sir Garnet Wolseley was appointed as High Commissioner to the island; the 42nd Regiment were selected to form the first garrison for the new possession.

The regiment left their post on Malta and set sail for Cyprus where they landed at Larnaca on 22nd July 1878, after landing the regiment began their march to barracks at Camp Chiflik Pasha and it was during this march that Samuel died from heat exhaustion at the age of 40.

He was buried close to where he died and a wooden cross was erected to mark his grave.

Three years later, Commissioner of Kyrenia, Colonel Scott Stevenson formerly of the Black Watch, learned that the Greek farmer who owned the land on which Sergeant McGaw was buried, had removed the wooden grave marker and had ploughed the land over the grave.

Colonel Stevenson, exhumed the remains and placed them in a coffin which was taken to Kyrenia where it was reburied in the English Cemetery. The grave was then marked with an ancient sarcophagus and is alongside the graves of other members of the Regiment who died in the campaign.

Samuel's Victoria Cross Medal is on public display at the Imperial War Museum in London, as part of the Lord Ashcroft collection.

Figure 146a. Grave of Samuel McGaw

Mark Sever Bell
4th February 1874 (VC No. 340)

Gazetted: 31st March 1874 24082/1921

Rank and Unit: Lieutenant – Royal Engineers

Citation

For his distinguished bravery, and zealous, resolute, and self-devoted conduct at the battle of Ordahsu, on the 4th February, 1874, whilst serving under the immediate orders of Colonel Sir John Chetham McLeod, K.C.B., of the 42nd Regiment, who commanded the Advanced Guard.

Sir John McLeod was an eye witness of his gallant find distinguished conduct on the occasion, and considers that this Officer's fearless and resolute bearing, being always in the front, urging on and encouraging an unarmed working party of Fantee labourers, who were exposed not only to the fire of the Enemy, but to the wild and irregular fire of the Native Troops in the rear, contributed very materially to the success of the day. By his example, he made these men do what no European party was ever required to do in warfare, namely, to work under fire in the face of the Enemy without a covering party.

Biography

Mark was born on 15th May 1843 in Sydney, Australia to father Hutchinson a Customs House Agent and mother Emily (née Royes). He was the 4th born of six children with older brothers George Hougham born on 9th October 1838 (who died before his first birthday) and Hutchinson Royes born in 1841; a younger brother John Hougham was born in 1845. He also had an older sister Emily Elizabeth born in 1840 and a younger sister Ann Maria born in 1847.

After his father died in 1847, Mark's mother moved the family back to England, probably sometime in 1849, and set up home in Islington London.

On 31st March 1851, the family moved to the island of Jersey.

Mark was privately educated before attending King's College in London and the Royal School of Military Engineering at Chatham.

On his graduating from Chatham, Mark was commissioned as a Lieutenant in the Royal Engineers on 25th June 1862.[235]

During 1865 to 1866, Mark served in the Bhutan (Duar) War, in charge of a unit of Royal Engineers and Bengal Sappers and Miners; for his service during the war he was awarded the India General Service Medal (1854–95) with clasp for Bhutan.

235 *London Gazette* – 22640/3368

Figure 147. Mark Sever Bell

In 1868, Mark served as Assistant Field Engineer during the Black Mountain (Hazara) Expedition; for his service he received a mention in despatches and was awarded the North West Frontier clasp to his India General Service Medal (1854–95).

On 10th May 1869, Mark was seconded to the Public Works Department in India[236] but on 2nd November 1871 was placed back on the effective list[237] and in 1871 and 1872 was based in Calcutta.

Following the outbreak of hostilities on the Gold Coast, Mark was appointed as Adjutant to the Brigade of Royal Engineers sent to take part in the 3rd Ashanti War.

After arriving off the Gold Coast on the 10th October 1873, Mark was part of the force despatched towards Coomassie, the Ashanti capital, early in the new year.

It was during the Battle of Ordahsu on 4th February 1874, that Mark performed the deeds for which he would later be awarded the Victoria Cross; the first recipient to have been born in Australia.

For his service during the war, Mark was awarded the Ashanti Medal (1873–74) with clasp for Coomassie and received a mention in despatches.

In 1874, after leaving the Gold Coast, Mark was based at the Carlisle Fort in Cork, Ireland and on 19th August 1874 was promoted to the rank of Captain.[238]

Mark was presented with his Victoria Cross Medal by Queen Victoria on 26th November 1874 at an investiture held at Windsor Castle.

On 27th May 1875, Mark was married to Angelina Helen (née Dickenson) at Cricklade in Wiltshire, the couple had two

236 *London Gazette* – 23535/5049
237 *London Gazette* – 23791/4467
238 *London Gazette* – 24123/4072

sons; Mark Fector Hougham born at Dover on 21st March 1876 who would die at the age of 17 in 1894 and Charles who was born in Farnham in September 1877 but died within the month.

During 1875 and 1876, Mark served at the Guildford Battery in Dover and in 1877 attended the Staff College at Farnborough, passing out in December 1878.

Mark's wife Angelina died on 28th March 1879, after just less than four years of marriage.

In 1880, Mark was appointed to the staff position of Assistant Quartermaster General Intelligence and on 25th June 1882 was promoted to the rank of Major[239] as an Intelligence Officer at Horse Guards.

Mark received a brevet promotion to the rank of Lieutenant-Colonel on 29th October 1884[240] and on 26th April 1885 was appointed to the position of Deputy Quartermaster General Intelligence.[241]

During 1886–87 Mark served as Intelligence Officer during the 3rd Anglo-Burmese war and was awarded the Burma (1885–87) clasp for his India General Service Medal.

On 16th March 1887, Mark was appointed as an Aide-de-Camp to Queen Victoria and received a brevet promotion to the rank of Colonel.[242]

Mark was awarded the Queen Victoria Jubilee Medal (1887) in 1887.

Mark was promoted to the rank of Lieutenant-Colonel on 10th May 1889.[243]

In 1889, Mark had the honour of being the first person to be awarded the MacGregor Gold Medal by the United Service Institution of India. The medal which is awarded for valuable military reconnaissance was instituted in 1888 to honour the memory of Major-General Sir Charles MacGregor who founded the institute.

On 16th April 1890, Mark was married to Nora Margaret (née Boger) at Knightsbridge in London, the couple would have three children; Anthony Harley Mark born in 1892 who would be awarded the Military Cross, Robert de Hougham Mark born on 16th November 1895 at Stoke Domerel, Plymouth who would be killed in action on 3rd September 1916 at the age of 20 and Ianthe Joan de Hougham born in 1899 at Devonport.

In 1890, Mark was appointed as a Fellow of King's College in London.

239 *London Gazette* – 25122/2965
240 *London Gazette* – 25409/4655
241 *London Gazette* – 25498/3652
242 *London Gazette* – 25683/1559
243 *London Gazette* – 25933/2626

On the 3rd of June 1893, Mark was appointed as an Ordinary Member 3rd Class (Companion) of the Military Division of the Most Honourable Order of the Bath.[244]

From 1894 until 1898, Mark had the staff appointment as commander of the Royal Engineers Western Division and was based at Portsmouth.

On 10th May 1894, after having completed five years as a Regimental Lieutenant-Colonel and being in ill health, Mark was placed on the half pay list.[245]

Mark was placed on retirement pay on 15th May 1900, after 38 years of army service.[246]

On 26th June 1906, Mark aged 63, died at his home Earlywood Lodge, Ascot in Berkshire and was buried three days later in All Souls Churchyard in South Ascot.

Mark's Victoria Cross Medal is on public display at the Royal Engineers Museum in Chatham.

Figure 147a. Grave of Mark Sever Bell

244 *London Gazette* – 26409/3252
245 *London Gazette* – 26510/2693
246 *London Gazette* – 27192/3073

George Nicholas Channer
20th December 1875 (VC No. 341)

Gazetted: 14th April 1876 24314/2476

Rank and Unit: Captain – Bengal Staff Corps – attached to 1st Gurka Rifles

Citation

For having, with the greatest gallantry, been the first to jump into the Enemy's Stockade, to which he had been dispatched with a small party of the 1st Ghoorkha Light Infantry, on the afternoon of the 20th December, 1875, by the Officer commanding the Malacca Column, to procure intelligence as to its strength, position, etc.

Major Channer got completely in rear of the Enemy's position, and finding himself so close that he could hear the voices of the men inside, who were cooking at the time, and keeping no look out, he beckoned to his men, and the whole party stole quietly forward to within a few paces of the Stockade. On jumping in, he shot the first man dead with his revolver, and his party then came up, and entered the Stockade, which was of a most formidable nature, surrounded by a bamboo palisade about seven yards within was a log-house, loop-holed, with two narrow entrances, and trees laid latitudinally, to the thickness of two feet.

The Officer commanding reports that if Major Channer, by his foresight, coolness, and intrepidity, had not taken this Stockade, a great loss of life must have occurred, as from the fact of his being unable to bring guns to bear on it, from the steepness of the hill, and the density of the jungle, it must have been taken at the point of the bayonet.

Biography

George was born on 7th January 1843 in Allahabad, India to father George Girdwood, a Colonel in the Royal Artillery and mother Susan (née Kendall). He had an older sister, Elizabeth Clara Kendall born on 9th October 1840 and a younger brother Bernard born on 20th September 1846.

Following a period at Truro Grammar School, George completed his formal education at Cheltenham College which he attended from September 1856 until June 1859.

Soon after leaving college, George at the age of 16 enlisted in the Indian Army and on 4th September 1859 was commissioned as an Ensign[247] on the General List of Infantry Officers, assigned to the 2nd Bengal Native Infantry Regiment.

247 *London Gazette* – 22828/1356

Figure 148. George Nicholas Channer

On the 25th May 1861, George was promoted to the rank of Lieutenant[248] on the Indian Army General List of Infantry Officers.

At some stage, probably in 1862, George was briefly attached to the 89th Regiment of Foot, however, he had left the regiment when he saw his first active service during the Umbeyla Expedition on the North West Frontier of India during 1863–64.

George saw action on 16th/17th December 1863 when Malka, the capital of the Sitana rebels, was captured and destroyed. He also served with General Wilde's column during operations in Jadur in early 1864.

For his service during the war, George was awarded the India General Service Medal (1854–95) with clasp for Umbeyla.

At some stage after the war, George was attached to the 95th Regiment of Foot for a short time.

On the 1st February 1867, George was transferred from the 95th Regiment of Foot as a probationer to the Indian Army Staff Corps.[249]

George was appointed as Quartermaster to the 35th Bengal Native Infantry on 5th March 1867 and then from 30th December 1869, served in the same capacity with the 2nd Bengal Native Infantry.

George was promoted to the rank of Captain on 4th September 1871.[250]

During 1870–71, George saw service during the Lushai Expedition on the North West Frontier of India, however, it

248 *London Gazette* – 22732/2406 – no fewer than 8 announcements appear in the gazette with different dates but this is the latest.

249 *London Gazette* – 23214/553

250 *London Gazette* – 23847/1797

appears that he was not awarded the Lushai clasp to his India General Service Medal.

George was married to Annie Isabella (née Watson) at Lewisham in London on 29th June 1872, the couple would go on to have 10 children; however, two sons would die at an early age.

The surviving children were; George Kendall born on 5th October 1873 at Dharmsala in India, Hugh Watson born on 23rd February 1878 at Dharmsala, Annie Ethel Dora born on 22nd February at Dharmsala, Mary Eva born on 1st November 1880 at Norwood in London, Edith Janie born on 9th February 1882 at Rawal Pindi in India, Isabella Hayward born on 7th November 1883 at Umbeyla in India, George Ralf born on 19th December 1884 at 40 Argyll Road in Kensington and Lewis Trevor born on 29th January 1887 at 13 Norham Gardens in Oxford.

On the 16th March 1873, George was transferred to the 1st Goorkha Regiment and it was with this regiment that he took part in the Perak Expedition to the Malay Peninsula.

During the war, George was with the Malacca column and took part in operations at Sungei Ujong, Terrachi and Sri-Mentani.

It was during the storming and capture of the stockades at the Burkit Putus Pass on 20th December 1875 that George performed the deeds for which he would later be awarded the Victoria Cross.

For his service during the war, George received a mention in despatches and was awarded the clasp for Perak to add to his India General Service Medal (1854–95).

On 12th April 1876, George received a brevet promotion to the rank of Major.[251]

George was presented with his Victoria Cross medal at some time during 1876 in India.

Serving with the 20th Punjab Infantry, as part of the Punjab Frontier Force, George saw action in 1877–78 while taking part in the Jowaki Expedition.

For his service during the war, George was awarded the clasp for Jowaki (1877–78) to add to his India General Service Medal (1854–95).

On the 24th January 1878, George was appointed to the command of the 29th Bengal Native Infantry.

In 1878–1880, George served in the 2nd Anglo-Afghan War in command of the 29th Bengal Native Infantry which was part of the 1st Infantry Brigade commanded by General Alexander H. Cobbe as part of the Kurram Valley Field Force commanded by Major General Roberts.

George was involved in the capture of Peiwar Kotal on 2nd December 1878.

251 *London Gazette* – 24313/2416

For his service during the war, George received a mention in despatches and was awarded the Afghanistan Medal (1878–80) with clasp for Peiwar Kotal.

On 4th September 1879, George was promoted to the rank of Major.[252]

George received a brevet promotion to the rank of Lieutenant-Colonel on 22nd November 1879.[253]

On the 12th July 1882, George was appointed to the command of the 23rd Bengal Native Infantry (Punjab Pioneers).

On 22nd November 1883, George received a brevet promotion to the rank of Colonel.[254]

George was appointed to the command of the 14th Bengal Native Infantry (Ferozepore) on 31st May 1884.

George was promoted to the rank of Lieutenant-Colonel on 4th September 1885.[255]

On the 12th January 1887, George was appointed to the command of the Rawalpindi Brigade with the local rank of Brigadier-General.

In 1888, George was appointed to the command of the 1st Brigade of the Hazara Field Force commanded by General John McQueen as part of the Black Mountain Expedition. This was a short lived expedition with active operations taking place between 3rd October and 18th November 1888.

For his service during the war, George received a mention in despatches and was awarded the clasp for Hazara 1888 to add to his India General Service Medal (1854–95).

George was appointed as an Ordinary Member 3rd Class (Companion) of the Military Division of the Most Honourable Order of the Bath on 10th April 1889.[256]

After the war, George returned to his command at Jalandhar and on 22nd April 1892, George was appointed to the command of a 2nd Class District (Assam) in India with the local rank of Brigadier General and the substantive rank of Colonel.[257]

On the 27th April 1893, George was promoted to the rank of Major-General.[258]

During the Chitral Campaign in 1895, George was appointed to the command of the Reserve Brigade which was not involved in any of the action.

George received a brevet promotion to the rank of Lieutenant-General on 9th November 1896.[259]

252 *London Gazette* – 24784/6495
253 *London Gazette* – 24785/6587
254 *London Gazette* – 25317/747
255 *London Gazette* – 25530/5245
256 *London Gazette* – 25923/2098
257 *London Gazette* – 26315/4494
258 *London Gazette* – 26448/5695
259 *London Gazette* – 26795/6275

On 11th December 1896, George resigned from his position on the Indian Staff as a commander of the Assam District.[260]

George was promoted to the rank of General on 12th January 1899.[261]

On 9th November 1901, after 42 years of service, George was placed on the Unemployed Supernumerary List.[262]

George died at his home in Buckleigh, Westward Ho! Devon on 13th December 1905 at the age of 62, following a long period of illness and was buried in the East-The-Water Cemetery in Bideford on the 16th December 1905.

George's Victoria Cross medal is not on public display, believed to be held within the family.

Figure 148a. Grave of George Nicholas Channer

260 *London Gazette* – 26839/1947
261 *London Gazette* – 27046/535
262 *London Gazette* – 27388/8918

Andrew Scott

26th July 1877 (VC No. 342)

Gazetted: 18th January 1878 24544/272

Rank and Unit: Captain – Bengal Staff Corps

Citation

For his gallant conduct at Quetta, on the 26th July, 1877, whilst serving in the 4th Sikh Infantry, on the occasion of an attack by some Pathan Coolies on Lieutenants Hewson and Kunhardt, of the Royal Engineers.

On the evening of that day, Captain Scott, whilst on duty at the regimental parade ground of the 4th Sikh Infantry at Quetta, hearing an alarm that British Officers were being killed, spontaneously rushed to the rescue, and finding Lieutenant Hewson cut down, and Lieutenant Kunhardt retiring, hard-pressed and wounded, and only protected by Sepoy Ruchpal Singh, of the above-mentioned Regiment, fell on the assailants, and with his own hand bayonetted two men, and closed with a third, who fell with him to the ground, and was killed by Sepoys of the Regiment.

This act of courage and devotion saved the life of Lieutenant Kunhardt.

Biography

Andrew was born on 22nd August 1840, probably at Lucknow in India,[263] to father John a Major in the Indian Army and mother Harriet.

On the 4th March 1860, Andrew began his army career when he was commissioned as an Ensign in the Indian Army and was placed on the General Infantry Officers List.

Andrew was promoted to the rank of Lieutenant, on the General Infantry Officers List, on 1st January 1862.[264]

Andrew saw his first active service during the Umbeyla Expedition on the North West Frontier of India during 1863–64.

For his service during the war, Andrew was awarded the India General Service Medal (1854–95) with clasp for Umbeyla.

On 6th June 1865, Andrew was attached to the 4th Sikh Infantry Regiment and it was with this regiment that he saw service in the Bhutan (Duar) War (1865–66).

For his service during the war, Andrew was awarded the clasp for Bhutan to add to his India General Service Medal (1854–95).

263 Many sources quote a birthplace of Devon, however, as Andrew was christened on 27th October 1840 in Lucknow, less than two months after his birth, this is unlikely and I think Lucknow is more probable.
264 *London Gazette* – 22625/2495

On the 4th August 1871, Andrew was appointed as a wing officer with the 4th Sikh Infantry Regiment.

Andrew was promoted to the rank of Captain on the Bengal Staff Corps on 4th March 1872.[265]

It was at Quetta on 26th July 1877, that Andrew performed the deeds for which he was later awarded the Victoria Cross; the last of the awards "not in the face of the enemy".

Andrew was presented with his Victoria Cross medal on 15th April 1878 at a ceremony in India.

In 1878–1880, Andrew served in the 2nd Anglo-Afghan War as a Brigade Major with the Kurram Valley Field Force commanded by Major General Roberts and later with the Kabul Field Force in 1878/79.

Andrew was involved in the capture of Peiwar Kotal on 2nd December 1878.

For his service during the war, Andrew was awarded the Afghanistan Medal (1878–80) with clasp for Peiwar Kotal.

On 22nd November 1879, Andrew received a brevet promotion to the rank of Major.[266]

Andrew was promoted to the rank of Major on 4th March 1880.[267]

Andrew was killed in action at Srinagar in Kashmir on 5th September 1882 and was buried on the next day in the Kashmir Cemetery.

The location of Andrew's Victoria Cross medal is unknown.

265 *London Gazette* – 23889/3777

266 *London Gazette* – 24785/6587

267 *London Gazette* – 24847/3177

Hans Garrett Moore
29th December 1877 (VC No. 343)

Gazetted: 27th June 1879 24738/4143

Rank and Unit: Major – 88th Regiment of Foot

Citation

For his gallant conduct in risking his own life in endeavouring to save the life of Private Giese, of the Frontier Armed Mounted Police, on the occasion of the action with the Gaikas, near Komgha, on the 29th December, 1877.

It is reported that when a small body of Mounted Police were forced to retire before overwhelming numbers of the enemy, Major Moore observed that Private Giese was unable to mount his horse, and was thereby left at the mercy of the Kaffirs.

Perceiving the man's danger, Major Moore rode back alone into the midst of the enemy and did not desist in his endeavour to save the man until the latter was killed, Major Moore having shot two Kaffirs and received an assegai wound in the arm during his gallant attempt.

Biography

Hans was born on 31st March 1834 at the Richmond Barracks, Dublin in Ireland to father Garrett a Captain in the 88th Regiment of Foot and mother Charlotte (née Butler).[268]

After his initial education at the famous Banagher Royal School, Hans entered Trinity College in Dublin in 1850 at the age of 16.

At the age of 21, Hans volunteered to join the army and on 7th June 1855 was commissioned as an Ensign in the 59th Regiment of Foot.[269]

Only a few weeks later on 13th July 1855, Hans was transferred to his father's regiment the 88th Regiment of Foot.[270]

Hans progressed his status in the regiment when he purchased a commission as Lieutenant on 26th October 1855.[271]

In June 1857, Hans and the regiment moved from their base at Aldershot to Portsmouth in preparation for service in India.

In July 1857, the regiment was despatched in four detachments on board *HMS Ulysses*, *HMS Surrey*, *HMS Calabar* and *HMS Cambodia* and by the end of November all of the

268 His nephew, also called Garrett won the Grand National in 1879 on "Liberator".

269 *London Gazette* – 21726/2217

270 *London Gazette* – 21745/2696

271 *London Gazette* – 21804/3951

Figure 150. Hans Garrett Moore

regiment had been disembarked at Calcutta to help subdue the mutiny.

During the mutiny, Hans was involved in action at Bhognapore, the siege of Lucknow, the siege of Kalpi, action at Selimpore on 23rd September 1858 when he was slightly wounded, action at Jummoo on 8th October 1858 and the capture of the forts at Birwa on 21st October 1858 where he was once again slightly wounded.

For his service during the mutiny Hans was awarded the India Mutiny Medal with clasp for Central India.

While at Lucknow, Hans saved the life of a native coolie who had stumbled and fallen in the river Gumti, without hesitation and still fully clothed he dove into the river and pulled the man to safety.

After the end of the mutiny, the regiment served as the garrison at Delhi for almost two years until in early 1861, after an outbreak of "Delhi Boils", the regiment was moved in order to improve its general health.

On 2nd April 1861, the regiment moved to Shahjehanpore where they exchanged stations with the 82nd Regiment of Foot.

On the 18th August 1863, Hans was appointed as adjutant to the 88th Regiment of Foot.[272]

In November 1863, the regiment were moved to Cawnpore where during the following year they suffered badly from outbreaks of cholera.

In early 1867, the regiment moved to Rawalpindi until November 1867 when they moved to Peshawar.

In January 1870, the regiment was moved to Calaba, which was to be their last station in India as on 16th November 1870 they boarded *HMS Jumna* at Bombay and set sail for England, ending a 13 year tour of duty in India.

272 *London Gazette* – 22794/6387

Of the 52 officers who arrived in India with the regiment in 1857, Hans was one of only two to have completed the full tour, the other being his commanding officer.

Hans was promoted to the rank of Captain on 19th June 1872[273] and had to relinquish his position as adjutant.

Eager to be back in action, Hans volunteered for special services during the Ashanti War (1873–74) and was employed in raising a force in the Wassawand and Denkera country on the left flank of the main advance. He was involved in the Battle of Amoaful on 31st January 1874 and the capture of the Ashanti capital Coomassie on 6th February.

For his service during the war, Hans was awarded the Ashantee Medal (1873–74) with clasp for Coomassie.

On the 1st April 1874, Hans received a brevet promotion to the rank of Major.[274]

Hans served in the ninth Cape Frontier War during 1877–78, taking part in the Kaffir Campaign and the 1st Geleka Campaign during which he led his regiment from 22nd November until 3rd December 1877.

It was on the 29th December at Draaibosch, near Komgha, that Hans performed the deeds for which he would later be awarded the Victoria Cross, the first awarded for action on South African soil.

During the action Hans received a severe wound to his arm from an assegai, which remained embedded in his arm until he returned to camp for medical attention. He refused early offers to remove the spear to prevent blood loss. His horse, which received three bullet wounds, had to be destroyed.

Despite his wound he continued to lead the regiment the next day during a further attack on the town.

In August 1878, Hans led smaller columns in operations in the Komgha, Chichaba and Transkei districts and was involved in the pursuit of Chief Kreli and his followers.

For his service during the war, Hans was awarded the South Africa Medal (1877–79) with clasp for 1877–8.

On the 9th March 1878, Hans received a brevet promotion to the rank of Lieutenant-Colonel.[275]

Hans was promoted to the rank of Major on 6th June 1878 and was transferred to the Half Pay list.[276]

On 15th March 1879, Hans was transferred to the 93rd Regiment of Foot as a Major from the Half Pay list.[277]

Hans was presented with his Victoria Cross Medal on 6th September 1879, by General Lord Napier, the Governor of Gibraltar.

273 *London Gazette* – 23878/3301
274 *London Gazette* – 24098/2780
275 *London Gazette* – 24559/1885
276 *London Gazette* – 24591/3590
277 *London Gazette* – 24694/2169

Hans was promoted to the rank of Colonel, on 29th April 1882.[278]

On 1st August 1882 Hans was appointed as Provost Marshal (Assistant Adjutant and Quartermaster General) to the Expeditionary force to Egypt.

During the war, Hans was involved in the Battle of Kassassin on 28th August 1882 and the Battle of Tel-el-Kebir on 13th September 1882.

For his service during the war, Hans was awarded the Egypt Medal (1882–89) with clasp for Tel-el-Kebir and the Khedive's Star (1882 – Egypt).

Hans was also appointed as a member 3rd class (Commander) of the Order of Osmanieh by the Turkish government.

Hans was appointed as an Ordinary Member of the 3rd Class (Companion) of the Military Division of the Most Honourable Order of the Bath on 17th November 1882.[279]

On 1st January 1884, Hans was promoted to the rank of Lieutenant-Colonel.[280]

After over 33 years of service, Hans was retired to pension from the army on 11th January 1888.[281]

On leaving the army, Hans returned to his home in Ireland.

On the 6th October 1889, Hans and his stoker Patrick Byrne, left Portumna Bay in Tipperary in his steam yacht *Foam* for a short trip to dine with General Cooper.

Figure 150a. Grave of Hans Garrett Moore

278 *London Gazette* – 25104/2078
279 *London Gazette* – 25169/5166
280 *London Gazette* – 25314/488
281 *London Gazette* – 25775/305

After dining with the General, Hans returned to his yacht during a violent storm and wanting to ensure that his boat was correctly secured, set off in a row boat to check the yacht's line which was attached to a buoy.

In the strong winds, Hans was unable to row back to his boat and was slowly pushed out into Dronineer Bay, where his boat overturned and he was drowned.

His body was found near Buggaun Island on the next morning, Hans was buried in the Mount Jerome Cemetery in Dublin.

Hans's Victoria Cross Medal is on public display at the Africana Library in Johannesburg, South Africa.

John Cook
2nd December 1878 (VC No. 344)

Gazetted: 18th March 1879 24697/2241

Rank and Unit: Captain – Bengal Staff Corps assigned to 5th Gurka Rifles

Citation

For a signal act of valour at the action of the Peiwar Kotal on the 2nd December 1878, in having, during a very heavy, fire, charged out of the entrenchments with such impetuosity that the enemy broke and fled; when, perceiving, at the close of the melee, the danger of Major Galbraith, Assistant Adjutant-General, Kurum Column Field Force, who was in personal conflict with an Afghan soldier, Captain Cook distracted his attention to himself, and aiming a sword cut which the Douranee avoided, sprang upon him, and, grasping his throat, grappled with him.

They both fell to the ground. The Douranee, a most powerful man, still endeavouring to use his rifle, seized Captain Cook's arm in his teeth until the struggle was ended by the man being shot through the head.

Biography

John was born in Edinburgh on 28th August 1843, to Alexander Shank a Scottish Advocate and Sheriff and mother Jane (née Stirling).

The second of seven children, all born in Edinburgh, John had an older brother George baptised on 9th August 1842, four younger brothers; Alexander baptised on 30th December 1847, Harry baptised on 11th July 1851 and Walter born in 1857.[282] John also had two younger sisters, Elizabeth baptised on 18th October 1844 and Diana baptised on 5th April 1846.

After his initial education at the Edinburgh Academy, John attended the Scottish Naval and Military Academy from 1856 to 1858, followed by attendance at Dr. Glennie Greig's preparatory school in Walthamstow from 1858 until 1859.

John's career in the military had been determined at an early age, his father obtained a nomination for him to attend the East India Company military seminary at Addiscombe when he was only 11 years old. John attended Addiscombe from 1859 until 1860, being one of the last pupils to attend under the old nomination system.

282 Walter was nominated for an award of the Victoria Cross but this was not granted.

Figure 151. John Cook

On graduating from Addiscombe, John received a commission as Ensign on the General Infantry Officers List of the Bengal Army on 19th December 1860.[283]

In early 1861, at the age of 18, John was despatched to India and spent his initial months of service assigned to the 4th Bengal European Regiment.

On 1st January 1862, John was promoted to the rank of Lieutenant and transferred to the 3rd Sikh Infantry Regiment[284] and joined his new regiment at Genda in Oudh.

In September 1863, John and the regiment moved to Rawalpindi where a force was being assembled for the Umbeyla Campaign and on the 5th December joined the 2nd Brigade of the Eusafzai Field Force.

John took part in the Battle of Umbeyla on 15th–16th December after which he was assigned to the force of General Wilde sent against the Sittana tribesman, which destroyed their capital at Malka.

For his service during the war, John received a mention in despatches (for leading a bayonet charge) and was awarded the India General Service Medal (1854–95) with clasp for Umbeyla.

After the war, the regiment resumed their duties as part of the Punjab Frontier Force and in November 1864, John was appointed as adjutant to the regiment.

In August 1868, the regiment was moved to Abbottabad, where a force was being assembled for an expedition against the Hazara tribesmen on the North West Frontier.

283 *London Gazette* – 22828/1355

284 *London Gazette* – 22639/3323 & 22710/947, initial date of promotion was 29th March 1862, however, after four further changes this was eventually pre-dated to the 1st January 1862.

John served in the Hazara (Black Mountain) expedition during 1868 and for his service was awarded the North West Frontier clasp for his India General Service Medal (1854–95).

In early 1870, John with the benefit of a medical certificate began a period of home leave and returned to England, returning to India in April 1871.

On the 19th December 1872, John was promoted to the rank of Captain in the Bengal Staff Corps and a few months later, on 27th March 1873,[285] was transferred to the 5th Ghurkha Rifles as a Wing Commander.

The 5th Ghurkhas were ordered to make ready for active service on the 24th September 1878 and in October they moved from Abbottabad to Thal where they joined the Kurram Field Force commanded by General Sir Frederick Roberts and were assigned to the 2nd Brigade under the command of General Thewall, to take part in the 2nd Anglo-Afghan War.

It was during the Battle of Peiwar Kotal on 2nd December 1878, that John performed the deeds for which he would later be awarded the Victoria Cross on the slopes of the Spingawai Kotal (White Cow) pass.

On 10th December 1878, John also saw action during the taking of the Monghyr pass and afterwards spent most of the summer with General Thewall's force based at Ali Khel near Kabul.

John was presented with his Victoria Cross Medal by General Sir Frederick Roberts VC at Ali Khel on 24th May 1879, during a parade to celebrate the Queen's birthday.

The siege and ultimate massacre of British forces (including the British Resident Sir Pierre Louise Bonaparte Cavagnari) at Kabul on the 3rd of September 1879, rekindled hostilities during the war and John together with the rest of General Thewall's force was assigned to the Kabul Field Force under the command of General Sir Frederick Roberts.

John took part in the Battle of Charasiab on 6th October 1879 and on 12th October Kabul was reoccupied by British forces.

On 22nd November 1879, John received a brevet promotion to the rank of Major in the Bengal Staff Corps.[286]

On the 11th December 1879, fighting alongside his brother Walter, John was involved in an action near Argundeh, where as part of the rear-guard he prevented the Afghan forces from seizing the Brigade's baggage. During the action, Walter was wounded in the chest and sent to Sherpur for treatment.

John was involved in action to take the Taht-i-Shah peak, on the following day despite having received a serious blow to the head on the day before. It was during this attack that John was struck by a bullet which passed through the bone of his left leg, just below the knee. After spending the night in the open, John was taken to the hospital at Sherpur the next day where despite treatment he died of his wound on 19th December 1879 at the age of 36.

For his service during the war, John received a mention in despatches and was awarded the Afghanistan Medal (1878–80) with clasps for Peiwar Kotal, Charisia and Kabul.

On 21st December 1879, John was buried at the Sherpur British Cemetery, known locally as the Gara Kabar (White Graveyard).

John's Victoria Cross Medal is on public display at the Imperial War Museum in London as part of the Lord Ashcroft collection.

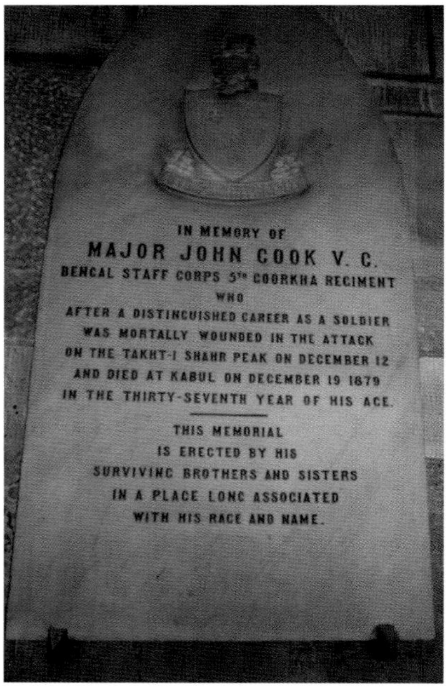

Figure 151a. Memorial to John Cook

285 *London Gazette* – 23962/1714
286 *London Gazette* – 24785/6587

Reginald Clare Hart
31st January 1879 (VC No. 345)

Gazetted: 10th June 1879 24732/3830

Rank and Unit: Lieutenant – Royal Engineers

Citation

For his gallant conduct in risking his own life in endeavouring to save the life of a private soldier. The Lieutenant-General commanding the 2nd Division Peshawar Field Force, reports that when on convoy duty with that Force on 31st January, 1879, Lieutenant Hart, of the Royal Engineers, took the initiative in running some 1,200 yards to the rescue of a wounded Sowar of the 13th Bengal Lancers in a river bed exposed to the fire of the enemy, of unknown strength, from both flanks, and also from a party in the river bed. Lieutenant Hart reached the wounded Sowar, drove off the enemy, and brought him under cover with the aid of some soldiers who accompanied him on the way.

Biography

Reginald was born on 11th June 1848 at Drewsborough House, Scarriff, Co Clare in Ireland to father Henry George[287] a Captain with the 49th Regiment of Foot and mother Francis Alicia (née Okes).

Reginald was the 2nd youngest of seven children, with three older sisters; Jane Margaret born on 24th January 1834 in Calcutta, Frances Alicia born on 24th April 1840 in London and Isabel Clare born on 4th June 1846 in Ireland; older brothers Holt William born on 27th June 1838 at Clifton in England and Arthur Fitzroy born on 4th May 1844 at Portsmouth and younger brother Horatio Holt born in 1850.

From February 1860 until December 1861, Reginald was educated at Marlborough College and then from January 1862 until June 1866 at Cheltenham College.

On leaving Cheltenham College, Reginald enrolled in the Royal Military Academy at Woolwich to begin his training as an army engineer.

On 13th June 1869, after graduating from the Royal Military Academy, Reginald was commissioned in the Royal Engineers with the temporary rank of Lieutenant,[288] the rank was made permanent five days later on 18th January 1869.[289]

287 Would later attain the rank of Lieutenant-General, and is famous as the author, editor, and proprietor of *Harts Army List*, an unofficial publication recording the details of the army service of officers.

288 *London Gazette* – 23458/164

289 *London Gazette* – 23745/2697

Figure 152. Reginald Clare Hart

Reginald spent most of the first three years of his army service based in England; however, on 27th July 1869 while on a visit to France he rescued a Frenchman from drowning in the Boulogne-sur-Mer harbour. For this brave act he was awarded the Royal Humane Society Medal (Silver), a medallion from the Mayor of Boulogne and the Medal of Honour (1st Class) by the French President.

Reginald was also present, as an observer, at the Siege of Paris during the Commune War of 1871.

On 6th August 1872, Reginald was married to Charlotte Augusta (née Seton-Synnot) at Louth in Ireland.

The couple would have seven children; twin boys, Henry[290] and Harold Charles born at Allahabad on 30th March 1874, Henry Francis born on 7th June 1876 at Ambala City,[291] Annie Rosabel Clare was born on 31st August 1880 at Aldershot, Reginald Seton was born on 27th June 1882 at Aldershot, Sylvia Agnes Alicia was born on 31st May 1885 at Dagshai in India and Norman Synnot was born on 24th March 1888 at Ranikhet in India.

In October 1878, Reginald left England for India and on his arrival took up a position with the Bengal Sappers and Miners.

Reginald was employed as an Assistant Garrison Instructor at Umbeyla from September 1874 until March 1878 when he returned to England on sick leave, returning to India in December 1878.

In 1879, Reginald was awarded a 1st Class Certificate in Musketry from the school at Hythe.

Reginald served in the 2nd phase of the 2nd Anglo-Afghan War in 1879, attached to the 24th Punjab Infantry the regiment was part of the Khyber Field Force.

290 Unfortunately Henry died on the day that he was born.

291 Like his namesake, Henry Francis died at an early age on 17th August 1876, surviving for less than 10 weeks.

It was on 31st January 1879, during the 2nd Bazar Valley Expedition, that Reginald performed the deeds for which he would later be awarded the Victoria Cross.

For his service during the war, Reginald received a mention in despatches and was awarded the Afghanistan Medal (1878–80).

Reginald was presented with his Victoria Cross Medal by Queen Victoria on 9th December 1879, at a ceremony at Windsor Castle.

In 1880, Reginald passed out from the Service College, passing his examinations with distinction, without having attended the normal two year course of instruction and was attached to the 1st Division of the Peshawar Field Force.

On 16th February 1881, Reginald was sent to West Africa where he served on the Special Service Staff of Sir Samuel Rowe, the Governor and Commander-in-Chief of the West Coast of Africa, during the Ashanti War.

Reginald was promoted to the rank of Captain on 1st July 1881[292] and for some time served in the Intelligence Department at Horse Guards.

On the 18th January 1882, Reginald received a brevet promotion to the rank of Major.[293]

From the 4th August 1882 until 5th November 1882, Reginald served in the Egyptian War as Aide-de-Camp to Major-General Graham, commander of the expeditionary force.

Reginald saw action at the reconnaissance of El-Magfar on 5th August, The Battle of Kassassin on 28th August and the Battle of Tel-el-Kebir on 13th September.

For his service during the war, Reginald received two mentions in Despatches and was awarded the Egypt Medal (1882–89) with clasp for Tel-el-Kebir, he was also awarded the Khedive's Star (1882) and was appointed as a Knight (4th Class) of the Order of Osmanieh by Turkey.

Reginald received a brevet promotion to the rank of Lieutenant-Colonel on 18th November 1882.[294]

In 1884, Reginald returned to India and on 15th December 1884, he saved the life of a Gunner who had been knocked off a pontoon bridge into the Ganges Canal at Roorkee. As he got the Gunner to safety on the canal bank, Reginald himself was in danger of drowning and was hauled to safety by Sergeant James Mills of the Royal Engineers.

For this second selfless act of saving a man for drowning, Reginald was awarded a silver clasp to his Royal Humane Society Medal.

On 18th December 1884, Reginald was appointed as Executive Engineer (4th Class) at Ambala.

292 *London Gazette* – 24999/3679
293 *London Gazette* – 25061/187
294 *London Gazette* – 25169/5174

Reginald was appointed as Garrison Instructor at Ranikhet on 31st October 1885.

On 20th May 1896, Reginald was appointed as an Ordinary Member 3rd Class (Companion) of the Military Division of the Most Honourable Order of the Bath.[295]

On 18th November 1886, Reginald received a brevet promotion to the rank of Colonel.[296]

Reginald was promoted to the rank of Major on 23rd November 1887.[297]

On 20th July 1889, Reginald was appointed as Director of Military Education in India, based at Simla.

Reginald was appointed to the command of a 2nd Class District (Belgaum) in India on 2nd March 1896 with the local rank of Brigadier General.

In 1897, Reginald was awarded the Queen Victoria Diamond Jubilee Medal.

During the Tirah Campaign (1897–98) Reginald served as commander of the 1st Brigade and was present at the capture of the Sampagha Pass on 29th October and the capture of the Arhanga Pass on 31st October. He was also involved in operations in the Waran Valley and Bazar Valley during December 1897.

For his service during the war, Reginald was twice mentioned in despatches and was awarded the India General Service Medal (1895–1902) with clasps for Punjab Frontier (1897–98) and Tirah (1897–98).

On the 5th October 1899, Reginald was appointed to the command of the 1st Class District of Quetta with the temporary rank of Major-General until 1st April 1901.

Reginald was appointed as an Ordinary Member 2nd Class (Knight Commander) of the Military Division of the Most Honourable Order of the Bath on 16th May 1899.[298]

During 1901–02, Reginald was involved in campaigns on the North West Frontier of India against the Mahsud, for this service he was awarded the clasp for Waziristan (1901–02) to add to his India General Service Medal (1895–1902).

On 9th December 1902, Reginald was promoted to the rank of Major-General and left India to take up his appointment as General Officer Commanding the Thames District and commandant of the School of Military Engineering[299] a position that he would hold until 19th December 1906.

On 21st October 1904, Reginald was appointed as a Knight Commander of the Royal Victorian Order.[300]

295 *London Gazette* – 26741/3053
296 *London Gazette* – 25645/5530
297 *London Gazette* – 25764/6799
298 *London Gazette* – 27080/3102
299 *London Gazette* – 27512/6
300 *London Gazette* – 27729/7023

Reginald was appointed to the command of the Cape Colony District on 30th November 1907.[301]

On 18th November 1908, Reginald was promoted to the rank of Lieutenant-General.[302]

Reginald was appointed as the commander in chief of the troops in South Africa on 9th March 1912,[303] a position that he would hold until 18th April 1914.

On 16th May 1914, Reginald was promoted to the rank of General.[304]

Reginald was appointed as the Lieutenant-Governor of Guernsey on 18th November 1914[305] a position that he would hold until 14th June 1918,[306] on relinquishing the appointment he received the thanks of His Majesty's Government for his services "during a very critical and difficult period."

On 16th June 1918, after 49 years of service and having reached the mandatory age, Reginald was placed on retirement pay.[307]

Reginald was appointed as an Ordinary Member 1st Class (Knight Grand Cross) of the Military Division of the Most Honourable Order of the Bath on the 3rd June 1831.[308]

On 10th October 1931, Reginald died at his home at 39 West Cliff Road, Bournemouth aged 83 and was buried in St Mary's Churchyard Cemetery, Netherby in Dorset.

Figure 152a. Grave of Reginald Clare Hart

301 *London Gazette* – 28087/8607
302 *London Gazette* – 28197/8408
303 *London Gazette* – 28590/1917
304 *London Gazette* – 28831/3928
305 *London Gazette* – 28981/9538
306 *London Gazette* – 30747/7064
307 *London Gazette* – 30773/7713
308 *London Gazette* – 33722/3625

Reginald's Victoria Cross Medal is on public display at the Imperial War Museum in London as part of the Lord Ashcroft collection.

Edward Pemberton Leach
17th March 1879 (VC No. 346)

Gazetted: 9th December 1879 24790/7265

Rank and Unit: Captain – Royal Engineers

Citation

For having, in action with the Shinwarris near Maidanah, Afghanistan, on the 17th March, 1879, when covering the retirement of the Survey Escort who were carrying Lieutenant Barclay, 45th Sikhs, mortally wounded, behaved with the utmost gallantry in charging, with some men of the 45th. Sikhs, a very much larger number of the enemy.

In this encounter Captain Leach killed two or three of the enemy himself, and he received a severe wound from an Afghan knife in the left arm. Captain Leach's determination and gallantry in this affair, in attacking and driving back the enemy from the last position, saved the whole party from annihilation.

Figure 153. Edward Pemberton Leach

Biography

Edward was born on 2nd April 1847 at Londonderry in Ireland to father George Archibald, a Lieutenant-Colonel in the Royal Engineers[309] and mother Emily (née Pemberton).

The second born of eight children, Edward had an older brother George born on 28th May 1845; five younger brothers Henry born on 10th October 1848, Harold born on 14 April 1851, Herbert born on 17th April 1853, Reginald born on 3rd January 1855 and Claude born on 18th March 1858; he also had a younger sister Helen born on 5th August 1863.

Edward was educated at Highgate School in London and afterwards attended the Royal Military Academy at Woolwich as a gentleman cadet.

On graduating from the Royal Military Academy, Edward received a commission in the Royal Engineers with the temporary rank of Lieutenant[310] on 17th April 1866, this was subsequently made permanent.[311]

After graduating from the Royal Military Academy at Woolwich, Edward attended the Royal College of Military Engineering at Chatham until 1868.

After graduating from Chatham, Edward left for India in November 1868 and in March 1869 took up command of a detachment of Bengal Sappers and Miners at Rawalpindi a position that he would hold until 25th February 1870 when he was seconded to the India Public Works Department[312] at Morar in Central India.

On 3rd November 1871, Edward was transferred back to the effective list and was appointed to the Indian Archaeological Survey team.[313]

During 1871–72, Edward served with the Cachar Column in the Lushai Expeditionary Force and for his service was awarded the India General Service Medal (1854–95) with clasp for Lushai.

From November 1877, Edward spent a period on furlough in England and on his return to India in 1878 served as Private Secretary to Sir James Caird the India Famine Commissioner during his tour of India following the great Indian famine of 1876–77.

Edward was promoted to the rank of Captain on 31st December 1878.[314]

With the outbreak of the 2nd Anglo-Afghan war, Edward joined the Khyber Survey party and it was while leading a survey in the Shinwari country on 17th March 1879, that he performed the deeds for which he would later be awarded the Victoria Cross. During the action Edward received a severe knife wound to his left arm.

On 22nd November 1879, Edward received a brevet promotion to the rank of Major.[315]

Towards the end of 1879, Edward was invalided home to England and on 9th December 1879 was presented with his Victoria Cross Medal by Queen Victoria at an investiture held at Windsor Castle.

309 On leaving the army George joined the civil service and became Secretary to the Board of Agriculture.
310 *London Gazette* – 23103/2462
311 *London Gazette* – 23435/5597
312 *London Gazette* – 23633/3353
313 *London Gazette* – 23791/4467
314 *London Gazette* – 24671/347
315 *London Gazette* – 24785/6587

In March 1880, Edward returned to India and the war, joining the Kandahar Field Force under the command of General Primrose.

In June 1880, Edward performed a reconnaissance of Giriskht in Helmand Province and on 4th June joined General Burrows column as a galloper and was involved in the Battle of Maiwand on 27th July 1880, during which his horse was wounded.

Edward was involved in the retreat to Kandahar, where he was appointed as Brigade Major and was part of the force commanded by Sir Frederick Roberts that finally defeated the Afghan forces.

For his service during the war, Edward received four mentions in despatches and was awarded the Afghanistan Medal (1878–80) with clasp for Kandahar.

On 2nd March 1881, Edward received a brevet promotion to the rank of Lieutenant-Colonel.[316]

Edward was married to Lady Elizabeth Maty (née Bazely) at Cirencester some time during 1883, the couple would have three children; Lilian Vera Pemberton born in 1883, Gordon Pemberton born on 2nd August 1885[317] and Elsie Pemberton born on 30th June 1888.

Edward was promoted to the rank of Colonel on 2nd March 1885.[318]

On 1st July 1885, Edward was appointed as a Colonel on the Staff in Egypt.[319]

Edward was appointed as an Ordinary Member 3rd Class (Companion) of the Military Division of the Most Honourable Order of the Bath on 25th August 1885.[320]

During 1885, Edward took part in the war in Egypt serving with the Suakin Expedition (commanded by General Sir Gerald Graham VC) and taking part in the Battle of Tamai on 13th March and Battle of Tofrek on 22nd March 1885, he also served in command of a brigade at Korosko during 1885–86 and commanded the British Brigade at Assouan from 1886 until 1887.

For his service during the war, Edward was twice mentioned in despatches and was awarded the Egypt Medal (1882–89) with clasps for Suakin 1885 and Tofrek. He was also awarded the Khedive's Star (1882) by the government of Egypt.

On 17th April 1886, Edward was promoted to the rank of Major.[321]

After the war in Egypt, Edward returned to England and took up a position as commandant of the Harbour Defences, based at Plymouth.

316 *London Gazette* – 24944/976

317 A Captain in the Royal Artillery, Gordon was killed in action at Gallipoli on 19th August 1915.

318 *London Gazette* – 25452/1198

319 *London Gazette* – 25489/3122

320 *London Gazette* – 25505/4050

321 *London Gazette* – 25579/1899

Edward received a promotion to the rank of Lieutenant-Colonel on 5th December 1892.[322]

On 2nd April 1900, Edward received a temporary appointment as Major-General on the Staff with command of the 9th Division, 3rd Army Corps in Belfast.[323]

Edward was promoted to the rank of Lieutenant-General on 3rd April 1905.[324]

On 6th December 1905, Edward was appointed General Officer Commanding-in-Chief (2nd Class) and was given command of the troops in Scotland.[325]

Edward was appointed as a Knight Commander of the Royal Victorian Order on 23rd October 1906.[326]

On 25th June 1909, Edward was appointed as an Ordinary Member 2nd Class (Knight Commander) of the Military Division of the Most Honourable Order of the Bath.[327]

Edward was promoted to the rank of General on 31st August 1910.[328]

On 4th September 1912, after 46 years of service, Edward was retired from the army to pension.[329]

After leaving the army, Edward took up residence at 29 Palace Gate in London, however, it was at Caddenbbia on Lake Como in Italy that Edward died on 26th April 1913 at the age of 66. He was later buried in the Grienza Cemetery in Caddenbbia.

Edwards Victoria Cross Medal is on public display at the Royal Engineers Museum in Chatham.

Figure 153a. Grave of Edward Pemberton Leach

322 *London Gazette* – 26351/7161

323 *London Gazette* – 27183/2506

324 *London Gazette* – 27781/2548

325 *London Gazette* – 27865/9088

326 *London Gazette* – 27960/7108

327 *London Gazette* – 28263/4854

328 *London Gazette* – 28415/6544

329 *London Gazette* – 28641/6538

Walter Richard Pollock Hamilton
2nd April 1879 (VC No. 347)

Figure 154. Walter Richard Pollock Hamilton

Gazetted: 7th October 1879 24768/5777

Rank and Unit: Lieutenant – Bengal Staff Corps – attached to Corps of Guides

Citation

For conspicuous gallantry during the action at Futtehabad on the 2nd April, 1879, in leading on the Guide Cavalry in a charge against very superior numbers of the enemy, and particularly at a critical moment when his, Commanding Officer (Major Wigram Battye) fell, Lieutenant Hamilton, then the only Officer left with the Regiment, assumed command and cheered on his men to avenge Major Battye's death.

In this charge Lieutenant Hamilton, seeing Sowar Dowlut Ram down, and attacked by three of the enemy, whilst entangled with his horse (which had been killed) rushed to the rescue, and followed by a few of his men cut down all three and saved the life of Sowar Dowlut Ram.

Biography

Walter was born on 18th August 1856 at Inistioge, Co Kilkenny in Ireland, to father Alexander a Justice of the Peace and mother Emma (née Pollock).

The fourth born of seven sons, Walter had three older brothers; Frederick Alexander Pollock born on 20th August 1852, Charles Pollock born on 9th October 1853 and Horace George Pollock born on 6th November 1854; he also had three younger brothers Alexander Pollock born on 8th July 1858, Robert Pollock born on 31st May 1860 and Archibald Pollock born on 17th September 1861; all the children were born in Inistioge.

Walter was educated at the Eagle House School in Wimbledon and then Felstead School in Essex.

On 28th February 1874, Walter enlisted in the army and was commissioned as a 2nd Lieutenant in the 70th Regiment of Foot.[330]

After spending a few months in the Depot in England, Walter joined his regiment in India in October 1874 and was stationed at Rawalpindi.

On 28th November 1876, Walter was promoted to the rank of Lieutenant[331] and appointed as a probationer in the Indian Staff Corps.[332]

330 *London Gazette* – 24069/890
331 *London Gazette* – 24367/5203
332 *London Gazette* – 24388/6531

Following his promotion to Lieutenant, Walter was offered and accepted a commission in the Queen's Corps of Guides and was assigned to the cavalry.

From 30th August 1877 until 30th January 1878, Walter served with the Punjab Field Force in the Jowaki Expedition. Walter served as Aide-de-Camp to General C. P. Keyes who commanded the Kohat column.

Walter also saw action at the Battle of Skhakat on 14th March 1878.

For his service during the war, Walter was awarded the India General Service Medal (1854–95) with clasp for Jowaki 1877–78.

In October 1878, with a worsening situation in Afghanistan, Walter and the Corps of Guides was moved to Jamrud at the mouth of the Khyber pass where they reconnoitred the area for the next six weeks.

Walter was involved in both of the initial campaigns of the 2nd Anglo-Afghan war and was present at the capture of Ali Musjid.

In March 1879, Walter commanded an escort of Guides on duty with the survey party led by Lieutenant Leach and were involved in the action during which Lieutenant Leach performed the deeds for which he was awarded the Victoria Cross.

Towards the end of March, Walter took part in the advance on Futtehabad, led by General Gough's brigade and it was during the Battle of Futtehabad on 2nd April 1879 that he performed the deeds for which he would later be awarded the Victoria Cross.

Following the treaty of Gundamuk, signed on 2nd May 1879, which ended the first phase of the war the British Minister, Sir Louis Cavagnari set out to establish a British Embassy in Kabul, as agreed under the terms of the treaty.

Walter was appointed as Military Attaché to the Minister and commanded the escort of 77 men from the Corps of Guides (25 Cavalry and 52 Infantry) which accompanied the party on their journey to Kabul. Sir Louise Cavagnari was also accompanied by Surgeon A. H. Kelly of the Guides as medical officer and his political assistant Mr W. Jenkyns.

Their arrival at Kabul on 24th July received a cordial welcome and for the following month all appeared to be going well, however, at the end of August, when the Amir changed over the regiments forming his garrison the first indication of trouble ahead became apparent.

As the newly arriving troops marched through the city, they called out abuse to the British, their embassy and Sir louise Cavagnari.

Warnings were also received that the new troops planned to attack the Residency and sack the treasury as they had not been paid by the Amir for several months.

On 3rd September, without any further indication, about 5,000 Afghan troops, supported by many of the local population mounted an attack on the British Embassy, despite the protection afforded by the treaty.

With only four British Officers and just over 70 native troops at his disposal, Walter bravely attempted to defend the Residency against insurmountable odds.

Suffering heavy casualties, Walter managed to hold off the Afghans for over five hours and when two enemy guns were brought to bear, only 100 yards from the Residency walls he mounted a charge with 12 of his men in an attempt to capture the guns.

Walter and his men managed to capture the guns and kill the gunners but did not have the manpower to drag them back to the Residency, so they were soon recaptured by the Afghan troops.

It was during a second attempt to capture the guns that Walter was killed; subsequently Sir Louise Cavagnari and all the occupants of the Residency were also killed but the action inflicted heavy casualties on the Afghans, about 600 were killed.

It is thought that Walter was buried in an unmarked grave in the Embassy gardens.

For his service during the war, Walter was awarded the Afghanistan Medal (1878–80).

The War Office sent Walter's Victoria Cross medal to his father by registered post on 25th October 1979.

Walter's Victoria Cross Medal is on public display at the Imperial War Museum in London as part of the Lord Ashcroft collection.

The recommendation for the award of a Victoria Cross to Walter was forwarded to the India Office on 15th May 1879 and they forwarded the papers to Horse Guards on 22nd July. On 28th July, General Horsford, the Military Secretary, wrote to the Private Under Secretary at the War Office to inform him that the Duke of Cambridge recommended that the India Office should be advised that Walter's act did not come within the regulations for the VC.

The decision was confirmed by Lord Stanley the Secretary of State for India on 6th August, however, Lord Cranbrook advised that the Governor General of India and the Commander in Chief of forces in India both thought that the case for Walter was similar to that for both Captain John Cook and Lieutenant Reginald Hart and they had both been awarded the medal.

This argument, appears to have had the desire effect on the Duke of Cambridge for on 16th September, General Dillon wrote again to the Private Under Secretary saying that the proposal had now been accepted and on 19th September Lord Stanley agreed to put the recommendation to the Queen.

There was one last twist to the tale, the letter accompanying the request to the Queen was pre-dated to 1st September (two days before Walter was killed at Kabul) "*... so as to avoid creating an awkward precedent in giving the decoration after death.*"

Garrett O'Moore Creagh
21st April 1879 (VC No. 348)

Gazetted: 7th October 1879 24768/5777

Rank and Unit: Captain – Bengal Staff Corps

Citation

On the 21st April Captain Creagh was detached from Dakka with two Companies of his Battalion to protect the village of Kam Dakka on the Cabul River, against a threatened incursion of the Mohmunds, and reached that place the same night. On the following morning the detachment, 150 men, was attacked by the Mobmunds in overwhelming numbers, about 1,500; and the inhabitants of Kam Dakka having themselves taken part with the enemy, Captain Creagh found himself under the necessity of retiring from the village. He took up a position in a cemetery not far off, which he made as defensible as circumstances would admit of and this position he held against all the efforts of the enemy, repeatedly repulsing them with the bayonet until three o'clock in the afternoon, when he was relieved by a detachment sent for the purpose from Dakka. The enemy were then finally repulsed, and being charged by a troop of the 10th Bengal Lancers, under the command of Captain D. M. Strong, were routed and broken, and great numbers of them driven into the river.

The Commander-in-Chief in India has expressed his opinion that but for the coolness, determination, and gallantry of the highest order, and the admirable conduct which Captain Creagh displayed on this occasion the detachment under his command would, in all probability, have been cut off and destroyed.

Biography

Garrett was born on 2nd April 1848 at Cahirbane, Co Clare in Ireland to Father James a retired Royal Navy Captain and mother Grace Emily (née O'Moore).

He was the fourth born son and one of nine children with five brothers; James, Vandeleur, Boyle Purdon, Edward Fitzgerald and Arthur Richard and three sisters; Augustine, Anne Vandeleur and Mary Emily.

Garrett was privately educated at home until 1863 when his mother moved to France, he then attended Mr Burney's preparatory school in Gosport as a boarder.

Following an open examination, which he passed, Garrett was enrolled as a Gentleman Cadet at the Royal Military Academy at Sandhurst in July 1865, just after his 17th birthday.

Figure 155. Garrett O'Moore Creagh

On graduating from Sandhurst, Garrett purchased a commission of Ensign with the 31st Regiment of Foot on 2nd October 1866;[333] however, he was immediately transferred to the 95th Regiment of Foot.[334]

As his regiment was currently on service in India, Garrett spent the initial years of his army career at the regimental depot in Pembroke Dock near Milford Haven.

After, just over two years at the Depot, Garrett was ordered to join his regiment in India and set sail from Portsmouth on board *HMS Malabar* on 7th January 1869, with a detachment of 100 men bound for Bombay.

His voyage on *HMS Malabar*, was one of the first to use the new route to India, via the Suez Canal, arrived at Bombay on 13th February 1869, and after disembarking the detachment proceeded by rail to Deolali.

After arriving at Deolali, due to a local outbreak of cholera, the detachment with the rest of the garrison was placed under quarantine in order to stop the spread of the disease and then due to the hot and wet summer season it was not until early November that they received orders to join the regiment at Mhow.

Following a 200 mile rail journey to Khandwa and a short march, Garrett finally joined his regiment at Mhow, however, the stay at Mhow was to be short lived as in early 1870 the regiment received orders that they would soon be despatched to Bombay in preparation for a return to England.

With his regiment set to return to England Garrett, who wished to stay in India, sat the examination for the Indian Staff Corps and applied for a position within the Bengal Staff Corps.

333 *London Gazette* – 23169/5390
334 *London Gazette* – 23169/5291

Garrett was appointed as a Lieutenant in the Bombay Staff Corps on 16th February 1870;[335] he had requested a position with a cavalry unit in the Punjab Frontier Force, however, he was assigned to the Marine Battalion of the Bombay Light Infantry, stationed in Bombay City.

After a short time with the Marine Battalion, Garrett was transferred to the 25th Bombay Native Light Infantry and relocated to Dhulia where on 16th February 1871 he completed his year of probationary service.

Soon after completing his probationary service, Garrett received a surprising appointment as Officiating Adjutant to the Deoli Irregular Force in Rajputana, which he took up in March 1871, taking his place on the station staff under the command of Colonel Macdonald.

At the end of July, the officer for whom Garrett was officiating returned to his duties and Garrett was appointed as Adjutant to the Merwara Battalion stationed at Ajmir.

On 3rd May 1871, having completed his transfer to the staff of the Indian Army, Garrett was granted the value of his commission.[336]

In the early part of the hot season of 1873, Garrett was struck down by a virulent fever and when he was sufficiently recovered to travel was sent to Bombay to be examined by a medical board. The board ordered Garrett home on an 18 month sick furlough, which he spent in Ireland at Birr.

In 1873, Garrett was married to Mary Letitia Longfield (née Brereton) a cousin, at Parsonstown in Ireland; unfortunately the marriage was short lived as Mary died in 1875 from cholera; their infant daughter, May Geraldine, was taken back to Ireland by a colleague's wife.

Garrett returned to Ajmir in the Autumn of 1874 and during the winter season he commanded the escort during Viceroy Lord Northbrook's four day visit to Jaipur.

In the winter of 1875/76, HRH The Prince of Wales (later to become King Edward VII) visited India and during his visit to Agra and Jaipur, Garrett commanded the local escort.

On 2nd October 1878, having completed 12 years of service, Garrett was promoted to the rank of Captain[337] and was appointed as the officiating Commandant of the Merwara Battalion, the tenure of the incumbent having expired and the new commander Major F. Boileau being unable to take up his new appointment immediately.

With the outbreak of war in Afghanistan, Garrett volunteered the battalion for service and took part in the 2nd Anglo-Afghan war with the Peshawar Valley Field Force commanded by General Sir Samuel J. Browne and on 21st November 1878 took part in the Battle of Ali Masjid.

At the end of November, Garrett and the Battalion, now commanded by Major Boileau, joined the 2nd Brigade commanded by General Maude VC and took part in the Bazar Valley Expedition to quell the Zakka Khel Afridi tribesmen.

In March 1879, Garrett was sent with a small force to occupy the fort at Kam Dakka which he did with little initial difficulty, however, as time progressed the villagers became more hostile and when reinforced besieged the British force.

It was during action on 21st April, to ward of the repeated attacks by the Afghans, that Garrett performed the deeds for which he would later be awarded the Victoria Cross.

After the village was relieved by a force sent by General Maude, Garrett remained at Kam Dakka until the end of May facilitating the line of communications.

When the treaty of Gundamuk, ending the first phase of the war, was signed on 2nd May the Indian Government lost no time in issuing orders for the withdrawal of the Peshawar Valley Field Force.

Despite the dangers of travelling during the hot season, the troops were forced to return to their bases in June 1879 and many men were lost due to cholera and heat exhaustion, however, Garrett's regiment suffered less than many of the regiments.

On arriving back at the base in Ajmer, Garrett took a leave into the Himalayan jungles to escape the heat.

With the start of the 2nd Phase of the war, following the slaughter of the British Mission at Kabul, on 3rd September 1879, Garrett volunteered his services and was appointed as Deputy Assistant Adjutant General to General Gordon, commanding the Kurram Valley Field Force.

Head quartered at Ali Khel, the field force was responsible for the security of the Kurram and Hariob valleys, while General Roberts led the Kabul Field Force to retake Kabul.

Initially, Garrett was involved in supervising improvements to the defences of Ali Khel, much needed as the perimeter had been reduced to accommodate the smaller garrison force.

These defences proved to be invaluable during a strong Afghan attack on 14th October which was repulsed by the British forces.

When General Gordon was replaced by General John Watson as commander of the Field Force, Garrett was promoted to the position of Assistant Quartermaster General.

On 22nd November 1879, Garrett received a brevet promotion to the rank of Major in recognition of his service during the war.[338]

335 *London Gazette* – 23747/2795

336 *London Gazette* – 23733/2124

337 *London Gazette* – 24667/119

338 *London Gazette* – 24785/6587

Soon afterwards, Garrett was involved in a successful expedition against the Zaimukhts a Pathan tribe with their stronghold at Zawa which ended in December 1879.

In 1880, Garrett was involved in the Chan Kanni Expedition and was present at the Battle of Ali Khel on 19th April 1880.

For his service during the war, Garrett twice received a mention in despatches and was awarded the Afghanistan Medal (1878–80).

At the end of the war, with the breakup of the Kurram Field Force, Garrett returned to Ajmir in November 1880, where he rejoined the Merwara Battalion and was appointed as Brigade-Major, second in command of the regiment.

On 1st April 1882, Garrett was appointed to the command of the Merwara Battalion (44th Infantry).

After 20 years of service in the army, Garrett was promoted to the rank of Major on 2nd October 1886.[339]

On 15th April 1890, Garrett was appointed to the command of the 29th Bombay Native Infantry (2nd Baluchi) Regiment and took up station at Loralai in Baluchistan.

In September 1890, Garrett and his regiment were involved in the Zhob Valley and the Kidarzai Expeditions as part of the many campaigns against the warring tribes of the North West Frontier of India. Garrett received a mention in despatches for each of these expeditions.

At the end of these expeditions, Garrett started 18 months of home leave in England and in April 1891 he was married to Elizabeth Lillah (née Reade) who he had met in India; their only child, a son Duncan Vandeleur[340] was born on 16th May 1892 while the couple were still in England.

Duncan pursued a military career, like his father and rose to the rank of Lieutenant-Colonel and was awarded the Military Cross for action during World War I.

In September 1892, Garrett and his family returned to India and he took up command of his regiment that was now stationed at Hyderabad.

Garrett was promoted to the rank of Lieutenant-Colonel on 2nd October 1892[341] and soon afterwards was appointed as the station commander at Hyderabad.

During the hot weather of 1893, Garrett moved his family to the hills at Simla and in the summer of 1894 moved them to the hills around Kasauli.

During the winter of 1895–95 the regiment was moved back to Loralai and on the 23rd February 1895, Garrett was appointed to the command of that station.

339 *London Gazette* – 25656/6371
340 On 10th September 1923, following the death of his father, Duncan changed his christian names to Michael O'Moore by deed poll.
341 *London Gazette* – 26354/7398

Garrett's return to Loralai was short lived as on 1st November 1895 he was appointed as Assistant Adjutant-General of the Poona Division.[342]

On the 17th March 1896, Garret was appointed as Assistant Quartermaster-General of the Bombay Army.[343]

Soon after taking up his appointment plague broke out in Bombay which soon spread to Poona, Lord Sandhurst, the Governor of Bombay asked Garrett to take charge of plague operations in Poona, a duty that he performed in addition to his military responsibilities.

After six months of hard and diligent work, the plague at Poona was finally brought under control and eliminated. Because of his success at Poona, the Governor of Bombay requested that Garrett be made available to take charge of the plague operations within the city, however, General Sir Charles Nairne (the commander-in-chief of forces in India) refused this request.

Garrett was promoted to the rank of Colonel on 2nd October 1896.[344]

On 7th August 1898, was appointed as the Political Resident and General Officer Commanding at Aden and on 22nd February 1899 was appointed to the command of a 2nd class district in India with the temporary rank of Brigadier-General.[345]

In the summer of 1900, Garrett received a telegram informing him that he had been appointed to command a brigade in the expeditionary force, commanded by General Sir A. P. Palmer, that was being raised in India to be despatched to China to suppress the Boxer Rebellion.

On 13th August 1900, Garrett was appointed to the command of the 2nd Brigade of the Expeditionary Force, with the local rank of Major-General while on duty in China.[346]

Garrett's Brigade of four battalions was assembled at Bombay and after arriving at Hong-Kong were despatched to Shanghai which was thought to be threatened by Boxer forces, as part of the North China Field Force.

After the Boxer Protocol was signed on 7th September 1901, Garrett was ordered to proceed to Tientsin and take up his role of General Officer Commanding the British forces in China.[347]

For his service during the war, Garrett was awarded the China War Medal (1900).

On 26th June 1902, Garrett was appointed as an Ordinary Member 3rd Class (Companion) of the Military Division of the Most Honourable Order of the Bath.[348]

342 *London Gazette* – 26721/1682
343 *London Gazette* – 26752/3705
344 *London Gazette* – 26809/5
345 *London Gazette* – 27085/3521
346 *London Gazette* – 27230/5766
347 *London Gazette* – 27357/6172
348 *London Gazette* – 27448/4190

Garrett was promoted to the rank of Major-General on 5th July 1902.[349]

In the summer of 1902, Garrett attended the annual army manoeuvres in Japan; Japan had been a British ally during the Boxer Rebellion. During the visit, the Emperor advised Garrett that he wished to decorate him for his service during the war and would do so once he had received the required approval of King Edward VII.

The King gave his approval and Garrett was duly awarded the Order of the Rising Sun (2nd Class) on his return to Tientsin later in the year.

During the winter of 1902/03, Garrett spent some time in England on home leave and finally left China in July 1903, having on 16th March 1903 been appointed to the command of a 1st Class District (Mhow) in India.[350]

On 26th June 1903, Garrett was appointed as an Ordinary Member 2nd Class (Knight Commander) of the Military Division of the Most Honourable Order of the Bath.[351]

Garrett spent six months on leave in England before returning to India and taking up his command of the 2nd Division based at Mhow in January 1904.

On the 13th May 1904, Garrett was appointed as Honorary Colonel of the 44th Merwara Infantry (2nd Baluchi).[352]

In the summer of 1905, Garrett was transferred to the command of the Rawal Pindi division and soon afterwards on 26th September 1905 was promoted to the rank of Lieutenant-General.[353]

In the summer of 1907, Garrett was offered the role of Secretary to the Military Department of the London Office and was ordered to London.

After sitting as a member of an Anglo-Japanese Military Committee, Garrett took up his appointment on 11th December 1907, having been promoted to the rank of General.[354]

On 25th June 1909, Garrett was appointed as an Ordinary Member 1st Class (Knight Grand Cross) of the Military Division of the Most Honourable Order of the Bath.[355]

Following the retirement of Lord Kitchener from the office, Garrett was appointed as Commander-in-Chief of forces in India on 10th September 1909[356] and was a member of the Viceroy's Council.

349 *London Gazette* – 27583/4902
350 *London Gazette* – 27632/28
351 *London Gazette* – 27448/4190
352 *London Gazette* – 27676/3090
353 *London Gazette* – 27877/545
354 *London Gazette* – 28142/4070
355 *London Gazette* – 28263/4853
356 *London Gazette* – 28290/7047

On 30th November 1911, Garrett was appointed as a Knight of Grace in the Grand Priory Order of the Hospital of St John of Jerusalem in England.[357]

Garrett was appointed as an Aide-de-Camp to King George V on 2nd December 1911[358] and ten days later was appointed as a Knight Grand Commander in the Most Exalted Order of the Star of India.[359]

Garrett attended the Delhi Durbar in late December 1911, when King George V was present to recognise his succession as Emperor of India and was later awarded the Delhi Durbar Medal (1911) to celebrate the occasion.

On 16th February 1912, Garrett was appointed as an honorary Colonel of the 129th Duke of Connaught's Own Baluchis.[360]

Garrett was replaced as Commander-in-Chief India by General Sir Beauchamp Duff on 8th March 1914[361] and a few weeks later on 4th May 1914 after over 48 years of service he retired from the army.[362]

On leaving the army, Garrett returned to England and established a home at 65 Albert Hall Mansions, South Kensington, London.

In his retirement, Garrett became an author, writing his autobiography and with Edith M. Humphris wrote the VC & DSO A Complete Record 1856–1920, which even today is an important reference work for those interested in the recipients of the Victoria Cross and Distinguished Service Order.

On 9th August 1923, at the age of 75, Garrett died at his home 65 Albert Hall Mansions and was buried two days later in East Sheen Cemetery in Surrey.

Garrett's Victoria Cross medal is on public display at the National Army Museum, Chelsea in London.

Figure 155a. Grave of Garrett O'Moore Creagh

357 *London Gazette* – 28555/9067
358 *London Gazette* – 28556/9173
359 *London Gazette* – 28559/9356
360 *London Gazette* – 28581/1177
361 *London Gazette* – 28812/2254
362 *London Gazette* – 28832/4012

George Stuart White
6th October 1879 (VC No. 349)

Gazetted: 3rd June 1881 24981/2859

Rank and Unit: Major – 92nd Regiment of Foot

Citation

For conspicuous bravery during the engagement at Charasiab on the 6th October, 1879, when, finding that the artillery and rifle fire failed to dislodge the enemy from a fortified hill which it was necessary to capture, Major White led an attack upon it in person.

Advancing with two companies of his regiment; and climbing from one steep ledge to another, he came upon a body of the enemy, strongly posted, and outnumbering his force by about 8 to 1. His men being much exhausted, and immediate action being necessary, Major White took a rifle, and, going on by himself, shot the leader of the enemy. This act so intimidated the rest that they fled round the side of the hill, and the position was won.

Again, on the 1st September, 1880, at the battle of Candahar, Major White, in leading, the final charge, under a heavy fire from the enemy, who held a strong position and were supported by two guns, rode straight up to within a few yards of them, and seeing the guns, dashed forward and secured one, immediately after which the enemy retired.

Biography

George was born on 6th July 1835 at Rock Castle near the fishing village of Port Stewart, Co Antrim in Northern Ireland to father James Robert and mother Frances (née Stuart).

George was the second of three sons with older brother James born on 9th September 1832 and younger brother John born on 16th July 1839. He also had six sisters; Francis Anne, Jane Eleanor, Victoria Isabella, Elizabeth and two others.

George was educated at home until just before his 9th birthday in 1844 when he was sent to the Bromsgrove School in England which he attended with his older brother. George did not settle at the school and it was only a few months before he returned to the family home in Ireland.

In January 1847, George now over 11 years of age attended the King William's College on the Isle of Man where due to his prowess as a swimmer he was given the nickname "White Duck".

Initially George was drawn to the sea and wanted to be a sailor, however, this was discouraged by his father as the family tradition was to serve in the army.

Figure 156. George Stuart White

In July 1850, at the age of 15, George entered the Royal Military College at Sandhurst as a gentleman cadet.

On graduating from Sandhurst, George was commissioned as an Ensign in the 27th Regiment of Foot (Inniskillings) at Dublin on 4th November 1853.[363]

George spent his first months of army service at the Royal Barracks in Dublin but in June 1854 received orders to make ready for deployment to India.

The war with Russia had just broken out and George, along with most of the regiment, was disappointed that they were going to India rather than the Crimea.

On 16th June, George who was now a Grenadier, left Dublin for Cork and on 20th June 1854 boarded the transport *Charlotte* and set sail for Calcutta via the Cape of Good Hope.

The *Charlotte* reached Algoa Bay, off the South Africa coast, on 19th September 1854 and was anchored in the bay while a small party was allowed ashore.

George remained onboard until early evening when he was relieved of duty and despite the heavy swells he went ashore.

The next evening, during a heavy storm, the *Charlotte* broke her moorings and was driven onto rocks in an inaccessible part of the bay; despite not being close to the shore, great efforts were made to effect a rescue, ropes were fired by rockets and the life boat was launched but to no avail.

In the early morning of the 21st September, the *Charlotte* broke in two and the aft part was driven further up the rocks, closer to the shore. Being closer, George and others were able to start and rescue the survivors with over 100 being saved.

Unfortunately 120 soles perished; 62 enlisted men, 11 women, 29 children and 18 crew members.

363 *London Gazette* – 21491/2961

The survivors of the disaster eventually reached Cape Town, where they waited for a replacement vessel to be engaged to complete their journey. The merchant ship *Maidstone* was engaged and after a journey of 6 months, George and his detachment of the regiment were anchored off Calcutta on 6th January 1855.

George was promoted to the rank of Lieutenant on 29th January 1855.[364]

Sometime during January 1855, the detachment left Calcutta bound for Sealkot in the Punjab, where the regiment was to be based; the 1,000 mile journey took three months to complete and they arrived on 30th March to the cheers of the rest of the regiment.

Sometime in 1856 the regiment was moved to Nowshera on the North West Frontier and were stationed there at the outbreak of the mutiny, on 8th July 1857, George was part of a detachment despatched to hold the old fort at Attock.

In March 1858, the regiment were replaced at Nowshera by the 81st Regiment of Foot and despatched to Umbeyla in the hills, where they arrived in early May.

During his time at Umbeyla, George studied for the entrance examinations to the Staff College back in England and for a time acted as Adjutant and Instructor of Musketry.

The regiments time during the mutiny was spent on securing the Punjab, where they disarmed several regiments of the Bengal Army to prevent their mutiny.

For his service during the mutiny, George was awarded the Indian Mutiny Medal (1857–58), without clasps.

In April 1859, George took time out from duties at Umbeyla to attend a course at the Musketry School at Sealkot, where he obtained a 1st Class certificate as Instructor of Musketry, passing out at the head of his class.

In early 1860, George was appointed to the staff as Deputy Assistant Quartermaster-General of the army and was posted to Allahabad.

Unhappy with his staff role at Allahabad, George returned to England on home leave on 16th October 1860 and after a period of rest and recuperation, joined his regiment's second battalion currently on station in Ireland in Cork.

On 10th July 1863, George advanced his position in the regiment when he purchased the commission as Captain[365] and soon afterwards on 4th August 1863, transferred to the 92nd Regiment of Foot (Gordon Highlanders) by way of exchange.[366]

Initially George was based in Edinburgh with the 92nd until 25th May 1864 when the regiment was moved to Glasgow where they remained for about one year.

364 *London Gazette* – 21719/2014
365 *London Gazette* – 22752/3453
366 *London Gazette* – 22759/3905

On 6th March 1865, George and the regiment boarded ship on the Clyde and set sail for Portsmouth on their way to the Camp at Aldershot where they arrived on 10th March.

After spending a year at Aldershot, the regiment were once again on their travels setting sail for Ireland on 1st March 1866 and after a brief stay at the Curragh Camp arrived at Dublin on 10th March.

The regiment's time in Ireland was quite fraught as they were involved in policing actions during the civil disturbances known as the Fenian riots.

In late 1867, the regiment were put on notice for a posting to India and on 25th January 1868, George and the regiment boarded the troopship *Crocodile* bound for India.

The regiment disembarked at Alexandria on 8th February and after making their way to Suez boarded the troopship *Malabar* on 10th February and set sail for Bombay.

After arriving off Bombay on 26th February, the regiment was transhipped to Karachi and then made their way overland to Jalundhur in the Punjab where they arrived on 30th March 1868.

On 1st April 1871, George set sail from Bombay on a merchant ship bound for Naples to begin an 18 month home leave, most of which he spent at the family home in Ireland.

On 8th October 1872, George began his journey to return to India arriving at Bombay on 31st October where he continued by rail and rejoined his regiment at the hill station of Chakrata but soon afterwards was sent to the hill station at Masuri on Court-martial duty.

After a short spell at Masuri, George returned to Chakrata where he spent the winter and in May 1873 was sent to Simla, the largest of the hill stations which served as the summer headquarters for the Indian Government.

On 22nd November, the regiment left Simla bound for Multan, which was one of the hottest and least favoured of all stations in India, where they arrived on 13th December 1873.

On arrival at Multan, they found that the 41st Regiment of Foot still occupied the barracks as they had been delayed in their departure to duties at Aden.

As a consequence, George and the regiment had to endure a miserable period in tents until the 41st finally departed on the 30th December.

On 24th December 1873, George was promoted to the rank of Major.[367]

George was married to Amelia Maria (née Baly) the daughter of the Archdeacon of Calcutta on 31st October 1874 at Simla and after a short honeymoon returned to Multan to set up home.

367 *London Gazette* – 24055/239

The couple would go on to have six children; Rose born on 5th December 1876 at Delhi, James Robert born on 22nd May 1879 at Richmond, May Constance born on 1st May 1883 at Southsea, Amy Gladys Stuart born in 1886 at Richmond and Georgina Mary born on 30th December 1895 at Calcutta.

Due to two senior officers having taken leave, George found himself in temporary command of the regiment from 24th March 1876 until 1st November 1876.

On the 2nd November 1876, the regiment left Multan bound for Delhi where they arrived on the 19th December 1876 and on 1st January 1877 took part in the "Imperial Assemblage" being held to commemorate the proclamation of Queen Victoria as Empress of India.

For a short period between 20th December 1876 and 8th March 1877, George was again in temporary command of the regiment.

On 12th March 1878, George and his family left India for a period of home leave in England.

In December 1878, the 92nd Regiment received orders to join General Roberts expeditionary force being assembled at the Shutargardan Pass for service in the 2nd Anglo-Afghan War.

After receiving a telegram to rejoin his regiment, George left England on 30th January 1879, leaving his wife and child behind.

George arrived back in India on 21st February 1879 and after joining his regiment, assembled as part of the 2nd Brigade, commanded by General H. Forbes, on 18th April 1879.

Hostilities ended on 26th May 1879, with the signing of the Gandamak treaty so the regiment saw no action during the first phase of the war. The regiment were based at Au Kheyl deployed on small reconnaissance and survey escort missions until September, while George was on duty at Simla.

On 24th September, following the massacre of Sir Louis Cavagnari and his diplomatic mission at Kabul, George rejoined the Regiment and now with the 1st Brigade, commanded by General Macpherson, part of the Kurram Valley Field Force was involved in the advance to retake Kabul.

It was during the Battle of Charisia on 6th October 1879, his first significant action, that George performed the deeds for which he would later be awarded the Victoria Cross.

The defeat of the Afghan army at Charisia forced them to abandon their resistance and Kabul was taken unopposed on 13th October 1879.

In November 1879, George commanded a wing of the regiment as part of a force commanded by General Baker despatched to the Chardeh Valley to chase down the fleeing Afghan Army and after the operations returned with the regiment to Sherpur on 1st December.

On 13th December 1879, George led the advance party in the capture of Takht-i-Shah and the taking of the Asmai Heights on the following day.

By 15th December the whole of the British force, around 7,000 men, was concentrated in the cantonment at Sherpur where they were immediately surrounded by an Afghan force numbering about 50,000 Afghan troops.

The besieged British forces managed to fight off the few attempts by the Afghans to enter Sherpur and on the 23rd December after a serious attempt was strongly repulsed, the enemy gave up their attempts and dispersed, ending the siege.

George and the regiment remained at Sherpur during the winter months with little action taking place until the Battle of Childuktean on 25th April 1880, when he once again led the regiment into action; the last action in Northern Afghanistan.

In the spring of 1880, following a general election in England which resulted in a change of government, the Marquis of Ripon was appointed as Viceroy of India and on 6th May, George received a telegram from him offering the position of Military Secretary.

George left Kabul on 8th May and returned to India to take up this new appointment and arrived at Simla on 16th May to await the arrival of the new Viceroy.

On 26th May, George left Simla for Bombay where on 31st May he met Lord Ripon at Government House and afterwards returned to Inverarm, the Military Secretaries house in Simla.

Lord Ripon received news of the British defeat at Maiwand and the subsequent siege of Kandahar on 28th July 1880 and immediately ordered General Roberts at Kabul to go to the relief of Kandahar.

With this new conflict in Afghanistan, George was eager to join his regiment on the march to Kandahar and offered his resignation to Lord Ripon to allow him to do so. Wishing to retain George's services as Military Secretary, Lord Ripon did not accept his resignation but allowed him a leave of absence so that he could join his regiment.

On 5th August 1880, George left Simla and arrived back in Afghanistan, near Kabul on five days later on 10th August.

After joining up with General Roberts force, George was with the regiment on the march to Kandahar and it was during the Battle of Kandahar on 1st September 1880 that he performed the deeds which form the second action in his Victoria Cross citation.

On 12th September 1880, as soon as the fighting was over, George began his return to India and by 21st September had returned to his duties at Simla.

For his service during the war, George received mentions in despatches and was awarded the Afghanistan Medal (1878–80) with clasps for Charisia, Kabul and Kandahar he was also awarded the Kabul to Kandahar Star (1881).

On 28th September 1880, the 92nd Regiment received orders to return and make their way to India as the start of their journey back to England, however, after reaching Allahabad on 6th January 1881 they received a change of orders which now directed the regiment to Natal to help quell the Boer uprising.

Once again, with his regiment going to war, George applied to join them, however, despite the support of Lord Ripon this was refused and he had to continue with his Military Secretary duties at Simla.

On 22nd February 1881, George was appointed as an Ordinary Member 3rd Class (Companion) of the Most Honourable Order of the Bath.[368]

George received a brevet promotion to the rank of Lieutenant-Colonel on 1st July 1881.[369]

George was presented with his Victoria Cross Medal on 4th October 1881 by the Viceroy of India, the Marquis of Ripon at a ceremony held in Simla, on the North West Frontier of India.

On 28th October 1881, in succession to Colonel Parker, George was appointed to the command of the 92nd Highlanders,[370] on half pay.

George relinquished his position as Military Secretary on 30th November 1881 and left India for England to take up his regimental command.

The 92nd Highlanders left South Africa towards the end of 1881 and arrived at Portsmouth on 30th January 1882 where they were quartered in the Anglesey Barracks.

On the 6th October 1882, the regiment left Portsmouth and on the 9th October were installed as the garrison at Edinburgh Castle.

The regiment left Edinburgh on 30th June 1884 and proceeded by rail to Greenock where they boarded *HMS Assistance* bound for Devonport and took up residence in the Raglan Barracks.

On the 8th February 1885, George received orders to proceed to Egypt as soon as possible to join the Nile Expeditionary Force and left England on the evening of 13th February.

On 13th February 1885 George was placed on half pay.[371]

George was appointed to the role of Assistant Adjutant General and Quartermaster General to the force on 19th February 1885 and moved from half pay.[372]

368 *London Gazette* – 24944/976
369 *London Gazette* – 24999/3686
370 *London Gazette* – 25096/1740
371 *London Gazette* – 25450/1092
372 *London Gazette* – 25469/2160

On 2nd March 1885, George was promoted to the rank of Colonel.[373]

General Dormer was appointed to the command of the Advanced Field Force in the Sudan in May 1885 and George was appointed as his Adjutant-General. When the field force was broken up on 1st June 1885, George applied for home leave and by the 30th June 1885 was back in England.

For his service during the war, George was awarded the Egypt Medal (1882–89) with clasp for the Nile (1884–85), he was also awarded the Khedive's Star (1884–86).

During his brief period of leave in England, George spent time with his wife and family who had been living at his in-laws home at Key during his time in Egypt but this was short lived as on 14th August after only six weeks in England he set out for India, to join his new command the Kampti Brigade in Central India.

On the 2nd September 1885, George was appointed to the command of a brigade (Kampti) with the local rank of Brigadier-General.[374]

In October 1885, with trouble brewing in Burma, George offered his services and was appointed to the command of the 2nd Brigade in the Burma Expeditionary Force, commanded by General Harry Prendergast.

On the 3rd November, George set sail from Madras and arrived off the mouth of the Irrawaddy river four days later.

On 9th November, after the British demands had been rejected by King Thibaw, the Expeditionary Force set off upriver from Rangoon towards the capital at Mandalay in a flotilla of river steamers.

When the force reached the outskirts of Mandalay, on 28th November 1885, King Thibaw had no alternative but to offer the surrender of his forces.

After occupying Mandalay, George was given responsibility for securing the king in his palace while the extensive forts and defences were dismantled and on 21st December was given command of the city while General Prendergast led an expedition up the river Bhamo.

On 1st January 1886, Lord Dufferin, the Viceroy of India, formally annexed Burma as part of British India.

George was appointed to the command of troops in Upper Burma, with the local rank of Major-General, on 1st April 1886.[375]

On 25th November 1886, George was appointed as an Ordinary Member 2nd Class (Knight Commander) of the Most Honourable Order of the Bath.[376]

373 *London Gazette* – 25448/922
374 *London Gazette* – 25521/4833, 25561/851
375 *London Gazette* – 25573/1536
376 *London Gazette* – 25650/5975

For the next two years, George was involved in the pacification of Burma and the gradual transfer of control from the military to the civil authorities.

For distinguished service in the field, George was promoted to the rank of Major-General on 1st July 1887.[377]

For his services during the 3rd Anglo-Burmese war, George was awarded the India General Service Medal (1854–95) with clasp for Burma (1885–87).

On 10th April 1888, George left Burma for three months leave in England and after a three year separation was reunited with his wife and children in May 1888.

On 15th June 1888, George left England to resume his duties in Burma, arriving at Bombay on 2nd July and was back in his headquarters at Mandalay on 27th July 1888.

On 1st April 1889, George was appointed to the command of a 1st Class District in India[378] (Quetta) and took up his command in Baluchistan on 3rd May 1889.

The Zhob Valley was a piece of no man's land, about the size of Switzerland, that occupied one of the passes between India and Afghanistan. For some years, Sir Robert Sandeman, the governor of Baluchistan had petitioned the Indian Government to annex this strategic piece of land and eventually in December 1889, his wish was granted.

Not losing any time, Sir Robert Sandeman arranged an expedition to the Zhob Valley in January 1890. With troops led by George, the valley was occupied and without a shot being fired it was annexed as part of the British protectorate.

George led further operations between November 1890 and January 1891, during which the peaks on the Afghanistan border were secured.

For the remainder of 1891 and during 1892 everything was quiet at Quetta and in late November 1892, George set out for a short period of home leave.

When George arrived at Suez a telegram was waiting for him offering the appointment of Commander-in-Chief India in succession to Lord Roberts, which he immediately accepted.

On 6th March 1893, George was appointed as Knight Grand Commander of the Most Eminent Order of the Indian Empire.[379]

George set sail, with his wife, for India in March 1893 and arrived at Bombay in early April; he was formally appointed to the post of Commander-in-Chief of forces in India, with the temporary rank of Lieutenant-General and the local rank of General, on 8th April 1893.[380]

377 *London Gazette* – 25761/6376
378 *London Gazette* – 25964/4394
379 *London Gazette* – 26381/1539
380 *London Gazette* – 26405/3002

George was appointed as honorary Colonel to the 2nd Volunteer Battalion of the Prince Albert's Somerset Light Infantry on 9th June 1894.[381]

On 1st April 1895, George was promoted to the rank of Lieutenant-General, supernumerary to the establishment.[382]

George was appointed as an Additional Member 1st Class (Knights Grand Cross) of the Military Division of the Most Honourable Order of the Bath on 22nd June 1897.[383]

On 28th June 1897, George was appointed as Colonel of the 92nd Gordon Highlanders.[384]

George received the Queen Victoria Jubilee Medal in 1897.

During his time as Commander-in-Chief, George oversaw several operations against tribes on the North West Frontier and was responsible for reorganising a unified command of forces in India following the abolition of the presidential army structure.

George was appointed as a Knight Grand Commander of the Most Exalted Order of the Star of India on 11th January 1898.[385]

It was intended that George would relinquish his command of forces in India during November 1897, however, when his replacement General Sir William Lockhart requested home leave to recover from illness, he agreed to remain in the post until April 1898.

This arrangement was to change as in early February 1898, George fell from his horse while out hunting and broke his leg in seven places which resulted in his being sent home, he arrived back in England towards the end of April.

On 15th October 1898, George was appointed as Quartermaster-General of the British Army[386] and took up his position on the War Office Staff at Whitehall as one of the five principal officers under the Secretary of War Lord Lansdowne.

In the summer of 1899 trouble was brewing with the Boer Republics of South Africa and war looked imminent.

George was offered the position of Governor of Gibraltar, by Lord Wolseley the Commander-in-Chief of the British Army on 12th July 1899, however, with the worsening situation in South Africa, he was advised by Lord Wolseley on 6th September to make himself ready for service to South Africa instead.

On the 16th September 1899, George was appointed to the staff as a Lieutenant-General with command of the troops in Natal.[387]

On the same day George set sail from Southampton, on board *HMS Tantallon Castle*, to take up his new position and arrived

381 *London Gazette* – 26520/3319
382 *London Gazette* – 26626/2944
383 *London Gazette* – 26867/3567
384 *London Gazette* – 26884/4673
385 *London Gazette* – 26928/164
386 *London Gazette* – 27014/5989
387 *London Gazette* – 27117/5693

off Capetown on 3rd October and reached Durban, the main port of Natal, on the morning of 7th October.

George's role was to defend the Natal Colony, while an invasion force to be commanded by General Sir Redvers Buller was assembled in England.

Three battalions of troops (6,000 men) were sent from India to boost his force to 14,000 and although it was about one third the number of men in the Boer Army, was thought to be sufficient to prevent an invasion.

George arrived at Ladysmith, where the bulk of his forces were concentrated, on 11th October, the day that the Second Boer War was declared.

On his arrival at Ladysmith, George first turned his attention to strengthening the defences of the town and stockpiling supplies of food.

Once Ladysmith was secured, George turned his attention to the invading column of Boers who had crossed into Natal from the Orange Free State and was heading for Ladysmith, further columns had also crossed the border from the Transvaal.

George's available forces were split across two positions, two thirds of his men were with George at Ladysmith while the other third, under the command of General Penn Symons, was 40 miles away at Dundee.

On 20th October 1899, the Boer army mounted an attack against Dundee and were defeated at the Battle of Talana, unfortunately the British commander General Penn Symons was killed during the action.

George led a force of his troops from Ladysmith against columns of Boers from the Transvaal who had occupied Elandslaagte and defeated them in battle on 21st October 1899.

On 24th October, George led half of his troops against the Boers at Rietfontein although George defeated the Boers this was mainly a diversionary strike to allow Major Yule's force, retreating from Dundee, to enter Ladysmith unmolested.

The columns of troops from the Orange Free State and those from the Transvaal joined up on 29th October and began to encircle Ladysmith; by 2nd November the town was under siege.

George commanded the garrison at Ladysmith throughout the 119 days of the siege until they were relieved by a force commanded by General Buller on 1st March 1900.

During the last few weeks of the Siege, George nearly 65 years of age, suffered ill health due to several bouts of fever and when the siege was ended he applied for home leave in England to regain his health.

For his service in South Africa, George was awarded the Queen's South Africa Medal (1899–1902) with clasps for Elandslaagte and Defence of Ladysmith.

His leave was granted and by the end of March 1900 George was in Capetown, where he met his son, now serving with the Gordon Highlanders. After a few days stay in Capetown, George set sail for England on board the transport *Dunvegan Castle* and arrived at Portsmouth on 14th April, where he received a rapturous reception.

After attending numerous receptions and dinners in London, George was able to return to his home in Ireland.

George was appointed as a Knight Grand Cross of the Royal Victorian Order on 7th May 1900.[388]

On 30th May 1900, George was appointed as Governor of Gibraltar and Commander-in-Chief of troops on Gibraltar.[389]

In early July 1900, George left England for Gibraltar where he arrived on the 11th July and was sworn in as Governor and Commander in Chief of the City and Garrison.

George was appointed as an Ordinary Member 1st Class (Knight Grand Cross) of the Most Distinguished Order of St Michael and St George on 19th April 1901.[390]

In 1902, George was awarded the King Edward VII Coronation Medal in honour of the new monarch ascending to the throne.

In April 1903, King Edward VII made a visit to Gibraltar, the first British monarch to do so and at the end of the visit informed George of his intention to promote him to Field-Marshal, stating that *"Nobody has deserved it better, and there has been no more loyal soldier to his sovereign and his country"*.

On 8th April 1903, George was promoted to the rank of Field-Marshal.[391]

Ending his time on foreign service, George left Gibraltar at the end of his Governorship on 13th June 1905 and returned to England.

George was appointed as Governor of the Royal Hospital at Chelsea on 17th June 1905[392] and was also appointed as Commissioner of the Duke of York's Royal Military School at Guston, near Dover.

On 30th June 1905, George was awarded the Order of Merit.[393]

In 1908, George was awarded the Franz Joseph I Jubilee Gold Medal (Austria).

George was awarded the King George V Coronation Medal in 1911, in honour of the new monarch ascending to the throne.

After suffering a long illness, George died on 24th June 1912 at the Royal Hospital Chelsea and was buried in the family plot

388 *London Gazette* – 27192/3070
389 *London Gazette* – 27198/3498
390 *London Gazette* – 27306/2698
391 *London Gazette* – 27547/2693
392 *London Gazette* – 27813/4631
393 *London Gazette* – 27811/4549

at Broughshane Presbyterian Churchyard, Ballymena in Co Antrim, Ireland.

George's Victoria Cross Medal is on public display at the Gordon Highlanders Museum, Aberdeen in Scotland.

Figure 156a. Grave of George Stuart White

Euston Henry Sartorius
24th October 1879 (VC No. 350)

Gazetted: 17th May 1881 24973/2553

Rank and Unit: Captain – 59th Regiment of Foot

Citation

For conspicuous bravery during the action at Sliah-jui, on the 24th October, 1879, in leading a party of five or six men of the 59th Regiment against a body of the enemy, of unknown strength, occupying an almost inaccessible position on the top of a precipitous hill.

The nature of the ground made any sort of regular formation impossible, and Captain Sartorius had to bear the first brunt of the attack from the whole body of the enemy, who fell upon him and his men as they gained the top of the precipitous pathway; but the gallant and determined bearing of this Officer, emulated as it was by his men, led to the most perfect success, and the surviving occupants of the hill top. seven in number, were all killed.

In this encounter Captain Sartorius was wounded by sword cuts to both hands, and one of his men was killed.

Biography

Euston was born on 6th June 1844 at Sintra in Portugal the 3rd child of father George Rose, Admiral of the Fleet and mother Sophia (née Lamb).

One of six children, Euston had two older brothers George Conrad born on 2nd April 1840 and Reginald William born on 8th May 1841.[394] He also had three younger sisters; Rose born in 1846, Emily born in 1849 and Kate born in 1850.

In 1855, while his family remained in Portugal, Euston and his older brother Reginald were sent as boarders to the Victoria College on the island of Jersey to complete their education.

Euston also attended the Royal Navy School at Newcross before joining the Royal Military College at Sandhurst as a Gentleman Cadet.

After graduating from the Royal Military Academy at Sandhurst, Euston was commissioned as an Ensign in the 59th Regiment of Foot on 8th July 1862.[395]

394 Reginald was also awarded a Victoria Cross for service in 1st Ashanti War on 17th January 1874, making them one of only four sets of brothers to receive the award.

395 *London Gazette* – 22642/3434

Figure 157. Euston Henry Sartorius

Euston was promoted to the rank of Lieutenant on 18th July 1865.[396]

On 29th June 1869, Euston was awarded the Royal Humane Society Bronze Medal for saving the lives of three girls, from drowning, at Broadstairs in Kent.

In December 1870, Euston passed out from the Army Staff College and on 23rd February 1871 was appointed as an instructor in Military Surveying at the Royal Military College, Sandhurst.

Euston was placed on the supernumerary list of his regiment on 12th February 1873 while serving as an instructor in Military Surveying at the Royal Military College, Sandhurst.[397]

On 30th September 1874, while still on the supernumerary list, Euston was promoted to the rank of Captain.[398]

Euston was married to Emily Jane (née Cook) at Richmond in Surrey on 22nd December 1874; the couple would go on to have two daughters Elfrida Elsie born in 1876 and Daisy Augusta born 20th December 1877, both of whom were born in India. They also had a son Euston Francis Frederick born in Preston Lancashire on 22nd March 1882 who died at the Battle of Neuve Chappelle on 5th April 1915, during the Great War.

On 31st January 1875, Euston left his position as instructor at the Royal Military College and after over 12 years of home service, finally embarked on his first period of foreign service when he joined his regiment in India on 1st February 1875.

Euston was removed from the Supernumerary List and returned to his regiment role as a Captain on 9th June 1877.[399]

396 *London Gazette* – 22992/3578
397 *London Gazette* – 23947/586
398 *London Gazette* – 24138/4652
399 *London Gazette* – 24477/3899

Euston saw his first active service when from 12th December 1878 he served with his regiment as part of the 2nd Infantry Brigade (commanded by General W. Hughes) of the 1st Division (commanded by General Donald Stewart) of the Kandahar Field Force in the 2nd Anglo-Afghan war.

In January 1879, Euston was involved in the capture of Kalat-i-Ghilzai and saw action at Tazi.

It was at Shahjui on 24th October 1879, that Euston performed the deeds for which he would later be awarded the Victoria Cross, during the action he was seriously wounded with sword cuts to both hand; he would subsequently lose the use of his left hand.

For his service during the war, Euston received two mentions in despatches and was awarded the Afghanistan Medal (1878–80).

At the end of the war, Euston returned to India on 24th December 1879 for a short time before returning to England on 28th February 1880.

From 16th December 1880 until 9th September 1881, Euston served as the Adjutant to the 3rd Regimental District.

On 2nd March 1881, for his service during the war in Afghanistan, Euston received a brevet promotion to the rank of Major.[400]

Euston was presented with his Victoria Cross Medal by Queen Victoria at a ceremony held in Windsor Castle on 1st July 1881.

On 1st July 1881, Euston was promoted to the rank of Major and took up his position with the East Lancashire regiment,[401] newly formed by the amalgamation of the 30th and 59th Regiments of Foot as part of the Cardwell reforms.

Euston was appointed to the staff post of Deputy Assistant Adjutant and Quartermaster General at Aldershot on the 11th April 1882.[402]

On 1st August 1882, Euston was appointed as Deputy Assistant Adjutant and Quartermaster General to the Egypt Expeditionary Force[403] sent to the war with Egypt.

For his service during the war, Euston received a mention in despatches and was awarded the Egypt Medal (1882–89) and the Khedive's Star (1882–91).

On 17th November 1882, for his service in Egypt, Euston was awarded the Order of the Osmanieh (Knight 4th Class) by Turkey[404] and received a brevet promotion to the rank of Lieutenant-Colonel.[405]

400 *London Gazette* – 24994/977
401 *London Gazette* – 24999/3683
402 *London Gazette* – 25093/1587
403 *London Gazette* – 25134/3581
404 *London Gazette* – 25169/5168
405 *London Gazette* – 25169/5173

After the war in Egypt, Euston returned to England and on 27th November 1882 resumed his staff role as Deputy Assistant Adjutant and Quartermaster General, at Aldershot.[406]

On 18th November 1886, Euston was promoted to the rank of Colonel.[407]

Euston was promoted to the rank of Lieutenant-Colonel on 11th April 1887 and placed on the half-pay list.[408]

On 21st August 1889, Euston was appointed to the staff position of Assistant Adjutant General of the Southern District at Portsmouth and was removed from the half pay list.[409]

On completion of his period in office as Assistant Adjutant General on 21st August 1894, Euston was returned to the half-pay list.[410]

Euston was appointed to the staff position as Military Attaché to Tokyo on 6th May 1896[411] and was removed from the half pay list; on the completion of his term of office on 18th February 1897 he returned to the half pay list.[412]

On 20th May 1896, Euston was appointed as an Ordinary Member 3rd Class (Companion) of the Military Division of the Most Honourable Order of the Bath.[413]

In 1897, Euston was awarded the Queen Victoria Jubilee Medal.

Euston was promoted to the rank of Major-General on 1st April 1899.[414]

In 1902, Euston was awarded the King Edward VII Coronation Medal.

Euston succeeded his father as Count of Penha Firme (Portugal) on 20th June 1903.

Euston was appointed as Honorary Colonel of the Prince of Wales Volunteers (South Lancs.) and the City of London Territorial Forces on 26th November 1909.[415]

In 1911, Euston was awarded the King George V Coronation Medal.

After a short illness, Euston died on 19th February 1925 aged 80 at his home the Old Swan House, 17 Chelsea Embankment in London and was buried at the St Peter and St Paul Churchyard in Ewhurst, Surrey.

Euston's Victoria Cross Medal is on public display at the National Army Museum, Chelsea in London.

406 *London Gazette* – 25175/6250
407 *London Gazette* – 25645/5529
408 *London Gazette* – 25760/6227
409 *London Gazette* – 25961/4269
410 *London Gazette* – 26544/4868
411 *London Gazette* – 26740/2989
412 *London Gazette* – 26848/2369
413 *London Gazette* – 26741/3053
414 *London Gazette* – 27074/2630
415 *London Gazette* – 28316/9415

James Williams Adams
11th December 1879 (VC No. 351)

Gazetted: 26th August 1881 25008/4393

Rank and Unit: Bengal Ecclesiastical Department – Chaplain to Kabul Field Force

Citation

During the action at Killa Kazi, on the 11th December, 1879, some men of the 9th Lancers having fallen, with their horses, into a Wide and and deep "nullah" or ditch, and the enemy being close upon them, the Reverend J. W. Adams rushed into the water (which filled the ditch), dragged the horses from off the men upon whom they were lying, and extricated them, he being at the time under a heavy fire, and up to his waist in water.

At this time the Afghans were pressing on very rapidly, the leading men getting within a few yards of Mr. Adams, who having let go his horse in order to render more effectual assistance, had eventually to escape on foot.

Biography

James was born on 24th November 1839 at Cork in Ireland to father Thomas O'Brion a local Justice of the Peace and mother Elizabeth (née Williams).

After being educated at the Hamblin & Porter's Grammar School in Cork, James attended Trinity College in Dublin from where he graduated in 1861 with a BA degree.

James began a period of theological education after leaving university and was ordained as a Deacon in 1863 and a Priest in 1864.

After being ordained as a Priest, James served as Curate to Reverend J. Warren at Hyde in Hampshire until 1865 when he moved to Shallenbrook Hill in Berkshire.

In October 1866, James moved to India and became a chaplain under Bishop Milman at Calcutta.

Suffering from a fever, James spent some time in Ceylon on sick leave to recover his health.

In October 1868, James was formally appointed as a Chaplain in the Bengal Ecclesiastical Department of the Indian Army and was posted to Peshawar.

From March to December 1870, James spent time at Allahabad after which he returned to Peshawar and from December 1872 until March 1873 was Chaplain at the Camp of Exercise at Army HQ.

James left Peshawar in March 1874, for a period of service in Kashmir, however, during his stay he had a sabbatical from

Figure 158. James Williams Adams

January 1876 at Meerut and in December 1876 attended the Cavalry and Artillery camp at Delhi for the Durbar and the visit from the Prince of Wales.

In January 1877, James was chaplain at Chakrata until sometime in 1878 when he became chaplain of Jubbulpore and Allahabad.

James saw his first active service during the 2nd Anglo-Afghan war when he was appointed as chaplain to the Kurram Field Force in November 1878.

James was present at the Battle of Peiwar Kotal on 28th/29th November 1878 and at the Battle of Charisia on 6th October 1879.

It was during action at Killa Kazi on 11th December 1879, that James performed the deeds for which he would later be awarded the Victoria Cross.

On 23rd December 1879, James was present at the recapture of Kabul.

James was with the forces of General Sir Frederick Roberts on the famous march from Kabul to Kandahar in August 1880 and at the Battle of Kandahar on 1st September 1880.

For his services during the war, James was awarded the Afghanistan Medal (1878–80) with clasps for Peiwar Kotal, Charisia, Kabul and Kandahar. He also received the Kabul to Kandahar Star (1880).

After the war, James returned to England for a period of home leave and on 16th August 1881 was married to Alice Mary (née Willshire) at Iver Heath in Buckinghamshire; the couple would have a daughter, Edith Juliet Mary born on 10th August 1882 in Lucknow, India.

James was presented with his Victoria Cross Medal by Queen Victoria on 1st December 1881 at a ceremony held at Windsor Castle.

The initial proposal for the award of the Victoria Cross to James, forwarded by the India Office to the War Office was rejected; on 26th March 1881, Lieutenant-General Whitmore, the Military Secretary, wrote stating that "... the Rev J. W. Adams was not eligible as he holds no military commission."

Undaunted, the India Office replied that James should be considered for the award as a civilian, quoting the cases of Mr Mangles, Mr McDonnell and Mr Kavanagh. Again the proposal was rejected, as technically James was not a civilian as he worked as a Chaplain in the Bengal Ecclesiastical Department of the Indian Army.

However, sense prevailed and on 6th August 1881, Queen Victoria signed a Royal Warrant that granted eligibility for the award to members of Indian Ecclesiastical Establishments; it was under the terms of this new warrant that the award to James was approved, the first and only person to receive the award under this provision. He was the fifth and last civilian recipient of the award.

In 1882, James returned to India with his wife and resumed service as a Chaplain at Lucknow.

James was next posted to the hill station of Naini Tal on February 1883 where he spent the next three years in the Himalayas.

For a short time in November/December 1885, James spent time with the expeditionary forces in Burma during the 3rd Anglo-Burmese war.

James was awarded the Indian General Service Medal (1854–95) with clasp for Burma 1885–7, for his service during the war.

After the war, James returned to Lucknow where he served until October 1886 when after having completed 20 years of service with the Ecclesiastical Department he retired and returned to England.

On his return to England, James took up the position of Vicar at Postwick near Norwich which he held until 1894.

James gave up his position at Postwick due to ill health and he spent the next two years on the island of Jersey recuperating.

On recovering his health, James took up the position as Vicar of Stow Bardolph in 1896 which he held until 1902.

On 7th May 1900, James was appointed as Honorary Chaplain to His Royal Highness the Prince of Wales[416] and following his ascension to the throne was appointed as Honorary Chaplain to King Edward VII on 23rd July 1901.[417]

James was appointed as one of the 12 Chaplains Ordinary to King Edward VII on 31st October 1901.[418]

In 1902, James received the King Edward VII Coronation Medal.

416 *London Gazette* – 27190/2920
417 *London Gazette* – 27336/4839
418 *London Gazette* – 27370/7045

After leaving the church at Stow Bardolph, in 1902, James became rector at St Mary's, Ashwell near Oakham in Rutland and it was here on 20th October 1903, at the age of 63, that he died and was buried four days later in St Mary's Old Churchyard, Ashwell.

James's Victoria Cross Medal is not on public display as it is believed to be in private hands.

Figure 158a. Grave of James Williams Adams

William Henry Dick-Cunyngham
13th December 1879 (VC No. 352)

Gazetted: 18th October 1881 25027/5140

Rank and Unit: Lieutenant – 92nd Regiment of Foot

Citation

For the conspicuous gallantry and coolness displayed by him on the 13th December, 1879, at the attack on the Sherpur Pass, in Afghanistan, in having exposed himself to the full fire of the enemy, and by his example and encouragement rallied the men who, having been beaten back were, at the moment, wavering at the top of the hill.

Biography

William was born on 16th June 1851 at Prestonfield in Edinburgh to father Sir William Hammer, the 6th Baronet of Prestonfields and 8th of Lambrughton, and mother Susan (née Alston-Stewart).

He was the youngest of five sons with older brothers; Robert Keith Alexander born on 21st December 1836, William Bouverie born on 12th February 1842, James born on 27th December 1845 and Alexander born on 2nd January 1848. He also had four sisters; Charlotte Emily born in 1838, Margaret Alice born in 1853, Susan Wilhamena born in 1868 and Harriet Christina Montagu.

From 1860 until 1866, William was educated at Trinity College, Glenalmond in Perthshire, Scotland.

At the age of 15, William enrolled in the Royal Military College at Sandhurst as a gentleman cadet and following his graduation was commissioned as a sub-lieutenant in the 92nd Regiment of Foot on 17th February 1872.[419]

After spending his first few months of service in England, William was despatched to join his regiment at Chukrata, India in January 1873 and on 17th February 1873 he was promoted to the rank of Lieutenant.[420]

On 22nd November 1873, William and the regiment set out on a 495 mile march to their new station at Multan, where they arrived on 13th January 1874.

William was appointed as Adjutant to a wing of the regiment in January 1877, a position that he would hold until April 1878.

In December 1878, the regiment was moved to Kohat in readiness to join the Kabul Field Force commanded by General

419 *London Gazette* – 23828/595
420 *London Gazette* – 24068/828

Figure 159. William Henry Dick Cunyngham

Sir Frederick Roberts, which was being prepared for action in the 2nd Anglo-Afghan War.

On 25th March 1878, the regiment was moved to Alikhel where it arrived on 18th April, however, before they could be deployed the first phase of the war was ended on 8th May with the signing of the treaty of Gandamak.

Hostilities were resumed in early September 1878, following the murder of the British Envoy Mr Cavagnari and his deputation as they took up residence at Kabul.

The whole of the Kabul field force was now assembled in the Logar Valley and on 2nd October they began their advance on Kabul.

Initially, William served with the transport department of the Quetta Field Force, commanded by General Sir Donald Stewart, on the advance to Kandahar and its subsequent occupation on 8th January 1879. He was also part of General Stewart's staff during the advance on Kalat-i-Ghilzai and served with the Thul Chotiali Force commanded by General Biddulph.

After rejoining the 92nd Highlanders, William served as part of the Korum Valley Field Force and was present at the Battle of Ali Kheyl on 14th October.

In November 1879, William was involved in the Maidan Expedition.

William took part in operations around Kabul during December 1879, and it was during an attack on the Sherpur Pass on 13th December 1879 that he performed the deeds for which he would later be awarded the Victoria Cross.

On 23rd December 1879, William was present at the recapture of Kabul and on 25th April 1880, at the Battle of Childukhtean.

William was with the forces of General Sir Frederick Roberts on the famous march from Kabul to Kandahar in August 1880 and at the Battle of Kandahar on 1st September 1880.

For his services during the war, William received two mentions in despatches and was awarded the Afghanistan Medal (1878–80) with clasps for Kabul and Kandahar. He also received the Kabul to Kandahar Star (1880).

On 28th September 1880, the regiment left Kandahar on their return to India and arrived at Meean Mir on 21st October.

William was appointed as adjutant to the regiment on 16th October 1880.

The regiment arrived at Cawnpore on 5th December 1880, under orders for their return to England, however, on 6th January 1881 they received new orders to proceed immediately to Natal instead to take part in the 1st Boer War, following the declaration of the Transvaal as a republic on 15th December by the Boers.

On 14th January 1881, William and the regiment boarded *HMS Crocodile* and set sail for South Africa where they arrived at Durban on 30th January and by the 16th February had established their camp at Newcastle.

After several defeats, the British signed an armistice on 6th March, followed by a peace treaty on 23rd March 1881 and with the Pretoria Convention of 3rd August, the British recognised the South Africa Republic and the Orange Free State.

William was promoted to the rank of Captain on 10th October 1881.[421]

William must have left South Africa in advance of his regiment as on 1st December 1881, he was presented with his Victoria Cross medal by Queen Victoria at a ceremony in Windsor Castle.

On 24th December 1881, the regiment boarded the *SS Calabria* at Durban and set sail for England, landing at Portsmouth on 30th January 1882 and were quartered in the Anglesea Barracks.

William retired from his post as adjutant on 25th February 1882.[422]

On 4th April 1883, William was married to Helen (née Wauchope) at St Mary's Cathedral in Edinburgh, the couple would have two children Audrey Helen born in 1884 and William Keith born in 1886. Tragically both children would die at a young age; William at the age of 11 was drowned on 11th September 1897 in Fraserburgh Bay will trying to rescue the eldest son of Lord Saltoun, who survived the incident. Audrey died on 12th February 1902 at the age of 18, after a long illness.

421 *London Gazette* – 25049/6710
422 *London Gazette* – 25075/771

William was seconded as Adjutant to the Auxiliary Forces on 1st December 1883[423] a position that he would hold until the 8th December 1888 and soon afterwards on 1st January 1889 resumed his post as Captain with the Gordon Highlanders.[424]

On 4th March 1891, William was promoted to the rank of Major and transferred to the Argyll & Sutherland Highlanders joining his regiment in India.[425]

William took up a staff position, with the Bengal Establishment, as a Station Staff Officer on 24th July 1893.[426]

On 30th October 1894, William was appointed as Deputy Assistant Adjutant General, within the Bengal Establishment,[427] a position that he would hold until 13th May 1896.

William was promoted to the rank of Lieutenant-Colonel on 12th February 1897 and was given the command of the 2nd Battalion Gordon Highlanders,[428] currently stationed at Aldershot.

On 22nd June 1897, William commanded the battalion during celebrations for Queen Victoria's diamond jubilee celebrations in London and was awarded the Queen Victoria Jubilee Medal.

William and the Battalion remained at Aldershot until 6th September 1898 when they boarded the transport *Nubia* at Southampton and set sail the next day for India where they landed at Bombay on 30th September.

Figure 159a.
Grave of William Henry Dick Cunyngham

With escalating troubles in South Africa, William and his Battalion were despatched from India sometime in mid-1899 to provide assistance if matters got out of hand; the 2nd Anglo-Boer war was declared on 11th October 1899.

William led his men at the Battle of Elandslaagte on 21st October 1899 and was shot in the leg in the early stages of the action. After being placed in a safe location by his men, William sat patiently for a few hours, smoking his pipe, until medical help arrived.

On 2nd November, soon after the victory at Elandslaagte, William and his battalion were part of the British force besieged at Ladysmith and it was here on 6th January 1900, after just having returned to active duties that William was again seriously wounded in a battle around Wagon Hill.

William died from his wound the next day on 7th January 1900 and was buried in the Town Cemetery in Ladysmith.

For his service during the war, William was awarded the Queen's South Africa Medal (1899–1902) with clasps for Elandslaagte and the Defence of Ladysmith.

William's Victoria Cross Medal is on public display at the Gordon Highlanders Museum in Aberdeen, Scotland.

423 *London Gazette* – 25293/6267
424 *London Gazette* – 25922/2018
425 *London Gazette* – 26140/1204
426 *London Gazette* – 26452/5956
427 *London Gazette* – 26590/343
428 *London Gazette* – 26822/838

Arthur George Hammond
14th December 1879 (VC No. 353)

Gazetted: 18th October 1881 25027/5140

Rank and Unit: Captain – Bengal Staff Corps – Queen's Own Corps of Guides

Citation

For conspicuous coolness and gallantry at the action on the Asmai Heights, near Kabul, on the 14th December, 1879, in defending the top of the hill with a rifle and fixed bayonet, against large numbers of the enemy, while the 72nd Highlanders and Guides were retiring; and again, on the retreat down the hill, in stopping to assist in carrying away a wounded Sepoy, the enemy being not sixty yards off, firing heavily all the time.

Figure 160. Arthur George Hammond

Biography

Arthur was born at Dawlish in Devon on 28th September 1843 to father Thomas John, a Major in HEIC Madras Army and mother Anne (née Warren). He was the fifth born of seven children, all boys, with brothers; Charles Edward born in 1837, Francis James born in 1838, Frederick born in 1840, Henry Albany born in 1842, Alfred George born in 1846 and William born in 1848.

From 1852, Arthur, like all of his brothers, was educated at the King Edward VI School at Sherborne in Dorset.

After completing his education at the King Edward VII school, Arthur was enrolled at the HEIC Military College at Addiscombe on 7th February 1861; his time at the college was short lived as he was commissioned as an Ensign in the Bengal Army on 7th June 1861.[429]

On 31st December 1861, Arthur arrived at Calcutta and was attached to the 82nd Regiment of Foot stationed at Delhi.

Arthur was promoted to the rank of Lieutenant in the Bengal Army on 13th August 1862,[430] however, this was later pre-dated to 19th May 1862.[431]

On 14th May 1862, Arthur was transferred to the Staff Corps of the Bengal Army.[432]

On 17th October 1862, Arthur was transferred to the 12th Bengal Native Infantry Regiment and less than a year later on 17th September 1863 was transferred to the Corps of Guides, part of the Punjab Frontier Force, based at Mardan.

429 *London Gazette* – 23489/2297
430 *London Gazette* – 22683/5568
431 *London Gazette* – 22770/4419
432 *London Gazette* – 23388/3245

Arthur was appointed as Quartermaster of the regiment in May 1864 and in November 1865 was appointed as a Wing Commander.

On 7th June 1873, Arthur was promoted to the rank of Captain in the Bengal Staff Corps.[433]

In late 1877, Arthur saw his first active service when he took part in the Jowaki Campaign (1877–78) against rebel tribesmen on the North West Frontier. He was involved in the capture of Payah and Jammu and the forcing of the Naru-Kula Pass and also saw action against the Ranizai village of Skhakat on 14th September 1878 and Utman Khel villages on 21st September 1878.

For his service during the campaign, Arthur received two mentions in despatches and was awarded the India General Service Medal with clasp for Jowaki (1877–78).

In late 1879, Arthur was back in action when his regiment was engaged during the 2nd Anglo-Afghan war and took part in the opening battle of the war at Ali Musjid (the narrowest part of the Khyber Pass) on 21st November 1878.

Arthur was involved in the fighting to capture Kabul, taking part in the Battle of Takht-i-Shah on 13th December 1879 and the Battle of Asmai Heights on the 14th December 1879, during which he performed the deeds for which he was later awarded the Victoria Cross.

He also took part in the 2nd Battle of Charisia on 25th April 1880.

For his service during the war, Arthur received a mention in despatches and was awarded the Afghanistan Medal (1878–80) with clasps for Ali Musjid and Kabul.

433 *London Gazette* – 24032/4855

On 7th June 1881, Arthur was promoted to the rank of Major.[434]

Queen Victoria presented Arthur with his Victoria Cross Medal on 1st December 1881 at an investiture held at Windsor Castle.

On 2nd June 1886, Arthur was married to Edith Jane (née Wright) at St George's Church in Campden Hill, London. The couple would go on to have three children; Edith Amber born on 7th June 1888 at Murree in the Punjab, India, Veronica Ruth born on 20th August 1889 also at Murree and Arthur Verney born on 16th October 1892 at Kensington in London, like his father he pursued a career in the army reaching the rank of Major-General and served with the Corps of Guides Cavalry.

Arthur was promoted to the rank of Lieutenant-Colonel on 7th June 1887.[435]

During the short Hazara Campaign, from 1st October 1888 until 13th November 1888, against tribes in the Black Mountains, Arthur commanded the 3rd Sikh Regiment as part of the Hazara Field Force.

For his service during the campaign, Arthur received a mention in despatches and was awarded the Hazara 1888 clasp to his India General Service Medal.

For his service during the Hazara Campaign of 1888, Arthur was appointed as a Companion of the Distinguished Service Order.[436]

On 12th February 1890, Arthur was appointed as an Aide-de-Camp to Queen Victoria with the brevet rank of Colonel.[437]

Arthur was appointed to the command of the Corps of Guides on 1st February 1891 and with the temporary rank of Brigadier-General was given the command of the Tilli column in the Black Mountain Field Force during the Hazara Campaign of 1891.

The main campaign was short lived, taking place during March to May 1891 and on the 9th June the majority of troops returned to their normal stations.

For his service during the campaign, Arthur received a mention in despatches and was awarded the Hazara 1891 clasp to his India General Service Medal.

From 17th July until 2nd December 1891, Arthur commanded the Hazara Field Force which remained in the Black Mountains until civil order and control was re-established.

434 *London Gazette* – 25003/4137
435 *London Gazette* – 25727/4242
436 *London Gazette* – 25923/2098
437 *London Gazette* – 26022/735

On 19th November 1891, Arthur was appointed as an Ordinary Member 3rd Class (Companion) of the Military Division of the Most Honourable Order of the Bath.[438]

In 1892, Arthur was awarded a Good Service Pension.

Arthur served as commander of the 2nd and 4th Brigades during the Isazai Expedition in 1892.

In 1895, Arthur served as commander of the 4th Brigade in the Chitral Relief Force commanded by General Sir Robert Low.

For his service during the expedition, Arthur was awarded the India Medal (1895–1902) with clasp for Chitral.

On 28th September 1895, Arthur relinquished his command of the Corps of Guides.

Arthur was promoted to the rank of Colonel on 11th February 1896.[439]

In 1897, Arthur was awarded the Queen Victoria Diamond Jubilee Medal.

During 1897–98, Arthur took part in the Tirah Campaign as part of the force commanded by General Sir William Stephen Alexander Lockhart. Initial Arthur served in command of the Peshawar column and later in command of the 3rd Brigade of the Khyber Field Force.

For his service during the campaign, Arthur received a mention in despatches and was awarded the Punjab Frontier and Tirah clasps to his India Medal.

Figure 160a. Grave of Arthur George Hammond

438 *London Gazette* – 26226/6229
439 *London Gazette* – 26736/2647

On 28th September 1900, Arthur was placed on the unemployed supernumerary list.[440]

Now effectively retired from the army, after nearly 40 years service, Arthur returned to England and took up residence at Sherbourne House in Camberley, Surrey.

On 1st January 1903, Arthur was appointed as an Ordinary Member 2nd Class (Knight Commander) of the Military Division of the Most Honourable Order of the Bath.[441]

Arthur died at his home in Camberley on 20th April 1919 at the age of 75 and was buried in St Michael's Churchyard in Camberley.

Arthur's Victoria Cross Medal is on public display at the Imperial War Museum in London as part of the Lord Ashcroft collection.

440 *London Gazette* – 27237/6255
441 *London Gazette* – 27511/4

William John Vousden
14th December 1879 (VC No. 354)

Gazetted: 18th October 1881 25027/5140

Rank and Unit: Captain – 5th Punjab Cavalry, Bengal Staff Corps

Citation

For the exceptional gallantry displayed by him on the 14th December, 1879, on the Koh Asmai Heights, near Kabul, in charging, with a small party, into the centre of the line of the retreating Kohistani force, by whom they were greatly outnumbered, and who did their utmost to close round them. After rapidly charging through and through the enemy, backwards and forwards, several times, they swept off round the opposite side of the village and joined the rest of the Troop.

Biography

William was born on 20th September 1845 at Perth in Scotland, the only child of father Thomas, a Captain in the Indian Army and mother Catharine (née Harrigan); his father was remarried in 1863 to Mary Jane (née Burkitt).

William was educated at Dr Hill's School in Woolwich and then from March 1858 until 1862 (when he was expelled for refusing to accept a punishment) at King's School in Canterbury.

After leaving the King's School, William was enrolled as a Gentleman Cadet in the Royal Military Academy at Sandhurst

Figure 161. William John Vousden

and following his graduation was commissioned as an Ensign in the 35th Regiment of Foot on 8th January 1864[442] and soon afterwards joined his regiment in India.

On the 4th October 1867, William was promoted to the rank of Lieutenant and transferred to the 5th Cavalry Regiment in the Punjab Frontier Force.[443]

William was promoted to the rank of Captain, in the Bengal Staff Corps on 8th January 1876.[444]

In late 1877, William saw his first active service when he took part in the Jowaki Campaign (1877–78) against rebel tribesmen on the North West Frontier. He was involved in the capture of Jammu.

For his service during the campaign, William was awarded the India General Service Medal with clasp for Jowaki (1877–78).

In early 1879, William was back in action when his regiment was engaged during the 2nd Anglo-Afghan war as part of the Khort Valley Expedition, taking part in the Battle of Matun on 7th January 1879.

William was also involved in the advance by General Roberts to recapture Kabul and on 27th September was involved at the Battle of Karatigi where he had his horse shot out from under him.

He was also involved in the Battle of Charisia on the 6th of October, and the Battle of Kabul on the 8th October 1879.

It was during the Battle of Asmai Heights on the 14th December 1879, that William performed the deeds for which he was later awarded the Victoria Cross.

For his service during the war, William received three mentions in despatches and was awarded the Afghanistan Medal (1878–80) with clasps for Charisia and Kabul.

On 2nd March 1881, William received a brevet promotion to Major for his service in Afghanistan.[445]

William was appointed as Adjutant to the Behar Mounted Rifles in September 1881, a position that he held until 22nd June 1883 when he was appointed as a Squadron Commander in the 5th Cavalry.

On 24th May 1882, William was presented with his Victoria Cross Medal by the Honourable A. R. Thompson, the Lieutenant-Governor of Bengal.

On 8th January 1884, William was promoted to the rank of Major.[446]

William was promoted to the rank of Lieutenant-Colonel on 8th January 1890.[447]

On 22nd June 1890, William was appointed to the command of the 5th Cavalry Regiment.

During January and February 1891, William led his regiment as part of the field force involved in the Miranzai Expedition against warring tribes on the North West Frontier of India.

Towards the end of 1891, William was married to Emmeline Mary Eden (Née Drummond) the widow of Colonel Edward Harris Steel, at St George's, Hanover Square in London.

William received a brevet promotion to the rank of Colonel on 26th July 1894.[448]

On the 17th March 1897, William was appointed to the command of the Sealkote Station.

During the Tirah Campaign (1897–98) William was appointed as base commandant for the line of communications.

For his service during the campaign, Arthur received a mention in despatches and was awarded the India Medal with clasps for Punjab Frontier and Tirah.

William was promoted to the rank of Colonel on 5th January 1899[449] and was given command of the Kohat Kurram Field Force for operations on the North West Frontier.

On 23rd May 1900, William was appointed as an Ordinary Member 3rd Class (Companion) of the Military Division of the Most Honourable Order of the Bath.[450]

William was given command of the Kalakand Punjab Field Force, with the temporary rank of Brigadier-General on 17th August 1900.

On the 1st April 1901, William was appointed to the command of a 2nd Class District in India, with the temporary rank of Brigadier-General.[451]

William was appointed to the command of the Punjab Frontier Force, with the local rank of Major-General on 3rd April 1901.[452]

On 18th October 1901, William was appointed as Inspector General of Cavalry[453] with the temporary rank of Major-General.[454]

William died on 12th November 1902, at the age of 57, from severe dysentery while serving at Lahore and was buried the next day in Lahore Cemetery.

The location of William's Victoria Cross Medal is unknown, believed to be in private hands.

442 *London Gazette* – 22820/724
443 *London Gazette* – 23613/2438
444 *London Gazette* – 24331/3247
445 *London Gazette* – 25022/4938
446 *London Gazette* – 25328/1260
447 *London Gazette* – 26031/1331
448 *London Gazette* – 26591/416
449 *London Gazette* – 27066/2082
450 *London Gazette* – 27195/3327
451 *London Gazette* – 27335/4782
452 *London Gazette* – 27308/2860
453 *London Gazette* – 27469/5611
454 *London Gazette* – 27377/7397

George Sellar
14th December 1879 (VC No. 355)

Gazetted: 18th October 1881 25027/5140

Rank and Unit: Lance-Corporal No. 1499 – 72nd Regiment of Foot

Citation

For conspicuous gallantry displayed by him at the assault on the Asmai Heights, round Kabul, on the 14th December, 1879, in having in a marked manner led the attack, under a heavy fire, and dashing on in front of the party up the slope, engaged in a desperate conflict with an Afghan who sprang out to meet him. In this encounter Lance-Corporal Sellar was severely wounded.

Biography

George was born in December 1850 at Wellington Terrace, Keith in Banffshire, Scotland to father George and Mother Ann (née Grant), he had a brother Alexander and sister Elspet.

It is believed that George enlisted in the army some time in 1869 and joined his regiment the 72nd Regiment of Foot who were stationed at Dublin in Ireland.

George spent the first years on his army service in Ireland, based at Dublin, Limerick and finally Cork from where on 21st February 1871, he set sail with the regiment for India.

Initially, George was stationed at Umbeyla until 1873 when the regiment moved to Peshawar followed by moves to Nowshera in 1875, Cherat a few months later and finally the hill station at Sealkote in 1876.

George saw his first active service when in November 1878 the regiment was despatch to Afghanistan to take part in the 2nd Anglo-Afghan War, where he was present at the Battle of Peiwar Kotal on 28th/29th November 1878, at the Battle of Charisiab on 6th October 1879 at the Battle of Charasiab on the 6th of October, and the Battle of Kabul on the 8th October 1879.

It was during the Battle of Asmai Heights on the 14th December 1879, that George performed the deeds for which he was later awarded the Victoria Cross, he was severely wounded during the action.

George was with the forces of General Sir Frederick Roberts on the famous march from Kabul to Kandahar in August 1880 and at the Battle of Kandahar on 1st September 1880.

For his service during the war, George was awarded the Afghanistan Medal (1878–80) with clasps for Peiwar Kotal, Charisia, Kabul and Kandahar. He was also awarded the Kabul to Kandahar Star.

Figure 162. George Sellar

In November 1880, George returned to India with his regiment and was based at Mean Meer near Lucknow.

George was presented with his Victoria Cross Medal on 14th December 1881 by Lieutenant-General Charles Robert Cureton, the General Officer Commanding the province of Oudh, at Lucknow.

On 25th February 1882, George and the regiment left India bound for Aden where they were to form the garrison.

George and the regiment were sent to Egypt on 2nd August 1882, where as part of the Indian Contingent commanded by General Sir Herbert Macpherson VC formed up with the Expeditionary Force commanded by General Sir Garnet Wolseley to take part in the Anglo-Egyptian War.

Figure 162a. Grave of George Sellar

George took part in the Battle of Tel-el-Kebir on 13th September 1882, which proved to be the decisive battle of the war.

For his service during the war, George was awarded the Egypt Medal (1882–89) with clasp for Tel-el-Kebir and the Khedive's Star (1882–91).

On 15th October 1883, George and the regiment returned to England where they were stationed at Parkhurst until 1885 when they were moved to the camp at Aldershot.

George returned to Scotland in 1886 when the regiment was posted to Glasgow until 1887 when he was appointed as Sergeant Instructor to the Lairg company of the 1st Sutherland and Caithness Highland Rifle Volunteers.

It was while stationed at Lairg, that George died on 1st November 1889 at the age of 38 and was buried in the Lairg Cemetery.

George's Victoria Cross Medal is on public display at the Queen Own Highlanders Regimental Museum at Fort George, Inverness in Scotland.

Patrick Mullane
27th July 1880 (VC No. 356)

Gazetted: 17th May 1881 24973/2553

Rank and Unit: Sergeant No. 2884 – Royal Horse Artillery

Citation

For conspicuous bravery during the action at Maiwand, on the 27th July, 1880, in endeavouring to save the life of Driver Pickwell Istead. This Non-Commissioned Officer, when the battery to which he belonged, was on the point of retiring, and the enemy were within ten or fifteen yards, unhesitatingly ran back about two yards and picking up Driver Istead, placed him on the limber, where, unfortunately, he died almost immediately.

Again, during the retreat, Sergeant Mullane volunteered to procure water for the wounded, and succeeded in doing so by going into one of the villages in which so many men lost their lives.

Biography

Patrick was born on 17th September 1858 at Ahmednuggur, Deccan in India to father Patrick, a Private in the 2nd Artillery Reserve, and mother Marguerite.

Based upon his discharge date and length of service, it would appear that Patrick enlisted in the army on 19th November 1867 and was enrolled as Private No. 2884 in the Royal Horse Artillery.

At some stage, Patrick was deployed to India and as a Sergeant took part in the 2nd Anglo-Afghan war in 1878–80. It was during the disastrous defeat at the Battle of Maiwand on 27th July 1880 that he performed the deeds for which he would later be awarded the Victoria Cross.

Patrick took part in the Battle of Kandahar on 1st September 1880.

For his service during the war, Patrick was awarded the Afghanistan Medal (1878–80) with clasp for Kandahar.

After the war, Patrick returned to India and on 11th July 1881 was presented with his Victoria Cross Medal by Lord Roberts VC at a ceremony held on Poona racecourse.

It is believed that Patrick returned to England some time in 1882 or 1883 and on 27th December 1884 he was married to Sarah Ann (née Harvey) at Plumstead in London and in 1886 they had a daughter Dorothy Kathleen born in Canterbury.

By 1891, the couple were living at the South Deans Barracks in Great Yarmouth but in c1894 after ten years of marriage the couple separated.

Figure 163. Patrick Mullane

After just over 28 years of service Patrick, now with the rank of Regimental Sergeant-Major, was discharged from the army to pension and went to live at 91 Pollock Road in Southwark, London.

For his lengthy service, Patrick was awarded the Meritorious Service Medal and the Army Long Service and Good Conduct Medal.

With the outbreak of the Great War, Patrick, now aged 54, enlisted with the army reserve and was assigned as a Sergeant-Major with the 92nd Royal Field Artillery at Deepcut Barracks in Camberley.

On 27th November 1914, Patrick was transferred to the 100th Brigade of the Royal Field Artillery until 27th January 1915 when he was discharged have been declared unfit for further service.

Figure 163a. Grave of Patrick Mullane

Patrick died at his home 31 Coronation Street, Plaistow in London, where he lived with his sister, on 20th November 1919 at the age of 61. He was buried a week late on 27th November 1919 in St Patrick's Cemetery, Langthorne Road, Leytonstone, London.

The whereabouts of Patrick's Victoria Cross Medal is unknown, believed to be in private hands.

James Collis
28th July 1880 (VC No. 357)

Figure 164. James Collis

Gazetted: 17th May 1881 24973/2553[455]

Rank and Unit: Gunner – Royal Horse Artillery

Citation

For conspicuous bravery during the retreat from Maiwand to Kandahar, on the 28th July, 1880, when the Officer commanding the battery was endeavouring to bring on a limber, with wounded men, under a cross fire, in running forward and drawing the enemy's fire on himself, thus taking off their attention from the limber.

Biography

James was born in Cambridge on 19th April 1856 to father William, a coal porter, and mother Mary.

James had an older sister, Ann Maria who was baptised on 7th September 1851, an older brother Henry who was born on 25th July 1853 and a younger brother Walter who was born on 24th April 1860.

The three brothers were all baptised at St Giles in Cambridge on 5th January 1862, while the family lived at 3 Kettles Yard, St Peters in Cambridge.

For a time, up until 1869, James was apprenticed as a groom at Newmarket.

Sometime in 1872 James joined the army and was enlisted as a private in the 2nd Battalion of the 32nd Regiment the Duke of Cornwall's Light Infantry.

At some stage, James transferred to the Royal Horse Artillery and was sent overseas to serve in India where from November 1878 until September 1880 he served in the 2nd Anglo-Afghan war.

It was during this war on 28th July 1880, at the time of the retreat following the Battle of Maiwand that James performed the deeds for which he would later be awarded the Victoria Cross.

For his service during the war, James was awarded the Afghanistan Medal with Kandahar Bar.

On the 6th May 1881, James was discharged from the Royal Horse Artillery and joined the Bombay Police Force as a constable.

James was presented with his Victoria Cross medal by Sir Frederick (later Lord) Roberts, himself a recipient of the Victoria Cross, at a ceremony held at Poona Racecourse on 11th July 1881.

455 The *London Gazette* entry erroneously names James as Colliss and the engraving on his Victoria Cross medal perpetuates this error.

On the 14th March 1882, at the Girgaum Mission Church, in Bombay, James was married to Adele Grace Skuse, a widow and the daughter of William Henry Woodham.

The couple would go on to have four children; Arthur Henry baptised on 5th January 1883, Elsie May baptised on 5th May 1884, William Edward John baptised on 8th January 1886 and Robert George born on the 7th October 1887 and baptised on 3rd December 1887.

James continued his career in the Bombay Police, rising to the rank of inspector until sometime in 1884 when he returned to the UK.

It is unclear whether James was dismissed from the Bombay Police or not, however, he did leave under a cloud when it was discovered that several of his cases which should have been solved remained undetected, it was suggested that he had received money to keep them open.

On the 15th September 1887, James re-enlisted in the army at Bury St Edmunds, for a period of 7 years followed by a reserve of a further 5 years, and joined the Suffolk Regiment.

As part of his service with the regiment, James returned to India on 25th September 1888 but in 1891 was discharged, having contracted rheumatic fever, and returned to England leaving his wife and family in India.

For some time James worked for the Corp of Commissioners but was discharged after complaints that too many "sisters" were visiting him.

After leaving the Corp of Commissioners, James was employed as a constable by the London County Council with duties to police a park in Lewisham. To supplement his income, James charged local prostitutes a fee to conduct their trade in the park.

On 26th February 1893, James was married to Mary (née Goddard) at St Paul's Chapel of Ease, St John's Hill in Battersea, later in the year James spent three months in Charing Cross hospital, having suffered a reoccurrence of rheumatic fever.

Sometime in 1895, after James had thrown out Mary from the family home when she became pregnant and "as he had another girl to take her place" (who had consented to marry him) Mary discovered that James was still married to Adele who was still living in India and reported the matter to the police.

James was arrested at his home in Dunstan's Road, East Dulwich and when questioned by the police, James stated that as he had not seen his wife for years he thought that he was free to remarry.

At his trial, at the Old Bailey on 26th November 1895, James who was wearing the uniform of the West Kent Rifle Volunteers was convicted of Bigamy, despite a defence of insanity and was sentenced to 18 months hard labour. He was told that had it not been for his service in Afghanistan he would have received a more serious sentence of 'penal servitude'.

In summing up the judge stated that this was one of the worst cases of bigamy to have come before his court as James had married three women, been engaged to a fourth and was now seducing a fifth woman.

Under the terms of clause 15 of the originating warrant of the Victoria Cross, having been awarded a sentence greater than 6 months, James was required to forfeit his Victoria Cross Medal and would lose his pension and his name would be removed from the medal roll.

A Royal Warrant to implement the forfeiture was issued on the 18th November 1895, one of only eight to have been issued.

Having fallen on hard times, James had pawned his medal for eight shillings and the Metropolitan Police redeemed the medal and returned it to the War Office who paid the redemption fee.

After leaving prison, in May 1897 it was not long before James was once again brought before the court, this time for indecent assault upon two young girls.

James, now employed as a labourer, was arrested at his home, 6 Johnston Street in Westminster and was indicted for indecently assaulting Kathleen Emily Smith aged 12 on 25th September and Mary Evelyn Oxley aged 13 on the 9th October, following visits to their parents.

At his trial at the Old Bailey on 13th November 1897, James was convicted and sentenced to 2 years hard labour.

On leaving prison, James moved to Bury St Edmonds where he held several jobs, however, in 1912 he was a resident in the Cambridge workhouse.

On the 25th November 1914, at the start of the First World War, James now aged 58, re-enlisted in the Suffolk Regiment and served as a Drill Instructor at the regimental depot.

Unfortunately, James continued to experience poor health and on the 6th August 1917 was given an honourable discharge from the army on medical grounds, suffering from Bright's Disease, an inflammation of the kidneys.

Having been discharged for medical reasons, James was awarded the Silver War Badge on 8th August 1917 in recognition of his service.

Less than a year later, on 28th June 1918, James died of a heart attack at the Anti Vivisection Hospital in Battersea, London and was buried in an unmarked mass grave for the poor in Wandsworth Cemetery, aged 62.

James was buried with full military honours, however, his family did not attend the funeral.

After his death, his sister petitioned the king George V to have her brother's name restored to the Victoria Cross register, the king did not accede to her wishes but wrote "... that most certainly Gunner Collis's name should be inscribed with those of other VCs on the tablets of the Royal Artillery Victoria Cross memorial".

The king had been sympathetic to the wishes of the family, however, the Secretary of State for War, Winston Churchill, was opposed, stating that as Collis had pawned his medals he placed little value on them and his family had waited nearly 25 years before raising their grievance.

In 1920 the Secretary of State for War approved amendments to the Royal Warrant for the Victoria Cross, specifying that only 'treason, cowardice, felony or an infamous crime' should lead to forfeiture of the award, however, the amendments were not retrospective.

Figure 164a. Grave of James Collis

It was not until 1953 that the War Office issued a list of VCs which included Gunner Collis and the seven other forfeitures.

On 22 May 1998, a Commonwealth War Graves Commission headstone was erected to mark James's grave in Wandsworth Cemetery.

James's Victoria Cross medal is on public display at the Imperial War Museum, part of the Lord Ashcroft collection.

William St Lucien Chase
16th August 1880 (VC No. 358)

Gazetted: 7th October 1881 25023/4990

Rank and Unit: Lieutenant – 28th Bombay Native Infantry – Bombay Staff Corps

Citation

For conspicuous gallantry on the occasion of the sortie from Kandahar, on the 16th August, 1880, against the village of Deh Khoja, in having rescued and carried for a distance of over 200 yards, under the fire of the enemy, a wounded soldier, Private Massey, of the Royal Fusiliers, who had taken shelter in a blockhouse. Several times they were compelled to rest, but they persevered in bringing him to a place of safety. Private Ashford rendered Lieutenant Chase every assistance, and remained with him throughout.

Biography

William was born on 2nd July 1856 at St Lucia in the British West Indies to father Richard Henry, a Captain in the War Office Control Department, serving as Commissioner of Ordnance and mother Susan Ifill (neé Buhot).

He was the oldest of seven children, with two sisters Alice Howell born in 1858 and Ethel Annie Buhot born in 1861 and four brothers Richard Henry born in 1860, Ernest Edward born in 1863, Lionel Berkles born in 1865 and Frederick Augustus born in 1868. Apart from Frederick who was born in Purfleet in Essex all of his other brothers and sisters were born in Barbados.

William was privately educated and then enrolled as a gentleman cadet at the Royal Military College at Sandhurst.

On graduating from Sandhurst, William was commissioned as a sub-lieutenant with the 15th Regiment of Foot on 10th September 1875[456] and soon afterwards joined his regiment in India.

William spent his first two years of service at the regimental HQ in Bombay and during this time he sat and passed with distinction the examinations to join the Staff Corps of the Bombay army.

On 31st May 1878, William was accepted as a probationer in the Bombay Staff Corps[457] and on 28th June 1878 was promoted to Lieutenant with an effective date of 10th September 1875.[458]

With the Bombay Staff Corps, William served at the stations in Poona, Almadabad, Baroda and Surat.

456 *London Gazette* – 24244/4452
457 *London Gazette* – 25615/4715
458 *London Gazette* – 24599/3834

Figure 165. William St Lucien Chase

On 29th September 1879, William was appointed as Quartermaster to the 28th Bombay Native Infantry Regiment and as part of the Kandahar Field Force, commanded by General Sir Donald Stewart, saw his first active service during the 2nd Anglo-Afghan War.

William was involved in actions at Chaman, Gatai and throughout the defence of Kandahar but it was during an ill-fated sortie on the village of Deh Khoja on 16th August 1880 that he performed the deeds for which he would later be awarded the Victoria Cross.

Following the Battle of Kandahar on 1st September 1880, William was given command of the post at Killa Abdullah until relieved in November 1880.

In January 1881, William was given command of the post at Gatai, guarding the lines of communication, where he remained until the Kandahar Field Force passed through on their return to India.

For his service during the war, William received a mention in despatches and was awarded the Afghanistan Medal (1878–80) with clasp for Kandahar.

On 23rd January 1882, William was presented with his Victoria Cross Medal by the General Officer Commanding at Poona in India.

On 1st November 1882, Willaim was appointed as Deputy Assistant Adjutant-General at Bombay.

During 1884, William was involved in the Zhob Valley Campaign and received a mention in despatches.

On 19th December 1884 was appointed as Deputy Assistant Quartermaster-General of the Sind District, a position that he held until 10th December 1887.

William was promoted to the rank of Captain on 10th September 1886.[459]

On 28th August 1889, William was appointed as a wing commander of the 28th Bombay Native Infantry (Pioneers) and took part in the Chin Lusai Expedition to Burma where he was involved in the advance on Fort Haka.

For his service during the expedition, William received a mention in despatches and was awarded the India General Service Medal (1854–95) with clasp for Chin Lushai.

On 24th February 1893, William was appointed as 2nd in command of the 28th Bombay Native Infantry and took part in the Naga Hills and Manipur Campaign.

William was promoted to the rank of Major on 10th September 1895.[460]

During 1897 and 1898, William served on the North-West Frontier in actions against the Orakzai and Afridi tribes, taking part in the Mohamand Expedition and the Tirah Campaign, taking part in the capture of the Sampagha Pass on 29th October 1897, operations around Dataoi on 24th November and operations in the Bara Valley from 7th to 11th December 1897.

For his services on the North-West Frontier, William received several mentions in despatches and was awarded the India Medal (1895–1902) with clasps for Punjab Frontier (1897–98) and Tirah (1897–98).

On 10th June 1899, William was appointed to the command of the 7th Bombay Native Infantry Regiment with the temporary rank of Lieutenant-Colonel.[461]

On 1st July 1901, William was married to Dorothy (neé Steele), who was previously married to Robert Nathaniel Burn of the Indian Public Works Department, at Lahore.

William was appointed to the rank of Lieutenant-Colonel on 10th September 1901.[462]

On 24th February 1902, William was appointed to the command of the 128th Bombay Native Infantry (Pioneers).

William was appointed as an Ordinary Member 3rd Class (Companion) of the Military Division of the Most Honourable Order of the Bath on 26th June 1903.[463]

On 10th September 1904, William received a brevet promotion to the rank of Colonel.[464]

William was promoted to the rank of Colonel[465] and appointed

459 *London Gazette* – 25649/5795
460 *London Gazette* – 26682/6356
461 *London Gazette* – 27132/6603
462 *London Gazette* – 27380/8094
463 *London Gazette* – 27568/4009
464 *London Gazette* – 27759/655
465 *London Gazette* – 28013/2577

as Assistant Adjutant General of the 4th Division at Quetta on 10th April 1906.[466]

On 24th June 1908, at the age of 51, William died from brain disease at Quetta and was buried in the English section of Quetta Cemetery.

William's Victoria Cross Medal is on public display at the Army Museum of Western Australia in Fremantle, Australia.

466 *London Gazette* – 27928/4556

Thomas Elsdon Ashford
16th August 1880 (VC No. 359)

Gazetted: 7th October 1881 25023/4990

Rank and Unit: Private No. 1317 – 7th Regiment of Foot (Royal Fusiliers)

Citation

For conspicuous gallantry on the occasion of the sortie from Kandahar, on the 16th August, 1880, against the village of Deh Khoja, in having rescued and carried for a distance of over 200 yards, under the fire of the enemy, a wounded soldier, Private Massey, of the Royal Fusiliers, who had taken shelter in a blockhouse. Several times they were compelled to rest, but they persevered in bringing him to a place of safety. Private Ashford rendered Lieutenant Chase every assistance, and remained with him throughout.

Biography

Thomas was born some time in 1859 at 2 Peck's Cottage, All Saints, Newmarket in Cambridgeshire; the illegitimate son of father Thomas a boot maker and Jane Elsdon, his parents were subsequently married in 1861.

At the age of 18, Thomas left his job as a baker and on 12th June 1877 enlisted in the army at Woolwich and was assigned as Private 1317 to the 49th Infantry Brigade.

On the 14th June 1877, Thomas was transferred to the 2nd Battalion of the 7th Regiment of Foot (Royal Fusiliers).

After a month at Woolwich, Thomas was posted to Ireland on 14th June 1877 to join his regiment at Dublin until 20th April 1878 when he was posted to Templemore in Co Tipperary.

On 9th March 1879, Thomas set sail from Ireland on board *HMS Eurua* bound for India and his first period of overseas service; initially stationed at Ahmednagar, where he arrived on 11th April 1879 he was posted to Bombay on 27th November 1879.

On 6th February 1880, Thomas left India with his regiment to take part in the 2nd Anglo-Afghan war as a unit within the Kandahar Field Force commanded by General Sir Donald Stewart.

After arriving at Kandahar on 24th April 1880, Thomas and his regiment were part of the garrison which was besieged in the town by a large force of Afghans.

It was during an ill-fated sortie on the village of Deh Khoja on 16th August 1880 that Thomas performed the deeds for which he would later be awarded the Victoria Cross.

Thomas and the 7th Regiment of Foot were involved in the Battle of Kandahar on 1st September 1880.

Figure 166. Thomas Elsdon Ashford

On 8th May 1881, Thomas and his regiment began their journey to return to India and arrived at Madras on 29th May 1881.

Thomas was presented with his Victoria Cross Medal by General Lord Roberts VC on 13th December 1881 in a ceremony at Madras and two weeks later on 27th December 1881, was moved to Bellary.

On the 3rd June 1882, Thomas was promoted to the rank of Lance-Corporal, however, on the 31st July 1882 at his own request he reverted back to the rank of Private.

Thomas was hospitalised from 1st July 1882 until 27th July 1882 for the treatment of Primary Syphilis, he was hospitalised again from 16th March 1883 until 10th April 1883 for further treatment for Primary Syphilis.

As preparation for their return to England, Thomas and the Regiment were sent to the transit camp at Deolali on 17th November 1883.

On 22nd January 1884, Thomas and the regiment boarded *HMS Euphrates* and set sail for England, arriving at Portsmouth on 19th February 1884.

Thomas was transferred to the Class "B" Army Reserve on 24th February 1884, to complete the remainder of his fixed term of enlistment and served as a private in the 12th Regimental District until 1st June 1884 when he was transferred to the 7/57 Regimental District.

Having completed his fixed period of a 12 year enlistment, Thomas was discharged from the army at Hounslow on 13th June 1889 at the age of 30 years and 6 months.

After leaving the army, Thomas briefly tried his hand at farming at Hallerton in Leicestershire but soon moved to Thringstone in Leicestershire where he became a postman (believed to be the first and only postal worker entitled to wear the Victoria Cross).

On 29th January 1891, Thomas was married to Betsy Ann (née Sisson) at Thringstone and soon afterwards set up home in Skinners Lane in the nearby village of Whitwick.

The couple would have two daughters; possibly Lillian Minnie born in 1892 and Gertrude Sophia born in 1895.

On 26th December 1912, Thomas took to his bed with bronchitis and died at the age of 53 or 54 on 21st February 1913 and was buried on 4th March in Whitwick Cemetery.

His Victoria Cross Medal is on public display at the Royal Fusiliers Museum in the Tower of London, bequeathed by the family in 1992.

Figure 166a. Grave of Thomas Elsdon Ashford

Teignmouth Melvill
22nd January 1879 (VC No. 360)

Gazetted: 2nd May 1879 24717/3178
15th January 1907 27986/325

Rank and Unit: Lieutenant – 1st Battalion 24th Regiment of Foot

Citation

Lieutenant Melville, of the 1st Battalion 24th Foot, on account of the gallant efforts made by him to save the Queen's Colour of his Regiment after the disaster at Isandhlwana, and also Lieutenant Coghill, 1st Battalion 24th Foot, on account of his heroic conduct in endeavouring to save his brother officer's life, would have been recommended to Her Majesty for the Victoria Cross had they survived.

15th January 1907
The KING has been graciously pleased to approve of the Decoration of the Victoria Cross being delivered to the representatives of the under mentioned Officers and men who fell in the performance of acts of valour, and with reference to whom it was notified in the London Gazette that they would have been recommended to Her late Majesty for the Victoria Cross had they survived:—

Biography

Teignmouth was born on 8th September 1842 at 4 Clarendon Place, Islington in London to father Philip, Military Secretary to the East India Company and mother Eliza (née Sandys).

One of 11 children, Teignmouth had one older brother, Philip Sandys born on 19th November 1827 and nine sisters; Eliza Mary born c1828, Emily Hester born in 1830, Caroline born in 1832, Mary Augusta born in 1833, Helen born in 1836, Eliza Sandys born in 1838, Claudia Sophia born in 1839, Elizabeth Cory born in 1844 and Georgina Catherine born in 1847.

Teignmouth attended Cheltenham College until January 1856 when he attended Harrow School until leaving in February 1858.

From 1861 until 1864, Teignmouth attended Trinity College, Cambridge on 9th February 1865, his attainment of a BA degree was announced.

On 20th October 1865, at the age of 23 Teignmouth started on a career in the army when he purchased a commission as Ensign in the 1st Battalion of the 24th Regiment of Foot.[467]

467 *London Gazette* – 23027/4942

Figure 167. Teignmouth Melvill

After his enlistment, Teignmouth joined his regiment at Dublin in Ireland where they were quartered in the Beggars Bush Barracks.

In February 1866, Teignmouth and his regiment were relocated to the Curragh Camp until 16th August 1866 when they moved to Belfast in preparation for deployment on overseas service.

Teignmouth and the regiment boarded *SS Pennsylvania* at Belfast on 30th September and set sail for Malta where they arrived on 12th October 1866 but due to Asiatic cholera being present in the UK were placed in quarantine for 15 days before being allowed to occupy the barracks at Fort Verdana.

In February 1868, the regiment moved to the Floriana Barracks until September 1868 when they move to Fort Ricasoli; during this time the Enfield rifle was replaced with the new Snider Rifle.

Teignmouth was sent as part of a one company detachment to Salvatore, where the officers of the regiment had created the Malta Racecourse.[468]

Teignmouth advanced his position within the regiment when on 2nd December 1868, he purchased a commission as Lieutenant.[469]

During April to June 1871, Teignmouth attended the Staff College.

On 29th February 1872, the regiment boarded the troopship *Jumna* and set sail for Gibraltar where they arrived on 5th March 1872 and were accommodated in the Europa Flats and Windmill Hill.

463 The first race on the course was between Teignmouth and an officer from another regiment.

469 *London Gazette* – 23446/6404

Following the death, from pneumonia, of the incumbent Lieutenant Corcor, Teignmouth was appointed as Adjutant on 7th March 1873.[470]

On 28th November 1874, Teignmouth with the Headquarters of the regiment boarded the troopship *Himalaya* and set sail for the Cape Colony where they landed at Cape Town on 2nd January 1875.

Teignmouth was married to Sarah Elizabeth (née Reed) at Port Elizabeth in February 1876; the couple had two children both born in Cape Town, Teignmouth Philip born on 13th February 1877 and Charles William born on 5th September 1878.

Both boys would enter the army and have distinguished careers; Teignmouth Philip attained the rank of Lieutenant-Colonel and was awarded the DSO, Charles William attained the rank of Brigadier-General and was also awarded the DSO together with a CB and CMG.

The battalion boarded *HMS Orontes* at Cape Town on 3rd August 1877 bound for East London where they landed on 6th–7th August and proceeded by rail to King William's Town.

With news of increasing disturbances in the Cape Colony, Teignmouth who had passed his entrance examinations and was now attending the Staff College in England, requested and obtained permission to rejoin his regiment in South Africa.

In August 1877, Colonel Glyn, commander of the battalion and the Eastern Frontier military district, despatched Teignmouth to report on the state of affairs at Gcalekaland and the Idutywa Reserve where there had been disturbances.

Teignmouth was present at the Butterworth river on 3rd October 1877, when colonial forces engaged the Galekas driving them from their villages which were then burnt to the ground; following the action he returned to King William's Town.

Teignmouth served with the headquarters column during the remainder of the Gaika-Galeka War which ended on the 28th June 1878 when the Colonial Government proclaimed an amnesty.

At the start of the Zulu War, in December 1878, Teignmouth and the battalion moved to Helpmakaar, on a high plateau overlooking the junction of the Blood and Buffalo rivers, where the invasion force was being assembled.

The invasion force was awaiting the expiry of the ultimatum delivered to Cetywayo to dismantle his army or face the invasion of his territory.

Teignmouth and his battalion, with the 3rd Column commanded by Colonel Glyn, were moved down to Rorke's Drift, where at Rorke's Farm a commissariat depot and base hospital, was to be established. Lieutenant Gonville Bromhead and company "B" of the 2nd Battalion, 24th Regiment of Foot was assigned to guard the station.

With the expiry of the ultimatum on 11th January 1879, the main invasion force crossed the Buffalo River and by nightfall had established a camp in Zululand.

Opposite Helpmakaar, was the Ingutu mountain where Chief Sirayo, one of Chief Cetywayo's principal men, had his kraal, it was here on 12th January 1879 that the first engagement of the war took place.

Teignmouth and the battalion were part of the force which attacked and captured, Sirayo's Kraal and then returned to Rorke's Drift.

On the 20th January 1879, leaving Lieutenant Bromhead and his men to guard the station, Colonel Glyn and the remainder of the 3rd Column left Rorke's Drift for Isandhlwana, about nine miles away, where they established a camp.

The camp at Isandhlwana was attacked on 22nd January by the Zulus and being outnumbered by at least six to one the British force was severely defeated with almost everyone being killed – from the 1st Battalion of the 24th only six men would survive the battle.

When it was clear that the battle was lost, Colonel Pulleine the commander of the forces at Isandhlwana ordered Teignmouth to try and rescue the regimental colours, by breaking through the cordon of Zulu warriors on horseback.

Teignmouth managed to break out from the encirclement of Zulus and was soon joined by Lieutenant Coghill, also on horseback. Finding the route to Rorke's Drift cut off by the Zulus,

Figure 167a. Grave of Teignmouth Melvill

470 *London Gazette* – 23969/2043

the pair rode on to the Buffalo River, which formed the border between Zululand and Natal.

Lieutenant Coghill managed to cross the swollen river, however, Teignmouth who was hampered by the colours got into difficulty and would have been swept away had Lieutenant Coghill not returned to help him across. During the crossing the colours were swept away but were subsequently recovered some six weeks later.

Having reached the Natal side of the river, the pair probably thought themselves to be safe, however, under threat from the Zulus who by now had reached the river bank, they were both killed at a place called Fugitives' Drift.

For his action in trying to save the regimental colours, Teignmouth was later awarded the Victoria Cross, one of the first to be awarded posthumously.

The local farmer, Mr George Bunting, placed the pair in a rough grave but a party from Rorke's Drift came and reburied the pair on 14th April 1879.

For his service during the war, Teignmouth was awarded the South Africa Medal (1877–79) with the 1877–8–9 clasp.

In February 1907, Teignmouth's Victoria Cross Medal was sent to his widow Sarah.

Teignmouth's Victoria Cross Medal is on public display at the South Wales Borderers Museum in Powys, Wales.

Nevill Josiah Aylmer Coghill
22nd January 1879 (VC No. 361)

Gazetted: 2nd May 1879 24717/3178
15th January 1907 27986/325

Rank and Unit: Lieutenant – 1st Battalion 24th Regiment of Foot

Citation

Lieutenant Melville, of the 1st Battalion 24th Foot, on account of the gallant efforts made by him to save the Queen's Colour of his Regiment after the disaster at Isandhlwana, and also Lieutenant Coghill, 1st Battalion 24th Foot, on account of his heroic conduct in endeavouring to save his brother officer's life, would have been recommended to Her Majesty for the Victoria Cross had they survived.

15th January 1907
The KING has been graciously pleased to approve of the Decoration of the Victoria Cross being delivered to the representatives of the under mentioned Officers and men who fell in the performance of acts of valour, and with reference to whom it was notified in the London Gazette that they would have been recommended to Her late Majesty for the Victoria Cross had they survived:—

Biography

Nevill was born on 25th January 1852 at Drumcondra in the County of Dublin in Ireland to father Sir John Joscelyn 4th Baron of Glen Barrahane and mother Catherine Frances (née Plunket); the oldest of seven children he had three brothers, Edgerton Bush born on 7th February 1853, Gerald Cramer born on 26th September 1854 and Claude Plunket born on 13th November 1859. He also had three sisters, Ethel Charlotte born in 1860, Beatrice Anna born in 1862 and Violet Alice Penrose born on 8th February 1868.

At the early age of 13, Nevill began his preparations for a career in the army when in 1865 he was enrolled in the East India Company Military Academy at Haileybury in Hertfordshire.

After graduating from Haileybury in 1869, Nevill returned to the family home in Ireland and on 13th May 1871 was commissioned as a supernumerary Lieutenant in the Dublin County Militia.

On the 26th January 1873, Nevill was commissioned as a sub-Lieutenant in the 24th Regiment of Foot[471] in the British

471 *London Gazette* – 23952/784

Figure 168. Nevill Josiah Aylmer Coghill

army and soon afterwards on 26th February was promoted to the rank of Lieutenant.[472]

Nevill set sail on 22nd May 1874, to join his regiment on garrison duties at Gibraltar but during November 1874 he returned to Brecon in Wales on depot duties.

In January 1876, Nevill set sail from Southampton on board *SS European* bound for South Africa and after arriving at Cape Town on 16th February 1876 was appointed as Aide-de-Camp to General Sir Arthur Cunynghame.

In his capacity as ADC to General Sir Arthur Cunynghame, Nevill served in the Gaika-Galeka War of 1877–78 and received a mention in despatches.

In March 1878, Nevill returned to England for a short period of home leave and on his return to the cape on board the troopship *Tyne*, he took up the position as Orderly Officer to Colonel Glyn, commandant of the regiment.

Later in 1878, Nevill was appointed as Aide-de-Camp to Sir Bartle Frere the High Commissioner for South Africa and Governor of the Cape Colony, however, in January 1879 he was granted six weeks of leave so that he could join his regiment for the invasion of Zululand.

On rejoining his regiment, Nevill took up the position of Aide-de-Camp to Colonel Glyn and was part of the 3rd Column which set up camp at Isandhlwana on 20th January 1879.

Having injured his leg the day before and being unable to mount his horse unassisted, Nevill did not travel with the recognisance column led by Colonel Glyn which left Isandhlwana on 21st January but remained in camp.

472 *London Gazette* – 24236/4073

The camp at Isandhlwana was attacked on 22nd January by the Zulus and being outnumbered by at least six to one the British force was severely defeated with almost everyone being killed – from the 1st Battalion of the 24th only six men would survive the battle.

When it was clear that the battle was lost, Colonel Pulleine the commander of the forces at Isandhlwana ordered his adjutant Lieutenant Melvill to try and rescue the regimental colours, by breaking through the cordon of Zulu warriors on horseback.

Soon after breaking through the Zulu line himself, Neville who was also on horseback, caught up with Lieutenant Melville and followed his route of escape. Finding the route to Rorke's Drift cut off by the Zulus, the pair rode on to the Buffalo River, which formed the border between Zululand and Natal.

Nevill managed to cross the swollen river, however, Lieutenant Melvill who was hampered by the colours got into difficulty and would have been swept away had he not returned to help him across.

During the crossing the colours were swept away but were subsequently recovered some six weeks later.

Having reached the Natal side of the river, the pair probably thought themselves to be safe, however, under threat from the Zulus who by now had reached the river bank, they were both killed at a place called Fugitives' Drift.

For his action in trying to save the life of Lieutenant Melvill and having assisted in the rescue of the colours, Nevill was later awarded the Victoria Cross, one of the first to be awarded posthumously.

Figure 168a. Monument erected on the spot where Melvill and Coghill died

The local farmer, Mr George Bunting, placed the pair in a rough grave but a party from Rorke's Drift came and reburied the pair on 14th April 1879.

For his service during the war, Nevill was awarded the South Africa Medal (1877–79) with the 1877-8-9 clasp.

On 6th February 1907, Nevill's Victoria Cross Medal was sent to his brother Egerton, who was now the 5th Baron.

Nevill's Victoria Cross Medal is on public display at the South Wales Borderers Museum in Powys, Wales.

Samuel Wassall
22nd January 1879 (VC No. 362)

Gazetted: 17th June 1879 24734/3966

Rank and Unit: Private No. 427 – 80th Regiment of Foot

Citation

For his gallant conduct in having, at the imminent risk of his own life, saved that of Private Westwood, of the same regiment. On the 22nd January, 1879, when the Camp at Isandhlwana was taken by the enemy, Private Wassail retreated towards the Buffalo River, in which he saw a comrade struggling, and apparently drowning. He rode to the bank, dismounted, leaving his horse on the Zulu side, rescued the man from the stream, and again mounted his horse, dragging Private Westwood across the river under a heavy shower of bullets.

Biography

Samuel was born on 28th July 1856 at 11 The Court, Alcester Street, Deritend, Aston in Birmingham to father Thomas, a wire worker and mother Elizabeth (née Silk); he had an older brother William born in 1845.

At the age of 18, Samuel who was working as an apprentice to a dyer enlisted in the army at Dudley on 28th November 1874 and on 1st December was posted as Private No. 427 with the 80th Regiment of Foot.

Samuel set sail on board the *SS Kashgar* on 11th November 1875 to join his regiment on station duty in Hong Kong and sometime in 1876 was moved with the regiment to Singapore.

In 1877, the regiment was moved to South Africa, with the main force stationed at King Williams Town, on 14th May 1877 Samuel was with a detachment sent to Newcastle.

Later in the year, the regiment was moved to Pietermaritzburg in Natal and for a time served in the Gaika-Galeka War which ended on the 28th June 1878 when the Colonial Government proclaimed an amnesty.

For a time, Samuel was attached to the Mounted Infantry know as "Carrington's Horse".

With the expiry of an ultimatum on 11th January 1879, the Zulu War commenced and Samuel and his regiment were part of the main invasion force that crossed the Buffalo River and by nightfall had established a camp in Zululand.

It was during the retreat following the disaster at the Battle of Isandhlwana on 22nd January 1879, that Samuel performed the deeds for which he was later awarded the Victoria Cross.

Samuel was involved in the Battle of Hlobane on 28th March 1879 and the decisive Battle of Ulundi on 4th July 1879.

Figure 169. Samuel Wassall

On 11th September 1879, Samuel was presented with his Victoria Cross Medal by Lord Wolseley at a ceremony in Utrecht.

For his service during the war, Samuel was awarded the South Africa Medal (1877–79) with clasp for 1877–8–9.

In April 1880, Samuel and the regiment left South Africa and were posted to Ireland where they were stationed at Dublin until 1881 when they were moved to Kerry.

On 10th April 1882, Samuel was married to Rebecca (née Round) at St Matthew's Church in Barrow-in-Furness: the couple would go on to have eight children; John Thomas born in 1883, Flora born in 1885, Louisa born in 1887, Albert born in 1890, Ernest born in 1893, Clara born in 1895, Minnie born in 1897 and Henry born in 1903 – all children were born in Barrow-in-Furness.

In 1883, Samuel moved back to England with the regiment and was stationed at Lichfield until 1884 when the regiment moved to Manchester, followed by a move to Plymouth in 1886.

Having completed his fixed term of engagement, Samuel was discharged from the Army at Lichfield on 20th November 1886.

After leaving the army, Samuel set up home with his family at Melbourne Street in Barrow-in-Furness where he obtained employment as a labourer in the Electrical Department of the Barrow Shipyard.

In 1891, Samuel and his family shared a house at 28 Exmouth Street with his brother William.

Samuel was proud to take part in ceremonial occasions as an ex-serviceman representative and often laid the ex-serviceman's wreath on Armistice Day.

On 17th May 1917, Samuel was one of several ex-servicemen presented to King George V when he visited Barrow.

Samuel was one of 34 Victoria Cross recipients that attended a garden party, held by King George V at Buckingham Palace on 26th June 1920.

At some stage Samuel moved his family to 34 Lyon Street in Barrow and it was while living there that he died at North Lonsdale Hospital in Barrow on 31st January 1927 at the age of 70.

Samuel was buried in the Barrow Cemetery in Barrow-in-Furness in an unmarked grave, after a funeral with full military honours; the local Royal Legion paid the funeral costs and the fees for the upkeep of the grave.

Samuel's Victoria Cross Medal is on public display at the Staffordshire Regimental Museum at Whittington Barracks in Lichfield, Staffordshire.

Figure 169a. Grave of Samuel Wassall

John Rouse Merriot Chard
22nd/23rd January 1879 (VC No. 363)

Gazetted: 2nd May 1879 24717/3177

Rank and Unit: Lieutenant – Royal Engineers

Citation

For their gallant conduct at the defence of Rorke's Drift, on the occasion of the attack by the Zulus on the 22nd and 23rd January, 1879.

The Lieutenant-General commanding the troops reports that, had it not been for the fine example and excellent behaviour of these two Officers under the most trying circumstances, the defence of Rorke's Drift post would not have been conducted with that intelligence and tenacity which so essentially characterised it.

The Lieutenant-General adds, that its success must, in a great degree, be attributable to the two young Officers who exercised the Chief Command on the occasion in question.

Biography

John was born at Boxhill, Pennycross near Plymouth on 21st December 1847 to father William Wheaton a landed proprietor and mother Jane (née Brimacombe). He was one of eight children with two brothers William born in 1842 who would rise to the rank of Colonel with the 7th Royal Fusiliers and Charles born in 1857 who became a vicar and five sisters; Charlotte born in 1841, Mary born in 1845, Jane born in 1850, Florence born in 1855 and Margaret born in 1859.

By 1851, John and his family had moved to Mount Tamar, St Budeaux, Plympton St Mary, in Plymouth.

Initially John was educated at the Plymouth New Grammar School followed by a period at Cheltenham Grammar School.

After a short time with a private tutor, John entered the Royal Military Academy at Woolwich for his initial training as a military engineer and after graduation was commissioned in the Royal Engineers on 15th July 1868, with the temporary rank of Lieutenant.[473]

John spent two years at the Military Engineering Academy at Chatham, to complete his professional training after which, on 21st October 1870, his temporary rank as Lieutenant was made permanent with an effective date of 15th July 1868.[474]

473 *London Gazette* – 23400/3941
474 *London Gazette* – 23670/4554

Figure 170. John Rouse Merriot Chard

On graduating from Chatham, in October 1870, John was sent to Bermuda where for the next three years he was employed in the construction of fortifications for the defence of the Naval Dockyard and anchorage at Hamilton.

From February 1874 until April 1875, John was on duty at Malta, helping with the construction of forts.

At the end of his time in Malta, John returned to England in April 1875 and after a period of leave, had short deployments at Aldershot and Chatham before taking up a position at Devonport in September 1875.

John returned to Aldershot in April 1878 for a short time before proceeding to Chatham in preparation for deployment overseas.

On 2nd December 1878, John set sail from Gravesend bound for South Africa with the 5th Field Company of Royal Engineers, commanded by Captain Walker Parke Jones.

After arriving at Durban on 4th January 1879, the engineers were ordered to join the No. 3 Column, commanded by Colonel Richard Glyn, in preparation for the invasion of Zululand.

Due to the lack of transportation, No. 5 Field Company could not immediately head out from Durban, so John was despatched with a small detachment of sappers (including his orderly Driver Charles Robson) to join up with No. 3 column and provide any needed assistance.

John and his men arrived at Rorke's Drift on 19th January 1879 and was given responsibility for operation of a pontoon bridge system across the river Buffalo, to assist in the advance of the British force into Zululand.

After war was declared on 11th January, the British force crossed the Buffalo River into Zululand and by 20th January the No. 3 Column had established themselves at Isandhlwana about ten miles from Rorke's Drift.

Rorke's Drift, a former mission station, was being used by the British forces as a hospital and supplies depot and when the majority of the troops moved out to Isandhlwana, John was left in command, by Major Spalding, of the small detachment guarding the station.

Altogether, the garrison was made up of 139 officers, NCOs and men, of whom 11 were, in practical terms, non-combatants and 35 were sick and in hospital, leaving a total of two officers and 91 NCOs and men fit for operational duties.

On the morning of 22nd January 1879, John was at the camp at Isandhlwana, however, when news arrived of approaching Zulu forces, he returned to Rorke's Drift to prepare his command for a possible attack.

It was during the defence of Rorke's Drift that John performed the deeds for which he would later be awarded the Victoria Cross.

On 23rd January 1879, John received a promotion to the rank of Captain,[475] supernumerary to the establishment and was awarded a brevet promotion to the rank of Major[476] in recognition of his defence at Rorke's Drift.

Following the events of 22nd/23rd January at Rorke's Drift, John remained in the immediate area and joined up with No. 5 Field Company of the Royal Engineers when they arrived at Helpmakaar on 26th January 1879.

John was probably involved in improving the defences at Rorke's Drift and the construction of new forts at Helpmakaar and Nevill on the Buffalo River.

On 17th February 1879, John, like many of his comrades, was struck down by enteric fever and was sent to Ladysmith for treatment.

A local newspaper, the "Natal Colonist" prematurely reported his death in May 1879, however, John made a full recovery leaving Ladysmith on 27th April and rejoined his unit at Landsman's Drift near Dundee on 29th April.

John was involved in preparations for a second invasion of Zululand and on 3rd June was part of the Ulundi Column, together with the No. 5 Field Company, that advanced into Zululand and was involved in the Battle of Ulundi on 4th July where the Zulus were finally defeated.

On 15th July, while returning from Ulundi, John met up with the new Commander-in-Chief, General Sir Garnet Wolseley, at the Inkwenken Camp near St Paul's Mission Station where at a special parade he was presented with his Victoria Cross Medal.

For his service during the war, John was awarded the South Africa Medal (1878–79) with clasp for 1879.

475 *London Gazette* – 24698/2309
476 *London Gazette* – 24698/2310

On 1st August 1879, John received orders to return to the UK and after boarding the National Line steamship *Egypt*, landed at Portsmouth on 2nd October 1879.

On his arrival, John was presented with a telegram from Queen Victoria which welcomed him home and invited him visit her at Balmoral.

John was in great demand and attended several civic receptions; at Taunton and North Curry on 3rd October and Chatham and Brompton on 9th October.

From the 12th to 14th October, John visited Queen Victoria at Balmoral Castle where he created a very favourable impression and was presented with a signet ring by the Queen.

John attended many receptions across the country before returning to his duties at Devonport at the end of January 1880.

On 16th May 1881, John was moved from the Supernumerary List as a Captain within the establishment of the Royal Engineers.[477]

John was posted to Cyprus in December 1881 and after a six year tour returned to England in March 1887.

On 17th July 1886, John was promoted to the rank of Major.[478]

John was posted to the Fulwood Barracks at Preston in April 1887 where he remained until he was posted to Singapore in December 1892.

On 4th April 1893, John was promoted to the rank of Lieutenant-Colonel,[479] which was later pre-dated to 8th January 1893.[480]

John returned to England in January 1896 and in September was appointed as the Commanding Royal Engineer for the Perth District in Scotland.

Once again John was invited to visit the Queen at Balmoral; however, due to illness he was unable to attend.

John, a lifetime pipe smoker was diagnosed with mouth cancer and in November 1896, he had an operation at Edinburgh.

On 8th January 1897, John received a brevet promotion to the rank of Colonel.[481]

John had a second operation at Edinburgh in March 1897, during which his tongue was removed, however, in a third visit to Edinburgh in August an examination confirmed that the cancer was terminal.

On the 8th August, John took sick leave from the army and went to live with his younger brother Charles at the Rectory in Hatch Beauchamp where he was the local vicar.

477 *London Gazette* – 24979/2746
478 *London Gazette* – 25611/3621
479 *London Gazette* – 26393/2292
480 *London Gazette* – 26423/4048
481 *London Gazette* – 26819/622

In 1897, John was awarded the Queen Victoria Diamond Jubilee Medal.

John died on 1st November 1897, aged 49, at his brother's home and was buried on 5th November in the Parish Churchyard of St John the Baptist at Hatch Beauchamp.

Queen Victoria, who had sent several letters to the Reverend Chard, enquiring after his brother's health sent a wreath to the funeral bearing a note in her own handwriting which stated *"A mark of Admiration and regard for a brave soldier from his Sovereign Victoria R.I."*.

Colonel Edward Browne VC also sent a wreath, on behalf of the 24th Regiment of Foot, as because of official duties he was unable to attend

John's Victoria Cross Medal is on public display at the Imperial War Museum in London as part of the Lord Ashcroft collection.

The medal was purchased by Stanley Baker, who played John in the film *'Zulu'* in 1872, when it was thought to be a copy. After Stanley Baker died, the medal changed hands several times and following analysis of the metal in 1985 was deemed to be the original.

Figure 170a. Grave of John Rouse Merriot Chard

Gonville Bromhead

22nd/23rd January 1879 (VC No. 364)

Gazetted: 2nd May 1879 24717/3177

Rank and Unit: Lieutenant – 2nd Battalion, 24th Regiment of Foot

Citation

For their gallant conduct at the defence of Rorke's Drift, on the occasion of the attack by the Zulus on the 22nd and 23rd January, 1879.

The Lieutenant-General commanding the troops reports that, had it not been for the fine example and excellent behaviour of these two Officers under the most trying circumstances, the defence of Rorke's Drift post would not have been conducted with that intelligence and tenacity which so essentially characterised it.

The Lieutenant-General adds, that its success must, in a great degree, be attributable to the two young Officers who exercised the Chief Command on the occasion in question.

Biography

Gonville was born on 29th August 1845 in Versailles, France to Edmund de Gonville the 3rd Baron of Thurlby a Major in the 54th Regiment of Foot and mother Judith Christine Cahill (née Wood).

He was the youngest son and one of seven children with three sisters, Hellen Morrison born in 1826, Alice Margaret born in 1830 and Francis Judith born in 1847 and three brothers; Edward born on 21st March 1832, Benjamin Parnell born on 22nd October 1838 and Charles James born on 15th September 1840.

He was born into a family with a strong military tradition,[482] going back to his great grandfather who served as an Ensign with General James Wolfe at Quebec in 1779. His grandfather attained the rank of Lieutenant-General and his uncle was in command of the 77th Regiment of Foot.

The family tradition of military service was continued by Gonville and his brothers with Edward rising to the rank of Captain and Benjamine and Charles were both Colonels.

Gonville was educated at the Thomas Magnus School in Newark-on-Trent.

On 20th April 1867, at the age of 21, Gonville began his military career when he purchased a commission as Ensign in the 2nd Battalion of the 24th Regiment of Foot.[483]

482 The family were also founders of the Gonville and Caius College at Cambridge.

483 *London Gazette* – 23243/2370

Figure 171. Gonville Bromhead

Gonville's first months of service were spent in England until 11th December 1868 when he set sail to join his regiment who were stationed at Secunderabad in India.

On 1st November 1871, Gonville was promoted to the rank of Lieutenant.[484]

On 2nd April 1872, Gonville was back in England, having returned ahead of the Battalion which had departed aboard the troopship *Euphrates* on 2nd December and arrived at Portsmouth on 26th January 1873 and proceeded to Warley in Essex.

In December 1873, Gonville and the regiment were moved to Aldershot where they were quartered in the North Camp until August 1875 when they moved to the Citadel at Dover.

On the 4th December, Gonville attended the School of Musketry at Hythe where he obtained a 1st Class Certificate.

The battalion left Dover on 21st June 1877 and moved to Chatham and early in the new year, on 28th January 1878 received orders to make ready for deployment to South Africa.

On 2nd February 1878, Gonville and the battalion boarded the troopship *HMS Himalaya* at Portsmouth and set sail for South Africa where on 11th March they disembarked at East London and by 14th March had moved off to King William's Town.

Soon after arriving at King William's Town, the battalion was despatched by company to various posts as part of the forces taking part in the later stages of the Gaika-Galeka War (the 9th Kaffir War) which ended on the 28th June 1878 when the Colonial Government proclaimed an amnesty.

Gonville, with "E" company was posted to the Perie Mission Station.

On 29th April 1878, Gonville and "E" company moved to Baillie's Grave to join other companies of the battalion for an attack on the rebel position at Intala Ka Udoda which took place on the next day.

Gonville and "E" company remained at Baillie's Grave to provide protection for the British Artillery.

After the successful British attack, Gonville and "E" Company moved up to Intala Ka Udoda to help construct earthworks, known as Fort Black.

On 2nd June 1878, Gonville was part of the force commanded by Major Black ordered to relieve the 90th Light Infantry on the Gozo Heights, who had been ordered to Natal.

After the armistice was signed the posts held by the 24th Regiment were gradually handed over to Colonial Troops and by 12th July were assembled at a camp in the Buffalo Poort bush.

On 19th July the regiment received orders to proceed to Natal, where war with Cetywayo, the Zulu king was imminent. The regiment set sail, in two detachments, from East London on 24th and 26th July and after landing at Durban assembled at Pietermaritzburg on 6th August 1878.

After a period of about three months at Pietermaritzburg, where they were refitted and underwent periods of training, the forces began to move towards the border with Zululand in preparation for an invasion.

Gonville, with the 2nd Battalion 24th Regiment, was moved to Greytown in November and then on to Helpmakaar where the invasion force was being assembled and were assigned to the 3rd Column commanded by Colonel R. T. Glyn.

When the ultimatum to Cetywayo, to disband his army, went unanswered, Colonel Glyn and the 3rd Column advanced to Rorke's Drift and Gonville, now in command of "B" company was ordered to guard Rorke's Farm which had been appropriated as a commissariat depot and a base hospital.

Colonel Glyn and the remainder of the 3rd Column set off for Isandhlwana about nine miles away where a British camp was established on 20th January 1879.

It was on 22nd/23rd January 1879, during the defence of Rorke's Drift, that Gonville performed the deeds for which he would later be awarded the Victoria Cross.

On 23rd January 1879, for his actions at Rorke's Drift, Gonville was promoted to the rank of Captain and received a brevet promotion to the rank of Major.[485]

The second battalion remained at Rorke's Drift until mid-April when half of the men, including Gonville who was now in command of Companies "G" and "H", were moved to Dundee.

Gonville and his command were later moved to Landsman's Drift and then to Kopjie Alleine where a strong fort was constructed.

484 *London Gazette* – 23812/5870

485 *London Gazette* – 24698/2310

On 28th July 1879, when the 2nd division was broken up, Gonville with Companies "F" and "H" were assigned as special escort to General Sir Garnet Wolseley, who had replaced Lord Chelmsford as commander of the British forces.

Gonville was presented with his Victoria Cross Medal on 11th August 1879 at a special parade at Utrecht in the Transvaal by General Sir Garnet Wolseley, the High Commissioner and General Officer Commanding troops in South Africa.

For his service during the Zulu War, Gonville received two mentions in despatches and was awarded the South Africa Medal (1877–79) with clasp for 1877-8-9.

On 9th September 1879, the battalion received orders directing them to Gibraltar and on 29th September began the 250 mile march towards Pietermaritzburg which they reached on 14th October.

The battalion resumed its march on 21st October and after some delay at the Camp in Pinetown, the battalion boarded *SS Ontario* on 12th January 1880 bound for Gibraltar where they arrived on 12th February and were quartered in the Casemate Barracks.

In June 1880, Gonville had an audience with Queen Victoria, during which she presented him with a portrait of herself.

On 31st July, following the disaster at the Battle of Maiwand in Afghanistan, the battalion received orders to make ready for a deployment to India and on 12th August 1880 boarded *HMS Orontes* and set sail for Bombay where they arrived on 1st September 1880.

The next day the battalion moved to Poonah but two weeks later on 15th September they set out for Secunderabad by rail.

On 17th April 1881, Gonville returned to England for a period of home leave and set out on his return to the regiment in India, from Portsmouth on board *HMS Serapis* on 2nd January 1883.

During his time in England, Gonville attended the School of Musketry at Hythe between 1st October and 5th December 1882 where he was awarded a 1st Class Extra Certificate.

Gonville was promoted to the rank of Major on 4th April 1883.[486]

On 31st December 1883, the battalion left Secunderabad and after spending a month in the Camp of Exercise at Bangalore were despatched by rail to Fort St George at Madras.

Gonville left India on 27th October 1886, bound for Burma, where Upper Burma had recently been annexed to the Indian Empire and on 2nd December, now in command of the left wing of the battalion moved to Tonghoo.

For the next two years, until November 1888, the Battalion was involved in the pacification of Upper Burma, on 24th May 1888, Gonville returned to India ahead of the battalion.

For his service in Burma, Gonville was awarded the India General Service Medal (1854–95) with clasps for Burma 1885–87 and Burma 1887–89.

In March 1889, Gonville was with the battalion at Ranikhet until November 1890 when they moved to Allahabad.

It was while based at Camp Dabhaura in Allahabad, that on 9th February 1891, Gonville at the age of 46, died from typhoid (enteric fever) and was buried in the New Cantonment Cemetery at Allahabad.

Gonville's Victoria Cross Medal is on public display at the South Wales Borderers Museum in Brecon, Powys, Wales.

Figure 171a. Grave of Gonvill Bromhead

486 *London Gazette* – 25250/3532

James Henry Reynolds
22nd/23rd January 1879 (VC No. 365)

Gazetted: 17th June 1879 24734/3966

Rank and Unit: Surgeon-Major – Army Medical Department

Citation

For the conspicuous bravery, during the attack at Rorke's Drift on the 22nd and 23rd January, 1879, which he exhibited in his constant attention to the wounded under fire, and in his voluntarily conveying ammunition from the store to the defenders of the Hospital, whereby he exposed himself to a cross-fire from the enemy both in going and returning.

Figure 172. James Henry Reynolds

Biography

James was born on 3rd February 1844 at Kingstown, Co Dublin in Ireland, the second son to father Laurence a local Justice of the Peace.

From 1855 to 1860, James attended the St Vincent College of the Castleknock School in Dublin before attending Trinity College, Dublin University to study medicine. He obtained his Bachelor of Medicine in 1864 and Bachelor of Surgery in 1867, leaving the university on 14th January 1868.

James began his career in the army on 31st March 1868, when at the age of 24 he was commissioned as an Assistant Surgeon on the staff of the Army Medical Department.[487]

On 24th March 1869, James was transferred from his staff position to the 36th Regiment of Foot as Assistant Surgeon[488] and soon afterwards, joined his regiment who were on service in India.

During his time in India, the regiment suffered a severe outbreak of cholera which James helped to contain and treat the inflicted before being invalided home in 1870. For his service in helping to manage the cholera outbreak, James received the thanks of the commanding officer, Lord Sandhurst.

On 7th December 1870, James was transferred from the 36th Regiment of Foot to a staff position.[489]

James was promoted to the rank of Surgeon on 1st March 1873 when the rank of Assistant-Surgeon was abolished.

With increasing hostilities in the Cape Colony, James was despatched to South Africa where he arrived in August 1874.

Attached to the 1st Battalion of the 24th Regiment of Foot, James took part in the Griqualand Campaign in the diamond fields, during 1875.

487 *London Gazette* – 23422/4994
488 *London Gazette* – 23481/1877
489 *London Gazette* – 23685/5660

James served alongside the 24th and 88th Regiments during the Kaffir War of 1877–78 and was present at the Battle of Mpetu in January 1878.

With the outbreak of the Zulu War in December 1878, James was appointed as a medical officer for the Central Column of the invasion force, commanded by Lord Chelmsford.

The Central Column crossed the Buffalo River into Zululand on 11th January 1879 and arrived at Rorke's Drift before moving on towards Isandhlwana; James remained at the mission station to take charge of the hospital that had been established there.

As the column departed, James said farewell to two good friends, Surgeon-Major Peter Shepard and Lieutenant Edgar Anstey of the 24th Regiment of Foot, both of whom would be killed during the Battle of Isandhlwana on 22nd January. Lieutenant Anstey left his dog Pip, a fox terrier, with James.

It was during the defence of Rorke's Drift on 22nd/23rd January that James performed the deeds for which he would later be awarded the Victoria Cross.

James was promoted to the rank of Surgeon-Major, effective 23rd January 1879, in recognition of his service at Rorke's Drift.[490]

It was not until 17th June 1879, that James was gazetted for the award, this was following questions raised in the House of Commons as to why he had not been included in the original list of Rorke's Drift recipients that were announced on 2nd May 1879.

After the defence, James remained for some weeks at Rorke's Drift where he continued to care for the sick.

490 *London Gazette* – 24698/2310

James was present at the British camp at Fort Nolela for the final battle of the war at Ulundi on 4th July 1879.

For his service during the war, James received a mention in despatches and was awarded the South Africa Medal (1877–79) with clasp for 1877–8–9.

James was presented with his Victoria Cross Medal by General Sir Garnet Wolseley at a parade held on 16th July 1879 at St Paul's in Zululand.

On 17th July 1879, the British Medical Association awarded James the Gold Medal for his services at Rorke's Drift.

After the close of the war, James returned to England on board the troopship *Eagle*, which landed at Spithead on 2nd October 1879.

On 17th December 1879, James was appointed as an honorary doctor of law by Trinity College, Dublin University and he was appointed as an honorary Fellow of the Royal College of Physicians, Ireland.

Soon after arriving back in England, James was appointed as Senior Medical Officer for an expedition to go to the aid of Captain James Cunningham Boycott[491] during the "Irish Land War" of 1880.

James was married to Elizabeth (née McCormick) on 22nd September 1880 at Glenageary, Co Wicklow; the couple would go on to have four children a daughter and three sons; George Cormac born in 1881, Percival born in 1884 and Henry Laurence born in 1885. All of the three sons joined the army and saw service during the great war as privates – George and Percival were both killed in action.

On 1st April 1887, James was promoted to the rank of Lieutenant-Colonel and on 25th December 1892 was promoted to Brigade-Surgeon.[492]

After 27 years of service, James retired from the army on 8th January 1896[493] but immediately took up the position of Senior Medical Officer with the Army Clothing Factory at Pimlico in London, which he held until May 1905.

For some time afterwards, James had his own medical practice in London.

At the beginning of 1929, James underwent 10 days of Radium treatment for cancer, which fortunately was successful and avoided the need for surgery.

In November 1929, James was the oldest of three Victoria Cross recipients who attended a dinner to commemorate the 50th anniversary of the Zulu War, hosted by the Prince of Wales in the Royal Gallery of the House of Lords.

James died at the Empire Nursing Home, Victoria in London on 4th March 1932 at the age of 88 and was buried in St Mary's Roman Catholic Cemetery, Harrow Road, London.

James's Victoria Cross Medal is on public display at the Royal Army Medical Corps Museum, Keogh Barracks, Aldershot, Hampshire.

Figure 172a. Grave of James Henry Reynolds

491 The word boycott, meaning "an act of voluntarily abstaining from using, buying, or dealing with a person" is named after him.

492 *London Gazette* – 26366/413

493 *London Gazette* – 26697/83

James Langley Dalton

22nd/23rd January 1879 (VC No. 366)

Gazetted: 18th November 1879 24784/6494

Rank and Unit: Acting Assistant Commissary – Commissariat and Transport Department

Citation

For his conspicuous gallantry during the attack on Rorke's Drift Post by the Zulus on the night of the 22nd January, 1879, when he actively superintended the work of defence, and was amongst the foremost of those who received the first attack at the corner of the hospital, where the deadliness of his fire did great execution, and the mad rush of the Zulus met its first check, and where by his cool courage he saved the life of a man of the Army Hospital Corps by shooting the Zulu, who, having seized the muzzle of the man's rifle, was in the act of assegaing him.

This Officer, to whose energy much of the defence of the place was due, was severely wounded during the contest, but still continued to give the same example of cool courage.

Biography

James was born around December 1832, in the St Andrews Parish of London,[494] it is possible that he was actually born in Ireland to father Charles and mother Hannah (née Langley) and that the family moved to London when he was very young.

Just before his 18th birthday, James left his job as an assistant in a stationers shop and joined the army at London and was enlisted as Private No. 965 in the 85th Regiment of Foot. Soon after his enlistment, James joined his regiment who were serving at Waterford in Ireland.

After spending about six months in Ireland, James returned with the regiment to England where he was stationed at Preston, Hull and Portsmouth.

In March 1853, James and the regiment boarded the troopship *Marion* and set sail for Mauritius where they were to form the garrison.

Soon after his arrival on Mauritius, James was promoted to the rank of Corporal on 1st July 1853 and on 17th September 1855 he was promoted to the rank of Sergeant.

In February 1856, James left Mauritius bound for South Africa where he took part in the eighth Cape Frontier War and returned to England in July 1858.

494 Exact confirmed details are not known, these are from his army discharge papers.

Figure 173. James Langley Dalton

On 20th December 1859, James re-engaged, at Pembroke Dock, for a further fixed period of service in the army.

James was transferred to the Commissariat Staff Corp at Aldershot, with the rank of Corporal on 1st April 1862 and on 1st January 1863 had been promoted back to the rank of Sergeant.

On 1st June 1863, James was promoted to Colour Sergeant and sometime during the following year attended the School of Musketry at Hythe.

James was promoted to the rank of Master Sergeant on 7th February 1866 and performed the role of a clerk and from April 1867 was stationed at Portsmouth.

In 1868, James saw service in Canada and was initially based in Quebec and then with General Sir Garnet Wolseley on the Red River Expedition in 1870.

On 1st April 1870, the Commissariat Staff Corp became part of the Army Service Corps and James's rank was changed to 2nd Class Staff Sergeant but on 1st July 1870 he was promoted to the rank of 1st Class Staff Sergeant.

After having spent just short of three years in Canada, James returned to England in 1871 and on 20th November 1871, after 22 years of service retired from the army. For his service, James was awarded the Army Long Service and Good Conduct Medal.

After spending some time in England, in 1877 James moved to South Africa, probably expecting a peaceful retirement, however, with the outbreak of the 9th Cape Frontier War, he volunteered his services and on 13th December 1877 was appointed as Acting Assistant Commissary, a civilian position with a temporary commission.

Having been posted to Ibeka, James was in charge of the stores depot responsible for supplying food, ammunition and equipment to the British forces in the field. For his efficient and effective handling of his responsibilities, he received a mention in despatches, the only civilian to be mentioned.

After the end of the war, James once again left the army, however, with the outbreak of the Zulu War he offered his services again and was appointed Sub-Assistant Commissary at Fort Napier, Pietmaritzburg on 21st November 1878.

James was with the Invasion force that crossed from Natal into Zululand and in January 1879, and with Assistant Commissary Walter Dunne, assistant storekeeper Louis Byrne and Corporal Francis Wood was responsible for the set-up of the stores at Rorke's Drift.

It was on 22nd/23rd January, during the defence of Rorke's Drift, that James performed the deeds for which he would later be awarded the Victoria Cross, during which he was severely wounded in the right shoulder. James spent some time in the hospital at Rorke's Drift where his wound was treated by Surgeon Reynolds.

For his service during the war, James was awarded the South Africa Medal (1877–79) with clasps for 1877–8 and 1879.

On 21st March 1879, in recognition of his service at Rorke's Drift, James was commissioned as Sub-Assistant Commissary on-half pay in the Army Service Corps, with an effective date of 13th December 1877.[495]

In October 1879, when the 2nd Battalion of the 24th Regiment were marching through the streets of Pietermaritzburg, James was amongst the crowds cheering them on. When men from Company "B" spotted him, one of them shouted "Why there's Mr Dalton cheering us! We ought to be cheering him! He was the best man there!" – James was hauled out of the crowd and made to march with the men.

James was presented with his Victoria Cross Medal by General Hugh Clifford VC, on 16th January 1880 during a special parade at Pietermaritzburg.

On 31st January 1880, James was promoted to the rank of Quartermaster on the staff of the Army Commissariat and Transport department,[496] however, in February he set sail on his return to England.

On reaching England, James retired from the army on 1st April 1880[497] and as a consequence his promotion to Quartermaster was cancelled.[498]

In 1884, James returned to South Africa where, during the gold rush of 1884–87, he prospected for gold in the Transvaal; he owned 1,500 shares in the Little Bess Mine at Barberton.

Just before Christmas in 1886, James went to stay with an old army friend John Williams who ran the Grosvenor Hotel in Port Elizabeth.

James appeared to be in good health but after spending a day in bed he suddenly died in his room on 7th January 1887 at the age of 54. He was buried in the Russell Road, Roman Catholic Cemetery in Port Elizabeth.

James's Victoria Cross Medal is on public display at the Royal Logistics Corps Museum, Blackdown, Camberley in Surrey.

Figure 173a. Grave of James Langley Dalton

495 *London Gazette* – 24698/2310

496 *London Gazette* – 24822/2017

497 *London Gazette* – 24829/2361

498 *London Gazette* – 24829/2360

William Wilson Allen (Allan)
22nd/23rd January 1879 (VC No. 367)

Figure 174. William Wilson Allen

Gazetted: 2nd May 1879 24717/3178

Rank and Unit: Corporal No. 1240 – 2nd Battalion 24th Regiment of Foot

Citation

It was chiefly due to the courageous conduct of these men that communication with the hospital was kept up at all. Holding together at all costs a most dangerous post, raked in reverse by the enemy's fire from the hill, they were both severely wounded, but their determined conduct enabled the patients to be withdrawn from the hospital, and when incapacitated by their wounds from fighting, they continued, as soon as their wounds had been dressed, to serve out ammunition to their comrades during the night.

Biography

William was born in the small village of Kyloe, near Berwick-upon-Tweed sometime around 1843.

At about 15 years of age, William lied about his age and enlisted in the army at York on 27th October 1859 and was enrolled as Private No. 1240, in the 2nd Battalion of 24th Regiment of Foot currently based at Aldershot.

On 31st December 1859, the battalion moved to Portsmouth and on 13th March 1860 boarded the troopship *Donald McKay* and set sail for Mauritius where they landed on 23rd May 1860.

In October 1865, the regiment was posted to Burma and landed at Rangoon by detachments in December 1865.

The battalion left Burma from Rangoon at the end of 1868 for India and arrived at their station at Secunderabad on 16th February 1869 where they remained until November 1872.

On 14th November 1872, the battalion left Secunderabad on a march to Bombay, where on 2nd/3rd December they boarded the troopship *Euphrates* bound for England, arriving at Portsmouth on 26th January 1873.

William moved with the depot companies to Brecon on 21st April 1874 and on 18th May was promoted to the rank of Lance-Corporal.

On 16th August 1876, William was married to Sarah Ann (née Reeves) at Brecon; the couple would go on to have seven children.

After gaining his 2nd Class Certificate of Education, William was appointed as assistant School Master at the Brecon Barracks in 1876 and on 6th July 1877 was promoted to the rank of Corporal.

With a deterioration of affairs on the east frontier of the Cape Colony, the call went out for reinforcements and on 28th January 1878, the 2nd Battalion was placed on readiness for deployment to South Africa.

William was recalled to the battalion and on 2nd February set out on board the troopship *HMS Himalaya* bound for the Cape where they landed at East London on 9th March 1878.

As part of company "B", William moved to the defence of King William's Town and was stationed at Hudson's Store, in the defensive line. In the middle of March the company were involved in an attack on the Rebula heights and drove the rebels through Hayne's mill before returning to Baillie's Grave.

In May 1878, William and "B" company were involved in operations on Mount Kempt were they remained until the war was ended with a general amnesty on 28th June 1878.

On 22nd May 1878, William was promoted to the rank of Lance-Sergeant, however, on 21st October 1878 after having been found drunk while on duty, he was reduced back to the rank of Corporal.

With preparations underway for the invasion of Zululand, the battalion were ordered to Natal and after setting sail from King William's Town on 24th–26th July landed at Durban and marched to Pietermaritzburg where they arrived on 6th August 1878.

On 11th January 1879, William with his battalion were part of the 3rd invasion column, commanded by Colonel R. T. Glyn, that crossed into Zululand after the expiry of the ultimatum issued to the Zulu Chief Cetywayo to dismantle his armies.

When the bulk of the column moved off to a camp at Isandhlwana, William and company "B", under the command of Lieutenant Gonville Bromhead were detached to guard the mission station at Rorke's Drift which had been set up by the army as a supply base and hospital.

It was during the defence of Rorke's Drift on 22nd/23rd January, that William performed the deeds for which he would later be awarded the Victoria Cross.

During the defence, William was seriously wounded by a bullet wound in his left shoulder, which was initially treated by Surgeon James Reynolds VC, in the hospital that he had so courageously helped to defend.

William remained at Rorke's Drift until the middle of April 1879 and then returned to England on board the troopship *Tamar* and on reaching home was sent to the Military Hospital at Netley where he received further medical treatment for his wounded arm.

For his service during the war, William was awarded the South Africa Medal with clasp for 1877–8–9.

On 25th October 1879, William attended a victory celebration at Portland Hall, Portsea held by the people of Portsmouth on behalf of the servicemen who had served in the Zulu War.

Although still somewhat incapacitated by his wounded shoulder, William served with the 3rd South Wales Borderers Militia at Brecon.

William was presented with his Victoria Cross Medal by Queen Victoria on 9th December 1879 at an investiture held at Windsor Castle.

On 11th June 1880, William was appointed as a provisional Sergeant and saw service at the Colchester Depot before moving to the Brecon Depot.

Figure 174a. Grave of William Wilson Allen

William was promoted to Sergeant in 1886 and appointed as Instructor of Musketry to "C" Company, 4th Battalion, South Wales Borderers based at Monmouth.

It was while serving at Monmouth that William contracted influenza during the epidemic of 1890 and died from complications on 12th March 1890 at the age of 46. He was buried five days later in Monmouth Cemetery.

A fund was set up to help look after his widow and seven children however, this did not prevent his widow having to sell his Victoria Cross Medal to help with the care of the children.

William's Victoria Cross Medal is on public display at the South Wales Borderers Museum at Brecon, Powys in Wales.

Christian Ferdinand (Frederick) Schiess
22nd/23rd January 1879 (VC No. 368)

Gazetted: 2nd December 1879 24788/7148

Rank and Unit: Corporal – Natal Native Contingent

Citation

For conspicuous gallantry in the defence of Rorke's Drift Post on the night of the 22nd January, 1879, when, in spite of his having been wounded in the foot a few days previously, he greatly distinguished himself when the Garrison were repulsing, with the bayonet, a series of desperate assaults made by the Zulus, and displayed great activity and devoted gallantry throughout the defence.

On one occasion when the Garrison had retired to the inner line of defence, and the Zulus occupied the wall of mealie bags which had been abandoned, he crept along the wall, without any order, to dislodge a Zulu who was shooting better than usual and succeeded in killing him, and two others, before he, the Corporal, returned to the inner, defence.

Biography

Christian, who preferred to be called Frederick, was born on 7th April 1856 at Bergdorf in the canton of Berne in Switzerland to father Niclaus, a stonecutter and mother Anna (née Ruchti). After both of his parents died, Frederick was brought up with his sisters in the municipal orphanage at Herisau near Appenzell.

At the outbreak of the Franco-Prussian War in July 1870, Frederick enlisted with the French army, although he was only 15 years of age at the time, and probably saw action at the Battle of Villersexel on 9th January 1871 and the Battle of Lisaine on 15th January 1871.

After the end of the war in May 1871, Frederick continued to serve in the army of General Charles-Denis Bourbaki for a further five years before taking his discharge and returning to Switzerland in 1876.

At the time Frederick returned to Switzerland, agents of the Cape Government were recruiting Swiss labourers and farmers to emigrate to the Cape on a state aided scheme.

At some time in mid 1877, Frederick with a group of emigrants boarded *HMS Adele* at Hamburg and set sail for the Cape where they arrived at East London on 21st August 1877.

Almost as soon as he arrived in South Africa, Frederick volunteered to join the South African colonial army at the start of the 9th Cape Frontier war against the Xhosa tribes. Because of his previous military experience Colonel Durnford appointed Frederick as a Corporal in the 2nd Battalion of the 3rd Regiment of the Natal Native Infantry.

At the end of the war, Frederick, without a trade, worked for a short time as an itinerate labourer in King William's Town.

With the build-up to the invasion of Zululand, Frederick volunteered once more and rejoined the Natal Native Infantry as a Corporal.

Soon after the start of the war, Frederick was sent to the hospital at Rorke's Drift in January 1879, suffering from an injury to his leg. Accounts of his injury differ, with two possibilities each having their own supporters; the first is that Frederick was sent to the hospital with badly infected feet caused by ill fitting boots; the second is that he was wounded in the foot and leg by an assegai during the attack on Chief Sirayo's kraal on 12th January 1879; the first engagement of the war.

The following wording in the official Victoria Cross citation, "*... in spite of his having been wounded in the foot a few days previously ...*", although not conclusive, would appear to support the latter proposition.

Whatever, the cause of his injury, Frederick was in the hospital at Rorke's Drift on 22nd January 1879 and it was during the defence of the mission station that he performed the deeds for which he would later be awarded the Victoria Cross, having received a further wound to his foot.

Frederick continued to serve until the end of the Zulu War in 1881, having joined Lonsdale's Horse on 24th January 1880.

On 3rd February 1880, Frederick was presented with his Victoria Cross Medal by General Lord Garnet Wolsely at a special parade in Pietermaritzburg.

Frederick was the last of the Rorke's Drift men to be sanctioned for the award of the Victoria Cross and only after intensive campaigning on his behalf. He was the first soldier serving with the South African Forces to receive the award and the only person of Swiss nationality.

For his service during the war, Frederick was awarded the South Africa Medal with the 1877–8–9 clasp.

At the end of the Zulu War, Frederick found work in the telegraph office in Durban for a time, however, when he became unemployed he was unable to find work and became destitute.

In late 1884 he was found on the streets of Cape Town, suffering from exposure and malnutrition, by men from the Royal Navy. The men gave him food and offered him a berth on their ship *HMS Serapis* which was returning to England.

Frederick gladly accepted the offer, however, during the voyage his health deteriorated and he died on 14th December 1884 at the age of 28 and was buried at sea off the coast of Angola.

Frederick's Victoria Cross Medal was on his person when he died and the Captain of *HMS Serapis* arranged for it to be returned to the War Office after they arrived in England. The medal is now on public display at the National Army Museum, Chelsea in London.

Alfred Henry Hook
22nd/23rd January 1879 (VC No. 369)

Gazetted: 2nd May 1879 24717/3178

Rank and Unit: Private No. 1373 – 2nd Battalion 24th Regiment of Foot

Citation

Private John Williams was posted with Private Joseph Williams, and Private William Horrigan, 1st Battalion 24th Regiment, in a distant room of the hospital, which they held for more than an hour, so long as they had a round of ammunition left: as communication was for the time cut off, the Zulus were enabled to advance and burst open the door; they dragged out Private Joseph Williams and two of the patients, and assagied them. Whilst the Zulus were occupied with the slaughter of these men a lull took place, during which Private John Williams, who, with two patients, were the only men now left alive in this ward, succeeded in knocking a hole in the partition, and in taking the two patients into the next ward, where he found Private Hook.

These two men together, one man working whilst the other fought and held the enemy at bay with his bayonet, broke through three more partitions, and were thus enabled to bring eight patients through a small window into the inner line of defence.

Biography

Alfred was born on 6th August 1850 at Alney, Churcham near Gloucester to father Henry a rural labourer (woodcutter) and mother Eleanor (née Higgs). Alfred was the oldest of six children with two brothers; James born in 1855 and Henry Daniel born in 1857; and three sisters Mary Rebecca born in 1852, Ellen born in 1860 and Emily born in 1863.

The family lived at "Birdwood", known locally as Hook's farm, at Alney near Churcham.

Alfred had very little formal education and for most of his life could not read or write, at the age of 11 he was working as a rural labourer (woodcutter) alongside his father.

On 1st May 1869, at the age of 18, Alfred left his job as a rural labourer and enlisted with the Royal Monmouthshire Militia.

Alfred was married to Comfort (née Jones) at Aston Ingham, near Newent in Herefordshire on 20th December 1870; the couple would go on to have four children, Raymond John born in 1871, Mary Henrietta born in 1874, Julianna born in 1876 and Julien born in 1877.

Figure 176. Alfred Henry Hook

In 1871 the couple lived in Drybridge street in Monmouth.

After five years of service, Alfred left the Royal Monmouthshire Militia in May 1874 and for the next three years presumably worked as an itinerate labourer.

With troubles in his marriage, Alfred left his wife and family and on 13th March 1877, at the age of 26, enlisted in the army at Monmouth and was engaged as Private No. 1373 in the 2nd Battalion of the 24th Regiment of Foot and was posted to duties at Dover Citadel.

With a deterioration of affairs on the east frontier of the Cape Colony, the call went out for reinforcements and on 28th January 1878, the 2nd Battalion was placed on readiness for deployment to South Africa.

On 2nd February, Alfred and the battalion set sail on board the troopship *HMS Himalaya* bound for the Cape where they landed at East London on 9th March 1878.

As part of company "B", Alfred moved to the defence of King William's Town and was stationed at Hudson's Store, in the defensive line.

In the middle of March the company were involved in an attack on the Rebula heights and drove the rebels through Hayne's mill before returning to Baillie's Grave.

In May 1878, Alfred and "B" company were involved in operations on Mount Kempt were they remained until the war was ended with a general amnesty on 28th June 1878.

With preparations underway for the invasion of Zululand, the battalion were ordered to Natal and after setting sail from King William's Town on 24th–26th July landed at Durban and marched to Pietermaritzburg where they arrived on 6th August 1878.

On 11th January 1879, Alfred with his battalion were part of the 3rd invasion column, commanded by Colonel R. T. Glyn, that crossed into Zululand after the expiry of the ultimatum issued to the Zulu Chief Cetywayo to dismantle his armies.

When the bulk of the column moved off to a camp at Isandhlwana, Alfred and company "B", under the command of Lieutenant Gonville Bromhead were detached to guard the mission station at Rorke's Drift which had been set up by the army as a supply base and hospital.

Alfred who was a teetotaller and a Methodist lay preacher, was assigned as cook to the hospital.

It was during the defence of Rorke's Drift on 22nd/23rd January, that Alfred performed the deeds for which he would later be awarded the Victoria Cross. During the action he received a spear wound to the scalp which would cause him trouble in later years.

After the defence, "B" Company remained at Rorke's Drift and Alfred was appointed as batman to Major Wilson Black, who would go on to command the 1st Battalion.

On 3rd August 1879, Alfred was presented with his Victoria Cross Medal at Rorke's Drift by General Sir Garnet Wolseley the General Officer Commanding troops in South Africa.

For his service during the war, Alfred was awarded the South Africa Medal with clasp for 1877–8–9.

On 9th September 1879, the Battalion received orders to go to Gibraltar and after a march of 250 miles reached Pietermaritzburg on 14th November, where they received a tremendous welcome.

After some delay while awaiting transportation the battalion set sail on *SS Ontario* and reached Gibraltar on 12th February 1880 where they were quartered in the Casemate barracks.

On 25th June 1880, after having served just over three years of his enlistment period Alfred purchased his discharge from the army at a cost of £18 and returned to England.

On his return to England, Alfred moved to Monmouth, where he was employed as a live-in servant (groom) for Dr George Willis a GP and surgeon.

At some stage, Alfred moved to London and was living in lodgings at Sydenham Hill near Crystal Palace when on 26th December 1881 he was employed as a labourer at the British Museum and at some time later was appointed as cloakroom attendant at the museum.

In April 1888, Alfred joined the 1st Volunteer Battalion of the Royal Fusiliers and served as a Sergeant Instructor of Musketry for almost 20 years.

While in London, Alfred continued to pursue two of his passions as a member of the Loyal St James Lodge of Oddfellows and as a Corporal with the Bloomsbury Rifle Volunteer Club (a silver plated memorial trophy bearing his name was later presented to the British Museum Rifle Association).

In November 1896, Alfred petitioned for a divorce from his wife Comfort, who had remarried at Gloucester in 1895, to David Meyrick who was noted as a co-respondent.

The divorce was granted in January 1897 and on 10th April 1897, Alfred was married at St Andrews Church in Islington to Ada Letitia (née Taylor); the couple would go on to have two children Victoria Catherine born in 1899 and Letitia Jean born in 1902.

In 1901, Alfred was living with his family at 15 Sealy Street in Islington while working as a cloakroom attendant at the British Museum.

Due to ill health, Alfred retired from his job at the British Museum on 31st December 1904 and was granted a gratuity; he moved with his family back to Gloucester and set up home at 2 Osborn Villas, Rosebury Avenue. In January 1905, Alfred retired from his position with the 1st Volunteer Battalion of the Royal Fusiliers.

On his arrival back in Gloucester, Alfred became a member of the Phoenix Lodge of Oddfellows.

Alfred did not have long to enjoy his retirement as he died at home, from tuberculosis on 12th March 1905 at the age of 54. He was buried six days later on 18th March at St Andrew's Parish Churchyard in Churcham; a fellow Rorke's Drift Victoria Cross recipient Frederick Hitch attended the funeral.

Alfred's Victoria Cross Medal is on public display at the South Wales Borderers Museum in Brecon, Powys, Wales.

Figure 176a. Grave of Alfred Henry Hook

William Jones
22nd/23rd January 1879 (VC No. 370)

Gazetted: 2nd May 1879 24717/3178

Rank and Unit: Private No. 593 – 2nd Battalion 24th Regiment of Foot

Citation

In another ward, facing the hill, Private William Jones and Private Robert Jones defended the post to the last, until six out of the seven patients it contained had been removed.

The seventh, Sergeant Maxfield, 2nd Battalion 24th Regiment, was delirious from fever. Although they had previously dressed him, they were unable to induce him to move. When Private Robert Jones returned to endeavour to carry him away, he found him being stabbed by the Zulus as he lay on his bed.

Biography

William was born in 1839 at Evesham in Worcestershire to father James a builder's labourer.

At the age of 19, William left his job as an apprentice shoemaker and on 22nd December 1858 enlisted in the army at Birmingham and was engaged as Private No. 593 in the newly formed 2nd Battalion of the 24th Regiment of Foot (raised at Sheffield on 3rd June 1858).

On 9th June 1859, William moved with the Battalion to Aldershot and soon afterwards on 1st September 1859 he was promoted to the rank of Corporal.

On 31st December 1859, following a fracas with some of the Tower Hamlets Militia on Christmas day, William and the batalion were moved from the camp at Aldershot and sent to Portsmouth where some days later they boarded the troopship *Urgent* and set sail for Cork where they arrived on 7th January 1860.

The battalion's stay in Ireland was short lived; on 13th March 1860 they boarded the troopship *Donald McKay* and set sail for Mauritius where they landed on 23rd May 1860.

On 5th September 1860, William was reduced in rank back to Private and served 8 days in prison for having been found drunk while on duty.

William and the Battalion boarded the ships *Devonport* and *Star of India* on 5th & 6th October at Port Louis and set sail for British Burma where they landed at Rangoon between 2nd and 10th December 1865.

On 1st January 1869, William re-engaged at Rangoon for a further fixed term of service in the army and on the same day

Figure 177. William Jones

began the journey to Secunderabad in India which was to be their new station.

Travelling via Madras, the battalion reached Secunderabad on 16th February 1869 where they remained until November 1872 before starting out on their return journey back to England.

The battalion set out on their march to Bombay on 14th November 1872 and on 2nd–3rd December boarded the troopship *Euphrates* and after a voyage via the Suez canal landed at Portsmouth on 26th January 1873 and proceeded to their station at Warley.

On 19th December 1873, the regiment was moved to the camp at Aldershot.

While based at Aldershot William was married to Elizabeth (née Goddard) on 25th July 1875 at the Wesleyan Methodist Church in nearby Farnham; the couple had a son William born on 18th November 1876 at Dover.

On the day after his marriage William and the Battalion were moved to Dover where they formed the garrison being stationed in the Citadel and on 21st June 1877 were posted to Chatham.

With the situation on the Eastern Frontier of the Cape Colony coming to a head, William and the battalion were put on alert on 28th January 1878 for deployment to the Cape.

On 1st February 1878, the battalion left Chatham by rail for Portsmouth and on the next day boarded the troopship *Himalaya* and set sail for South Africa. William was accompanied by his wife, however, his young son was left in England under the care of his maternal grandparents, Charles and Harriet Goddard.

After a good voyage, William and "B" Company was one of the first to be landed at East London on 9th March 1878 and by 14th March was at his assigned station in the defensive line guarding King William's Town. His wife and the other families were sent to the safety of Durban.

As part of company "B", William moved to the defence of King William's Town and was stationed at Hudson's Store, in the defensive line. In the middle of March the company were involved in an attack on the Rebula heights and drove the rebels through Hayne's mill before returning to Baillie's Grave.

In May 1878, William and "B" company were involved in operations on Mount Kempt were they remained until the war was ended with a general amnesty on 28th June 1878.

With preparations underway for the invasion of Zululand, the battalion were ordered to Natal and after setting sail from King William's Town on 24th–26th July landed at Durban.

On arriving at Durban, William discovered that his wife was gravely ill, suffering from tuberculosis and while the rest of the Battalion set out to join the invasion force he was given a leave of absence to care for his wife.

While caring for his wife in Duban, William supplemented his income by working as a cobbler, repairing shoes.

Unfortunately William's wife Elizabeth died on 11th October 1878 and after the funeral he began the journey to rejoin his regiment, eventually meeting up with them at Rorke's Drift by the middle of January 1879.

It was during the defence of Rorke's Drift on 22nd/23rd January 1879 that William performed the deeds for which he would later be awarded the Victoria Cross.

William remained at Rorke's Drift until the middle of April 1879 and then on 4th July 1879 took part in the Battle of Ulundi.

For his service during the war, William was awarded the South Africa Medal with clasp for 1877–8–9.

After the end of the War, William was at Pietermaritzburg where the battalion had just received orders for their deployment to Gibraltar. It was while at Pietermaritzburg, that William was examined by a medical tribunal on 3rd September 1879, where he was diagnosed as suffering from chronic rheumatism and ordered home.

Not long after returning to England, William was admitted to the Royal Military Hospital at Netley for treatment of his arthritis.

William was presented with his Victoria Cross Medal by Queen Victoria on 13th January 1880 at a ceremony held in Windsor Castle.

As a result of his arthritis diagnosis, William was declared unfit for further service and on 2nd February 1880, after over 21 years of service, was discharged from the army with the award of the Army Long Service and Good Conduct Medal.

After leaving the army, William moved to 174 Lupin Street in Birmingham and during the 1881 census was shown as a warehouseman, being a visitor to the home of Charles and Elizabeth

Frodham who were living at Court 3, 6 Love Lane, Duddeston in Aston with their five children.

William had great difficulties in finding continuous employment in Birmingham and for a time performed with Hamilton's Pansterorama in Rochdale, where dressed in his uniform he recited his experiences at Rorke's Drift.

By 1891, William was living as a boarder at 8 Luxton Street, Duddleston in Aston with Elizabeth Frodsham and her now seven children; Elizabeth's husband Charles had moved out.

In 1892, William toured Lancashire with the Buffalo Bill Wild West Show where he performed as a narrator during an enactment of the battle at Rorke's Drift.

On 16th July 1901, William married Elizabeth Frodsham (née Walters) now a widow, at St Augustine's Church in Newton Heath, Manchester.

Due to his bad health, William still had great difficulty in finding employment and in 1910 was forced to pawn his Victoria Cross Medal for the sum of £6, to help feed his family.

William was found wandering, in an "impoverished condition" in 1912 and his wife Elizabeth had to collect him from the Bridge Street Workhouse in Salford and return with him to their home at 72 Sanderson Street, Collyhurst in Manchester.

William died at his stepdaughter's home at 6 Brompton Street, Ardwick in Manchester on 15th April 1913 at the age of 73. He was buried in an unmarked pauper's grave, with military honours, in the Philips Park Cemetery in Bradford, Manchester; a headstone was erected in 2007.

William's Victoria Cross Medal is on public display at the South Wales Borderers Museum, Brecon, Powys in Wales.

Figure 177a. Grave of William Jones

Robert Jones

22nd/23rd January 1879 (VC No. 371)

Gazetted: 2nd May 1879 24717/3178

Rank and Unit: Private No. 716 – 2nd Battalion 24th Regiment of Foot

Citation

In another ward, facing the hill, Private William Jones and Private Robert Jones defended the post to the last, until six out of the seven patients it contained had been removed.

The seventh, Sergeant Maxfield, 2nd Battalion 24th Regiment, was delirious from fever. Although they had previously dressed him, they were unable to induce him to move. When Private Robert Jones returned to endeavour to carry him away, he found him being stabbed by the Zulus as he lay on his bed.

Biography

Robert was born at Tynewydd, Clytha near Raglan in Monmouthshire on 19th August 1857 to father Robert a farm labourer and mother Hannah (née Fryer). He was one of 16 children with nine brothers and six sisters.

Robert worked as a farm labourer, alongside his father, until on 12th January 1876 at the age of 18 and much against his family's wishes he enlisted in the army at Brecon.

On 28th January 1876, Robert had been assigned as Private No. 716 to Company "B" in the 2nd battalion of the 24th Regiment of Foot and joined his regiment on garrison duties at the Dover Citadel.

On 21st June 1877, the battalion were posted to Chatham but with the situation on the Eastern Frontier of the Cape Colony coming to a head, Robert and the battalion were put on alert on 28th January 1878 for deployment to the Cape.

On 1st February 1878, the battalion left Chatham by rail for Portsmouth and on the next day boarded the troopship *Himalaya* and set sail for South Africa.

After a good voyage, Robert and "B" Company was amongst the first troops to be landed at East London on 9th March 1878 and by 14th March was at his assigned station in the defensive line guarding King William's Town.

As part of company "B", Robert moved to the defence of King William's Town and was stationed at Hudson's Store, in the defensive line. In the middle of March the company were involved in an attack on the Rebula heights and drove the rebels through Hayne's mill before returning to Baillie's Grave.

Figure 178. Robert Jones

In May 1878, Robert and "B" company were involved in operations on Mount Kempt were they remained until the war was ended with a general amnesty on 28th June 1878.

On 18th July 1878, Robert was tried for being drunk while on guard duty and having been found guilty served 14 days in prison.

With preparations underway for the invasion of Zululand, the battalion were ordered to Natal and after setting sail from King William's Town on 24th–26th July landed at Durban and marched to Pietermaritzburg where they arrived on 6th August 1878.

On 11th January 1879, Robert with his battalion were part of the 3rd invasion column, commanded by Colonel R. T. Glyn, that crossed into Zululand after the expiry of the ultimatum issued to the Zulu Chief Cetywayo to dismantle his armies.

When the bulk of the column moved off to a camp at Isandhlwana, Robert and company "B", under the command of Lieutenant Gonville Bromhead were detached to guard the mission station at Rorke's Drift which had been set up by the army as a supply base and hospital.

It was during the defence of Rorke's Drift on 22nd/23rd January 1879 that Robert performed the deeds for which he would later be awarded the Victoria Cross. During the action Robert received three spear wounds, two to his right side and one to the left, he also received a bullet wound.

Robert remained at Rorke's Drift until the middle of April 1879 and then on 4th July 1879 took part in the Battle of Ulundi.

For his service during the war, Robert was awarded the South Africa Medal with clasp for 1877–8–9.

On 9th September 1879, the Battalion received orders to go to Gibraltar and after a march of 250 miles reached Pietermaritzburg on 14th November, where they received a tremendous welcome.

Robert was presented with his Victoria Cross Medal by General Sir Garnet Wolseley, the GOC of troops in South Africa, at a ceremony held at Utrecht in the Transvaal on 11th September 1879.

After some delay while awaiting transportation the battalion set sail on *SS Ontario* and reached Gibraltar on 12th February 1880 where they were quartered in the Casemate barracks.

On 31st July, following the disaster at the Battle of Maiwand in Afghanistan, the battalion received orders to make ready for a deployment to India and on 12th August 1880 boarded *SS Orontes* and set sail for Bombay where they arrived on 1st September 1880.

The next day the battalion moved to Poonah but two weeks later on 15th September they set out for Secunderabad by rail where they would remain until the end of 1883.

Robert left India in advance of the battalion and by 1st July 1881 was serving with the depot companies at Brecon.

On 27th January 1882, Robert was transferred to the 1st Class Army Reserve until 2nd August 1882 when he was recalled to army service with his old regiment which was now named the South Wales Border Regiment.

Robert was once again transferred to the Army Reserve on 7th February 1883.

On 7th January 1885, Robert was married to Elizabeth (née Hopkins) at Llantilio near Abergavenny; the couple would go on to have five children, Robert, Ellen, Mary, Rose and May.

Robert was discharged from the army, at the end of his enlistment period, on 26th January 1888 and he moved his family to Peterchurch in Herefordshire where they set up home in Rose Cottage.

Robert found work as a grounds man on the estate of Major de la Hay of Crossways House.

Although he was a good father to his children and a talented amateur poet, Robert still suffered from his experiences and wounds from the Zulu War, experiencing severe head pains from one of the wounds and having nightmares about the attack on Rorke's Drift.

In August 1898, he suffered a collapse and although he quickly recovered, his wife noticed a change in his personality and he began to drink more heavily.

On 6th September 1898, on reaching his place of work, Richard borrowed a shotgun and two cartridges, saying that he was going out to shoot vermin (crows).

A few minutes later gunshot fire was heard and Robert was discovered in Major de la Hay's garden, dead from a shot to the head.

An inquest returned a verdict of suicide, while of unsound mind; this was strongly disputed by the family who believed his death was the result of a tragic accident as he was crossing uneven ground and the shotgun had a hair trigger.

Although suicide generally excluded a burial on consecrated soil an exception was made in Robert's case because of his Victoria Cross, however, the following conditions were applied, his coffin was not allowed through the main churchyard entrance and had to be passed over a wall and his headstone had to face in the opposite direction to all of the other headstones in the churchyard.

Robert was buried on 8th September 1898 in St Peter's Churchyard, Peterchurch.

Robert's Victoria Cross Medal is on public display at the Imperial War Museum in London as part of the Lord Ashcroft collection.

Figure 178a. Grave of Robert Jones

John Williams (Fielding)
22nd/23rd January 1879 (VC No. 372)

Gazetted: 2nd May 1879 24717/3177

Rank and Unit: Private No. 716 – 2nd Battalion 24th Regiment of Foot

Citation

Private John Williams was posted with Private Joseph Williams, and Private William Horrigan, 1st Battalion 24th Regiment, in a distant room of the hospital, which they held for more than an hour, so long as they had a round of ammunition left: as communication was for the time cut off, the Zulus were enabled to advance and burst open the door; they dragged out Private Joseph Williams and two of the patients, and assagaied them.

Whilst the Zulus were occupied with the slaughter of these men a lull took place, during which Private John Williams, who, with two patients, were the only men now left alive in this ward, succeeded in knocking a hole in the partition, and in taking the two patients into the next ward, where he found Private Hook.

These two men together, one man working, whilst the other fought and held the enemy at bay with his bayonet, broke through three more partitions, and were thus enabled to bring eight patients through a small window into the inner line of defence.

Biography

John was born at Merthyr Road, Abergavenny on 24th May 1857 to father Michael and mother Margaret (née Godsil) and was the second of ten children.

In 1862 the family moved to Cwmbran and in 1865, John at the age of 8 was employed in the Patent Nut and Bolt Factory in the town.

In February 1877, just before his 20th birthday, John embarked upon his career in the army when he enlisted with the Royal Monmouthshire Militia. To prevent his family discovering that he had joined the army he enlisted under the name of John Williams, the name that he used throughout his army life.

John enlisted with the 24th Regiment of Foot at Monmouth on 27th May 1877 and was assigned to "B" Company as Private No. 1393 Williams.

On 21st June 1877, John joined the battalion at Chatham but with the situation on the Eastern Frontier of the Cape Colony

Figure 179. John Williams

coming to a head, John and the battalion were put on alert on 28th January 1878 for deployment to the Cape.

On 1st February 1878, the battalion left Chatham by rail for Portsmouth and on the next day boarded the troopship *Himalaya* and set sail for South Africa.

After a good voyage, John and "B" Company were amongst the first troops to be landed at East London on 9th March 1878 and by 14th March was at his assigned station in the defensive line guarding King William's Town.

As part of company "B", John moved to the defence of King William's Town and was stationed at Hudson's Store, in the defensive line. In the middle of March the company were involved in an attack on the Rebula heights and drove the rebels through Hayne's mill before returning to Baillie's Grave.

In May 1878, John and "B" company were involved in operations on Mount Kempt were they remained until the war was ended with a general amnesty on 28th June 1878.

With preparations underway for the invasion of Zululand, the battalion were ordered to Natal and after setting sail from King William's Town on 24th–26th July landed at Durban and marched to Pietermaritzburg where they arrived on 6th August 1878.

On 11th January 1879, John with his battalion were part of the 3rd invasion column, commanded by Colonel R. T. Glyn, that crossed into Zululand after the expiry of the ultimatum issued to the Zulu Chief Cetywayo to dismantle his armies.

When the bulk of the column moved off to a camp at Isandhlwana, John and company "B", under the command of Lieutenant Gonville Bromhead were detached to guard the mission station at Rorke's Drift which had been set up by the army as a supply base and hospital.

It was during the defence of Rorke's Drift on 22nd/23rd January 1879 that John performed the deeds for which he would later be awarded the Victoria Cross.

John remained at Rorke's Drift until the middle of April 1879 and then on 4th July 1879 took part in the Battle of Ulundi.

For his service during the war, John was awarded the South Africa Medal with clasp for 1877–8–9.

On 9th September 1879, the Battalion received orders to go to Gibraltar and after a march of 250 miles reached Pietermaritzburg on 14th November, where they received a tremendous welcome.

After some delay while awaiting transportation the battalion set sail on *SS Ontario* and reached Gibraltar on 12th February 1880 where they were quartered in the Casemate barracks.

On 1st March 1880, John was presented with his Victoria Cross Medal on the Almeda Parade Ground at Gibraltar by Major-General Anderson the General Officer Commanding troops in Gibraltar.

On 31st July, following the disaster at the Battle of Maiwand in Afghanistan, the battalion received orders to make ready for a deployment to India and on 12th August 1880 boarded *SS Orontes* and set sail for Bombay where they arrived on 1st September 1880.

The next day the battalion moved to Poonah but two weeks later on 15th September they set out for Secunderabad by rail where they would remain until the end of 1883.

In October 1883, John was returned to England ahead of his battalion and was discharged to the army reserve where he served as a Sergeant with the 3rd Volunteer Battalion of the South Wales Borderers.

John was married to Elizabeth (née Murphy) at Pontypool in Monmouthshire some time in 1884; the couple would go on to have three sons and two daughters. One son, Thomas, was killed on 26th September 1914 during the retreat from Mons, while serving as Private No. 8391 with the 1st Battalion of the South Wales Borderers.

After 16 years of army service, John was discharged from the reserve on 22nd May 1893.

With the outbreak of the Great War, John volunteered his services and was employed in a civilian capacity at Brecon Barracks where he assisted with recruitment; he served in this capacity until 1920 when he was discharged suffering from bronchitis.

On 26th June 1920, John attended a garden party for Victoria Cross recipients, hosted by King George V at Buckingham Palace.

John attended a dinner for Victoria Cross recipients, at the House of Lords which was hosted by the Prince of Wales.

John was a member of the Union Jack Club at Newport.

For a time John lived at 146 Llantarnam Road in Cwmbran and after the death of his wife at the home of his daughter Margaret at 28 Cocker Avenue in Cwmbran.

It was on 25th November 1832, while visiting another daughter at her home Tycoch in Cwmbran that John died of heart failure at the age of 75, the last surviving Rorke's Drift Victoria Cross recipient.

After lying in state at the Wesley Street Catholic Church, he was buried on 29th November 1932 in St Michael's Churchyard, Llanfhiagel, Llantarnam in Monmouthshire, Wales.

Company Sergeant Major John H. Williams VC DCM MM, a close personal friend attended the funeral representing the Ebbw Vale British Legion.

John's Victoria Cross medal is on public display at the South Wales Borderers Museum, Brecon, Powys in Wales.

Figure 179a. Grave of John Williams

Frederick Hitch

22nd/23rd January 1879 (VC No. 373)

Gazetted: 2nd May 1879 24717/3178

Rank and Unit: Private No. 1362 – 2nd Battalion 24th Regiment of Foot

Citation

It was chiefly due to the courageous conduct of these men that communication with the hospital was kept up at all. Holding together at all costs a most dangerous post, raked in reverse by the enemy's fire from the hill, they were both severely wounded, but their determined conduct enabled the patients to be withdrawn from the hospital, and when incapacitated by their wounds from fighting, they continued, as soon as their wounds had been dressed, to serve out ammunition to their comrades during the night.

Biography

Frederick was born on 29th November 1856 at Chase Side, New Southgate, a hamlet in Edmonton in London, to father John a shoemaker and mother Sarah (née Champress). He was the second youngest of eleven children with six brothers; Samuel born in 1841, Henry born in 1842, John born in 1850, Edward born in 1852, Walter William born in 1853 and younger brother Charles born in 1861. He also had four older sisters; Susan born in 1844 but died in 1845, Sarah born in 1846, Jane born in 1848 and Elizabeth born in 1855.

Frederick, who had little or no formal education was illiterate and it wasn't until his later years that he learnt to read and write.

While working as a bricklayer's labourer, Frederick appeared before the magistrates at Westminster Police Court on 7th March 1877 and having been found guilty of an unknown offence[499] was given the option of joining the army instead of serving a prison sentence – he chose the army.

Frederick was enlisted in the army on the same day and was assigned as Private No. 1362, in company "B" of the 2nd Battalion of the 24th Regiment of Foot and on 11th May 1877 joined his regiment on duty at Chatham.

With the situation on the Eastern Frontier of the Cape Colony coming to a head, Frederick and the battalion were put on alert on 28th January 1878 for deployment to the Cape.

499 The offence must have been relatively minor as he appeared before the Police Court rather than the Sessions or Crown Court.

Figure 180. Frederick Hitch

On 1st February 1878, the battalion left Chatham by rail for Portsmouth and on the next day boarded the troopship *Himalaya* and set sail for South Africa.

After a good voyage, Frederick and "B" Company was amongst the first troops to be landed at East London on 9th March 1878 and by 14th March was at his assigned station in the defensive line guarding King William's Town.

As part of company "B", Frederick moved to the defence of King William's Town and was stationed at Hudson's Store, in the defensive line. In the middle of March the company were involved in an attack on the Rebula heights and drove the rebels through Hayne's mill before returning to Baillie's Grave.

In May 1878, Frederick and "B" company were involved in operations on Mount Kempt were they remained until the war was ended with a general amnesty on 28th June 1878.

With preparations underway for the invasion of Zululand, the battalion were ordered to Natal and after setting sail from King William's Town on 24th–26th July landed at Durban and marched to Pietermaritzburg where they arrived on 6th August 1878.

On 11th January 1879, Frederick with his battalion were part of the 3rd invasion column, commanded by Colonel R. T. Glyn, that crossed into Zululand after the expiry of the ultimatum issued to the Zulu Chief Cetywayo to dismantle his armies.

When the bulk of the column moved off to a camp at Isandhlwana, Frederick and company "B", under the command of Lieutenant Gonville Bromhead were detached to guard the mission station at Rorke's Drift which had been set up by the army as a supply base and hospital.

It was during the defence of Rorke's Drift on 22nd/23rd January 1879 that Frederick performed the deeds for which he would later be awarded the Victoria Cross. During the action Frederick was badly wounded by a bullet which shattered his shoulder.

He was initially treated for his wound at Rorke's Drift by Surgeon Reynolds's VC, who removed 39 pieces of bone from the wound.

Frederick with many of the other injured soldiers was sent to Helpmakaar where he received further treatment from Surgeon D. Blair Brown before being sent to Durban where on board *SS Tamar*, he set sail for England.

For his service during the war, John was awarded the South Africa Medal with clasp for 1877–8–9.

On his arrival back in England Frederick was sent to the Royal Military Hospital at Netley near Southampton where he arrived on 10th June 1879.

Frederick was presented with his Victoria Cross Medal on 12th August 1879, at Netley by Queen Victoria who had travelled to the hospital from Osborne House, accompanied by Princess Beatrice.

Due to his wound, Frederick was considered unfit for further service and was invalided out of the army on 25th August 1879.

On his discharge, Frederick stated that he intended to find work as a bricklayer's labourer, however, with his wounded arm being almost useless it was unlikely that he would ever perform this type of work again.

Fortunately, within five weeks of his discharge, Frederick was given work as a Commissionaire in the Corps of Commissionaires which had been founded in 1859 by Captain Sir Edward Walter.

In July 1881, Frederick was married to Emily (née Meurisse) at Kensington in London; the couple would go on to have eight children; three sons, Frederick born in 1883, Charles born in 1885 and Willie born in 1889 and five daughters, Louise born in 1887, Florence born in 1891, Winifred born in 1894, Dorothy May born in 1901 and Selina born in 1903.

Initially the couple lived at Portchester Square but then were accommodated in the family quarters of the Corps of Commissioners at Exchange Court, just off the Strand.

At some stage, Frederick and his family lived above a pub the "Durweston Arms" on Little Durweston Street, off Crawford Street and for a period it appear that it was operated by him as the sign above the door stated "F. Hitch VC" to be the publican. It appears that Frederick obtained his liquor licence on 7th October 1893 but this was forfeited a few months later on 23rd July 1894.

In addition to his job with the Corps of Commissioners, Frederick also did work for the Imperial Institute in South Kensington as a messenger and caretaker.

It was while working at the Imperial Institute in July 1901, that Frederick fell from a ladder and was knocked unconscious; he awoke in the Charing Cross Hospital and asked about his Victoria Cross Medal which was pinned to his tunic and had been left at the Institute.

A messenger was sent to collect his tunic and medal, however, although the tunic was found the medal was missing and to-date has not reappeared.

Soon afterwards, Frederick stopped working for the Institute which accepted no responsibility for the loss of the medal and in fact may have thought that he had staged the accident to cover up his sale of the medal. At this time Frederick was living with his family at Epirius Mews behind Fulham Broadway.

At some time around the turn of the century, Frederick set up a small transport business in Chiswick, operating horse drawn cabs, apparently a fellow Victoria Cross recipient Joseph Farmer,[500] who also worked at the Corps of Commissioners, was an occasional driver.

In 1908, Frederick received a replacement for his stolen Victoria Cross, following a request from his son to the Army Council; however, he had to pay three pounds seven shillings and six pence for the privilege.

In 1910, with the decline in the popularity of the horse drawn cabs in favour of the new motorised "Taxicabs",[501] Frederick joined the London General Cab Company as a driver.

For a period of time after the death of his wife, Frederick lived as a lodger with his daughter Louisa at her home Flat 12, Pond House Place in Chelsea.

On the 5th January 1813, during a strike of the London taxi drivers, Frederick was in the garden of his lodgings at 62 Cranbrook Road, talking to one of his neighbours when he collapsed.

On the next day his landlady discovered that he had died during the night, of pneumonia and heart failure at the age of 57.

Five days later on 11th January 1913, Frederick was buried in the Chiswick Old Cemetery in St Nicholas's Churchyard. His coffin was carried to the cemetery on board his taxi cab which was hauled by 24 of his fellow cab drivers; over 1,500 London Taxi Drivers attended the funeral as did John Williams VC a comrade from Rorke's Drift.

Frederick's Victoria Cross Medal is on public display at the South Wales Borders Museum in Brecon.

Figure 180a. Memorial to Frederick Hitch

500 Joseph was awarded his VC for action on 27th February 1881, during the Boer War.

501 So called because of the Taximeter with which they were fitted.

Anthony Clarke Booth
12th March 1879 (VC No. 374)

Gazetted: 24th February 1880 24814/832

Rank and Unit: Sergeant No. 919 – 80th Regiment of Foot

Citation

For his gallant conduct on the 12th March, 1879, during the Zulu attack on the Intombi River, in having, when considerably outnumbered by the enemy, rallied a few men on the south bank of the river, and covered the retreat of fifty soldiers and others for a distance of three miles.

The Officer Commanding 80th Regiment reports that, had it not been for the coolness displayed by this Non-commissioned Officer, not one man would have escaped.

Figure 181. Anthony Clarke Booth

Biography

Anthony was born on 21st April 1846 at Carrington, Basford near Nottingham to father William a lace maker and mother Sarah (née Clarke). He was one of six children with an older brother Herbert born in 1841 and four sisters, Mary born in 1842, Sarah born in 1844, Lucy born in 1850 and Emily Ann born in 1852.

It is probable that, from his birth until joining the army, Anthony lived at Bulwell Lane, Club Row, Carrington, Basford near Nottingham.

On 28th October 1864 at the age of 18½ Anthony left his job as an apprentice tailor and enlisted in the Army, at Sheffield. He had previously tried to enlist with the Royal Marines but had been rejected on medical grounds.

He was assigned as Private No. 919 in the 80th Regiment of Foot on 31st October 1864 and joined his regiment at Bullevant, Co Cork in Ireland on 10th November 1864.

In March 1865, Anthony and the regiment were moved to Chatham in Kent but after a few months were transferred to the recently opened Tregantle Fort in Devon, part of the new defences for Portsmouth.

Anthony was promoted to the rank of Corporal on 1st July 1865, however, a few weeks later, after being confined for improper conduct, he was reduced in rank back to Private on 4th September 1865.

On 18th September 1866, Anthony was married to Lucy (née O'Brien) at Stoke Damerel, near Portsmouth. The couple would go on to have seven children; one daughter Florence born in 1873 at Hong Kong and six sons;[502] Herbert born in 1867 at Portland, Anthony born in 1868 at Fleetwood, William born in 1870 at Belfast, Harry Charles born in 1875 at Hong Kong, Andrew born in 1881 at Dublin and Albert born in 1883 at Tralee in Ireland.

In 1866, the regiment was posted to Portland until 1867 when they were moved to Aldershot before moving to Fleetwood in 1868.

In 1869, the regiment was posted to Ireland and was initially stationed at Birr in Co Tipperary, where on 20th April 1869, Anthony was once again promoted to the rank of Corporal.

The regiment moved to Belfast in 1870 and it was here on 5th September 1871 that Anthony re-engaged after the completion of his initial period of enlistment to extend the period to 21 years.

On 1st January 1872, Anthony was promoted to the rank of Sergeant and soon afterwards on 12th January 1872 boarded the troopship *Orontes* and set sail for his first period of overseas service in the Straits Settlements in Malaya.

Anthony served with his regiment at Singapore until 27th November 1872 when he was seconded to the Commissariat Department and sent to Hong Kong to serve as acting Barrack Sergeant.

Following the assassination of Mr James W. W. Birch, the first British Resident of Perak, in November 1875 Anthony and his regiment were amongst the troops sent to Perak to quell the civil unrest; during the Perak War he saw action in Perak, Malacca and Rassa.

For his service during the war, Anthony was awarded the India General Service Medal (1854) with clasp for Perak.

On 15th February 1876, Anthony was back on Commissariat Duties at Singapore.

Anthony was promoted to the rank of Colour Sergeant on 3rd April 1876.

502 Four of his six sons would also go on to serve with the 80th Regiment of Foot

On 11th March 1877, Anthony and the regiment set sail for South Africa, where trouble was brewing on the eastern borders of the Cape Colony, and landed at East London.

In June 1878, after leaving his wife and family at Pietermaritzburg, Anthony and the regiment were despatched to Pretoria where they arrived on 15th August 1878.

Anthony was involved in the first invasion of Zululand in early January 1879 and on 9th February 1879 was part of an escort for a convoy of stores being despatched to Luneberg.

On the 11th February 1879, Anthony reverted back to the rank of Sergeant.

It was on 12th March 1879, during the Battle of Intombi, when the convoy was attacked by about 500 Zulu warriors, that Anthony performed the deeds for which he would later be awarded the Victoria Cross.[503]

On the day after the battle, Anthony was once again elevated to the rank of Colour Sergeant.

Antony was also involved in the second invasion of Zululand and took part in the decisive Battle of Ulundi on 4th July 1879, which ended the war.

For his service during the war, Anthony was awarded the South Africa Medal with clasp for 1878–79.

On 11th May 1880, Anthony and his family boarded the troopship *Orontes* at Cape Town and set sail for home arriving at Dublin towards the end of the month where they were quartered in the Richmond barracks.

Anthony was presented with his Victoria Cross Medal on 26th June 1880 by Queen Victoria in a ceremony held at Windsor Castle.

On 19th October 1881, Anthony once again reverted back to the rank of Sergeant.

Anthony was presented with the Army Long Service and Good Conduct Medal on 1st July 1883 and in September moved with the regiment from Dublin to Lichfield.

On 15th March 1884, Anthony was once again promoted back to the rank of Colour Sergeant.

While serving at Lichfield, Anthony spent 32 days in hospital, between 1st April 1885 and 2nd May 1885, suffering from pneumonia.

Towards the end of 1885, between 6th–11th October, Anthony spent a further six days in hospital at Fleetwood, suffering from dyspepsia.

In 1886, Anthony spent a further two periods in hospital at Lichfield; 12 days between 5th–17th February for bronchitis and 8 days between 6th–13th August when he suffered from bronchial catarrh.

503 Anthony was initially recommended for an award of the DCM, however, on the insistance of Lord Chelsford this was changed to a recommendation for the award of a Victoria Cross.

Anthony spent a further period in hospital at Lichfield for 10 days between 26 March 1888 and 4th April 1888, again suffering from bronchitis.

On 16th May 1888, Anthony was transferred to 1st Volunteer Battalion of the South Staffordshire Regiment as Colour Sergeant for "C" company and a Sergeant Drill Instructor.

Based at Brierly Hill in Staffordshire, Anthony set up home at 19 William Street in Brierly Hill.

On 30th April 1898, after over 33 years of service, Anthony was retired to pension at Lichfield.

Anthony died at his home in Brierley Hill on 8th December 1899 from Jaundice following rheumatic fever and at the age of 53 was buried four days later in St Michael's RC Churchyard in Brierely Hill.

His Victoria Cross Medal is on public display at the Staffordshire Regimental Museum, Whittington Barrack in Lichfield, Staffordshire.

Figure 181a. Grave of Anthony Clarke Booth

Redvers Henry Buller
28th March 1879 (VC No. 375)

Gazetted: 17th June 1879 24734/3966

Rank and Unit: Captain and Brevet Lieutenant-Colonel – 60th Rifles

Citation

For his gallant conduct at the retreat at Inhlobana, on the 28th March, 1879, in having assisted, whilst hotly pursued by Zulus, in rescuing Captain C. D'Arcy, of the Frontier Light Horse, who was retiring on foot, and carrying him on his horse until he overtook the rear guard.

Also for having on the same date and under the same circumstances, conveyed Lieutenant C. Everitt, of the Frontier Light Horse, whose horse had been killed under him, to a place of safely.

Later on, Colonel Buller, in the same manner, saved a trooper of the Frontier Light Horse, whose horse was completely exhausted, and who otherwise would have been killed by the Zulus, who were within 80 yards of him.

Biography

Redvers was born on 7th December 1839 at Downes House, Crediton in Devon to father John Wentworth a Liberal Member of Parliament and mother Charlotte Juliana Jane (née Molyneux-Howard). His father also ran the family estates which extended to some 5,000 acres and brought in a sizable income.

He was one of eleven children with six brothers; James Howard born in 1835, Ernest Wentworth born in 1841, Herbert Molyneux born in 1843, Arthur Tremayne born in 1850, Mowbray Charles born in 1851 and Audley Cecil born in 1853. He also had four sisters; Julia Elizabeth, Adele Catherine, Henrietta Isabella and Alice Mary.

At the age of seven Redvers was sent to a boarding school in Exmouth run by Reverend John Penrose where he started his formal education, before spending a short time at Eton and completing his education at Harrow.

Sometime in 1857 while spending time at the family home, Redvers severely injured his leg while chopping wood, the local doctor actually advised amputation. Although he recovered from the injury and retained his leg, Redvers never fully got over the injury which caused him some troubles for the rest of his life.

Figure 182. Redvers Henry Buller

Having decided on a career in the army, on 23rd May 1858, Redvers purchase a commission as Ensign in the 60th Regiment[504] and on 14th July joined the rifles depot at Winchester.

On 7th January 1859, Redvers set out on his journey to join his regiment in India; after *HMS Ceylon* conveyed him to Alexandria he crossed the desert to Suez and boarded *HMS Alma* for the voyage to India where he joined the headquarters of the 1st Battalion on station at Benares.

On 28th February 1860, Redvers and the regiment set sail from India, on board *HMS Hougoumont* bound for China, in the build-up to the second Opium War.

After spending some time in the Stanley Barracks at Hong Kong the regiment departed on 24th July and landed at Peh-Tang on 1st August 1860, as part of the Anglo-French invasion force.

With the force commanded by Sir James Hope Grant, Redvers was involved in the third Battle of Taku Forts on 12th–21st August 1860 and the occupation of Peking on 13th October 1860, which ended the war.

For his service during the war, Redvers was awarded the 2nd China War Medal (1857–60) with clasps for Taku Forts (1860) and Peking (1860).

Although he was untouched by the fighting in China, Redvers had a bad experience when a horse kicked him in the mouth; he lost his front teeth which would render his speech to be indistinct for the rest of his life. He also nearly lost his life through drowning.

Redvers and his regiment were the last to leave Peking on 9th November when they moved to Tientsin to spend the winter.

In September 1861, the regiment left China and on 2nd November 1861 set sail, from Hong Kong, on board *SS Simdon*

504 *London Gazette* – 22142/2518

for England; after a voyage via the Cape of Good Hope, Redvers arrived back in England on 24th February 1862 where the battalion was stationed in the Cambridge Barracks at Portsmouth.

On 9th December 1862, Redvers advanced his position in the regiment when he purchased a commission as Lieutenant[505] and was despatched to join the 4th Battalion on duty in Canada based at Quebec.

During his time in Canada, Redvers served under Colonel Robert Beaufoy Hawley from whom he learned much of the skill of soldiering and modern army practices.

Redvers was placed in charge of the "Look Outs" in 1867, these were 15 posts on the Canadian border with the USA, established to prevent deserters escaping to America. This was an arduous command which involved Redvers covering over 1,000 miles each month by horse as he inspected each of his commands.

In 1868, when the Adjutant Lieutenant Brownrigg departed on a long leave, Redvers was persuaded to undertake the role on an acting basis.

In 1869, the battalion returned to England, however, after Redvers purchased a commission as Captain on 28th May 1870[506] he was posted to the 1st battalion and returned to Canada where they were stationed at Toronto.

Redvers joined the battalion, at Thunder Bay on 10th June 1870, just in time to take part in the Red River Expedition, Commanded by Colonel Garnet Wolseley.

The objective of the Expedition was to oust Louis Riel and his French speaking Métis who had established an illegal provisional government at the Red River Colony with their main base at Fort Garry.

Fort Garry was in a very remote location and from Thunder Bay it required a hazardous river journey of about 650 miles. It was during this journey that Redvers was nearly drowned but was saved by his servant called Lemar.

The expedition reached Fort Garry on 21st August 1870 and entered unopposed; Louis Reil and his supporters having fled just before the British arrival.

The expeditionary force returned to Montreal via their arrival route, however, General Wolseley gave Redvers the job of taking a party via an alternative route known as Snow's Road to evaluate its usefulness. Having successfully completed his task, Redvers arrived back at Montreal in mid-October.

Soon after arriving at Montreal, Redvers was returned to England.

For his service during the campaigns in Canada, Redvers was awarded the Canadian General Service Medal (1866–70) with clasps for Fenian Raid 1866, Fenian Raid 1870 and Red River 1870.

Towards the end of 1871, Redvers entered the Staff College and in August 1873, while on the continent studying the battlefields of the Franco-Prussian war had a premonition that General Wolseley needed him.

On returning to England Redvers discovered that General Wolseley had indeed been trying to contact him, for an appointment on his staff for the upcoming Ashanti Expedition; he was appointed as Deputy Assistant Adjutant and Quartermaster General with responsibility for intelligence.

General Wolseley and his Staff set sail on board *SS Ambriz* from Liverpool on 12th September 1873 bound for West Africa and the start of the 3rd Anglo-Ashanti War.

The *SS Ambriz* reached Sierra Leone on 29th September and General Wolseley assumed command of the British forces in the West Africa settlements. On 2nd October, General Welseley established his headquarters at Cape Coast Castle on the Gold Coast.

Within two weeks of landing on the Gold Coast, Redvers intelligence services was bearing fruit and on 14th October resulted in an attack on Elmina and surrounding villages where large stock of Ashanti stores were found and destroyed.

On 25th October Redvers succumbed to fever and dysentery and was hospitalised on board *HMS Simoom*, by the end of the first week in November, General Welseley and 7 out of 10 of his staff officers were also struck down and hospitalised.

By the 4th December, the Ashanti army had been forced back across the Prah river and the first phase of the war was completed.

Following the landing of the main expeditionary force in January 1874, the British fought the Battle of Amoaful on 31st January and occupied the Ashanti capital Coomassie on 4th February, the King have recently abandoned the place.

On 3rd February, during the march towards Coomassie, Redvers received a bullet wound to his right shoulder.

For his service during the war, Redvers received mentions in despatches and was awarded the Ashantee Medal (1873–74) with clasp for Coomassie. The war was ended with the treaty of Fomena signed in July 1874.

While on his journey to the coast to make ready for his return to England, Redvers was struck down by Cape fever and had to spend a few days on board *HMS Argus* for treatment before boarding *HMS Simoom* for his return to England.

For his service during the war, Redvers was appointed as an Ordinary Member 3rd Class (Companion) of the Military Division of the Most Honourable Order of the Bath on 31st March 1874.[507]

505 *London Gazette* – 22688/6269

506 *London Gazette* – 23619/2745

507 *London Gazette* – 24082/1921

On the next day he also received a brevet promotion to the rank of Major.[508]

With the death of his older brother James on 13th October 1874, Redvers inherited the family estates.

From 1st April 1874, on his return from western Africa, Redvers worked as Deputy Assistant Adjutant General working under Sir Richard Airey at the War Office in Horse Guards.

On 30th January 1878, Redvers was appointed to special service with General Thesiger who was off to replace General Sir Arthur Cunynghame as commander of troops in the Cape Colony.

General Thesiger and his team set sail from Plymouth on board *SS American* on 1st February 1878 and set sail for South Africa, landing at Cape Town on 25th February 1878.

During the 9th Kaffir War, Redvers initially served as Staff Officer to Commander Frost, a civilian in charge of Colonial Irregular forces at Kabousie. This unusual arrangement only lasted about five weeks as on 22nd April, Redvers was given command of the Frontier Light Horse.

Redvers led the Frontier Light Horse in operations against the Gaika tribesmen in the Perie Bush surrounding King William's Town until the campaign came to a close in June 1878.

On 7th July 1878. Redvers and the Frontier Light Horse were despatched to Natal in the Transvaal, to assist with the mounting troubles with the Zulu nation.

By 23rd August, the Frontier Light Horse had arrived at Pietermaritzburg and soon afterwards joined Colonel Evelyn Wood VC at Utrecht.

Redvers received a brevet promotion to the rank of Lieutenant-Colonel on 11th November 1878.[509]

On 11th January 1879, Redvers and the Frontier Light Horse were part of the 4th Column, commanded by Colonel Evelyn Wood, of the force that invaded Zululand.

Redvers and his regiment were at Bemba's Kop on the Blood River acting in support of the advance of the centre column, however, after the disaster at Isandhlwana the planned attack on the Zulu capital Ulundi was abandoned and the force moved to Kambula to await reinforcements from England.

With the second phase of hostilities, it was during an attack on Inhlobana Mountain on 28th March 1879, that Redvers performed the deeds for which he would later be awarded the Victoria Cross; saving the lives of Captain D'Arcy, Lieutenant Everitt and Trooper Rundall.

On the following day, Redvers was part of the force involved in the Battle of Kambula where the British force of 2,100 men successfully fought off about 22,000 Zulu warriors.

508 *London Gazette* – 24082/1925
509 *London Gazette* – 24650/6683

On 4th July 1879, Redvers took part in the decisive Battle of Ulundi where he commanded the mounted troops.

For his service during the war, Redvers received several mentions in despatches and was awarded the South Africa Medal (1977–79) with clasp for 1878–79.

On 5th August 1879, Redvers boarded *SS German* at Cape Town and set sail for home, arriving at Plymouth on 26th August 1879.

Following the inheritance of the family estate, Redvers was appointed as a Commissioner for Land Tax and other Rates and Taxes for the county of Devon on 19th August 1879.[510]

Not long after his return to England, Redvers was invited to visit Queen Victoria at Balmoral on 9th September and during the visit the Queen presented him with his Victoria Cross Medal.

Soon after the visit he was appointed as an Aide-de-Camp to Queen Victoria on 27th September with the rank of Colonel.[511]

Due to the vagaries of the system, even though Redvers had a rank of Colonel in the Army, his regimental rank was still only that of Captain and on 12th September 1879, he was returned to the regimental roll of the 60th Rifles after his secondment to South Africa.[512]

On 19th December 1879, Redvers was appointed as an Ordinary Member 3rd Class (Companion) of the Most Distinguished Order of St Michael and St George,[513] bestowed for his services in the Amatola Mountains.

Redvers was promoted to the rank of Major on 13th March 1880.[514]

On 8th April 1880, Redvers was placed on half pay and appointed as Assistant Adjutant and Quartermaster General of the North Britain Division,[515] a position that he held until 1st July 1880 when he was transferred, in the same capacity to Aldershot.[516]

In early 1881, Redvers was about to board ship and join the 2nd Battalion of the 60th Rifles on service in Afghanistan when the Duke of Cambridge countermanded these orders and on 24th February 1881 appointed him to the post of Deputy Adjutant and Quartermaster General to the forces in South Africa.

After reaching South Africa, Redvers was directed to Newcastle, where on 12th March he was appointed as Chief of Staff to General Sir Evelyn Wood; a few days later he was promoted to

510 *London Gazette* – 24753/5048
511 *London Gazette* – 24765/5652
512 *London Gazette* – 24783/6427
513 *London Gazette* – 24793/7483
514 *London Gazette* – 24822/2016
515 *London Gazette* – 24832/2440
516 *London Gazette* – 24857/3590

Brigadier-General with the local rank of Major-General while in South Africa.[517]

Redvers had arrived in South Africa just as the 1st Boer War came to a close, on 23rd March 1881 when General Wood was instructed by London to conclude a peace.

General Wood was the acting Governor of Natal as well as the Commander in Chief of troops in South Africa, and now as his second in command Redvers acted as administrator of the colony while the General was away in Pretoria.

With little likelihood of a flare-up of trouble with the Boers, as a treaty had finally been ratified, Redvers left South Africa on 6th December 1881 and arrived back in England early in the new year.

Redvers spent the first seven month of 1882, looking after affairs at the family estates.

On 10th August 1882, Redvers was married to Lady Audrey Jane Charlotte (née Townsend) the widow of Grenville Theophilus Howard, at St Margaret's in Westminster, London. The couple would go on to have a daughter, Audrey Charlotte Georgiana who was baptised on 3rd September 1883.

On 21st August, while on his honeymoon in Belgium, Redvers received a letter from General Sir Garnet Wolseley, requesting that he join him in Egypt. Returning to England that evening Redvers left London on 25th August on his way to Ismailia where an Expeditionary Force was being assembled.

After arriving at Port Said six days later, Redvers boarded *HMS Hecla* which transported him to Ismailia, via the Suez Canal, where he arrived on 1st September and on the next day was appointed as Chief of the Intelligence Department by General Wolseley.

Redvers reconnoitred Egyptian positions and on 13th September 1882 was present at the Battle of Tel-el-Kebir.

For his service during this phase of the Anglo-Egyptian war, Redvers received several mentions in despatches and was awarded the Egypt Medal (1882–89) with clasp for Tel-el-Kebir. He was also appointed as a Commander of the 3rd Class of the Order of Osmanieh by Turkey and was awarded the Khedive's Star (1882) by Egypt.

On 1st October 1882, Redvers left from Cairo to return to England and after an absence of only six weeks was back at home by 10th October 1882.

On 24th November 1882, Redvers was appointed as an Ordinary Member 2nd Class (Knight Commander) of the Most Distinguished Order of St Michael and St George,[518] bestowed for his services in Egypt.

Redvers was appointed Assistant Adjutant-General on the staff at the War Office on 22nd July 1883.[519]

On the 9th February 1884, Redvers received orders to join the Expeditionary Force under the command of General Sir Gerald Graham VC, that was being assembled to invade the Sudan.

Redvers, who had been appointed as commander of the 1st Infantry Brigade boarded *HMS Helicon* on 12th February and set sail for Alexandria where after some delays he landed on 21st February. On the next day he boarded *SS Damanhour* and by 27th February had arrived at the bay of Trinkitat where the invasion force was still being assembled.

On 29th February, Redvers took part in the Battle of El Teb and on 13th March 1884 at the Battle of Tamai was instrumental in avoiding a potential disaster by quickly re-forming his troops and those of the 2nd Battalion after a sudden charge by the Sudanese tribesmen.

For his service during the war in Sudan, Redvers was awarded the clasps for El-Teb-Tamai and Suakin 1884 to his Egypt Medal (1882–89).

Redvers left Egypt on board *SS Utopia* on 1st April 1884 and arrived back in London about two weeks later and after a short holiday resumed his role as Assistant Adjutant-General at the War Office.

On 21st May 1884, he also received a brevet promotion to the rank of Major-General for his distinguished service in the Sudan.[520]

By the end of August 1884, the British Government had finally agreed to mount an expedition to relieve General Charles Gordon who was besieged at Khartoum and appointed Lord Wolseley as overall commander.

On 26th August 1884, General Wolseley appointed Redvers as the Chief of Staff to the expedition with the primary responsibility to transport the expeditionary force up the river Nile to Korti which was to be the assembly point for the attack on Khartoum.

On the same day, Redvers left for Trieste where on 29th August he boarded the *SS Espero* and set sail for Alexandria where he landed on 9th September.

Redvers arrived at Cairo on 3rd September and on the 27th September accompanied General Wolseley and his staff on their journey to Wadi Halfa where they arrived on the 5th October 1884.

On 16th November, General Wolseley received a letter from General Gordon informing him that his supplies would last only until the 14th December.

517 *London Gazette* – 24960/1734
518 *London Gazette* – 25171/5319
519 *London Gazette* – 25248/3426
520 *London Gazette* – 25356/2278

Redvers estimated that the relief force would not be assembled at Korti until 22nd January 1885, so it was agreed to send an expedition of the Camel Corps, under the command of Colonel Sir Herbert Stewart across the desert to Metemmeh and from there up river to Khartoum.

On 28th January 1885, General Wolseley received news that Colonel Stewart and his deputy Colonel Burnaby had both been killed and the expedition was stalled at Metemmeh which had been reinforced by Mahdist forces from Khartoum.

On the next day, having handed over his duties as Chief of Staff to Sir Evelyn Wood VC, Redvers left Korti, instructed by General Wolseley to take over the command of the desert expedition.

On 3rd February 1885, Redvers reached Gakdul where he receive the news that after a siege which had started on 18th March 1884, Khartoum had fallen on 26th January 1885 and General Gordon and his garrison had all been slaughtered.

Redvers joined up with the desert column at Gubat on 11th February with orders that now required him to abandon the advance on Khartoum and return to Korti.

With Khartoum having fallen to the Mahdi forces, the garrison at Gubat was threatened by a force of 10,000 men, so Redvers had little alternative but to evacuate the town and retreat back over the desert to Korti.

At Korti, Redvers reverted to his duties as Chief of Staff until on 11th May orders were received from London to withdraw all British troops from the Sudan and finally in the Autumn he managed to return back to England.

For his service during this part of the war in Sudan, Redvers received several mentions in despatches and was awarded the clasp for Nile (1884–85) to his Egypt Medal (1882–89).

On 25th August 1885, Redvers was appointed as an Extra Member 2nd Class (Knight Commander) of the Military Division of the Most Honourable Order of the Bath.[521]

Redvers was appointed as Deputy Adjutant-General to the forces on 1st November 1885 and took up his position at the War Office.[522]

On 24th August 1886, Redvers was sent to Ireland where he was employed in a civil capacity as head of Police in Kerry and Clare to restore law and order in Co Kerry and reorganise the police force.

Redvers was appointed as Under-Secretary for Ireland with a position on the Irish Privy Council, on 15th November 1886 and moved to Dublin.

Redvers returned to military duties on 15th October 1887 when he was appointed as Quartermaster-General at the War Office[523] with the rank of Major-General.

521 *London Gazette* – 25505/4050
522 *London Gazette* – 25524/4980
523 *London Gazette* – 25840/4013

During his time at the War Office, Redvers did much to reorganise the army supply and transport departments, culminating in the creation of the Army Service Corps on 11th December 1888.

On 1st October 1890, Redvers was appointed as Adjutant-General to the forces with the temporary rank of Lieutenant-General,[524] in succession to Lord Wolseley.

Redvers was promoted to the rank of Lieutenant-General on 1st April 1891[525] and on 29th April was given the temporary rank of General while serving in his position as Adjutant-General.[526]

On 4th May 1892, Redvers was appointed as Honorary Colonel to the 1st Volunteer Battalion of the Devonshire Regiment.[527]

In 1893, Redvers was offered the position of Commander-in-Chief in India to succeed Lord Roberts, due to personal reasons the offer was declined.

On 26th May 1894, Redvers was appointed as an Ordinary Member, 1st Class (Knight Grand Cross) of the Military Division of the Most Honourable Order of the Bath.[528]

Redvers was appointed as Colonel Commandant of the Kings Royal Rifle Corps on 13th July 1895.[529]

In 1895, with the upcoming retirement of HRH the Duke of Cambridge, Redvers was offered the position of Commander-in-Chief of the British Army; as a matter of principal Redvers declined the offer as he believed that a better suited candidate was Lord Wolseley and he would not be a party to him being superseded.

The government of the day refused to nominate Lord Wolseley, however, the government fell and the new government did appoint Lord Wolseley to the position.

On 24th June 1896, Redvers was promoted to the rank of General.[530]

Redvers continued in the position of Adjutant-General until his term expired on 31st September 1897 and he was replaced the next day by General Sir Evelyn Wood VC.[531]

In celebration of Queen Victoria's Jubilee, Redvers was awarded the Queen Victoria Jubilee Medal in 1897.

On 1st February 1898, Redvers was appointed to the committee that was making arrangements for the British participation in the 1900 Paris Exhibition.[532]

524 *London Gazette* – 26088/4998
525 *London Gazette* – 26152/2061
526 *London Gazette* – 26156/2311
527 *London Gazette* – 26284/2555
528 *London Gazette* – 26516/3115
529 *London Gazette* – 26643/3946
530 *London Gazette* – 26759/4095
531 *London Gazette* – 26895/5321
532 *London Gazette* – 26935/673

Redvers was appointed to the Staff position of Commander of troops at Aldershot on 9th October 1898.[533]

In the spring and summer of 1899, when war with the South African Republic seemed to be unavoidable, Redvers was advised in June that he had been selected as Commander-in-Chief of South African forces in the event of a conflict.

What became known as the 2nd Boer War was officially declared on 11th October 1899 and would last until 31st May 1902.

Finally, on 9th October 1899, Redvers was appointed as General Commander-in-Chief of British forces in South Africa[534] and on 14th October set sail from Southampton bound for the Cape where he arrived at Cape Town on 30th October.

When Redvers arrived at the Cape, matters were dire; almost all of the 15,000 men designated to defend southern Natal, together with his Chief of Staff and other staff officers, were besieged in Ladysmith and the whole of the colony lay at the mercy of the Boers.

In the Cape Colony, things were not much better with the Boers occupying the northern territories.

Redvers had left England with a mission to make an attack on the Boer Transvaal Colony but in reality his first priority was to secure the British Colonies of the Cape and Natal before anything else.

It soon became obvious that Redvers needed to be closer to the main seat of war in Natal, so he left Cape Town and landed at Durban on 25th November where reinforcements arrived just in time to save Maritzburg and check the advance of the Boers.

On 17th December 1899, Lord Roberts was appointed to succeed Redvers as Commander-in-Chief of Forces in South Africa but he would not arrive in the colony until 9th February 1900.

Redvers retained command of the troops in the Natal colony.

The relief of Ladysmith was Redvers next objective, however, he suffered three setbacks with defeats at the Battle of Colenso on 15th December 1889, the Battle of Spion Kop on 23rd–24th January 1900 and the Battle of Vaal Krantz on 5th–7th February 1900.[535]

Victory at the Battle of Tugela Heights on 14th–17th February 1900 paved the way for the final relief of Ladysmith on 28th February 1900 after 118 days besieged.

While Lord Roberts, with large reinforcements from England concentrated on clearing the Cape Colony, including the relief of Kimberley on 15th February 1900 after 124 days of siege and the relief of Mafeking on 17th May 1900 after 217 days of siege, Redvers set out to clear Natal.

On 18th May 1900, Newcastle was back in British hands and after extensive operations the Boers had been cleared from most of northern Natal.

In June 1900, Redvers and his force advanced into the Transvaal and had notable success against strong positions at Alleman's Nek and Laing's Nek.

After further operations in the Transvaal, Redvers relinquished command of the Natal Field Force on 10th October 1900 and on 24th October set sail for England from Cape Town arriving at Southampton on 9th November 1900.

For his service during the war, Redvers was awarded the Queen's South Africa Medal (1899–1902) with clasps for Cape Colony, Tugela Heights, Orange Free State, Relief of Ladysmith, Laing's Nek and Belfast.

On 17th November, soon after his return to England, Redvers met with Queen Victoria at Windsor Castle.

On 10th January 1901, Redvers resumed his position as Commander of the troops at Aldershot.[536]

Redvers was appointed as an Ordinary Member 1st Class (Knight Grand Cross) of the Most Distinguished Order of St Michael and St George on 19th April 1901.[537]

On 1st October 1901, following the merger of the Aldershot command into the 1st Army Corps, Redvers was given command of the Corps.[538]

The appointment was criticised in the press and the War Office did little to defend Redvers and would not allow him to defend himself. On 10th October 1901, at a public lunch he made a speech which caused the government to remove him from his command.

Although he was still on the active list, Redvers military career was now over and he retired to the family estate at Downes on which he now concentrated his attention.

On 23rd October 1906, after over 48 years of service, Redvers was formally discharged from the army when he was placed on retirement pay.[539]

Redvers at the age of 68 died at his home, Downes House, Crediton on 2nd June 1908 from bladder and liver cancer and was buried with military honours three days later at the Churchyard of the Holy Cross, Crediton.

His Victoria Cross Medal is on public display at the Royal Green Jackets Museum in Winchester.

533 *London Gazette* – 27013/5921

534 *London Gazette* – 27126/6178

535 Winston Churchill was acting as a war correspondent in South Africa during this time.

536 *London Gazette* – 27267/396

537 *London Gazette* – 27306/2698

538 *London Gazette* – 27360/6400

539 *London Gazette* – 27960/7113

William Knox Leet
28th March 1879 (VC No. 376)

Gazetted: 17th June 1879 24734/3966

Rank and Unit: Major – 1st Battalion 13th Regiment of Foot

Citation

For his gallant conduct, on the 28th March, 1879, in rescuing from the Zulus Lieutenant A. M. Smith, of the Frontier Light Horse, during the retreat from the Inhlobana.

Lieutenant Smith whilst on foot, his horse having been shot, was closely pursued by the Zulus, and would have been killed had not Major Leet taken him upon his horse and rode with him, under the fire of the enemy, to a place of safety.

Figure 183. William Knox Leet

Biography

William was born on 3rd November 1833 at Dalkey in Co Dublin, Ireland to father Edward Patrick who was rector at the local church, his mother Sarah (née Knox) was the daughter of a wealthy businessman.

He was the last born of seven children with four brothers and two sisters; all of his brothers had military careers three in the Army and one in the Royal Navy.

After graduating from Trinity College, Dublin, William decided on a career in the army and was commissioned as an Ensign in the 13th Light Infantry on 4th July 1855.[540]

On 1st February 1856, William advanced his position within the regiment when he purchased a commission as Lieutenant.[541]

William saw his first overseas service when on 16th March 1856, the regiment was posted to Malta on garrison duties. From 20th June 1856 the regiment was transferred to Gibraltar where they remained until 9th July 1856 when they returned to England.

After a short time back in England, William and the regiment departed for South Africa to the Cape Colony where they remained until 5th November 1857 before being deployed to India.

From 22nd August 1857 until 1st August 1858, William was acting paymaster for the regiment.

William saw his first active service after arriving at Calcutta where he was involved in the latter stages of the Indian Mutiny in various operations under General Lord Mark Kerr.

During 1858, William served as Staff Officer to Major Cox in Field Forces for operations in Central India and Trans-Gogra, including Gorakhpur and Oudh.

540 *London Gazette* – 21741/2597
541 *London Gazette* – 21845/366

William took part in the Battle of Amorah on 25th April 1858 and again on 31st May at the Battle of Nuggar on 9th June 1858.

On 2nd August 1858, William was appointed as Adjutant to the regiment.[542]

William saw further action at Jugdespore on 28th October 1858, at Toolespore on 23rd December 1858 and actions at Bootwall on 25th and 28th March 1859.

For his service during the mutiny, William received two mentions in despatches and was awarded the Indian Mutiny Medal (1857–58).

From 21st January 1863 until 8th October 1863, William served as the station staff officer at Dum Dum.

William and the regiment returned to England on 3rd March 1864 and soon afterwards he resigned from his position as Adjutant on 21st June 1864.[543]

His resignation was probably in anticipation of promotion to the rank of Captain, which he purchased on 4th November 1864.[544]

From 1st August 1867 until 10th March 1869, William served as an Instructor in Musketry.

William spent a short time with the garrison in Gibraltar from 20th August 1870 until 29th September 1871 when he returned to England and was appointed as Captain Instructor at the School of Musketry at Hythe on 30th September 1871 a position that he held until 30th June 1872.

On 12th April 1871, William was married to Charlotte Elizabeth Anne (née Sherlock) at the Church of the Holy Trinity in Cork, Ireland; the couple would have two children, Bertie Fielding Knox born on 26th April 1873 at Maughal in Co Cork and

542 *London Gazette* – 22187/4317
543 *London Gazette* – 22865/3168
544 *London Gazette* – 22908/5207

Dedley Knox born on 2nd June 1881 at the Raglan Barracks in Devonport.

On 1st July 1872, William was appointed to the position of Deputy Assistant Adjutant and Quartermaster General of the Cork District in Ireland.

When the 1st Battalion set sail from South Africa in 1875, as William was in command of two depot companies from the 2nd Battalion he had to remain at his post in Ireland until 30th September 1877.

On 1st October 1877, William received a brevet promotion to the rank of Major[545] and on 24th November 1877 was removed from the supernumerary list and posted back to his regiment the 1st Battalion of the 13th Regiment of Foot with the rank of Captain.[546]

William, now back on the regiment's strength was posted to join them in South Africa where he arrived on 14th May 1878 having been promoted to the rank of Major on 1st May 1878.[547]

In October 1878, William took part in the Sekukuni Campaign and in December marched to Utrecht where they joined column no.4 commanded by General Evelyn Wood for the upcoming invasion of Zululand.

On 7th February 1879, William was placed in command of a unit called "Wood's Irregulars" who were a group of disaffected Zulus prepared to fight against King Cetywayo.

Before the column was involved in the hostilities, William had the misfortune to wrench his knee during a tug-of-war competition between officers of the 13th and 90th Regiments of Foot. When the troops moved out to attack Hlobane on 28th March 1879, William was ordered to stay behind, because of his injured leg, however, he insisted in taking part and led his unit into battle.

It was during the Battle of Hlobane on 28th March 1879, that William performed the deeds for which he was later awarded the Victoria Cross, after saving the life of Lieutenant A. Metcalf-Smith. William himself would probably have lost his life but for the selfless action of Lieutenant Duncombe who was killed while holding back the Zulu warriors and giving William time to escape.

Despite his injury, William also led the Irregulars during the Battle of Kambula on the following day.

William commanded the Irregulars until 5th May 1879 and returned to England on 5th September 1879, for his service during the war he received mentions in despatches and was awarded the South Africa Medal (1877–79) with clasp for 1878–79.

545 *London Gazette* – 24508/5463
546 *London Gazette* – 24532/7251
547 *London Gazette* – 24585/3242

On 29th November 1879, while based at the Raglan Barracks in Devonport, William received a brevet promotion to the rank of Lieutenant-Colonel.[548]

William was presented with his Victoria Cross Medal by Queen Victoria on 9th December 1879, at a ceremony held at Windsor Castle.

On 1st July 1881, William was promoted to the rank of Lieutenant-Colonel and on 1st May 1883[549] was appointed to the command of the 2nd Battalion of the Regiment.[550]

William was promoted to the rank of Colonel on 29th November 1883.[551]

On 2nd November 1885, William and his battalion left England for India as part of the Burma Expeditionary Force for the 3rd Anglo-Burmese War.

For his service during the war, William received mentions in despatches and was awarded the India General Service Medal (1854–95) with clasp for Burma (1885–87).

Having completed four years service in command of a battalion and being over the mandatory retirement age, William was retired to pension on 1st May 1887 with the honorary rank of Major-General.[552]

Figure 183a. Grave of William Knox Leet

548 *London Gazette* – 24787/6840
549 *London Gazette* – 24999/3681
550 *London Gazette* – 25247/3378
551 *London Gazette* – 25297/6523
552 *London Gazette* – 25704/2924

With effect from 1st July 1887, William was appointed as an Ordinary Member 3rd Class (Companion) of the Military Division of the Most Honourable Order of the Bath.[553]

On retiring from the army, after over 22 years of service William moved to South London and it was at his home Grove House in Great Chart, near Ashford in Kent, that on 29th June 1898 he died at the age of 65 and was buried in the St Mary the Virgin Churchyard in Great Chart.

William's Victoria Cross medal is on public display at the Somerset Light Infantry Museum, Taunton, Somerset.

553 *London Gazette* – 25812/2466

Henry Lysons
28th March 1879 (VC No. 377)

Gazetted: 7th April 1882 25093/1586

Rank and Unit: Sub-Lieutenant – 90th Light Infantry (Perthshire Volunteers)

Citation

On the 28th March, 1879, during the assault of the Inhlobane Mountain, Sir Evelyn Wood ordered the dislodgment of certain Zulus (who were causing the Troops much loss) from strong natural caves commanding the position in which some of the wounded were lying.

Some delay occurring in the execution of the orders issued, Captain the Honourable Ronald Campbell, Coldstream Guards, followed by Lieutenant Lysons, Aide-de-Camp, and Private Fowler, ran forward in the most determined manner, and advanced over a mass of fallen boulders, and between walls of rock, which led to a cave in which the enemy lay hidden.

It being impossible for two men to walk abreast, the assailants were consequently obliged to keep in single file, and as Captain Campbell was leading, he arrived first at the mouth of the cave, from which the Zulus were firing, and there met his death, Lieutenant Lysons and Private Fowler, who were following close behind him, immediately dashed at the cave, from which led several subterranean passages, and firing into the chasm below, succeeded in forcing the

Figure 184. Henry Lysons

occupants to forsake their stronghold. Lieutenant Lysons remained at the cave's mouth for some minutes after the attack, during which time Captain Campbell's body was carried down the slopes.

Biography

Henry was born on 13th July 1858 at Morden, Kingston-upon-Thames, the 2nd son of father Daniel a distinguished army officer and mother Harriet Sophia (née Bridges).

One of five children, Henry had four brothers; Daniel born on 15th July 1857, Arthur born in 1859 who died in 1861, Charles born on 8th April 1960 and Frederick born on 3rd June 1861.

After completing his education at Wellington College in Sandhurst, Henry enlisted in the Kings Own 1st Staffordshire Militia on 31st July 1875 and was commissioned as a 2nd Lieutenant.[554]

On 21st July 1877, Henry was promoted to the rank of Lieutenant.[555]

Henry left the Militia and enlisted with the regular army on 11th May 1878 and was commissioned as a Sub-Lieutenant with the 90th Light Infantry (Perthshire Volunteers).[556]

Soon after his enlistment, Henry left England on 4th July 1878 to join his regiment in South Africa at the Cape Colony.

On 15th December 1878, Henry was appointed as Orderly Officer on the staff of General Evelyn Wood, the commander of the 4th column designated for the invasion of Zululand, and served in this capacity throughout his stay in South Africa.

On 24th January 1879, Henry was involved in the Battle of Zungen Nek one of the first actions in the Zulu War.

It was during the Battle of Hlobane Mountain on 28th March 1879 that Henry performed the deeds for which he would later be awarded the Victoria Cross.

Henry also took part in the Battle of Kambula on 29th March 1879 and the decisive Battle of Ulundi on 4th July 1879.

Henry returned to England with the regiment on 31st July 1879, for his service during the war he received mentions in despatches and was awarded the South Africa Medal (1877–79) with clasp for 1879.

On 15th December 1879, Henry was promoted to the rank of Lieutenant[557] and soon afterwards on 2nd January 1880 set sail for India where the regiment was to serve in Bengal.

Soon after arriving in India, Henry was appointed as Adjutant to the regiment on 21st July 1880.[558]

On the 1st July 1881, the 90th Light Infantry was merged with the 26th Regiment of Foot to form the 2nd Battalion Cameronians (Scottish Rifles).

Henry was presented with his Victoria Cross Medal by Colonel Craig commanding officer at Cawnpore on 18th August 1882.

On 20th November 1882, Henry relinquished his position as Adjutant of the regiment.[559]

Henry left India on 21st December 1882 and with the regiment returned to duties in England.

On 26th May 1884, Henry was seconded for service with the Egyptian Army,[560] and joined his unit soon afterwards in Cairo.

During his time in Egypt, Henry was involved in the Sudan Campaign and the abortive attempt to relieve General Gordon besieged in Khartoum.

For his service during the war, Henry was awarded the Egypt Medal (1882–89) with clasp for The Nile (1884–85). He was also awarded the Khedive's Star (1882) by the Egyptian government.

On 4th October 1885, Henry had relinquished his post with the Egyptian Army and by 10th October 1885 had been moved from the supernumerary list back to the regimental strength.[561]

Henry was seconded to the Staff and appointed as Aide-de-Camp to Brigadier-General J. H. Dunne, the Officer Commanding at Aldershot on 1st February 1886.[562]

While still serving on the Staff, Henry was promoted to the rank of Captain on 23rd June 1886.[563]

On 31st March 1887, Henry relinquished his post as Aide-de-Camp and on 1st June 1887 was appointed as Garrison Adjutant at Dublin.

Henry was moved from the Supernumerary List on 4th April 1888 and was transferred back to the regimental strength of the 2nd Battalion Cameronians.[564]

Henry relinquished his post as Garrison Adjutant at Dublin on 31st January 1889 and at the start of 1890 attended the Staff College at Sandhurst from which he passed out in December 1890.

On 22nd June 1891, Henry was seconded to the Staff and appointed as an Extra Aide-de-Camp to General Sir Evelyn Wood VC, the Officer Commanding at Aldershot,[565] a position that he held until 8th October 1893.

Henry was transferred from the supernumerary list back onto the regimental strength as Captain on 10th October 1893.[566]

554 *London Gazette* – 24232/3818
555 *London Gazette* – 24487/4417
556 *London Gazette* – 24580/2990
557 *London Gazette* – 24845/3068
558 *London Gazette* – 24908/6354
559 *London Gazette* – 25193/535
560 *London Gazette* – 25384/3533
561 *London Gazette* – 25534/5585
562 *London Gazette* – 25599/2978, 25605/3278
563 *London Gazette* – 25614/3795
564 *London Gazette* – 25852/4736
565 *London Gazette* – 26180/3596, 26185/3872
566 *London Gazette* – 26462/6987

On 15th November 1895, Henry was once again seconded to the Staff and appointed as Deputy Assistant Adjutant-General of the Western Command.[567]

In the last quarter of 1897, Henry was married to Vanda Louis (née Treffry) at St Austell in Cornwall.

On 6th April 1898, Henry was promoted to the rank of Major with the Royal Fusiliers (City of London Regiment)[568] and on 14th November 1898 relinquished his position as Deputy Assistant Adjutant-General of the Western Command on the expiry of his term of office.[569]

Henry was promoted to the rank of Lieutenant-Colonel on 12th December 1900 and appointed to the command of the 1st Battalion, the Bedford Regiment.[570]

On 10th February 1904, Henry was appointed as an Ordinary Member 3rd Class (Companion) of the Military Division of the Most Honourable Order of the Bath and on the same day received a brevet promotion to the rank of Colonel.[571]

Henry was appointed as Assistant Quartermaster-General with the rank of Colonel on the staff of the Madras Command in India on 23rd July 1904.[572]

On 30th November 1905, Henry relinquished his staff appointment in India and was given the honorary rank of Major-General,[573] after 28 years of service he retired from the army on half pay on 10th January 1906.

Henry died at his home, 3 Mandeville Place, Marylebone in London on 24th July 1907 and was buried in St Peter's Churchyard, Rodmarton near Cirencester in Gloucestershire.

His Victoria Cross Medal is on public display at the Cameronians Regimental Museum, Hamilton, Lanarkshire in Scotland.

Figure 184a. Grave of Henry Lysons

567 *London Gazette* – 26681/6253, 26683/6671
568 *London Gazette* – 26954/2211
569 *London Gazette* – 27025/6938
570 *London Gazette* – 27255/8377
571 *London Gazette* – 27655/1543
572 *London Gazette* – 27736/7477
573 *London Gazette* – 27912/3248

Edmund John Fowler
28th March 1879 (VC No. 378)

Gazetted: 7th April 1882 25093/1586

Rank and Unit: Private No. 1317 – 90th Light Infantry (Perthshire Volunteers)

Citation

On the 28th March, 1879, during the assault of the Inhlobane Mountain, Sir Evelyn Wood ordered the dislodgment of certain Zulus (who were causing the Troops much loss) from strong natural caves commanding the position in which some of the wounded were lying.

Some delay occurring in the execution of the orders issued, Captain the Honourable Ronald Campbell, Coldstream Guards, followed by Lieutenant Lysons, Aide-de-Camp, and Private Fowler, ran forward in the most determined manner, and advanced over a mass of fallen boulders, and between walls of rock, which led to a cave in which the enemy lay hidden.

It being impossible for two men to walk abreast, the assailants were consequently obliged to keep in single file, and as Captain Campbell was leading, he arrived first at the mouth of the cave, from which the Zulus were firing, and there met his death, Lieutenant Lysons and Private Fowler, who were following close behind him, immediately dashed at the cave, from which led several subterranean passages, and firing into the chasm below, succeeded in forcing the occupants to forsake their stronghold. Lieutenant Lysons remained at the cave's mouth for some minutes after the attack, during which time Captain Campbell's body was carried down the slopes.

Biography

Edmund was born during February 1861 at Crook, Waterford in Ireland to father John and mother Bridget.

On 17th March 1977, at the age of 16 but telling the army that he was 18, Edmund left his job as a butler and enlisted in the army at Waterford where he was assigned to the 90th Light Infantry as Private No. 1317.

After being stationed at Limerick for a few weeks, Edmund moved to Portsmouth on 20th April 1877 and then to Aldershot on 28th June 1877.

On the 9th February 1878, Edmund and the regiment were sent to South Africa where they took part in the Cape Frontier War.

Figure 185. Edmund John Fowler

In December 1878, Edmund and the regiment were assigned to the 4th column designated for the invasion of Zululand, commanded by General Evelyn Wood.

On 24th January 1879, Edmund was involved in the Battle of Zungen Nek one of the first actions in the Zulu War.

It was during the Battle of Hlobane Mountain on 28th March 1879 that Edmund performed the deeds for which he would later be awarded the Victoria Cross.

Edmund also took part in the Battle of Kambula on 29th March 1879 and the decisive Battle of Ulundi on 4th July 1879.

Edmund returned to England with the regiment on 31st July 1879, for his service during the war he received mentions in despatches and was awarded the South Africa Medal (1877–79) with clasp for 1877–8–7.

On 29th January 1880, at Netley, Edmund requested to be discharged from the army and after paying £18 this was effected on 24th February 1880 and he left the army with just less than three years of service.

Edmund re-enlisted in the army at Chatham on 14th February 1882 and was enrolled in the 2nd Battalion of the Royal Irish Regiment as Private No. 373.

On 13th May 1882, Edmund was presented with his Victoria Cross Medal by Queen Victoria at Windsor Castle.

Edmund set sail on board *SS City of Paris* on 11th August 1882 bound for Egypt.

During his time in Egypt, Edmund was involved in the Sudan Campaign and the abortive attempt to relieve General Gordon besieged in Khartoum.

For his service during the war, Edmund was awarded the Egypt Medal (1882–89) with clasp for The Nile (1884–85). He was also awarded the Khedive's Star (1882) by the Egyptian government.

On 19th February 1883, Edmund spent a short time on duty at Malta before returning to England on 28th May 1883 when he was stationed at Aldershot.

Edmund was married to Mary (née Maguire) on 8th July 1883, the couple would go on to have six children; Mary born in 1888 at Plymouth, William born in 1889 in Ireland, Catherine born in1890 at Devonport, Margaret born in 1895 at Birr in Ireland, Patrick born in 1897 at Hamilton in Scotland and Annie born in 1900 at Hamilton.

Edmund left England on 11th September 1883 bound for India, arriving on station at Meerut on 11th November 1883.

On 7th May 1884, Edmund spent 56 days in hospital with Enteric fever and at a medical board on 18th October 1884 it was suggested that he needed a change of climate in order to improve his condition.

Edmund was ordered home on 2nd November 1884 and a few days later he boarded *MS Jumna* on 21st November and set sail for England.

After arriving back in England, Edmund was sent to the military hospital at Netley on 19th December 1884 where for the next 13 days he received treatment for his condition.

On his discharge from hospital, Edmund was transferred to the 1st Battalion Royal Irish Regiment and was posted to Clonmel in Ireland where he arrived on 5th January 1885.

On 2nd February 1889, Edmund extended his period of service to 12 years and a few weeks later on 14th March 1889 was promoted to the rank of Lance-Corporal.

Edmund and the Battalion were posted to Colchester on 10th May 1889 and on 1st June 1889 he was promoted to the rank of Corporal.

On 10th September 1891, Edmund was promoted to the rank of Sergeant and a few weeks later on 9th November 1891 was posted back to Ireland where he was stationed at the Curragh Camp.

Edmund was transferred to the 3rd Battalion (Wexford Militia) of the Royal Irish Regiment on 12th May 1892.

On 21st April 1893, Edmund once again extended his period of service, this time to 21 years.

Edmund was transferred back to the 1st Battalion of the Royal Irish Regiment on 25th July 1894 and on 11th August 1894 was posted to Birr.

On 31st October 1894, Edmund was posted to Limerick and from 20th May 1895 spent 17 days in hospital for treatment of leg ulcers. The leg ulcers, resulting from his Enteric fever while serving in India would continue to plague him for the rest of his service.

Edmund had a further 8 days of treatment for his leg ulcers, in the hospital at Limerick, from 19th June 1895 and had yet more treatment for 21 days starting on 10th December 1895.

On 16th March 1896, Edmund was transferred to the 3rd Battalion Cameronians (Scottish Rifles) and was posted to Hamilton in Scotland where he arrived on 21st March 1896.

Edmund was posted to Lanark on 3rd April 1897 where he was hospitalised for 59 days during which he received his most extensive treatment yet for his leg ulcers, including skin grafts. After his treatment, Edmund returned to Hamilton on 31st May 1897.

On 14th May 1898, Edmund was promoted to the rank of Colour-Sergeant.

By now Edmund's leg ulcers were becoming chronic and following a further 89 days in hospital at Hamilton from 31st July 1898 he was called before a medical board at Edinburgh on 15th November 1898.

The medical board judged that Edmund was unfit for further service and on 13th February 1900, after 18 years of service, he was discharged from the army.

On leaving the army, Edmund moved with his family to Colchester where he lived at Middlewhich Cottage, Old Heath, St Giles and worked as the landlord of the Cups Hotel Tap public house.

Soon afterwards he purchased a pub, the "Live and Let Live" on Stanwell Street; on 13th February 1901, because of his military record, Edmund was acquitted by Colchester Magistrates for selling a gallon of beer (to a Sergeant from the Essex Regiment) after 11 O'clock in contravention of the licensing hours.

Edmund sold his Victoria Cross Medal by auction at Sotheby's in February 1906 for the sum of £42.

At some time after this Edmund purchased a green grocers shop (which was damaged by fire in 1910) and by 1911 was living at 11 Priory Street in Colchester.

Figure 185a. Grave of Edmund John Fowler

At some time Edmund served on the town council.

Edmund died at his home on Brerechurch Road, St Giles on 26th March 1926, at the age of 65, and was buried five days later in Colchester Cemetery.

His Victoria Cross Medal is on public display at the Cameronians Regimental Museum, Hamilton, Lanarkshire in Scotland.

Edward Stevenson Browne
29th March 1879 (VC No. 379)

Gazetted: 17th June 1879 24734/3966

Rank and Unit: Lieutenant – 1st Battalion, 24th Regiment of Foot

Citation

For his gallant conduct, on the 29th March, 1879, when the Mounted Infantry were being driven in by the enemy at Inhlobana, in galloping back and twice assisting on his horse (under heavy fire and within a few yards of the enemy) one of the mounted men, who must otherwise have fallen into the enemy's hands.

Biography

Edward was born on 23rd December 1852 in Cambridge to father Salwey a Captain in the Durham Light Infantry[574] and mother Elizabeth (née Stevenson) who was born in Quebec Canada.

He was the oldest of three children with a brother Henry born in 1855 and a sister Louisa born in 1857.

After his father's death on 24th July 1859, the family moved to 13 Regent Street, East Teignmouth in Devon.

Details of Edward's early education are unknown, however, he attended the Royal Military Academy at Sandhurst as a cadet from 2nd August 1869 until 31st December 1870.

On 23rd September 1871 Edward enlisted in the army and was commissioned as an Ensign in the 1st Battalion of the 24th Regiment of Foot.[575]

Only a few weeks after his enlistment, Edward was promoted to the rank of Lieutenant on 1st November 1871, this was subsequently antedated to 28th October 1871.[576]

On 6th January 1872, Edward set sail from England bound for Malta, to join his regiment who had been serving as the garrison since 1866.

After spending only a short time at Malta, Edward embarked with the battalion on board the Indian troopship *Jumna* and on 29th February 1872 set sail for Gibraltar, where they arrived on 5th March 1872.

On 28th November 1874, Edward with the head-quarters of the battalion boarded the troopship *Himalaya* and set sail for the Cape of Good Hope and landed at Cape Town on 2nd January 1875.

574 His father was studying for a BA at Cambridge University at the time of his birth.

575 *London Gazette* – 23778/4029

576 *London Gazette* – 23812/5870, 23876/3199

Figure 186. Edward Stevenson Browne

A detachment of about 100 men under the command of Captain E. B. Sawbridge was despatched from Cape Town on 6th May 1875 to Griqualand West to subdue disorder in the diamond fields.

On 15th May 1875, Edward was part of a second detachment under the command of Colonel R. T. Glyn also despatched to the diamond fields as a mounted infantry unit.

The two detachments from the 24th joined up at Hope Town on 12th June 1875 and on19th June entered Griqualand West and proceeded to the diamond fields at Kimberley where on their arrival the ringleaders of the disaffected miners were arrested.

Moving on to Barkley, where they arrived on 2nd July 1875 and remained in camp until 11th October when they began the return journey to Cape Town where they arrived in early November.

On 21st April 1877, Edward was one of the men selected to form a mounted infantry corps and was despatched to the Transvaal, which had recently been annexed by the Cape Colony, where they were stationed at Victoria.

With the return of Lieutenant F. Carrington to Cape Town, Edward was given temporary command of the 1st Squadron of the Mounted Infantry on 20th November 1877, a position that he would hold until 31st August 1878.

In August 1878, Edward returned to Pretoria where he was placed in command of the headquarters squadron of Mounted Infantry and under the command of Major J. C. Russell of the 12th Lancers was part of the force engaged in the Sekukuni Expedition.

In December 1878, Edward and the Mounted Infantry moved to the Zululand border and was attached to the 3rd Column of the invasion force commanded by Colonel R. T. Glyn.

On 5th January 1879, Edward was once again given temporary command of the 1st Squadron of Mounted Infantry a position that he would hold until 20th August 1879.

Major J. C. Russell was once again in overall command of the Mounted Infantry and led them in the action at Sirayo's Kraal, the first action of the war, on 12th January 1879.

Part of the Mounted Infantry squadron, about 28 men, was wiped out at the disastrous Battle of Isandhlwana on 22nd January 1879, however, Edward avoided the catastrophe as, with Major Russell and about 80 men, he was accompanying Lord Chelmsford and Colonel Glyn and missed the battle.

Edward took part in the Battle of Inhlobane on 28th March 1879 and at the Battle of Kambula on the next day, where he performed the deeds for which he would later be awarded the Victoria Cross.

On 4th July 1879, Edward was also present at the Battle of Ulundi when the Zulu capital was captured and effectively ended the war.

The battalion received orders on 26th July 1879 to march to Durban and prepare for a return to England and after proceeding via Dundee, Graytown and Pietermaritzburg arrived at Pine Town where they set up camp.

It was at Pine Town on 22nd August 1879, during a special parade that Edward was presented with his Victoria Cross Medal by General Sir Garnett Wolseley, the High Commissioner and General Officer Commanding of British Forces in South Africa.

For his service during the wars in South Africa, Edward received two mentions in despatches and was awarded the South Africa Medal (1877–79) with clasp for 1878–9.

On 27th August, Edward and the battalion boarded the transport *Egypt* and set sail for England, landing at Portsmouth on 2nd October, they marched to the New Barracks in Gosport.

Edward was married to Annie (née Maxton), the widow of Captain Wright of the 106th Regiment of Foot, on 6th November 1879 at Edinburgh, the couple would go on to have four children; Edward Dennis born on 25th August 1880 at Gosport, Ethel Winifred born on 13th November 1881 at Abergavenny, Maurice born on 13th December 1884 at Abergavenny and Elle Maxton born on 9th February 1889 at Dublin.

On 19th May 1880, Edward was promoted to the rank of Captain.[577]

As a consequence of a reorganisation of the army, on 1st July 1881 the 24th Regiment of Foot was redesignated as the South Wales Borderers, at this time Edward was with the 1st Battalion stationed at Colchester.

577 *London Gazette* – 24892/5286

On 19th September 1881, Edward was appointed as Adjutant to the 4th Monmouth Rifle Volunteer Battalion of the regiment,[578] based at Pontypool.

Edward was promoted to the rank of Major on 2nd November 1885.[579]

On 20th September 1886 with his term of office having expired, Edward was released from his position as Adjutant to the 4th Monmouth Rifle Volunteer Battalion of the regiment.[580]

Edward, now with the 2nd Battalion, left England on 3rd May 1889 to join the battalion on duty at Bareilly in India and in November 1890 was moved to Allahabad.

On 3rd November 1891, Edward was seconded to the India Staff Corps and appointed as Deputy Assistant Adjutant-General of Musketry for the Bengal Establishment[581] a position that he would hold until 8th May 1892.[582]

After relinquishing his post on the India Staff Corps, Edward left India to rejoin his battalion on duty at Portsdown in England.

Edward was promoted to the rank of Lieutenant-Colonel on 8th April 1893.[583]

In 1897, the battalion moved to Pembroke in Wales and on 8th April 1897 Edward was promoted to the rank of Colonel and was given command of the 24th Regimental District (the South Wales Borderers) at Brecon.[584]

Edward was awarded the Queen Victoria Jubilee Medal in 1897.

On 4th March 1900, Edward was appointed as Assistant Adjutant-General for the North East District.[585]

Edward was appointed to the command of the 25th Infantry Brigade of the 5th Army Corps, with the temporary rank of Brigadier-General, on 7th September 1902[586] and stationed at York.

On the 3rd December 1902, Edward was appointed as Honorary Colonel of the 2nd Volunteer Battalion of the West Yorkshire Regiment.[587]

Edward was appointed to the command of the 11th Brigade, 2nd Army Corps, Southern Command at Portsmouth on 10th November 1903.[588]

On 24th June 1904, Edward was appointed as an Ordinary Member 3rd Class (Companion) of the Military Division of the Most Honourable Order of the Bath.[589]

Edward relinquished his Command of the 11th Brigade on 4th December 1906[590] and after a career of 35 years retired from the army.

On 16th July 1907, Edward died at his home, La Rouvenaz, Commune du Chatelard, Montreaux in Switzerland, from chronic heart disease at the age of 54.

He was buried in the Protestant Section of Clarens Cemetery, Chemin de Muraz, in Montreaux; his grave was reused in 1991 and the original gravestone was broken up.

Edwards Victoria Cross Medal is on public display at the South Wales Borderers Museum, Brecon, Powys in Wales.

578 *London Gazette* – 25026/5090
579 *London Gazette* – 25561/850
580 *London Gazette* – 25626/4472
581 *London Gazette* – 26248/319
582 *London Gazette* – 26308/4129
583 *London Gazette* – 26423/4049
584 *London Gazette* – 26841/2077
585 *London Gazette* – 27173/1713
586 *London Gazette* – 27474/5964
587 *London Gazette* – 27500/8369
588 *London Gazette* – 27617/7033
589 *London Gazette* – 27688/4008
590 *London Gazette* – 27974/8648

William Leslie De La Poer Beresford
3rd July 1879 (VC No. 380)

Gazetted: 9th September 1879 24760/5395

Rank and Unit: Captain – 9th Lancers

Citation

For gallant conduct in having at great personal risk, during the retirement of the reconnoitring party across the "White Umvolosi River" on 3rd July last, turned to assist Sergeant Fitzmaurice, 1st Battalion 24th Foot (whose horse had fallen with him), mounted him behind him on his horse, and brought him away in safety under the close fire of the Zulus who were in great force, and coming on quickly.

Lord William Beresford's position was rendered most dangerous from the fact that Sergeant Fitzmaurice twice nearly pulled him from his horse.

Figure 187. William Leslie De La Poer Beresford

Biography

William was born on 20th July 1847 at Mullaghbrack, Markethall in Co Armagh Ireland to father John[591] who was the local Rector and mother Christina (née Leslie).

He was the third born of five children, with brothers; John Henry born on 21st May 1844 who had a career in the army and was a Member of Parliament, Charles William born on 10th February 1846 who had a distinguished career in the Royal Navy, reaching the rank of Admiral who was also a Member of Parliament, Marcus Talbot born on 25th December 1848 who had a career in the army and Delaval James born on 19th January 1862 who had a career in the army.

William's initial formal education was at the Reverend Dr Renau's Preparatory School at Bayford which he attended until moving to Eton in 1858.

In 1863, at the age of 16, William left Eton and moved to Bonn in Germany to study French and German under his tutor Dr Perry.

During the spring of 1866, during a walking holiday in the Swiss Tyrol, William was instrumental in saving the life of his tutor Dr Perry, by going for help to a village when the doctor had fallen over a ledge and was suspended from a small tree which had saved him from a further fall.

After three years with Dr Perry, William returned to Ireland where several private tutors helped to prepare him for his chosen career in the army and on 8th June 1867, at the age of 20, he purchased a commission as Cornet in the 14th Hussars but was immediately transferred to the 9th Lancers.[592]

Initially William joined his regiment at the Island Bridge Barracks in Dublin before being moved to Cahir near Waterford which allowed him to spend his free time at the family home at Curraghmore.

In 1868, William and his regiment returned to England where they were stationed at Newbridge until 1869 when they moved to Hounslow and then to Aldershot in 1870.

On 6th July 1870, William advanced his position in the regiment when he purchased a commission as Lieutenant.[593]

In 1872, the regiment moved to Woolwich for six months before moving to York and then in 1874 to Colchester.

Having been informed as early as March 1874 regarding a move to India, it was not until January 1875 that William and the regiment boarded trains for Portsmouth where they boarded the troopship *Euphrates* and set sail for India, arriving at Bombay on 12th February 1875.

By 9th March 1875, the regiment had arrived at their new station at Sealkote where they relieved the 5th Lancers who were returning home.

William was appointed as Aide-de-Camp to Lord Northbrook, Viceroy of India, on 7th December 1875 and was moved

591 On 29th March 1859, John succeeded his brother to become the 4th Marquess of Waterford

592 *London Gazette* – 23260/3228

593 *London Gazette* – 23631/3266

to Calcutta. When Lord Lytton replaced Lord Northbrook on 12th April 1876, William remained on the staff as Aide-de-Camp to the new Viceroy.

William spent the summer of 1876 in Simla, the summer residence of the government and on 27th December 1876 was promoted to the rank of Captain.[594]

On 1st January 1877, William was with the government officials gathered at Delhi for the proclamation of Queen Victoria as the Empress of India.

Towards the end of 1877, Lord Lytton appointed General C. P. Keyes to the command of a Punjab Field Force to subdue the tribes on the North West Frontier, William obtained permission from Lord Lytton to accompany the force.

During the resulting Jowaki Expedition (30th August 1877 to 30th January 1878) William saw his first active service, after which he returned to his duties in Calcutta.

William keenly followed the exploits of the 9th Lancers during the Second Anglo-Afghan War and following the resumption of hostilities, after the murder of the British envoy Mr Cavagnari in Kabul, he requested a leave of absence so that he could join his regiment and take part in the action.

William caught up with his regiment, part of the force commanded by General Sir Samuel J. Browne VC, in time to take part in the Battle of Ali Musjid on 21st November 1878. Soon after Christmas 1878, William returned to his duties in Calcutta as his months leave of absence came to an end.

For his service during the war, William received a mention in despatches and was awarded the Afghanistan Medal (1878–80) with clasp for Ali Musjid.

William was following the events unfolding in South Africa leading up to the Zulu War and after the debacle at the Battle of Isandhlwana was eager to take part in the fighting and again requested a leave of absence, this time for six months.

His leave of absence having been granted, William departed for South Africa and after arriving at Durban in the middle of April 1879 managed to secure the position as Aide-de-Camp to Colonel Redvers Buller to replace Captain Ronald Cambell who had recently been killed in battle.

William joined up with Colonel Buller at Kambula where he was in command of the irregular Cavalry, part of Sir Evelyn Wood's force.

By the 1st of July the force was in the Valley of Umveloosi, opposite the kraal of the Ulundi King and it was on 3rd July 1879, during an attack on Ulundi that William performed the deeds for which he would later be awarded the Victoria Cross.

594 *London Gazette* – 24424/922

For his service during the war, William received a mention in despatches and was awarded the South Africa Medal (1877–79) with clasp for 1879.

After the war, with some leave time still remaining, William decided to make a short visit to England before returning to his duties in India.

As his ship reached Plymouth, the Prince of Wales, who was on board ship in the sound with William's brother Charles, was amongst the first to welcome William and deliver the command from Queen Victoria to proceed to Osborne House on the Isle of Wight.

It was at Osbourne House that William was presented with his Victoria Cross Medal by Queen Victoria on 24th August 1879. During the investiture, William advised the Queen that he could not in honour receive the award unless it was shared with Sergeant O'Toole who he believed deserved greater credit for the action. On his advice the Queen later bestowed the Victoria Cross on Sergeant O'Toole.

After spending only 18 days in England and Ireland, William began the return to India to resume his duties with Lord Lytton.

In the spring of 1880, there was a change of government in England and the new Liberal Prime Minister, Mr Gladstone soon took steps to reverse Lord Lytton's policy regarding Afghanistan, causing him to resign his office as Viceroy of India on 8th June 1880. In his stead, Lord Ripon was appointed as the new Viceroy. Lord Ripon retained the services of William as one of his Aides-de-Camp.

Under the tenure of Lord Ripon, William served under the Military Secretary Major George White VC until he was replaced by Major John Ardagh who only lasted for a short time after which on 28th December 1881, William was offered the position, which he gladly accepted.

In November 1884, Lord Ripon left India and from 13th December 1884 was replaced as the Viceroy of India by the Earl of Dufferin, again William was retained in his position as Aide-de-Camp and Military Secretary by the new Viceroy.

On 15th December 1884, William was promoted to the rank of Major.[595]

After a bad fall while racing at the Calcutta meeting in January 1885, William returned to London for a few months leave to recuperate, returning to India in April 1885.

On 1st January 1886, William was appointed as a Companion of the Most Eminent Order of the Indian Empire.[596]

595 *London Gazette* – 25455/1375
596 *London Gazette* – 25545/5

On 3rd February 1886, after Burma had been annexed by British India on 1st January 1886, William accompanied Lord Dufferin on an Expedition to the new colony.

For his service during the later part of the third Anglo-Burmese War, William received a mention in despatches and was awarded the India General Service Medal (1854–95) with clasp Burma 1885–7.

On 1st July 1887, William received a brevet promotion to the rank of Lieutenant-Colonel for his service during the Burma war.[597]

Lord Dufferin was replaced by Lord Lansdown as Viceroy of India on 10th December 1888 and once again William was retained as Military Secretary to the new Viceroy.

On 3rd December 1890, William was promoted to the rank of Lieutenant-Colonel and placed on half pay.[598]

William was removed from the half pay list and promoted to the rank of Colonel on 1st January 1891.[599]

On the 1st January 1894, William was appointed as a Knight Commander of the Most Eminent Order of the Indian Empire.[600]

William vacated his position as Military Secretary to the Viceroy on 27th January 1894 and was placed on half pay[601] bringing to an end his army career of 27 years; a few weeks later he returned to England.

In June 1894, William was a guest of Lily, the Duchess of Marlborough, at Deepdene in Dorking as part of a party going to Ascot Races.

In September 1894, William returned to India for a few months to attend to some business matters and on his return his engagement to Lily the Duchess of Marlborough was announced.

On 30th April 1895, William was married to Lilian (née Warren) the daughter of Cicero Price, a Commodore in the US Navy, at St George's Church, Hanover Square in London.

This was Lilian's third marriage, having first been married to Louis Hammersley. a wealthy businessman from New York, who left his wife a large fortune and secondly to George Charles Spencer-Churchill, the 8th Duke of Marlborough, who had died in 1892.

The couple would have one child, William Warren born on 4th February 1897.

Throughout his life, William had a passion for horse racing, which during his time in the army in India he was able to enjoy to the full, with great success as an owner and as a rider.

A terrible accident in December 1896, after a fall while riding with the Warnham Stag Hounds which shattered his pelvis, brought his riding exploits to an end, however, he continued in horse racing as an owner.

As an owner, William was very successful, between 1896 and 1900 his stable won 158 races with prize money amounting to over £88,000, however, he only had success in one "Classic" the 1899 1,000 Guineas at Newmarket which he won with his horse Sibola.

William died on 28th December 1900 at Deepdene in Dorking at the age of 53 from dysentery and peritonitis leading to heat failure. He was buried in the family vault at Clonagam Churchyard, Curraghmore, Co Waterford in Ireland on 3rd January 1901.

Williams Victoria Cross Medal is believed to be retained by the family and is not on public display.

Figure 187a. Grave of William Leslie De La Poer Beresford

597 *London Gazette* – 25761/6476
598 *London Gazette* – 26111/6802
599 *London Gazette* – 26126/362
600 *London Gazette* – 26472/2
601 *London Gazette* – 26494/1526

Henry Cecil Dudgeon D'Arcy
3rd July 1879 (VC No. 381)

Gazetted: 10th October 1879 24769/5830

Rank and Unit: Captain – Cape Frontier Light Horse

Citation

For his gallant conduct on the 3rd July, 1879, during the reconnaissance made before Ulundi by the Mounted Corps, in endeavouring to rescue Trooper Raubenheim, of the Frontier Light Horse, who fell, from his horse as the troops were retiring.

Captain D'Arcy, though the Zulus, were close upon them, waited for the man to mount behind him; the horse kicked them both off and though much hurt by the fall and quite alone, Captain D'Arcy coolly endeavoured to lift, the trooper, who was stunned, on to the horse and it was only when he found that he had not strength, to do so that he mounted and rode off.

His escape was miraculous as the Zulus had actually closed upon him.

Biography

Henry was born on 11th August 1850 at Wanganui on the North Island of New Zealand where his father Oliver Barker was serving as a Major with the 65th Regiment of Foot, his mother was Martha (née Buck).

The 7th of nine children, Henry was the 5th son with siblings: Oliver George born in 1834 in Ireland who died on 20th December 1837 at the age of 3; Oliver George Wynyard born on 22nd November 1838 at Kilkenny in Ireland; Ellen Constance who was born in Jersey on 28th November 1840; Edward Stuckley Hill born on 7th February 1844 in Leeds; Richard Keats Henry born on 19th November 1846 at Northfleet in Kent; Angelica Martha born on 4th April 1849 at Wanganui in New Zealand; William John McCleverty born in London during 1856 but died on 3rd May 1863 at 7 years old and Annie Rosalie Eva born on 4th September 1858 born in Kensington, London.

At some time in 1856, Henry returned to England with his family when his father was placed on the unattached list.

In October 1859, after his father purchased a commission with the 18th Regiment of Foot, Henry and his family moved to the Cape Colony in South Africa where his father was stationed on the frontier of British Kaffrarian.

For a time Henry was employed as a clerk in the Civil Service at Grahamstown in the Cape Colony, however, in 1877 with the outbreak of hostilities on the frontier, he was eager to undertake military service for his adopted country.

Figure 188. Henry Cecil Dudgeon D'Arcy

In early 1877, he submitted his resignation to the Civil Service and without waiting for a response enlisted with the Albany Mounted Volunteers as a Trooper and was soon promoted to the rank of Sergeant-Major.

On 20th December 1877, Henry joined the Cape Frontier Light Horse, at King William's Town, as a Sergeant-Major and a few days later on 26th December he was joined in the unit by his childhood friend Edmund O'Toole.

Soon after joining the Cape Frontier Light Horse, Henry received news that his resignation from the Civil Service had not been accepted and that he had been appointed as Justice of the Peace and Inspector of Licences for King William's Town and Peddie.

For a time, Henry was able to carry out his Civil Service duties concurrent with his military service, until he went off to war.

Henry served with the unit, under the command of Major Redvers Buller, in the 9th Frontier War when in July 1878 they moved to Pietermaritzburg and on into Sekhukhuneland for operations against the Pedi in the Transvaal.

With the start of the Anglo-Zulu war, Henry and the unit, now under the command of Captain Robert Johnston Barton, were attached to No. 4 Column of the invasion force as part of Sir Evelyn Wood's flying column.

On 20th January 1879, Henry saw action on Zunewini Mountain and the unit acted as rearguard during the Battle of Hlobane on 28th March 1879,[602] where they suffered heavy losses. They were also involved in the Battle of Kambula on 29th March.

602 Henry was one of six men recommended for their action during the battle but was turned down because he did not belong to an Imperial Regiment (the others Buller, Leet, Browne, Lysons and Fowler all received the award).

In April, Henry was promoted to Captain (Commander) and given command of the regiment when Major Redvers Buller was given command of all the mounted volunteers.

It was on 3rd July 1879, during a reconnaissance in force across the White Mflozi, on the day before the Battle of Ulundi, that Henry performed the deeds for which he would later be awarded the Victoria Cross.

With the breakup of Wood's Flying Column in late July 1879, the unit was assigned to Baker Russell's column until they were disbanded in September 1879 at Pietermaritzburg.

For his service during the war, Henry was awarded the South Africa Medal (1877–79) with clasp for 1879.

Henry was presented with his Victoria Cross Medal on 10th December 1879 at Pretoria by General Sir Garnet Wolseley.

After the presentation at Pretoria, Henry returned to Pietermaritzburg where he became so ill that he was unable to attend his father's funeral on 3rd February 1880, at King William's Town.

On 15th May 1880, Henry had recovered sufficiently to take up the commission of Captain in the recently formed Cape Mounted Riflemen.

In July 1880, Henry led units of the Cape Mounted Riflemen to Basutoland where they took part in the Basuto (Gun) War from September 1880 until April 1881. During the war Henry was involved in the relief of Mafeteng and the relief of Mohalis Hoek.

Due to ill health, Henry sold his commission and resigned from the army on 15th April 1881 and returned to King William's Town where he bought a small farm at Stutterheim.

Being depressed by his illness, Henry turned to drink and was almost certainly an alcoholic when on 4th August 1881 he went to stay with the Reverend Taberer and his wife (friends of his parents) at the St Matthews mission station at Keiskama Hoek, where he hoped that the mountain air would revive his health.

After dinner on the day after his arrival, Henry retired to his bed early saying that he felt very tired, however, in the morning his bed was found to be empty and had not been slept in.

After conducting his Sunday service, the Reverend led a small search party to look for Henry but to no avail so he informed the Stutterheim and King William's Town police of his disappearance and more extensive searches were carried out over the next few days.

On the 11th August, the police received news that a woman had seen a man matching Henry's description, walking off alone into the Perie Bush but after further searching without success hopes of finding Henry alive receded and the search was finally called off.

On 28th December 1881, the remains of a man were found at the bottom of a cliff in the Amatola forest about six miles from the mission station and by a distinctive signet ring and gold hunter watch were identified to be those of Henry.

The body was recovered and on 3rd January 1882, Henry was buried in the family plot at King William's Town cemetery.

Henry's Victoria Cross Medal is not on public display, believed to be in the hands of his family.

On 11th September 1992, an unsubstantiated report was printed in the *Daily Telegraph* which purported that Henry had faked his death by leaving his ring and watch on the remains of a man that he had found dead in the snow.

The report was based upon the tale of a man (a cricketer) from Newcastle in Natal who claimed that 56 years after his reported death he recognised Henry from a photograph and when confronted the man begged him to remain silent as he "*... wished to remain dead to the world*".

Figure 188a. Grave of Henry Cecil Dudgeon D'Arcy

Edmund O'Toole

3rd July 1879 (VC No. 382)

Gazetted: 10th October 1879 24769/5830

Rank and Unit: Sergeant – Cape Frontier Light Horse

Citation

For his conspicuous, courage and bravery on several occasions during the campaign, and especially for his conduct on the 3rd July, 1879, at the close of the reconnaissance before Ulundi, in assisting, to rescue Sergeant Fitzmaurice 1st Battalion 24th Mounted Infantry, whose horse fell and rolled on him, as the troops retired before great numbers of the enemy. When lifted up behind him by Lord William Beresford the man, being half stunned by the fall, could not hold on, and he must have been left had not Sergeant O'Toole, who was keeping-back the advancing Zulus, given up his carbine and assisted to hold Sergeant Fitzmaurice on the horse.

At the time the Zulus were rapidly, closing on them, and there was no armed man between them and Sergeant O'Toole.

Figure 189. Edmund O'Toole

Biography

The origins of Edmund are unclear with some sources claiming a place of birth as Grahamstown, Cape Colony, South Africa, however, with no supporting documentation.

The details which I believe to be correct, because of the supporting documentation, are as detailed below.

It is probable that Edmund was born as Edmond Joseph Toole during 1848 (baptised in Dublin on 23rd July 1848) at Bray in Co Wicklow in Ireland to father Charles Laurence Toole and mother Mary Helena (née Burke). It should be noted that the surname O'Toole and Toole were completely interchangeable at the time.

Edmond was one of eight children with siblings; Charles born in 1841, William born in 1843, Francis Xavier born in 1844, Luke born in 1846, Francis Laurence born in 1850, Henry born in 1853 and Mary born in 1855.

At some stage, (probably in the early 1850s) Edmund and his family moved to England and in 1861 were living in the village of Esh in Co Durham. Edmund and his brother Luke were attending Ushaw College in Co Durham during 1861, his older brother William having attended the college from 1854 until 1859.

It is probable that Edmund and his family moved to the Cape Colony in South Africa at sometime around 1867.

At some stage the family moved to King William's Town in the Eastern Cape and with the increasing levels of unrest on the frontier Edmund was one of the 200 volunteers who joined the Frontier Light Horse on 26th December 1877, when it was founded by Lieutenant Frederick Carrington.

Edmund served with the unit, under the command of Major Redvers Buller, in the 9th Frontier War when in July 1878 they moved to Pietermaritzburg and on into Sekhukhuneland for operations against the Pedi.

With the start of the Anglo Zulu war, Edmund and the unit, now under the command of Captain Robert Johnston Barton, were attached to No. 4 Column of the invasion force as part of Sir Evelyn Wood's Flying Column.

On 20th January 1879, during action on Zunewini Mountain, Edmund helped Trooper Hartley who had been unseated from his horse.

The unit acted as rearguard during the Battle of Hlobane on 28th March 1879, where they suffered heavy losses. They were also involved in the Battle of Kambula on 29th March during which Edmund gave assistance to Trooper Elliot who had been unseated from his horse.

It was on 3rd July 1879, during a reconnaissance in force across the White Mflozi, on the day before the Battle of Ulundi, that Edmund performed the deeds for which he would later be awarded the Victoria Cross.

With the breakup of Wood's Flying Column in late July 1879, the unit was assigned to Baker Russell's column until they were disbanded in September 1879.

For his service during the war, Edmund was awarded the South Africa Medal (1877–79) with clasp for 1879.

Edmund was presented with his Victoria Cross Medal on 16th January 1880 at Fort Napier, Pietermaritzburg by Major-General Clifford VC.

With the military situation in Basutoland and the Transkei deteriorating and conflict escalating to the districts of Herschel, Barkly East, Griqualand East and Maclear; Edmund enlisted on 15th October 1880 with the Herschel Native Contingent and was commissioned as Captain.

Edmund was involved during the Basotho and Transkei rebellions until 1882.

In 1890, Cecil Rhodes decided, as a private venture, to invade, occupy and settle Mashonaland and he raised the Mashonaland Pioneer Column as a private army to accomplish this task. The Pioneers would provide the military force to conquer the land and afterwards would settle the land, occupying and farming the 3,000 acres which they would be granted.

Edmund joined Troop "A", commanded by Major Maurice Heany, an American, at Mafeking where the Pioneer Force was being assembled, sometime in early 1890.

The Pioneer Column left Mafeking on 18th May 1890 and headed north, their initial task being to construct a road through the country and by 11th August had crossed the Tokwi River and were close to their objective of the fertile plains of the highlands.

Having reached the high veldt, the first post in Mashonaland, Fort Victoria, was created in open countryside.

On 12th September 1890, the expedition was halted, where the town of Salisbury now stands, and in the name of the Queen all the land in South Central Africa, not claimed by any civilized power, was annexed to the Empire.

After building a fort at Salisbury, the Pioneer force was disbanded on 30th September 1890; having built a road 400 miles in length, created four forts and annexed Mashonaland (what would become Rhodesia) without a life having been lost.

For his part in the Pioneer Column, Edmund was granted land at Hartfield Hill near Salisbury which he called "Toole Farm" which he tried to cultivate, however, his crops were wiped out by torrential rains.

After the failure of his crops, Edmund sold his farm and is thought to have gone to work for Lionel Cripps at his farm "Cloudlands", but after repeatedly being found drunk was dismissed and returned to Salisbury where he died soon afterwards some time in 1891.[603]

His year of death is disputed as some sources indicate that he tried to enlist in the army in August 1900 to fight in the 2nd Boer War but was rejected because of his age.

In any event, the exact time and location of his death, as well as the place of his burial is currently unknown as is the location of his Victoria Cross Medal.

603 In the book "Northward Trek" by Stanley Portal Hyatt, which is an account of the Mashonaland Expedition, it is reported that Edmund died at Salisbury in 1891.

Richard Kirby Ridgeway
22nd November 1879 (VC No. 383)

Gazetted: 11th May 1880 24843/2968

Rank and Unit: Captain – Bengal Staff Corps – 44th Ghurkha Rifles

Citation

For conspicuous gallantry throughout the 'attack ' on Konoma, on the 22nd November, 1879, more especially in the final assault, when, under a heavy fire from the enemy, he rushed up to a barricade and attempted to tear down the planking surrounding it, to enable him to effect an entrance, in which act he received a very severe rifle shot wound in the left shoulder.

Biography

Richard was born at Oldcastle in Co Meath, Ireland on 18th August 1848 to father Richard a doctor and Fellow of the Royal College of Surgeons and mother Annette (née Adams).

Richard was privately educated before attending the Royal Military College at Sandhurst where upon graduation he was commissioned as an Ensign in the 2nd Regiment of Foot on 8th January 1868.[604]

Only a few weeks after his enlistment, Richard was transferred to the 96th Regiment of Foot.[605]

Figure 190. Richard Kirby Ridgeway

604 *London Gazette* – 23340/54
605 *London Gazette* – 23344/277

On 14th February 1870, Richard was promoted to the rank of Lieutenant.[606]

Richard was appointed to the Indian Army and assigned to the 43rd Bengal Native Light Infantry on 6th January 1872.

Richard was appointed as a probationer in the Bengal Staff Corps on 9th March 1872[607] and on 30th April 1873 received the full value for his commission when his transfer to the Bengal Staff Corps was finalized.[608]

On the 17th May 1873, Richards rank as Lieutenant was confirmed in the Bengal Staff Corps to be effective 14th February 1870.[609]

Richard was married to Emily Maria (Amy) (née Fallon) on 12th July 1871 at Dinapore in India; the couple would have one child a daughter, on 1st March 1881 born at Castlecor in Ireland but unfortunately she was stillborn.

Richard was appointed as adjutant to the 44th Bengal Native Light Infantry regiment on 3rd July 1874.

Following the murder of Lieutenant Holcombe and his survey party at Ninu on 2nd February 1875, Richard, with a detachment of the 44th Bengal Native Light Infantry, was part of the force led by Colonel J. M. Nuttall which left Dibrugarh on 27th February to avenge the attack.

After destroying the villages involved and capturing some of the individuals most directly involved the expedition returned to Dibrugarh on 11th April 1875.

On 13th October 1879, Mr. Damant, the political agent, was killed while visiting the Naga village of Konoma. Captain Reid and the garrison of 43rd Assam Light Infantry, at the village of Kohima was also besieged by Naga tribesmen.

Lieutenant-Colonel Johnstone, the political agent at Manipur, with a force of 2,000 levies relieved Kohima on 26th October 1879 but was not allowed to press on to Konoma and take retribution for the killing of Mr. Damant.

Brigadier-General Nation, Commander in Chief of forces in Assam, began to assemble an expeditionary force at Piphima on 14th November 1879.

Richard and the 44th Bengal Native Light Infantry were at Goalundo, on their way to take part in the Afghan War, were ordered to be part of the expedition against the Naga Hill tribe.

It was during the attack on Konoma on 22nd November 1879, that Richard performed the deeds for which he would later be awarded the Victoria Cross; during the action he was seriously wounded in the right shoulder.

606 *London Gazette* – 23619/2745
607 *London Gazette* – 23838/1359
608 *London Gazette* – 23971/2128
609 *London Gazette* – 23977/2494

For his service during the expedition, Richard received a mention in despatches and was awarded the India General Service Medal (1854–1895) with clasp for Naga 1879–80.

Richard returned to Ireland for treatment to his wound and a period of recovery and on 8th January was promoted to the rank of Captain.[610]

On 6th March 1880, Richard was appointed as 2nd in Command of the 44th Bengal Native Light Infantry.

Owing to his wound, Richard was unable to attend an investiture and his Victoria Cross Medal was sent by registered post to him at his home in Ireland by the War Office on 2nd June 1880.

In December 1883, Richard passed out from the Staff College.

Richard was appointed as Deputy Assistant Quartermaster-General of the Oudh division on 23rd June 1885.[611]

On 8th January 1888, Richard was promoted to the rank of Major.[612]

Richard was appointed as a District Officer 1st Class at Army Headquarters on 23rd April 1889.[613]

After the fixed term of five years, Richard's appointment as Deputy Assistant Quartermaster-General of the Oudh division expired on 23rd June 1890.[614]

On 1st January 1891, Richard was appointed to the command of the 44th Ghurkha Rifles.

Richard commanded his regiment during the Anglo-Manipur War which lasted between 31st March 1891 and 27th April 1891.

For his service during the war, Richard received a mention in despatches and was awarded the NE Frontier 1891 clasp for his India General Service Medal.

On 8th January 1894, Richard was promoted to the rank of Lieutenant-Colonel.[615]

Richard was appointed as Assistant Adjutant-General to the district of Peshawar on 29th April 1895.[616]

During the Tirah Expedition (10th June 1897 – April 1898) Richard served as Assistant Adjutant-General to the 2nd Division of the Tirah Field Force commanded by General Sir William Lockhart.

For his service during the Expedition, Richard was awarded the India Medal (1895–1902) with clasps for Punjab Frontier 1897–98, Samana 1897 and Tirah 1897–98 and after the war he returned to his position in the district of Peshawar.

610 *London Gazette* – 24824/2139
611 *London Gazette* – 25510/4279
612 *London Gazette* – 25798/1710
613 *London Gazette* – 25966/4527
614 *London Gazette* – 26083/4726
615 *London Gazette* – 26499/1832
616 *London Gazette* – 26645/4103

On 8th January 1898, Richard was promoted to the rank of Colonel.[617]

After completing his five year term of office, Richard vacated his position as Assistant Adjutant-General of the Peshawar District on 1st April 1900.[618]

Richard was appointed as an Ordinary Member 3rd Class (Companion) of the Military Division of the Most Honourable Order of the Bath on 30th June 1905.[619]

On 15th December 1905, Richard was placed on the Unemployed Supernumerary List[620] and a few weeks later on 9th January 1906 retired from the army after 37 years of service.[621]

Richard died at the Grand Hotel in Harrogate, Yorkshire on 11th October 1924 and was cremated at the Lawnswood Crematorium in Leeds four days later; his ashes were scattered in the crematorium grounds.

Richard's Victoria Cross Medal is not on public display, it is believed to be in the hands of his family.

617 *London Gazette* – 27008/5653
618 *London Gazette* – 27222/5176
619 *London Gazette* – 27811/4548
620 *London Gazette* – 27864/9012
621 *London Gazette* – 27900/2338

Robert George Scott
8th April 1879 (VC No. 384)

Gazetted: 1st October 1880 24887/5113

Rank and Unit: Sergeant – Cape Mounted Rifles

Citation

For conspicuous gallantry and devotion during an attack on Morosi's Mountain, on the 8th April, 1879, in volunteering, to throw time fuse shells, as hand grenades, over a line of stone barricades, from behind which, the enemy, were bringing a heavy fire to bear on the Colonial Troops, and which it was impossible effectually to return.

After causing all the men of his party to retire under cover, lest the shell should burst prematurely, by which precaution many lives were in all probability saved, Sergeant Scott advanced in a most deliberate manner under a heavy fire, and, having got under the wall, made two attempts to throw shells over it.

At the second attempt, owing to some defect in the fuse, which he had just lighted, the shell exploded almost in Sergeant Scott's hands, blowing his right hand to pieces, and wounding him severely in the left leg.

Biography

Robert was born on 22nd April 1857 at Whittlesey near Peterborough, Cambridgeshire to father Robert Charles a Fleet Surgeon in the Royal Navy and mother Mary Elizabeth (née Sinclair). He

Figure 191. Robert George Scott

was the oldest of four children with siblings; Mary Helen born in 1862, Alexander Francis born in 1868 and John Henry born in 1869.

Between 1870 and 1871, Robert attended Epsom College followed by time at Aberdeen Grammar School.

In the 1870s the government in the Cape Colony were offering significant inducements for men aged between 18 and 30 to join their armed forces. With agents in England, the offer included free transportation to the colony and it was probably through such a scheme that Robert left England for South Africa sometime in early 1876.

On 26th September 1876, Robert was enlisted into the Frontier Armed and Mounted Police at King William's Town, the unit was renamed as the Cape Mounted Rifles in 1878.

From September 1877 until June 1878, Robert was involved in the 9th Cape Frontier War (Xhosa War) against the Gcaleka and Gaika tribes in the Transkei.

Following the Xhosa War, Robert with the Cape Mounted Rifles took part in the Morosi Campaign against the Basuto tribe in the northern Transvaal from March to November 1879.

It was during the Battle of Morosi Mountain on 8th April 1879, that Robert performed the deeds for which he would later be awarded the Victoria Cross. During the action, he was severely wounded in the left leg and had most of his right hand blown away.

For his service in the war, Robert was awarded the South Africa Medal (1877–79) with clasp for 1877–8–9.

It would appear that Robert returned to England for treatment of his wounds and in September 1879 he received a commission as Lieutenant.

Robert was presented with his Victoria Cross Medal by Queen Victoria on 17th December 1880 at an investiture held at Windsor Castle.

The 1881 census, shows Robert living in London as a retired army officer, however, within the next few years he must have returned to South Africa and established a residence at Kimberley, possibly working in the diamond fields.

Robert was married to Constance Mary (née Daniell) at Kimberley on 8th April 1884; the couple would go on to have four children, Dulcie Mary, John Dayrell Sinclair, Robert Falkines Sinclair and Guy Sinclair.

At the start of the 2nd Boer War, Robert was still living in Kimberley, possibly working for the de Beers mining company and from 14th October 1899 until 15th February 1900 was besieged within the town by the Boers.

On 18th October 1899, soon after the 124 day siege started, Robert was commissioned as a Major in the Kimberley Light Horse and helped to defend the town.

In February 1900, after the siege was lifted, Robert formed Scott's Railway Guards,[622] an irregular unit charged with protecting the railway lines between Kimberley and Mafeking to allow the safe passage of supplies.

Robert resigned his commission with the Kimberley Light Horse on 25th March 1900 and assumed the rank of Lieutenant-Colonel in command of the Scott Railway Guards until the unit was disbanded on 31st May 1902.

For his service during the war, Robert received a mention in despatches and was awarded the Queen's South Africa Medal (1899–1902) with clasps for Cape Colony, Orange Free State and Transvaal. He was also awarded the King's South Africa Medal (1901–02) with clasps for South Africa 1901 and South Africa 1902.

On 27th September 1901, for his service during the war in South Africa, Robert was appointed as a Companion of the Distinguished Service Order.[623]

Robert set sail for England in June 1902, at the end of the hostilities, however, at some stage he returned to his home in Kimberley.

Despite bad health, Robert volunteered his services on the outbreak of the Great War and formed the Kimberley Central Commando which with the rank of Lieutenant-Colonel he led throughout the German South West Africa Campaign.

During the war, the commando operated in the region of the Kalahari, and took part in the engagement at Uppington. The hardships entailed by the campaign accentuated his illness, and he died on the 3rd of Oct. 1918, near Wynberg and was buried in the Plumstead Cemetery at Wynberg.

For his service during the Great War, Robert received a mention in despatches and was awarded the 1915–1915 Star, the British War Medal (1914–20) and the Victory Medal (1914–19).

Robert's Victoria Cross Medal is not on public display, as it is presumed to be in the hands of his family.

622 Also known as the Cape Railway sharpshooters and Scott's Sharpshooters.
623 *London Gazette* – 27359/6330

Peter Brown
8th April 1879 (VC No. 385)

Figure 192. Peter Brown

Gazetted: 13th April 1880 24833/2510

Rank and Unit: Trooper – Cape Mounted Rifles

Citation

Trooper Peter Brown, during the assault on Morosi's Mountain on 8th April, 1879, whilst lying under cover waiting for the order to re-commence the advance, heard two men, who had been wounded some time before, crying out for water.

Trooper Brown carried a water-bottle to these men, under a heavy fire, to an adjacent rock to which they had crept for shelter.

Whilst giving the first man water he was wounded severely in the right thigh, and immediately afterwards a bullet shattered his right arm, the use of which he has never recovered.

Biography

Unfortunately very little is known regarding Peter who was reputedly born in Sweden. If Sweden is in fact his birthplace then his name Peter Brown is a name he adopted when he emigrated to South Africa.

Peter's date of birth is also in doubt with sources stating a year of birth as 1862, 1837 or 1832 the date quoted on his death certificate.

Nor knowing the origins of the other dates, I have assumed a date of birth as December 1832 as per his death certificate.

At some stage, Peter and possibly his family emigrated from Sweden to the Cape colony in South Africa and settled in or near King William's Town.

At some stage probably around 1865, Peter enlisted with the Frontier Armed and Mounted Police who were headquartered at King William's Town, the unit was renamed as the Cape Mounted Rifles in 1878.

From September 1877 until June 1878, Peter was involved in the 9th Cape Frontier War (Xhosa War) against the Gcaleka and Gaika tribes in the Transkei.

Following the Xhosa War, Peter with the Cape Mounted Rifles took part in the Morosi Campaign against the Basuto tribe in the northern Transvaal from March to November 1879.

It was during the Battle of Morosi Mountain on 8th April 1879, that Peter performed the deeds for which he would later be awarded the Victoria Cross. During the action, he was severely wounded in the leg and arm, which he subsequently lost the use of.

For his service in the war, Peter was awarded the South Africa Medal (1877–79) with clasp for 1877-8-9.

Robert was presented with his Victoria Cross Medal by Lord Wolseley sometime during 1880 at a parade at King William's Town.

At some stage in 1880, after 15 years of service, Peter was retired to pension as a result of his wounds.

Peter died of Bright's disease on 11th September 1894, aged 62, at the home of a friend Joseph Smiles, 1 Primrose Street in Cape Town, where he lived and was buried in the Woltmade Cemetery in Cape Town.

His plot was later reused and now has a headstone for George Edward and Kevin George Abrahams.

Peter's Victoria Cross Medal is on public display at the Amathole Museum, King Williams Town, Cape Province, South Africa.

Edmund Baron Hartley
5th June 1879 (VC No. 386)

Figure 193. Edmund Baron Hartley

Gazetted: 7th October 1881 25023/4990

Rank and Unit: Surgeon-Major – Cape Mounted Rifles

Citation

For conspicuous gallantry displayed by him in attending the wounded, under fire, at the unsuccessful attack on Morosi's Mountain, in Basutoland, on the 5th June, 1879; and for having proceeded into the open ground, under a heavy fire, and carried in his arms, from an exposed position, Corporal A. Jones, of the Cape Mounted Riflemen, who was wounded.

While conducting him to a place of safety the Corporal was again wounded. The Surgeon-Major then returned under the severe fire of the enemy in order to dress the wounds of other men of the storming party.

Biography

Edmund was born on 6th May 1847 at Ivybridge in Devon to father Edmund who was a surgeon and mother Sophia (née Baron); he was the oldest of five children with brothers Francis born in 1850, Frederick William born in 1852, Arthur Charles born in 1853 and Ernest Basset born in 1855.

From 1867 to 1869, Edmund work as a clerk for HM Inland Revenue Department after which he decided to follow his father into a medical career.

Edmund commenced his medical training at St George's Hospital Medical School in 1869 and graduated as a Member of the Royal College of Surgeons in 1874.

At some time in 1874, Edmund was married to Constance Ellen (née Aldridge) at Holborn in London.

In 1874, after his graduation, Edmund emigrated to South Africa and secured the position as District Surgeon of British Basutoland, apparently the first British medical man to serve in the country; he held this position until 1877.

After leaving Basutoland, Edmund was commissioned as a Surgeon with the Frontier Armed Mounted Police at King William's Town in 1877; the unit was renamed as the Cape Mounted Riflemen in August 1878 and he was appointed as Principal Medical Officer to the unit.

From 1877 until 1879, Edmund served in the Cape Frontier Wars and saw action in the Gcaleka, Gaika, Morosi and Tempu Campaigns.

It was on 5th June 1879, during the Battle at Morosi's Mountain, that Edmund performed the deeds for which he would later be awarded the Victoria Cross.

For his service during the war, Edmund received several mentions in despatches and was awarded the South Africa Medal (1877–79) with clasp for 1877–8–9.

Soon after the end of the war, Edmund returned to the UK to continue his medical studies and in 1880 graduated as a Licentiate of the Royal College of Physicians at Edinburgh.

On his return to South Africa, Edmund, as Principal Medical Officer to the Cape Mounted Rifles, took part in the Basuto Gun War from 1880 until 1881 during which he received two mentions in despatches and at some stage was promoted to the rank of Surgeon-Major.

Edmund was presented with his Victoria Cross Medal on 3rd December 1881 by Brigadier-General Charles M. Clarke in South Africa.

For a period between 1882 and 1883, Edmund served as Principal Medical Officer to forces in Basutoland commanded by General Charles Gordon.

In 1897, Edmund with the Cape Mounted Rifles took part in the suppression of the Bechuanaland Rebellion, during which he was wounded.

For his service during the war, Edmund received a mention in despatches and was awarded the Cape of Good Hope General Service Medal (1880–97) with clasps for Bechuanaland, Basutoland and Transkei.

Edmund served in the 2nd Boer War from 11th October 1899 to 11th June 1902 initial as commanding officer of the Bearer Company supporting the Highland Brigade and subsequently as Principal Medical Officer to the Colonial Forces.

On the advance to the relief of Kimberley, Edmund was involved in the Battle of Belmont and Graspon also known as

Enslin on 23rd to 25th November 1899. He was also involved in the Battle of Magersfontein on 11th December 1899.

On 19th April 1901, Edmund, now with the rank of Lieutenant-Colonel, was appointed as a member of the 3rd Class (Companion) of the Most Distinguished Order of Saint Michael and Saint George.[624]

For his service during the war, Edmund received mentions in despatches and was awarded the Queen's South Africa Medal (1899–1902) with clasps for Cape Colony, Transvaal and Wittebergen; he was also awarded the King's South Africa Medal (1901–02) with clasps for South Africa 1901 and South Africa 1902.

After the war, Edmund was promoted to the rank of Colonel and founded and commanded the Cape Medical Corps.

Edmund retired from the army in 1903, after over 25 years of service, and at some stage returned to England.

From 1910 to 1912, Edmund was in command of six Voluntary Aid Detachments in Somerset and with the outbreak of the Great War was secretary of the Voluntary Aid Detachment Hospital at Seaton in Devon.

Edmund died at his home in Ash near Aldershot from heart failure following a period of influenza and was buried in Brookwood Cemetery near Woking.

On 29th May 1919, after his death, Edmund was appointed as a Knight of Grace in the Order of the Hospital of Saint John of Jerusalem in England.[625]

His Victoria Cross medal is on public display at the Army Medical Services Museum in Aldershot.

Figure 193a. Grave of Edmund Baron Hartley

624 *London Gazette* – 27306/2698
625 *London Gazette* – 31380/7064

Francis Fitzpatrick
28th November 1879 (VC No. 387)

Gazetted: 24th February 1880 24814/832

Rank and Unit: Private No. 5268 – 94th Regiment of Foot

Citation

In recognition of their gallant conduct during the attack on Sekukuni's Town on the 28th November last, in carrying out of action Lieutenant Dewar, 1st Dragoon Guards, when badly wounded.

At the time when he received his wound, Lieutenant Dewar had with him only Privates Flawn and Fitzpatrick, and six of the Native Contingent, and, being incapable of moving without assistance, the natives proceeded to carry him down the hill, when about thirty of the enemy appeared in pursuit about 40 yards in the rear, whereupon the men of the Native Contingent deserted Lieutenant Dewar, who must have been killed but for the devoted gallantry of Privates Flawn and Fitzpatrick, who carried him alternately, one covering the retreat and firing on the enemy.

Biography

Francis was born some time during 1859 at Tullycorbet, Co Monaghan in Ireland, unfortunately he is one of those brave Irish soldiers about whom very little is known.

Figure 194. Francis Fitzpatrick

At some stage, Francis moved from Ireland to the United Kingdom and probably went to live in Scotland in common with many of his countrymen at this time.

Francis enlisted in the British army, at sometime around 1876, and joined the 94th Regiment of Foot as Private No. 5268.

On 26th February 1879, Francis and his regiment set sail from Southampton bound for the Cape Colony.

During his time in South Africa Francis saw service in the Zulu War and the 1st Boer War; it was on 28th November 1879 during an attack on Sekuni Town, in the Basuto Gun War, that Francis performed the deeds for which he was later awarded the Victoria Cross.

For his service in South Africa Francis was awarded the South Africa Medal (1877–79) with clasp for 1879.

Francis was presented with his Victoria Cross Medal on 17th September 1880 by Lieutenant P. R. Anstruther at Lydenburg, Transvaal in South Africa.

During his time in South Africa, Francis was also involved in the 1st Boer War and it was on 20th December 1880, during the Battle of Bronkers Spruit, the opening battle of the war, that he lost his Victoria Cross Medal which was replaced by the War Office in June 1881.

The original medal was later found in the effects of a comrade who had been killed and was returned to the War Office on 18th August 1881.

On 22nd April 1882, Francis arrived back in England with the regiment and soon afterwards was discharged to army reserve service with the Duke of Cornwall's Light Infantry.

Francis was discharged from the army on 10th May 1888, after completing his 12 year service period.

On leaving the army, Francis returned to live in Glasgow, where at some stage he was married.

At some stage Francis re-enlisted with the Argyll and Sutherland Highlanders and took part in the 2nd Boer War for which he was awarded the Queen's South Africa Medal (1899–1902) with clasps for Cape Colony and South Africa 1902.

At the age of 73, Francis died at Glasgow on 10th July 1933 and was buried a week later on 17th July at St Kentigen's Cemetery, Glasgow in an unmarked grave; a headstone was erected in July 2014.

Francis's medals are on public display at the National Army Museum in Chelsea, London.

Thomas Flawn
28th November 1879 (VC No. 388)

Gazetted: 24th February 1880 24814/832

Rank and Unit: Private – 94th Regiment of Foot

Citation

In recognition of their gallant conduct during the attack on Sekukuni's Town on the 28th November last, in carrying out of action Lieutenant Dewar, 1st Dragoon Guards, when badly wounded.

At the time when he received his wound, Lieutenant Dewar had with him only Privates Flawn and Fitzpatrick, and six of the Native Contingent,' and, being incapable of moving without assistance, the natives proceeded to carry him down the hill, when about thirty of the enemy appeared in pursuit about 40 yards in the rear, whereupon the men of the Native Contingent deserted Lieutenant Dewar, who must have been killed but for the devoted gallantry of Privates Flawn and Fitzpatrick, who carried him alternately, one covering the retreat and firing on the enemy.

Biography

Thomas was born on 22nd December 1857 at Finedon, Irthlingborough, Northamptonshire to father Thomas, an agricultural labourer, and mother Fanny (née Campion). He was one of four children with brothers Samuel born in 1854, William born in 1856 and sister Elizabeth born in 1869.

Thomas was educated at the Church School in Finedon but by the age of 13 was working as an agricultural labourer, like his father.

On 28th October 1876, at the age of 18, Thomas enlisted in the army at Leeds, for 6 years of army service followed by 6 years in the army reserve and was assigned as a Private in the 25th Regiment of Foot.

Thomas was transferred to the 26th Regiment of Foot on 31st August 1877 and then on 19th February 1879 to the 94th Regiment of Foot who were on orders for overseas service in South Africa.

On 26th February 1879, Thomas and his regiment set sail from Southampton bound for the Cape Colony.

During his time in South Africa Thomas saw service in the Zulu War and the 1st Boer War; it was on 28th November 1879 during an attack on Sekuni Town, in the Basuto Gun War, that Thomas performed the deeds for which he was later awarded the Victoria Cross.

Figure 195. Thomas Flawn

For his service in South Africa Thomas was awarded the South Africa Medal (1877–79) with clasp for 1879.

Thomas was presented with his Victoria Cross Medal on 17th September 1880 by Lieutenant P. R. Anstruther at Lydenburg, Transvaal in South Africa.

On 22nd April 1882, Thomas arrived back in England with the regiment and on 27th January 1883 was discharged to the 1st Class Army Reserve.

Thomas was married to Mary Elizabeth (née Barley) at Wellingborough on 26th February 1883.

On 27th October 1888, after having completed his 12 years of service, Thomas was discharged from the army and soon afterwards obtained employment as a stoker at the Woolwich Arsenal.

Figure 195a. Grave of Thomas Flawn

Thomas's wife Mary died on 25th November 1894 and sometime in 1895 he was remarried to Mary Ann (née Hayes).

The 1911 census shows that Thomas was living with his wife at 3 Oakly Villa, Olven Road in Plumstead, London and was still working at the Woolwich Arsenal as a stoker.

It was at his home in Plumstead, on 19th January 1925, that Thomas died at the age of 67 and was buried in Plumstead Cemetery.

Thomas's Victoria Cross Medal is not on public display, believed to be in the hands of a private collector.

John Frederick McCrea
14th January 1881 (VC No. 389)

Figure 196. John Frederick McCrea

Gazetted: 28th June 1881 24989/3239

Rank and Unit: Surgeon – 1st Cape Mounted Yeomanry

Citation

For his conspicuous bravery during the severely contested engagement with the Basutos on the 14th January, 1881, at Tweefontein, near Thaba Tsen, when, after the enemy had charged the Burghers in the most determined manner, forcing them to retire with a loss of sixteen killed and twenty-one wounded, Surgeon McCrea went out for some distance, under a heavy fire, and, with the assistance of Captain Huxton of the Mafeteng Contingent, conveyed a wounded Burgher named Aircamp to the shelter of a large ant-heap, and having placed him in a position of safety returned to the Ambulance for a stretcher. Whilst on his way thither Surgeon McCrea was severely wounded in the right breast by a bullet, notwithstanding which, he continued to perform his duties at the Ambulance, and again assisted to bring in several wounded men, continuing afterwards to attend the wounded during the remainder of the day, and scarcely taking time to dress his own wound, which he was obliged to do himself, there being no other Medical Officer in the Field.

Had it not been for this gallantry and devotion to his duty on the part of Surgeon McCrea, the sufferings of the wounded would undoubtedly have been much aggravated, and greater loss of life might very probably have ensued.

Biography

John was born on 1st April 1854 at Fort St George, Madras in India where his father Captain Herbert Taylor was serving as Paymaster to the 43rd Regiment of Foot; his mother Elizabeth Dobree (née Corey) was heavily pregnant with John, when the family were moved from the Cape Colony to India where they arrived on 30th January 1854 only weeks before his birth.

The middle child of three, John had an older brother Herbert Corey Howes who was born on 28th November 1851 at St Peter Port in Guernsey and a younger sister Elizabeth Charlotte born on 20th June 1855 at Kamptee in India.

A few days after the birth of his sister, his mother died on 6th July 1855 and when his father died on 28th July 1855, John and his brother and sister were sent to live with his aunt Charlotte at St Peter Port, in Guernsey.

John was initially educated at Elizabeth College in St Peter Port and then studied medicine at Guy's Hospital in London where he qualified as a Member of the Royal College of Surgeons in 1878, at the age of 24.

In 1879, John moved to South Africa and obtained employment as a civilian surgeon at the Military Hospital in Cape Town.

In 1880, John moved to Fort Beaufort where he intended to settle, however, in August 1880 he enlisted as a Surgeon with the 1st Regiment of the Cape Mounted Yeomanry.

Not long after joining the regiment, John saw his first active service during the Basuto (Gun) war when he was sent to Basutoland as part of the force sent to the relief of Mafeteng.

John was involved in action at Kalabani when his batman was killed while riding at his side.

It was on 14th January 1881, while in support of a patrol towards the Thaba Tsueu mountain, that John performed the deeds at Tweefontein for which he would later be awarded the Victoria Cross. During the action, John was wounded by a bullet to the left chest and being the only medical officer on the field had to dress his own wound.

Following the end of the war in 1881, the Cape Mounted Yeomanry were disbanded and John was transferred to the Cape Infantry Regiment as Surgeon.

John was presented with his Victoria Cross medal on 25th October 1881 by Brigadier-General Charles M. Clarke, Commander of the South African Colonial Forces, at a special parade held in King William's Town, Natal.

On 2nd February 1882, John was promoted to the rank of Surgeon-Major and was transferred to the Cape Mounted Rifles, stationed at Kokstad.

It was some time in 1887, while serving at Kokstad, that he was married to Elizabeth Antoinette (née Watermeyer), the couple would have no children.

While still serving at Kokstad, John died from lung inflammation after a bout of influenza on 16th July 1894 a few weeks after his 40th birthday and was buried in the Kokstad Cemetery.

John's Victoria Cross Medal is on public display at the Imperial War Museum in London as part of the Lord Ashcroft collection.

Figure 196a. Grave of John Frederick McCrea

James Murray

16th January 1881 (VC No. 390)

Gazetted: 11th March 1882 25084/1130

Rank and Unit: Lance-Corporal – 2nd Battalion Connaught Rangers

Citation

For their gallant conduct during an engagement with the Boers at Elandsfontein on the 16th January, 1881, in advancing for 500 yards, under a very heavy fire from a party of about 60 Boers, to bring out of action a private of the 21st Foot who had been severely wounded; in attempting which Lance-Corporal Murray was himself severely wounded.

Biography

James was born in the parish of St Michael's in Cork City, Ireland during February 1859; unfortunately very little is known about his life outside his Victoria Cross exploits.

It is likely that James moved to England to escape the privations existing in Ireland and probably during 1876/1877 enlisted with the 94th Regiment of Foot as a Private.

On 26th February 1879, James and his regiment set sail from Southampton bound for the Cape Colony.

During his time in South Africa James saw service in the Zulu War and the 1st Boer War; it was on 16th January 1881, during the Battle of Elandsfontein in the 1st Boer War, that James (now a

Figure 197. James Murray

Lance-Corporal) performed the deeds for which he was later awarded the Victoria Cross.

James was severely wounded, by a bullet which entered his right side and exited near his spine, during the action and was taken prisoner by the Boers but released under a flag of truce a few days later.

For his service in South Africa James was awarded the South Africa Medal (1877–79) with clasp for 1879.

Due to the serious nature of his wound, James was probably returned to England for treatment and recuperation and was possibly discharged from further service in the army.

James was presented with his Victoria Cross Medal on 15th May 1882 by Queen Victoria in a ceremony held at Windsor Castle.

In recognition of his service in South Africa, James was awarded the King George VI Coronation Medal in 1937.

At some stage, James returned to his native Ireland and it was on 19th July 1942 (at the age of 83) that he died at his home in Dublin and was buried in the Glasnevin Cemetery in an unmarked grave (a headstone was erected in the 1990s).

James's Victoria Cross Medal is on public display at the National Army Museum in Chelsea, London.

Figure 197a. Grave of James Murray

John Danaher (Danagher)

16th January 1881 (VC No. 391)

Gazetted: 11th March 1882 25084/1130

Rank and Unit: Trooper – Nourse's (Transvaal) Horse

Citation

For their gallant conduct during an engagement with the Boers at Elandsfontein on the 16th January, 1881, in advancing for 500 yards, under a very heavy fire from a party of about 60 Boers, to bring out of action a private of the 21st Foot who had been severely wounded; in attempting which Lance-Corporal Murray was himself severely wounded.

Biography

John was born on 25th June 1860 at Limerick in Ireland to father Patrick and mother Bridget (née Tuohy).

John received his education at the Christian Brothers School in Limerick and in 1880, at the age of 20, he emigrated to South Africa to seek his fortune.

Following the outbreak of the 1st Boer (Transvaal) War on 16th December 1880, John enlisted as a trooper with the Nourse's Horse, a colonial unit raised to help with the defence of Pretoria which was soon besieged by the Boers.

It was on 16th January 1881, while riding with a column commanded by Colonel Gildea, at the Battle of Elandsfontein that John performed the deeds for which he would later be awarded the Victoria Cross.

Following the end of the Siege of Pretoria, Nourse's Horse was disbanded and John joined the 2nd Battalion of the Connaught Rangers on 23rd April 1881.

In 1882, John with his new regiment returned to Ireland and were stationed at Fermoy.

John was presented with his Victoria Cross Medal on 23rd August 1882 by Earl Spencer, the 5th Earl and Viceroy of Ireland, at a special parade held at the Curragh Camp.

In 1885, John moved to Templemore in Co Tipperary where in the following year he was married to Bridget (née Connolly), the couple would have 12 children; John Joseph, Patrick Stephen, Francis, George, Martin, Arthur, Hector, Bernard, Ambrose, Michael, Sonny and Agnes Maude.

John and the regiment moved to Portsmouth in 1887 and then to Aldershot in 1889 in preparation for deployment to Malta later in the year.

From Malta, John was deployed to Cyprus in 1892 and then to Egypt in 1895, Sudan in 1896 and to India in 1897 where he

Figure 198. John Danaher

served at Meerut until 1903, Ahmednagar until 1906 and finally at Poona.

In 1908, after nearly 20 years of foreign service, John returned to Ireland where he was stationed at Tipperary.

Soon after his return to the United Kingdom, John retired from the army after 27 years of service and retired to Portsmouth; he was awarded the Army Long Service and Good Conduct medal.

In 1911, John embarked on a career as a publican when he became the licensee of "The Falcon" public house at 74 King's Road in Southsea.

In 1918, John became the licensee of the "Dog and Duck" public house at 115 Fratton Road, in Portsmouth and it was while living here that he died at St Mary's Hospital, Milton on 9th January 1919 and was buried six days later at the Milton Cemetery in Portsmouth.

John's Victoria Cross Medal is on public display at the National Army Museum in Chelsea, London.

Figure 198a. Grave of John Danaher

Alan Richard Hill (Hill-Walker)
28th January 1881 (VC No. 392)

Figure 199. Alan Richard Hill

Gazetted: 14th March 1882 25084/1130

Rank and Unit: Ensign (Sub-Lieutenant) – 58th Regiment of Foot

Citation

For gallant conduct at the action of Laing's Nek on the 28th January, 1881, in having, after the retreat was ordered, remained behind and endeavoured to carry out of action Lieutenant Baillie, of the same Corps, who was lying on the ground severely wounded.

Being unable to lift that officer into the saddle, he carried him in his arms until Lieutenant Baillie was shot dead. Lieutenant Hill then brought a wounded man out of action on his horse, after which he returned and rescued another. All these acts being performed under a heavy fire.

Biography

Alan was born on 12th July 1859 at Northallerton in Yorkshire to father Thomas, a former Captain in the army who was the founding Chief Constable of the North Riding of Yorkshire and mother Frances Mirriam (née Walker).

He was the oldest of three children with sister Maude born in 1861 and brother Cecil born in 1862.

After having been educated at Richmond, Alan joined the North York Militia some time in 1876 as an Ensign (sub-Lieutenant) and on 12th July 1876 was promoted to the rank of Lieutenant.[626]

On 22nd February 1879, Alan was commissioned as an Ensign (sub-Lieutenant) in the 58th Regiment of Foot[627] and four days later on 26th February 1879 set sail, with his new regiment, for South Africa to take part in the Zulu War.

For his service during the Zulu War, Alan was awarded the South Africa Medal (1877–79) with clasp for 1879.

After the Zulu War, Alan and his regiment were moved to the Transvaal and served throughout the 1st Boer (Transvaal) War.

It was on 28th January 1881, during the Battle of Laing's Nek, one of the first major battles of the war, that Alan performed the deeds for which he would later be awarded the Victoria Cross.

During this battle, the 58th Regiment gained the distinction of being the last regiment to carry its regimental colours into battle.

On the day after the battle, Alan was promoted to the rank of Lieutenant.[628]

Alan also saw action during the Battle of Ingogo (Battle of Schuinshoogte) on 8th February 1881 and the decisive Battle of Majuba Hill on 27th February, where the British were soundly beaten by the Boers and Alan was severely wounded by a bullet which shattered his right elbow.

For a while, after the battle, Alan was reported as missing in action.

For his service during the 1st Boer War, Alan received a mention in despatches, however, no campaign medal was issued for this conflict.

On 1st July 1881, as part of the Childers's army reforms, the 48th Regiment was merged with the 58th Regiment and became respectively the 1st and 2nd Brigades of the Northamptonshire Regiment.

With his new regiment, Alan set sail from South Africa on 4th August 1881 for the United Kingdom and was posted to Ireland, stationed at Tipperary.

On 13th May 1882, Alan was presented with his Victoria Cross Medal by Queen Victoria at an investiture held at Windsor Castle.

Now with the 1st Brigade, Alan returned to South Africa on 3rd May 1883 and served in Natal and Cape Town until returning to England on 21st September 1885 to be stationed at Preston.

On 1st September 1886, Alan was promoted to the rank of Captain.[629]

Alan was appointed as Adjutant to the 3rd and 4th Battalions of the Northampton Militia on 6th October 1887[630] a pos-

626 *London Gazette* – 24557/1770
627 *London Gazette* – 24681/870
628 *London Gazette* – 24965/2001
629 *London Gazette* – 25631/4835
630 *London Gazette* – 25749/5654

ition that he held until 1st October 1892 when his term of office expired.[631]

On 5th November 1892, Alan was despatched to India to take up the position of station officer at Bangalore.

Alan was promoted to the rank of Major on 22nd September 1896 and in 1897 was moved to Secunderabad where for a short time he served as officiating Assistant Adjutant General to Mandalay.

Together with his battalion, Alan was part of the 4th Brigade, commanded by General R. Westmacott in the Tirah Field Force, commanded by General Sir William Lockhart that took part in operations on the North West Frontier of India during 1897 to 1898.

For his service during these campaigns, Alan was awarded the India Medal (1895–1902) with clasps for Punjab Frontier 1897–98 and Tirah 1897–98.

After the war, Alan moved to Fyzabad in 1899 and on 12th October 1901, after over 26 years of service he retired from the army and moved back to England where he lived at 15 High Street, Agnesgate, Ripon in Yorkshire with his widowed mother and his sister.

In April 1902, Alan was married to Muriel Lilias Oliphant (née Walker) at Kirby Wiske in Yorkshire, the couple would go on to have two children; Thomas Harry born on 29th August 1904 who had a career in the Royal Navy and as Lieutenant-Commander, captain of *HMS Pintail*, was killed in action on 1st November 1940; their other son Gerald Alan was born *c.*1910 and like his father attained the rank of Major in the Northamptonshire regiment.

Not long after his marriage, Alan changed his surname to Hill-Walker, the name born by his children.

To celebrate the occasion of the coronation, Alan was awarded the King George VI Coronation medal in 1937.

Alan died at his home in Thirsk on 21st April 1944, at the age of 83 and was buried in St Michael and All Angels Churchyard in Maunby, North Yorkshire.

Alan's Victoria Cross medal is on public display at the Imperial War Museum in London, as part of the Lord Ashcroft collection.

Figure 199a. Grave of Alan Richard Hill

631 *London Gazette* – 26331/5561

John Doogan
28th January 1881 (VC No. 393)

Figure 200. John Doogan

Gazetted: 14th March 1882 25084/1130

Rank and Unit: Private No. 1401 – 1st Dragoon Guards

Citation

For gallant conduct during the action of Laing's Nek on the 28th January, 1881. During the charge of the mounted men Private Doogan, servant to Major Brownlow, 1st Dragoon Guards, seeing that officer (whose horse had been shot) dismounted and among the Boers, rode up and (though himself severely wounded) dismounted and pressed Major Brownlow to take his horse, receiving another wound while trying to induce him to accept it.

Biography

John was born on 23rd March 1853 at Aughrim in Co Galway, Ireland.

On 10th June 1875, at the age of 22, John enlisted as Private No. 1401 in the 1st Dragoon Guards of the British army.

In late 1878, John was part of a detachment from the regiment sent to South Africa for service in the Zulu war and on 4th July 1879 took part in the Battle of Ulundi during which a patrol led by Major Marter from the regiment captured the Zulu king Chief Cetywayo.

At the end of the war, John and the regiment were moved to Natal and took part in the 1st Boer (Transvaal) War.

It was during the Battle of Laing's Nek on 28th January 1881 that John performed the deeds for which he would later be awarded the Victoria Cross. While saving the life of Major Brownlow,[632] for whom John served as batman, he was seriously wounded twice, with bullets to the leg and wrist.

Due to his wounds, John took no further part in the war and was sent back to England for treatment.

For his service in South Africa, John was awarded the South Africa Medal (1877–79) with clasp for 1879.

After treatment at the Netley Military Hospital, John was discharged from the army to pension on 28th June 1881 being considered to be unfit for further service due to the severity of the wound to his wrist.

John was presented with his Victoria Cross Medal by the Superintendant of Pensions at Cork on 23rd May 1882; he was due to be presented with the medal by Queen Victoria on 13th May at Windsor Castle but his address could not be found in time to send out the invitation.

In 1882, John was married to Mary (née Evans) at Welshpool in Montgomeryshire, the couple would go on to have ten children; Mary born in 1882, Sarah born in 1883, Alice born in 1885, Fanny born in 1887, Ada born in 1888, John Jack born in 1889, William born in 1890, Margaret born in 1892, Albert born in 1893 and Richard born in 1894.

All of the children except Alice, who was born in Ireland, were born in Welshpool; John Jack and Richard would subsequently be killed in action during World War I. At some stage, most of the children returned to Ireland and lived in or around Cork; William moved to Shrewsbury in Shropshire.

After leaving the army, John, due to his damaged wrist, had trouble gaining employment to the extent that on 14th February 1884 Mr Charles Watkin Williams-Wynn, a prominent Barrister living in Welshpool, sent a letter to the editor of the local Morning Post newspaper outlining his plight and seeking offers of employment on his behalf.

It is probable that some time in 1884/85, John spent time back in Ireland and was possibly employed as a Constable in the Royal Irish Constabulary.

By 1891, John was living with his wife and three children at 3 Mill Place in Welshpool and was employed as a Mail Driver for the General Post Office.

In 1901, John and his wife were living at Church Cottage, Churchend, Shinfield, Wokingham in Berkshire and John was employed as a butler.

On 25th October 1915, it was reported that John, who was living at Cause Mountain near Westbury in Shropshire and now too old for active service, had been appointed as an additional recruiting Sergeant for Shropshire.

632 When Major Brownley died in 1926, at the age of 84, after having been run down by a car, John was bequeathed £20/year in his will.

After the death of his wife Mary in 1924, John moved to Shropshire near to where his son William was living and from 1829 was living at Mitchell's Fold, Stapley Hill near Munsterly where he ran a farm and engaged Martha Maria Roberts as his housekeeper.

Despite his housekeeper being 39 years younger, the couple were married at the Welshpool Registry Office on 16th September 1929.

Somehow the marriage was discovered to be bigamous, and Martha, who claimed to be a widow when she was engaged by John, appeared at the Shropshire Assizes on 20th February 1930 charged with bigamy.

The evidence showed that Martha was married to David Philip Roberts on 8th November 1923 at Wrexham. In her defence, Martha claimed that she had only lived with Mr Roberts for a few weeks, had last seen him in 1929 and had heard rumours that he was dead.

The marriage to John was annulled, however, instead of the usual custodial sentence for bigamy, Martha was only bound-over for the sum of £10 and released.

On 1st April 1933, John, who was now 70 years old, was married for the third time to Elizabeth (née Evans) at Welshpool – Bessie was only 22 years old.

John was awarded the King George VI Coronation Medal in 1937.

In 1937, John gave up his smallholding at Stapely Hill and retired to Folkestone in Kent, where in 1939 he was living at 12 New Dover Road with his wife Elizabeth.

In 1939, John was appointed as a life time member of the South Africa Veteran Association at Folkestone.

John died at his home, 5 Folly Road in Folkestone, on 24th January 1940 at the age of 87 and was buried two days later in the Shorncliffe Military Cemetery in Folkestone.

Figure 200a. Grave of John Doogan

Soon after the end of World War II, in accordance with John's wishes, the family donated his Victoria Cross Medal to his regiment, where for years it was on display in the Sergeants mess at Cardiff Castle.

Between 15th June and 7th July 1956 an exhibition was held at Marlborough House in London, to celebrate the centenary of the Victoria Cross; 198 Victoria Cross Medals, including John's, were on display during the exhibition.

At the end of the exhibition, an attempt was made to return John's medal to the regiment, however, by now they were on service in Malaya, so the medal was placed in the vault of a London bank for safe keeping.

Apparently forgotten, the medal languished in the bank vault for 41 years before eventually being returned to the regiment in 1997; the medal is now on public display at the Queen's Dragoon Guards Regimental Museum in Cardiff.

James Osborne
22nd February 1881 (VC No. 394)

Gazetted: 14th March 1882 25084/1130

Rank and Unit: Private No. 911 – 58th Regiment of Foot

Citation

For his gallant conduct at Wesselstroom, on the 22nd February, 1881, in riding, under a heavy fire, towards a party of 42 Boers, picking up Private Mayes, who was lying wounded, – and carrying him safely into camp.

Figure 201. James Osborne

Biography

James was born on 13th April 1857 at Wigginton, near Tring in Hertfordshire to father John and mother Mary; he had two brothers, William and Frederick.

It would appear that James had little or no formal education as he was illiterate throughout his life.

On 4th November 1876, James left his job as a labourer and enlisted as Private No. 5441 in the Hertfordshire Militia.

James received a conditional discharge from the Hertfordshire Militia towards the end of 1877, the condition being that he enlist with the regular army; this he did on 1st January 1877 at Gosport when he joined the 16th Regiment of Foot as Private No. 911.

On 24th March 1878, James was transferred to the 58th Regiment of Foot and on 26th February 1879 set sail, with his regiment, for South Africa to take part in the Zulu War.

For his service during the Zulu War, James was awarded the South Africa Medal (1877–79) with clasp for 1879.

After the Zulu War, James and his regiment were moved to the Transvaal and served throughout the 1st Boer (Transvaal) War.

On 28th January 1881, James to part in the Battle of Laing's Nek, one of the first major battles of the war. It was during this battle, the 58th Regiment gained the distinction of being the last regiment to carry its regimental colours into battle.

It was during the Battle of Wesselstroom on 22nd February 1881, that James performed the deeds for which he would later be awarded the Victoria Cross.

James also saw action during the Battle of Ingogo (Battle of Schuinshoogte) on 8th February 1881 and the decisive Battle of Majuba Hill on 27th February, where the British were soundly beaten by the Boers.

On 1st July 1881, as part of the Childers's army reforms, the 48th Regiment was merged with the 58th Regiment and became respectively the 1st and 2nd Brigades of the Northamptonshire Regiment.

James was presented with his Victoria Cross Medal on 26th April 1882 at a special parade at Fort Napia in Natal.

Having completed his period of service in the regular army, James boarded the *SS Arab* on 23rd March 1883 and set sail for home, arriving back in England on 26th April 1883.

On 10th May 1883, under the terms of his enlistment having completed 6 years (6 years and 129 days) in the regular army, James was transferred to the Army Reserve.

James was married to Rhoda (née Collier) at Wigginton on 8th September 1883, the couple would go on to have three children; Mary Elizabeth born in 1886, John born in 1892 and Edith born in 1895.

On 31st December 1888, having spent 5 years and 236 days in the Army Reserve, James was discharged from the army having completed the 12 years of his period of limited engagement.

After leaving the army, James and his family set up home at Clay Hill in Wigginton and for the next 26 years he was employed as a labourer on the Rothschild Estate until 1913 when a stroke left him partially paralysed.

On 1st February 1928, at the age of 70, James died at his home in Clay Hill and was buried in St Bartholomew's Parish Churchyard in Wigginton.

After his death and in accordance with his wishes, James's Victoria Cross Medal was donated to his regiment.

At the outbreak of World War II, the regiment were stationed at Ballykinler in Ireland and in the middle of October 1939, with the regiment being moved back to England, James's Victoria Cross and the regimental silver were lodged with the Ulster Bank on York Street in Belfast for safe keeping.

During a German bombing raid on the town on the night of 4th–5th May 1941, the Ulster Bank was substantially damaged and James's medals and the regimental silver were destroyed.

It was not until 1964 that James's daughter Edith learned that her father's medal had been destroyed but it was not until 2008 that a formal request for an official replacement was made by his granddaughter Mrs Rhoda Whitehouse.

The request was turned down on the grounds that as a granddaughter, Mrs Whitehouse was not the direct next of kin of the recipient.

The decision was perhaps coloured by the fact that a replacement VC provided to the family of Sergeant Thomas Byrne in 1976, had been sold by the family for £700 two years later.

Figure 201a. Grave of James Osborne

Joseph John Farmer

27th February 1881 (VC No. 395)

Gazetted: 17th May 1881 24973/2553

Rank and Unit: Lance-Corporal No. 4030 – Army Hospital Corps

Citation

For conspicuous bravery during the engagement with the Boers at the Majuba Mountain, on the 27th February, 1881, when he showed a spirit of self-abnegation and an example of cool courage which cannot be too highly commended. While the Boers closed with the British troops near the wells, Corporal Farmer held a white flag over the wounded, and when the arm holding the flag was shot through, he called out that he had "another." He then raised the flag with the other arm, and continued to do so until that also was-pierced with a bullet.

Biography

Joseph was born on 5th May 1854 at Clerkenwell in London to father Thomas, a stable hand and mother Julia, he was the youngest of three children with sister Julia born in 1846 and brother Thomas born in 1849.

He was educated in local schools at Kings Cross until the age of 10 when he started an apprenticeship in the building trade.

In 1868, at the age of 14, Joseph became a merchant seaman, initially as a boy and later as an Able Seaman he served on several British and American merchant ships and visited many countries; France, Spain, Italy, Greece, the Bay of Bengal, China, South America and South Africa.

Figure 202. Joseph John Farmer

His time in the merchant navy was not without incident, he was twice shipwrecked, once in 1875 off the Isle of Wight and again the next year in a hurricane off Hong Kong.

Ten years later in February 1878, Joseph landed at Liverpool, having completed what would be his last voyage as a merchant seaman, from Liverpool he returned to London where he contracted smallpox and was hospitalised in the Hampstead Smallpox hospital.

One day during his stay in the hospital a delirious patent named Freeman tried to escape by jumping through a window and seriously cut himself, Joseph saved his life by preventing his escape, restraining him with a Lawn Tennis net.

At the time of his discharge from the hospital, Joseph was given employment as a night porter at the hospital, to look after the delirious patients but due to a reduction in staff was discharged in August 1878.

On leaving the Hampstead Smallpox Hospital, Joseph was briefly employed at the Banstead Asylum as an attendant until on 27th February 1879, eager to pursue a medical career he enlisted in the Army Medical Corps as Private No. 4030.

After joining the Army Medical Corps, Joseph was sent to Aldershot and attended courses in Anatomy and Ambulance work, following which he was sent with reinforcements to the Cape Colony in South Africa.

Initially Joseph served as batman to Surgeon Major Hector but after a short time was sent to Ladysmith where he served under Surgeon Major Babington, treating the wounded from the Battle of Ulundi.

Joseph was next sent to Newcastle, where for a time he acted as an ambulance man ferrying convalescents to either Pietermaritzburg or Utrecht.

During his time in South Africa, Joseph's conduct was not always exemplary; he appeared in the regimental defaulter's book on several occasions for being absent from parade, drunk on duty and insubordination. He was also found guilty of a civil offence in Pietermaritzburg for breaking windows and causing a disturbance on Commercial Road.

At the outbreak of the 1st Boer War, Joseph helped General Colly in fitting out a field hospital and helped treat the wounded from the Battle of Laing's Nek on 28th January 1881.

It was during the Battle of Majuba Hill on 27th February 1881, that Joseph performed the deeds for which he would later be awarded the Victoria Cross; during the action he was seriously wounded in both arms.

For his service during the war, Joseph was awarded the South Africa Medal (1877–79) without clasp.

Due to the severity of his wounds, Joseph was sent to Newcastle and after a medical examination of 8th April was sent back to England where on 16th August 1881, at Netley Military Hospital he was discharged from the army, judged to be unfit for further service.

On 9th August 1881, just prior to his discharge, Joseph was presented with his Victoria Cross medal by Queen Victoria at an investiture held at Osborne House on the Isle of Wight.

On leaving the army, Joseph moved to Camden Town and was employed as a Sergeant in the Corps of Commissioners on 1st September 1881 and moved to Fulham.

While working at the Corps of Commissioners, Joseph became a close friend of Frederick Hitch VC and attended his funeral on 11th January 1913 and at some time after his death was a witness at the marriage of one of his daughters, Emily on 2nd April 1913.[633]

On 9th October 1881, Joseph was married to Emily (née Saggers) at the Old Parish Church in St Pancreas; the couple would go on to have five sons; Joseph born in 1883, Frederick born in 1885, Thomas born in 1887, Henry born in 1890 and Frank born in 1894 they also had two daughters.

By 1901, Joseph and his family were living at 169, Wandsworth Bridge Road in Fulham and life was quite hard as during the winter, due to his wounds, he was often prevented from carrying out his work as a house painter. On 14th July 1901, he wrote to the Secretary of State for War, explaining his plight and requesting and increase in his pension from one to two shillings per day.; he was granted an increase of sixpence a day.

Figure 202a. Grave of Joseph John Farmer

633 Some sources state that Fred and Joseph met at Rorke's Drift, which is highly unlikely and Joseph was certainly not one of the Rorke's Drift defenders.

In 1903, Joseph gave up his work as a house painter and went to work as a Gatekeeper for a factory in Fulham, where he was to work for the next 25 years until he retired at the age of 74.

While living at 27 Rectory Road in Fulham, Joseph died at Mount Vernon Hospital, Northwood from bronchopneumonia, carcinoma of the pharynx and malignant glands in the neck; he was 76 years old.

Joseph received a military funeral at Brompton Cemetery and a boulder from Majuba Mountain was later used as part of his headstone.

Joseph's Victoria Cross Medal is on public display at the Army Medical Services Museum, Keogh Barracks, Mytchett in Surrey.

Israel Harding
11th July 1882 (VC No. 396)

Gazetted: 15th September 1882 25147/4260

Rank and Unit: Gunner – Royal Navy – *HMS Alexandra*

Citation

At about nine o'clock, on the morning of the 11th July, whilst Her Majesty's Ship "Alexandra" was engaging the Forts at Alexandria, a 10-inch spherical shell passed through the ship's side and lodged on the main deck. Mr. Harding hearing the shout "there is a live shell just above the hatchway," rushed up the ladder from below, and, observing that the fuze was burning, took some water from a tub standing near, and threw it over the projectile, then picked up the shell and put it into the tub.

Had the shell burst, it would probably have destroyed many lives.

Biography

Israel was born on 21st October 1833[634] at Portsmouth to father John, a Queen's Pilot and mother Sophia (née Martin); he had two older sisters, Sarah born in 1816 and Sophia born in 1819, he also had a younger brother William born in 1836.

Figure 203. Israel Harding

634 Inexplicably, Israel's Royal Navy papers show a date of birth of 21st October 1829, later amended to 26th December 1829.

Israel was educated privately at the Victoria School above the Bethel Chapel in Bath Square, Portsmouth until the age of 11.

Having learnt the rudiments of navigation, Israel joined his father on board the *SS Echo* on 11th February 1846 and began an apprenticeship to become a Pilot.

On 16th March 1849, at the age of 16, Israel enlisted in the Royal Navy and was assigned as an Ordinary Seaman to *HMS Arrogant*, commanded by Captain Robert Fitzroy, on the Home station at Portsmouth. On 29th February 1852, Israel attained the rank of Able Seaman.

Israel saw further service on *HMS Arrogant* under Captain Robert Spencer Robinson and Captain Stephen Grenville Fremantle until 26th September 1852 when he transferred to *HMS Excellent* which was the Royal Navy Gunnery School based in Portsmouth, commanded by Captain Henry Ducie Chads.

On 10th January 1853, Israel was married to Harriet (née Ellis) at St Mary's Church in Portsea, the couple would have three children; Sophia born in 1856, Joseph born in 1859 and Harriet born in 1861. After nearly 20 years of marriage the couple were divorced in 1872 as a result of his wife's adultery with a Mr George Sutton.

Israel volunteered for a seven year period of continuous and general service with the navy on 1st July 1853 while at *HMS Exellent* where he continued to serve until 24th December 1853 (apart from a period between 7th November and 6th December which he spent in prison).

On 25th December 1853, having completed his training at the Royal Navy Gunnery School, having gained his seaman gunners certificate on 28th June 1853, Israel joined *HMS Cressy* as an Ordinary Seaman and served under Captain Richard Laird Warren as part of the Baltic Fleet in the Crimean (Russian) War.

Israel was promoted to the 2nd Class Petty Officer position of Captain of the Mizzen Top on 28th January 1854.

In early April 1854, *HMS Cressy* formed up with the rest of the British Baltic Fleet and entered the Baltic sea intent on disrupting the Russian shipping.

HMS Cressy experienced early success when she captured the Russian Brig *Patrioten* on 15th April 1854.

In July 1854, the British Fleet was supplemented by French warships when they assembled at Baro Sound.

On 18th March 1855, *HMS Cressy* had to go to Spithead for repairs, however, returned to the Baltic in time to take part in the bombardment of the Russian Naval Yards and Fortress at Sveaborg, near Helsinki, in August 1855.

For his service during the war, Israel was awarded the Baltic Medal (1854–55).

After the war ended, Israel with *HMS Cressy* returned to service on the Mediterranean Station and on 1st January 1857 he was promoted to the rank of Captain of the Fore Top.

HMS Cressy returned to England on 14th May 1857 and the next day Israel returned to *HMS Excellent* for further gunnery training.

Having completed his training, Israel joined *HMS Algiers* on 16th February 1859 and served under Captain George William Douglas O'Callaghan, as part of the Channel Squadron until 20th March 1860.

After a period of just over 12 years of service, Israel was promoted to the Warrant Officer rank of Gunner 3rd Class on 21st March 1860 and was transferred for a short period to *HMS Excellent*.

On 31st May 1860, Israel was transferred to *HMS Barracouta* as a Gunner and initially served under Commander William Wood in operations on the North America and West Indies Station.

Israel continued his service on board *HMS Barracouta*, on the North America and West Indies Station commanded by Commander George John Malcolm from 24th August 1861 and Commander John D'Arcy from 13th November 1863, until 23rd November 1864 when she returned to England and the crew was paid off at Sheerness.

For a short time until 30th November, Israel was with *HMS Cumberland*, a Stationary Ship at Sheerness, until he was posted back to *HMS Excellent* on 1st December 1864.

On 26th July 1865. Israel left *HMS Excellent* and joined *HMS Industry* on the following day, under the command of Master Commander Edward Charles Taylor Youel, the store ship was on particular service at home for several months.

Israel was promoted to the rank of Gunner 2nd Class on 23rd December 1865 and continued to serve with *HMS Industry*; from 1st January, the ship now under the command of Staff Commander Charles James Polkinghorne saw service off the west coast of Africa.

On 9th December 1868, Israel was once again assigned to *HMS Excellent* where he served until 20th July 1869.

From 21st July 1869 until 20th August 1869, Israel spent a short time with *HMS Asia*, a stationary ship at Plymouth until he joined *HMS Gladiator* on 21st August 1869 and saw service on the South American Station under the command of Captain Norman Bernard Bedingfield.

Sometime in 1871, Israel was placed in charge of a Royal Navy party, sent ashore in Rio de Janeiro to help extinguish a fire at the military arsenal in the city; for his part in the action he was awarded a Brazilian Medal (probably the Dom Pedro II Silver Medal) and a testimonial letter from the Princess Imperial Regent of Brazil.

After returning to England and having been paid off at Plymouth on 20th February 1872 Israel once again returned to *HMS Excellent* the following day where he remained until 4th October 1873; having been promoted to the rank of Gunner 1st Class on 7th July 1873.

On leaving *HMS Excellent*, Israel again spent a short time on the stationary ship *HMS Asia* until 20th November 1873, while awaiting his next deployment and during this period, on 10th November 1873 he was married to Emma Annette (née Nunn) at Woolwich Parish Church. The couple would go on to have four daughters; Emma Castopa born in 1878, Louisa born in 1879, Annette born in 1880 and Victoria Maude born in 1884.

On 21st November 1873, Israel was assigned to *HMS Victor Emanuel* commanded by Captain George Henry Parkin and took part in the 3rd Anglo-Ashanti war, where they served as a hospital ship off Cape Coast Castile. *HMS Victor Emanuel* then served as a receiving ship at Hong Kong where they arrived on 11th December 1874 to relieve *HMS Princess Charlotte*.

For his service during the war, Israel was awarded the Ashantee Medal (1873–74).

In July 1875, Commodore John Edward Parish took over the command of *HMS Victor Emanuel* and Israel continued his service at Hong Kong until 27th December 1875 when he returned to England.

On 28th December 1875, Israel was once again assigned to *HMS Excellent* and was initially on leave until 13th February 1876.

Israel continued with *HMS Excellent* until 7th July 1876 when on the following day he was assigned to *HMS Castor*, the drill ship for the Royal Navy Reserve, commanded by Commander Charles Gudgeon Nelson, at North Shields.

On 15th July 1879, Israel left *HMS Castor* and returned to *HMS Excellent* where he served until 4th February 1880 and on the following day was assigned to *HMS Alexandra* under the command of Captain Lord Walter Talbot Kerr which went to service on the Mediterranean Station and served as the flagship to Vice-Admiral Frederick Beauchamp Paget Seymore.

It was on 11th July 1882, during the bombardment of Alexandria during the Anglo-Egyptian War, with Captain Charles Frederick Hotham now in command of *HMS Alexandra*, that Israel performed the deeds for which he would later be awarded the Victoria Cross. In recognition of his bravery, Israel was immediately promoted to the rank of Chief Gunner.

For his service during the war, Israel received a mention in despatches and was awarded the Egypt Medal (1882–89) with clasp for Alexandria 11th July. He was also awarded the Khedive's Star (1882–89).

After the war, *HMS Alexandra* continued her service on the Mediterranean Station and during a short visit to Malta Israel was presented with his Victoria Cross Medal on 14th October 1882 by Lord Alcester, Admiral Sir Frederick Beauchamp Seymor the Commander in Chief Malta.

Israel returned to England on board *SS Nepal* on 31st January 1883 and from 1st February 1883 was assigned to the stationary ship *HMS Asia* before being assigned to *HMS Duke of Wellington*, the flagship of the port Admiral at Portsmouth, commanded by Captain Charles John Rowley, on 21st December 1883.

From 24th October 1884, Israel continued his service with *HMS Duke of Wellington*, now commanded by Captain Philip Howard Colomb until 8th February 1885 when after over 36 years of service he was discharged from the navy to pension.

After leaving the Royal Navy, Israel lived in Portsmouth and continued his life at sea with a career in the Merchant navy; he also pursued his passion for photography and in 1891 was Vice President of the Southsea Photographic Society. He was also the honorary Agent and Receiving Officer for the Portsmouth branch of the Shipwrecked Fishermen and Mariner's Royal Benevolent Society.

Following the vacancy resulting from the death of Chief Gunner A. Ward, Israel was awarded the Greenwich Hospital Pension of £35 per year on 24th November 1902.

On 13th November 1903, while serving as Chief Mate on the *SS Magnolia* on a voyage from Brazil to Bergen, Israel was the sole survivor when the ship sunk just off the Faroe Islands.

The Captain, his wife and 25 crew members took to the boats when the ship floundered and were never seen again; Israel

Figure 203a. Grave of Israel Harding

decided to stay with the ship and when it sank grasped a floating spar and was rescued two hours later by a trawler from Hull.

After this incident, it appears that Israel was working as a trawler man out of Grimsby and at the start of the Great War he offered his services via the National Reserve Organisation and despite being 80 years old was accepted; possibly the oldest person to serve during the war.

Israel was engaged on minesweeping duties in the North Sea and Atlantic Ocean and during this time he was sunk three times his ship either hitting a mine or being torpedoed.

It was in September 1915, during operations in the Dardanelles, that Israel was sunk for a fourth time and 11 of the crew of 13 were lost with only Israel and the cook surviving, however, Israel's leg was broken and he was sent home to hospital in Southampton and then to a convalescence home at Withernsea.

Israel died on 22nd May 1917, at the age of 83, while on a visit to his daughter's home at Silkstead House, Billinghurst in Sussex and was buried four days later in the Highland Road Cemetery in Portsmouth.

Israel's Victoria Cross Medal is on public display at the Imperial War museum as part of the Lord Ashcroft collection.

Frederick Corbett (David Embleton)
5th August 1882 (VC No. 397)

Gazetted: 16th February 1883 25199/859

Rank and Unit: Private No. 3804 – 3rd Battalion Kings Royal Rifle Corps

Citation

During the reconnaissance upon Kafr Dowar, on 5th August, 1882, the Mounted Infantry, with which Private Corbett was serving, came under a hot fire from the enemy and suffered some loss, including Lieutenant Howard-Vyse, mortally wounded. This officer fell in the open, and there being then no time to move him, Private Corbett asked and obtained permission to remain by him, and though under a constant fire, he sat down and endeavoured to stop the bleeding of this officer's wounds, until the Mounted Infantry received orders to retire, when he rendered valuable assistance in carrying him off the field.

Biography

Frederick was born as David Embleton on 17th September 1853 at Maldon in Essex to father William who was a baker and mother Jane; he had an older brother William born in 1850 and a younger brother Joseph born in 1856.

Nothing is known of Frederick's life before he joined the army, however, for a period, probably since his 18th birthday, he was a private in "G" company of the 2nd Essex Regiment of Volunteers where he was regarded as the best shot in the company and excellent at drill.

On or around 8th April 1879,[635] Frederick enlisted in the regular army and was posted as Private No. 3804 in the 60th Rifles. For some unknown reason, he enlisted as Frederick Corbett, a name that he would use for the rest of his life, rather than his given name of David Embleton.

It is likely that Frederick spent the early part of his enlistment in England, probably at the depot in Colchester until he was sent to South Africa, as part of a new draft, on 20th April 1881.

Following the Childers army reforms, the 60th Rifles was renamed as the Kings Royal Rifle Corps on 1st July 1881.

Frederick was with his battalion at Capetown when orders were received for their despatch to Egypt and on 22nd February

635 In Frederick's Royal Artillery discharge papers it is recorded that he had previous service of 4 years and 66 days in the 60th Rifles – taking his discharge from the 60th Rifles as 13th June 1883 gives an enlistment date of 8th April 1879.

Figure 204. Frederick Corbett

1882 he boarded *HMS Orontes* and arrived at Alexandria on 17th July 1882 after a voyage via Malta and Cyprus.

Frederick was appointed as batman to Lieutenant Henry Granville Lindsey Howard Vyse and accompanied him on an operation to protect a train sent to wreck the railway at Mallaha Junction on 22nd July 1882 and it was during this patrol that he saw his first action, preventing enemy cavalry from attacking the train.

It was on 5th August 1882, during a reconnaissance at Kafr-el-Duar, that Frederick performed the deeds for which he would later be awarded the Victoria Cross.[636]

Frederick took part in the Battle of Tel-el-Kebir on 13th September 1882 and shortly afterwards on 14th November 1882 was attached to the Military Police.

For his service during the war, Frederick was awarded the Egypt Medal (1882–89) with clasp for Tel-el-Kebir; he was also awarded the Khedive's Star (1882).

Frederick was presented with his Victoria Cross Medal on 2nd March 1883, by Lord Napier of Magdala, the Commander in Chief Gibraltar at a parade on Abdin Square, Cairo.

Soon after receiving his medal, Frederick was returned to England and on 13th June 1883 was discharged from the army; some sources say that the discharge was for medical reasons but his Chelsea discharge papers state that he purchased his discharge.

It is reported that after leaving the army, Frederick fell in with bad company and began to drink heavily, at some time in 1883 he sold his Victoria Cross Medal to fund his drinking, however, he did commission two unofficial copies to use on ceremonial occasions.

636 In a letter dated 4th January 1883, Frederick was recommended for the award of the Distinguished Conduct Medal but this was later upgrade to an award of the Victoria Cross.

Despite having been rejected by a medical board on 2nd October 1883, Frederick reapplied and on 13th December 1883 was enlisted as Driver No. 40396, in the Royal Artillery at Woolwich.

After spending a short time at the depot in Woolwich, Frederick was assigned to B Brigade on 1st January 1884 and after the brigade had been despatched to Egypt on 26th February 1884, to take part in the Suakin Campaign, he was appointed to the command of "C" Battery on 1st March 1884.

After returning to England on 4th June 1884, Frederick was soon in trouble with the authorities after being absent without leave between 12th July 1884 and 23rd July 1884.

After returning to his Brigade, Frederick spent the next five days on remand awaiting court martial and after being tried on 30th July 1884, at Aldershot, and being convicted of being AWOL, theft and embezzlement from an officer, spent the next 28 days until 26th August 1884 in a military prison.

Having been convicted of a serious crime, a Royal Warrant was issued on 30th July 1884 which, under the terms of clause 15 of the originating Warrant, stripped Frederick of his Victoria Cross Medal and pension; becoming one of only eight men to have forfeited the award.

On leaving prison, Frederick was returned to duties with his brigade for a few days before being transferred to the depot at Woolwich on 1st September 1884.

On 9th October 1884, when B Brigade was despatched for service in India, Frederick was transferred back to the Brigade and sailed with them to India and on 1st November was assigned to the command of "E" battery.

The brigade arrived on station at Bangalore on 22nd November 1884 and served there until 9th November 1885 when they were transferred to Secunderabad.

During his time in India, Frederick had many visits to hospital, mainly for treatment of varicose veins in his legs but also for venereal disease and ague.

From 12th February 1887 until 27th February 1887, Frederick spent 16 days on remand awaiting trial.

At his court martial on 28th February 1887, Frederick was tried and convicted of losing and neglect of his equipment and theft from his comrades and was sentenced to 84 days imprisonment, which he served in the Secunderabad Military Prison.

Having served his sentence, Frederick returned to duty with the battalion on 23rd May 1887 until 6th September 1889, when he spent 11 day on remand while awaiting his third court martial.

On the 17th September 1889, Frederick was tried and convicted of striking a superior officer and was again sentenced to 84 days imprisonment, which was served in the Secunderabad Military Prison.

Released from prison, Frederick was again returned to duty with the brigade on 10th December 1889 and a few days later on 31st December 1889, the brigade was moved to duties at Mhow.

Towards the end of 1890, with the condition of his legs deteriorating, a medical examination determined that he was no longer fit for service and on 6th November 1890 he boarded *HMS Malabar* bound for England.

On the 1st December 1890, Frederick arrived back in England and after a further medical board at Woolwich was discharged from the army on 6th January 1891, without pension, being deemed to be unfit for further military service.

Probably as a result of his poor health, Frederick had difficulty in finding work and without the benefit of a pension had to resort to the workhouse as a means of support.

On 12th March 1896, at Greenwich Police Court, Frederick was charged with refusing to work at the Greenwich Union Casual Workhouse, he was remanded on his promise that he would go to the Church Army who would find him work.

Frederick was again in trouble with the law when on 14th April 1899, at the Petty Sessions in Colchester, he pleaded guilty to breaking the shop window of Mr George Dennis, a grocer on the high street. In mitigation, Frederick stated that he bore Mr Dennis no malice and that he broke the window because he was drunk. He was fined and ordered to pay costs and compensation to Mr Dennis for a replacement window.

On 14th September 1904, at Bow Street, Frederick was convicted of breaking a window in the door of the War Office and was sentenced to one month of hard labour.

This incident was probably the result of a local newspaper report, which outlined the details of concerns regarding the ownership of the Victoria Cross Medal which had been awarded to Frederick.

In 1903, a Victoria Cross bearing the name of Frederick Corbett came into the possession of Mr Mansfield, a clerk with Kingsbury Urban District Council; he contacted the War Office regarding his intention of returning the medal to Frederick or his family.

Mr Mansfield was informed that as the award had been forfeited and that Frederick's name had been erased from the Victoria Cross Register, the medal should not be delivered to Frederick or his family under any circumstances.

Unsure as to whether he was allowed to retain the medal or if he should return it to the War Office, Mr Mansfield contacted the War Office again and received the reply that "*... in view of Corbett having sold his VC at a time when he was not subject to the Army Act,*[637] *Mr Mansfield was entitled to retain it.*"

637 The Army Discipline and Regulations Act 1879 made it illegal to sell medals while serving in the army.

Frederick was upset by the newspaper report as it was the first time that the forfeiture of his Victoria Cross had been made public, he was also angry at the War Office believing that they were responsible for his troubles.

On 25th September 1912, at the age of 59, Frederick died from brain cancer in the Maldon Union Workhouse Infirmary and was buried five days later in an unmarked grave at the London Road Cemetery in Maldon.

Frederick's Victoria Cross Medal is on public display at the Royal Green Jackets Museum in Winchester.

Figure 204a. Grave of Frederick Corbett

William Mordaunt Marsh Edwards
13th September 1882 (VC No. 398)

Figure 205. William Mordant Marsh Edwards

Gazetted: 13th February 1883 25198/792

Rank and Unit: Lieutenant – 2nd Battalion Highland Light Infantry

Citation

For the conspicuous bravery displayed by him during the battle of Tel-el-Kebir, on the 13th September, 1882, in leading a party of the Highland Light Infantry to storm a redoubt. Lieutenant Edwards (who was in advance of his party) with great gallantry rushed alone into the battery, killed the Artillery Officer in charge, and was himself knocked down by a gunner with a rammer, and only rescued by the timely arrival of three men of his Regiment.

Biography

William was born on 7th May 1855, at Hardingham Hall in Norfolk to father Henry William Bartholomew, the High Sheriff of Norfolk and mother Caroline Georgiana (née Marsh); he was the second born of six children with an older sister Ellen Lucy born in 1853 and younger siblings, Constance Catherine born in 1858, Madelain Margaret Marsh born in 1859 but died at 4 years old, Gertrude Louisa born in 1861 but died at 3 months old, Ernest Marshall Lambe born in 1863 and Mildred Virtue born in 1868.

After being educated at Rottingdean and Eton, William was admitted to Trinity College, Cambridge on 28th February 1874.

Instead of completing his degree course, William took and passed the Army Entrance examination and on 22nd March 1876 was commissioned as a sub-Lieutenant and placed on the unattached list.[638]

With effect from his enlistment date, William was later transferred to the 74th Regiment of Foot[639] and promoted to the rank of Lieutenant.[640]

On 2nd December 1976, William with his regiment boarded *HMS Orontes* and set sail for his first overseas deployment to the Straits Settlements.[641]

The headquarters and two companies were landed at Penang on 9th January 1877 and further units were deployed to Malacca on 15th January and Singapore on 18th January 1877.

638 *London Gazette* – 24307/2015

639 *London Gazette* – 24404/219

640 *London Gazette* – 24599/3835

641 The Straits Settlements was a crown colony on the Malayan Peninsular that consisted of the Malacca, Dinging, Penang (Prince of Wales Island) and Singapore (including Christmas Island and the Cocos (Keeling) Islands) colonies.

When the 80th Regiment of Foot left Singapore for the Cape Colony in March 1877, the 74th Highlanders moved their headquarters from Penang to Singapore.

In January 1878, William and the battalion boarded *HMS Tamar* and set sail for Hong Kong where they arrived on 29th January 1878 and occupied several barracks in the city.

The health of the battalion had been so badly affected by their time in Hong Kong by March 1879, that they were ordered back to the Straits Settlement where they landed at Singapore on 16th March 1879.

On 8th December 1879, William and the battalion boarded *HMS Orontes* and set sail for home, arriving at Greenock on 21st January 1880 from where they proceeded by train to Glasgow to be stationed in the Maryhill Barracks.

The battalion remained in Glasgow until 26th May 1881 when they proceeded by rail and steamer to Portsmouth and then to Aldershot where they took up residence in the permanent infantry barracks.

On 1st July 1881, as a result of the Childers's army reforms, the 74th was merged with the 71st to become the Highland Light Infantry, with the 74th designated as the 2nd battalion.

With the outbreak of hostilities in Egypt, the 2nd battalion Highland Light Infantry became the first of the Childers's merged regiments to be deployed on foreign service.

On 8th August 1881, William with his battalion boarded *SS France* at Plymouth bound for Egypt, were landed at Alexandria on 20th August and despatched to the camp at Ramleh where they became part of the 3rd or Highland Brigade of the 2nd Division of the Egyptian Field Force commanded by General Sir E. B. Hamley.

William and the battalion remained at Ramleh, guarding the left flank of the British position until 30th August 1882 when they set sail for Ismailia where they arrived on the 2nd September and on 9th September marched off to Kassassin where forces were being assembled for an attack on the Egyptian forces at Tel-el-Kebir.

It was on 13th September 1882, during the Battle of Tel-el-Kebir that William performed the deeds for which he was later awarded the Victoria Cross; during the action he was seriously wounded.[642]

After the battle, the battalion was moved to Cairo, where they remained for the remainder of their stay in Egypt.

On the 5th February 1883, William and the regiment boarded *HMS Serapis* at Alexandria and set sail for home, arriving at Plymouth on 18th February, where they set up quarters.

For his service during the war, William was awarded the Egypt Medal (1882–89) with clasp for Tel-el-Kebir, he was also awarded the Khedive's Star (1882).

William was presented with his Victoria Cross Medal by Queen Victoria on 23rd February 1883 at an investiture held at Windsor Castle.

After a short time at home, William and the battalion was once again despatched to foreign service and on 1st October 1884 boarded *HMS Serapis* at Portsmouth and set sail for India where they reached Bombay on 29th October and arrived at their station at Umbeyla on 7th/8th November 1884.

On 12th March 1885, the battalion was moved to Rawal Pindi for manoeuvres and reviews and attended the camp of exercise at Delhi between December 1885 and January 1886, after which they moved to Dagshai until 3rd November 1886 when they were moved back to Umbeyla.

William was promoted to the rank of Captain on 23rd March 1887.[643]

In 1889, William and the battalion were transferred to Peshawar and it was while stationed here that he was married to Alice (née Norton), the daughter of General Edward Nugent Norton, on 1st November 1889 at St John's Church in Peshawar.

In February 1900, William returned home with the battalion and was stationed at Hamilton in Lanarkshire when the couple had their only child; Barth Mordaunt Marsh was born on 30th March 1891.

William was appointed as Adjutant to the 3rd Battalion Highland Light Infantry on 1st January 1892,[644] a position that he would hold until his retirement from the army.

642 *London Gazette* – 25154/4558
643 *London Gazette* – 25716/3498
644 *London Gazette* – 26250/426

On 4th September 1895, William was promoted to the rank of Major.[645]

After just over 20 years of service, William retired from the army on 11th November 1896[646] and returned to live with his family at the family home at Hardingham Hall in Norfolk.

On 19th February 1899, upon the nomination of Lord Belper, William was appointed as one of the Honourable Corps of Gentlemen-at-Arms to Queen Victoria.[647]

William was commissioned as Deputy Lieutenant of the County of Norfolk on 13th August 1900[648] and at some stage he was also appointed as a Justice of the Peace.

In 1902, William was awarded the King Edward VII Coronation Medal.

With the death of his father on 11th June 1909, William, as the oldest son, inherited the family estate at Hardingham Hall.

In 1911, William was awarded the King George V Coronation Medal.

William died at Hardingham Hall on 17th September 1912, at the age of 57 and was buried in St George's Churchyard in Hardingham.

William's Victoria Cross Medal is not on public display, believed to be in private hands.

Figure 205a. Grave of William Mordant Marsh Edwards

645 *London Gazette* – 26658/4970
646 *London Gazette* – 26793/6126
647 *London Gazette* – 27067/2159
648 *London Gazette* – 27222/5180

Arthur Knyvet Wilson
29th February 1884 (VC No. 399)

Gazetted: 21st May 1884 25356/2277

Rank and Unit: Captain – Royal Navy – Naval Brigade

Citation

This Officer, on the staff of Rear-Admiral Sir William Hewett, at the battle of El-Teb, on the 29th February, attached himself during the advance to the right half battery, Naval Brigade, in the place of Lieutenant Royds, R.N., mortally wounded. As the troops closed on the enemy's Krupp battery the Aralis charged out on the corner of the square and on the detachment who were dragging the Gardner gun. Captain Wilson then sprang to the front and engaged in single combat with some of the enemy, thus protecting his detachment till some men of the York and Lancaster Regiment came to his assistance with their bayonets. But for the action of this Officer Sir Redvers Buller thinks that one or more of his detachment must have been speared.

Captain Wilson was wounded but remained with the half battery during the day.

Biography

Arthur was born at Swaffham in Norfolk on 4th March 1842 to father George a Commander (later Rear-Admiral) in the Royal Navy and mother Agnes Mary (née Yonge) the daughter of the Vicar at Swaffham.

He was the third born of five children with older brothers William born in 1838 and Roland born in 1841 and younger sisters Edith born in 1844 and Katherine born in 1846.

Arthur's two older brothers both attended Eton on scholarships and in order to be near the boys, the family moved to Eaton and then Windsor where in 1851 they lived at Brunswick Place, New Windsor. In 1852, at the age of 10, having failed to secure a scholarship, Arthur attended Eaton as a day-boy.

With the outbreak of the Crimean War in 1854, prospects on employment in the Royal Navy were looking favourable, so after some coaching from his father Arthur sat the Naval Cadet examinations at Portsmouth in 1855, which he passed on 11th June 1855.

On 29th June 1855, Arthur joined *HMS Victory* as a Naval Cadet under the command of Captain George Thomas Gordon, which was serving as the flag-ship to Rear-Admiral Thomas John Cochrane at Portsmouth.

Figure 206. Arthur Knyvet Wilson

Arthur joined *HMS Powerful* on 9th July 1855, under the command of Captain George Mansel, as a supernumerary for transfer to the Black Sea and at Malta on 7th August boarded the troopship *HMS Himalaya* to continue his journey to the Crimea.

After arriving at Balaklava, later in the month, Arthur was transferred via *HMS Sphinx* and *HMS Royal Albert* to *HMS Algiers* where under the command of Captain Charles Talbot he served in operations in the Black Sea towards the end of the Crimean War; taking part in the bombardments of Sevastopol in September 1855 and of Kinburn in October 1855.

For his service during the Crimean War, Arthur was awarded the Crimea Medal (1854–56) with clasp for Sevastopol, he was also awarded the Turkish Crimea Medal (1855–56) and the Order of the Medjidieh (3rd Class) by the Turkish Government.

At the end of the war, *HMS Algiers* was sent to Malta for a refit and in March 1856 returned to England where after spending a week on board *HMS Rodney*, commanded by his father, Arthur was appointed to *HMS Colossus* under the command of Captain Harry Keppel a relative and friend of the family.

HMS Colossus was sent on a return trip to the Crimea, however, Arthur did not make the return journey on *HMS Colossus* as, after reaching Balaklava he went ashore to look for the lost dog belonging to an army officer and by the time that he had found the dog and returned to the dock, *HMS Colossus* had set sail for home.

After making his return to England via another ship, Arthur was transferred to *HMS Raleigh*, on 17th September 1856, to be reunited with Captain Harry Kepple who now commanded this vessel for service on the China Station.

On the way to her station, *HMS Raleigh* stopped briefly at Madeira on 8th December 1856 before rounding the Cape on the way to Hong Kong to join up with the Commander-in-Chief.

On 15th March 1857, while on the approach to Macao, *HMS Raleigh* struck a rock and was beached on soft mud where she eventually sank; fortunately all hands were saved.

After three days on shore, Arthur was part of a large party of officers and men from *HMS Raleigh* sent to Hong Kong to join *HMS Calcutta* commanded by Captain William King Hall, which was the flagship of Rear-Admiral Michael Seymour who was the Commander-in-Chief of the station.

With *HMS Calcutta*, was involved in the 2nd Anglo-China (Arrow) War; after spending most of the summer in harbour at Hong Kong, Arthur was assigned to a field gun in November 1857 and finally saw action during the bombardment of Canton on 14th December which led to the capture of the city on 1st January 1858.

On 20th May 1858, Arthur was involved in the first Battle of the Taku Forts and for his action received a mention in despatches.

For his service during the war, Arthur was awarded the Second China War Medal (1857–60) with clasps for Canton 1857 and Taku Forts 1858.

In October 1858, with a break in the hostilities, *HMS Calcutta* returned to Hong Kong and in January 1859 received orders to return home; after leaving Hong Kong in mid-March she arrived at Devonport on 13th August 1859 where Arthur and the crew were paid off.

After 6 weeks leave, spent mainly with his family in Dieppe, Arthur joined *HMS Topaze* under the command of Captain John Welbore Sunderland Spencer at the beginning of October 1859 and by the middle of the month set sail for duty on the Pacific station.

HMS Topaze crossed the Atlantic and after replenishing her supplies of coal at Rio de Janeiro made her way via the Magellan Straits into the Pacific and arrived at Esquimalt on the coast of Canada which was the headquarters of the Pacific Station.

Arthur spent the next year at Esquimalt, mainly on harbour duties and on his 19th birthday took further naval examinations on 4th March 1861, which he passed and being awarded a first class certificate continued his service with *HMS Topaze* as acting sub-Lieutenant.

After a further 2½ years of service on the Pacific station, *HMS Topaze* set sail for home and on the return journey, when a vacancy for Lieutenant arose, Arthur was appointed as acting Lieutenant.

Arthur was paid off when *HMS Topaze* landed at Portsmouth on 31st December 1863 and after only three days of leave he entered the Naval College at Portsmouth to prepare for further examinations.

After passing his examinations with great success, Arthur was promoted to the rank of Lieutenant which was back dated to 11th December 1861.

Soon after his promotion to Lieutenant, Arthur joined *HMS Gladiator* on 10th March 1864, under the command of Captain Francis Henry Shortt followed from 15th June 1865 by Captain Elphinstone D'Oyly D'Auvergne Aplin.

HMS Gladiator was employed on "particular service" i.e. under the direct control of the Admiralty to transport troops or stores, search for a wreck or any other emergency duty.

It was while serving on *HMS Gladiator*, that Arthur received the sad news of the death of his brother William who was killed in a fall from mount Rifflehorn in Switzerland on 11th July 1865.

After serving on *HMS Gladiator* for two years, Arthur attended a Lieutenant Gunnery course at *HMS Excellent* on Whale Island from 2nd April 1866.

In early 1867, Arthur was invited to join a mission to Japan under the command of Commander Richard Tracey a one of several Royal Navy officers being sent by the British Government to Yedo (Tokyo) where they were to help train young Japanese Navy Officers.

Arthur left for Japan on board *HMS Rodney* in May 1867 and after transferring to a mail steamer at Hong Kong arrived at Yokohama on 23rd October 1867.

The school opened on 1st January 1868, however, the opportunity for teaching was short lived as when war broke out between the Tycoon and Mikado factions in Japan, to preserve the strict British neutrality the school was closed on 5th March 1868 and the British party returned to Yokohama.

With no prospect of the school being reopened, Arthur and the British party finally left Japan and arrived back in England during December 1868.

On 1st January 1869, Arthur was appointed as first Lieutenant to *HMS Britannia*, a training ship at Dartmouth.

Arthur was appointed, together with Captain William Arthur and Captain Morgan Singer, on 12th May 1870 to a committee based at *HMS Excellent* to investigate the properties of a torpedo designed by a Mr Whitehead.

As Mr Whitehead was delayed for a time in France, due to the outbreak of the Franco-Prussian War, Arthur was assigned for a short time to *HMS Royal Sovereign* while she acted as guard ship at Cowes while Queen Victoria was on a visit to Osborne House.

During this duty, Arthur had the pleasure of giving his sovereign, and Prince Arthur and Princesses Louise and Beatrice, a guided tour of the ship.

On 31st August 1870, the torpedo trial finally got underway on the Medway with great success, the first firing with an armed warhead sank the target hulk.

After the end of the torpedo trial, Arthur was appointed to *HMS Caledonia* and on 25th September 1870 joined *HMS*

Lord Warden, commanded by Captain Thomas Brandreth, as gunnery Lieutenant during his passage to the Mediterranean to join his new ship. On the voyage, Arthur worked with Lieutenant Kane, the gunnery officer, on experiments with submarine mines.

Arthur joined his new ship *HMS Caledonia*, commanded by Captain Thomas Cochran, off Syracuse in December 1870 and was involved in the abortive attempt to save *HMS Psyche* which sank off Catania on 15th December 1870.

On 11th May 1871, Captain Chandos Scudamore Stanhope took over the command of *HMS Caledonia*, however, his tenure was short lived as he died from smallpox on 7th July 1871 and was replaced the next day by Captain Charles Pringle.

During the summer of 1872, *HMS Caledonia* took part in an exercise with the combined Mediterranean and Channel fleets off the west coast of Spain, after which the crew was paid off and Arthur returned to England in September 1872.

On 16th October 1872, Arthur was appointed as first Lieutenant to *HMS Narcissus*, which under the command of Captain John Ommanney Hopkins was the flagship to Rear-Admiral Frederick Archbald Campbell the commander-in-chief of the six ship detached squadron.

The squadron, which was used as a vehicle for the further training of naval officers, had no fixed station set sail from Plymouth for the West Indies on 15th January 1873.

After touching base at Trinidad, the squadron patrolled the islands until June when at Bermuda they had a refit before proceeding to Halifax Nova Scotia where they were quickly ordered to proceed to Gibraltar.

On 18th September 1873, Arthur received his long awaited promotion to the rank of Commander[649] and returned to England sometime in December 1873 (in time for his brother's wedding on 27th December).

On 9th December 1873, Arthur was appointed as Executive Officer to *HMS Raleigh* under the command of Captain George Tryon which was to be part of a detached squadron. As the ship was recently commissioned, she required fitting out and went on sea trial so did not join the rest of the squadron at Gibraltar until 8th November 1873.

From Gibraltar, the squadron undertook a voyage around the south Atlantic visiting the Falkland Islands and the Cape Colony and after a short journey to transport General Sir Garnet Wolseley (the governor and commander-in-chief of the Cape Colony) and his staff from Cape Town to Durban *HMS Raleigh* rejoined the squadron at St Helena before returning to Gibraltar by mid-June 1875.

649 *London Gazette* – 24018/4255

Soon after arriving at Gibraltar, the squadron received orders that they were to act as the escort to the Prince of Wales, on board *HMS Serapis*, on his visit to India.

On 14th July 1875, the squadron left Gibraltar and arrived at Bombay on 22nd October, with the Prince on board *HMS Serapis* arriving a few days later on 8th November 1875.

After the Prince of Wales arrival in India, his itinerary required a sea voyage from Bombay to Calcutta via Ceylon and *HMS Raleigh* was ordered to act as guard ship to *HMS Serapis* on her journey.

When *HMS Serapis* left Ceylon for Calcutta, *HMS Raleigh* was relieved of her escort duties and set sail for Madras and eventually returned to Bombay.

On 9th February 1876, while stationed at Bombay, Arthur received the news that he was being posted to *HMS Vernon*; he left India by mail steamer at the beginning of March and was back in London by 25th March 1876.

Arthur took up his appointment as Executive Officer on board *HMS Vernon* on 26th April 1876, under the command of Captain William Arthur, the ship was the recently formed torpedo school at Portsmouth.

In 1879, during his visit to England, Alexander Graham Bell visited *HMS Vernon* and helped adapt a telephone for improved communications between divers and those on shore or on board ship.

On 20th April 1880, following a strong recommendation by Captain William Arthur some nine months earlier, Arthur was promoted to the rank of Captain.[650]

During the time that Arthur was waiting to be appointed to his first command he produced an updated torpedo manual which was a summary of his last four years of work.

On 5th March 1881, Arthur was appointed to the command of *HMS Hecla* and on 25th March 1881 joined his first command at Malta.

For the next few months, Arthur commanded his ship on fleet exercises and drills across the Mediterranean and Adriatic until returning to Spithead on 13th May 1882 for a replacement crew.

Following her refit at Spithead, it was intended that *HMS Hecla* would join the Channel Squadron, however, with the worsening situation in Egypt, Arthur and his ship was deployed to Malta where they arrived on 1st July 1882.

HMS Hecla left Malta on 7th July 1882 with orders to join the British Fleet assembled off Alexandria at the start of the Anglo-Egyptian war; she arrived at Alexandria on 11th July half an hour before the start of the British bombardment of the city.

650 *London Gazette* – 24840/2786

After the bombardment, *HMS Hecla* was fitted out as a magazine ship and was used to resupply the rest of the fleet with munitions.

When the British seized the Suez Canal, *HMS Hecla* was moved to Lake Timsah where she formed part of the canal guard and on 26th September, following the end of the war she set sail for Malta on 26th September for a refit.

For his service during the war, Arthur was awarded the Egypt Medal (1882–89) with clasp for Alexandria 11th July, he was also awarded the Khedive's Star (1882).

The refit at Malta was completed within three weeks and by the end of October 1882, *HMS Hecla* was at Port Said, where in addition to his command of the ship Arthur was appointed Commandant of the town with a garrison of 240 Marines and orders to maintain order in the town.

On the 6th November *HMS Invincible* arrived at Port Said and took over responsibility for the town and the next morning Arthur set sail for Corfu and Fiume to witness the demonstration of a new type of torpedo.

HMS Hecla returned to England, arriving at Spithead on 31st March 1883 and after a few weeks at Portsmouth was attached to the Channel Fleet for exercises in mining and countermining.

At the end of November 1883, *HMS Hecla* returned to duties in the Mediterranean and after a short visit to Fiume to see a demonstration of the latest torpedo improvements proceeded to Malta.

On 8th February 1884, Arthur received orders to board a detachment of 240 marines and proceed to Port Said, in response to troubles breaking out in the Sudan. After arriving at Port Said on 12th February, the marines were transferred to *HMS Orontes* and 170 men bound for London were loaded on board *HMS Hecla* for transfer home.

HMS Hecla left Port Said bound for home, on 16th February, however, on 21st February Arthur came across *HMS Neera*, beached on reefs with the 19th Hussars on board. Coming alongside *HMS Neera* many of the troops were transferred to *HMS Hecla*, with the remainder being boarded on other ships which had also come to the rescue.

With his new charges, Arthur set sail for Trinkitat, where General Gerald Graham was assembling a force to go to the relief of Tokar, arriving on the evening of 23rd February 1884.

Arthur sent 25 men from *HMS Hecla*, with a Gardiner gun, to join the Naval Brigade at Fort Baker on 28th February, in preparation for an assault on El Teb planned for the following day.

It was on the 29th February 1884, while serving with the Naval Brigade at the Battle of El Teb, in the Sudan that Arthur performed the deeds for which he would later be awarded the Victoria Cross, during the action he was wounded by a sabre slash to the head.

During the next few weeks, *HMS Hecla* was anchored off the Port of Suakin and Arthur provided working parties, from his crew, to assist with duties in the port.

By the beginning of April it was obvious that there was no further role for the ship in the remainder of the campaign as it drew to a close, so *HMS Hecla* set sail for Malta where she arrived on 21st April 1884.

For his service during the war, Arthur was awarded the clasp for El Teb and Suakin 1884, to add to his Egypt Medal (1882–89).

Soon after the arrival at Malta, *HMS Hecla* together with *HMS Inflexible* carried out some long postponed torpedo experiments and then Arthur with *HMS Hecla* set sail for their return to England, arriving at Spithead on 10th May 1884.

After spending a few days completing his official duties, Arthur returned to his home town of Swaffham where, following the announcement of his Victoria Cross award, he received a warm welcome.

On 6th June 1884, Arthur was presented with his Victoria Cross medal by Admiral Sir Geoffrey Hornby, at Southsea Common in Portsmouth.

On 26th June, *HMS Hecla* was involved in two weeks of mining exercises at Berehaven after which she joined the rest of the squadron at Portland for further exercises.

HMS Hecla returned to Portsmouth on 31st July 1884 and Arthur handed over his command and after a short holiday took up new duties as Chairman of the Torpedo Discharge Committee.

On 24th February 1885, Arthur was appointed as Flag Captain to Admiral Sir Walter James Hunt-Grubbe at the Cape of Good Hope, and was given command of his old ship *HMS Raleigh* which was to be the Admiral's flag ship.

After completing commissioning trials at Plymouth, Arthur and *HMS Raleigh* set sail on 29th March 1885, with the Admiral on board, bound for the Cape Station, where she arrived at Simon's Town on 13th May.

As flagship, *HMS Raleigh* spent much of her time in harbour at Simon's Town but in December 1885 had a brief visit to Port Elizabeth for the opening of an exhibition held by the Cape Governor.

In January 1886, *HMS Raleigh* conveyed the Admiral on his annual tour of the colony, returning to Simon's Town at the end of March following which Arthur took a short leave.

The remainder of 1886, was similar to the previous year, with much time spent in the harbour at Simon's Town, however, in June 1886, *HMS Raleigh* had a short tour putting in at Port Elizabeth, East London and Durban.

In November 1886, *HMS Raleigh* transported the High Commissioner Sir Hercules Robinson to Mauritius for an enquiry into the administration of the colony and on her return to the Cape in December, Arthur received the news that he had been appointed to a newly created post as Director of Torpedoes at the Admiralty.

In February 1887, Arthur accompanied the Admiral on his annual voyage around the Cape Colony, however, when *HMS Raleigh* reached St Helena he relinquished his command to his successor, boarded a mail steamer and set sail for home to take up his new appointment.

After arriving at Southampton on 2nd March 1887, Arthur reported to the Admiralty and found that his role was now Assistant Director of Torpedoes, reporting to Captain Fisher the Director of Naval Ordnance who would now act as Director of Naval Ordnance and Torpedoes.

Arthur took up his duties at the Admiralty on 20th April 1887 and was soon in attendance at various torpedo trials and experiments.

On 21st June 1887, Arthur was appointed as an Ordinary Member 3rd Class (Companion) of the Military Division of the Most Honourable Order of the Bath.[651]

Apart from a short spell as commander of *HMS Imperieuse*, during the Naval Review to celebrate the Queen's Jubilee, Arthur continued in his role as Assistant Director of Torpedoes until 1st January 1889 when he was appointed as Captain of *HMS Vernon*, part of the torpedo school at Portsmouth.

In July 1889, with the torpedo schools closed while reserve ships were mobilised for manoeuvres, Arthur served as Flag Captain to Rear Admiral Tracey on board *HMS Rodney* until September 1889.

Arthur was appointed to the command of *HMS Sans Pareil*, a new battleship under commissioning at Chatham, on 9th February 1892, destined for service on the Mediterranean Station.

On 14th February 1892, Arthur was appointed as a Naval Aide-de-Camp to Queen Victoria, a post that he would hold until he attained flag rank on 20th June 1895.[652]

HMS Sans Pareil left England on 6th March 1892, bound for the Mediterranean and after her sea trials and some remedial work at Malta took her place with the fleet at the end of May.

On 22nd June 1893, while on exercises off Tripoli, Arthur was a witness to the collision between *HMS Victoria* and *HMS Camperdown* which resulted in the sinking of *HMS Victoria*, the death of 358 men (half her crew) and the death of Rear-Admiral Sir George Tryon, the commander of the Mediterranean fleet.

651 *London Gazette* – 25712/3362

652 *London Gazette* – 26264/1275

When the new commander in chief, Admiral Sir Michael Seymour, reached Malta, *HMS Sans Pareil* was ordered to Malta and Arthur was appointed as Flag Captain, until the new flagship *HMS Ramillies* arrived on station.

Arthur was subsequently called as a witness held on board *HMS Hibernia*, in Malta on 17th July 1893 at which the cause of the collision was put down to the orders of the deceased Rear-Admiral.

On 9th February 1895, having completed the normal period of a commission, Arthur was informed that *HMS Sans Pareil* was to be replaced by *HMS Barfleur* and on 14th March left Malta to meet the replacement at Gibraltar where they met on 23rd March.

HMS Sans Pareil arrived home at Sheerness on 29th March and the crew was paid off on 17th April 1895.

After leaving *HMS Sans Pareil*, Arthur spent the next two months on holiday with friends in Norfolk, however, in June he was offered the command of an experimental Torpedo Squadron, to test the capabilities of the newly developed torpedo-boat destroyer.

Before Arthur was able to take up his new command he received an unexpected surprise when he was promoted to the flag rank of Rear-Admiral on 20th June 1895.[653]

Towards the end of July 1895, the experimental squadron was assembled at Plymouth and Arthur selected *HMS Hermione* as his flagship and on 28th July left port for exercises.

In the summer of 1896, Arthur was appointed to act as Rear-Admiral 2nd in command of the Reserve Fleet during the annual Navy Manoeuvres and selected his previous command *HMS Sans Pareil* as his flagship.

In August, at the end of the manoeuvres, Arthur was placed in charge of a small mission sent to Mauritius to select a suitable site for constructing a dry dock large enough to take a battleship.

After spending four months to select a site to the north of Grand Port, Arthur returned to England only to find that the Admiralty had decided on a site at Simon's Town in the Cape Colony.

Arthur was awarded the Queen Victoria Golden Jubilee Medal in 1897 and was appointed as Controller of the Navy by the First Sea Lord, taking up his duties on 23rd August 1897 with responsibility for a large programme of refits and new builds.

After over three years of successful, but sometimes acrimonious, times as Controller of the Navy Arthur was appointed to the command of the Channel Squadron and on 18th April 1901, hoisted his flag on *HMS Majestic* at Portsmouth.

653 *London Gazette* – 26637/3692

A few days later Arthur sailed to join his squadron at Berehaven off the coast of Ireland for exercises before the squadron returned to Portsmouth for refits and leave before the annual Navy Manoeuvres.

On 24th May 1901, Arthur was promoted to the rank of Vice-Admiral.[654]

In June 1901, the Channel Squadron reassembled at Portland and took part in the annual Navy Manoeuvres after which they joined the Mediterranean fleet off Lagos on the coast of Portugal for further exercises.

After the exercises, the Channel Squadron returned to Berehaven and on 26th September resumed normal duties.

Arthur was appointed as an Ordinary Member 2nd Class (Knight Commander) of the Military Division of the Most Honourable Order of the Bath on 26th June 1902,[655] during the year he was also awarded the King Edward VII Coronation Medal.

Arthur's last cruise with the Channel Squadron, left Berehaven on 18th February, bound for operations off the coast of Spain and as his term of command was about to expire, returned to Portsmouth where on 13th April 1903 he transferred his command to Lord Charles Beresford.

Towards the end of May, Arthur was appointed to his new command as Commander in Chief of the Home Fleet and on 21st May hoisted his flag on his new flagship *HMS Revenge* at Portsmouth.

The Home fleet was mainly involved in duties around the coasts of Great Britain but also was involved in joint exercises with the Channel and Mediterranean fleets.

On 11th August 1903, Arthur was appointed as a Knight Commander of the Royal Victorian Order.[656]

After a visit to the new Submarine School at Portsmouth in December 1903, Arthur proposed that the Home Fleet should be involved in an exercise to develop tactics on how to engage these new vessels.

Arthur's suggested exercise against submarines, eventually took place in March 1904 off Spithead, these ended prematurely on 18th March when a submarine was accidentally rammed and sunk by a mail steamer.

On 5th April 1904, with *HMS Revenge* in dock at Portsmouth for her annual refit, Arthur struck his flag and went on leave and on his return hoisted his flag on *HMS Exmouth*, his new flagship, on 13th June 1904 at Portland.

In December 1904, Arthur became involved in a project to build a Sailors Home at Weymouth, helping with the fundraising and later as chairman of the Building Committee, seeing the project to a successful completion being opened by the 1st Lord of the Admiralty, Lord Tweedmouth in March 1907.

On 14th December `1904, changes by the Admiralty designated the Home Fleet as the Channel Fleet, with the former Channel Fleet now designated as the Atlantic Fleet.

On 24th February 1905, Arthur was promoted to the rank of Admiral[657] and continued with his command of the newly designated Channel Fleet.

During a visit to the Netherlands, Arthur and many of his flag officers were invited by Queen Wilhelmina to attend a dinner at her palace at Het Loo where he was appointed as a Knight Grand Cross of the Order of the Lion.

On 11th August 1905, Arthur was appointed as a Knight Grand Cross of the Royal Victorian Order.[658]

During a tour which took in Germany and Denmark, on 8th September 1905 while anchored off Copenhagen, Arthur and his flag officers received an invitation from King Christian to visit the king at his palace at Bernsdorff where he was appointed as a Knight Grand Cross of the Order of Dannebrog.

On 9th November 1906, Arthur was appointed as an Ordinary Member 1st Class (Knight Grand Cross) of the Military Division of the Most Honourable Order of the Bath.[659]

Arthur set sail for the last time as Commander of the Channel Fleet on 12th December 1906 and returned to Weymouth on 22nd February 1907 where he completed his final act of command by taking part in the opening ceremony for the Sailors Home.

On 1st March 1907, during an audience with King Edward VII, at which Arthur was due to resign his command, having reached the mandatory retirement age of 65, he was surprised when the King handed him a commission as Admiral-of-the-Fleet.[660]

Arthur left *HMS Revenge* on 4th March 1907, after having handed over his command and after nearly 52 years of service went to live with his sister at Beech Cottage in Swaffham, expecting that his Navy career was now at an end.

In his retirement, Arthur learned to drive a motor car and after moving with his sister into the nearby Manor House at Swaffham took up golf and created a nine hole course on waste ground just outside the town.

In November 1907, Arthur was asked by the Admiralty to oversee some experiments with an Aim Corrector, invented by Mr. Pollen which he eagerly accepted.

Arthur was invited by Prime Minister Herbert Henry Asquith to become a member of the Committee of Imperial Defence in

654 *London Gazette* – 27318/3637
655 *London Gazette* – 27448/4189
656 *London Gazette* – 27586/5057
657 *London Gazette* – 27769/1503
658 *London Gazette* – 27826/5532
659 *London Gazette* – 27965/7551
660 *London Gazette* – 28001/1574

April 1909 and acted as the Chief Umpire during the annual Navy Manoeuvres during the summer.

On 6th November 1909, Arthur was invited to attend an audience with King Edward VII at Sandringham where the King offered him the post of First Lord of the Admiralty, soon to be vacated by Sir John Fisher.

Arthur was initially reluctant to accept the offer, but was eventually persuaded by the King to accept the appointment which was formally offered on 20th November and announced in the London Gazette on 2nd December 1909.

On 27th December 1909, Arthur spent a week at Sandringham as a guest of the King and on 25th January 1910 took up his appointment as 1st Sea Lord after having been appointed as a Commissioner of the Lord High Admiral of the United Kingdom[661] (the Admiralty Board), under the First Lord, Reginald McKenna.

On 27 January 1910, Arthur moved to his official residence at 16 Queen Anne's Gate but later moved to Mall House.

Arthur was subsequently reappointed to the Commission of the Lord High Admiral on 20th December 1910[662] and 25th March 1911.[663]

During 1911, Arthur was awarded the King George V Coronation Medal.

On 24th October 1911, on his return to duties following a holiday, Arthur learned that Reginald McKenna was to be replaced as First Lord by Mr Winston Churchill and soon afterwards he was advised that he would be replaced as 1st Sea Lord.

The new Admiralty Board was sworn in on 5th December 1911 and on 13th December Arthur returned to Swaffham for a second period of retirement.

Arthur was offered a peerage, however, after having obtained the permission of the King, he graciously declined the offer.

On 4th March 1912, his 70th birthday, Arthur was placed on the retirement list.[664]

Arthur was appointed as a member of the Order of Merit by King George V[665] on 8th March 1912 and in June received a degree as Doctor of Civil Law from Oxford University.

Soon after the outbreak of the Great War, Prince Louis resigned as 1st Sea Lord on 28th August 1912 and Winston Churchill appointed Lord Fisher as his replacement.

Arthur was offered the position as Chief of the Naval War Staff to assist Lord Fisher, however, he declined but agreed to assist in an unpaid and unofficial capacity and was accepted as such working with the Naval War Staff Group.

With growing tension between Lord Fisher and Mr Churchill, regarding the conduct of operations, Lord Fisher tendered his resignation as First Sea Lord on 15th May 1915 and left office without waiting to brief his replacement.

Eager not to leave an important gap in the Naval Command, Mr Churchill offered the position of First Sea Lord to Arthur, however, before this could be approved Mr Churchill was replaced as First Lord of the Admiralty by Mr Arthur Balfour and Sir Henry Jackson was appointed as First Sea Lord – Arthur continued in his unofficial capacity as a member of the Naval War Staff Group.

On 1st January 1917, Arthur underwent an operation to remove a cataract which was impairing the sight of one eye, however, after only one week of convalescence was back at work at the Admiralty.

Finally on 18th August 1918, Arthur retired from his duties for the last time and returned to his home at Swaffham.

On 29th October 1919, on the death of his brother Roland, Arthur succeeded his brother to become the 3rd Baronet of Delhi.[666]

Arthur attended a garden party at Buckingham Palace, to which all holders of the Victoria Cross had been invited on 26th

Figure 206a.
Grave of Arthur Knyvet Wilson

661 *London Gazette* – 28333/689
662 *London Gazette* – 28449/9547
663 *London Gazette* – 28479/2421
664 *London Gazette* – 28558/1747
665 *London Gazette* – 28588/1743

666 Sir Archdale Wilson was created as the 1st Baronet of Delhi in 1858 after his defence of Delhi during the Indian Mutiny, having died without heirs the Baronetsy passed to his brothers line.

June 1920, 63 years to the day since the first medals were presented by Queen Victoria in Hyde Park.

In addition to his many awards and decorations previously mentioned, at some stage Arthur was also appointed as a Grand Officer of the Legion of Honour by France and as a Grand Cross of the Order of Naval Merit by Spain.

At the age of 79, Arthur died of heart failure following pneumonia, on 25th May 1921 at Beech Cottage in Swaffham and was buried with military honours at Swaffham Church five days later.

Arthur's Victoria Cross Medal is on public display at the National Royal Navy Museum in Portsmouth.

William Thomas Marshall
29th February 1884 (VC No. 400)

Gazetted: 21st May 1884 25356/2278

Rank and Unit: Quartermaster Sergeant – 19th Hussars

Citation

For his conspicuous bravery during the Cavalry charge at El-Teb, on 29th February last, in bringing Lieutenant-Colonel Barrow, 19th Hussars, out of action. That officer having been severely wounded, and his horse killed, was on the ground surrounded by the enemy, when Quartermaster-Sergeant Marshall, who stayed behind with him, seized his hand and dragged him through the enemy back, to the regiment.

Had Lieutenant-Colonel Barrow been left behind he must have been killed.

Biography

William was born on 5th December 1854 at Newark in Nottinghamshire to father John Richard, a stone mason, and mother Mary (née Briggs). He was the oldest of five children with brothers Walter born in 1858, John Richard born in 1863 and Charles born in 1869, he also had a sister Julia born in 1861 who died in 1863.

On 20th July 1873, at the age of 18 William enlisted in the British Army as a trooper with the 19th Hussars.

William was initially stationed at Aldershot and then from the end of June 1875 the regiment was moved to Leeds with detachments at Preston and Bury.

In June 1876, the regiment moved to Ireland and saw service during the "Boycott" campaign and the Land League conspiracy in support of the civil powers.

In June 1882, the regiment received orders to return to England and while on the march to Aldershot, where they arrived on 14th July 1882, they received news of their immediate posting to Egypt on active service.

As part of a force being assembled at Alexandria, under the command of General Sir Garnet Wolseley, on 10th August 1882, William and the regiment boarded the transports *Assyrian Monarch* and *Montreal* at Southampton and set sail for Egypt.

William and the regiment arrived at Ismailia on 24th August 1882, too late to take part in the opening actions of the Anglo-Egyptian War during which the British forces secured the Suez Canal.

The 19th Hussars were deployed as divisional troops, William with the right wing under Colonel Coghill was assigned to the

Figure 207. William Thomas Marshall

1st Division, commanded by General Willis while the left wing under Colonel Webster was assigned to the 2nd Division commanded by General Sir E. Hamley.

On 13th September 1882, William took part in the Battle of Tel-el-Kebir and seized the railway station and bridge, cutting off many of the fleeing enemy.

The next day, Cairo was taken and the war was over, the regiment was stationed at Cairo.

For his service during the war, William was awarded the Egypt Medal (1882–89) with clasp for Tel-el-Kebir, and the Khedive's Star.

In November 1883, the regiment was notified to make ready for a return to England, however, events in the Sudan, leading up to the Mahdist war soon changed these plans.

On 17th February 1884, William and the regiment boarded the transports *Osiris* and *Neera* at Cairo and set sail for Trinkitat where the *Osiris* landed on 22nd February.

The *Neera* was less fortunate as she struck a rock off Suakin and was totally wrecked, although all the men and horses were saved and eventually reached Trinkitat on 25th February.

The regiment, together with the 10th Hussars and mounted infantry were assigned to a cavalry force commanded by Colonel Herbert Stewart and on 28th February 1884 this force moved to Fort Baker.

On the 29th February 1884, William and the regiment were involved in the Battle of El Teb and it was during this action that he performed the deeds for which he would later be awarded the Victoria Cross.

On 6th March 1884, the regiment boarded transports at Trinkitat and were landed at Suakin on the next day.

William and the regiment fought in the Battle of Tamai on 13 March 1884, this was against about 10,000 Mahdist soldiers, mainly from the Hadendoa tribe, who due to their unique hair style were known by the British Soldiers as "Fuzzy Wuzzies".

On 1st April 1884, with their objectives achieved, William and the regiment boarded transports at Suakin and set sail for Cairo where they landed on 6th April 1884.

For his service during the war, William received a mention in despatches and was awarded the clasps for Suakin 1884 and El Tab / Tamai to add to his Egypt Medal (1882–89).

William's Victoria Cross medal was sent out to Egypt in May 1884, with the intention that it should be presented by Colonel A. G. Webster the commanding officer of the 19th Hussars, however, by the time the medal arrived, William had already left for England.

A replacement medal was rapidly struck by Hancock's and was presented to William by Queen Victoria on 3rd July 1884 at an investiture held at Windsor Castle, the original medal was eventually returned to the War Office.

During 1884–85, some troops of the 19th Hussars took part in the Nile Expedition, to go to the relief of General Gordon at Khartoum, however, it is not known if William was one of those involved.

One of the casualties during the Nile Expedition was Quartermaster Lima, who was killed on 20th January 1885, William was commissioned as his replacement on the same day.

The force involved in the Nile Expedition were reunited with the regiment at Cairo on 14th August 1885.

On 19th May 1887, William and the regiment boarded the transports *Geelong* and *Iona* at Alexandria and set sail for England, landing at Harwich and Woolwich on 6th–7th June, from where they moved to Norwich with a detachment at Colchester.

In April 1888, the regiment was moved to Hounslow, Hampton Court and Kensington until June 1889 when they moved to Aldershot.

On 27th October 1890, the General Officer Commanding at Aldershot wrote to the War Office, concerning William's Victoria Cross pension, which due to previous interpretations of the originating Warrant would cease following his commission as Quartermaster; by now William was an honorary Lieutenant.

On 6th November, General Harman, the Military Secretary, wrote to the Financial Secretary that he did not believe that it was the intention of the Warrant to deprive a soldier of his pension when he was subsequently commissioned.

It was finally agreed by the Secretary of State Mr Stanhope, that soldiers who were subsequently commissioned should retain their Victoria Cross pension as from 1st April 1890.

On 1st September 1891, William and the regiment boarded *HMS Euphrates* at Portsmouth and set sail for India arriving at

Bombay on 28th September where they were forwarded by train to Secunderabad where they relieved the 7th Hussars.

In November 1891, the regiment was moved by train to Bangalore where they remained until October 1896 when they were transferred back to Secunderabad and soon afterwards returned to England.

On 20th January 1893, William received an honorary promotion to the rank of Captain.

The regiment were soon on foreign service once again when in September 1899 they were posted to the Cape Colony in South Africa and were serving at Ladysmith at the outbreak of the 2nd Boer War on 12th October 1899.

William and the regiment were involved in the Battle of Rietfontein on 24th October 1899 and the Battle of Lombard's Kop on 30th October, which was an unsuccessful operation to prevent the siege of Ladysmith.

From 2nd November 1899 to 28th February 1900, William and his regiment were besieged at Ladysmith until relieved by forces led by General Redvers Buller.

William was involved with his regiment in operations in Natal from March 1900 until June 1900, culminating in the Battle of Laing's Nek on 2nd to 9th June.

From July 1900 until 31st May 1902, William was involved in operations in the Transvaal and the Orange River Colony.

For his service during the war, William was awarded the Queen's South Africa Medal (1899–1902) with clasp for Defence of Ladysmith, Orange Free State, Transvaal and Laing's Nek.

On 24th October 1900, William was married to Lydia Louise (née Wiseman) at Ipswich, the couple would have three children, a daughter Violet and two sons.

Following the war, William and the regiment remained in South Africa until 1904 when they returned to England.

On 26th May 1905, William was transferred from the 19th Hussars, assigned to Aldershot as Camp Quartermaster, with honorary rank of Major.

After 34 years of service, William retired from the army to pension on 19th January 1907.

On leaving the army William and his family moved to Scotland where he was employed by the Weems's Bay Tramway Company.

William continued his association with the military, serving as Secretary of the County of Fife Territorial Force Association from 1st March 1908 until his death.

From 1908 until 1914, William also served as the Honorary County Secretary of the Fife branch of the British Red Cross Society.

On 11th September 1920, William died at his home in 16 Townsend Crescent, Kirkcaldy at the age of 65 and was buried in the Bennochy Road Cemetery in Kirkcaldy.

William's Victoria Cross medal is on public display at the Discovery Museum (home of the 15th/19th King's Royal Hussars Museum) in Newcastle-upon-Tyne.

Figure 207a. Grave of William Thomas Marshall

Percival Scrope Marling
13th March 1884 (VC No. 401)

Gazetted: 21st May 1884 25356/2278

Rank and Unit: Lieutenant – 60th Rifles

Citation

For his conspicuous bravery at the battle of Tamai, on 13th March last, in risking his life to save that of Private Morley, Royal Sussex Regiment, who, having been shot, was lifted and placed in front of Lieutenant Marling on his horse. He fell off almost immediately, when Lieutenant Marling dismounted, and gave up his horse for the purpose of carrying off Private Morley, the enemy pressing close on to them until they succeeded in carrying him about 80 yards to a place of comparative safety.

Figure 208. Percival Scrope Marling

Biography

Percival was born on 6th March 1861 at Stanley House, King's Stanley in Stroud, Gloucestershire to father William Henry a woollen cloth manufacturer[667] and mother Mary Emily (née Abraham), he was the oldest of four children with three younger brothers; Charles Murray born on 3rd December 1862, Samuel Stanley born on 20th September 1864 and William John Paley born on 23rd October 1865.

From 1870, Percival attended a preparatory school at Eagle House, Wimbledon run by Rev Dr Huntingford and Rev Arthur Malon until in January 1875 when at the age of 13 he attended Harrow School where he was a member of Randall's House.

At the end of the summer term in 1878, Percival left Harrow and on 20th September 1878 started at a cramming school at Northcott in Ealing to prepare for his Army entrance examinations.

In October 1878, Percival passed the preliminary entry examination for the Royal Military College at Sandhurst but failed the final examination in December.

After a brief holiday at home, over the Christmas period, Percival returned to Northcott in January 1879 for further preparation and in July he passed the entry examination for Sandhurst, coming 103rd out of the 105 applicants who were accepted.

Percival entered the Royal Military College at Sandhurst in September 1879 and in July 1880, passed out and on 11th August 1880 was commissioned as a 2nd Lieutenant in the 3rd battalion of the 60th Kings Royal Rifles.[668]

667 The family business had been in operation for three generations and had large factories at Ebley and Stanley.

668 *London Gazette* – 24872/4366

After only a few weeks of service, Percival began his first period of foreign service when on 15th October 1880 he boarded the transport *Dunrobin Castle* at Dartmouth, with his battalion and set sail for the Cape Colony.

The battalion arrived at Cape Town on 7th November and on 11th November boarded the transport *Melrose* and set sail for Durban where they arrived on 16th November 1880.

By rail and then road, the battalion left proceeded from Durban to Maritzburgh where they arrived on 25th November and took up residence in the barracks at Fort Napier.

On 19th December 1880, the Boers captured Heidelburgh and declared a republic, thus signalling the start of the 1st Boer War with Britain.

To help counter the threat, Percival and the battalion left Fort Napier on 1st January 1881 and made their way to Newcastle, where they arrived on 25th January. At Newcastle General Sir George Pomeroy Colley was assembling a force to attack the Boers and as part of this force Percival and the battalion were involved in the Battle of Laing's Nek on 28th January 1881 and the Battle of Ingogo on 8th February 1881.

Percival was also involved in the British defeat at the Battle of Majuba, which proved to be the decisive battle of the war; a peace treaty was signed at O'Neil's Farm on 23rd March 1881.

Just after the end of the war, from 29th March until 6th April, Percival was hospitalised suffering from dysentery.

On 1st July 1881, as part of the Childers's Army reforms, the 60th Kings Royal Rifles was renamed as the King's Royal Rifle Corps and on the same day Percival was promoted to the rank of Lieutenant.

After the war, Percival and his regiment spent some months in the Cape Colony before boarding *HMS Orontes* at Durban on 23rd February 1882 and set sail for Malta where they landed at Valetta on 3rd April and were installed in the Baviére barracks.

Only three months after arriving at Malta, Percival and the regiment were once again despatched on active service boarding *HMS Agincourt* on 8th July 1882 setting sail for Egypt where they arrived at Alexandria on 18th July to take part in the Anglo-Egyptian War.

After some minor actions around Alexandria, Percival and the battalion boarded *HMS Euphrates* on 18th August and set sail for Ismailia, where they landed two days later.

As part of the force commanded by General Wolseley, Percival and the battalion took part in the Battle of Kassassin on 9th September 1882 and the Battle of Tel-el-Kebir on 13th September after which the British were in total control of the Suez canal.

For his part in the war, Percival was awarded the Egypt Medal (1882–89) with clasp for Tel-el-Kebir, he was also awarded the Khedive's Star by Egypt.

For the next few months after the war, Percival spent his time split between Cairo and Ismailia apart from a period in January 1883 which he spent on board a hospital ship at Alexandria suffering from a further bout of dysentery.

On 24th April 1883, Percival and several of his fellow officers boarded the P&O ship *Poona* at Suez bound for England and a period of home leave.

After arriving at Plymouth on 10th May, Percival spent most of his leave in London until in July he was recalled to the regiment, which was suffering greatly from an epidemic of cholera.

Percival boarded a mail steamer at Marseilles and after landing at Alexandria on 1st August 1883 was despatched to Suez where the regiment was encamped.

On 31st December 1883, Percival was transferred to the Mounted Infantry based at Abbassia, to replace an officer who had transferred to the Egyptian army.

The Mounted Infantry received orders on 13th February 1884 to take part in the Suakin Expedition to the Sudan and go to the relief of the garrison at Tokar.

Percival, with the Mounted Infantry, set off by rail on 15th February and arrived at Suez the next day where they boarded *HMS Orontes* and set sail for the Sudan, landing at Trinkitat on 23rd February.

As part of the force commanded by General Sir Gerald Graham (VC), Percival and the Mounted Infantry fought in the Battle of El Teb on 29th February 1884 and the relief of Tokar on the next day.

It was during the Battle of Tamai on 13th March 1884, that Percival performed the deeds for which he would later be awarded the Victoria Cross.

For his part in the Suakin Expedition, Percival received two mentions in despatches and was awarded the Suakin 1884 and El Teb/Tamai clasps to his Egypt Medal (1882–89).

On 21st March 1884, the Expeditionary force was broken up and by 4th April, Percival who was now acting as Quartermaster was back in the camp at Abbassia in Cairo.

Percival was presented with his Victoria Cross medal, sometime in early July, by General Sir F. C. A. Stephenson the General Officer Commanding troops in Egypt at a ceremony held in Cairo.

On 15th July 1884, soon after receiving his medal, Percival left Egypt for a period of leave in England, however, after only three weeks at home he received a telegram ordering his immediate return to Egypt.

Leaving England at the end of September 1884, Percival rejoined his unit, now renamed the Mounted Infantry Camel Corps at Wadi Halfa on 26th October 1884.

In December 1884, the Mounted Infantry Camel Corps received orders that they were assigned to the force of 7,000 men, under the command of Lord Wolseley, sent as the Nile Expedition to go to the relief of Khartoum, where General Gordon was besieged.

The relief force under the command of General Garnet Wolseley proceeded up the Nile by river steamers and while the bulk of the force continued up river by smaller boats, Percival and the Mounted Infantry Camel Corps were assigned to the desert column.

The desert column was a force of about 1,500 men under the command of General Sir Hubert Stewart that would cross the Bayuda desert on camels avoiding the waterfalls on the Nile.

On 30th December 1884, the Desert Column left Korti and after crossing the desert encountered a force of about 12,000 Mahdist on 16th January 1885.

On the following day, Percival took part in the Battle of Abu Klea; after the battle, the desert column pressed on to Khartoum which they reached on 28th January 1885, only to learn that General Gordon had been killed two days earlier and that the Mahdist forces now occupied the city.

Learning of the news, the British Government decided to withdraw the troops from the Sudan and by 15th July 1885, Percival and his unit were back in quarters at Cairo.

For his service in Egypt, Percival was awarded clasps for The Nile 1884–85 and Abu Klea to add to his Egypt Medal (1882–89).

On 30th July 1885, the Mounted Infantry was disbanded and Percival returned to the 60th Rifles based at Alexandria, however, at the end of August he received order to proceed to Cairo and help reform the Mounted Infantry.

Percival was appointed to the Re-mount Committee in September and in this capacity helped to secure horses for the reformed unit.

On 1st November 1885, Percival was formerly seconded to the Mounted Infantry[669] and given command of a Company and on 1st January 1886 was given the temporary rank of Captain while in command of a company.[670]

In April 1886, Percival set sail from Alexandria on three months home leave and after spending time in Venice, Paris and London, returned back to duty in Cairo on 1st August 1886.

Following an offer from the Duke of Cambridge, Percival was transferred to the 18th Hussars with the rank of Captain on 22nd December 1886.[671]

Percival left Cairo in February 1887 and after spending a short time in London joined his new regiment at their headquarters in Cahir, Tipperary, Ireland on 20th March 1887.

On 30th May 1887, Percival and the regiment left Ireland and after landing at Avonmouth, marched to the Aldershot North Camp where they were encamped on Farnborough Common.

At the end of August until the end of September, Percival attended a musketry course at Hythe and in early 1889 was appointed as Magistrate for Monmouth.

On the 8th August 1889, the regiment moved to the camp at Shorncliffe in preparation for their deployment to India.

Percival and the regiment boarded the troopship *HMS Malaba* at Portsmouth on 20th November 1889 and set sail for India arriving at Bombay on 17th December and at Mhow on 22nd December.

On 1st May, Percival attended a Garrison course at Poona as part of his preparations for promotion to Major and in August commanded the first Mounted Infantry School to be held in India, which lasted for six weeks. At the end of the school, Percival passed his examinations in Engineering.

On 27th April 1891, Percival received a telegram from Colonel Hood (later Lord Bridport) with an offer to become Adjutant of the West Somerset Yeomanry,[672] which he accepted.

Percival left India, to take up his new appointment in August and arrived at Taunton to take up his new role on 19th September 1891.

A year later, Percival was granted permission to resign from his position as Adjutant and after a period of sick leave left England to return to his regiment, now stationed at Umbeyla, where he arrived just before Christmas 1892.

On 9th July 1894, Percival left Calcutta bound for Colombo in Ceylon at the start of a period of leave where he intended to visit Japan, however, after missing his connection to Japan at Colombo he boarded *HMS Himalaya* on 14th August and sailed to Australia instead, visiting Melbourne and Sydney before returning to Umbeyla.

In August 1895, after three years in India, Percival was granted a year of home leave which he mainly spent in London. Having been elected to the MCC at the beginning of 1896, Percival played cricket for the club during the summer of 1896.

Percival was promoted to the rank of Major on 12th August 1896[673] and in October was appointed to the command of the 18th Hussars Depot at Aldershot.

In April 1898, Percival had a very bad fall from his horse while hunting and spent several months at the family home in Sudbury recovering. In November 1898, acting on his doctors advice to seek warmer climes, with his brother Jack, Percival spent several weeks in Rome, Naples and on the French Riviera before returning to England in January 1899.

Percival was married to Beatrice Caroline (née Beaumont) at Buckland Court in Surrey on 18th May 1899 and set off on his honeymoon in Paris and Switzerland.

With news of the impending hostilities in South Africa and his regiment's expected despatch to the war zone, Percival cut short his honeymoon and returned to England in June 1889 and hastily attended a medical board in London, which certified him as being fit for active service.

On 24th June 1899, Percival set sail with his wife on board *Tantallon Castle* bound for Cape Town, in his luggage was a confidential package from the War Office (which contained the Plan of Campaign in the event of war breaking out in the Transvaal) which was to be handed to General Sir William Butler in Cape Town.

Percival arrived at Cape Town on 11th July 1899 and after handing over the package to General Sir William Butler set sail two days later for Durban where he arrived on 20th July and then made his way to join the regiment (who had arrived in South Africa from India some months earlier) at Ladysmith on 25th July 1899.

Due to his previous experience in South Africa (during the 1st Boer War), Percival was selected by the General to carry out a recognisance of Laing's Nek and Majuba hill which took place between 12th and 18th August 1889.

On 25th September, Percival and the regiment were assigned to the Glencoe Field Force, commanded by Colonel Pickwood of the Royal Artillery, which was sent to Dundee in the northern territories of Natal.

669 *London Gazette* – 25542/6193
670 *London Gazette* – 25545/9
671 *London Gazette* – 25657/6435
672 *London Gazette* – 26203/4990
673 *London Gazette* – 26767/4573

The force at Dundee was expanded in October 1899 and General Penn Symons took over direct command of what was now the Glencoe Division.

On 12th October 1899, following the expiry of ultimatums, the 2nd Boer War commenced and the Boers immediately went on the offensive.

Percival and his regiment were involved in the Battle of Talana Hill on 20th October but despite their victory against the Boers it was decided to withdraw the forces from Dundee and fall back on Ladysmith.

On 25th October 1899, after several forced marches, Percival, leading the advanced guard reached Ladysmith and on 30th October was involved in the unsuccessful Battle of Lombard's Kop which was a British attempt to prevent the town being besieged.

On 1st November 1899, the day before the Boers managed to besiege Ladysmith, Percival managed to send his wife Beatrice to the relative safety of Pietermaritzburg where she was to stay with the Governor.

From 2nd November 1899, for the next 118 days until 28th February 1900, Percival was one of the besieged force that defended Ladysmith until relieved by a force commanded by General Sir Redvers Buller (VC).

It should be noted that Percival spent much of the siege outside of Ladysmith; on 9th of December he was placed on the sick list with a very high fever and on 24th December was sent by train to the Hospital at Intombi, which was considered to be neutral ground. Here he suffered further from fever and a severe bout of dysentery and did not return to Ladysmith until the siege was lifted.

On 3rd March 1900, Beatrice returned to Ladysmith, one of the last of the ladies to leave she was one of the first to return.

Still on sick leave, Percival left with Beatrice for Durban on 31st March, to continue his recuperation, however, he contracted enteric fever and a medical board on 24th April was ordered home.

After arriving at Southampton on 30th May, Percival spent several weeks at Buckland Court with his in-laws until July when he was sent by his doctors to Plombiéres, a sanatorium in Vosges, France, however, his dysentery persisted and he did not return to England until the end of September 1900.

At a medical board in Bristol, during January 1901, Percival was deemed unfit for service but after obtaining a certificate from an eminent London doctor was finally pronounced fit by a later medical board.

On 25th February 1901, Percival and his wife boarded the transport *Oratava* and set sail for South Africa where they arrived off Cape Town on 15th March 1901 and rejoined his regiment at Piet Retief on 10th April and took over the command from Major Laming while Colonel Knox was absent.

For the next few months, generally as part of the force commanded by General Walter Kitchener, Percival and his men were involved in various operations across the Transvaal.

On 13th February 1902, Percival went on leave and visited his wife at Dundee where, because of the worsening situation he made arrangements for her return to England.

Following the death from pneumonia of General Knox in England, Percival was promoted to the rank of Lieutenant-Colonel on 19th February 1902[674] and took over command of the regiment.

Percival returned to the regiment on 2nd March in time to set off on the Orange River Colony Expedition, commanded by General Plumer on the following evening.

At the end of the first gruelling march, Percival suffered a reoccurrence of his dysentery and on 5th March was sent to the hospital in Pretoria but rejoined the regiment at Vlaklaagte on 13th April.

Percival continued to lead the regiment in operations in the Orange River Colony and on the Natal Zululand border until the war ended when peace was signed on 31st May 1902.

For his service during the wars in Egypt, Percival received two mentions in despatches and was awarded the Queen's South Africa Medal (1899–1902) with clasps for Cape Colony, Talana, Defence of Ladysmith, Orange Free State and Transvaal. He was also awarded the King's South Africa Medal (1901–02) with clasps for South Africa 1901 and South Africa 1902.

On 26th June 1902, Percival was appointed as an Additional Member 3rd Class (Companion) on the Military Division of the Most Honourable Order of the Bath.[675]

When news arrived that the regiment would remain in South Africa until at least September, Percival's wife Beatrice set sail on board the transport *Plassey* on 10th July to join her husband in the Cape Colony.

On his travels down to Durban to meet his wife, Percival was again struck down with dysentery and when he arrived at Durban a Medical Board sent him to a sanatorium at Berea, where after her arrival on 12th August Beatrice joined him.

Doctors advised Percival that he should return to England, but wishing to travel back with his regiment he boarded the transport *Canada* on 31st August and set sail for Durban where they arrived on 4th September 1902.

After arriving at Durban, the transport arrangements for the regiments return home were very confused and in the end

674 *London Gazette* – 27426/2601
675 *London Gazette* – 27448/4192

Percival, with his wife and some of the other officers of the 18th Hussars left Durban on board the transport *Cecilia* on September 18th and arrived at Southampton on 8th October 1902.

The bulk of the regiment boarded the transport *Englishman* on 20th September and arrived at Southampton on 31st October and proceeded to the South Cavalry Barracks at Aldershot.

In October 1903, Percival and the regiment were moved to York and on 20th October 1903 he was appointed as Deputy Lieutenant of Gloucestershire.[676]

In 1904, Percival gifted a site at Tidenham near Chepstow to the Regiment for two cottages, built by subscription, to be used as rent free accommodation by wounded soldiers of the Regiment; he also undertook to pay all operating expenses and upkeep for the properties for the remainder of his life.

Percival received a brevet promotion to the rank of Colonel on 19th February 1905[677] and exactly a year later on 19th February 1906, having completed his term of office was placed on half pay and relieved from the command of the 18th Hussars.[678]

After leaving the 18th Hussars, Percival moved with his wife to the family home at Stanley Park and soon afterwards was asked to stand as the Conservative candidate for the Forest of Dean, which he declined.

In April 1906, Percival was elected to the Gloucestershire County Council and was also appointed as Chairman of the Lydney Petty Sessions.

On 23rd February 1907, Percival was promoted to the rank of Colonel.[679]

In 1907, Percival was appointed as Commissioner of the Boy Scouts for the Forest of Dean.

Percival received a telegram from Sir John French in November 1908, offering him the command of the Potchefstroom District in South Africa, with the temporary rank of Brigadier-General; the appointment was confirmed to be effective from 2nd January 1909.[680]

On 1st January 1909, Percival and his wife boarded the transport *Saxon* and set sail for South Africa where they arrived at Cape Town on 19th January 1909.

Percival's time with his new command was short lived, as while on manoeuvres in June 1909 he had a bad fall from his horse and still suffering from the effects in October was ordered home.

At the end of November 1909, Percival and his wife boarded the liner *Durham Castle* and set sail for England and on his arrival he was placed in a Nursing Home.

Due to his continued ill health, after nearly 30 years of service, Percival was retired from the army to pension on 29th January 1910.[681]

In September 1910, Percival was re-elected to the Gloucestershire County Council, having resigned his position when he was posted to South Africa in January 1909.

Following the declaration of war on 4th August 1914, Percival travelled to London and offered his services; while awaiting a response he joined his friend General Anderson, recently appointed to the command of East Coast Mounted Infantry, at Bury St Edmunds to help out on an unofficial basis.

In September 1914, Percival was appointed to the command of 123 interpreters being sent to France and on 18th September boarded *SS Gloucester Castle* for the journey, however, due to having to wait for *HMS Edinburgh Castle*, their escort, they did not arrive at Marseilles until 26th September.

Percival was still with the interpreters when they were transferred to Orleans on 19th October but soon afterwards joined the HQ Staff of the Indian Army Corps in France at Bethune in northern France.

On 1st January 1915, Percival was appointed as Provost-Marshal to the Indian Corps but while on leave in England suffered from a high fever, resulting from influenza and severe rheumatism and in May a medical board decided that he was unfit for foreign service. Due to repeated illnesses he would not return to duty.

For his service during the Great War, Percival was awarded the 1914 Star[682] with clasp for 5th Aug – 22nd Nov 1914, the British War Medal (1914–20) and the Victory Medal (1914–19).

With the death of his father, at the age of 84, on 19th October 1919, Percival succeeded to the title of 3rd Baronet Marling of Stanley Park and Sudbury Park, County of Gloucester.

On 26th July 1920, Percival attended a garden party at Buckingham Palace, hosted by King George V for recipients of the Victoria Cross.

Percival was nominated for the position of Sheriff of Gloucestershire on 13th November 1922[683] and was appointed to the position on 12th March 1923.[684]

In his retirement, Percival spent much of his time travelling with long trips to South Africa and Australia in addition to many across Europe.

On 28th February 1934, Percival was appointed as Honorary Colonel to the 5th Battalion of the Gloucestershire Regiment in the Territorial Army.[685]

676 *London Gazette* – 27608/6441
677 *London Gazette* – 27766/1282
678 *London Gazette* – 27887/1225
679 *London Gazette* – 27998/1283
680 *London Gazette* – 28214/315
681 *London Gazette* – 28333/693
682 Mons Star
683 *London Gazette* – 32768/8104
684 *London Gazette* – 32805/1989
685 *London Gazette* – 34028/1347

Percival was awarded the King George V Silver Jubilee Medal in 1835.

On 29th May 1936, at the age of 75, Percival died at the family home at Stanley Park and was buried in the family vault at All Saints Church in Selsey near Stroud.

Percival's Victoria Cross Medal is on public display at the Imperial War Museum in London as part of the Lord Ashcroft collection.

Figure 208a. Grave of Percival Scrope Marling

Thomas Edwards
13th March 1884 (VC No. 402)

Gazetted: 21st May 1884 25356/2278

Rank and Unit: Private No. 235 – 1st Battalion Black Watch (Royal Highlanders)

Citation

For the conspicuous bravery displayed by him in defence of one of the guns of the Naval Brigade, at the battle of Tamai, on 13th March, 1884. This man (who was attached to the Naval Brigade as Mule Driver) was beside the gun with Lieutenant Almack, R.N., and a blue jacket. Both the latter were killed, and Edwards, after bayonetting two Arabs, and himself receiving a wound with a spear, rejoined the ranks with his mules, and subsequently did good service in remaining by his gun throughout the action.

Biography

Thomas was born on 19th April 1863 at Brill, Aylesbury, Buckinghamshire to father Jasper and mother Jessie.

On 3rd December 1880, at the age of 20, Thomas left his job as a farm labourer and enlisted in the British Army at York, he was assigned to the 6th Infantry Brigade for his training and general service.

Thomas was transferred to the 1st Battalion of the newly formed[686] Black Watch (Royal Highlanders) as Private No. 235 on 15th August 1881.

Initially based at Edinburgh, on 7th August 1882, Thomas and his battalion set sail for Egypt to take part in the Anglo-Egyptian War.

After landing at Alexandria on 20th August and being assigned to the Highland Brigade, commanded by General Sir Archibald Alison, part of General Hamley's 2nd Division, they re-embarked and landed at Ismailia on 1st September 1882.

On 11th September, the brigade was moved to Kassassin where General Wolseley was assembling a strike force and on 13th September 1882, Thomas saw his first action during the Battle of Tel-el-Kebir.

After the battle, the Highland Brigade was encamped at Ghezireh until November, when Thomas and the battalion were moved into barracks at Cairo.

During 1883, the battalion spent time at Suez and Heluan before returning to Cairo.

686 As part of the Childers Army reforms, the 42nd and 73rd highland regiments were merged to form the 1st and 2nd Battalions respectively of the Black Watch (Royal Higlanders) on 1st July 1881.

Figure 209. Thomas Edwards

With increasing tension in the Sudan, as the Mahdist War once again flared up, Thomas and the battalion were posted to the 2nd Infantry Brigade, commanded by General Davis, in early 1884.

As part of the Sudan Campaign, the force was assembled at Suakim from where they were shipped to Trinkitat and on 29th February 1884 took part in the 2nd Battle of El-Teb.

It was at the Battle of Tamai on 13th March 1884, that Thomas performed the deeds for which he would later be awarded the Victoria Cross, he received a spear wound during the action.

After the battle, as it was impossible to pursue the Mahdist forces any further, the force returned to Suakim where they boarded ship and returned to Cairo.

Following much delay, the British Government finally decided to send an expedition to go to the relief of General Gordon, who was besieged at Khartoum.

Thomas and the battalion were assigned to the force of 7,000 men, under the command of Lord Wolseley, sent as the Nile Expedition to go to the relief of Khartoum.

After proceeding by train to Assiout, the battalion boarded two steamers and four barges and set off up the Nile to Assouan which they reached on 6th October 1884.

In November, the Nile Expedition boarded 84 whale boats as the river was now difficult to navigate, in fact even these boats had to be man hauled over many cataracts and other obstructions.

On 24th January 1885, the battalion advanced from Hamdab as part of the 3,000 strong River Column under the command of General Earle and on 9th February reached Dalka Island where they camped about a mile from a strong enemy position at Kirbekan.

Thomas and the battalion were part of the force which engaged the enemy in the Battle of Kirbekan on 10th February 1885.

While the River Column was advancing up the Nile another column crossed desert and reached Khartoum on 28th January 1885, only to learn that General Gordon had been killed two days earlier and that the Mahdist forces now occupied the city.

Learning of the news, the British Government decided to withdraw the troops from the Sudan and by 27th June 1886, Thomas and the battalion were back in their quarters at Cairo,

For his service in Egypt, Thomas was awarded the Egypt Medal (1882–89) with clasps for Tel-el-Kebir, Suakin 1884, El Teb / Tamai, The Nile 1884–85 and Kirbekan. He was also awarded the Khedive's Star by Egypt.

On 1st May 1886, Thomas and the battalion left Egypt bound for Malta where they formed the garrison until 24th December 1886 when they moved to Gibraltar.

After having completed his initial enlistment term of 12 years, Thomas was retired to the reserves on 1st December 1892.

After leaving the Army, Thomas moved to York where at some stage he was married and had two children, a son and a daughter.

Towards the end of his life, perhaps after the death of his wife in 1943, Thomas moved to Essex where he lived at 2 Cross Road, Woodford Bridge, it was here on 27th March 1953 at the age of 89 that he died from bronchitis.

After a Service at St Paul's Church[687] in Woodford Bridge, Thomas was buried at St Mary's Churchyard, Chigwell in an unmarked grave (a headstone was erected in March 2001).

Thomas's Victoria Cross Medal is on public display at the Black Watch Museum in Balhousie Castle, Perth Scotland.

Figure 209a. Grave of Thomas Edwards

687 St Paul's at Woodford Bridge had no churchyard, hence the burial at St Mary's in Chigwell.

Alfred Smith
17th January 1885 (VC No. 403)

Gazetted: 12th May 1885 25469/2156

Rank and Unit: Gunner No. 23641 – Royal Artillery Regiment

Citation

At the Action of Abu Klea, on the 17th January last, when the enemy charged, the square fell back a short distance, leaving Lieutenant Guthrie, Royal Artillery, with his gun, in a comparatively unprotected position. At this moment a native rushed at Lieutenant Guthrie with a spear and would in all probability have killed that officer, who had no weapon in his hand at the time (being engaged in superintending the working of his gun), when Gunner Smith with a gun handspike warded off the thrust, thus giving Lieutenant Guthrie time to draw his sword, and with a blow bring the assailant to his knees, but as the latter fell he made a wild thrust at the Officer with a long knife, which Gunner Smith again warded off, not however before the native had managed to inflict a wound in Lieutenant Guthrie's thigh. Before the Soudani could repeat the thrust Gunner Smith killed him with the handspike and thus for the time saved the life of his Officer, though the latter unfortunately died some days afterwards of his wound.

Figure 210. Alfred Smith

Biography

Alfred[688] was born some time during 1861 in London, unfortunately nothing is known of his early life.

At some time, probably in 1879 when he reached the age of 18, Alfred enlisted in the British Army and was enrolled as Gunner No. 23641 in the 1st Battery of the Southern Division of the Royal Regiment of Artillery.

It is likely that after spending some time in England at Woolwich, Alfred saw foreign service at Gibraltar, the Channel Islands and Malta.

In September 1884, Alfred and his battery where despatched to Egypt and after their arrival at Cairo were assigned to the force of 7,000 men, under the command of Lord Wolseley, sent as the Nile Expedition to go to the relief of Khartoum, where General Gordon was besieged.

The relief force under the command of General Garnet Wolseley proceeded up the Nile by river steamers and while the bulk of the force continued up river by smaller boats, Alfred and half his battery were assigned to the desert column.

The desert column was a force of about 1,500 men under the command of General Sir Hubert Stewart that would cross the desert on camels avoiding the waterfalls on the Nile.

Alfred and the battery, equipped with 2.5" RML Mountain Guns (the "screw gun") and Gardner machine guns were attached to a small Naval Brigade composed of men from *HMS Alexandra*.

On 30th December 1884, the Desert Column left Korti and after crossing the desert encountered a force of about 12,000 Mahdist on 16th January 1885.

It was during the Battle of Abu Klea, on the following day, that Alfred performed the deeds for which he would later be awarded the Victoria Cross.

After the battle, the desert column pressed on to Khartoum which they reached on 28th January 1885, only to learn that General Gordon had been killed two days earlier and that the Mahdist forces now occupied the city.

Learning of the news, the British Government decided to withdraw the troops from the Sudan and by July 1885, Alfred and his battery were back in quarters at Cairo.

For his service in Egypt, Alfred was awarded the Egypt Medal (1882–89) with clasps for The Nile 1884–85 and Abu Klea. He was also awarded the Khedive's Star by Egypt.

Alfred was presented with his Victoria Cross Medal on 3rd August 1885 by General Sir F. C. A. Stephenson, the General Officer Commanding troops in Egypt, at a ceremony in Cairo.

After his service in Egypt and the Sudan, Alfred and the battery were moved back to Malta and it was here on 4th December 1889 that he left the army and returned to England.

At some stage, Alfred was married to Elizabeth, who shares his grave.

688 His Victoria Cross citation in the *London Gazette* mistakenly refers to Albert Smith.

Alfred died at his home at Harger Road in Plumstead in Kent on 6th January 1932 at the age of 71 and was buried in Plumstead Cemetery in an unmarked grave, a headstone was erected in 1986.

His Victoria Cross medal was on public display at the Royal Artillery Museum, Woolwich, however, this is now closed but is planned to be rehoused in a new purpose built Salisbury Plain Heritage Centre, close to the Royal Artillery home at Larkhill on Salisbury Plain, which is planned to be opened to the public in the Spring of 2019.

Figure 210a. Grave of Alfred Smith

John Crimmin

1st January 1889 (VC No. 404)

Gazetted: 17th September 1889 25975/4989

Rank and Unit: Surgeon – Bombay Medical Service – Indian Army

Citation

Lieutenant Tighe, 27th Bombay Infantry (to the Mounted Infantry of which Corps Surgeon Crimmin was attached) states that in the action near Lwekaw, Eastern Karenni, on the 1st January last, four men charged with him into the midst of a large body of the enemy who were moving off from the Karen left flank, and two men fell to the ground wounded. He saw Surgeon Crimmin attending one of the men about 200 yards to the rear. Karens were round the party in every direction, and he saw several fire at Surgeon Crimmin and the wounded man. A Sepoy then galloped up to Surgeon Crimmin, and the latter joined the fighting line which then came up. Lieutenant Tighe further states that very shortly afterwards they were engaged in driving the enemy from small clumps of trees and bamboo, in which the Karens took shelter. Near one of these clumps he saw Surgeon Crimmin attending a wounded man. Several Karens rushed out at him. Surgeon Crimmin thrust his sword through one of them and attacked a second, a third Karen then dropped from the fire of a Sepoy, upon which the remaining Karens fled.

Biography

John was born on 19th March 1859 at Kilballyowen, Bruff in Co Limerick, Ireland to father Michael and mother Nancy (née Malloy).

Figure 211. John Crimmin

John studied medicine at Dublin and qualified as a Licentiate of the Royal College of Surgeons (Ireland) in 1879 and a Licentiate of Kings and Queen College of Physicians in 1882.

While living at 1 Zion Road, Rathfarnham in Dublin, John applied to the India Office for a position with the Medical Service of the Indian Army.

On 21st August 1882, John took and passed a qualifying examination in London, being placed eighth out of the applicants[689] and was appointed as a Surgeon in the Indian Medical Department of the Bombay Army on 30th September 1882.[690]

In 1885 John served as the Regimental Surgeon to 4th Bombay Infantry (Rifle Corps) until 1886 when he became Regimental Surgeon to 27th Bombay Light Infantry (1st Balooch Battalion) and was posted to Burma in September 1886 at the end of the 3rd Anglo-Burma War.

John's first two years in Burma were mainly taken up with the suppression of bandits until in September 1888, when the Chief of the Eastern Karenni (one of the Shan states) started trouble and an expedition was mounted to capture him.

John, as Senior Medical Officer, was part of the Karen Field Force despatched on 29th December 1888 for this purpose.

It was on 1st January 1889, during their first encounter with the Karenni tribesmen at the village of Ngakyaing, near Lwekaw, that John performed the deeds for which he would later be awarded the Victoria Cross; the first member of the Indian Army Medical Service to receive the award.

John was also involved in the actions to force the Nanko Defile and to capture Saw Lon, the eastern Karenni capital, on 8th January 1889.

For his service in Burma, John received a mention in despatches and was awarded the India General Service Medal with clasp for Burma (1887–89).

After the war John returned to India and in September 1889 was appointed as the Civil Surgeon at Shikarpur.

At some time in 1889 after his return to India, John was presented with his Victoria Cross Medal by the Duke of Connaught the Commander in Chief of forces in Burma.

John was promoted to the rank of Surgeon-Major on 30th September 1894,[691] having previously been promoted to the rank of Surgeon-Captain.

John was appointed as the Civil Surgeon to Rutnagherry from 30th September 1894 and from 4th November 1898 was Acting Health Officer for the Port of Bombay.

From 3rd July 1900, John was appointed as the Health Officer for the Port of Bombay.

On 29th October 1900, John was married to Julia Mary Josephine (née Lennan) at St Joseph's Church in Terenure, Dublin. The couple would go on to have five children; Mary Josephine born on 19th August 1901, Nora Frances born on 27th August 1903, Winifred Julia born on 14th August 1904, John Frances born on 18th June 1906 and George William born on 2nd February 1908.[692]

John was appointed as a Companion of the Most Eminent Order of the Indian Empire on 1st January 1901.[693]

On 30th September 1902, John was promoted to the rank of Lieutenant-Colonel.[694]

At some stage before 1908, John was awarded the Volunteer Officers Decoration (VD) for long service.

In 1911, John was appointed as Principal Medical Officer to the Kohat Brigade on the North West Frontier.

John was appointed as an Ordinary Member 3rd Class (Companion) of the Military Division of the Most Honourable Order of the Bath on 3rd June 1913.[695]

On 1st October 1913, John was promoted to the rank of Colonel.[696]

Just after the start of the Great War, John was appointed as Assistant Director of Medical Services in India, based at Kohat on the North West Frontier, on 22nd October 1914, a position that he would hold throughout the war.

On 18th February 1916, John was appointed as an Honorary Physician to King George V.[697]

After 37 years of service, John retired from the army, due to ill health,[698] on 25th February 1919,[699] this was later post-dated to 27th March 1919.[700]

On leaving the army, John returned to England and took up residence at Allandale, Chepstow road in Croydon, London.

John attended a garden party, for surviving recipients of the Victoria Cross, hosted by King George V at Buckingham Palace on 26th June 1920, 77 years to the day since Queen Victoria presented the first Victoria Cross Medals at Hyde Park.

John's wife Julia, died on 21st January 1932 at the age of 73.

689 He subsequently took a further examination at the Royal Military Hospital at Netley in February 1883 and his score combined with the London examination placed him fifth of the applicants.

690 *London Gazette* – 25215/1633

691 *London Gazette* – 26580/7453

692 Both of John's sons would pursue a military career and attain the rank of Lieutenant-Colonel, like his father before him George was a member of the Royal Army Medical Corps.

693 *London Gazette* – 27261/2

694 *London Gazette* – 27516/313

695 *London Gazette* – 28723/3904

696 *London Gazette* – 28782/9258

697 *London Gazette* – 29597/5289

698 *London Gazette* – 32899/588

699 *London Gazette* – 31574/12037

700 *London Gazette* – 32518/9061

In January 1838, at the age of 78, John was knocked down by a car, not far from his home in Croydon and suffered head injuries and shock.

At some stage, John moved from Croydon to Woodbury House, Bath Road, Wells in Somerset and this was where he died on 20th February 1945, at the age of 85, after a short illness and was buried in the Wells Cemetery.

The location of John's Victoria Cross Medal is unknown, believed to be in private hands.

Figure 211 a. Grave of John Crimmin

Ferdinand Simeon Le Quesne[701]
4th May 1889 (VC No. 405)

Gazetted: 29th October 1889 25988/5721

Rank and Unit: Surgeon – Army Medical Service

Citation

Displayed conspicuous bravery and devotion to duty during the attack on the village of Tartan, by a Column of the Chin Field Force, on the 4th May last, in having remained for the space of about ten minutes, in a very exposed position (within five yards, of the loop-holed stockade from which the enemy were firing), dressing with perfect coolness and self-possession the wounds from which Second Lieutenant Michel, Norfolk Regiment, shortly afterwards died.

Surgeon Le Quesne was himself severely wounded later on whilst attending to the wounds of another Officer.

Biography

Ferdinand was born on 25th December 1863 at St Helier, Jersey in the Channel Islands to father Giffard Nicholas a merchant and ship-owner who as a Lieutenant-Colonel commanded the Royal Jersey Artillery and mother Augusta Wilhelmina (née Simeon).

He was the fourth born and third son of seven children with three sisters and three brothers; Frances Wilhelmina born in 1852, Augustus Simeon born in 1853, Gifford Simeon born

Figure 212. Ferdinand Simeon Le Quense

701 The name Le Quesne means "The Oak Tree" and originates on the island of Jersey, Le Quesnes are known to have lived on Jersey for over 700 years.

in 1861, Augusta Simeon born in 1862, Albert Simeon born in 1866 and Mated J. born in 1867.

After his initial education in the Channel Islands, Ferdinand attended King's College Hospital in London for his medical training where he qualified as a licentiate of the Society of Apothecaries in 1885 and as a Member of the Royal College of Surgeons and a licentiate of the Royal College of Physicians in 1886.

At the end of his medical education, Ferdinand enlisted in the army and was commissioned as a Captain Surgeon in the Army Medical Service on 28th July 1886.[702]

On joining the army, Ferdinand was attached to the 2nd battalion of the Norfolk Regiment, as regimental Surgeon, who were serving in India at Sitapur and Benares.

In October 1888, Ferdinand and the regiment was ordered to Burma, to take part in the later stages of the 3rd Anglo-Burma War and on 1st November they boarded *HMS Canning* at Calcutta and set sail for Rangoon where they arrived on the 6th November 1888.

At Rangoon the regiment boarded river steamers and sailed up the Irrawaddy to Mandalay where they arrived on 17th November to relieve the 2nd battalion Royal Munster Fusiliers.

On 22nd December, Ferdinand was part of a detachment of 200 men from the regiment, commanded by Major Shepherd, sent as reinforcements to the force of General Sir George Stuart White (VC), operating against the Chin tribes.

The detachment arrived in time to be involved in the capture of the village of Siyin, in the midst of the Chin Hills where Fort White was built and occupied by the British troops on 9th April 1889.

It was on 4th May, during an operation to destroy the village of Tartan that had been rebuilt by the Chin forces, that Ferdinand performed the deeds for which he would later be awarded the Victoria Cross; during the action he was seriously wounded in the left arm.

Ferdinand was presented with his Victoria Cross Medal by General B. L. Gordon at Rangoon on 18th February 1890.

Having recovered from his wounds, Ferdinand took part in further operations in Burma, including the campaigns with the Chin-Lushai Field Force in 1890, the Wuntho Field Force in 1891 and the Kaukwee Expedition.

For his services during the war in Burma, Frederick received two mentions in despatches and was awarded the India General Service Medal (1854–95) with clasps for Burma (1887–89), Chin Lushai 1889–90 and Burma (1889–92).

702 *London Gazette* – 25620/4177

Frederick returned to England in 1893, however, a year later he was again serving in India, initially in Bengal and then in the Punjab.

On 28th July 1898, Ferdinand was promoted to the rank of Surgeon Major.[703]

In November 1901, Ferdinand was posted to service in the Cape Colony, towards the end of the 2nd Boer War where he served until the end of the war at the end of May 1902.

For his service during the war, Frederick received a mention in despatches and was awarded the Queen's South Africa Medal (1899–1902) with clasps for Cape Colony, South Africa 1901 and South Africa 1902.

At the end of the war, Frederick returned to England where he spent two years before returning to service in Bengal, India.

On 28th July 1906, Ferdinand was promoted to the rank of Surgeon Lieutenant-Colonel.[704]

In 1909, Ferdinand left India and returned to England at the outbreak of war in 1914, he joined the British Expeditionary Force and served during the Great War until his retirement, after 30 years of service in 1918.

For his service during the Great War, Ferdinand was awarded the 1914 Star, British War Medal (1914–20) and the Victory Medal (1914–19).

During his retirement, Ferdinand pursued his recreations of shooting, racquets and lawn tennis but also undertook various

Figure 212a. Grave of Ferdinand Simeon Le Quesne

703 *London Gazette* – 26994/4770
704 *London Gazette* – 27938/5459

medical interests being appointed to the post of Honorary Surgeon to the Metropolitan Hospital in London.

In 1937, Ferdinand was awarded the King George VI Coronation Medal.

Ferdinand died at his home, 6 Victoria Square, Clifton, Bristol at the age of 86 on 14th April 1950 and was buried at Canford Cemetery, Westbury-on-Tryn in Bristol five days later.

Frederick's Victoria Cross Medal is on public display at the Jersey Museum, St Helier, Jersey.

BIBLIOGRAPHY AND SOURCES

Wherever possible I have tried to use contemporary or near contemporary sources during the research of this volume, a task made much easier in this Internet age. I have drawn the information from newspapers, books, regimental records and other official and unofficial sources and documents too numerous to mention here.

Bibliography

The Egyptian Soudan its loss and recovery (Alford and Sword 1898)
The British Empire (Basil-Williams 1928)
Transvaal War (Bellairs 1885)
The conflict of east and west in Egypt (Bowen 1887)
The Ashanti War (Brackenbury 1874)
Taeping Rebellion (Brine 1862)
Narrative of the late war in New Zealand (Carey 1863)
History of the Zulu War (Colenso 1880)
The New Zealand Wars (Cowan 1922)
The Pacification of Burma (Cresthwaite 1912)
South Africa and the Transvaal War (Creswicke 1900)
My command in South Africa (Cunynghame 1880)
Sudan Campaign (d'Entragues 1886)
The Afghan Wars (Forbes 1892)
The war in New Zealand (Gudgeon 1879)
History of the Transvaal (Haggard 1899)
The Second Afghan War (Hanna 1899)
The Afghan War (Hensman 1889)
British Expedition to Abyssinia (Hozier 1869)
Outram and Havelock's Persian Campaign (Hunt 1858)
The Second Afghan War (India Defence Ministry 1907)
Basuto Rebellion, Civil War and Reconstruction (Kagan 1973)
The Arrow war with China (Leavenworth 1901)
Kafir and Zulu Wars (Parr 1880)
The Ashantee Campaign (Reade 1874)
Bhotan and the Dooar War (Rennie 1866)
Coomassie and Magdala (Stanley 1874)
Ti-Ping Revolution (Lin Te 1866)
The Egyptian War of 1882 (Vogt 1883)
History of Kathiawad (Wilberforce-Bell 1916)
History of the Zulu War (Wilmot 1880)
The "Ever Victorious Army" (Wilson 1868)
Lushai Expedition (Woodthorpe 1873)

Sources

In addition to the books listed in the Bibliography, which were all retrieved via Archive.Org the following sources were utilised to some extent or another:

BritishBattles.Com – a very useful and comprehensive site covering a wide variety of British battles – many of the maps in this volume are included with permission of the copyright John Fawkes.

Memorial to Valour – another excellent site from which most of the photographs of recipient graves and memorials were taken with kind permission.

The London Gazette and Findmypast were indispensible in pulling together the recipient biographies.

INDEX

U

V

W

Z